International Handbook of Research on Children's Literacy, Learning, and Culture

International Handbook of Research on Children's Literacy, Learning, and Culture

Edited by

Kathy Hall, Teresa Cremin,
Barbara Comber, and Luis C. Moll

WILEY-BLACKWELL

A John Wiley & Sons, Ltd., Publication

This edition first published 2013
© John Wiley & Sons, Ltd

Wiley-Blackwell is an imprint of John Wiley & Sons, formed by the merger of Wiley's global Scientific, Technical and Medical business with Blackwell Publishing.

Registered Office
John Wiley & Sons Ltd, The Atrium, Southern Gate, Chichester, West Sussex, PO19 8SQ, UK

Editorial Offices
350 Main Street, Malden, MA 02148-5020, USA
9600 Garsington Road, Oxford, OX4 2DQ, UK
The Atrium, Southern Gate, Chichester, West Sussex, PO19 8SQ, UK

For details of our global editorial offices, for customer services, and for information about how to apply for permission to reuse the copyright material in this book please see our website at www.wiley.com/wiley-blackwell.

The right of Kathy Hall, Teresa Cremin, Barbara Comber, and Luis Moll to be identified as the authors of the editorial material in this work has been asserted in accordance with the UK Copyright, Designs and Patents Act 1988.

Library of Congress Cataloging-in-Publication Data applied for

A catalogue record for this book is available from the British Library.

Cover image: Paul Klee, Colour Shapes, 1914. Image by © The Barnes Foundation, Merion Station, Pennsylvania / Corbis
Cover design by Nicki Averill Design

Typeset in 10/12pt Galliard by Aptara Inc., New Delhi, India

1   2013

Contents

Notes on Contributors

The Editors

Kathy Hall is Professor and Head of the School of Education at University College, Cork. She researches and publishes in the areas of learning, literacy, and assessment and has co-edited and authored several books and research papers on these topics. She has recently co-edited two books on socio-cultural perspectives on learning: *Learning and Practice: Culture and Identities* (2008, Murphy and Soler); *Pedagogy and Practice: Agency and Identities* (2008, with Murphy) and edited a book arising from an ESRC-funded exploration of interdisciplinary perspectives on reading: *Interdisciplinary Perspectives on Learning to Read: Culture, Cognition and Pedagogy* (2010, with Goswami, Harrison, Ellis, and Soler). She is currently leading a knowledge exchange project on inclusion and pedagogy funded by the Irish Research Council and is working on a book with Curtin and Rutherford entitled *Networks of the Mind: A Critical Neurocultural Perspective on Learning*, to be published by Routledge in 2013.

Teresa Cremin is a Professor of Education (Literacy) at the Open University. She is a past President of the United Kingdom Literacy Association (UKLA) and a current Trustee and Board Member of Booktrust and the Poetry Archive in the UK. She is also joint coordinator of the British Educational Research Association Special Interest Group on Creativity, a member of the ESRC Peer Review College and currently Chair of the International Reading Association's Outstanding Dissertation Award committee. Teresa's socio-cultural research focuses on creativity in literacy teaching and learning, teachers' literate identities and practices as readers and writers, and the pedagogy and practice of reading and writing for pleasure. She is currently leading a project exploring storytelling and story acting in the early years and another examining young people's literary reading discussions in the context of extracurricular reading groups. Teresa has written and edited over 25 books and numerous research papers and professional texts, most recently *Writing Voices: Creating Communities of Writers* (2012, with Debra Myhill).

Barbara Comber is a Research Professor in the Faculty of Education at Queensland University of Technology. Her interests include literacy education and social justice, teachers' work and identities, place and space, and practitioner inquiry. She has recently co-edited two books: *The Hawke Legacy: Towards a Sustainable Society* (2009, with McKinnon) and *Literacies in Place: Teaching Environmental Communication* (2007, with Comber, Nixon, and Reid). She is currently conducting three Australian Research Council funded projects: 'Mandated literacy assessment and the reorganization of teachers' work'; 'New literacy demands in the middle years: Learning from design experiments'; and 'Educational leadership and turnaround literacy pedagogy'.

Luis C. Moll is Professor in the Language, Reading and Culture Program of the Department of Teaching, Learning and Sociocultural Studies, College of Education, The University of Arizona. His main research interest is the connection between culture, psychology, and education, especially as it relates to the education of children in at-risk conditions. His co-edited volume, *Funds of Knowledge: Theorizing Practices in Households, Communities, and Classrooms* (2005), received the 2006 Critics' Choice Award of the American Educational Studies Association. He was elected to membership of the (US) National Academy of Education (1998).

Contributors

Sandra Schamroth Abrams is an Assistant Professor in the Department of Curriculum and Instruction at St John's University in New York. Her interest in digital literacies and dynamic pedagogy fuels her research on virtual spaces and the identities and practices developed, maintained, and modified in online and offline social and academic contexts. Though Abrams primarily focuses on video games and learning, she recognizes the often symbiotic relationship among literacy practices, and, thus, examines digital narratives and multimodal representations to understand nuanced meaning-making at the seemingly irregular borders of digital and place-based environments. Along with Jennifer Rowsell, Abrams co-edited the NSSE volume, *Rethinking Identity and Literacy Education in the 21st Century* (2011), and she has published journal articles and book chapters that continue to explore the elements of behavior and learning, and the power and pedagogy shaping student understanding.

Florencia Alam received a BA in Language from the University of Buenos Aires. She is currently working on Master's and PhD degrees in Discourse Analysis at the University of Buenos Aires and has obtained a doctoral scholarship from the CONICET (National Council of Scientific Research of Argentina). Her research is focused on interactions between children.

Evelyn Arizpe is a Lecturer in Children's Literature at the School of Education, University of Glasgow. She is program leader for the MEd in Children's Literature and Literacies and has taught and published widely in the areas of literacies, reader response to picture books, and children's literature. She is co-author, with Morag Styles, of *Children Reading Pictures: Interpreting Visual Texts* (2003) and *Reading Lessons from the Eighteenth Century: Mothers, Children and Texts* (2006). Also with Morag Styles, she has co-edited *Acts of Reading: Teachers, Texts and Childhood* (2009). She has a particular interest in Mexican children's books and children's literature about Latin America. She is project leader for 'Visual Journeys', an international project based on research in Spain, Australia, and the United States that investigates immigrant children's responses to wordless picture books. In the UK, the research was funded by a grant from the United Kingdom Literacy Association (UKLA); the follow-up project was funded by the Esmée Fairbairn Foundation.

Georgina Barton is a Lecturer in the School of Education and Professional Studies at Griffith University, Australia. For over 20 years Dr Barton has been a classroom teacher and literacy educator in schools. She has worked with teachers, particularly in socio-disadvantaged areas, in developing literacy programs to improve students' outcomes. She is also an Arts teacher, a researcher, and a practitioner, having performed both nationally and internationally in various music ensembles. She is currently researching in the area of Arts literacy and aesthetics education. Her other work focuses on multiliteracies, modalities, arts and music education, ethnomusicology, and teacher education.

Catherine Beavis is a Professor of Education at Griffith University, Australia. She teaches and researches in the areas of English and literacy curricula, and around digital culture, young people, and new media. Her work has a particular focus on the changing nature of text and literacy, and the implications of young people's experience of the online world for contemporary English and Literacy curricula. Her research looks particularly at computer or video games and young people's engagement with them, exploring the ways in which games work as new textual worlds for players, embodying and extending 'new' literate and multimodal literacies and stretching and changing expectations about 'reading,' narrative, and participation. Her work explores the role of game-play in young people's lives, connections between game-play and constructions of identity and community, and games as the spaces within which young people play. She has a keen interest in what might be learned about students' experience of digital texts such as video games in their out-of-school lives that might in turn enrich contemporary classroom curriculum and pedagogy. Publications include *Teaching the English Subjects: Essays on English Curriculum History and Australian schooling* (edited with Bill Green), *P(ICT)ures of English: Teachers, Learners and Technology* (edited with Cal Durant), and *Doing Literacy Online: Teaching, Learning and Playing in an Electronic World* (edited with Ilana Snyder). Publications in press include *Digital Games: Literacy in Action* (edited with Joanne O'Mara and Lisa McNeice) and *Literacy in 3D* (edited with Bill Green).

Shirley Brice Heath, Margery Bailey Professor of English and Dramatic Literature and Professor of Linguistics, Emerita, Stanford University, studies learning environments within families and under-resourced communities. A linguistic anthropologist, she is best known for her longitudinal research on language socialization within families and community settings. She also studies situations in which project work by artists and scientists is taking place. This research, carried out in studios, rehearsal zones, and laboratories, has demonstrated the importance of sustained visual attentiveness, embodiment, and the envisionment of a future outcome to project work. Her recent research is informed by cognitive neuroscience research that can supplement explanations of learning documented through observations and recordings of behavior. She is the author of the classic *Ways with Words: Language, Life, and Work in Communities and Classrooms* (Cambridge University Press, 1983/1996) and the sequel volume, *Words at Work and Play: Three Decades in Family and Community Life* (Cambridge University Press, 2012).

Cathy Burnett is Senior Lecturer in Primary English at Sheffield Hallam University, UK, where she leads the Language and Literacy Research and Scholarship Group and co-leads the Teacher Education Research and Scholarship Group. Her research focuses on relationships between literacies within and beyond formal educational contexts, with a particular emphasis on the social practices emerging around new technologies in classrooms. She is interested in how children negotiate meaning through and around digital texts, using theories of space to explore meaning making across on/offline contexts. Her published work has also explored the continuities and discontinuities between pre-service teachers' literacy practices in different domains of their lives and considered the barriers and possibilities that teachers associate with using new texts in schools. She is co-editor of the United Kingdom Literacy Association journal, *Literacy*.

Brian Cambourne is a Principal Fellow in the Faculty of Education at the University of Wollongong, Australia. Since 1980 Brian has been researching how learning, especially literacy learning, occurs. His current research interests have continued this tradition, and center on the re-examination of the concept of 'learning' through a 'biological-cum-evolutionary' lens rather than the traditional psychological lens. One outcome of this has been the reframing of 'knowledge' as 'the sum total of all the meanings constructed using a range of abstract symbol systems.' He is currently engaged in several schools, helping teachers develop discourse that reflects this way of framing 'learning' and monitoring how this discourse affects their pedagogies and their students' knowledge building. Recent publications that reflect these interests include chapters in: *Changing Literacies for Changing Times* (2009); *Defying Convention, Inventing the Future in Literacy Research and Practice* (2010); and *Reading Researchers in Search of Common Ground* (2012).

Victoria Carrington took up a Chair in Education in the School of Education and Lifelong Learning at the University of East Anglia in March 2010. Before joining UEA, she held a Research SA Chair at the University of South Australia and has held posts at the University of Plymouth, the University of Queensland, and the University of Tasmania. Victoria writes extensively in the fields of sociology of literacy and education and has a particular interest in the impact of new digital media on literacy practices. She is co-editor of the international journal *Discourse: Studies in the Cultural Politics of Education* and sits on the editorial boards of a number of international journals. With Associate Professor Aaron Koh, she is the editor of a new book series *Cultural Studies and Transdisciplinarity in Education*. Recent publications include: 'Literacy-lite in BarbieGirls' (2010) in the *British Journal of Sociology of Education* (with K. Hodgetts); *Digital literacies: Social Learning and Classroom Practice* (2009, with M. Robinson); and 'The contemporary gothic: Literacy and childhood in unsettled times' in the *Journal of Early Childhood Literacy* (2012).

Eveline Chan is a Senior Lecturer in English and Literacies Education in the School of Education, Australia. Eveline has worked in language education for over two decades, in teacher preparation programs in the areas of language and literacy development and TESOL, and in teaching students from non-English speaking backgrounds in school and tertiary contexts. Her research interests include literacy pedagogy and assessment, classroom discourse analysis, multimodal representations of curriculum knowledge, image-language interaction in multimodal texts, and reading in hypertext environments. She has served as the assistant editor of *English for Specific Purposes: An International Research Journal* and continues to review articles submitted to various peer-reviewed, scholarly publications in her areas of expertise. Eveline's recent publications include a chapter in: *Semiotic margins: Meaning in Multimodalities* (2011), and 'Image-language interaction in online reading environments: Challenges for students' reading comprehension' in *The Australian Educational Researcher* (2011, with Len Unsworth).

Johanne Clifton was, until recently, Head teacher at Allens Croft Primary School. She was appointed in 2006, and has a passionate commitment to the use of literature in raising standards in literacy. On arriving at Allens Croft, she found that the school had a strong sense of community values but was struggling with raising standards of achievement. Through working with creative practitioners, staff and parents, the school developed a clear ethos of creative learning and partnership in order to develop an engaging and relevant curriculum through which children were excited by learning and so able to achieve high standards in writing. She has since moved to Billesley Primary school, also in Birmingham.

Cassandra S. Coddington, PhD, is a graduate of the University of Maryland, College Park with a degree in Human Development Education. She has worked with the Reading Engagement Project, Concept-Oriented Reading Instruction (CORI), and Reading Engagement for Adolescent Learners (REAL) at the University of Maryland; the Center for Research on Atypical Development and Learning (CRADL) at Georgia State University; and the Mobile Youth Survey (MYS) at the University of Alabama. She has co-authored research on reading and engagement published in *Reading Psychology*, the *Journal of Learning Disabilities*, and the *Journal of Literacy Research*, and has edited three handbook chapters. She is currently a postdoctoral researcher at the University of Alabama in Tuscaloosa in the College of Human Environmental Sciences, working on the Mobile Youth Survey. The MYS is a 14-year longitudinal survey study of 10- to 18-year-old low-income African-American youth's behaviors and affects. She is currently studying predictors and contextual factors associated with academic resiliency in African-American adolescents from high-poverty communities. Of particular interest is the relationship between early reading success and later academic success and the role of engagement in that association.

Catherine Compton-Lilly is an Associate Professor in Curriculum and Instruction at the University of Wisconsin Madison. Dr Compton-Lilly teaches courses in literacy studies and works with professional development schools in Madison. She is the author of *Reading Families: The Literate Lives of Urban Children* (2003), *Rereading Families* (2007), and *Reading Time: The Literate Lives of Urban Secondary Students and their Families* (2012). In these books she describes her experiences in following eight of her former first grade students through middle school. She is currently writing about the high school experiences of these same students. Dr Compton-Lilly has authored articles in the *Reading Research Quarterly*, *Research in the Teaching of English*, *The Reading Teacher*, *Journal of Early Childhood Literacy*, and *Language Arts*. She engages in longitudinal research projects. Her interests include examining how time operates as a contextual factor in children's lives as they progress through school and construct their identities as students and readers. In an ongoing study, Dr Compton-Lilly is working with a team of graduate students to follow 15 children from immigrant families from primary school through high school. She is currently the editor-in-chief of *Networks: An Online Journal for Teacher Research*.

Alicia Curtin is a Lecturer in the School of Education, University College, Cork. Her research interests center on adolescent literacies and identities in both school and non-school contexts. Her research also explores socio-cultural and neuroscientific understandings of learning and the implications of these understandings for everyday practice. She is currently working on a knowledge exchange project on inclusion and pedagogy funded by the Irish Research Council and is co-authoring a book entitled *Networks of the Mind: A Critical Neurocultural Perspective on Learning*, to be published in 2013.

Sophie Dewayani graduated in 2011 from the University of Illinois at Urbana-Champaign where she completed her dissertation on the literacy practices of street children in Bandung, Indonesia. She will continue her research on the literacy practices of under-represented children in Indonesia, especially those related to the use of popular culture. Currently, she is an Adjunct Lecturer in Bandung Institute of Technology and Indonesia University of Education.

Clare Dowdall is a Lecturer in Education at Plymouth University where she works mainly with PGCE students in the areas of language and literacy. She has published several articles and book chapters on children's use of social networking sites as platforms to perform identity through textual artifact construction. Her key research interests include children's text production and design in the digital age, and the tensions that can be perceived between the formal curriculum for young children's education and their creation of and engagement with texts in their own online spaces. Currently she is involved in a joint project researching urban textual landscapes with Victoria Carrington. Recent publications include: 'Impressions, improvisations and compositions: Reframing children's text production in the digital age,' in *Literacy – Literacy and Identity Special Issue* (2009); chapters in *Digital Literacies, Social Learning and Classroom Practices* (2009, with M. Robinson) and *Play, Creativity and Digital Cultures* (2008); and (2006) 'Dissonance between the digitally created words of school and home', in *Literacy* (2006).

Bernadette Dwyer is a Lecturer in Literacy Studies in Education at St Patrick's College, Dublin City University. Bernadette currently teaches at undergraduate and postgraduate levels in the Education Department of the college. She is also involved in a range of continuing professional development courses with teachers. Previously a classroom teacher, with over 23 years of teaching experience, she has taught at all levels of the primary school, including in Learning Support. She has also taught in a variety of school settings including in high-poverty districts. She earned her PhD at the University of Nottingham in 2010. Her doctoral dissertation: 'Scaffolding Internet reading: A study of a disadvantaged school community in Ireland', focused on the integration of the new literacies of the Internet within an inquiry-based classroom curriculum in a disadvantaged school setting. Her research work currently focuses on the development of new literacies, particularly online reading comprehension processes; digital tools that support the development of reading, writing, communication, and deep learning across the content areas; and supporting struggling readers from disadvantaged communities in an online environment.

Anne Haas Dyson is currently a Professor of Education at the University of Illinois at Urbana-Champaign. She studies the childhood cultures and literacy learning of young schoolchildren. Among her publications are *Social Worlds of Children Learning to Write in an Urban Primary School*, which was awarded NCTE's David Russell Award for Distinguished Research, *Writing Superheroes, The Brothers and Sisters Learn to Write: Popular Literacies in Childhood and School Cultures*, and, with Celia Genishi, *Children, Language, and Literacy: Diverse Learners in Diverse Times*.

Sue Ellis studied Linguistics and Language Pathology at the University of Essex and is currently Reader in Education at the University of Strathclyde, where she teaches undergraduate and postgraduate courses on literacy development and literacy pedagogy. Her research interests are in literacy and literacy policy implementation. Recent funded projects have focused on support models for children with language impairment in mainstream classrooms; formative assessment in the writing curriculum; and on developing genre pedagogies in primary and secondary schools. She is interested in the ways in which different epistemological understandings of language and literacy can enhance teachers' empirical knowledge base for making decisions about literacy teaching and learning in schools. She is a member of the editorial boards of *Child Language Teaching and Therapy* and the United Kingdom Literacy Association (UKLA) journal, *Literacy*, and sits on the publications committee of the International Reading Association. She coordinates the Language and Literacy Special Interest Group of the British Educational Research Association and is the UKLA representative on the International Development in

Europe Committee and on the Committee for Linguistics in Education. Her most recent book is *Applied Linguistics and Primary Teaching* (2001, with Elspeth McCartney).

Moisés Esteban-Guitart is an Associate Professor in the Department of Psychology at the University of Girona (Spain). He received his doctorate from the University of Barcelona and did pre-doctoral visits at the Intercultural University of Chiapas (México) and Leeds University. He conducted postdoctoral studies at the Institute for Cultural Research and Education (California) and has been a visiting scholar in the Department of Teaching, Learning, and Sociocultural Studies at the University of Arizona. His research addresses the connections between culture, identity, and education, especially in relation to the construction of identity in multicultural settings such as in Chiapas (indigenous and *mestizos* students) and in Catalonia, Spain (immigrant populations). He has studied how identity processes take place in the broader social contexts of school, family, and community life, and attempted to establish pedagogical relationships between these settings. He is a member of the International Society for Cultural and Activity Research.

Maureen Farrell is a Senior Lecturer at the University of Glasgow, School of Education. She has been a researcher and teacher, working in schools and FE colleges for 12 years before becoming a teacher educator. She has been a program leader and Associate Dean with responsibility for all Initial Teacher Education programs and is on the teaching team for the MEd in Children's Literature and Literacies. She gained her PhD in Scottish Children's Literature in 2008. Her research interests and publications are mainly in that field, though recently she has also worked on both the 'Visual Journeys' and 'Journeys from Images to Words' projects with Evelyn Arizpe and Julie McAdam.

Peter Freebody is a Professorial Research Fellow at the University of Sydney, and is based in the Faculty of Education and Social Work. He is a Fellow of the Academy of the Social Sciences in Australia. His research and teaching interests are literacy education, educational disadvantage, classroom interaction, and research methodology. He has authored and edited books, journal articles, and chapters on these topics, including invited entries in international handbooks and encyclopedias. He has served on Australian regional, state, and national advisory groups in the areas of literacy education and curriculum design. He was evaluator of the Australian national online curriculum initiative conducted by the Australian Curriculum Corporation, and a co-founder of the Centre for Research in Pedagogy and Practice at the National Institute of Education, Singapore. He is currently a member of the New South Wales State Ministerial Advisory Group for Literacy and Numeracy, the Australian Commonwealth Government's National Literacy and Numeracy Expert Group, and the International Reading Association's Literacy Research Panel. Recent publications include chapters in *The Handbook of Research on Teaching the English Language Arts* (2010); *Literacy and Social Responsibility: Multiple Perspectives* (2010); and *The International Handbook of Reading Research* (2011).

Toni Gennrich teaches in the School of Education at the University of the Witwatersrand, Johannesburg, South Africa. Her teaching and research are in the areas of media literacy, academic literacy, teacher identity, and drama teaching. She has written material for educational supplements in newspapers and has presented material for students on television. She is currently working on a PhD on teachers' literate habits.

Perry Gilmore, PhD, a sociolinguist and educational anthropologist, is Professor of Language, Reading and Culture and Second Language Acquisition and Teaching faculty at the University of Arizona. She is also Professor Emerita at the University of Alaska, Fairbanks where she maintains an affiliate faculty position at the Alaska Native Language Center. She has conducted communication, language, and literacy research in a wide variety of urban and rural settings in the US, Russia, Africa, and Australia. Interest in language and communication has led her to explore a wide range of questions on the origin, nature, and development of interaction and communication, including: field studies of nonhuman primate communication in the West Indies and East Africa; pidginization and creolization of languages; social aspects of literacy acquisition; and Indigenous language and culture regenesis. She is the author of numerous ethnographic studies and co-editor of several major ethnography collections including *Children In and Out of School: Ethnography and Education*; *The Acquisition of Literacy: Ethnographic Perspectives*; and *Indigenous Epistemologies and Education: Self-Determination, Anthropology and Human Rights*. Gilmore is a past President of the Council on Anthropology and Education.

Bill Green is Professor of Education in the School of Teacher Education and Strategic Research Professor in the Research Institute for Professional Practice, Learning and Education (RIPPLE) at Charles Sturt University, Australia. His research interests are focused on curriculum inquiry and literacy studies, English teaching and curriculum history, doctoral research education, education for rural-regional sustainability, and practice theory and professional education. He has a longstanding interest, in particular, in literacy and technology, and more generally in technocultural studies in education. His publications include a number of significant edited volumes, including *The Insistence of the Letter: Literacy Studies and Curriculum Theorizing* (1993), *Teaching the English Subjects: Essays on English Curriculum History and Australian Schooling* (1996, with Catherine Beavis), and more recently *Understanding and Researching Professional Practice* (2009). He also co-authored with Colin Lankshear and Ilana Snyder *Teachers and Technoliteracy: Managing Literacy, Technology and Learning in Schools* (2000). Publications in press and forthcoming include *Literacy in 3D: A Multidimensional Perspective in Literacy Education* (co-edited with Catherine Beavis) and *Rethinking Rural Literacies: Transnational Perspectives* (Palgrave Macmillan, 2013), co-edited with Michael Corbett. He is co-editor of the UK-based journal *Changing English: Studies in Culture and Education*, and among his recent activities is a Special Issue of *English Teaching; Practice and Critique* entitled 'English(es) and the Sense of Place', co-edited with Urszula Clark.

Erica Hateley teaches and researches children's and adolescent literature in the School of Cultural and Language Studies in Education at Queensland University of Technology, Australia. She is the author of *Shakespeare in Children's Literature: Gender and Cultural Capital* (2009) and is currently undertaking research into Australian children's book awards.

Jennifer I. Hathaway is an Assistant Professor in the Department of Reading and Elementary Education at the University of North Carolina at Charlotte, where she teaches elementary reading methods courses at the undergraduate and graduate levels. She received her PhD at Vanderbilt University after teaching in elementary schools for several years. Her research interests include teachers' beliefs, teacher education, and professional development for teachers. She is also interested in supporting struggling readers' learning and is part of a research team working to improve young readers' comprehension. She has served as the chairperson of the Disabled Reader Special Interest Group of the International Reading Association since 2009.

Hilary Janks is a Professor in the School of Education at the University of the Witwatersrand, Johannesburg. She is the editor and an author of the *Critical Language Awareness* series of workbooks and the author of *Literacy and Power* (2009). Her teaching and research are in the areas of language education in multilingual classrooms, language policy, and critical literacy. Her work is committed to a search for equity and social justice in contexts of poverty.

Rebecca Jesson is a Research Fellow in the School of Curriculum and Pedagogy at the University of Auckland, and is a Senior Researcher with the Woolf Fisher Research Centre. Her research focuses on raising achievement in literacy in diverse communities in New Zealand. A specific focus is the pedagogy of writing and building teachers' pedagogical content knowledge for writing using the theories of intertextuality and transfer as the impetus for refinements to writing instruction.

Stephanie Jones is concerned about women disciplining one another in service of a neoliberal state that excludes and exploits women. She is also Associate Professor at the University of Georgia where she teaches undergraduate and graduate courses on ethnographic and place-based teaching for social change, feminist theory and pedagogy, social class and poverty, early childhood education, and literacy. She is co-director of the Red Clay Writing Project, a site of the National Writing Project, and of the CLASSroom project for assembling class-sensitive pedagogies and ending classism in schools. Stephanie's scholarly interests sit at the intersections of social class, gender, place, bodies, and critical literacies, and she is currently working with the comics medium to transform a three-year study of feminist pedagogy in teacher education into a graphic book. Recent publications include: 'Negotiating mothering identities: Ethnographic and intergenerational insights to social class and gender in a high-poverty US context', in *Gender and Education*; 'Making sense of injustices in a classed world: Working-poor girls' discursive practices and critical literacies', in *Pedagogies: An International Journal*; 'Speaking of bodies in justice-oriented, feminist teacher education' (with Hilary Hughes-Decatur), in the *Journal of Teacher Education*; and 'The precarious nature of social class-sensitivity in literacy: A social, autobiographic, and pedagogical project' (with Mark Vagle), in *Curriculum Inquiry*. She serves on the editorial review boards for: *Language Arts*; *English Teaching: Practice and Critique*; *Reading and Writing Quarterly*; and the *Journal of Adolescent and Adult Literacy*.

Tanya Kaefer is Research Fellow at the University of Michigan. Dr Kaefer earned her doctoral degree in developmental psychology from Duke University in 2009. She studies reading development and the influence of content knowledge on early literacy skills.

Barbara Kamler is Emeritus Professor at Deakin University, Melbourne and Honorary Professor at the University of Sydney. She has researched extensively on the theory and practice of writing across the life span, from early childhood to old age, in primary, secondary, university, and community contexts. Her work with teacher researchers has used writing as a form of social action and identity formation to achieve socially just literacy outcomes. She currently runs *Writing Designs*, a program that offers seminars, workshops, and writing retreats to help doctoral and early career academics develop authoritative writing and a robust publication record. Recent book publications include *Helping Doctoral Students Write: Pedagogies for Supervision* (with Pat Thomson, 2006); *Publishing Pedagogies for the Doctorate and Beyond* (co-edited with Claire Aitchison and Alison Lee, 2010) and; *Writing for Peer Refereed Journals: Strategies for Success* (with Pat Thomson, 2012.)

Eithne Kennedy is a teacher educator at St Patrick's College, Drumcondra, Dublin, where she teaches on a range of literacy courses at undergraduate and postgraduate level. Prior to joining the college faculty, she was a classroom teacher for many years in Dublin and the US. Her doctoral research, which focused on raising literacy achievement in disadvantaged schools, was awarded the International Reading Association's Outstanding Dissertation Award in 2010. As the director of the Write to Read research initiative, a St Patrick's College, School and Community Literacy project, she works collaboratively with schools and communities to design and implement research-based approaches to literacy instruction aimed at raising achievement in ways that motivate and engage children as readers, writers, and thinkers. She has authored and co-authored several publications in the field including policy papers on literacy, articles for *The Reading Teacher*, *Reading Research Quarterly*, and her first book, *Raising Literacy Achievement in High-Poverty Schools: An Evidence-Based Approach* (2012). She regularly presents at national and international conferences including RAI, UKLA, LRA, and IRA. She is a past President and current executive committee member of the Reading Association of Ireland.

Julie Kiggins is Sub Dean in the Faculty of Education, University of Wollongong. She is an experienced senior lecturer with high-level involvement in and coordination of mainstream teacher education and an alternative teacher education program – the Knowledge Building Community program (KBC). The KBC program achieved recognition via national and international conference presentations, book chapters, and journal publications as well as favorable reviews in the Ramsey Report: *Quality Matters* (2000) and the NSW Inquiry into Public Education conducted by Professor Tony Vinson (2001). It was tabled in the NSW Parliamentary Enquiry into the Recruitment and Training of Teachers (2005) and the National Inquiry into Teacher Education (2006). In 2006, she was awarded the Vice Chancellor's Early Career Academic Award for Outstanding Contribution to Teaching and Learning. Together with Brian Cambourne she won a Carrick Citation for Outstanding Contributions to Student Learning and a Carrick Australian University Teaching Award for a program that Enhances Student Learning in the Innovation in Curricula, Learning, and Teaching category for the Knowledge Building Community Program.

Karl Kitching is a Lecturer in the School of Education, University College, Cork. From his experiences of primary schools he developed his research interests in literacy, migrant education, and the politics of racism, schooling, and nation-building. He has published recent pieces on these themes in the journals *Race Ethnicity and Education*, *Power and Education*, *Irish Educational Studies*, and the books *Race and Intersectionality in Education* (with Bhopal and Preston, 2012), *Pedagogy, Oppression and Transformation in a 'Post-Critical' Climate* (O'Shea and O'Brien, 2011) and *The Changing Faces of Ireland* (with Darmody, Tyrrell, and Song, 2010). He is currently finishing a paper titled 'Where is she from if she's not making her Communion?', which examines the politics of religion, secularism, childhood, and nation-building in the Irish public school system.

Rachael Levy is Lecturer in Early Childhood Education at the University of Sheffield. She directs and teaches on the Early Childhood Education strand of the University's EdD program and is Course Director for the MA in Educational Studies, which is run in Malta. Rachael's research interests focus on the factors that influence young children's attitudes and beliefs about literacy. She is especially interested in understanding how constructions of reading are influenced by children's home and school discourses, including the impact of technological change within communication practices in society. Issues of confidence and motivation for learning are also inherent factors within Rachael's research. In particular, she is concerned with developing an understanding of the factors that influence young children's confidence and attitudes toward themselves as learners. Rachael is also interested in gender studies and has explored young boys' and girls' attitudes toward aspects of literacy. She has recently published

Young Children Reading at Home and at School (2011), which reports extensive research that challenges existing approaches to the teaching of reading and encourages the reader to reflect on the ways in which practice needs to be developed to promote young children's confidence and motivation for reading. She has also published a variety of journal articles and book chapters. Rachael reviews articles for several journals and is currently the editor for the UKLA minibook series.

Guofang Li is an Associate Professor of Second Language and Literacy Education in the Department of Teacher Education, Michigan State University. Li's research focuses on immigrant students' home literacy practices and their relationships to schooling framed around issues of culture, race, class, and gender; Asian immigrants' education, their social processes of learning, and the impact of the 'model minority' myth on language and literacy development; and research-based practices in ESL/EFL education. Li has published nine books and over 60 journal articles and book chapters. Her recent works include: *Best Practices in ELL Instruction* (2010, with P. Edwards); *Multicultural Families, Home Literacies, and Mainstream Schooling* (2009); *Model Minority Myths Revisited: An Interdisciplinary Approach to Demystifying Asian American Education Experiences* (2008); and *Culturally Contested Literacies: America's 'Rainbow Underclass' and Urban Schools* (2008). Li is the recipient of the 2011 Publication Award of the Association of Chinese Professors of Social Sciences in the US (ACPSS), the 2010 Early Career Award at the American Educational Research Association (AERA), the 2008 Division G Early Career Award of AERA, and the 2006 Ed Fry Book Award of the National Reading Conference.

Karen Littleton is Professor of Psychology in Education at the Open University, where she directs the Centre for Research in Education and Educational Technology. Her research addresses the complex interrelationship between context and cognition and highlights that ways of thinking are embedded in the use of language in social context. She has a particular interest in the use of language in the classroom. In collaboration with colleagues (notably Professor Neil Mercer, University of Cambridge, UK; Dr Lyn Dawes, University of Northampton, UK; and Professor Rupert Wegerif, University of Exeter, UK) she has developed a distinctive line of research concerned with understanding how classroom dialogue contributes to children's intellectual development. A former editor of the *International Journal of Educational Research* and the *European Association for Research on Learning and Instruction*'s book series, Karen is currently editor of the Routledge *Psychology of Education* book series. She serves on the editorial boards of *Educational Research Review*, *Journal of Computer Assisted Learning*, and *International Journal of Educational Research*. Her most recent books are *Educational Dialogues* (2010, with Christine Howe), *International Handbook of Psychology in Education* (2010, with Clare Wood and Judith Kleine Staarman), and *Orchestrating Inquiry Learning* (2012, with Eileen Scanlon and Mike Sharples).

Margaret Mackey is a Professor in the School of Library and Information Studies at the University of Alberta. She teaches, researches, and publishes widely in the area of multimodal literacies and youth culture. Her most recent book is *Narrative Pleasures in Young Adult Novels, Films, and Video Games* (2011).

Jackie Marsh is Professor of Education at the University of Sheffield. Her research interests center on the role and nature of popular culture, media, and new technologies in young children's literacy development, both in- and out-of-school. She is also interested in how teachers can develop literacy curricula and pedagogy appropriate for the digital age. Jackie has been involved in a number of research projects that have explored these issues, funded by bodies such as the Arts and Humanities Research Council (AHRC), British Academy, BBC, and the Esmée Fairbairn Foundation. Jackie is currently involved in research on the history of childhood and play, based on the archive of material that the folklorists Iona and Peter Opie deposited at the Bodleian Library. Her recent publications include *Children, Media and Playground Cultures: Ethnographic Studies of School Playtimes* (with Willett, Richards, Burn, and Bishop, in press), *Children's Virtual Play Worlds: Culture, Learning and Participation* (co-edited with J. Burke, in press), and *Virtual Literacies: Interactive Spaces for Children and Young People* (co-edited with Merchant, Gillen, and Davies, in press). She is also currently involved in editing, with Joanne Larson, a second edition of the *Handbook of Early Childhood Literacy*. Jackie is an editor of the *Journal of Early Childhood Literacy*.

Janet Maybin is a Senior Lecturer in Language and Communication at the Open University. Originally trained as a social anthropologist, she has written extensively for Open University courses and also researches and writes on children's and adults' informal language and literacy practices, focusing currently on voice and creativity. Recent publications include *Children's Voices: Talk, Knowledge and Identity* (2006), *The Art of English: Everyday Texts and Practices* (edited with J. Swann, 2006), *Children's Literature: Approaches and Territories* (edited with N.J. Watson, 2009) and *The Routledge Companion to English Language Studies* (edited with J. Swann, 2009).

Julie McAdam is a University Teacher at the University of Glasgow, School of Education. She has been involved in literacy teaching and establishing teacher education programs in international settings, such as Egypt, Portugal, Hungary, UAE, and Scotland. She has worked as a researcher on funded projects on teacher identity, mentoring, and visual literacy. Her most recent work has been with children newly arrived in Scotland in both the 'Visual Journeys' and 'Journeys from Images to Words' projects with Evelyn Arizpe and Maureen Farrell.

Stuart McNaughton is Director of the Woolf Fisher Research Centre at the University of Auckland. His research focuses on literacy and language development, including the design of effective instruction and educational programs for culturally and linguistically diverse populations. His current research focuses on the properties of effective teaching of literacy and language in the context of research-based interventions with clusters of schools, including a focus on literacy across and within content areas.

Neil Mercer is Professor of Education at the University of Cambridge, where he is also Chair of the Psychology and Education Group and Vice President of the college Hughes Hall. Previously, he was Professor of Language and Communications at the Open University. He is a psychologist with particular interests in the development of children's language and reasoning, classroom talk, and the application of digital technology in schools. His research with colleagues generated the 'Thinking Together' practical approach to talk for learning, and he has worked extensively with teachers, researchers, and educational policy makers on its application in schools. Formerly editor of the journals *Learning and Instruction* and *The International Journal of Educational Research*, he is now an editor of the journal *Learning, Culture and Social Interaction*. His most recent books are *Exploring Talk in School* (with Steve Hodgkinson, 2008) and *Dialogue and the Development of Children's Thinking* (with Karen Littleton, 2007).

Guy Merchant is Professor of Literacy in Education, and research lead for the Department of Teacher Education at Sheffield Hallam University. His research focuses on the relationship between children and young people, new technology and literacy, and he has published widely in this area. *Web 2.0 for Schools: Learning and Social Participation* (2009), co-written with Julia Davies, has been influential in charting the way forward for new literacies in education. Guy is also lead editor of *Virtual Literacies: Interactive Spaces for Children and Young People* (2012), a collection that includes recent empirical research on virtual worlds and online spaces in and beyond educational institutions, and contains international studies from the UK, North America, and Australasia. He is a founding editor of the *Journal of Early Childhood Literacy*, and a member of the editorial board of *Literacy*. He is also active in literacy education and professional work, including writing curriculum materials and professional publications. He is research convener for the United Kingdom Literacy Association and a member of the association's Executive Committee and National Council.

Kathy A. Mills is involved in language and literacy education at the Queensland University of Technology. Dr Mills has published educational research widely in multiliteracies, multimodality, reading comprehension, new pedagogies, critical ethnography, and literacy assessment. Dr Mills is currently part of a research team investigating a print and digital literacy educational reform funded by the Australian Research Council for students from low socio-economic and Indigenous backgrounds. Mills is the author of four books, most recently *The Multiliteracies Classroom*. She has published in international journals that include *Review of Educational Research, Linguistics and Education, Journal of Adolescent and Adult Literacy*, and the *Australian Educational Researcher*. Dr Mills serves internationally on the executive committee of the AERA Writing and Literacies SIG, and is a review board member of *The Reading Teacher*.

Elizabeth Birr Moje is Associate Dean for Research and an Arthur F. Thurnau Professor in the School of Education at the University of Michigan, Ann Arbor. Moje also serves as a Faculty Associate in the University's Institute for Social Research, Latino/a Studies, and the Joint Program in English and Education. She teaches undergraduate and graduate courses in secondary and adolescent literacy, literacy and cultural theory, and qualitative and mixed research methods. Her research interests focus on the intersection between the literacies and texts youth are asked to learn in the disciplines and the literacies and texts they experience outside school. In addition, Moje studies how youth make cultures and enact identities from their home and community literacies, and from ethnic cultures, popular cultures, and school cultures. These research interests stem from the start of her career when she taught history, biology, and drama at high schools in Colorado and Michigan. Her current research focuses on communities and schools in Detroit, Michigan. She also engages in literacy professional development with teachers in Detroit and around the world.

Susan B. Neuman is a Professor in Educational Studies specializing in early literacy development. Previously, she served as the US Assistant Secretary for Elementary and Secondary Education. In her role as Assistant Secretary, she established the Early Reading First program, developed the Early Childhood Educator Professional Development Program and was responsible for all activities in Title I of the Elementary and Secondary Act. Along with Linda Gambrell, she is the incoming editor of *Reading Research Quarterly*, the most prestigious journal in reading research. Her research and teaching interests include early childhood policy, curriculum, and early reading instruction for pre-Kindergarten through Grade 3 children who live in poverty. She has written over 100 articles, and authored and edited 11 books, including the *Handbook of Early Literacy Research* (vols I, II, III) with David Dickinson, *Changing the Odds for Children at Risk* (2009), *Educating the Other America* (2008), and *Multimedia and Literacy Development* (2008).

Helen Nixon is Associate Professor of Education in the Children and Youth Research Centre at Queensland University of Technology in Brisbane, Australia. Her research interests include young people's relationships with place, their meaning-making using new media, and the implications of the changing landscape of communication for literacy curricula and pedagogy. A recent book co-authored with Sue Nichols, Jennifer Rowsell, and Sophia Rainbird is *Resourcing Early Learners: New Networks, New Actors* (2012) published by Routledge.

Kate Pahl is a Reader in Literacies in Education at the University of Sheffield. Her work focuses on literacy in home and community contexts. She has conducted a number of research projects that focus on the nature of home writing practices, drawing on collaborative methodologies. She has increasingly focused on the co-production of research with communities, for example, through her research projects, including *Language as Talisman* funded by the AHRC's Connected Communities program. She is the Deputy Director of the Research Exchange for the Social Sciences at the University of Sheffield, with a focus on community university partnerships. Kate has written widely in the field of arts practice, literacy and language in communities, and ethnography. She is the author of *Literacy and Education: Understanding the New Literacy Studies in the Classroom* (with Jennifer Rowsell, 2nd edn, 2012) as well as *Artifactual Literacies: Every Object Tells a Story* (2010, with Jennifer Rowsell). Kate is the Director of the EdD in Literacy and Language at the University of Sheffield. Her book *The Uses of Literacy Revisited: Materialising Literacies in Communities* is to be published in 2014.

Judy Parr is Professor of Education at the University of Auckland. Within literacy, her particular expertise is in writing, encompassing how writing develops, the cultural tools of written literacy, considerations of instructional issues like teacher knowledge and practice and, in particular, assessment of written language. A major focus of her research concerns school change and improvement in order to ensure effective practice and raise achievement in literacy for under-served students.

Ashley M. Pinkham is a Research Fellow at the University of Michigan. Dr Pinkham completed her doctoral studies in cognitive-developmental psychology at the University of Virginia in 2009. Her research focuses on sources of children's knowledge acquisition and conceptual development, including observational learning, adult–child conversations, and book-reading experiences.

Taffy E. Raphael, PhD, is Professor of Literacy Education at the University of Illinois at Chicago and President of SchoolRise LLC. Her research includes strategy instruction in comprehension and writing, and frameworks for literacy curriculum and instruction (e.g., QAR, Book Club Plus). She directed Partnership READ (2002–2011), a school–university partnership to improve literacy instruction through professional development, recognized by the American Association of Colleges of Teacher Education's 2006 Best Practices Award for Effective Partnerships. She has published several books and over 100 articles and chapters. She received the International Reading Association's Outstanding Teacher Educator in Reading Award in 1997, the 2007 University of Illinois at Urbana-Champaign Distinguished Alumni Award, the 2011 University of North Carolina at Greensboro Distinguished Alumni Award, and the 2008 National Reading Conference Oscar Causey Award for Lifetime Contributions to Literacy Research. She has been a Fellow of the National Council of Research in Language and Literacy since 1996 and member of the Reading Hall of Fame since 2002. She served on the Board of Directors of International Reading Association (2007–2010) and on the Board of Directors (1987–1989), as Treasurer (1989–1992), and as President (1999–2000) of the Literacy Research Association (formerly National Reading Conference).

Iliana Reyes (PhD, UC Berkeley) is an Associate Professor in the Department of Teaching, Learning, and Sociocultural Studies at the University of Arizona. She is also a faculty member in the following programs: Language, Reading and Culture, Early Childhood Education, SLAT (Second Language and Acquisition Teaching), and the Center for Latin American Studies. She is the Director of the Early Childhood LiBRO (Literacy and Biliteracy Resource Office) project, a resource collection that provides undergraduate and graduate students and teachers with updated research materials and early literacy development bilingual books to be used in the classroom with preschool and elementary educators and children. Her research encompasses a range of key issues in the areas of early childhood, early language and literacy development, biliteracy, and, more recently, the Reggio Emilia approach and inquiry in young children. Dr Reyes has also examined family and student engagement with immigrant families and their learning experiences outside the classroom and how these provide opportunities for young children to explore their *100 Languages* (Malaguzzi, 1993) and use these to express their knowledge and theories about their worlds.

Victoria J. Risko is Professor Emerita, Vanderbilt University and the 2011–2012 President of the International Reading Association. She is a former classroom teacher and reading specialist and for years has collaborated with classroom teachers and curriculum specialists to provide literacy instruction that makes a difference for students, especially students who experience reading difficulties. She has taught prospective teachers, and Master's and doctoral students, at Vanderbilt University. Her research focuses on teacher education, reading comprehension and meaningful learning, and uses of cases and multimedia environments to enhance learning, especially the learning of diverse and struggling learners. She has received teaching and research awards and in May 2011 was inducted into the Hall of Fame, International Reading Association. She is co-author of *Declaration of Readers' Rights* (2007, with JoAnn Bass, Sheryl Dasinger, Laurie Elish-Piper, and Mona Matthews); *Collaboration for Diverse Learners* (2001, with Karen Bromley); and *Be that Teacher! Breaking the Cycle for Struggling Readers* (2012, with Doris Walker-Dalhouse).

Celia R. Rosemberg is a researcher at the National Council for Scientific and Technical Research of Argentina (CONICET) and a Professor in the School of Philosophy and Literature at the University of Buenos Aires. She was awarded her PhD in Education from the University of Buenos Aires and specializes in early literacy development. Her work, carried out within a psycholinguistic and socio-cultural framework, aims to study and promote literacy in children living in different socio-cultural contexts.

Lisa Schwartz is a Postdoctoral Research Associate at the University of Colorado, Boulder. She has worked with youth from diverse racial, working-class, and immigrant backgrounds. Currently, she works with Dr Kris Gutiérrez and a team on the Connected Learning Research Network (CLRN). Her dissertation research reflects the accumulation of her experience as a researcher, educator, and designer of digital learning environments. She has presented numerous papers and has journal articles in preparation as well as a chapter in *Time and Space in Literacy Research* (with Nogueron-Liu and González, forthcoming).

Kristy Shackelford is a former elementary school teacher, a mother of two, and a doctoral student at the University of Georgia. She teaches undergraduate courses in early childhood education and helps future teachers perceive themselves as cultural beings who are shaped by – and can shape – social forces constituting privilege and marginalization. Her teaching goals include creating spaces for personal and collective transformations, and helping students see themselves as powerful advocates for themselves as educators, and for traditionally marginalized children and families. Kristy is also a facilitator and researcher for the CLASSroom project, aimed at building class-sensitive pedagogies and ending classism in schools. Her research interests include feminist theory, social class, and children's literature, and the construction of working-class mothers in school-based discourses. Her personal experiences of being a girl living between social classes, a mother, and a teacher working with mothers struggling to make ends meet motivate her to build solidarity among women inside and outside educational institutions.

Margaret Shane is a professional librarian for the Alberta Teachers' Association and a PhD student in the Department of Secondary Education at the University of Alberta. Her current research interests are reading theory, multimodal literacies, semiotics and philosophy in youth and media culture.

Margaret Sheehy is an Associate Professor in the Reading Department at University at Albany – State University of New York. Her current work concentrates on classroom literacy practices with a real interest in the various ways teachers and students build disciplinary content knowledge together. To that end, she has been teaching a supplemental instruction course (supplemental to social studies and language arts courses in general education classrooms) in an urban high school, working with young people who do not do well in school but have an interest in achievement nonetheless. She will continue piloting this course for the next several years and publish when she feels she can make a contribution to disciplinary learning. She remains interested in and informed by spatial theories and geography. Margi Sheehy's most recent significant publication is a book based largely on David Harvey's and Henri Lefebvre's ideas about space, *Place Stories: Time Space and Literacy in Two Classrooms* (2010).

Gerry Shiel is a Research Fellow at the Educational Research Centre, St Patrick's College, Dublin. He currently works on national and international studies, including the OECD Programme for International Student Assessment (PISA), and on test development. He also teaches courses on reading literacy as part of the MEd Programme at St Patrick's College. His research interests include the assessment of literacy and teacher professional development. Recent publications include *Reading Literacy in PISA 2009: A Guide for Teachers* (with Rachel Perkins, Gráinne Moran, and Jude Cosgrove, 2011) and *Oral Language in Early Childhood and Primary Education: Children 3–8 Years* (with Áine Cregan, Anne McGough, and Peter Archer, 2012). Gerry is currently Chair of the Federation of European Literacy Associations (FELA) and is a member of the Implementation Group for Ireland's National Literacy and Numeracy Strategy 2011–2020.

Sandra Soto-Santiago is a doctoral student in the Department of Teaching, Learning, and Sociocultural Studies, College of Education, The University of Arizona. Her research interests include qualitative research methods, teaching English as a second language, migration and education, and transnationalism and education. Her dissertation addresses the return migration of Puerto Rican youths from the US to the island, part of the transnational flow of this population, and the consequences for educational policy and practices.

Alejandra Stein received a PhD in Language from the National University of Córdoba (Argentina). She specializes in early and family literacy. She has obtained a doctoral and a postdoctoral scholarship from the CONICET (National Council of Scientific Research of Argentina). She currently teaches at the University of Buenos Aires, Argentina.

Pat Thomson PSM PhD is Professor of Education in the School of Education, the University of Nottingham, Director of the Centre for Advanced Studies in the faculties of Arts, Humanities, and Social Sciences, Director of the Centre for Research in Schools and Communities, and editor of the *Educational Action Research Journal*. She was for 20 years a Head teacher of disadvantaged schools in South Australia. She remains committed to thinking about how schools can change to become more engaging and inclusive; her research mainly focuses on the arts and creativity in school and community change. Her most recent publications include *Writing for Peer Reviewed Journals: Strategies for Getting Published* (with Barbara Kamler, 2012); *The Routledge International Handbook of Creative Learning* (edited with Julian Sefton Green, Ken Jones, and Liora Bresler, 2011); and *Changing Schools: Alternative Ways to Make a World Of Difference* (with Terry Wrigley and Bob Lingard, 2011).

Christopher S. Walsh is a Senior Lecturer at the Open University. He has researched primary and secondary teacher education with specializations in literacy, new technologies, multimodality, and international development. His research investigates the ways in which English and literacy education might benefit from examining digital games to improve the teaching of print and multimodal forms of literacy. He is also currently involved in large-scale teacher professional development programs in Bangladesh and India where the projects are using mobile phones within a robust program of work-based teacher professional development. Recent co-edited book publications include *Transforming Practice: Critical Issues in Equity, Diversity and Education* (with J. Soler and A. Craft, 2012) and *Equality, Participation and Inclusion: Diverse Perspectives* (with J. Rix, M. Nind, K. Sheehy, and K. Simmons, 2010). He has published widely in the field of literacy, with articles in the *Journal of Research in Reading, Literacy, The Australian Journal of Language and Literacy*, and the *Journal of Adult and Adolescent Literacy*. He also edits the international peer-reviewed journal *Digital Culture & Education (DCE)*.

Catherine M. Weber, PhD, is an Assistant Professor in the Mary Lou Fulton Teachers College at Arizona State University. She is a former elementary teacher and literacy coach who has spent the majority of her career working with diverse learners in high-poverty urban settings. She served as the Assistant Director of Partnership READ at the University of Illinois at Chicago. In this role, she supported teachers, curriculum leaders, and administrators to develop the skills necessary to create and sustain whole-school literacy improvements. She has presented to teacher and researcher audiences at national and international conferences. She is a member of the Literacy Research Association, American Educational Research Association, Arizona Reading Association, and the International Reading Association. Dr Weber's research interests include teacher education and professional development, urban school reform, and teacher's conceptions of literacy and how those conceptions influence curriculum and pedagogy.

Leisy T. Wyman is an Associate Professor in the Language, Reading, and Culture program and affiliate faculty member in American Indian Studies and Second Language Acquisition and Teaching at the University of Arizona. As a teacher-researcher and linguistic anthropologist of education, she has collaborated with Yup'ik adults and youth on books of Yup'ik elders' narratives. Additional works include the book *Youth Culture, Language Endangerment and Linguistic Survivance* (2012), a theme issue on Indigenous youth language for the *Journal of Language, Identity and Education* (with McCarty, 2009), and a book in progress on Indigenous youth language in North America (edited with McCarty and Nicholas).

Dylan Yamada-Rice is Lecturer in Early Childhood Education at the University of Sheffield. Her research interests are concerned with early childhood literacy, multimodal communication practices, and visual and multimodal research methods. Dylan is in the final stages of a PhD funded by the Economic and Social Research Council (ESRC) that focuses on young children's interaction with, and comprehension of, the visual mode as one aspect of contemporary multimodality. Her previous research has explored children's access to digital technologies that foreground the visual mode and has examined the way in which family members support engagement with digital technologies using the visual mode in the urban landscapes of Tokyo and London. Previously, she worked and studied for more than a decade in Japan; first, in the faculty of Japanese Art History at Kyoto University and then as an Assistant Director of an international preschool in Tokyo. Her previous postgraduate work was awarded the United Kingdom Literacy Association (UKLA) Postgraduate Research Award (2010). Dylan has published a number of journal articles and book chapters.

List of Reviewers

Peter Afflerbach, Albany State University of New York
Dorit Aram, Tel Aviv University
Richard Beach, University of Minnesota
Eve Bearne, formerly University of Cambridge
Cathy Burnett, Sheffield Hallam University
Jon Carpentieri, Institute of Education, London
Michelle Commeryas, University of Georgia
Teresa Cremin, the Open University
Alicia Curtin, University College, Cork
Julia Davies, University of Sheffield
Clare Dowdall, University of Plymouth
Joel Dworin, University of Texas, El Paso
Marie Emmitt, Australian Catholic University, Melbourne
Cyndi Giorgis, University of Nevada, Las Vegas
Yetta Goodman, University of Arizona
Margaret Grigorenko, Cedarville University, Ohio
Carmel Hinchion, University of Limerick
Jim Hoffman, Texas University
Hilary Janks, University of the Witwatersrand, Johannesburg
Ken Jones, Goldsmiths, University of London
Barbara Kamler, Deakin University, Melbourne and University of Sydney
Marjorie Kinsella, University College, Cork
Susan Lutz Klauda, University of Maryland
Kristiina Kumpulainen, CICERO Learning, University of Helsinki
Mairtin Mac an Ghaill, Newman University College, Birmingham
Mary Macken-Horarik, University of New England, Armidale, Australia

Carmen Martínez-Roldán, Teachers College, Colombia University

Dixie D. Massey, University of Washington

Diane Mavers, Institute of Education, London

Jenny McDougall, Central Queensland University

Marilyn McKinney, University of Nevada

Guy Merchant, Sheffield Hallam University

Suzanne Mol, Leiden University

Kath Murdoch, University of Melbourne

Debra Myhill, University of Exeter

George Newell, Ohio State University

Helen Nixon, Queensland University of Technology, Australia

Marjorie Orellana, University of California

Kate Pahl, Sheffield University

David Parker, Director of Research and Impact, Creativity, Culture and Education, UK

Laavanya Parthasarathi, Trinity College, Dublin

Jo-Anne Reid, Charles Sturt University, Victoria, Australia

Mary Roe, Arizona State University

Rebecca Rogers, University of Missouri-St. Louis

Sylvia Rojas-Drummond, Universidad Nacional Autónoma de México

Deborah Rowe, Peabody College, Vanderbilt University

Jennifer Rowsell, Brock University

Robert Rueda, University of Southern California

Vanessa Rutherford, University College, Cork

Vivienne Smith, Strathclyde University

Margaret Somerville, University of Western Sydney

Morag Styles, Cambridge University

Pat Thomson, University of Nottingham

Vivian Vasquez, American University, Washington DC

Eva Vass, University of Bath

Christopher Walsh, the Open University

Linda Wold, Loyola University, Chicago

David Wray, Warwick University

Foreword

This handbook engages in an expansive conversation about consequential literacy learning and the forms of educational change needed to create equitable, sustainable, and robust learning ecologies. This volume is about all youth but, in particular, it is about youth from nondominant and vulnerable communities across the world – youth who must negotiate the additional set of developmental demands of poverty, of politics and policies gone awry, as well as of institutions, both social and formal, that persist in the social creation and organization of inequality.

Collectively, the chapters provide situated accounts of activity systems, tools, and practices that give and index meaning for humans. In this context, the editors and authors elaborate the ways language and a range of semiotic means mediate human activity and, in doing so, advance more expansive views of language and literacy learning, particularly new understandings of human neurobiological development and the affordances of new media.

Consistent with the orientation of many of the authors, I bring a cultural historical lens to my discussion of what I believe are the key contributions of this handbook. Although explicit discussions of learning in general are largely underspecified in this volume, with notable exceptions of the Heath, the Reyes and Esteban-Guitart, and the Littleton and Mercer chapters, for example, I would like to argue for an expanded view of learning as the organization of possible futures – one that requires a more interventionist stance to remediate the current conditions in which nondominant youth learn and appropriate multiple literacies in particular. As Freebody and colleagues remind us (this volume), programs of research, accountability frameworks, and the ways teachers are prepared have contributed, even if indirectly, to sustained inequality. As they note, the processes by which material, socio-economic, linguistic, and cultural differences continue to be silently but systematically converted into educational disadvantage amplify and consolidate inequalities in life trajectories.

Conceiving of learning as the development of new trajectories is fundamental to designing new possibilities, to remediate extant, and often reductive, understandings of students' linguistic repertoires of practice, their construction, both locally and historically, and their possibilities in processes of learning. In my own work (Gutiérrez, 2011), this involves employing a social scientific, historicizing inquiry that privileges the interpretation of learning situations across a minimum of two interacting activity systems, while foregrounding social practices, dynamic notions of culture, and human agency and trajectories toward transformative ends. This human science of learning aims to understand how to make life dignified for all human beings (O'Connor and Penuel, 2010).

From this perspective, I would like to draw some parallels with other current work to underscore and extend salient ideas across these chapters, as well as put forward some ideas that I believe need further examination and theorization in our field. Across the various discussions of literacies in a variety of communities, particularly multiliteracies and new media practices, is a view of literacy learning as being socially, culturally, and historically organized – one in which language and other semiotic means play central mediating roles.

In line with the view of colleagues in this volume, youths' literacy practices are understood to develop in particular social and located relationships. Pahl and Burnett, in particular, provide a richly situated view of new literacies, emphasizing the importance of examining contextualized multimodal literacy practices across a minimum of two activity systems, for example, home and community literacies, to develop more robust and useful theorizations of youths' literacy repertoires and the multiple literacies in which they engage. This work is aligned with other work in the Learning Sciences and New Media Studies that acknowledges the movement of people and tools across practices, noting that such movement is not linear, straightforward, or unproblematic. New research on Connected Learning funded by the MacArthur Foundation (Connected Learning Research Network, 2013) seeks to advance an approach to learning that leverages youths' repertoires toward consequential learning and productive pathways that have resonance for youths' life trajectories. In particular, a suite of designed studies examine how new media can support the development and sustainability of ecologies that support connected learning organized around robust and equitable ends. In this work, we employ an iterative model to develop, design, and assess new theories of connected learning.[1] One Connected Learning study examines children's new media practices across an after-school technology mediated change laboratory and their homes to document what new tools and practices 'travel' and what tools and practices are leveraged across spaces of use and meaning.[2]

The spatial turn in studies of literacy learning and in the learning sciences more broadly emphasizes how attending to space and place is important to understanding the situated nature of people's meaning-making and related practices (see Gilmore and Wyman; Sheehy; and Mills and Comber in this volume). Sheehy's human geography perspective, in particular, helps us understand that boundaries are both stable and permeable, allowing us to account for the ways in which youth leverage resources that 'flow in and out of their schools' (p. 409). This view is critical to understanding what processes, means, and tools open up and restrict boundaries. This spatial turn, then, challenges notions of practices as bounded and impermeable to shifts and change, directing us to follow 'cultural flows' (Hall, 2004, p. 109) and what takes hold, shifts, and is redesigned in that movement as people and practices travel across time and cultural spaces (Gutiérrez *et al.*, 2010).

In the context of migration, diaspora, and other forms of transnational and intercultural movement, studying and designing for possibility demands methodological tools fit for capturing the inherent complexity and creativity of human development. The mutual constitution of local and transnational literacy practices becomes salient in producing principled, respectful, and nuanced accounts of youths' literacy repertoires (Gutiérrez, Bien, and Selland, 2011). Pahl and Burnett capture this sensibility as they describe the important and diverse ways in which youth experience and navigate communities, as well as the dynamic flow of literacies 'within and across different locations' (p. 3, this volume). Here it might be instructive to imagine Edward Soja (2010) in this conversation, as he would probably remind us that space and place are different yet related. In particular, he would remind us that space is constitutive of and constitutes literacy practices at an ontological level. From this perspective, we must be mindful that separating the two analytically can lead to misunderstanding spatial practices.

In this regard, employing a spatial analysis within an activity theoretical approach would be helpful in illuminating the ways in which children's literacy practices are dynamically constituted across multiple activity systems – analysis that would, I believe, yield more expansive understandings of children's language and literacy practices. From this theoretical perspective, Shirin Vossoughi and I (Vossoughi and Gutiérrez, forthcoming) have proposed the methodological importance of multisited sensibilities informed by understandings of 'learning as movement' (Gutiérrez, 2008). Drawing from both single-sited and multisited traditions, a 'multisited sensibility' in ethnographic research on literacy learning includes identifying and employing the ways of looking, hearing, seeing, and knowing developed by humanist-oriented scholars and educational ethnographers that are needed to move beyond the hierarchies and limitations of the classic ethnographic template; traditional forms of ethnography that are not attuned to notions of both place-based learning and the importance of documenting the construction of youths' repertoires in hybrid and multimodal practices.

As noted in other work (Gutiérrez and Arzubiaga, 2012), one of the enduring criticisms of past anthropological work on communities is that it has not accounted sufficiently for the dynamic constitution of communities or the ongoing movement and flow occurring especially in communities experiencing migration and transmigration. The increased interest in studying the effects of rapid globalization, immigration, diasporic communities, and cultural communities in general, makes rethinking the ways we theorize and study communities compelling issues to address. However, we need to push on learning theories to help us better understand 'learning as movement.'

The privilege of working for decades with students from migrant farmworker backgrounds has made evident to me a significant lacuna in the Learning Sciences. Migrant students' accounts of their movement across borders, across familiar, new, and reorganized and hybridized practices, and their learning trajectories, call attention to underaddressed and unresolved questions in the Learning Sciences: How do we account for the learning and development embodied within and across the movement, the border and boundary crossing of students who migrate to and throughout the United States? What new capacities and identities are developed in this movement? To what extent do these capacities and identities travel and shift across settings? What new tools and dispositions emerge as resources in new and hybridized practices? How do we account for the repertoires of practice developed across time and space – locally and historically? What new educational arrangements provoke and support new capacities that extend students' repertoires of practice? (Gutiérrez, 2008, p. 150)

Of relevance to literacy learning, the focus of this volume, this view shifts our analytical focus from deficit explanations about individuals' capacities and practices to seek richer understandings of individuals' histories of involvement with literacy, that is, their repertoires of practice (Gutiérrez and Rogoff, 2003). In a multiliteracies context, the focus is on situating literacy practices, while also accounting for their historical influences, both proximal and distal.

Such approaches, as the authors in this volume note, are critical in capturing, understanding, and leveraging youths' repertoires toward new social futures. The growing disconnect between the interests and everyday practices of our nation's youth and formal schooling's approaches to engaging them in rigorous, meaningful, and relevant learning make new understandings of literacy learning more relevant. Of concern, there are social and cognitive, as well as personal, institutional, and economic, consequences to disconnected learning. Today's youth move across a range of contexts and produce artifacts that reflect the intercultural, hybrid, and multimodal discourses and practices of which they are part. These repertoires developed across the ecologies of interest and everyday life should be cultivated as an important dimension to learning.

As Kalantzis and Cope (2012) have elaborated, there are a variety of approaches to literacy: didactic, authentic, functional, and critical literacies but, as they argue, we must rethink these singular categories to understanding the deployment of literacy pedagogies in the plural.

From this perspective, literacy approaches that foster cross-fertilization of discourses and cross-cultural hybridity have significant affordances in promoting and valuing diversity (Kalantzis and Cope, 2011). For these multiliteracy scholars, navigating contemporary social spaces requires the application of not just one set of rules for meaning-making (literacy in the singular), but the negotiation of different literacies depending on the people and contexts encountered. There are, in other words, many literacies, and these vary according to cultural context, social purpose, life experience, personal interest, knowledge base, and so on. The key is not learning how to communicate in the one, right, way but how to negotiate these differences in meaning (Kalantzis and Cope, 2011, p. 1).

Here I take the opportunity to engage further in notions of navigation advanced in this volume and elsewhere to raise questions about whether such notions reflect or capture more expansive processes of learning and identity work – processes that have particular consequences for members of nondominant communities. I find Kalantzis and Cope's work instructive to this discussion. Navigation, they argue, necessarily involves navigating the plural, the multiliteracies that privilege the multiplicity of semiotic systems found across diverse cultural contexts and practices. In this way, each meaning exchange is a cross-cultural accomplishment. New technologies have made diversity and a multiplicity of semiotic systems and their affordances across more diverse cultural locations more salient (Janks, 1993).

Diversity is also a resource for the accomplishment of powerful literacies (Hamilton, 2012), or what I term socio-critical literacies, and serves as an organizing principle for the design of transformative ecologies and practices. In my own work (Gutiérrez, 2008), socio-critical literacies are historicizing literacies oriented toward critical social thought, the realization of the self as a socio-historical actor, and the development of a collective vision of new futures. From a decolonial perspective, this realization involves movement or world-traveling (Lugones, 2009) necessary for the survival and agency for women of color, for example, and/or shifting modes of ideologies (Cruz, 2012, pers. comm.; Sandoval, 2000). However, unlike notions of navigating, for women, particularly women of color, the concept of world-traveling is more forceful and nuanced, characteristics that remain unclear or absent in majoritarian views of navigation.

Here, I emphasize how such perspectives also must be theorized from the standpoint of nondominant and vulnerable communities to address the diversity in the processes of traveling across and within groups. Consider the construct of navigating from the perspective of women of color, for example, who at times are forced to 'travel' – to move across spaces – unwillingly, as acts of resistance, or for coalition building. At the same time, members of dominant communities can world-travel and remain tourists or voyeurs, without having to see themselves from the position of the nondominant or to travel as the nondominant. Of relevance here, traveling is inherently cross-cultural, as it involves movement toward the other, toward a plural self.

These processes are inherently hybrid; hybridity, however, is neither static nor telos. Hybridity involves the plural, anchored in and constructed in the borders, where hybridization occurs; hybridity, then, is a place maker. In these spaces and places, for example, bodies of the nondominant become animated, as these are the sites of the production of *mestizaje* and *caló* (Anzaldúa, 1987), where new languages, indeed hybrid languages, can emerge out of the gaze or surveillance, and control of dominant language ideologies. Hybrid practices, including hybrid language practices like *mestizaje*, are material realities. The discourses of third spaces are material and should not be understood as productions of the nondominant or the dominant, or its hybridity as the mixing of pure types. From this perspective, we must ask: Are not *caló* and other subaltern languages – languages constructed in third space/borderlands – reflections of creativity, of possibilities? It follows, then, that we would want to push on considerations of *mestizaje* and hybrid artifacts, for example, as dualisms, from considerations of hybridity as binary, as being in two worlds, as such social constructions result in notions of the hyphenated being in which assimilation is privileged. There is no hybridity in the hyphenated language, or in the hyphenated self.

Hybridity, from these perspectives, is not the property of nondominant communities, their practices, and their discourses, or the mixing of pure types, as such views normalize dominant group practices and discourses. Instead, it's 'hybridity all the way down,' as Renato Rosaldo describes, 'on the one hand, hybridity can imply a space betwixt and between two zones of purity in a manner that follows biological usage that distinguishes two discreet species and the hybrid pseudo species that results from their combination. . . . On the other hand, hybridity can be understood as the ongoing condition of all human cultures, which contain no zones of purity because they undergo continuous processes of transculturation (two-way borrowing and lending between cultures). Instead of hybridity versus purity, it is hybridity all the way down' (Rosaldo, 1995, p. xv, as cited in Cole, 2000).

In a talk honoring the contributions of Jerome Bruner, Michael Cole's (2000) elaborated discussion of hybridity and its misunderstanding is relevant here: 'it might be tempting to argue that the new, hybrid educational practices that we see springing up around us can easily be incorporated into the notion of hybridity as the mixing of pure types. However, as recent decades of research on classroom organization and culture have demonstrated, the "pure types" that competing theorists hurl at each other like epithets are themselves always made up of a variety of more local cultural practices. Moreover, the hybrids currently being produced cannot properly be considered "pseudo species." Rather, they, like the earliest mammals, are a new species of educational practice, eking out their existence in an environment dominated by educational practices that can be appropriately termed, dinosaurs. Perhaps, from their current humble beginnings, such fragile new species will come to dominate the educational world.'

In the same vein, one does not 'stay' in hybridity. Hybrid practices give rise to new practices and new spaces – third spaces, if you will. From this perspective, third spaces – collective zones of proximal development – are generative sites where people can organize, gather energy, develop new tools and practices, and engage in political strategy (Gutiérrez, 2008). These are particularly consequential spaces for youth from nondominant communities. Third spaces are sites of contradiction, possibility, ingenuity, and for the organization of new futures. In terms of literacy learning, following Vygotsky's notion of concept-formation, we can document in third spaces a reorganization – a movement, if you will – of everyday concepts *and* scientific or school-based concepts, a reorganization of everyday *and* school-based literacies (Vygotsky, 1978). From an activity theoretical view, this process necessarily involves a two-dimensional formation of negotiation and hybridization. So we might ask, do current notions of navigation accommodate this understanding of knowledge and identity formation in third spaces and its hybrid practices and tools?

This generative view of third spaces and hybrid designs underscores the dynamic nature of cultural practices and should help us develop static notions of cultural processes. Moreover, seeing hybrid spaces, third spaces, and cultural spaces in general as static, devoid of cultural processes, belies their possibilities as sites of ingenuity and creativity (McDermott and Raley, 2011). This kind of misunderstanding of cultural processes and artifacts is, I believe, what Moll and colleagues see as a core issue in their chapter. The concept of the 'funds of knowledge' is often misunderstood as inert knowledge rather than networks of productive exchange and knowledge production. Moll, Soto-Santiago, and Schwartz address this problematic in their chapter by illustrating how the borderlands themselves are dynamic spaces in which new forms of knowledge and practices are created. Using cases of transnational/return migration, the authors document how changes in immigration laws and the introduction of new media tools into these hybrid and dynamic contexts have both necessitated, as well as generated, new networks for the flow and appropriation of funds of knowledge needed for families' 'survival and advancement.' Following Moll and colleagues, dynamic notions of cultural processes and practices orient us to the stable and improvisational nature of cultural practices and to attend to the regularity and variance in communities' and members' literacies.

I hope the ideas I have advanced underscore the intent of this volume and its authors. I believe that, taken as a whole, the contributions argue the importance of designing for connected and consequential learning and the development of a new imagination about what kinds of tools and practices provide the context and supports for new forms of learning and new possibilities for today's youth. Undergirded by socio-cultural and *proleptic* views of learning – that is, learning organized for possible futures – the collective goal of this handbook is to engage youth in expansive forms of literacy activity in which peer, youth, and community cultures and their literacies are valued, leveraged, and extended.

Kris D. Gutiérrez
Inaugural Provost's Chair,
Professor of Learning Sciences and Literacy
University of Colorado, Boulder and
Professor Emerita, Social Research Methodology
University of California, Los Angeles

Notes

1. The Connected Learning Research Network, funded by the MacArthur Foundation, includes PI Mimi Ito, and CO-PIs Kris Gutiérrez, Sonia Livingstone, Bill Penuel, Jeanne Rhodes, Katie Salen, Juliet Schor, Julian Sefton-Green, and Craig Watkins.
2. This study involves PI Gutiérrez, Project Coordinator and Research Director, Lisa Schwartz, and a team of graduate students.

References

Anzaldúa, G. (1987) *Borderlands/La Frontera: The New Mestiza*. San Francisco, CA: Aunt Lute Books.
Cole, M. (2000) Bruner and hybridity. Paper presented at the Symposium Honoring Jerome Bruner. Annual Meeting of the American Anthropological Association. San Francisco, November 17, accessed November 23, 2012: http://lchc.ucsd.edu/People/MCole/brunerapa.html
Connected Learning Research Network (2012) accessed November 23, 2012: http://clrn.dmlhub.net/
Gutiérrez, K. (2008) Developing a Sociocritical literacy in the third space. *Reading Research Quarterly*, 43(2): 148–164.
Gutiérrez, K. (2011) AERA Presidential Address. Annual Meeting of the American Education Research Association Meeting, New Orleans, LA. April 10.
Gutiérrez, K., and Arzubiaga, A. (2012) An ecological and activity theoretic approach to understanding diasporic and non–dominant communities. In W. Tate (ed.) *Research on Schools, Neighborhood, and Communities*. New York: Rowman and Littlefield Publishers, Inc, pp. 203–216.
Gutiérrez, K., Bien, A., and Selland, M. (2011) Polylingual and polycultural learning ecologies: Mediating emergent academic literacies for dual language learners, *Journal of Early Childhood Literacy*, 11(2): 232–261.
Gutiérrez, K., Bien, A., Selland, M., and Pierce, D. (2010) Syncretic approaches to studying movement and hybridity in literacy practices. In D. Lapp and D. Fisher (eds) *Handbook of Research on Teaching the English Language Arts*, 3rd edn. New York: Routledge, pp. 415–419.

Gutiérrez, K., and Rogoff, B. (2003) Cultural ways of learning: Individual traits or repertoires of practice. *Educational Researcher*, 32(5): 19–25.

Hall, K. (2004) The ethnography of imagined communities: The cultural production of Sikh ethnicity in Britain. *The Annals of the American Academy of Political and Social Science*, 595(1): 108–120.

Hamilton, M. (2012) *Literacy and the Politics of Representation*. New York: Routledge.

Ito, M., Gutiérrez, K., Livingstone, S., Penuel, *et al.* (2013) *Connected Learning: An Agenda for Research and Design*. Irvine, CA: The Digital Media and Learning Research Hub Reports on Connected Learning.

Janks, H. (1993) *Language, Identity and Power*. Critical Language Awareness Series. Johannesburg: Hodder and Stoughton and Wits University Press.

Kalantzis, M., and Cope, B. (2011) *The Powers of Literacy: A Genre Approach to Teaching Writing*. London: Routledge.

Kalantzis, M., and Cope, B. (2012) *Literacies*. Cambridge: Cambridge University Press.

Lugones, M. (2009) Playfulness, 'world'–traveling, and loving perception. *Hypatia*, 2(2): 3–19.

McDermott, R., and Raley, J. (2011) Looking closely: Toward a natural history of human ingenuity. In E. Margolis and Luc Pawels (eds) *The Sage Handbook of Visual Research Methods*. Los Angeles: Sage, pp. 372–391.

O'Connor, K., and Penuel, W.R. (2010) Introduction: Principles of a human sciences approach to research on learning. In W.R. Penuel, K. O'Connor and National Society for Studies in Education (eds) *Learning Research as a Human Science*. New York: Teachers College Press, pp. 1–16.

Sandoval, C. (2000) *Methodology of the Oppressed*. Minneapolis: University of Minnesota Press.

Soja, E. (2010) *Seeking Spatial Justice*. Minneapolis: University of Minnesota Press.

Vossoughi, S., and Gutiérrez, K. (forthcoming) Toward a multi-sited ethnographic sensibility. In J. Vadeboncoeur (ed.) *National Society for Studies in Education Yearbook*. New York: Teachers College Press.

Vygotsky, L.S. (1978) *Mind in Society: The Development of Higher Psychological Processes*, eds and trans. M. Cole, V. John-Steiner, S. Scribner, and E. Souberman. Cambridge, MA: Harvard University Press.

Editors' Introduction

Literacy, Learning, and Culture

Kathy Hall, Teresa Cremin, Barbara Comber, and Luis C. Moll

We come together as editors to prepare an introduction to this international volume at a time of economic turbulence, new uncertainties about the future, and a growing demand on the part of most governments for further alignment of education with the economy. Literacy, in particular, is in the vanguard, for literacy only too frequently is positioned as a proxy for education. What are the purposes of literacy teaching and how is it to be achieved? What counts as literacy in 'new times,' in 'participatory culture' where people 'believe their contributions matter, and feel some degree of social connection with one another' (Abrams and Merchant, Chapter 23)? How can everyone be included as critical citizens of the world in whatever definition of literacy we endorse?

What fresh perspectives, new ways of thinking, and good ideas for the understanding of literacy are out there? What are the possibilities for the future? An exploration of these kinds of questions and their answers, however tentative, provides us, we believe, with our best defense against the uncertainties of our age. In some respects this is our overall purpose in the volume, to explore our understanding and future possibilities by bringing together critical reviews of the major theories, methods, and pedagogical advances that have taken place in the past 20 years in the field of literacy research at the primary/elementary school level. Each chapter in the volume is newly written for the Handbook while overall the book is intended to be a distillation of key thinking and theory which offers new directions for research in literacy. It aims to revisit current interpretations, make novel connections, frame new possibilities, and encourage researchers to pursue innovative and compelling lines of inquiry.

It is our view that the volume represents broadly the major lines of research inquiry on literacy. The structure and diverse authorship of the Handbook offers a wide range of perspectives on curricula and pedagogies as well as research insights into family and community literacies and teacher development and identities.

The book is organized into three interconnected parts, each of which is devoted to a major aspect of literacy education research, namely:

Part I Society, culture, and community
Part II School, culture, and pedagogy
Part III Teachers, culture, and identity

Part I brings together an interdisciplinary and international group of scholars to address issues of language and literacy learning as situated in and constitutive of multiple and diverse human activities. The authors, although far from monolithic, favor a socio-cultural framing of language and literacy practices, with a predilection for studying these practices in the actual, living, or concrete conditions of life, whether located in homes, classrooms, or digitally, in some sort of 'in-between' context. These authors also offer, as a central aspect of their scholarship, ideas for producing or leveraging cultural resources for positive changes in educational practice. These two aspects, attention to place, whether material or digital, especially given the situated nature of language and literacy learning, and a concern with delivering findings and insights that matter in practice, are intricately related and generally define the chapters in this section and in this volume. Mills and Comber (Chapter 30) state it well: 'Literacy research that ignores place may become abstract, disembodied, and decontextualized from local and global geographies, with their affordances and constraints for meaningful social action.'

The chapters featured in Part I explore a variety of issues, offering a broad view of human action as mediated by language, literacy, and other symbols systems. Hence the authors emphasize, in diverse ways, the variation of textual mediation in different kinds of activities, in or out of school, and whether such activities encourage, or not, the learning by adults or children of essential cultural resources for living. As Mackey and Shane (this volume) observe, a consequence of the 'the new fluidities of contemporary literacies,' is that 'the making of *textual* meaning has steadily become a more elaborate enterprise for young learners, who must absorb how to orchestrate an increasing variety of information channels.' As such, the authors explore in various ways the idea that human beings not only live *with* language but also *in* language, and in multiple other semiotic modes as well, as we exist in the constant and changing flow of our social interactions. In brief, we learn, as Vygotsky proposed long ago, that human beings create themselves through the mediation of social relations, tools or artifacts, emotionally-loaded lived experiences, and diverse socio-cultural contexts for living, all of which represent affordances and also constraints for learning and development. As Curtin and Hall (Chapter 9) write, the learning of language and literacy is always positioned 'within social, emotional, and cultural spheres,' and these help constitute both who we are and who we could be as human beings. However, this ecological perspective must also include the dynamic relation between brain and culture. These authors suggest, as does Heath in Chapter 14, that one cannot understand human development without also understanding neurobiological development. That people are inextricably biological and cultural historical must be axiomatic, whether one is studying 'mirror neurons' or language, literacy, and culture.

Pahl and Burnett's opening chapter proposes an ecological, interdisciplinary approach to study the 'multisitedness' of literacy and explore issues of the fluidity and hybridity of such spaces. This intersectional emphasis responds to unitary notions of the social circumstances of literacy, where domains of activity, such as home and school, are viewed and studied as separate literacy sites, rather than interconnected sites for study and action. As the authors explain, 'the *textual* dimension evoked through the words and images we encounter in texts and the *connected* dimensions generated as networked technologies link people, places, and texts rather than seeing these as separate spaces.' The chapter provides examples and discussion of literacy practices in relation to place, space, and time, taking into account multimodal uses of text, and addressing material and socio-cultural aspects of diverse ways with literacy that span both home and community settings.

Chapter 2 by Mackey and Shane also addresses issues of multimodal literacies and the 'new fluidities' of current literacies. The goal is to 'explore issues of mutating literacy possibilities and the kinds of critical scaffolding that benefit children who are growing up in this rapidly transforming landscape.' Given this diversity of multimodal options, the authors advocate developing a critical stance regarding the ideological and commercial manipulation of these options. After all, they assert, children's engagement with multimodal formats starts very early, and most likely precedes their engagement with print literacy. They concentrate on wealthy Western children, a sample that provides a view of the 'most intriguing' new literacies, such as using games and video content stored on their parents' mobile phones, or ready access to heavily marketed websites, gadgets, and toys that purport to enhance the child intellectually, that may also provide new insights into the class-based digital divide. In this complex context, they assert, where corporate priorities and framing of texts and advantages for children are common and forceful, parents may be at a loss as to how to provide critical guidance or understanding for their children, regardless of their class status.

Nixon and Hateley's chapter addresses the theme of play, especially what they call playing to learn. Young children in many parts of the world are now growing up in a digitalized play world, requiring a range of skills and understandings different from previous generations. The authors note that this is a rapidly changing ecology of play, a broad and fluid scene, where there is a tight relation between markets for books, toys, and digital media specially designed for children's play which all the while reassure parents that they are investing in their children's intellectual development. This is all highly commercialized, where appeals to parents to prepare their children for the future by buying these toys for learning are persuasive and children are increasingly viewed as 'consuming citizens' in this massive market. Although literacy learning is still critical in developing informed citizens, 'researchers committed to learning from and contributing to young people's agency and social opportunities need to pay attention to what is happening culturally when reading and playing and literacy and learning means tapping, touching, swiping, and scrolling and combining online and offline activities.'

Green and Beavis call for a reconceptualization of literacy education to account for 'new media,' featuring novel forms and practices 'that are being picked up by many young people, both children and adolescents, in such a way and to such a degree as to become their primary *modus operandi*, and key markers and makers of identity.' These are fundamentally new literacies or forms of semiosis, digitally mediated practices for making meaning in life, whose vitality must find its way into school settings for them to remain relevant to the students they teach. The challenge, then, is whether schooling in general, and literacy education in particular, is up to the task of educating the young who are immersed in a new media and information culture – whether it is congruent with the new media age and culture. The authors suggest that the time is ripe for a new formulation of what counts as literacy which considers the rapidly changing forms of textuality and technology, and determines what it might mean for schooling in this new century.

Thomson and Clifton report on a successful strategy, which features a school–university collaboration, to help a school create tighter bonds with its local community. At the heart of the strategy is identifying the community's needs while honoring local literacies and knowledge in the process, all with the goal of helping teachers define the children, families, and neighborhood as assets for instruction. This approach represents a direct challenge to narrow policy-directed approaches beholden to equally narrow outcome measures. It brings a humanizing, creative orientation to teaching and learning, connecting schooling to life by fostering the participation of 'institutions such as churches and social and sporting clubs and people with reservoirs of life/work knowledge and know-how, networks, experiences and literacies.' The strategy not only provides new opportunities for parent and student engagement, but for teacher involvement in motivating intellectual work, such as learning about real people in real circumstances, directly relevant to their goals as teaching professionals.

The connection between communities and schools is also the topic of the chapter by Rosemberg, Stein, and Alam, who summarize a novel and intricate research project conducted in both indigenous communities and marginalized urban areas in Argentina. At the heart of their work is the production of what they call 'ethnographic reading books.' As they describe them, these are texts for children inspired by the lives, stories, and activities within their communities. The characters and the details of the story emerge from their observations in the communities and interactions with local participants, both adults and children. A key aspect of these books is that they are 'bidialectical'; the narrator utilizes the standard dialect, in this instance Spanish, but the book's characters use their particular community's linguistic variation in their dialogue. The goal is for the children to find themselves in the written story, its illustrations, and its particular ways with language. As they explain it, 'knowledge of the local physical, social, and spiritual world is juxtaposed with scientific knowledge and school curriculum. This allows children to learn conventional scholastic information and scientific thinking skills, while also giving greater importance to local society and culture.'

Compton-Lilly discusses the importance of considering time, or temporality, in any analysis of social context, particularly in relation to literacy learning and schooling. This conceptualization of 'time as context,' as she writes, is a neglected or often merely implicit dimension of analysis, although it highlights the developmental aspects of the phenomena under study. In particular, temporality informs the formation of particular subjectivities in relation to engagement with social practices, that themselves change over time. In other analyses, it may clarify the 'significance of living during particular historical times, the social ties that temporally link lives, and the historically constructed mechanisms of socialization that surround and define people's experiences.' Time is a critical unit of study for any approach that seeks to understand the trajectories of literacy development and their relation to changing social situations for living or for going to school. It is what situates development in its historical context.

Carrington and Dowdall's chapter investigates the relation between media culture, which represents important contexts for early literacy development, and children's use of material artifacts in their creation of lifespaces for exploring ideas and developing creative practices. The chapter builds on an exploratory 'object ethnography,' in this instance of the well-known LEGO® blocks, and the use of these objects by two boys who 'construct spaceships, boats, houses, vehicles, and a range of other items.' The goal of the analysis is 'to situate artifacts and engagements with them in broader cultural, economic, and political narratives.' The use of such everyday artifacts, combined with broader media discourses, in a sense, spotlight how using the objects mediates creating or participating in fiction adventures through the media outlets. These objects embody the values of the designers, but children can actively redefine such objects to assemble their own practices and purposes as part of the creative process.

In their chapter Curtin and Hall elaborate on one of the principles of socio-cultural psychology, the intimate and reciprocal connection between brain and culture, in what they call the 'neurocultural network of learning.' As they put it, 'mind and body are inextricably linked through neural, cultural, and social networks.' As an example, they discuss the relationship between social interactions and what are known as 'mirror neurons.' These are those neurons that activate when a person performs an act or observes someone else performing the act. The latter point is the key to interest in this neuronal function. Because these neurons 'fire' based on similar actions by others, it is thus said that they 'mirror' those actions. The idea is that these neurons play an important role in helping understand the actions of others or in imitating others, both critical aspects for developing social relations or 'intersubjectivity' in life, although this is controversial. In other words, these neurons have a social base, and also provide a neurological structure for social actions. Hence the plasticity of the brain 'mirrors' the plasticity of learning in social life. The purpose of addressing this dynamic relation is to draw implications for literacy research and pedagogy. For example, their summary suggests that literacy provides a 'portable context,' one could say, for communication but also for mediating awareness or recognition of self and for facilitating a shared consciousness with others.

Gilmore and Wyman draw on their extensive involvement with language- and literacy-related issues with native communities in Alaska to provide what they call 'an ethnographic long-look,' a combined longitudinal assessment of their respective work spanning over three decades. Alaska natives, as their indigenous counterparts elsewhere, have been the object of long-standing policies of forced assimilation, in this case by the US state and federal government, with the goal of stripping them of their languages and cultural lifestyles; as the authors recount, it has been a political strategy of coercion, abuse, and domestication of native groups. These policies, however, have met with considerable and coordinated opposition, movements for self-determination, especially around establishing tribal sovereignty in offering forms of schooling that respond to, rather than disregard or condemn, native ways and languages. Their chapter, then, is about resistance and change, not about demise. Through the authors' combined retelling, they 'illustrate how people in the Alaska Native communities … have developed literacy practices in response to historically rooted language uses, ideologies, and circulating authoritative discourses as they also rapidly reshaped channels of communication to support unique ways of life, knowledge systems and, in many cases, endangered languages in new Indigenous networks and spaces.'

Li addresses the educational situation of Asian English language learners in the United States. Asians are now the largest immigrant group in the country, surpassing Hispanics. However, the label Asian (as does the label Hispanic) subsumes several groups with distinct and varied cultural experiences and languages, including within-group differences. With the interplay between culture and Asian ELL literacy learning in mind, Li advocates for an ambitious program of 'cultural translation' that would benefit teachers by informing and engaging them in critical practices that account for the diversity of Asian students, while also reflecting on the details of a sound pedagogy that is culturally informed. As she writes, Asian ELL students 'constitute different cultural codes, histories, languages, memories, and community narratives that are often gendered, classed, and raced.' As it is with other groups, diversity is the norm for Asians as well, regardless of popular perceptions about them as stellar or model students, who need little social or academic support.

Reyes and Esteban-Guitart offer a cross-national and cross-cultural overview of how children develop multiple literacies, especially in home and community settings, and the role of family members, teachers, and peers. Drawing on their work in the US southwest (Reyes) and in Catalonia, Spain (Esteban-Guitart), and from their knowledge of additional work in other locations, they also describe the literacy experiences of new generations of children from immigrant families in different parts of the world, and how they draw from the knowledge that they and their families bring from their ancestral homeland when they interact in their new host communities. In these communities, characterized by the presence of more than one language, and by multiple domains of activity, the development of biliteracy, or even multiple literacies, may be taken as a common cultural expression, usually involving various social practices and funds of knowledge as resources for learning and development; 'biliteracy and multiple literacies are here taken as the "normal" practice when communities learn how to effectively translate these "resources" into tools for children and their families to exchange knowledge and values. It is a move from a singular to multiple pathways to literacy.'

Moll, Soto-Santiago, and Schwartz discuss the 'funds of knowledge' approach, developed originally in the US southwest, as a way of documenting the lived experiences and production of knowledge by, mostly, working-class Latino families. Central to this approach is the participation of teachers as co-researchers, with the goal of developing curricular practices, especially around the teaching of literacy, that connect classroom activities to family funds of knowledge as a way of making lessons meaningful for the students. This chapter concentrates on how rapidly changing community conditions, especially those that threaten family stability and livelihood, compel researchers to address not only the existence of resources but also how households innovate to address their vulnerabilities. It draws on two case examples to illustrate the 'translocal' responses by youth from immigrant families to the changing and threatening political conditions that have altered their realities and those of their families. In one case the student is attempting the extraordinary feat of finishing her secondary schooling in both Mexico and the United States, knowing that the US government's anti-immigration policies have curtailed her opportunities for higher education. In the second case example, the student, whose parents have been deported, uses digital modalities and networks to seek and document the transnational experiences of other students similarly situated and to understand the consequences of such experiences for identity formation among youth. Both examples illustrate the need to consider how children and youth produce their own funds of knowledge that may be independent from the adults in the family.

Concerned with the diminished opportunities for play, Shirley Brice Heath starts her chapter with a historical overview of the changing nature of play, up to the opening of the twenty-first century, as found in the social organization of family life within what she calls 'mainstream households of modern economies.' She also points out the increasing limitations on play in schooling practices, especially during the early years, a restriction that coincides with the neoliberal emphasis on accountability and testing in education, which has closed the spaces for play within the curriculum. The subsequent sections concentrate on analyzing the cognitive consequences of the 'hand of play,' reminding us that the hand is not only an investigator and manipulator of the environment, but also a primary tool of representation in various forms of play. As she writes, 'Children who use their hands as they play undertake perception, action, and cognition simultaneously when they create representations. Cognition becomes grounded as young children engage in motor-dependent production of visual representations of what they are thinking, imagining, and planning.' In particular, she emphasizes the relation of socio-dramatic forms of play, with their diverse expressions of emotions and perspectives, to brain development, showing that every lived experience contributes to the shaping of neuronal networks, and thus to the plasticity of the brain and the flexibility of our thinking.

Part II: School, culture, and pedagogy, addresses literacy in schools and classrooms. It ranges widely in terms of focus and topic, attending to different language modes, digital literacies, children's literature, creativity, literacy and curriculum, and hybrid literacies. It attends to relatively new theoretical perspectives such as space and place pedagogies, critical race theory, and emotional investments linked to gender and class. It also ranges widely methodologically, incorporating narrative and systematic review of a relevant field, conceptual and framing studies, empirical case material, and longitudinal work.

The focus of an empirical review chapter by Neuman, Pinkham, and Kaefer stems from their concern about a drop in achievement that occurs for many children around the age of nine and which tends to grow steeper as they move into higher grades. This phenomenon they attribute to limitations in the word and world knowledge in early literacy and they review studies that explain the gap with reference to socio-economic status. Their analysis leads them to conclude that schools and teachers can address this gap through systematic and explicit attention to relevant word and world knowledge but that this should happen in the early childhood years that are seen as crucial to acquiring the foundational skills necessary for lifelong reading achievement. What is clear from their chapter is that economically poorer children, compared with their better-off peers, depend disproportionately on their teachers to provide them with the experiential and linguistic resources necessary to benefit from their schooling.

Extending this analysis in a more critical vein is the review chapter by Jesson, Parr, and McNaughton which challenges schools to consider the kind of experiences offered to learners in the writing classroom and the extent to which the lessons and tasks available align sufficiently with learners' lived experiences outside school. Drawing explicitly on socio-cultural perspectives, these authors highlight the significance of learners' intertextual histories as vital resources for their developing competence as writers. The evidence reviewed in their chapter points to the fact that without an understanding of the array of literacy knowledge that their learners may have, teachers may not recognize their learners' resources that are then denied as sources of cultural and instructional bridging. In drawing on such histories learners have permission to borrow from texts they encounter in a diverse range of contexts. Such a dialogic approach links writing with reading and promotes a critical literacy where texts are compared, contrasted, and critiqued, and where teachers 'revoice' children's knowledge by renaming it as a resource that has authority in school.

Complementing the chapter on writing is the multidisciplinary review by Ellis and Coddington of research on engagement in reading. This chapter examines definitions and measures of reading engagement in the existing literature and shows how this is a complex construct requiring pedagogies and interventions that are tailored, nuanced, and integrated into the range of school activities for learners. The evidence reviewed is compelling in relation to the need for intrinsic motivation, choice, collaborative tasks, a culture of risk-taking, and yet also requires determination and persistence. Of major significance in the studies reviewed is the theme of mastery over performance such that learners need to understand that the point of reading is to enhance one's life, not to 'show off' in class or please the teacher. In this regard, the authors signal the danger of the current (almost global) orientation toward skill-based, narrow, and technicist literacy curriculum and assessment policies and practices that potentially compromise the development of reading engagement as conceptualized here.

The language arts or literacy classroom without children's literature would be unimaginable but how is the role of children's literature understood in policy and practice? In their review of research on this topic, Arizpe, Farrell, and McAdam show how theory, practice, and research have shifted the perspective on its role from a 'treat' to a resource that aids in the exploration of the self, others, and knowledge of the world, and more recently to a core cultural artifact that can enable transformative practice. That children's literature is now part of a multimedia world through the integration of art and aesthetics, visual literacy, and multimodality more generally, adds to its power and role. On the practice front, their review shows how the metaphors of mirror, window, and door capture the reason why literacy educators value literature as central to their practice. As a mirror, children's literature offers new representations and understandings of the self; as a window, it offers alternative and possible worlds that learners can compare with what they see in the mirror, thus allowing for questioning of their own value system; and, as a door, children's literature offers the potential for reframing, recasting, and repositioning the reader as an active citizen of the world. Not for the first time in this volume, authors fear the orientation toward skills and the testing of narrow elements of literacy and how this utilitarian orientation challenges the potential that children's literature has for education.

In different ways the next four chapters focus on language as a mediator and resource for living and learning, and more specifically for creativity, peer relationships, improvisation, and identity performing. In different ways they draw on a range of disciplines, from anthropological to literary studies, and from childhood to neo-Vygotskian studies, all the while foregrounding the learner, the classroom, and the role of the teacher and curriculum.

First is 'Writing in Childhood Cultures' by Dyson and Dewayani. Challenging dominant models of writing pedagogy, it proffers a conceptual framework for composing as a mediator of childhood cultures as they emerge in school settings. Dyson's own considerable corpus of work is revisited here along with other studies to formulate the authors' conceptual framework based on three aspects: children's appropriation of cultural texts from their everyday lives, the textual processes through which literacy practices form and contribute to social relations and childhood practices, and, interconnections between childhood practices and writing in official classroom cultures. The chapter's premise is not that the unofficial world of childhood should somehow replace the official one of school culture but rather that the unofficial world should be recognized and the interplay between both be examined, researched, and more fully appreciated. That literacy, and composing more particularly, can afford playful, enriching, and pleasurable encounters with peers is central to the world that the various characters in the studies surveyed here are figuring, and the analysis is clear and compelling.

Second in this group of four is a thematic review by Cremin and Maybin on children's and teachers' creativity in and through language, a chapter that pays tribute to the work of Anne Haas Dyson and indeed that of Neil Mercer, the latter co-authoring the next chapter in this group. Creativity here is taken as process, not necessarily a creative product, and as such our attention is focused on themes like play and playfulness, spontaneity and innovation, narrative and collaboration, improvisation and the language of possibility ('what if' language), while a helpful distinction is drawn between creativity *in* and *through* language. This is an under-researched area and these authors identify several new directions that are ripe for further exploration and research. What is especially exciting and promising about their treatment of creativity is its lifelong nature in and through language such that teachers too are an important focus of research in relation to their creativity with language in the classroom.

Littleton and Mercer, in the next chapter, revisit the much-researched area of social interaction and classroom talk for learning. Their focus is primarily, though not exclusively, their own research and its antecedent base. Therefore the settings that are the subject of those studies are mainly classrooms in England. Dialogic teaching, exploratory talk, and educational dialogue are all defined, explored, and exemplified while their own 'thinking together' intervention program and its evaluation are also described with several suggestions offered for further socio-cultural research geared to investigating situationally sensitive accounts of productive educational dialogues.

Staying with the theme of language as a crucial mediator of learning, Freebody, Chan, and Barton pose a key question that forms the basis of their chapter: 'how are students' literacy resources worked up, worked on, put to work day to day – across the school years and across the curriculum areas?' As the question implies, their focus is how the literacy–curriculum relationship is carried out as opposed to how it ought to be carried out and their chapter incorporates fine-grained analysis of classroom interaction. These authors distinguish between two kinds of literacy demands facing students in school. One demand is the more obvious 'traditional' aspects, the other is the literacy demands of each curriculum domain and it is the latter that exercises the authors in their chapter. Echoing some of the points noted in the chapter by Neuman *et al.*, these authors challenge us to consider the 'pedagogical silences,' especially in the early/primary/elementary phases of education where too often literacy and curriculum are separated into distinct areas of study. Arising from their review, the authors identify specific areas meriting further investigation, not least of which is how each domain knowledge is represented in practice, how each uses communicational and knowledge-accessing technologies, and the implications for how to be a successful learner is those various domains.

Almost all the chapters in this international volume refer to multimedia, new technologies, and digital literacies in some way. However, the next three chapters in this part deal with digital technologies explicitly.

The first, entitled 'The Digital Challenge', by Schamroth Abrams and Merchant, is based on a systematic review of empirical literature published over an 11-year period (2000–2011) and bears on the integration of technology into the curriculum for 5–13 year olds. The title elegantly captures its thesis: that technology education continues to be considered through a traditional lens and much theoretical and empirical work remains to be done to evaluate the effective use of technology in the classroom. Their synthesis of the evidence points to a dearth of research on how educators are using digital resources in elementary and middle-school classrooms and a surprising lack of research on the use of mobile technologies for the age range studied. The authors report on the increasing recognition in classroom practice of how literacies are evolving as a result of digital communication, which is especially evident in how texts are produced and distributed. The authors go on to highlight the promises and challenges of technology for classrooms, noting in particular the need for far more studies, especially longitudinal studies, of practice.

In a narrative review of empirical work, Levy, Yamada-Rice, and Marsh identify three aspects as the focus of a more in-depth exploration: the use of Web 2.0 applications, film and television, and computer games in primary classrooms. Drawing primarily on European and Australian-based literature, they conclude that there is in evidence a range of good practice enabling young learners to become confident users and creators of digital texts. From their analysis a key challenge is assessment, since there are few models of progression in relation to the analysis and creation of multimodal texts that are available to teachers for describing their learners and for identifying next steps in a learning trajectory. The nature of feedback, dialogue, planning, and progression are all aspects that would appear to merit considerably more investigation.

The third in this trio on digital literacies is about developing online reading comprehension. Here Dwyer explores how online literacies impact on the development of learners' online reading comprehension and information-seeking skills and strategies. She begins by explaining what online text comprehension demands of the reader and what is required of the teacher in terms of effective pedagogies. For the learner the challenges include: planning and setting goals for online information searchers, generating search terms and investigating search results, and, locating, evaluating, and communicating online information. For the teacher, the 'digital divide' means that scaffolding Internet reading with struggling readers requires considerable pedagogic skill and this theme is explored through a case study analysis of the author's own research in a high-poverty setting.

The final group of chapters in this section overtly address, in various ways, the political contexts within which literacy teaching and learning occur, in tackling issues concerning race, class, gender, and location. Each of these chapters seeks to expand our conceptual tools for thinking about the politics of teaching and learning in culturally diverse classrooms.

Moje revisits ground-breaking work on 'hybridity' to examine what this metaphor allows us to understand and what it obscures. She suggests an alternative term, 'navigating,' as a more accurate description of the work people do to make sense and represent meaning in complex and changing contexts. She explains that navigation is an active process, requiring conscious strategy and tactics, and as such fosters a more dynamic and situated account of the ways literate identities are constituted and one that incorporates agency, rather than hybridity, which has a tendency to be seen as an unchanging state. Because 'hybridity' has been associated mainly with explaining the practices of marginalized groups, the concept loses some explanatory power and traditional binaries such as 'everyday' and 'academic' literacies remain dominant and unquestioned. Importantly she asks what it might take to teach and to research such navigation of literate practices and identities. Researchers clearly need to study the literate practices of groups and individuals across time and in different social and material contexts, recognizing the negotiation of literate identities as contingent and involving power relations.

Writing from the changing landscape of Irish education where multicultural and multiracial classrooms are recent phenomena, Kitching also explores the political aspects of navigating particular literacy worlds. While acknowledging the usefulness of 'funds of knowledge' and 'culturally responsive teaching' as productive frames for designing literacy pedagogies, his chapter puts issues of race center stage. Drawing on Critical Race Theory and Whiteness Studies, he conceptualizes literate identities as constituted by repertoires of cultural practices which incorporate, usually unspoken, racial practices. Like Moje he emphasizes that literacy lessons call for the embodied and situated performance of identity, whether that be in the context of a book discussion or simply getting the class to attend to the task at hand. Referring to an observation of an English class comprising a multiracial student population, he demonstrates the ways in which a group of white working-class boys and their white teacher dominate the discussion of a novel where different versions of spoken English are portrayed. Not only do the white boys dominate but they find unobtrusive ways of making racial slurs in the course of the discussion. Kitching calls on literacy scholars to consider the embodied nature of everyday practices in constructing unequal relations of power.

Jones and Shackelford also report their search for alternative interpretive resources for explaining how gender and class are implicated in constituting literate identities. Informed by feminist poststructuralist analyses they note that the emotional dimensions of literacy are frequently ignored. Like Kitching and Moje they explicitly contest the neutrality of literacy. Instead they focus on the psychosocial gains and losses associated with particular textual practices, in this case the portrayal by working-class girls of their relationships with their mothers. They argue that such texts should be read 'testimonially,' that is, underpinned by an understanding of specific ways of life and conditions whereby poor mothers are characterized by their daughters as strong, working, and powerful. Whereas dominant educational discourses often position working-class mothers in terms of deficit, these girls told of mothers who managed, led, worked, cared, and exercised power. Jones and Shackelford are able to provide such an account as they witnessed the emotional investments in the textual practices of a group of girls over an extended period of time in different educational contexts, an example of the kind of research called for by Moje.

Sheehy poses the question: 'What does human geography have to do with classrooms?' She explains that literacy research is enjoying a 'spatial turn' that stresses that classroom relationships are not only social, but also political and spatial. Context matters, but we need more complex understandings of contexts that foreground the resources available to different people in different places. Sheehy goes on to illuminate the macro processes that impact on school literacy practices, such as educational policy trends toward national standards and high-stakes testing. Importantly Sheehy demonstrates that such policies have uneven local effects and that inequitable educational opportunities can result for schools located in different places and serving different communities, in ways that relate to class and race, thereby reproducing the educational inequalities such policies purport to address. In terms of literacy practices this can result in an emphasis on decoding and direct instruction for poor students of color and self-selected literature discussions for more affluent student communities. The problem is that such choices can have long-term effects where educational trajectories are closed off for students who have been assigned to special or low track classes. Sheehy argues that a focus on place can help us discover which educational mechanisms make or sustain inequitable and divisive boundaries and those which are permeable. Further, she stresses that at this time literacy studies need research that explores migration and movement and teachers need to map how they and their students are positioned. Such spatial analytical processes are fundamental to educators' and students' agency.

Mills and Comber also note the spatial turn in literacy studies, arguing that it represents a rebalancing of the semiotic with the materiality of lived, embodied, and situated experience. Marginalization is often accomplished spatially; being seated at a desk near the teacher, going to a room for indigenous students, books for the special class on particular shelves in the library – material positionings that signal embodied relations of inclusion and exclusion. While

Mills and Comber demonstrate that the micropolitics of classroom interactions are integrally connected with space, place can also be seen as a rich resource for literacy learning and identity work. They review a number of studies incorporating place-based pedagogies where students were able to engage in critical literacy practices – design, research, and action – in and on local environments. As they make clear, stories of place are contested and it is in that multiplicity and contradiction that spaces are created for new learning. Networked technologies in the global communications environment allow for the production of new spaces for social and literate encounters, signaling the need for researchers to consider new relationships between text users, objects, and material as well as virtual spaces. In addition, they point out, there are new approaches for undertaking spatial analysis that allow literacy researchers to work differently with different kinds of data and look for different relationships.

In **Part III**, Teachers, culture, and identity, the lens turns from pedagogies of schooling toward pedagogies employed in the context of pre-service education and continuous professional development. Teachers' knowledge, beliefs, values, and literate identities are foregrounded and cutting-edge research on professionals' conceptions of literacy, literacy histories, cultural practices, and classroom experience is presented. Additionally, the ways in which these are made manifest in learning contexts and tasks in the classroom are considered. Many of the authors also note the significant influence of external factors such as high stakes assessment and prescribed curricula, which serve to compromise professional practice, not only creating contradictions between teachers' reported beliefs and their practices but also creating mixed messages about what counts as literacy. Other inconsistencies, contradictions, and dilemmas are also considered in relation to whole-school professional learning communities, professional development, and teacher research. Yet individually and collectively, the authors in this section, through their empirical and conceptual work and wide-ranging reviews of the field, demonstrate that despite the challenges of the past, novel and productive directions for the future exist, both for research and practice.

As Hathaway and Risko from the United States note, research into pre-service teachers' knowledge development and their associated beliefs represents a challenge, in part because researchers' conceptualizations of the dual constructs of knowledge and literacy-learning beliefs differ; some perceive them as distinct, others as intertwined. In recognizing the inherent complexity in this field and the potentially reciprocal nature of the teacher learning process, the authors consider some of the tools used to research teachers' beliefs, and after due consideration of these argue that 'it is imperative that teacher educators help pre-service teachers make their beliefs explicit.' In exploring ways forward they examine instruction and demonstrations that can foster knowing and believing, consider supportive learning conditions, and detail various methods and strategies that create dissonance in order to enable pre-service teachers to confront and even disrupt their beliefs and understandings.

Cambourne and Kiggins examine the drivers behind the persistent pressure to reform the way teachers are prepared to teach. In the process they highlight concerns about coherence, the perceived lack of relevance of the theoretical components in education programs, and the need to change traditional construals of 'knowledge,' 'knowing,' 'teaching,' and 'learning.' They draw parallels with the insistent calls for reform in the field of literacy education, 'a similarly contested field of inquiry' that they acknowledge is also 'characterized by a long history of acrimonious debate about so-called "best pedagogies of teaching reading and writing."' In reflecting on the longstanding epistemological debate around the kinds of knowledge and skills needed for teaching literacy, Cambourne and Kiggins offer examples from their Australian context of the ways in which (with a small proportion of a pre-service cohort) they sought to engage students in continual cycles of collegial construction and reconstruction of professional meanings, in part through the use of multiple symbol systems. In asserting that the professional learning culture that they created was 'significantly different from the traditional culture of university teaching and learning' they offer new ways forward for teacher education.

The focus on pre-service teachers' own engagement as literate individuals is developed further by Gennrich and Janks who show how the shifting nature of both literacy and contemporary curricula tend to disrupt teachers' 'pedagogic habitus,' though as they observe, such disruption may be embraced or resisted. In examining whether teachers need to be models of reading and writing, they note that the debate appears to ignore the demands of the curriculum, the fact that students bring different dispositions to literacy and different out-of-school literacy practices into the classroom. They also note that it fails to pay sufficient attention to contemporary literacy practices enabled by new technologies and the nature and form of literacy teachers' engagement in digital literacies. Using examples from South Africa, Gennrich and Janks explore the relationship between curriculum, policy, and teacher identity, and show how teacher education can intervene effectively in the development of literacy teachers. As in the previous chapters the innovative approach described and empirical work undertaken by these authors affords new insights both for researchers engaged in exploring the construction and enactment of pre-service teachers' literate identities, and for teachers and teacher educators who seek to extend their 'students' horizons of possibility and prowess,' particularly in response to their technological competence.

Weber and Raphael also attend to the challenge of teaching twenty-first century learners and the literacy identity shifts that may be required on the part of the profession at this time. Significantly however, these US authors widen the discussion to include an examination of the construction of collective identity within whole-school professional learning communities and present a professional development model for sustainable school change. In reasserting that 'teacher knowledge about changing societal demands is central to preparing students for full participation' as well as enabling them to contribute to public, community, and economic life, they detail the myriad of skills and tools students need to navigate new demands successfully, and examine the consequences for teachers' own knowledge, beliefs, and identities as literacy professionals. Through reviewing research on teacher change and development, they contend that 'successful models for professional development honor teachers' individual literacy identities, build on their strengths, and capitalize on the collective expertise of a professional learning community to make rigorous, sustainable change school-wide.' Additionally, they offer research-based principles that they argue are critical to creating and maintaining improvements in literacy teaching and learning, and describe professional development that attends to both individual growth and growth of collective identities.

Kennedy and Shiel from Ireland also foreground professional learning communities and examine the field in order to identify those forms of professional development that work most effectively to close the gap in literacy achievement. Critiquing courses and workshops in particular, they also evaluate literacy coaching, teacher research, and professional development undertaken for accreditation or qualification. In highlighting the value of collaborative inquiry, the authors note that 'outsiders can help schools evolve into professional learning communities by providing scaffolding as teachers adopt an "inquiry stance" to identifying the strengths and weaknesses of the school's literacy framework.' They also recommend embedding demonstrations and nonevaluative observations into educators' professional learning journeys and argue that early success and time for support, reflection, and evaluation is essential. Overall their review, which encompasses examination of a number of recent empirical studies in the area, suggests that in relation to bridging the gap, development work needs to be embedded in a school context and 'customized, collaborative, inquiry-based, grounded in content and pedagogical content strategies,' and with full attention paid to ongoing analysis of student data.

In the final chapter Walsh and Kamler, working in the UK and Australia respectively, consider the affordances of teacher research that links inquiry to democracy, social justice, and educational change. Deploying the metaphor of teachers 'turning around' to students, they review the history of teacher research, examine some of the consequences of such professional repositioning, and highlight studies in which students too become researchers of language and discourse, asserting that in this way both groups may 'gain proficiency in critical research methods,' and are better positioned to 'challenge authoritarian, racist, and gendered discourses encountered in school, media texts and their lived experience.' While recognizing the tensions and dilemmas involved in teacher and student research, their review, which also includes attention to research that 'turns around' to technology, identifies new directions and gaps in the field. In essence, Walsh and Kamler argue that in the light of the changing face of literacy, fostering a researchful disposition in both pre-service and professional development is critical, not only to challenge deficit assumptions about children's literacy, but in order for the profession to progress. Such a disposition, they assert, has the potential to foster educational change and offer an enriched social justice agenda for all.

The Handbook as a whole adopts the view that communication among scholars on the interrelated areas of literacy education documented will likewise enhance the potential for educational change, in part through generating intellectual energy, debate, and exploration of the application of research insights in diverse contexts. While it is common to think of a Handbook as an 'object,' its power is in its generative momentum, its ability to recreate interpretations, launch new directions, and encourage people to pursue innovative and compelling lines of inquiry. In the end it is this that may afford the book its capacity to move the field forward.

Part I
Society, Culture, and Community

Chapter 1
Literacies in Homes and Communities

Kate Pahl and Cathy Burnett

Introduction

This chapter explores how inter-disciplinary approaches support an understanding of new perspectives in relation to children and young people's literacy practices in homes and communities. In particular it explores the significance of the 'spatial turn' in new literacies research and explores new perspectives drawing on material cultural studies. Conceptualizing home and community literacies involves entering the social spaces of the home. It also involves studying the various places that children inhabit such as faith settings, youth clubs, libraries – and schools. Such work is important in highlighting the varied and multiple literacies in which children engage. At the same time there is a need to problematize bounded or unitary conceptions of 'home' or 'community.' Communities may be fluid or transitory or experienced in different ways by different children and literacies may move within and across different locations. All this is complicated further by the varied ways in which local and global spaces intersect (Massey, 2005). Children grow up in a place and this structures their literacy practices (Comber, 2010; Mackey, 2010). However, their practices are patterned by texts and artifacts that originate in other times and places (Robinson and Turnball, 2004). They also engage with virtual spaces (Marsh, 2010, 2011; Wohlwend, 2010) that are both local and global. Time moreover has a part to play in the way literacy practices are experienced in home and community contexts (Compton-Lilly, 2010). Literacies are also multilingual (Kenner, 2004) and multimodal (Kress, 1997) with a variety of scripts and representations that challenge conventional concepts of what 'counts' as literacy. All this challenges unitary notions of the situatedness of literacy and suggests that we need to see literacy as multisited.

In this chapter, we argue that we need an interdisciplinary framework to investigate this multisitedness and explore the fluidity and hybridity of spaces for literacy. We begin by mapping the field of new literacies in homes and communities, and locate the disciplines that inform this field. We then focus on the way in which 'context' as a way into understanding literacy in homes and communities is conceptualized and describe methodologies that look at context. We focus on the concept of 'situated literacies' (Barton, Hamilton, and Ivanic, 2000), as well as the crossing of literacy practices across home, school, and communities. Next, we

International Handbook of Research on Children's Literacy, Learning, and Culture, First Edition.
Edited by Kathy Hall, Teresa Cremin, Barbara Comber, and Luis C. Moll.
© 2013 John Wiley & Sons, Ltd. Published 2013 by John Wiley & Sons, Ltd.

explore how perspectives from different fields – linked to multimodality, material culture, and cultural geography – can contribute to an understanding of spaces for literacy. We conclude by signaling new directions in the field and suggesting some methodological directions to aid our insights. In particular we signal the importance of ecological approaches to literacy research (Nichols, Nixon, and Rowsell, 2009). We argue for an approach that combines a focus on spatial justice with a new literacies perspective that accounts for the diversity of literacy practices (Soja, 2010).

Mapping the Field

The field of literacies in homes and communities has been characterized by a number of different, but related strands. The first, and the most established, is the field commonly known as the New Literacy Studies (NLS) (Barton and Hamilton, 1998; Street, 2000). NLS has been characterized by a series of ethnographic studies of home and community literacy and language practices by such scholars as Shirley Brice Heath (Heath, 1983); Brian Street (1984) and David Barton and Mary Hamilton (1998). While NLS has continued to be dominant, it has broadened in scope. For example, recent work on urban literacies, related to specific sites such as Harlem (Kinloch, 2010) and Los Angeles (Morrell, 2008) as well as a focus on rural literacies, for example by Brooke (2003), has shown how literacy practices are shaped by socio-cultural and geographical factors, enabling an understanding of literacy that is, literally, 'from the feet up' (Mackey, 2010).

The second strand is research that opened out the concept of literacy to a broader concept of *communicative practices*. Researchers conducting ethnographic research particularly in home settings were observing a diversity of meaning making practices that included writing, but also speech, drawing, gesture, and model making (e.g., Kenner, 2000; Lancaster 2003; Pahl, 2002). These studies used the framework of *multimodality* to describe the ways in which children quite naturally drew on a variety of modes to make meaning in home settings. Their work was inspired by the work of Gunther Kress, most notably his seminal work *Before Writing: Rethinking the Paths to Literacy* (1997). Equally important in this strand was the highlighting of digital literacy practices together with popular cultural practices in homes and communities, particularly through the work of Jackie Marsh (2005, 2010, 2011) and Anne Haas Dyson (Dyson, 1993a, 2003). Dyson used the concept of 'remix' to describe how children drew on literate practices outside school and mixed them with in-school practices (Dyson, 2003). She used Bahktin's theories of texts as being dialogic, to recognize the intertextual nature of children's textual productions across sites (Dyson, 1993a). Dyson recognized the way in which children's textual productions, despite being composed at school, seep outside into the worlds of home and community.

Finally, a related but broader area in this field emerges from studies of homes and communities from a number of disciplines including anthropology (e.g., Miller, 2008; Pink 2004) sociology (e.g., Hurdley, 2006), cultural studies and English (e.g., Steedman 1982; Willis 2000) and cultural and critical geography (Christiansen and O'Brien, 2003; Soja, 2010). These studies broaden an understanding of material culture, lived experience, cultural identities, and spatial insights to inform research on literacy in homes and communities. While literacy was not the focus of these studies, we consider them to be important in providing a framework for thinking about how children come to make meaning in home and community settings. For example, when investigating the meanings of writing in the home, understanding where writing is situated, that is, in textiles, on walls, and in different material objects, helps broaden and deepen an understanding of writing practices. An edited collection on *The Anthropology of Writing*

(Barton and Papen, 2010) signals the need to describe, using social anthropology, everyday writing and make sense of the textually mediated nature of out-of-school writing practices.

What characterizes all of this research is a focus on literacy practices in relation to place and space, as well as an understanding of time, either through literacy practices as connected to contexts (NLS), or to the use of texts in specific ways (multimodality) or through an understanding of material and historical/socio-cultural practices in space (social anthropology/cultural geography/history). In what follows we consider what each field brings to the study of home and community literacies and then suggest ways that extending this focus on space and place may help us gain new insights.

Conceptualizing Context in Relation to Home and Community Literacies

Thinking about literacy practices in homes and communities requires attention to context. Duranti and Goodwin (1992, p. 4) argue that this process involves focusing on the relationships between the data and the much larger world of which they are a part. Street's (1984) understanding of literacy practices as ideological, that is situated within relations of power, and therefore subject to analysis of their situated-ness, is also vital. School constructs literacy in relation to a set of skills, and sometimes the 'ideological' nature is lost in the detail of schooled literacy practices (Street and Street, 1991).

This perspective highlights how literacy relates to practice, and to identities and discourses in homes and communities. Bourdieu's concept of 'habitus' highlights the concept of lived experience that is handed down over generations (Bourdieu, 1990). The timescales of a family's interaction with literacy practices are important contextually. A study by Pahl (2008) of a Turkish child's meaning making at home showed how the habitus was transformed across generations in the form of texts that were shaped by improvisations and cultural reworking. Bartlett and Holland (2002) describe identity as being about improvisation and fluidity, and highlight how an understanding of narratives and text making can uncover the transformation of the habitus across generations. For example, in a home of British Asian heritage, textiles played a part in the way in which writing was understood. A child was observed producing a piece of embroidery with her sister's name on it. At the same time, her aunt observed in that:

> The textile side of our heritage comes from the women in the family. We have older relatives that do appliqué, crochet, embroidery, sewing and knitting. From the girls' mother's side their grandmother's sister and cousin and from their father side his two cousins who live close by. My younger sister loves craft type of activities and buys the girls a lot of resources to do sewing and fabric work especially on birthdays, Christmas and Eid. (Written text from the girls' aunt, by email, August 2010: Pahl, 2012)

The comment from the girl's aunt situates the embroidery the girl produced within a heritage that merged textiles with culturally rich forms of meaning making.

Gee (1996) has looked at how discourse patterns of children outside school settings significantly differ from those in school settings. His work has been developed, for example, in Rebecca Rogers' study of the Treader Family (2003) and Catherine Compton-Lilly's work on family literacy across generations (Compton-Lilly, 2010; Compton-Lilly and Greene, 2011). These studies have looked at the rich resources within families that have been defined in negative terms by policy makers as being 'at risk.' Both Compton-Lilly and Rogers argue for a more fluid and multiple conceptualization of literacies as multilingual, multiple, and multi-modal to account for the diversity of literacy practices within families (Compton-Lilly, Rogers, and Lewis, 2012).

Research exploring discontinuities between literacies in home/community and school settings has demonstrated how certain literacies are privileged in educational contexts and highlighted the power relations they reflect and sustain (Hope, 2011; Levy, 2011). However, as Hull and Schultz (2002) argue, it is also important to study continuities. This means a different kind of methodology that traces the spaces children inhabit and highlights the 'flows of meaning' (Pahl and Rowsell, 2006, p. 2) that occur as practices, events, and texts across sites.

Considering such flows demands an attention to complex and fluid notions of context. Wohlwend (2009), for example, draws on Scollon's work on geosemiotics (Scollon, 2001) in her analysis of children's play in an early years setting. Highlighting the 'nexus of practices' circulating around this setting, she shows how home literacies may intersect with literacies associated with educational settings as children recruit new literacies to their play. Such work challenges binary distinctions between in/out of school and helps us understand how children's literacies sit within broader 'learning ecologies' (Barron, 2006).

Incorporating an ecological perspective into the study of literacy involves recognizing the 'Ariadne's threads' that extend outwards from texts to practices, while acknowledging the material reality of the text (Brandt and Clinton, 2002). Linking the threads together is partially the task of the ethnographer. These links can be between local and global contexts, or across home and school contexts. By drawing on an ecological understanding of literacy as nested within community contexts (see Neuman and Celano, 2001, 2006; Nichols, Nixon, and Rowsell, 2009) together with an ethnographic understanding of the home and home literacy practices (Pahl, 2002; Gregory, Long, and Volk, 2004) there emerges a complex picture of literacies across home and school, which flow in and out of context. This process is methodologically challenging as it requires an attention to the perspectives of the people within the research (Gregory and Ruby, 2011). Indeed, many of these studies, such as those carried out by Shirley Brice Heath, Brian Street, and Luis Moll, have relied upon ethnographic insights to enable 'emic' ways of conceptualizing literacy practices to be articulated; the 'etic' being the framing by the researcher and the 'emic' being the framing by the participants (Gonzalez, Moll, and Amanti, 2005, Heath and Street, 2008). This creates opportunities to use research tools that are congruent with everyday practices, such as film and photography (Pink, 2001, 2009). For example, in a recent study of literacy practices in a community library, Pahl and Allan (2011) asked the young people in their study about the research methodologies they wanted to use and developed the study with their methodological input.

Multimodality in Relation to Home and Community Literacies

To understand home and community literacies requires a wide-angle lens to 'see' what is there. This incorporates a multimodal perspective. Kress (1997) highlighted how children's meaning making at home drew on the 'stuff' that was to hand, the ensemble of resources that were within homes. Pahl (2002) likewise observed how children created multimodal texts from prayer beads, tissue paper, and small pieces of 'stuff' within the home. Pahl described this process with the expression 'ephemeral literacies.' More recently in a study of writing in the home and in the street, Pahl (2012) found that in households where, for example, there was a strong textile heritage or focus on color and form in gardening, the textual productions of children at home were shaped by these practices. By using the term 'multimodal literacies' to describe these forms (Flewitt, 2008), it becomes possible to include the plethora of communicative practices children engage with outside school.

One of the challenges for the researcher is to 'recognize' these practices. Literacy practices associated with 'school literacy' (Street and Street, 1991) particularly those that are salient in middle-class homes, such as book sharing, alphabetic literacy, and highly resourced craft activities, are easily recognized. However there is also a need for research that traces the less visible 'ephemeral literacies' in homes that are less visible to the eye of school and mainstream media. For example, as described above, a home which draws on Arabic print literacies as well as cultural traditions involving textiles and gardening might not have 'recognizable' literacy practices within it, but will contain rich and meaningful practices that could be translated into school literacy. Gregory and Ruby (2011) have written about the 'faith literacies' that children carry with them from mosques, temples, and other religious sites to home. Rosowsky (2008) has also described the liturgical literacies that can be found within the Mosque settings. Kenner (2004) has identified how these bilingual literacies are multimodal and demonstrated how a broader recognition of home literacies is possible if we recognize the ways in which children draw on multimodal sign systems to make meaning.

A multimodal perspective can be extended to incorporate the digital literacy practices children encounter in homes. Marsh (2005, 2010, 2011) has traced the way in which children's digital literacies online, such as Club Penguin, are associated with dancing to television and using a plethora of digital resources including mobile phones, digital toys, and online games. These practices encompass a variety of multimodal meaning making structures. Likewise Pahl (2005) watched the way in which the experience of playing online games then structures the way children create texts. Graham (2009) has looked at how the process of games playing affects the structuring of narrative texts in school. Popular cultural texts can become resources for meaning making in nursery settings as Wohlwend (2009) described, and can become anchors for play in the home (Pahl, 2005).

Material Cultural Studies Perspectives on Home and Community Literacies

Literacy practices in homes and communities can be understood as materially situated. By this, we mean that these practices are linked to material culture in homes (Miller, 2010; Pink, 2009). Studies have looked at the way in which the ecologies of literacy circulate across spaces but are linked together through textual practices (Neuman and Celano, 2001; Nichols, Nixon, and Rowsell, 2009). Homes are linked to other spaces through, for example, the objects and stories within them that might have travelled from other places (Pahl and Rowsell, 2010). Literacy as an activity can therefore be seen as a social process involving tools and people, which can lead to a variety of inscriptions, or entangled lines that then represent meanings (Ingold, 2007). In considering new literacies in home and community settings we can ask the question, how is writing materialized in everyday settings? In such settings, it is sometimes difficult to separate writing from the context from which it has arisen. Everyday writing can often get lost and can dissolve in the researcher's gaze, so entangled and enmeshed it is in cultural practices in everyday life (Pahl, 2002). In order to illustrate the ways in which literacies are materialized in home settings, what follows is an example from an ethnographic study of 'Writing in the Home and in the Street' (Steadman-Jones, Pahl, and Gould, 2010–2011):

> When I enter a home, in this case, a family of British Asian heritage, in an industrial northern town in the UK, these are the forms of writing I note. I drive my car up a narrow street of Victorian terraced houses, although this particular house I am to visit happens to be detached. I get out of my car, and walk up to the front porch. Over the door to the house, itself a late-Victorian detached house, built about 1901, is the name of the house inscribed in plaster on the outside. This was

written in the early years of the late twentieth century and is fixed, being inscribed in a stone-like substance. As I enter, there are framed, small, inscriptions over the doors, which are written in Arabic, as they relate to sections of the Koran and signify holy words. These inscriptions are also fixed. They were put up when they first came to the house, in December 2010. The family are British Asian Muslims. They therefore see the inscriptions as important to provide holy texts for their home.

I walk into the back of the house, where there is a cosy fireplace, and a computer and two sofas to sit on. The family have three children; one aged two years of age, one of eight and one of twelve, all girls. When I walk in, the things on the floor and on the seating area vary. Sometimes there are toys and small books. There are to be found fragments of script within the toys and artifacts strewn about the floor of the back living room. For example a board book for the youngest was inscribed with Arabic letters. Most recently, I encountered an, 'Etch-a-Sketch' on which the youngest writes. These objects are relatively fluid, in that they move about, and are sometimes visible, and sometimes are tidied away when the youngest is asleep and the mother does the housework. A computer is placed in the corner, on which the older girls do their homework and write stories and emails to me, and the mother sends orders for garden products. This computer is fixed. I can observe some fixed and settled forms of writing (writing on the house, inscription on the framed images, the computer with the sign of the maker) and some less fixed forms of writing including those that are fixed but put away (toy laptop, books, drawing materials) and some that are never permanent (the lines made by the child on her Etch-a-Sketch). [Kate Pahl, May 2011]

Within this space, script is present, but it is not always fixed. It flows throughout the household. Sometimes it is momentarily fixed, as the girls bring in a cloth bag with script embroidered on it, or the family might decide to consult Street View to look at neighboring streets. Stories and colored-in writing are found within the home and presented as examples of script that the girls produce at home. Script is often ephemerally located and flows within family life. These forms of writing are not often recognizable as the writing forms located within schooling. The writing in the home is linked to the epistemologies of those who created it, to the builder who marked the house, to the person who made the Arabic inscription that was then purchased, and displayed like a picture in the home, to the momentary trace of writing by the two year old on the 'Etch-a-Sketch,' to the colored stitches of the eldest as she embroiders her bag. Each of these forms of writing was contained within an epistemological space. The writing is also linked to other spaces – to the sewing club where the bag was written, to the library where the coloring activities took place. Literacy practices are linked across by invisible lines to other spaces and contexts. This provides the ecologies of writing. Some of this writing takes place between contexts or en route to other settings.

Spatial Perspectives in Conceptualizing Home and Community Literacies

This discussion of fluidity, multimodality, and materiality highlights the entangled nature of literacy. Home and community literacies are deeply embedded in social and cultural practices but at the same time, connected in multiple ways to other locations. In this section, we suggest ways forward in researching and conceptualizing this complexity. We argue that a perspective that emphasizes the fluidity and multiplicity of *space* offers rich opportunities for conceptualizing home and community literacies.

Over recent years, a 'spatial turn' in social theory has explored the significance of space to social action, highlighting its reflexive relationship to discourse, identity, and practice. Space has been seen as *socially produced* as practices and experiences are both influenced by and help to define its quality and boundaries (Lefebvre, 1991). This process of ongoing production means that spaces are not fixed. As Lefebvre noted, 'every spatial envelope implies a barrier between inside and out, but this barrier is always relative, and, as in the case of membranes, always permeable' (1991, p. 176). Therefore, although environments may have been designed (whether in contemporary or past times) to reflect certain assumptions, individuals' and groups' experience of such spaces may be more fluid. Massey's tripartite conceptualization of space helps to articulate this fluidity. She argues that space is: 'always under construction,' consists of 'coexisting trajectories,' and is a 'product of inter-relations' (Massey, 2005, p. 9). Massey's work challenges the boundaries of space in terms of time and location. It both highlights the significance of individual pathways and practices and recognizes the significance of broader structural forces. Rather than seeing homes or communities, for example, as defined or separate spaces contained within physical boundaries, we might see them as linked in multiple ways to other locations and relationships, produced through a complex interaction between the practices that enact them and the artifacts, identities, texts, and so forth that go alongside them. From this perspective, different trajectories and differently bounded spaces may open up to allow new kinds of interactions and relationships.

This focus on fluidity is particularly salient when investigating practices involving digital media. Research into digital practices has explored online identities and communities (Turkle, 1995; Thomas, 2007) and has considered how space and place are produced online (Burbules, 2004). Increasingly, however, studies have described the relationships *between* children and young people's activities in physical and virtual environments (Crowe and Bradford, 2006; Davidson, 2009; Marsh, 2010). In response, calls for a 'connective ethnography' recognize these relationships (Hine, 2000; Leander and McKim, 2003). Leander and McKim argue that literacies research should shift from 'identifying sites,' for literacy, to identify 'siting' as a productive process (Leander and McKim, 2003, p. 213). Rather than looking separately at online activity in 'online space,' this prompts us to look at how the online and offline intersect and how social spaces shift as a result of this (Burnett, 2011a).

This perspective, we argue, offers a valuable framework for looking at children's home/ community literacies. This may involve looking at how practices work across different dimensions (Burnett, 2011b), which include the *material* or physical dimension – the artifacts, including texts, buildings, and general 'stuff' associated with literacy practices in different contexts – the *textual* dimension evoked through the words and images we encounter in texts and the *connected* dimensions generated as networked technologies link people, places, and texts rather than seeing these as separate spaces. Exploring how texts, identities, and practices move across and between these dimensions may provide more nuanced notions of situatedness. This then requires a rethinking of literacy practices in homes and communities as the process of production is more about flows and shifts, and less about where a text is produced. Social space becomes both more salient and less fixed.

New Directions in Home and Community Literacies Research

In this review, we have argued for researching literacy practices in homes and communities through a lens that incorporates multimodality, materiality, multilingualism, and a sensory engagement with place and space. The consequence of this lens is a methodological focus on literacy as being meshed within other modalities and other communicative practices (Flewitt, 2008) and an attention to cultural practices in homes. It means paying attention to lost things, travelling, inscriptions, lines and traces, street literacies and oral stories, in short the complex, meshed 'stuff' of everyday cultural life (Ingold, 2007; Miller, 2010). This requires particular methodologies, which incorporate an ethnographic perspective that is situated and collabo-rative, participatory and visual (Lassiter, 2005; Pink, 2009), together with an understanding that methods and their practices construct reality (Law, 2004). This might involve making the familiar strange (Agar 1996; Heath and Street, 2008). An ecological approach to new literacies in homes and communities involves paying attention to sensory and embodied understandings of the world, through material cultural encounters (Ingold, 2007; Pink, 2009; Miller, 2010).

Building on the work cited above, we argue that effective methodologies for researching home and community literacies should incorporate children's epistemologies and recognize the inequalities in homes and communities in relation to access to literacy (Neuman and Celano, 2001) as well as access to digital technologies (Marsh, 2010, 2011). This highlights the significance of the policy background to how literacies in homes and communities are theorized and researched. Our thinking takes us into the realm of social and cultural geographies that map inequalities (Dorling and Thomas, 2011). By tracking the movement of literacy practices across sites, and the circulation of literacies between home, school, and community, research can locate the way certain literacies are privileged over others. Methodologies for doing this kind of research include the ecological methods used by Neuman and Celano (2001) and Nichols, Nixon, and Rowsell (2009) whereby literacy artifacts were located in particular hubs. Their work involved interviewing literacy sponsors or mediators and the focus was on access to literacy in communities. Some of this work includes understanding the nature of commercialized literacy texts (Nixon, 2011). Such work demonstrates how homes are not bounded spaces but networks resourced through other spaces such as libraries (Nichols, 2011). A study of home and community literacies needs to acknowledge the permeability of the home in accessing literacy.

All this has implications for language and literacy in educational settings. We see this in Dyson's ethnographic work exploring children's classroom interactions with, through, and around texts. These show how children may overlay classroom activities with relationships and interactions suited to varied social purposes, associated with both official and unofficial worlds (Dyson, 2008). Dyson demonstrates how children rework and renegotiate school-based activities in the light of their experiences beyond school and their own purposes within it. Home and community literacies become resources for establishing new kinds of meaning in classrooms. As she writes, 'Children are complex social actors in classroom worlds, and these ends influenced their ways of enacting, participating in, literacy events. They drew on diverse sorts of cultural materials as they worked towards varied ends' (Dyson, 1993b, p. 20). For Dyson, the challenge in responding to this complexity is to create a 'permeable curriculum' that recognizes and seeks to capitalize on intersections between teachers' and children's language and literacy experiences. A permeable curriculum would recognize the varied cultural materials children draw on in classrooms and find ways of enabling them to use, reflect upon, and build on these. As Dyson writes,

> Such a curriculum seeks to acknowledge and respect the complexity of children's social worlds and cultural materials. And it attempts not only to create bridges between worlds, but to support children's own naming and manipulating of dynamic relationships between worlds. (1993b, p. 28)

Teachers need to be aware of the 'schema' they bring to an understanding of what literacy is. Further research that gathers together the disparate fields of social anthropology, material cultural studies, New Literacy Studies, multimodality, and cultural geography is required to provide a lens that recognizes and values literacy practices in homes and communities. If literacy involves playing computer games, watching television, making a purse with craft activities and putting stickers on it, creating textiles with writing embroidery on it, or making models that are connected to stories, the process of recognition of those practices is more complex. Since home literacies are often embedded within multilingual scripts, craft activities, computer games, television programs, and oral stories it is important to widen the lens through which to recognize home literacy practices. A multidisciplinary lens is required to do that important work. We argue, in this review, for a bringing together of a lens that challenges contemporary 'tropes' of home literacy practices (for example, book sharing) and widens the scope of the ways in which home literacies are recognized so that this potential can be carried into the wider domains of school, workplace and community.

References

Agar, M. (1996) *The Professional Stranger: An Informal Introduction to Ethnography*, 2nd edn. New York: Academic Press.

Barron, B. (2006) Interest and Self-Sustained Learning as Catalysts of Development: A Learning Ecology Perspective. *Human Development*, 49: 193–224.

Bartlett, L., and Holland, D. (2002) Theorizing the space of literacy practices. *Ways of Knowing*, 2(1): 10–22.

Barton, M., and Hamilton, M. (1998) *Local Literacies: Reading and Writing in One Community*. London: Routledge.

Barton, D., Hamilton, M., and Ivanic, R. (eds) (2000) *Situated Literacies: Reading and Writing in Context*. London: Routledge.

Barton, D., and Papen, U. (eds) (2010) *The Anthropology of Writing*. London: Continuum Press.

Bourdieu, P. (1990) *The Logic of Practice*. Oxford: Blackwell.

Brandt, D., and Clinton, K. (2002) The limits of the local: Expanding perspectives of literacy as a social practice. *Journal of Literacy Research*, 34(3): 337–356.

Brooke, R.E. (ed.) (2003) *Rural Voices: Place-Conscious Education and the Teaching of Writing*. New York: Teachers College Press.

Burbules, N. (2004) Rethinking the virtual. *E-learning*, 1(2): 162–183.

Burnett, C. (2011a) Shifting and multiple spaces in classrooms: An argument for investigating learners' boundary-making around digital networked texts. *Journal of Literacy and Technology*, 12(3): 2–23.

Burnett, C. (2011b) The (Im)materiality of educational space: Interactions between material, connected and textual dimensions of networked technology use in schools. *E-Learning and Digital Media*, 8(3): 214–227.

Christiansen, P., and O'Brien, M. (eds) (2003) *Children in the City: Home, Neighbourhood and Community*. London: Routledge.

Comber, B. (2010) Critical literacies in place: Teachers who work for just and sustainable communities. In J. Lavia and M. Moore (eds) *Cross-Cultural Perspectives in Policy and Practice: Decolonizing Community Contexts*. London: Routledge, pp. 46–57.

Compton-Lilly, C. (2010) Considering time: In the field of family literacy and in the lives of families. In K. Dunsmore and D. Fisher (eds) *Bringing Literacy Home*. Newark, DE: International Reading Association, pp. 306–331.

Compton-Lilly, C., and Greene, S. (eds) (2011) *Bedtime Stories and Book Reports: Connecting Parent Involvement and Family Literacy*. New York: Teachers College Press.

Compton-Lilly, C., Rogers, R., and Lewis, T.Y. (2012) Analyzing epistemological considerations related to diversity: An Integrative critical literature review of family literacy scholarship. *Reading Research Quarterly*, 47(1): 33–60.

Crowe, N., and Bradford, S. (2006) 'Hanging out in runescape': Identity, work and leisure in the virtual playground. *Children's Geographies*, 4(3): 331–346.

Davidson, C. (2009) Young Children's engagement with digital texts and literacies in the home: Pressing matters for the teaching of English in the early years of schooling. *English Teaching: Practice and Critique*, 8(3): 36–54.

Dorling, D., and Thomas, B. (2011) *Bankrupt Britain: An Atlas of Social Change*. London: Policy Press.

Duranti, A., and Goodwin, C. (eds) (1992) *Rethinking Context: Language as an Interactive Phenomenon*. Cambridge: Cambridge University Press.

Dyson, A.H. (1993a) *Social Worlds of Children Learning to Write in an Urban Primary School*. New York: Teachers College Press.

Dyson, A.H. (1993b) *Negotiating a Permeable Curriculum: On Literacy, Diversity, and the Interplay of Children's and Teacher's Worlds*. Urbana, IL: National Council of Teachers of English.

Dyson, A.H. (2003) *The Brothers and Sisters Learn to Write: Popular Literacies in Childhood and School Cultures*. New York: Teachers College Press.

Dyson, A.H. (2008) Staying in the (curricular)Lines: Practice constraints and possibilities in childhood writing. *Written Communication*, 25: 119–159.

Flewitt, R. (2008) Multimodal Literacies. In J. Marsh and E. Hallet (eds) *Desirable Literacies: Approaches to Language and Literacy in the Early Years*. London: Sage, pp. 122–139.

Gee, J.P. (1996) *Social Linguistics and Literacies: Ideology in Discourses*, 2nd edn. London: Taylor and Francis.

Gonzalez, N., Moll, L., and Amanti, C. (eds) (2005) *Funds of Knowledge: Theorizing Practices in Households, Communities and Classrooms*. Mahwah, NJ: Lawrence Erlbaum Associates.

Graham, L. (2009) It was a challenge but we did it! Digital worlds in a primary classroom. *Literacy*, 43(2): 107–114.

Gregory, E., Long, S., and Volk, D. (eds) (2004) *Many Pathways to Literacy: Young Children Learning with Siblings, Grandparents, Peers, Communities*. London: Routledge.

Gregory, E., and Ruby, M. (2011) The 'insider/outsider' dilemma of ethnography: Working with young children and their families in cross-cultural contexts. *Journal of Early Childhood Research*, 9(2): 162–174.

Heath, S.B. (1983) *Ways with Words: Language, Life and Work in Communities and Classrooms*. Cambridge: Cambridge University Press.

Heath, S.B., and Street, B.V., with Molly Mills (2008) *On Ethnography: Approaches to Language and Literacy Research*. New York: Teachers College Press.

Hine, C. (2000) *Virtual Ethnography*. London: Sage.

Hope, J. (2011) New insights into family learning for refugees: Bonding, bridging and building transcultural capital. *Literacy*, 45(2): 91–96.

Hull, G., and Schultz, K. (2002) *School's Out: Bridging out of School Literacies with Classroom Practice*. New York and London: Teachers College Press.

Hurdley, R. (2006) Dismantling mantelpieces: Narrating identities and materializing culture in the home. *Sociology*, 40(4): 717–713.

Ingold, T. (2007) *Lines: A Brief History*. London: Routledge.

Kenner, C. (2000) *Home Pages: Literacy Links for Bilingual Children*. Stoke on Trent: Trentham Books.

Kenner, C. (2004) *Becoming Biliterate*. Stoke on Trent: Trentham Press.

Kinloch, V. (2010) *Harlem on Our Minds: Place, Race and the Literacies of Urban Youth*. New York: Teachers College Press.

Kress. G. (1997) *Before Writing: Rethinking the Paths to Literacy*. London: Routledge.

Lancaster, L. (2003) Beginning at the beginning: How a young child constructs time multimodally. In G. Kress, and C. Jewitt (eds), *Multimodal Literacy*. London: Peter Lang, pp. 107–122.

Lassiter, L.E. (2005) *The Chicago Guide to Collaborative Ethnography*. Chicago: University of Chicago Press.

Law, J. (2004) *After Method: Mess in Social Science Research*. London: Routledge.

Leander, K.M., and McKim, K.K. (2003) Tracing the everyday 'sitings' of adolescents on the Internet: A strategic adaptation of ethnography across online and offline spaces. *Education, Communication and Information*, 3(2): 211–240.

Lefebvre, H. (1991) *The Production of Space*, trans. D. Nicholson-Smith. Oxford: Blackwell.

Levy, R. (2011) *Young Children Reading At Home and At School*. London: Sage.

Mackey, M. (2010) Reading from the Feet Up: The Local Work of Literacy. *Children's Literature in Education*, 41: 323–339.

Marsh, J. (ed.) (2005) *Popular Culture, Media and Digital Literacies in Early Childhood*. London: Routledge/Falmer.

Marsh, J. (2010) Young children's play in online virtual worlds. *Journal of Early Childhood Research*, 8(1): 23–39.

Marsh, J. (2011) Young children's literacy practices in a virtual world: Establishing an online interaction order. *Reading Research Quarterly*, 42(6): 101–111.

Massey, D. (2005) *For Space*. London: Sage.

Miller, D. (2008) *The Comfort of Things*. Cambridge: Polity Press.

Miller, D. (2010) *Stuff*. London: Routledge.

Morrell, E. (2008) *Critical Literacy and Urban Youth: Pedagogies of Access Dissent and Liberation*. London and New York: Routledge.

Neuman, S., and Celano, D. (2001) Access to print in low-income and middle-income communities: An ecological study of four neighbourhoods. *Reading Research Quarterly*, 36(1): 8–26.

Neuman, S.B., and Celano, D. (2006) The knowledge gap: Implications of levelling the playing field for low-income and middle-income children. *Reading Research Quarterly*, 41(2): 176–201.

Nichols, S. (2011) Young children's literacy in the activity space of the library: A geosemiotic investigation. *Journal of Early Childhood Literacy*, 30(2): 164–189.

Nichols, S., Nixon, H., and Rowsell, J. (2009) Shaping the identities and practices in relation to early years literacy. *Literacy*, 43(2): 65–74.

Nixon, H. (2011) 'From bricks to clicks': Hybrid commercial spaces in the landscape of early literacy and learning. *Journal of Early Childhood Literacy*, 11(2): 114–140.

Pahl, K. (2002) Ephemera, mess and miscellaneous piles: Texts and practices in families. *Journal of Early Childhood Literacy*, 2(2): 145–165.

Pahl, K. (2005) Narrative spaces and multiple identities: Children's textual explorations of console games in home settings. In J. Marsh (ed.) *Popular Culture, Media and Digital Literacies in Early Childhood*. London: Routledge/Falmer, 126–145.

Pahl, K. (2008) Tracing habitus in texts and practices. In A. Luke and J. Albright (eds) *Pierre Bourdieu and Literacy Education*. London: Routledge, pp. 187–208.

Pahl, K. (2012) 'A reason to write': Exploring writing epistemologies in two contexts. *Pedagogies: An International Journal*, 7(3): 209–228.

Pahl, K., and Allan, C. (2011) I don't know what literacy is: Uncovering hidden literacies in a community library using ecological and participatory methodologies with children. *Journal of Early Childhood Literacy*, 11(2): 190–213.

Pahl, K., and Rowsell, J. (eds) (2006) *Travel Notes from the New Literacy Studies*. Clevedon: Multilingual Matters Ltd.

Pahl, K., and Rowsell, J. (2010) *Artifactual Literacies: Every Object Tells a Story*. New York: Teachers College Press.

Pink, S. (2001) *Doing Visual Ethnography*. London: Sage.

Pink, S. (2004) *Home Truths: Gender, Domestic Objects and Everyday Life*. Oxford: Berg.

Pink, S. (2009) *Doing Sensory Ethnography*. London: Sage.

Robinson, M., and Turnball, B. (2004) Bilingual children's uses of popular culture in text-making. In J. Marsh (ed.) *Popular Culture, New Media and Digital Literacy in Early Childhood*. Abingdon: RoutledgeFalmer, pp. 51–72.

Rogers, R. (2003) *A Critical Discourse Analysis of Family Literacy Practices: Power In and Out of Print*. Mahwah, NJ: Lawrence Erlbaum.

Rosowsky, A. (2008) *Heavenly Readings: Liturgical Literacy in a Multilingual Context*. Bristol: Multilingual Matters Ltd.

Scollon, R. (2001) *Mediated Discourse: The Nexus of Practice*. London: Routledge.

Soja, E. (2010) *Seeking Spatial Justice*. Minneapolis: University of Minnesota Press.

Steadman-Jones, R., Pahl, K., and Gould, W. (2010–2011) Writing in the Home and in the Street. Arts and Humanities Research Council Connected Communities grant AH/I507639/1, accessed November 28, 2012: www.sheffield.ac.uk/education/research/groups/csnl/writinghome

Steedman, C. (1982) *The Tidy House: Little Girls Writing*. London: Virago.

Street, B.V. (1984) *Literacy in Theory and Practice*. Cambridge: Cambridge University Press.

Street, B.V (2000) Literacy events and literacy practices: Theory and practice in the new literacy studies. In M. Martin-Jones and K. Jones (eds) *Multilingual Literacies: Reading and Writing Different Worlds*. Amsterdam/Philadelphia: John Benjamins Publishing Company, pp. 17–29.

Street, B.V., and Street, J. (1991) The schooling of literacy. In D. Barton and R. Ivanic (eds) *Writing in the Community*. London: Sage, pp. 143–166.

Thomas, A. (2007) *Youth Online: Identity and Literacy in the Digital Age*. New York: Peter Lang.

Turkle, S. (1995) *Life on the Screen: Identity in the Age of the Internet*. London: Phoenix.

Willis, P. (2000) *The Ethnographic Imagination*. Cambridge: Polity Press.

Wohlwend, K. (2009) Damsels in discourse: Girls consuming and producing identity texts through Disney Princess play. *Reading Research Quarterly*, 44(1): 57–83.

Wohlwend, K. (2010) A is for avatar: Young children in literacy 2.0 worlds and literacy 1.0 schools. *Language Arts*, 88(2): 144–152.

Chapter 2

Critical Multimodal Literacies

Synergistic Options and Opportunities

Margaret Mackey and Margaret Shane

Introduction

Today's children learn to interpret the world through a great variety of data sources. The making of *everyday* meaning has always been a complex exercise for children, involving many forms of sensory input. Over the past **30** years, the making of *textual* meaning has steadily become a more elaborate enterprise for young learners, who must absorb how to orchestrate an increasing variety of information channels. And the development of *critical* understanding must take place in the context of very sophisticated aesthetic, ideological, and commercial manipulation of multimodal options for young people.

In this chapter, we will explore the idea of critical multimodal literacies. All three of these words offer contested terms. The idea of criticality is the most complex challenge. Even the basic online dictionary built into our word-processing program gives contradictory information: not approving is the first definition of this term with a more positive second meaning of giving comments or judgments; the sixth meaning, undergoing change, is also germane. We will look at the connotations of suspicion (of not approving) that surround many ideas of critical literacy, as well as exploring the issues arising out of questions of judgment more broadly and positively conceived. The conflicted associations with the word 'critical' as it applies to young learners and consumers of various media will shape our approach to this work.

The other two words in our main heading are in flux, and their meanings are often mutually constituted. Effectively, all literacies are multimodal; the design of the page, the meaning-laden conventions of printed text, and the temporal rhythms of reading inflect print literacy with information beyond what is denoted by the black marks on the paper. Once we turn our attention away from the two-dimensional limits of the page to look at how young people actually behave with it, these qualities and affordances become evident. The printed words, the illustrations, even the white space, all serve as channels of meaning and interact productively with each other (see Kress and van Leeuwen, 1996).

The pleasures and powers of the illustrated page have been accessible at least to privileged children for centuries. The earliest children's picture book, *Orbis Sensualium Pictus*, produced by John Amos Comenius in 1658, incorporated two semiotic channels: words and

International Handbook of Research on Children's Literacy, Learning, and Culture, First Edition.
Edited by Kathy Hall, Teresa Cremin, Barbara Comber, and Luis C. Moll.
© 2013 John Wiley & Sons, Ltd. Published 2013 by John Wiley & Sons, Ltd.

images. Comenius prefaced his little book by identifying the pedagogical value of printed captions and representational images working in concert to support understanding in a mutually enhancing way.

> Which such Book... may (I hope) serve... To entice witty children to it... For it is apparent, that children (even from their infancy almost) are delighted with Pictures, and willingly please their eyes with these lights... This same little Book will serve to stir up the Attention, which is to be fastened upon things, and even to be sharpened more and more (Comenius, 1658, n.p.).

The polysemic qualities of a print literacy developed through the distinct temporal logic and visual grammar of picture books are reinforced and well understood (Kress, 2003; Serafini, 2011). Nevertheless, too many people still assume that the picture book's value is solely as a stepping-off point to the mature interpretation of pure text (Strasser and Seplocha, 2007). However, many contemporary children now engage first with numerous *different* multimodal formats before encountering print literacy; the picture book may well not be the first form of text they encounter. In terms of the understanding of textual conventions that they develop, some readers may consider books to be limited and static, offering narrower interpretive options.

At the outset of this chapter, we must make one proviso. The reality of our contemporary situation is that the most affluent children are engaged in the most intriguing new literacies; newspapers, for example, report an 'App Gap' between rich and poor families (*Daily Mail* Reporter, 2011, n.p.). While acknowledging the massive significance of socio-economic status, we have chosen to focus on the most far-reaching changes as they are manifest in the hands and in front of the eyes and ears of mainstream Western children in the upper income strata.

At the same time, it is vital to note that print literacies are also differentially accessible at home. A survey conducted by the National Literacy Trust in the United Kingdom in September 2011 revealed that one British child in three does not own a single book – a total of 3.8 million bookless children (Clarke and Poulton, 2011, p. 8). Almost certainly some of these children have access to a parent's mobile phone, tablet device, or home computer. The gulf between affluent and poor children is significant but it is more multifaceted than a simple digital divide.

For decades many children have approached book literacy via prior experience with television; now the situation is more complex, with screens of many sizes, powers, and functions featuring very early in children's daily lives. With due acknowledgement that not all children are in the ever-shifting, ill-defined digital vanguard, this chapter will explore issues of mutating literacy possibilities and the kinds of critical scaffolding that benefit children who are growing up in this rapidly transforming landscape.

An Analytical Framework

Frank Serafini offers an organizing image to help us think critically about these multiplying, shifting, and contradictory channels of meaning. He talks about three interconnected analytical perspectives, namely: (1) perceptual, (2) structural, and (3) ideological perspectives (2010, p. 88). In this chapter we propose to look at perceptual, structural, and ideological factors in the development of critical multimodal literacies. *Perceptual* perspectives allow interpreters to make subjective sense of what they observe. Serafini tells us that one's perceptions of multimodal texts are colored by prior knowledge, personal experiences, and socio-cultural and historical contexts of reception and production (Serafini, 2010, p. 88). Contemporary children amass knowledge and experiences in relatively new contexts of reception and production, so their perceptual priorities may differ from those of their elders. James Pope provides an example of this shift in perception and its implications. He points out that adult readers of interactive fictions make use of their understanding of narrative ingredients of a satisfying story at the same time as they draw on their awareness of what to expect from a good interface (Pope, 2010, p. 76). It is a question of *both/and* rather than *either/or*. Contemporary children will take many *both/and* perspectives for granted as they master a variety of formats and media. This flexibility shapes even the youngest learners' perceptual perspectives. Indeed, in some paradoxical ways, children's familiarity with a variety of media and modalities actually makes the book more visible to them; they are more explicitly aware of its affordances and limitations. This change is also a factor in their developing literacy.

The *structural* perspective involves awareness of conventions and how they are used to produce meaning (Serafini, 2010, p. 89). We argue that children's awareness of structural considerations has blossomed in the digital age and that the pedagogies that address issues of structure need to take this new knowledge into account.

Ideological considerations address how texts are *motivated* or developed to perform specific social actions or tasks (Serafini, 2010, p. 89, emphasis in original). We believe that although ever more children are in a position to develop expertise at a structural level, such knowledge may, paradoxically, blind them to the possibilities of more critical perspectives concerning the ideological shaping of their texts.

Background Issues

In homes where children have access to new literacies, the rate of change in domestic technologies is accelerating and affecting ever younger children. Babies and their parents, for example, discover that some digital forms call for less manual dexterity than the skill of turning book pages. The cognitive capacities of young children are remarkable, and new formats and tools may be actively designed to be baby-friendly. Even very young children register that they inhabit a world of representations. Children as young as 18-24 months exhibit the cognitive capacity to identify a two-dimensional image of themselves (Bard, 2006, p. 214). They acknowledge the content of other representations as well: 18-month-old children who hear a new word in relation to a picture of an object appreciate that the word refers to the real object, not simply to its picture (Ganea, Pickard, and DeLoache, 2008, p. 48).

Changing times require us to expand our thinking of these issues beyond the framework of babies and their board books. Today's infants have their own software programs, and learn to aim their clumsy fists at the keyboard for onscreen feedback and rewards including mouse-click dexterity training (Giggles, 2012, n.p.). They may communicate with distant family members via Skype and FaceTime. Toddlers swiftly become experts at locating games and video content on their parents' mobile phones. Their first experience of the written word may be a texted message from Daddy on the small screen rather than via the pages of a picture book. With all our capacity for domestic production of media texts, a very young child in the prosperous parts of the world can become a very sophisticated consumer – and indeed often co-producer – of media materials without ever moving very far beyond the real-world examples of family and friends. At an extremely young age, they learn the appeal of a complex rather than a singular text. Ruxandra Bularca expresses it this way: 'Digital reading seduces with its call for distributed attention' (2011, p. 139). Pope (2010) suggests that some of that distribution lies between the narrative content and the possibilities offered by the interface. Young children are learning to distribute their attention productively.

Today's affluent children have parents who grew up in a digital world, and are developing new forms of Rumsey's heritage literacy. In such a setting, certain practices, tools, and concepts are adapted, adopted, or alienated from use, depending on the context (Rumsey, 2009, p. 575). Such parents may mediate many forms of personal statement and connection for their children, even before birth, and many of these mediations involve forms of new literacy. For example, a common first appearance of a baby still *in utero* within the public world of private representations is the appearance of the ultrasound image on Facebook. Such parents regard their literate heritage as hybrid, and they are keen to inculcate their children into a world of multiple literacies. At the same time, many of these parents continue to valorize the importance of print-and-paper literacy as part of their hybrid systems. According to the *New York Times*, sales of e-books for children lag well behind those for adults, accounting for a mere 5 percent of total children's sales, radically less than adult sales (Richtel and Bosman, 2011, n.p.).

Most toddlers who live among many media-rich representations of their own *personal* world will also explore *externally* referenced materials (books, DVDs, games, Internet sites) that introduce them to imaginary worlds, which exist only inside the text(s). The child must then develop other ways of thinking about the power of representation, Not only can it give the child differently constructed access to the people familiar to her or him in daily life, it can also introduce that child to characters he or she has never met – and at some point that child will start to register that these characters may not have a real-life existence at all. In some cases, a child will know these personae only within the diegesis of the single book or television show or app; in other cases, a child will meet the character across a variety of media in the guise of toys, theme parks, domestic accoutrements, and other media.

These observations seem simple but their potential to ramify into complexity should not be underestimated. Children may develop ontological questions about the degree to which a fictional character is real when it is incarnated in their daily lives in the form of text-specific branded toys and regalia. Further crossover occurs if such branded toys are then recorded in the ubiquitous home videos that reside in the mobile phone; the recorded existence of these fictional characters among the representations of family life is thus reified. Perceptual and structural issues are merged in this scenario, and the ideological framing provided by the branded story and branded toy is not really open to critique on the part of the child who is invested in the reality of the toy and committed to the emotional importance of their relationship.

Videos and toys aimed explicitly at babies introduce questions of understanding to the very youngest consumers. *Baby Einstein*, for example, is certainly a major player in the world of infant media. In addition to educational videos for babies and a dedicated television program, the company produces a line of toys ostensibly designed to stimulate cognitive development (although they are now more careful than they used to be about how categorically they assert this connection). The market is huge. By the end of 2005, Baby Einstein had a presence in more than 30 countries and offered products in more than 25 different languages (Baby Einstein, n.d.)

Adult purchasers of all things developmental for babies and toddlers represent an enormous market and the notion of a young child advancing through the early stages of literacy by dint of branded scaffolding is often presented as an unquestioned good. Take, for example the discourse of the Leapfrog website, marketing its electronic gadgets and toys for various ages and (explicitly marketed) developmental stages. At three different stages, (0–12 months, 12–36 months, 3–5 years), learning challenges are addressed by marketing solutions as the following excerpts from the Leapfrog toy shop website demonstrate:

> Babies are naturally curious, and learn about the world around them using a developing set of new skills. Encourage their discoveries with a soft, personalized puppy like My Pal Scout or the award-winning Learn and Groove™ line of musical toys. (Leapfrog, 2012a)

There's no stopping little learners. And their minds are moving just as quickly – exploring numbers, letters, shapes and more! Keep up the momentum with our engaging toys, or books that magically come to life with the Tag™ Junior book pal. (Leapfrog, 2012b)

As children get ready for school, help set the stage! See how imagination and open-ended play combine with colors, counting and more in toys like Count and Draw and Count and Scan Shopper. Then discover more learning fun with our gaming handhelds. (Leapfrog, 2012c)

In such an approach both parental anxieties and also their delight in their small children's blossoming curiosity is tapped for the brand.

The numbers of sites linked to any Google search is not a form of definitive evidence by any critical standard, but it can serve as a rough marker. A Google search for baby software (December 4, 2011), returned 1,760,000,000 hits. No matter how you qualify such results with caveats about dead-ends and duplications and commercial over-kill, one-and-three-quarter-billion hits is a suggestive number. Simply navigating even the first one-tenth of 1 percent of that list (those being the most successful online marketers) calls for a formidable degree of critical literacy that many parents may not possess.

Many contemporary children, therefore, explore a multimediated and multirepresentational world long before the onset of schooling, through a context of domestic life and of play, even to the extent of making a plaything of the meta. One three-year-old, for example, internalized a hypertext storybook's mechanics to create a Click on Me game (Smith, 2002, p. 13). Cynthia Smith describes how James comprehended the structural role of the mouse:

James' internalization of the 'Click on' cause leading to a resulting effect was so complete as to influence his subconscious imagination in response to a nightmare. He said his dreams were like the computer. He could click on a scary dream or a good dream . . . he could use his 'dream mouse' to story the dream and click on a good dream. (2002, p. 7)

The complex relationship between James and the power of the click, coupled with those staggering numbers for baby software, raises fascinating and fundamental questions. What skills and assumptions, cultural capital, and understanding of representation do such digi-tots bring to bear on learning to read? What other kinds of media literacies spring from such a beginning? And how do children who meet so many forms of mediation so early in life view the power and potential of the book?

Young children must learn to navigate this multimodal world, developing ways of processing, enjoying, judging, and resisting a huge variety of texts and formats. We know too little about how they achieve the different stages of these new forms of literacy. Scholars such as Marsh (2005, 2008, 2011), Dyson (2003), Genishi and Dyson (2009), Plowman, Stephen, and McPake (2010), Tyner (2010), Wohlwend (2008, 2009, 2011) and Carrington and Robinson (2009), have investigated some of the ways in which children learn to come to terms with literacies that seem new to their elders but to the children themselves are simply part of the daily landscape. Their literate development occurs in a communicative network of great fluidity.

Daily life is more and more mediated; fictional characters are more frequently incarnated in furry and plastic forms and made a physical part of daily life (and perhaps remediated into the domestic record as well via home video or FaceTime exchanges, to take just two possibilities). Sometimes these tangible objects are mirrored or augmented by a walking, talking online version, as in the wildly successful Webkinz model where a branded stuffed toy is linked via a coded number to a matching online avatar (see Black (2010) for an interesting investigation into the Webkinz phenomenon). When we checked the website in January 2012, the company was inviting young Webkinz owners to participate in creating videos and exploring social media, a further layering of a complex ontology, or, in an alternative phrasing, an even more fragmented distribution of attention:

> Hey! It's Valarie VonScribe here, the official gossip and newz reporter for Webkinz. Over the holidays I've been watching tons of cool Webkinz videos on YouTube, and I've been following the official Webkinz Facebook page (http://facebook.com/Webkinz) where a few awesome KinzTubers have been featured.
>
> Webkinz fans who create videos using Webkinz Pets often refer to themselves as KinzTubers, and I consider myself one too! It's so much fun to create and share videos using a Webkinz cast because there are millions of things you can do, from pet adoption videos to Webkinz music videos and action movies. (Ganzworld, 2012).

Children's interpretive capacities develop in this complex context. To follow their development through the ever-proliferating channels of meaning now available to them, we need to consider how creative and critical understanding are built through, between, and in the absence of different channels of meaning. Three components are important: the elements of play and pleasure that enhance development; the implications of the commercial framework that is an essential component of many childhood fictions and much childhood play; and the place for developing a more critical awareness, in the broadest sense of the word critical.

Synergy, the Picture Book, and the Larger Multimodal Universe

The picture book has been associated with childhood for many centuries. Theoretical analysis of the polysemic nature of the picture book and empirical observations of how children learn to process it offer us models for exploring the new fluidities of contemporary literacies. Such work explores the importance of those multichannel affordances and the impact of being able to communicate more than one idea at a time (Lewis, 2001; Nikolajeva and Scott, 2001; Nodelman, 1988; Pullman, 1989). Lawrence Sipe uses the concept of *synergy* to explore the relationship between words and illustrations, and the open-ended qualities of this term make it particularly useful for exploring an expansive universe of textual channels.

> In a picture book, both the text and the illustration sequence would be incomplete without the other. They have a synergistic relationship in which the total effect depends not only on the union of the text and illustrations but also on the perceived interactions or transactions between these two parts (1998, pp. 98–99).

Sipe explores the words and the pictures in terms of their predominantly temporal or spatial natures. The verbal text drives us to read on in a linear way, where the illustrations seduce us into stopping to look (1998, p. 101). He suggests we manage this phenomenological experience through a process of oscillation. Whenever we move across sign systems, 'new meanings are produced,' because we interpret the text in terms of the pictures and the pictures in terms of the texts in a potentially never-ending sequence (1998, p. 102). These oscillations can create information out of the gaps between words and images.

Sipe's synergy develops out of the interaction between two channels of information. What happens when such channels multiply, duplicate, feedback, and invite or even drive participation? The television program for example, lends itself to linear viewing that may be disrupted by rewinds and reviewings if the program is recorded or streamed or reproduced in DVD.

A website actively encourages us to browse but we may become expert enough to move to our favorite sub-page in purposive, linear ways. To some extent, levels of linearity, of purpose, of distribution, and of synergy are in the hands of the interpreter, even the very youngest. Even toddlers can learn to oscillate.

Children must learn to make perceptual sense of all the texts available to them before they can develop further insights. In the course of moving between media formats, they almost certainly gain a more strongly developed structural sense of what is possible in one medium or another. It seems likely that the affordances of the book become more visible to children in such a context; as evidence for such an assertion it is possible to turn to the books themselves. An increasing number of picture books address the question of What can a book do? in explicit and/or oblique ways. *Press Here* by Hervé Tullet (2011/2010) is a book pretending to be an app. *It's a Book* (Smith, 2010) talks about what a book can and cannot offer. *We Are in a Book* (Willems, 2010) allows the characters to speak directly to the reader about the conditions of being a character on a page. *Wolves* (Gravett, 2005) goes one step further and plays textual games with the affordances of being a library book. Such books not only describe aspects of *bookness*, they assume that such issues will be meaningful to the children who are being addressed. When the book is no longer the only option its material qualities become more visible.

The Complexities of Reception and Participation

Questions of reception are extremely important for children who learn about multimedia stories in the context of their own decoding efforts. Children move from making explicit use of their own family's contextual explorations of the textual world to a context of play in which they practice the assembling of meaning in a variety of situations, many of them fictional. The process is anything but impersonal as Karen Wohlwend reminds us:

> Children use play to import opportunities for literacy performances and increase their participation within communities of practice.... Through play, children take up identities as literacy users in imagined communities.... Such play performances of more experienced readers allow them to mediate texts for themselves and others (2008, p. 128).

Play is – and remains – participatory by its very nature. What changes over time are the conditions of participation. Textual changes such as those we have noted above represent one element of those conditions; we explore texts according to the interpretive experience and expertise we have assembled from other texts in our lives. But our era of participation – and that toddler helping to text to Daddy stands at the start of a very long road – raises a number of important critical questions.

Stuart Poyntz describes what he calls a participation paradox:

> there are more opportunities than ever for children and youth to be actively involved with contemporary media environments, more ways for interventionist fans, local non-commercial producers, activists, and others to use screen resources to produce meaning in their own and others' lives.... On the other hand, then, it is of note that transnational media corporations are also adept and attentive to the ways that young people's participation can be nurtured for profitable ends.... For instance, any number of children's [online] play spaces and practices... now nurture children's creative expression and/or sense of responsibility through a sociality knit to the development of new products and to dynamic data maps that track kids' everyday lives (2010, p. 113).

Poyntz talks about children's play spaces in an unmarked sense. Diane Carver Sekeres produces a special definition of the play space that takes account of exactly the kind of commercial forces in children's textual worlds that Poyntz is describing. She talks about the kind of play space that is created by encountering branded fiction.

> What I am calling branded fiction books are those that are created synergistically, tethered to other products, and that draw on literacies other than reading words printed on paper. Brands are built by corporations mostly to create associations in consumers' minds between branded products and a desirable lifestyle; books are simply one product among many that attract the consumer to the brand. (2009, p. 400)

Branded fictions sell each other but at the same time they also sell a certain kind of play:

> When a corporation publishes stories with the idea of using them as one product in a line of goods, then it follows that a tween who engages with the branded fiction will be learning to consume as she purchases additional products of the line. The model for play is based on capitalist values of commercial exchange (2009, p. 405).

Sekeres is explicit about children developing multiliteracies in order to enter this play space. These skills are constructed through reading, playing with toys alone or with friends, using products alone or in community with family or friends, and spending time online interacting with games and people who have similar interests (2009, pp. 405–406).

Karen Wohlwend explores branded fiction through girls' consumption of Disney's ubiquitous Princess play-discourses and product ranges which collectively achieved global sales of $4 billion in 2007.

> Regular opportunities to play with toys during a writing workshop allowed children to improvise and revise character actions, layering new story meanings and identities onto old. Dolls and storyboards facilitated chains of animating and authoring, linking meanings from one event to the next as they played, wrote, replayed, and rewrote. The notion of production consumption explains how girls enthusiastically took up familiar media narratives, encountered social limitations in princess identities, improvised character actions, and revised story lines to produce counter narratives of their own. (2009, 57)

Whether or not scholars, teachers, librarians, and parents are willing to consider these branded products as literature, the fact remains that many children learn their most potent lessons about interpretation in the branded fiction play space. The corporate framing of many interpretative and productive activities thus becomes part of a child's textual toolkit.

Sipe's concept of synergy is open-ended, and can very easily be extended to incorporate not only the multimodal affordances of texts in many different media but also a developing awareness of branded fictions and even the very process of branding. Serafini provides language for discussing these developments. In addition to expanding their *perceptual* alertness, today's young people often evince an advanced *structural* sense as well. Many children have a sophisticated awareness both of branded content and also of some elements of the background decision-making that guides its production. Even James, at the age of three, is thinking beyond the story to the mouse-click that makes choice possible.

Numerous educational efforts explore the structural zone of diverse textual materials. Similarly, staples of the popular culture of contemporary childhood such as a DVD's bonus features encourage children to master the intricate chain of decision-making that goes into the composition of a film or a television series. These children, however, often remain uncritical; their *ideological* development remains rudimentary to the extent that this enlarged understanding simply makes them buy in more enthusiastically to the whole idea of commercial fiction-making. In Maaike Lauwaert's terms, children may apply all their developing interpretive skills and emotional commitment to the practice of becoming active residents in a brand's world (2009, p. 11).

The prospect of introducing a critical perspective in the face of such a wholehearted engagement may be very difficult for an observing adult to contemplate. Yet what Lauwaert terms the expansion pack and serial economy of children's fictional engagement (2009, p. 41) presents its own complexities. She is speaking of games but her terms apply to many forms of contemporary fiction whose internal logic is based on consumerist principles of gathering, trading, and accumulating (2009, p. 41). The extended popularity of Scholastic's *39 Clues* (Scholastic, 2008–2010, various authors) is a testimonial to the fact that children are happy to contribute hours of assembly to the development of a fictional universe. What is an appropriate pedagogy for addressing the questions raised by such an enterprise? Scholastic supplies its own teacher guides for the series, but acknowledgement or critique of Scholastic's own role in the production of this transmedia enterprise is absent from these guides (see Sekeres and Watson, 2011, for an interesting discussion of this series). What alternative pedagogical spaces can we create to enable the kinds of ideological discussion we need? And, how can we make these spaces respectful of the perceptual commitment and structural expertise that bind many children to their stories?

Developing Critical Understanding

All texts are produced for a variety of reasons, both private and public, and also within particular ideological, cultural, and commercial frameworks. To some extent, readers, viewers, players, and users may not pay much heed to the motivation that brings a text into being.

For example, how many interpreters bring an actively critical perspective to the meta-level supports that now often surround a text or a play space: the author's website, for example, or the producer's blog? Jennifer Gillan discusses the blog *Grey Matter* that accompanies the television show *Grey's Anatomy* and features the musings of its writers and producers. Gillan observes:

> Although they read like casual personal insights, the posts on *Grey Matter* were contractually obligated forms of expression and, as such, they fed into the network's attempt to control perception and circulation of its intellectual property and commentary upon it (2011, p. 230).

Yet even teachers – perhaps indeed especially teachers – may be susceptible to the author persona created on a website or a blog. The critical apparatus they bring to the initial text may shift to a less rigorous stance when it comes to exploring the many channels of background information. In a world where serious as well as populist authors all need to consider more sophisticated forms of self-marketing, those at the reception end need to be alert to ideological issues in the metatext and the paratext as well as the text itself.

Other forms of commercial address are less subtle, and it is interesting to consider how contemporary young people respond to an invitation to *join* rather than critique the corporate framework. One of us explored web responses to the television program *Felicity*. In one important example, a self-identified network executive invited *Felicity* fans to collaborate in creating a slogan for use in selling *Felicity* merchandise back to them (Mackey, 2003, p. 402). Eight fans responded with suggestions. Were they mere dupes of a sophisticated marketing system? Or, did they perceive themselves to be participating purposefully in the creation of the Felicity universe by pulling the levers of the infrastructure that creates and supports that fictional world? Do they see such marketing as interesting at a structural or an ideological level? Their response reads differently in each scenario. Discussing Lego users in terms that also apply to textual interpreters, Lauwaert says, 'In the many-to-many geography [of textual reception], the periphery gains in importance for the companies, has therefore more influence over the core but loses some of its autonomy' (2009, p. 67). By participating in *Felicity* merchandizing efforts, did these fans surrender some of their autonomy? It is doubtful that they would think so. How can they be introduced to a more critical perspective without thinking that it represents knee-jerk hostility to their beloved stories, one more wearisome example of that *not approving* connotation of criticality?

Ultimately, we are all implicated in the corporate framing of our texts. The strong case concerning the ideological infusion of aesthetic materials suggests that all efforts to develop a more mobile approach to artistic works in and of themselves serve the needs of corporate capitalism. Thomas Elsaesser makes just this case, using the example of complex mind-game films or puzzle films such as *Pulp Fiction*, *Memento*, and so forth:

> [M]edia consumption has become part of the affective labor required in modern (control) societies, in order to properly participate in the self-regulating mechanisms of ideological reproduction, for which retraining and learning are now a lifelong obligation. Undergoing tests – including the tests put up by mind-game films – thus constitutes a veritable ethics of the (post-bourgeois) self: to remain flexible, adaptive, and interactive, and above all, to know the rules of the game (2009, p. 34).

The outcome of such thinking, which some may find unduly pessimistic, is that despite our efforts to become more sophisticated, more critical, more astute and alert, we are only serving our corporate masters' interests after all. It may be that our notion of critical needs to be expanded to include the notion of resistance – but at what age do we invite children to start resisting their favorite fictions in the cause of retaining some autonomy in the face of those commercially inspired self-regulating mechanisms of ideological reproduction that sit on their bookshelves and in their toy cupboards? How do we import questions of critical engagement and resistance into their reading of beloved books and their use of other highly engaging media? Perhaps it is a sequential issue. Perhaps children learn about the perceptual questions that will allow them to interpret the mediated texts put before them, then go on to develop some structural expertise – and then, at a later stage in their childhood, can be introduced to ideological issues. Or perhaps it is an incremental project. Very young children can learn 'They make it look so appealing because they want you to buy it,' and develop a gradual understanding of the different rhetorical addresses that greet them every day. Analyzing the complexities of the Webkinz invitation (Black, 2010) to submit homemade videos of branded avatars will call for some subtle ideological thinking; making such critical analysis accessible to young KinzTubers represents an even greater challenge.

It is important not to confuse the structural and the ideological. For some decades now, media literacy education has paid a great deal of attention to structural issues. *All media are constructed* is usually item number one on any list of media literacy lessons. It is perhaps time to realize that this lesson, though still important, needs perhaps less attention than it used to do. Becoming structural experts, knowledgeable about every background detail of their chosen narrative, does not offer ideological immunity to children; the ideological elements of their relationship to their stories must be teased out separately.

The dominating ideology of consumerism infiltrating our children's reading is daunting. However, there is a precedent for such an overwhelming agenda. It is not so long since much of children's literate activity was filtered through the ideology of a variety of religions. The two approaches share a surprising degree of commonality. We actually have more experience with children's developing literacies being colonized by a particular ideology than we may sometimes suppose. As with the religious approach to children's literacy, the first challenge is simply to render the frame visible.

Conclusions

The capacity to assemble semiotic cues and clues and create some kind of salient personal meaning is a complex and highly pleasurable operation. Today's children are undoubtedly gaining early exposure to the joys and challenges of polyvalent text forms, in ways that allow them to oscillate not only among the various channels of communication but also between the perceptual and the structural zones. Being knowledgeable about how a favorite text has been created is almost a rite of passage for many young literates, who revel in their own expertise. Very often they are delighted to be respected for their deep knowledge, which accrues cultural capital among their peers. They are often equally thrilled to engage with the corporations that invite their responses and mine their data.

How to establish the significance of the ideological layer in Serafini's model is a complicated challenge. The satisfactions of the structural layer provide a sense of false security in a way – young readers (and sometimes their teachers too) who understand *so much* about the creation of their stories may not wish to consider that their intelligent responses are not sufficient to comprehend and/or resist the corporate priorities that often lie behind any decision to publish. Their new capacity to participate as experts in the structural zone of their stories may provide significant delight. They may resist a deeper approach that runs the risk of destroying their pleasure in the fictional universe they inhabit and understand so well. The alternative they perceive may be limited to the kind of cynicism that destroys all pleasure.

Expertise in the structural zone allows children to enjoy the pleasures of the meta, to know that they are able to look at their perceptual interpretations with a double eye. It should be relatively straightforward to move from structural to ideological considerations, to find equivalent fascination in exploring the assumptions and agendas that inform a given fiction. Many children, however, are more likely to resist such dissection of a beloved text set than they are likely to resist the text itself.

Today's young people are highly skilled at assembling and assessing multiple sources of data to create worlds of fictional pleasure. They are very well aware of the media studies mantra, all media are constructed; they absorb this idea with their early exploration of the DVD extra tracks. Finding ways to include the ideological zone as we explore the intellectual and affective pleasures of our texts remains a significant pedagogical challenge for all who care about young people and their stories.

References

Baby Einstein (n.d.) Website, accessed November 8, 2012: www.babyeinstein.com/en/our_story/history

Bard, K. (2006) Self-awareness in human and chimpanzee infants: What is measured and what is meant by the mark and mirror test? *Infancy*, 9(2): 191–219.

Black, R.W. (2010) The language of Webkinz: Early childhood literacy in an online virtual world. *Digital Culture and Education*, 2(1), 7–24, accessed November 8, 2012: www.digitalcultureandeducation. com/cms/wp-content/uploads/2010/05/dce1028_black_2010.pdf

Bularca, R. (2011) How the Internet taught me to read. *Caitele Echinox 20: Literature in the Digital Age*, 137–150.

Carrington, V., and Robinson, M. (eds) (2009) *Digital Literacies: Social Learning and Classroom Practices*. London: UKLA/Sage.

Clarke, C., and Poulton, L. (2011) *Book Ownership and its Relation to Reading Enjoyment, Attitudes, Behaviour and Attainment*. London: National Literacy Trust.

Comenius, J.A. (1658) *Orbis Sensualium Pictus*, 1887 edition accessed November 8, 2012: www. gutenberg.org/files/28299/28299-h/28299-h.htm#preface_ed

Daily Mail Reporter (2011) The 'App Gap' – a new gap between the rich kids and the poor. *Mail* Online, October 25, accessed December 4, 2011: www.dailymail.co.uk/news/article–2053460/App-Gap–The-New-Gap-Between-Rich-Poor-Kids.html

Dyson, A.H. (2003). 'Welcome to the jam': Popular culture, school literacy, and the making of childhoods. *Harvard Educational Review*, 73(3): 328–361.

Elsaesser, T. (2009) The mind-game film. In W. Buckland (ed.) *Puzzle Films: Complex Storytelling in Contemporary Cinema*. Chichester: Wiley-Blackwell, pp. 13–41.

Ganea, P.A., Pickard, M.B., and DeLoache, J.S. (2008) Transfer between picture books and the real world by very young children. *Journal of Cognition and Development*, 9: 46–66.

Ganzworld (2012) Website, accessed November 8, 2012: http://webkinznewz.ganzworld.com/polka-dot-cow-adoption-video-by-webkinz-fan/

Genishi, C., and Dyson, A.H. (2009) *Children, Language, and Literacy: Diverse Learners in Diverse Times*. New York: Teachers' College Press.

Giggles Computer Funtime for Baby (2012) Website, accessed November 8, 2012: www.giggles.net/

Gillan, J. (2011) *Television and New Media: Must-Click TV*. New York: Routledge.

Gravett, E. (2005) *Wolves*. Basingstoke: Macmillan Children's Books.

Kress, G. (2003) *Literacy in the New Media Age*. London: Routledge.

Kress, G., and van Leeuwen, T. (1996) *Reading Images: The Grammar of Visual Design*. London: Routledge.

Lauwaert, M. (2009) *The Place of Play: Toys and Digital Cultures*. Amsterdam: Amsterdam University Press.

Leapfrog (2012a) Baby Toys 0–12 months: Learning toys, accessed November 8, 2012: http://shop. leapfrog.com/leapfrog/jump/Baby-Toys-0–12-mo./category/lfBabyToys?q_facetTrail=9004% 3AlfBabyToysandcategoryNavIds=lfBabyToysandaddFacet=9004%3AlfBabyToys

Leapfrog (2012b) Toddler toys 12–36 months: Learning toys, accessed November 8, 2012: http://shop. leapfrog.com/leapfrog/jump/Toddler-Toys–12–36-mo.-/category/lfToddlerToys?q_facetTrail= 9004%3AlfToddlerToysandcategoryNavIds=lfToddlerToysandaddFacet=9004%3AlfToddlerToys

Leapfrog (2012c) Pre-school toys 3–5 years: Learning toys, accessed November 8, 2012: http://shop. leapfrog.com/leapfrog/jump/Preschool-Toys–3–5-yrs.-/category/lfPreschoolToys?q_facetTrail= 9004%3AlfPreschoolToysandcategoryNavIds=lfPreschoolToysandaddFacet=9004%3AlfPreschool Toys

Lewis, D. (2001) *Reading Contemporary Picturebooks: Picturing Text*. London: Routledge/Falmer.

Mackey, M. (2003) Television and the teenage literate: Discourses of Felicity. *College English*, 65(4): 389–410.

Marsh, J. (ed.) (2005) *Popular Culture, New Media and Digital Literacy in Early Childhood*. London: RoutledgeFalmer.

Marsh, J. (2008) Out-of-school play in online virtual worlds and the implications for literacy learning. Paper presented at the Centre for Studies in Literacy, Policy, and Learning Cultures, University of South Australia, July 2008, accessed November 8, 2012: www.unisa.edu.au

Marsh, J. (2011) Young children's literacy practices in a virtual world: Establishing an online interaction order. *Reading Research Quarterly*, 46(2): 101–118.

Nikolajeva, M., and Scott, C. (2001) *How Picturebooks Work*. New York: Garland.

Nodelman, P. (1988) *Words about Pictures: The Narrative Art of Children's Picture Books.* Athens: University of Georgia Press.

Plowman, L., Stephen, C., and McPake, J. (2010) *Growing Up with Technology: Young Children Learning in a Digital World.* London: Routledge.

Pope, J. (2010) Where do we go from here? Readers' responses to interactive fiction: Narrative structures, reading pleasure and the impact of interface design. *Convergence: The International Journal of Research into New Media Technologies*, 16(1): 75–94.

Poyntz, S.R. (2010, Winter) The participation paradox, or agency and sociality in contemporary youth cultures. *Jeunesse: Young People, Texts, Cultures*, 2(2): 110–119.

Pullman, P. (1989) Invisible pictures. *Signal: Approaches to Children's Books*, 60: 160–186.

Richtel, M., and J. Bosman. (2011) For their children, many e-book fans insist on paper. *New York Times*, November 20, accessed November 8, 2012: www.nytimes.com/2011/11/21/business/for-their-children-many-e-book-readers-insist-on-paper.html?_r=3andhp

Rumsey, S.K. (2009) Heritage literacy: Adoption, adaptation, and alienation of multimodal literacy tools. *College Composition and Communication*, 60(3): 573 –586.

Sekeres, D.C. (2009) The market child and branded fiction: A synergism of children's literature, consumer culture, and new literacies. *Reading Research Quarterly*, 44(4): 399–414.

Sekeres, D.C., and Watson, C. (2011) New literacies and multimediacy: The immersive universe of *The 39 Clues. Children's Literature in Education*, 42(3): 256–273.

Serafini, F. (2010) Reading multimodal texts: Perceptual, structural and ideological perspectives. *Children's Literature in Education*, 41(2): 85–104.

Serafini, F. (2011) Expanding perspectives for comprehending visual images in multimodal texts. *Journal of Adolescent and Adult Literacy*, 54(5): 342–350.

Sipe, L.R. (1998) How picture books work: A semiotically framed theory of text-picture relationships. *Children's Literature in Education*, 29(2): 97–108.

Smith, C.R. (2002) Click on me! An example of how a toddler used technology in play. *Journal of Early Childhood Literacy*, 2(5): 5–20.

Smith, L. (2010) *It's a Book.* New York: Roaring Brook Press.

Strasser, J., and Seplocha, H. (2007) Using picture books to support young children's literacy. *Childhood Education*, 83(4): 219–224.

Tullet, H. (2010/2011) *Press Here.* San Francisco: Chronicle Books.

Tyner, K. (ed.) (2010) *Media Literacy: New Agendas in Communication.* New York: Routledge.

Willems, M. (2010) *We Are In a Book!* New York: Hyperion Books for Children.

Wohlwend, K. (2008) Play as a literacy of possibilities: Expanding meanings in practices, materials, and spaces. *Language Arts*, 86(2): 127–136.

Wohlwend, K. (2009) Damsels in discourse: Girls consuming and producing identity texts through Disney princess play. *Reading Research Quarterly*, 44(1): 57–83.

Wohlwend, K. (2011) *Playing their Way into Literacies: Reading, Writing, and Belonging in the Early Childhood Classroom.* New York: Teachers' College Press.

Chapter 3

Books, Toys, and Tablets

Playing and Learning in the Age of Digital Media

Helen Nixon and Erica Hateley

Introduction

During a recent study of how parents source information about children's early learning, one of us made our first serious foray into a local store licensed to the global chain Toys 'R' Us. While walking the aisles, closely observing layout, signage, and stock, several things became obvious. First, large numbers of toys were labeled 'educational.' Second, many toys in that category were intended for children under the age of two years. These were further differentiated as intended for 'babies' or 'infants,' and sub-categorized on packaging or shelving using even smaller age increments (e.g., 0–3 months, 12–18 months, and so on). Third, many products were labeled as 'interactive' and 'learning' toys that promised to assist children's early learning and development. The activation of some of these toys relied on embedded computer chip technology and promised to 'connect' children with the home television, computer, and the Internet. These products were hybrids between a toy and a platform for digital media interaction. Closer inspection of toy packaging and other promotional material suggested that the industry had begun to invest heavily in developing highly differentiated children's markets for products that yoked together concepts of learning and development, the 'fun toy' that incorporates digital technology, and offline and online participation. In this chapter we explore the growth of this contemporary cultural phenomenon that now connects books, toys, and mobile digital media with children's play and learning.

Scholars in the fields of communication and cultural studies have for some time drawn attention to the influence of the toy and entertainment industries on the material artifacts of popular culture that children play with and the social practices that they engage in while doing so. Seminal studies in this regard have been Ellen Seiter's *Sold Separately* and Stephen Kline's *Out of the Garden*, both published in 1993 just as the Internet-capable multimedia 'personal computer' was becoming readily available and heavily promoted for domestic use (Nixon, 1998). Both these studies noted the rise of the child-consumer subject in the twentieth century and associated practices in which children's popular culture was 'sold separately' to the child and the parent (for discussions of these works see Buckingham (2000)

International Handbook of Research on Children's Literacy, Learning, and Culture, First Edition.
Edited by Kathy Hall, Teresa Cremin, Barbara Comber, and Luis C. Moll.
© 2013 John Wiley & Sons, Ltd. Published 2013 by John Wiley & Sons, Ltd.

and Kenway and Bullen (2001)). More recent research suggests that the children's market has grown significantly, and that children are now being addressed directly and through a wider range of media, and in a wider range of settings, than was previously the case (Buckingham, 2011).

It is not possible to know with any precision the extent of children's participation in popular culture and the cultures of the book and mobile digital media. Nor is it easy to get up-to-date estimates because information from market research is tightly held and expensive to access. However, according to a 2009 survey of over 2000 Americans aged 8 to 18 funded by the Kaiser Family Foundation (Rideout, Foehr, and Roberts, 2010), the use of every type of media increased in the decade 1999–2009 with the exception of the reading of print media. Nonetheless, time spent reading books (rather than magazines) 'remained steady, and actually increased slightly . . . (from 21 to 25 minutes a day)' (p. 2). That is, this study found that during the previous decade, *both* codex book reading *and* engagement with non-print media had been important in the lives of young people aged over 8 years.

This survey provided no information about the media use of children younger than 8 years. However, a similar sized survey of households with children aged between 0 and 6 years undertaken in the United Kingdom in 2004–2005 (Marsh *et al.*, 2005) reported that some children were engaging with the electronic media as part of their 'play' from the first months of life. This study found that most children in the sample had first watched television between the ages of 6 and 11 months and had turned it on by themselves by the age of two. Of those in the sample who had used a computer mouse to point and click, most had first done so by the age of three. In short, by 2005 young children were 'growing up in a digital world and develop[ing] a wide range of skills, knowledge and understanding of this world from birth' (Marsh *et al.*, 2005, p. 5). These studies suggested relatively high levels of exposure to electronic and digital media among children aged between 6 months and 10 years, with over 50 percent of all children over 8 years having exposure to mobile and 'personal' media.

Despite these figures, the commercial push to market smart toys and digital media for young babies, infants, and toddlers had until then come under relatively little scrutiny. However, concerns had been expressed by parent groups, psychologists, and early childhood educators (e.g., Levin, 1998; Schor, 2004) that mass-marketed toys, and electronic toys in particular, might inhibit children's capacity for open-ended play and, therefore, interfere with children's supposedly 'natural' curiosity and patterns of development. Diane Levin, author of a book about 'remote control childhood' (Levin, 1998) and founder of TRUCE (Teachers Resisting Unhealthy Children's Entertainment), is one high-profile advocate who has maintained a skeptical attitude towards electronic toys and the media/entertainment industries. On the topic of electronic toys she issued the following warning to literacy educators:

> Individualized, open-ended opportunities for play can be greatly hampered by the programmed response of mobile phones, scripts embedded in talking dolls, and the musical score that is a push-button away in an electronic busy-box. (Levin and Rosenquest, 2001, p. 2)

In contrast, other education scholars have taken a more sanguine approach, reminding readers of the history of 'moral panics' on the topic of children and popular culture, the complexities of the issue for society and researchers alike, and the paucity of evidence about the 'effects' of the cultural shift to digital media (e.g., Buckingham, 2000; Marsh, 2002). In a response to Levin's contention that children's play can be hampered by the use of electronic toys, early childhood educator Jackie Marsh (2002) adds a note of caution about such general assertions. Rather, Marsh argues that studies have shown that 'play takes shape in different families in different ways' (p. 134) and, further, that 'children do not always use toys in a routine or predictable manner' (p. 135). Indeed Marsh was an early advocate for the integration of electronic toys and new technologies into educational practice in the early years of life. Her argument that children should be assisted to participate with competence in the contemporary environment in which 'technological know-how is an essential foundation for a range of learning opportunities' (Marsh, 2002, p. 136) is as convincing today as it was a decade ago, perhaps even more so. However, just how teachers, parents and caregivers might best achieve this outcome remains unclear.

Political Economies of 'Edutainment' Media for Children

Children's cultural studies and media scholar David Buckingham has been at the forefront of studies of children's popular media cultures that pay equal attention to the analytic triad of industries, audiences, and texts. Of particular interest here are his studies of education, entertainment, and learning in the home undertaken with Margaret Scanlon (e.g., Buckingham and Scanlon, 2001, 2002, 2005) and his recent book *The Material Child* (Buckingham, 2011). Buckingham's research has demonstrated how the figure of 'the material child' has emerged within 'a complex web of economic, technological and cultural factors' (Buckingham, 2011, p. 89) and the significant part played by the media and cultural industries.

In one paper Buckingham and Scanlon (2005) analyze the then emerging market for 'edutainment' for children across three main industry sectors: print publishing, software and online learning. The study was conducted during a period of government policy initiatives in the United Kingdom and beyond that emphasized 'the importance of parental involvement in children's learning' and sought 'to extend the reach of schooling into children's leisure time' (p. 1). This research showed the effects on book publishing and retailing of a concentration of ownership among large, multinational companies. It highlighted a 'tendency towards vertical integration of publishing and retailing, partly through direct marketing and use of the Internet' (p. 2), and pointed to the narrowing effects on the diversity of material published associated with the government initiatives such as the introduction of the National Curriculum, the Numeracy and Literacy Hour and standardized testing. The authors also noted the dominance of the imperatives of national testing in the children's software market and suggested the likelihood of its equally strong influence on the then-emerging online learning market. Finally, the authors speculated that one possible outcome of all these developments was that 'the kinds of "informal" learning that might occur in the home will become increasingly "curricularised"' (Buckingham and Scanlon, 2001, p. 45) or allied to official pre-school and school curriculum. There is some evidence that this is happening in relation to the pre-school years market (Nichols, Nixon, and Rowsell, 2009; Nixon, 2011) but more research is needed in relation to the primary school age markets.

In the United States, investigative journalist Susan Thomas (2007) has examined the political economy of the popular media culture for very young children. Unlike Buckingham and Scanlon, she did not confine her study to 'educational' media and toys. Rather, she first traces the merging of the 'cult of the child-rearing expert and the marketing industry' (p. 41) that began to flourish in the first two decades of the twentieth century. Following that, she summarizes developments in the toy industry for young children between the late 1980s and early 2000s. Thomas highlights the significant influence during these years of scientific publications about infant neuropsychology, or 'brain science' (Nadesan, 2002), that was used by the US government to bolster the notion that cognitive development in the first three years of life was crucial for children's future success and the future of the nation's economy.

Drawing on published research and interviews she conducted with industry personnel, Thomas documents events that led to a situation in which 'today, to be competitive in the baby and toddler business, a toymaker's products must encourage "learning", or at least claim that they do' (2007, p. 9). She makes the argument that a complex set of economic, technological, and cultural factors accounts for what she calls 'the baby genius phenomenon' (cf. Hughes, 2005) – 'the widely held notion that infants and toddlers can be made smarter through exposure to the right products and programs' (p. 9). Here she notes the significance of the appearance of the Baby Einstein brand in 1996 and credits its founder, Julie Aigner-Clark, with first brokering 'the merger of two ideas: that a video or TV program can be *a good baby toy* and that a well-designed toy might *boost a baby's brain power*' (p. 9, italics added). Since then, Thomas writes:

> As the zero-to-three market has grown, so has a popular culture revolving around babies and toddlers. It includes formal classes and school (gymnastics, music, art, academics), the use of machines previously reserved for adults and kids (computers, VCRs, TV, DVRs, cell phones, digital cameras), and rigorous schedules to ensure that every moment offers an opportunity to 'learn' (2007, p. 4).

Despite cautions from educational researchers about the lack of 'brain science' research evidence from the study of human beings (as compared with laboratory animals) (Nadesan, 2002; MacNaughton, 2004), there is little doubt that the baby genius phenomenon became extremely lucrative for the toy and entertainment industries (Hughes, 2005). Further, it has been argued that, despite doubts raised, brain science continued to appeal to educators because it offered 'seductive facts and logic for early childhood educators' (MacNaughton, 2004, p. 92) who were looking for scientific 'proof' that accords importance to early childhood education. As MacNaughton points out, despite the limitations of brain science, 'the allure of its cause-and-effect logic' (2004, p. 101) led to the ideas continuing to have 'considerable currency and authority . . . [even being] promulgated by key international institutions such as the World Bank' (p. 92). Summing up the situation, she notes that 'questions of the brain' became 'big policy and big business' (p. 101). This observation is borne out by the advent of companies such as Genius Babies, online retailers supposedly geared toward toys designed 'to enrich your new baby's or child's learning skills while still being fun' (Genius Babies Inc., 1998–2012). Here the ideologies of playing to learn, and the need for lifelong learning from birth to ensure future success, are tightly connected and 'sold' to receptive parents and carers.

The Rise of Mobile Media 'Toys'

As already noted, the Baby Einstein phenomenon has been credited with promulgating the idea that a communication *medium* such as a book or video can be thought of *as a toy* (Thomas, 2007). Since that time the market for digital toys and hybrid web-toys that operate by connecting book, music, and toy artifacts with website participation has expanded and become interconnected with the mobile media market.

A survey of American children aged 0 to 8 years conducted in mid-2011 found that this group spends an average of about three hours a day with media of all kinds, including print media, screen media, and music. Most of that time is spent with screen media, and 27 percent of all screen time is spent with digital media: computers, hand-held and console video game players, and other interactive mobile devices such as cell phones, video iPods, and iPad-style tablet devices (Common Sense Media, 2011). This survey is interesting for the detail it provides about *mobile* media use among this age group:

> Half (52 percent) of all children now have access to one of the newer mobile devices at home: either a smartphone (41 percent), a video iPod (21 percent), or an iPad or other tablet device (8 percent). More than a quarter (29 percent) of all parents have down-loaded 'apps' (applications used on mobile devices) for their children to use. And more than a third (38 percent) of children have ever used one of these newer mobile devices, including 10 percent of 0- to 1-year-olds, 39 percent of 2- to 4-year-olds, and 52 percent of 5- to 8-year-olds. In a typical day, 11 percent of all 0- to 8-year olds use a cell phone, iPod, iPad, or similar device for media consumption, and those who do spend an average of :43 doing so. (Common Sense Media, 2011, p. 9)

Another study of the children's media and culture industries conducted for the Joan Ganz Cooney Centre has shown that four industries constitute the bulk of digital media products that children consume: toys, video games, computer software, and WWW destinations (Shuler, 2007, 2012). That is, market research now routinely aligns the formerly distinct category of *toys* with *digital media games* and *online participation*. A second point of interest is the finding that WWW destinations are increasingly likely to be accessed by children on *mobile* platforms such as mobile phones and tablets – wireless computers operated using touch technologies. For example, as the Silicon Valley toy company Nukotoys reports:

> We're building a new kind of toy company, redefining toys for today's digitally fascinated kids and engaged parents: children, who by age 3 navigate an iPad with ease; parents, who want to their kids to benefit from this fascination. As a company, we believe in giving kids fun, fantastical experiences that join online and real-world play. (Nukotoys, 2012)

According to market research conducted in the last quarter of 2011 (Neilsen, 2012 cited in Johnson, 2012), seven out of ten children under the age of 12 in a house with a tablet use them. In tablet-owning families 57 percent of children use educational applications and 77 percent play downloaded games on the tablet. However, there is also developing an increasingly wide digital divide with respect to digital media access among young children from different families, especially in regard to mobile touch or 'smart' media. For example, the US survey conducted by Common Sense Media (2011) referred to above notes 'the new "app gap" that has developed among young children,' with '38 percent of lower-income parents saying they did not even know what an app is compared to just 3 percent of higher-income parents' (p. 10). Similarly, concerns have been raised in the digital book industry that children's book publishers have been slow to publish e-books, and that many children will not have access to the devices required to read these books due to poverty (e.g., Greenfield, 2012). At the same time, companies continue to forge ahead developing book-toy-game-web hybrid products that operate by merging virtual and real world activities and can be activated on mobile devices such as tablets.

Digital Mobile Media Toys for Literacy Learning: The Case of LeapFrog™

While Thomas (2007) credits the Baby Einstein brand with making the baby genius phenomenon possible, she credits the LeapFrog™ company with 'pushing the baby genius movement forward' (p. 26). LeapFrog™ is a popular brand of electronic educational toy that has maintained a specific emphasis on supporting young children's literacy learning. LeapFrog™ Enterprises was founded by US lawyer, Michael Wood in 1995. Following input from a professor of education at Stanford University, Wood designed the first LeapFrog™ toy in the hope that it would help his young son to master phonics. Since that time many of the company's products have been designed in consultation with significant figures in the academic fields of education, psychology and technology in a bid to justify the company's slogan that 'LeapFrog™ puts learning first' and aims to 'help every child achieve his or her potential by delivering best-in-class curriculum through engaging content, age-appropriate technology-based platforms, and toys' (LeapFrog Enterprises, 2001–2010).

Since the release of the first LeapPad in 1999, the company has been marketing to children and parents, and schools and teachers, various 'learning systems' and 'personalized tools' for learning, including toy-web hybrids. The company sees three developments as central to its future success: the LeapPad, LeapFrog™ Learning Path, and LeapWorld (Chiasson, 2010). The 2012 version of the LeapPad is described as:

> the learning tablet just for kids. With a built-in camera, and a library of 100+ cartridge games and activities, the durable LeapPad features innovative apps that inspire creativity and turn reading into fun and games. It's a new way to learn, a new way to play – a new way to unlock your child's potential! (LeapFrog Enterprises, 2001–2012c)

Despite the centrality of a mobile digital device to the LeapFrog™ experience for children aged 4 to 9 years, the company retains a focus on conventional literacy activities such as reading and writing stories. In addition, however, when connected to the home computer, the LeapPad enables parents to see what and how their child has been learning to read, write, or 'create' stories using multimedia. That is, flows of data gleaned from a child's activities with the device are uploaded to the LeapFrog™ website and transformed into a semiotic representation of the child's so-called 'learning path' for parents to view. In effect, this provides parents with 'progress reports':

> Learning Path updates are available to give you details on the time your child spends playing with our reading or gaming systems, game questions answered, skills explored, etc. They also help you recognize areas where your child excels and areas where he/she may need more support. (LeapFrog Enterprises, 2001–2012a)

In this way, parents are encouraged and assisted to *monitor* and *measure* their children's learning 'development' and to assess this relative to a child's 'current age level.' In a climate of high-stakes testing of school-readiness, and mandated standardized testing in literacy and numeracy, this provides a potentially powerful incentive for parents to consider signing up for this online service to supplement their children's play.

A third key development for the company is LeapWorld™, described as 'a safe, online world for kids aged four to nine' in which all aspects of the pre-school and school curriculum are covered. By connecting their portable LeapFrog™ device to the Internet via the home computer, children can enter an online space where: '[e]xclusive online games and activities automatically adapt, so that as they play children can unlock math and literacy learning that is just right for their skill level' . . . 'on topics such as science, social studies and even life skills' (LeapFrog Enterprises, 2001–2012b). This initiative continues to support the expansion of privately funded educational provision that both bypasses and supposedly 'supports' school learning and also potentially widens the gap between those families who can and cannot afford to supplement their children's play and learning in this way.

Playing as Reading on the iPad: The Case of Little Golden Books

The integration of physical toys or books with digital add-ons and online connectivity is seen by the relevant industries as having great potential for expansion, especially given the extraordinary reception of the Apple iPad and the success of web-toy hybrids like WebKinz™ (Ganz, 2005–2012). Toy company Mattel, for example, has developed branded iPad apps for the character Barbie (Mattel Inc., 2011). It has also showcased its first 'Apptivity Action' game that consists of toys and an iPad app; a physical toy made of conductive plastic is 'recognized' by the iPad and used to interact with or play app games. Meanwhile established toy brands like Lego and book publishers such as Random House have been among the first to develop children's apps for the iPad in an emergent market.

It may be that the political economy of twentieth-century children's literature distinguished between the 'ready-made possible world' of canonical children's literature and basal readers, and the 'texts of popular culture . . . [which] rely heavily on a direct connection to the consumer and media world outside the text' (Luke, Carrington, and Kapitzke, 2003, p. 254). However, in the twenty-first century, such distinctions are breaking down in the face of the new market and cultural dominance of the iPad and similar tablet technologies. Indeed, in the ongoing linking and co-marketing of books, toys, and games as 'pedagogic commodities' (Luke, Carrington, and Kapitzke, 2003, p. 249), app/interactive e-books render canonical children's literature as popular culture texts connected to consumer and media worlds, and reflect the ongoing trend away from playing *at* reading to playing *as* reading discussed above.

From a literacy education point of view, it is worth noting that while the iPad is a new form of communications technology, having been launched in 2010, it differs from other e-reader technology in its alignment with codex-based interaction for readers. As Al-Yaqout (2011) notes, the iPad 'does not claim to offer an alternate mode of reading books. On the contrary, it appears as if its primary aim is to come as close as possible to the experiences had with the conventional codex picturebook' (p. 65). This extends to the fact that '[o]n the iPad, the turning of the page has been artfully constructed to mimic a hand movement reminiscent of the action a reader performs when navigating the pages of the codex text' (p. 68).

Of course, on an iPad, the hand movements needed to navigate content are not limited to this hand movement. So, while readers can swipe through or 'turn' the pages of an e-version of the story, they can also tap and drag visual elements to access or manipulate non-narrative features of the app. This is important, because it marks one of the primary distinctions between e-books (available for a variety of platforms, including personal computers, branded readers such as Kindle or Nook, etc., and for software installed on an iPad, as when users can download a Kindle app to an iPad in order to access Kindle-formatted e-books) and apps designed for the iPad platform that can combine such e-texts with multimodal features unavailable in codices or their digital equivalents.

An obvious example of a successful transition from canonical children's book to iPad interactive e-book/app is Beatrix Potter's *Peter Rabbit* (1902). The 2011 app version, *PopOut! The Tale of Peter Rabbit*, by Loud Crow Interactive, seeks to visually replicate images of a paper-based book while adapting it to the capabilities of the iPad (iTunes Preview, 2011b). *Peter Rabbit* offers a useful example not only because of its presence as an early success story of children's literature apps, but also because it has always carried the dual codings of canonicity and popularity: 'from its initial appearance, *The Tale of Peter Rabbit* has been plundered to sponsor an ever-expanding collection of consumables and collectibles' (Mackey, 1998, pp. xvii).

Within Loud Crow's app, there is not only a desire to reproduce the visual culture of the codex book (page numbers, the gutter replete with stitching marks, the paper grain), but also to 'app' the reading experience by including a voice-over narration/read-aloud function, background musical soundtrack, and moveable elements. On pages 10–11, for example, the rabbits can be jiggled, (just as throughout the app, movable textual elements visually resemble pull-tabs and pop-up elements from children's books of the past and elements from iPad games) and readers are alerted to the very engaging possibility of 'popping out' the falling blackberries by tapping them with a finger, rotating the iPad to make the berries roll around the screen, and finally to squash the berries by tapping on them again (iTunes Preview, 2011b). The potential for literacy learning when using such an app includes print literacy, visual literacy, app-based literacy (learning the controls of the specific app), and technological literacy, as readers/users/players engage physically and intellectually with the iPad.

To consider some of the textual and cultural repercussions of the convergence of the canonical and the popular, and the simultaneous convergence of corporate properties, brands and technologies, we turn to two examples of Little Golden Book apps. *The Poky Little Puppy* is a canonical children's book that has undergone a digital makeover for the iPad; *Barbie*[TM] *Princess Charm School* is an app based broadly on a popular Mattel toy, and specifically on a DVD film based on that property. Between them, these apps make visible the conflation of canonical and popular culture in a landscape tailor-made for the conflation of playing and learning.

Like other 'educational' resources for children, Little Golden Books were first marketed by appealing to socially aspirational and anxious caregivers (Pugh, 2009) who were concerned to acquire resources to support beginning readers (often but not exclusively young children). They were first published in 1942 to meet the (real or marketing-generated) needs of:

> a large unserved portion of the public – consisting of Americans who, though less educated and less prosperous than traditional book buyers, were eager to better themselves and their children – [who] could be reached only if good books were manufactured and sold far more cheaply than in the past. (Marcus, 2007, p. 30)

From the start Little Golden Books courted and represented pleasurable consumption (both in the sense of purchasing and of reading) combined with an educational goal focused on literacy as an element of social mobility. Little Golden Books has become a highly recognizable brand that continues to enjoy an emotionally engaged and intergenerational fan or customer base.

Of the initial series of twelve Little Golden Books, *The Poky Little Puppy* has enjoyed particular success. In 2001 *Publisher's Weekly* identified it as the best-selling children's book in the United States (Roback and Britton, 2001, p. 24) and the best-selling picture book of all time, and the same year the book won the Dr Toy 'Best Classic Toy Award' (Random House Children's Books, 1995–2012). *The Poky Little Puppy* (1942/1970), written by Janette Sebring Lowrey ([Kirkus Reviews, 2001] 1942/1970) and illustrated by Gustaf Tenggren, tells the story of a family of five puppies negotiating between their desires to explore their local environment and parental sanctions against doing so. This particular book 'sells' the same logic of educational entertainment that is claimed by the Little Golden Books as a whole. The claim is that the book not only helps beginning readers to develop their literary and visual literacies, it also depicts the protagonist engaging in reading activity that is connected with 'appropriate' social behavior that supports social conformity and cohesion.

Given the longevity and popularity of *The Poky Little Puppy*, it makes commercial and cultural sense that Random House used this book as the source for the first of its Golden Books apps for iPad launched in the United States in August 2011. The app version of *The Poky Little Puppy* is a commodity that potentially benefits each corporate participant – Apple Inc. and Random House – not only in terms of immediate sales, but also in terms of re-training their respective markets to incorporate dual corporate consumption. The collaboration enables

Apple to extend its iPad market share to caregivers and educators keen to see children 'learn while playing' while it enables Random House to articulate an existing market from owning texts published in one format to owning texts published in multiple formats.

The Poky Little Puppy app sells through Apple's app store for direct download to an iPad, iPhone, or iPod Touch via iTunes. The options for engaging with traditional and new textual elements in the app include the following:

> 'Auto-play' allows for continuous narration and features a pleasing adult female voice and automatic page turns. In this mode text words are highlighted as they are read. 'My Voice' prompts children to read and record their own narration. Both 'Sound Effects' and 'Narrator' can be switched on and off.... Delightful interactive features, which include a hissing snake, a chirping grasshopper, and musical flowers, complement the original art and are seamlessly integrated with the text and narration. Tapping an icon located in a corner of each screen will elicit a developmentally appropriate question encouraging children to identify colors, numbers, or objects. Correct answers are rewarded with a sticker that is stored in an album. (Sheridan, 2011)

The familiarity and authority of *The Poky Little Puppy* as a mainstay of US children's literature may well have contributed to the app being reviewed by major professional journals, including *School Library Journal* and *Kirkus*. These are mostly descriptive reviews, but much praise for 'educational goodies' (Kirkus Reviews, 2001), 'educational interactivity' (Healy, 2012), and 'delightful interactive features' (Sheridan, 2011) is present across the field. We suggest that such reviews now do the kind of cultural work that was formerly undertaken for the original Little Golden Books by 'the assurance that the entire series was being published under the supervision of "Dr. Mary Reed of Teachers' College, Columbia University"' (Marcus, 2007, p. 50). As Marcus notes, this 'educator's imprimatur, emblazoned on the copyright page of every Little Golden Book until the time of Reed's death in 1960, would soon become as well known a guarantor of excellence as the Good Housekeeping Seal of Approval' (2007, p. 50). While the Apple app store promotes itself as a democratic marketplace, the approval of 'key educational reviewers' is nonetheless mentioned within that marketplace, and presumably offers a sense of assurance to those contemporary purchasers who desire that children's interactions with iPads be as literary and as educational as possible.

Where the *The Poky Little Puppy* app works most obviously as an adaptation of an existing literary property (indicating a 'literature to popular culture' trajectory), another of the first Little Golden Books apps launched by Random House in 2011 reverses this trajectory to draw on a popular culture text and re-present it *as* literary. A wide variety of textual and material incarnations of *Barbie Princess Charm School* mark it as a corporate property par excellence that proliferates across a range of platforms and media. The organizing narrative of the property can be found on the straight-to-DVD animated film, released in 2011, and tells the story of Blair, who is plucked from waitressing to attend Princess Charm School. This plot turns on a 'special' individual taking advantage of a standardized pedagogical journey to achieve social mobility.

Among the many online games, books, toys, and e-texts associated with it, *Barbie Princess Charm School* offers a range of reading, playing, and learning pleasures for consumers. At the Barbie Princess Charm School website (Mattel Inc., 2012), visitors can consume a variety of advertising, activities, 'personalized' digital artifacts, and even attend Princess Charm School. A downloadable welcome kit outlines the Charm School schedule, which incorporates earning 'badges' that map onto key narrative events in the DVD film (such as poise, tea party skills, and tiara decoration), and leads visitors towards viewing a preview of the film and downloading the film's theme song (Mattel Inc., 2012). Of course, the website links to other areas within Mattel's Barbie online content, including its online shop front.

While the film and the website embed their narrative in a school setting, and thus conjure traditional school-related pedagogies, each is less explicitly interested in literacy than is the Random House iPad app, *Barbie*^{TM} *Princess Charm School*. By retelling in prose the narrative of the DVD, the app offers a more sustained literary narrative than any of the other incarnations we have explored. Its interactive features are similar to those in the *The Poky Little Puppy* app – users can access moveable illustrations, add their name and photograph to the text as owners, collect stickers, and so forth – and the app is thus aligned with other Random House Little Golden Book apps at the same time as being aligned with a range of *Barbie Princess Charm School* texts and artifacts (iTunes Preview, 2011a).

When read in juxtaposition with other iPad apps for children's literature, Little Golden Books apps, and Barbie Princess Charm School commodities, the *Barbie Princess Charm School* app reveals not only a convergence of playing, learning, and reading, but also of corporate interests as Apple, Mattel, and Random House collaborate to 'edutain' consumers, not only in playing, learning, or reading, but also in learning to consume (cf. Martens, 2005). This is not to say that users are passive stooges to corporate interests, but perhaps more usefully to point out that the gap between books, games, and toys, or the literary and the popular, has long been an arbitrary distinction based on technologies, economies of access and the sociology of 'taste' (Bourdieu, 1986). As *The Poky Little Puppy* acquires a twenty-first century sheen of digital play, and Barbie acquires a twenty-first century sheen of pedagogy, 'learning' and the literary, each basks in the glow of its newly acquired quality while retaining its original values: literary reassurance for caregivers meets playful pleasures for users, and anachronistic social values of gender and class are given a twenty-first century corporate makeover.

Just as the first Little Golden Books were marketed to adults anxious to build their children's literacy and, thus, to encourage future socio-economic success, the iPad is being marketed as a kind of crossover technology that represents educational and economic 'belonging.' The iPad materializes links between home and professional cultures, and home and school cultures; links which are widely understood to shape one's capacity for socio-economic participation, agency, and mobility. The iPad itself is an increasingly mobile and thus desirable example of communications technology, which in turn strengthens its symbolic value within and across home, school, and workplace cultures. The Little Golden Book apps are being designed to provide a nostalgic link with the visual culture of the original Little Golden Books, and also to establish a range of features and activities as newly-familiar and safe; inviting consumers to entrust their children's learning and play-time to the popular technology of the iPad.

Concluding Comments

We have attempted to canvass the constellation of cultural factors that are shaping a situation in which the industries and markets for books, toys, and digital media designed for children's play and learning have become tightly interconnected. In the process we have noted the expanding number of social spaces such as supermarkets and toy stores in which families now encounter invitations to learn about and participate in the literacy learning and development of children from birth until the early years of school and beyond (Nichols *et al.*, 2012). We have also examined cases of cross fertilization that has been occurring between the printed literary book and the popular digitally enhanced toy/game, and between both of these artifacts and branded websites and 'apps' designed for tablet style computers. In our view, exploring this cultural context and these particular phenomena in more depth should be on the agenda of media and literacy researchers alike.

One reason this topic falls within the province of literacy educators was first noted by Marsha Kinder when she argued that rich forms of transmedia *intertextuality* accompany such movements of characters and stories across multiple formats using digital technologies (Kinder, 1991). Developing research methods to trace the flows of intertextual references and modes of meaning-making that are potentially available to children while they participate in print and digital media cultures remains an ongoing challenge for the field of literacy studies.

Newly mobile and flexible technologies of literacy and play render much of children's lives as pedagogical environments, and encourage caregivers to identify themselves as pedagogical agents. At the same time, as Jack Zipes notes, '[c]hildren are not as literate as their parents were in the domain of literature, but their parents are also not as literate in the new technologies that are pivotal for their children's acquiring a distinct and distinguished habitus under present cultural and economic conditions' (2008, p. 24). The imperative is thus for adults versed in relatively stable print and literary cultures to address their own illiteracy in the new cultural environment as much as children's perceived illiteracies. As the relationship between young people, their cultural consumption, and the points of access and meaning-making become increasingly flexible and mobile, scholarly engagement with the very concept of literacy must be similarly flexible and mobile.

There is also an ongoing need for educational researchers to find ways to productively investigate what these developments actually mean for the children and their families who engage with such products and services. Many researchers working in the field of literacy studies have looked to ethnographic methods to provide a window onto the richly textured practices associated with making and communicating social meanings in everyday life. However, there are signs that the edutainment industries are now also using such methods for their own purposes. For example, Braiterman and Larvie (2002, p. 1) report on an industry-funded study that used 'rapid ethnography . . . combined with an iterative design process' to integrate 'knowledge of user motivation, sensitivities and tolerances' during the design of an 'early Internet-enabled toy.' Here methods such as making video-tapes during three-hourly visits to homes were used to fit with industry imperatives associated with 'compressed product cycles' (p. 2).

In her research discussed above, Thomas (2007) also describes the long-term use by 'educational' toy companies Playskool, Fisher Price, and LeapFrog™ of well-funded research 'labs,' overseen by academically distinguished researchers, to trial prototype toys with volunteer children and parents. Here, during the development of products, academic terminology from developmental psychology is used by industry to 'categorize milestones . . . and to suggest that little children will be learning academic subjects' (p. 48) when they play with particular toys. Companies like Disney and Mattel also commission ethnographies conducted in the home to help them market products to children. Thomas makes the point that today 'many advertising and marketing firms have ethnography divisions, often headed by an executive with a graduate degree in anthropology' (2007, p. 131). Further, she demonstrates how Vygotsky's concept of scaffolding – usually associated with school-based teaching and learning – has been enlisted by market researchers to enable them conduct in-depth, at-home interviews with children and to encourage them to complete journals about their 'dream electronic,' for example, in ways that the industry considers to be 'clear' and 'authentic' (p. 134). Thomas reports that market researchers credit these methods with assisting children to 'reflect on their routines and interests, and to begin to trust that the team is genuinely interested in their experiences and ideas' (p. 133). At the same time, these methods also assist industry to learn more about children's 'attachment to characters' and how this is connected with 'brand sensitivity and understanding' among different age groups (pp. 134–135).

In the context of this kind of industry-supported research, literacy researchers face significant challenges in securing funding and delineating and articulating distinctive research objectives and methods. Despite the changing artifacts and technologies enlisted by people to play, communicate, and learn, literacy continues to constitute a significant component of active social participation and informed citizenship. As children are inducted younger and younger into particular modes of literacy, and particular dispositions as 'consuming citizens,' researchers committed to learning from and contributing to young people's agency and social opportunities need to pay attention to what is happening culturally when reading and playing and literacy and learning means tapping, touching, swiping, and scrolling and combining online and offline activities.

References

Al-Yaqout, G. (2011) From slate to slate: What does the future hold for the picturebook series? *New Review of Children's Literature and Librarianship*, 17(1): 57–77.

Bourdieu, P. (1986) *Distinction: A Social Critique of the Judgement of Taste*, trans. R. Nice. London: Routledge.

Braiterman, J., and Larvie, P. (2002) Each sold separately: Ethnography as a tool for integrating online and offline use of educational toys. Human Factors Conference, Melbourne, Australia, accessed November 8, 2012: www.jaredresearch.com/portfolio/leapfrog/index.html

Buckingham, D. (2000) *After the Death of Childhood: Growing Up in the Age of Electronic Media*. Cambridge, UK: Polity Press.

Buckingham, D. (2011) *The Material Child: Growing Up in Consumer Culture*. Cambridge, UK: Polity Press.

Buckingham, D., and Scanlon, M. (2001) Parental pedagogies: An analysis of British 'edutainment' magazines for young children. *Journal of Early Childhood Literacy*, 1(3): 281–299.

Buckingham, D., and Scanlon, M. (2002) *Education, Entertainment and Learning in the Home*. Buckingham, UK: Open University Press.

Buckingham, D., and Scanlon, M. (2005) Selling learning: Towards a political economy of edutainment media. *Media, Culture and Society*, 27(1): 41–58.

Chiasson, W. (2010) LeapFrog Enterprises, Inc. Chief Executive Officer and President's 2009 Annual Report and 2010 Proxy Statement, accessed November 8, 2012: http://media.corporate-ir.net/media_files/irol/13/131670/LF2010/HTML2/default.htm

Common Sense Media (2011) Zero to eight: Children's media use in America. A Common Sense Media Research Study, accessed November 8, 2012: www.commonsensemedia.org/sites/default/files/research/zerotoeightfinal2011.pdf

Ganz (2005–2012) Webkinz website, accessed April 30, 2012: www.webkinz.com/

Genius Babies Inc. (1998–2012) 'Genius babies... smart baby gifts and toys', accessed November 8, 2012: www.geniusbabies.com/

Greenfield, J. (2012) When growth in children's e-books hits the poverty line. Digital Book World, 14 March, accessed November 8, 2012: www.digitalbookworld.com/2012/when-growth-in-childrens-e-books-hits-the-poverty-line/

Healy, C. (2012) The Poky Little Puppy. Common Sense Media. Online, accessed November 8, 2012: www.commonsensemedia.org/mobile-app-reviews/poky-little-puppy

Hughes, P. (2005) Baby, it's you: International capital discovers the under threes. *Contemporary Issues in Early Childhood*, 6(1) 30–40.

iTunes Preview (2011a) 'Barbie: Princess Charm School,' accessed April 30, 2012: http://itunes.apple.com/us/app/barbie-princess-charm-school/id455731362?mt=8

iTunes Preview (2011b) 'PopOut! The adventure of Peter Rabbit,' accessed November 8, 2012: http://itunes.apple.com/us/app/popout!-tale-peter-rabbit/id397864713?mt=8

Johnson, L. (2012) 57pc of children use tablets for educational apps: Nielsen. *Mobile Marketer*, accessed November 8, 2012: www.mobilemarketer.com/cms/news/research/12141.html

Kenway, J., and Bullen, E. (2001) *Consuming Children: Education-Entertainment-Advertising*. Buckingham UK: Open University Press.

Kinder, M. (1991) *Playing with Power in Movies, Television, and Video Games: From Muppet Babies to Teenage Mutant Ninja Turtles*. California: University of California Press.

Kirkus Reviews (2001) *The Poky Little Puppy*. Online. September 28, 2011, accessed November 8, 2012: www.kirkusreviews.com/book-reviews/janette-sebring-lowrey-1/poky-little-puppy/

Kline, S. (1993) *Out of the Garden: Toys and Children's Culture in the Age of TV Marketing*. London: Verso.

LeapFrog Enterprises (2001–2010) Investor relations, accessed November 8, 2012: http://www.leapfroginvestor.com/phoenix.zhtml?c=131670&p=irol-irhome

LeapFrog Enterprises (2001–2012a) Connect to your child's learning!, accessed November 8, 2012: www.leapfrog.com/en/get_connected/learning-path.html

LeapFrog Enterprises (2001–2012b) LeapWorld™ launches online learning, accessed November 8, 2012: www.leapfrog.com/en/home/about_us/leapfrog_press_room0/leapworldlaunch.html

LeapFrog Enterprises (2001–2012c) LeapPad The #1 learning tablet for kids, November 8, 2012: www.leapfrog.com/leappad/index.html#create_and_share

Levin, D. (1998) *Remote Control Childhood? Combating the Hazards of Media Culture*. Washington DC: National Association for the Education of Young Children.

Levin, D., and Rosenquest, B. (2001) The increasing role of electronic toys in the lives of infants and toddlers. *Contemporary Issues in Early Childhood*, 2(2): 242–246.

Lowrey, J.S. (1942/1970) *The Poky Little Puppy*, illustrated by G. Tenggren. New York: Random House.

Luke, A., Carrington, V., and Kapitzke, C. (2003) Textbooks and early childhood literacy. In N. Hall, J. Larson and J. Marsh (eds) *Handbook of Early Childhood Literacy*. London: Sage, pp. 249–257.

Mackey, M. (1998) *The Case of Peter Rabbit: Changing Conditions of Literature for Children*. New York: Garland.

MacNaughton, G. (2004) The politics of logic in early childhood research: A case of the brain, hard facts, trees and rhizomes. *The Australian Educational Researcher*, 31(3): 87–104.

Marcus, L. (2007) *Golden Legacy: How Golden Books won Children's Hearts, Changed Publishing Forever, and Became an American Icon Along the Way*. New York: Random House.

Marsh, J. (2002) Electronic toys: Why should we be concerned? A response to Levin and Rosenquest (2001). *Contemporary Issues in Early Childhood*, 3(1): 132–138.

Marsh, J., Brooks, G., Hughes, J., *et al.* (2005) Digital beginnings: Young children's use of popular culture, media and new technologies. Report of the 'Young Children's Use of Popular Culture, Media and New Technologies' study. Literacy Research Centre, University of Sheffield, UK.

Martens, L. (2005) Learning to consume – consuming to learn: Children at the interface between consumption and education. *British Journal of Sociology of Education*, 26(3): 343–357.

Mattel Inc. (2011) Mattel brands apps and mobile, accessed November 8, 2012: www.mattel.com/mobile-apps

Mattel Inc. (2012) Play like a Barbie Princess – videos, games, and activities for kids Barbie Princess Charm School, accessed November 8, 2012: www.barbie.com/princess-charm-school

Nadesan, M. (2002) Engineering the entrepreneurial infant: Brain science, infant development toys, and governmentality. *Cultural Studies*, 16(3): 401–432.

Nichols, S., Nixon, H., and Rowsell, J. (2009) The 'good' parent in relation to early childhood literacy: Symbolic terrain and lived practice. *Literacy*, 43(2): 65–74.

Nichols, S., Rowsell, J., Nixon, H., and Rainbird, S. (2012) *Resourcing Early Learners: New Networks, New Actors*. New York and London: Routledge.

Nixon, H. (1998) Fun and games are serious business. In J. Sefton-Green (ed.) *Digital Diversions: Youth Culture in the Age of Multimedia*. London: University College London Press, pp. 21–42.

Nixon, H. (2011) 'From bricks to clicks': Hybrid Commercial spaces in the landscape of early literacy and learning. *Journal of Early Childhood Literacy*, 11(2): 114–140.

Nukotoys (2012) Company: What we do, accessed April 30, 2012: www.nukotoys.com/company/parents-play/

Pugh, A. (2009) *Longing and Belonging: Parents, Children and Consumer Culture*. Berkeley: University of California Press.

Random House Children's Books (1995–2012) Little Golden Books timeline, accessed November 8, 2012: www.randomhouse.com/golden/lgb/timeline.html

Rideout, V., Foehr, U., and Roberts, D. (2010) *Generation M²: Media in the Lives of 8–18 Year-Olds*. Menlo Park, CA: Henry J. Kaiser Family Foundation.

Roback, D., and Britton, J. (eds) (2001) All-time bestselling children's books. *Publishers Weekly*, December 17, 24–32.

Schor, J. (2004) *Born to Buy: The Commercialized Child and the New Consumer Culture*. New York: Scribner.

Seiter, E. (1993) *Sold Separately. Parents and Children in Consumer Culture*. New Brunswick, New Jersey: Rutgers University Press.

Sheridan, R. (2011) Review of *Poky Little Puppy* for iOS. *School Library Journal*. Online. September 16, accessed November 8, 2012: http://blog.schoollibraryjournal.com/touchandgo/2011/09/16/review-of-pokey-little-puppy-for-i0s/

Shuler, C. (2007) D is for digital: An analysis of the children's interactive media environment with a focus on mass marketed products that promote learning. New York: The Joan Ganz Cooney Center at Sesame Workshop, accessed November 8, 2012: http://joanganzcooneycenter.org/Reports-2.html

Shuler, C. (2012) iLearn II: An analysis of the education category of the iTunes app store. New York: The Joan Ganz Cooney Center at Sesame Workshop, accessed November 8, 2012: http://joanganzcooneycenter.org/Reports-33.html

Thomas. S. (2007) *Buy, Buy Baby: How Consumer Culture Manipulates Parents and Harms Young Minds*. New York: Houghton Mifflin.

Zipes, J. (2008) *Relentless Progress: The Reconfiguration of Children's Literature, Fairy Tales, and Storytelling*. New York: Routledge.

Chapter 4

Literacy Education in the Age of New Media

Bill Green and Catherine Beavis

Introduction

In this the second decade of the twenty-first century, it becomes especially challenging to consider how best to (re)conceptualize literacy education, taking into account the new conditions of possibility and intelligibility for making meaning, locally and globally, and hence the changing nature of literacy, textuality, and communication. Especially significant in this regard is the emergence of what is here called *new media*, although other labels are sometimes used in different contexts. This is because, increasingly, attention is focused on and organized by distinctly new media forms and practices, now more often than not highly customized and collaborative. Moreover, it is these 'new' new media forms and practices that are being adopted by many young people, both children and adolescents, in such a way and to such a degree as to become their primary *modus operandi*, and key markers and makers of identity.

Two points can be made here. First, while the term 'new media' is more and more widely used, there is as yet no settled agreement about what it actually refers to nor about how it should be used. The term 'new,' in particular, can connote anything from a 'different' way of using and thinking about (existing) media forms, a way of catching a contemporary zeitgeist in a networked, globalized world, through to referencing specific new technologies and the forms they enable. The problematic nature of this term is discussed further below. Regardless of definitional difficulties, however, literacy education needs to attend to the phenomenon of 'new media,' and the literacies they generate and employ. Undoubtedly the 'new media,' however defined, call on a far wider range of communicative modalities than do traditional print (and oral) literacy. Similarly, they enable a wide range of digitally mediated literacy practices, and opportunities for those who engage with them, in whatever form, to read, create, respond, or otherwise interact and participate. These interactions have powerful implications for literacy education and what that might entail, both in the contemporary moment and in times to come.

Second, that young people are likely to have particular affinity with new technology and media is now such a familiar theme that it is easy to take it for granted. However, it remains a crucial consideration in thinking about literacy education today and tomorrow. Almost

International Handbook of Research on Children's Literacy, Learning, and Culture, First Edition.
Edited by Kathy Hall, Teresa Cremin, Barbara Comber, and Luis C. Moll.
© 2013 John Wiley & Sons, Ltd. Published 2013 by John Wiley & Sons, Ltd.

inevitably, there is a lag in culture and sensibility between those who are now presenting for school, with their distinctive interests, energies, and investments, and what is made available to them in school. Moreover, a clear distinction is emerging between education and schooling – between the historical apparatus of the popular state-run school, on the one hand, and the rich and varied educational opportunities provided by media, in all its new and burgeoning manifestations, on the other. Given this, literacy education, therefore, is now something that needs again to be questioned and examined. At the very least, it must be understood to entail both the formal provision of literacy teaching and learning within schools, *and* within or with respect to that wider, more informal field of the world beyond school. Conceptualizing literacy education in this way entails thinking about (re-)schooling and beyond. Taking all this on board means thinking differently about teachers and teaching, and about teacher education, as it does about learners and learning, and the young more generally, more or less from birth onwards, as the erstwhile 'natural' or assumed constituency of schooling.

In what follows, then, we focus on the question of literacy education itself – on how this is to be understood in the current and emerging age, how it is changing, and what it is for. We also engage the other key question here, that of what constitutes 'new media,' or rather, as Levinson (2009) puts it, 'new new media' – media forms emerging on the scene more or less constantly, and each time ever newer. This continual 'newness', of course, presents a challenge in itself for any account presented at a given moment in time.

Changing Literacy Education

A challenge immediately presents itself in speaking of literacy education today, and indeed tomorrow, or with reference to even the near future. To begin with, the very notion of 'literacy' needs to be interrogated, or at least carefully thought about. At issue here is the *object* of the educational enterprise, in this instance: what it is that literacy education is organized around, and addressed to – the 'what' of pedagogy. It may even be somewhat anachronistic to formulate this challenge in terms of 'literacy,' especially in considering the educational significance of new media forms and practices. This matter has been raised before, and it is salutary to observe the ways in which it has been recognized, conceptualized and spoken of over the past two decades at least. Observing that schools are traditionally and indeed historically '(verbal) language-bound institutions,' Green noted, in 1993, that the shift to a new digital-electronic order 'open[ed] up the possibility of asking about those forms of human semiosis which are currently slighted, if not suppressed, in the official discourse on curriculum and schooling' (Green, 1993, pp. 209–210). At that time, he argued that '[i]t may be inappropriate, of course, to employ the term "literacy" at all . . . unless it be expressly understood in a metaphorical sense, since many would want to argue that, strictly speaking, the notion of "literacy" is specific to written language,' and more broadly what has been called 'the written world' (Green, 1993, p. 210) – the world of logocentric modernity.

A decade later, Kress (2003a) similarly pointed to the questionable universality of the term 'literacy' in the context of globalization and the network society, moreover noting that 'other languages do not have such a word' (Kress, 2003a, p. 22). Moreover, for Kress (2003a, p. 23), '*literacy* is the term to use when we make messages using letters as the means of recording that message' – 'the term which refers to (the knowledge of) the use of the resource of writing' (Kress, 2003a, p. 24). In this regard, it is at least rhetorically appropriate to posit a distinction, as Wendy Morgan (1998) has done, between literacy and what she calls 'letteracy.' A highly significant, even momentous development has been the relatively recent but now extensive work on *multimodality*, in which Kress has been of course a leading figure (e.g., Kress *et al.*,

2001; Jewitt, 2009), and relatedly so-called 'multiliteracies' (Cope and Kalanztis, 2000). These concepts encompass an extension in the modes, or forms of semiosis, available largely though not at all exclusively through the new technologies of communication, information, (moving) image, and expression. At least potentially they represent what has been described as a radical expansion of the human sensorium (Green, 1993) and a profound transformation of the global semiotic landscape (Kress, 2003a). What this means educationally is that, rather than a more or less exclusive focus on print-alphabetic literacy, programmatically at the very least, attention needs to turn to developing *a repertoire of capabilities* in terms of both *mode* and *medium*. Whether this is properly framed within 'literacy' education may be debatable. Indeed, historically it is useful to trace a line from 'English teaching' to 'literacy education,' as the organizing site for such work, on to whatever it is that is emerging now, in 2013 and beyond, in the age of new media. This might be readily and appropriately described simply as media education, or media studies in education, if there were not a long history of struggle between rival curriculum fields and their various constituencies (Media vs English/Literacy). As well, there has been a curious lack of recognition, until very recently, of the extensive educational work done in 'media' (pre-computing, as it were) on the part of many associated with ICT.

The other side of the challenge of re-thinking literacy education takes up the issue of education itself: that is, how the purposes, forms and practices of education are changing, institutionally and otherwise, within a new globally networked digital-communication order. It may be timely indeed to rethink the structure of schooling, ranging from its early childhood ('pre-school') forms through the early years and subsequently of the primary school, with the middle years (however formalized) conceived as a transition phase into the junior secondary school, followed by high school more generally. Much debate has been generated over the past two decades about whether schooling in its current-traditional form is adequate to the task of educating the young, in a time increasingly characterized by new intensities of media and information culture (Selwyn, 2010). Certainly there can be little doubt that the overall structure and purpose of mass-compulsory ('popular') schooling needs to be reviewed and re-assessed. Schooling is increasingly uncoupled from *curriculum*, on the one hand, and from *literacy*, on the other – that is, schooling can no longer be identified either with curriculum at least in its conventional form, as school(-subject) knowledge, or with literacy as (simply) 'reading' and 'writing,' or how to make good use of 'texts.' This is not to be understood as an absolute dis-engagement, rather it is a *re-settlement*, whereby schooling is reimagined, in part – in particular, how it now relates to curriculum and literacy, together and separately. Learning, knowledge, identity-work, and what might be called communicative competency are no longer the (sole) province of the school, on this account, or the prime responsibility of teachers. But this does not mean that schools and teachers are no longer involved or engaged in such work: quite the contrary (e.g., Beavis, 2006; Burnett and Merchant, 2011; Green, 1993, pp. 208–209; O'Mara and Laidlaw, 2011; Walsh, 2010). Rather, the challenge is coming to terms with how that different role and function might be understood and managed.

Given a complex array of possible, probable, and preferred futures, Facer (2011) argues that what remains constant with regard to the prospects for digital literacy curriculum and pedagogy is the need for a focus on what she calls 'critical literacies.' Such a focus involves 'the capacity to ask questions about the values embedded in the tools and resources we use, to explore the kinds of identities and subjectivities they are encouraging, to examine the types of human relationship and social relationships they develop and to imagine and explore alternatives to such arrangements' (Facer, 2011, p. 237). Hence: '[A]t a time of constrained curriculum, where there is massive uncertainty about potential future developments, there is a strong case for arguing that we intensify our efforts to engender critical literacies through school settings' (Facer, 2011, p. 237). This certainly includes new media developments.

Right through the early years of schooling to the beginning of high school, and indeed into the junior and senior secondary years, that focus on 'critical literacy' should however be set alongside systematic and appropriate attention to the *operational* and *cultural* dimensions of literacy pedagogy, and to the integrated effect of all three dimensions – critical, cultural, and operational – working together (Green and Beavis, 2012). This means conceptualizing and organizing literacy curriculum in terms of a programmatic emphasis on authentic meaning-making and effective engagement with the world, specifically in ways congruent with the new media age. What is needed, then, is an informed sense of what might be an appropriate and desirable general repertoire of capabilities vis-à-vis mode and medium; and also the provision of opportunities and environments likely to promote children's reflexive practice in this regard.

New Literacies, New Media; or, What Constitutes the 'New'?

The three central issues at the core of this discussion are the questions of what constitutes 'literacy' in present times, what is encompassed by the term 'new media,' and what the implications are for teaching and learning due to the relationship between the two. To answer questions such as these, many literacy theorists and educators concerned with (new) media forms and their role in children's lives draw on the related fields of Media Studies and New Media Studies. They call on 'old media' core concepts such as 'texts, audiences and institutions' (e.g., Buckingham, 2003) or the circuit of culture – representation, identity, production, consumption and regulation (du Gay *et al.*, 1997) – and 'new media' interdisciplinary perspectives to provide insights into these 'new' communicative forms and the practices they enable and entail.

As often pointed out, for children and many adults who have never lived without 'new media' or 'new technologies,' such formulations are meaningless – they 'work, think and play within a new media environment as naturally as fish swim in the sea' (Lister *et al.*, 2009, p. xi). Yet, as Lister and his colleagues observe: 'One thing about which fish know exactly nothing is water, since they have no anti-environment which would enable them to see the element they live in' (p. xi). To pursue the analogy further, they argue, we need to explicitly focus on new media forms and literacies. Given the massive presence of these 'new' technologies and media in contemporary lives, they argue, the need is to make strange emergent forms of media and communication, along with the 'literacies' they entail.[1]

'Old media' as might be found in pre-digital Media Studies courses, for example, would likely include such things as books, magazines, films, newspapers, radio, photography, and television: a mixture, that is, of print and electronics, framed more or less exclusively in broadcast terms. What is meant by the term 'new media' is less easy to define. As Lister *et al.* (2009, p. 13) note:

> [T]he unifying term 'new media' actually refers to a wide range of changes in media production, distribution and use. These are changes that are technological, textual, conventional and cultural. Bearing this in mind, we nevertheless recognise that since the mid 1980s at least . . . a number of concepts have come to the fore which offer to define the key characteristics of the field of new media as a whole. We consider these here as some of the main terms in discourses about new media. These are: *digital, interactive, hypertextual, virtual, networked,* and *simulated*.[2]

Scholars of new media point to key differences and assumptions that characterize approaches to old and new media, and their study. The characteristics of these media forms, and the ways in which they are conceptualized, have significant implications for the ways in which new

Table 4.1 Significant conceptual debates between Media Studies and New Media Studies

Media Studies	New Media Studies
The effects of technology are socially determined	The nature of society is technologically determined
Active audiences	Interactive users
Interpretation	Experience
Spectatorship	Immersion
Representation	Simulation
Centralized media	Ubiquitous media
Consumer	Participant/co-creator
Work	Play

Source: Dovey and Kennedy (2006, p. 3)

literacies in turn are understood. Dovey and Kennedy (2006), for example, chart 'significant conceptual debates' between Media Studies and New Media Studies, with the study of new media forms – in their case, computer games – situated and produced *through* the tensions between them. Table 4.1 provides an overview of their analysis.

As a thumbnail sketch, this outline is at once illuminating and problematic, but it does provide a useful overview of underlying assumptions and principles across the two fields. Of particular relevance for literacy education are the ways in which relationships with media/new media are perceived, including a shift from seeing those who interact with media/new media as active audience to interactive users, and from consumers of forms such as film or television to participants or co-creators of forms such as websites and computer games. Of course there is much more crossover and fluidity across these categories than this table seems to imply, but collectively they have considerable significance for conceiving of literacy education in the present and coming age, alongside the literacy/new literacies and multimodal/multiliteracies frameworks mentioned earlier.

Examples of New Media forms include such things as blogs, wikis, YouTube, social networking sites such as Facebook and Myspace; virtual worlds such as Second Life, Twitter, photo-sharing sites such as Flickr, chat spaces, forums such as those surrounding online digital games, and Wikipedia (Levinson, 2009). Such forms or sites are accessed through a diversity of fixed, mobile, and ubiquitous forms of hardware, ranging from desktop computers through to iPads and smart phones.

Many of these 'new media' forms are gathered under the umbrella of Web 2.0. In considering Web 2.0-based versions of new media, as the table above foregrounds, what distinguishes them from old media, including old (digital) media, is primarily the capacity for users to participate and create content, rather than just 'read.' Davies and Merchant (2009) follow Lankshear and Knobel (2006) in thinking of Web 2.0 as 'best described as a developing trend or attitude.' Merchant (2009, p. 108; see also Davies and Merchant, 2009) describes four characteristic features of Web 2.0, in pointing to the potential and implications for literacy education and schools:

1   *Presence*: Web 2.0 spaces encourage users to develop an active presence through an online identity, profile or avatar;
2   *Modification*: Web 2.0 spaces usually allow a degree of personalization such as in the design of the user's home page and personal links, or in the creation of an on-screen avatar. Web 2.0 spaces may also be 'mashable' or interoperable;

3 *User-generated content*: Web 2.0 spaces are based on content which is generated within and by the community of users rather than provided by the site itself;
4 *Social Participation*: Web 2.0 spaces provide an invitation to participate… Just as user generated content makes us both producers and consumers, so with social participation we are simultaneously both performers and audience. (Merchant 2009, pp. 108–109)

As the above lists indicate, New Media are, at once, sites or spaces for participation and specific forms with particular features and affordances. They are spaces for text-mediated representation and interpretation, and also places for online interactions, meetings, and exchanges. This double-sided quality, and the accompanying ambiguities, bedevils attempts to restrict analysis and understanding of online interactions and behavior to being 'simply' about textual forms and dexterity, or 'simply' about personal interaction and behavior online. New media forms like digital games work as both text and action, with clear implications for literacy and English education (Apperley and Beavis, 2011; Beavis, O'Mara, and McNeice, 2012). As with other literacy practices, use is always contextual and socially situated. Using digital and online literacies quintessentially entails embodied social practice, for all their ostensibly 'disembodied' form. How does literacy education take account of dimensions such as these?

Digital or online literacies and literacy practices are intricately embedded in, and arise from, 'new media.' These terms, or others like them (e.g., multimedia/multimodal literacy, techno-literacy, electronic literacy), are used to describe the forms of literacy and literacy practices that young people (and others) engage with, in, and on the sites, forms and texts characterizing 'new media' and online space. Alvermann (2008, p. 9) defines online literacies as 'socially mediated ways of generating meaningful content through multiple modes of representation (e.g., language, imagery, sounds, embodied performances) to produce digital texts (e.g., blogs, wikis, zines, games, personal webpages) for dissemination in cyberspace.' Wikipedia, that exemplary 'new media' text/site, similarly describes 'new literacies' in terms of online social practice and activities:

> Commonly recognized examples of new literacies include such practices as instant messaging, blogging, maintaining a website, participating in online social networking spaces, creating and sharing music videos, podcasting and videocasting, photoshopping images and photo sharing, emailing, shopping online, digital storytelling, participating in online discussion lists, emailing and using online chat, conducting and collating online searches, reading, writing and commenting on fan fiction, processing and evaluating online information, creating and sharing digital mashups, etc. (Wikipedia, 2012)

Why theorize 'how attending to adolescents' online literacies might inform our work?' asks Alvermann (2008, p. 9), describing these as 'literacies so powerfully motivating that young people are more and more willing to invest a substantial amount of time and effort in creating content to share with others online.' There are various answers here, and not only in relation to those literacy forms that entail creating and sharing content online, although this in itself provides an important and persuasive opportunity to understand the sophisticated literacy knowledge and practices that many young people engage in, and which too often remain invisible in formal pedagogy and curriculum and also, importantly, in measures of literacy achievement. Another is that the kinds of communication, collaboration, and online textual practices that many young people engage in, out of school, powerfully shape their expectations of what learning and literate communication might be. Further, their engagement with such texts and technologies – the 'information' they find there, their interactions with others, and the kinds of opportunities, communities and behaviors they encounter, both benign and otherwise – shape their sense of themselves, of others, and of their world.

With respect to Education's utilitarian brief to prepare young people for the present and future world, there is a need to help them understand and master the various genres and conventions of literacy and literacy practice that characterize increasingly dominant modes of conducting local and global business, employment, advertising, leisure, government, and the economy. This concern, to help students become powerfully literate, creative, critical, *and* reflective, remains central to the role of English teachers and literacy educators, and to English and literacy curriculum in most parts of the English-speaking world.

Two kinds of research in the area of digital culture and new literacies are of particular interest to literacy educators. On the one hand are studies into what young people are doing as they engage in digital culture of various kinds in their leisure time. These studies provide insights into the nature of contemporary communication, including such things as engagement, collaboration and participation, the social, literacy and knowledge-building practices that are entailed in students' involvement with online worlds, and the ways in which meanings are made in these contexts, in particular through viewing literacy as design. Research of this kind is not so much about how teachers might make use in the classroom of the digital technologies and forms of cultural participation they explore, as about what might be learnt about young people, about learning, and about changing literacies. Indeed, an important principle for much work in this vein is, while being wary of either appropriation or domestication, to understand the *emergent* nature of these spaces and sites, and the forms of literacy, identity and community, among other things, that such participation enables and entails.

Thus, for example, Steinkhuehler's (2006, 2007) studies of game-play within the massively multiplayer online game *Lineage* provide highly-detailed and nuanced accounts of the ways in which multiple representational elements, together with social codes and conventions, and the manner in which one plays, all shape the online experience and the ways in which play proceeds. Through fine-grained textual analysis of ordinary moments of play, she demonstrates the ways in which gaming entails 'participation in a discourse' (Steinkhuehler, 2006) and 'a constellation of literacy practices' (Steinkhuehler 2007). Black's (2007) study of learners of English as an additional language, and also members of an online fan fiction site, mapped the ways in which participants with a shared passion for the Japanese animation series *Cardcaptor Sakura* were supported through the site and their activities on it, as readers, writers, reviewers, and more, to become adept and confident users of their new language (Black, 2007). Marsh's (2008) studies of young children playing *Club Penguin* provide insights into the ways in which virtual worlds 'offer young children a wide range of opportunities to decode, respond to and create multimodal texts in a playful space, significant activities in a new media age' (Marsh, 2008, p. 1). Gee's 36 principles of learning in *What Video Games Have to Teach Us about Learning and Literacy* were derived from observations and analysis of computer game-play. They range from how games work as a 'complete' learning environment, where 'all aspects of the learning environment (including ways in which the semiotic domain is designed and presented) are set up to encourage active and critical, not passive, learning' (Gee, 2007, p. 221), through to how games exemplify principles of design and the interconnectedness of elements within design, and the ways in which games may rely on distributed knowledge and collaborative problem-solving among players.

A second set of research studies with regard to new media and literacy education explores the incorporation of new media into specific classroom activities. Corio and colleagues (2008), for example, provide a wide range of discussion and examples of the classroom use of various digital forms. Alvermann (2010) includes studies of school-based work around Webkinz (Cowan, 2010), game-making in Media Studies classes (Dezuanni, 2010), and fantasy football in secondary English (Gutierrez and Beavis, 2010). Davies and Merchant (2009) includes discussion and examples of the use of Flickr, blogs, YouTube, wikis and virtual worlds, among other things, in schools. Willett, Robinson, and Marsh (2009) provide discussion and examples of a range of interactions with digital culture in and out of school, exploring ways in which children's creativity and play are configured within digital cultures, including commercialized spaces, and how this has been incorporated or addressed in school. In *Digital Games: Literacy in Action*, Beavis, O'Mara, and McNeice (2012) present a range of case studies of English and Media teachers working in various ways around literacy and computer games. Other examples abound.

Prospects and Problematics: Curriculum, Literacy, (New) Media

In the digital-electronic age, residual print-based conceptions of literacy are clearly no longer adequate to account for the ways in which communication occurs and through which meanings are made, and hence literacy curriculum and policy require radical revision and supplementation. The 'new literacies' tradition pioneered by Street (1995), Barton and Hamilton (1998) and others, within which largely ethnographic approaches to the study of literacies foreground the ways in which literacy works as social practice, continue to underpin much research into emergent forms of literacy in contemporary mobile and digital culture, and in young people's out-of-school textual worlds (e.g., Pahl and Rowsell, 2006; Street, Pahl, and Rowsell, 2009). Hand-in-hand with this tradition, ongoing work on 'multiliteracies' (Cope and Kalanztis, 2000) and the important view of 'literacy as design' noted earlier (Kress, 2003a) provide generative frameworks for researching literacies in the new media age.

The question at the heart of this chapter – what new media might mean for literacy education in the twenty-first century – raises further questions of various kinds.

What might the incorporation of digital texts and literacies, and the use of new media, in the classroom mean for what is understood by 'literacy,' and how both 'literacy' and subject English are understood and defined? What might it mean for the relationship between school-subjects more generally and the world outside school? What might it mean for English pedagogy, curriculum, and assessment? Which knowledge, in what form, and determined by whom, is to be considered centrally important, and what does this in turn mean for both cultural-heritage approaches to curriculum and understandings of what the role of schooling in the twenty-first century might be?

The degree to which addressing digital media and online literacies and literacy practices can or should be incorporated into English and literacy curriculum is open to debate. It is clear that an expanded notion of literacy and text[3] has implications for what constitutes the subject-field, if only at the level of considering what 'texts' might be studied or prescribed, and which 'literacies' to include in school and national assessment measures and regimes. Just as Kress, Green and others point to difficulties in retaining the term 'literacy' to refer to nonverbal semiotic elements and systems, such as those entailed in 'multimodal' forms of semiosis, preferring rather the terminology of 'design,' so both 'literacy' and 'English' may no longer serve to describe familiar subject-parameters. 'Digital' or 'online' literacies extend beyond verbally based forms to include the consideration of such things as images, sound, color, placement, foreground/background, space, size, movement, symbol and icons, and the meanings created across them, as well as meanings created through the juxtaposition of several screens, as happens typically in video games. Going further, the capacity to be a producer as well as reader of digital literacy may entail skills and understandings more readily seen, perhaps, as part of Technology Studies or Arts, rather than English/Literacy – the capacity to Photoshop images, for example, or to download images or music and create mash-ups, to manipulate sprites and the underlying algorithms to make short games, to create podcasts or blogs, to combine clothes, skin-types, race, gender, and coloring to make avatars, to present oneself as cool and in control in social networking sites through language, images, and connections, to create fan fictions and fan art, and post them online, and so forth.

Similarly, if the range of texts prescribed for study expands beyond the range of classic and popular literature – newspaper, film, television, advertisements, and so on – that typically constitutes much English and literacy curriculum to include websites, computer games, and digital literacies, how will the changed balance and proportion of attention given to different forms be received? Will correspondingly less time be given to traditional literary texts in order to make room for contemporary, nonprint forms? Would something be lost, as well as gained? The shift from 'telling the world to showing the world,' Kress (2003b) argues, leads to a profound reorientation in reading:

> The screen is organized and dominated by the image and its logic. The logic of (alphabetic) writing is the logic of time and sequence; the logic of image, on the other hand, is the logic of space and simultaneity. The logic of writing . . . is temporal and sequential; the elements of writing unfold in time and are related by sequence. By contrast, the elements of the image are present in spatial arrangements, and they are ordered by spatial relations (Kress, 2003b, p. 140).

The different kinds of attention brought to texts, and the different reading orientations, may mean that the deep reflection and introspection associated with complex literary texts gives way to forms of reading more outwardly directed, with greater attention to forms of presentation and the relationship between these:

> Imagination in the sense required by the demands of design – my imposition of order on the representational world, whether as text maker or as reader – is a move toward action in and on the outer world. One was a move to contemplation; the other is a move toward involvement in outward action (Kress, 2003b, p. 152).

A different set of questions concerns the dangers of appropriation and domestication attendant upon all incorporation of popular culture into the classroom, and unexamined assumptions that activities undertaken outside school remain the same when moved into this very different context, regardless of changed purposes, relationships, and autonomy. A related set of questions concerns whether students in fact welcome such transference in the name of relevance or engagement, or see it as a form of appropriation, and an attempt to colonize their private, out-of-school worlds. From a different angle, a fundamental question is whether all digital or online literacies are equally valuable to bring into school, or whether in fact some are not helpful, with doing so running the risk of undermining existing, valued forms of literacy. As many have noted, just because something exists outside the classroom does not necessarily mean it should be brought in.

Perhaps a bigger underlying question here concerns the nature of the relationship between new media texts, technologies, and literacies and existing iterations of 'literacy' and 'English.' If new media and the cultures and literacies they engender are merely 'add-ons,' not much will change. Properly acknowledging new media, and the spread and power of digital texts and technologies and online literacies, presages far-reaching change. As Leander (2010, p. 202) notes:

> the notions of 'students,' 'critical,' 'agency' and 'classroom' are fundamentally challenged. The result is that digital media and popular culture are not merely being 'connected' to classrooms, or not simply 'integrated' (as a project of domestication), but are rather actively reshaping our assumed genres and roles concerning pedagogy and schooling.

In conclusion, then: increasingly, literacy guidelines in many parts of the world call on teachers to incorporate attention to multimodal and electronic texts into their classrooms and curriculum. Curriculum guidelines addressing the 'new literacies' are structured around an expanded view of literacy that recognizes the changing and dynamic nature of text and textual forms, and call on research into the textual, communicative and cultural practices of young people as they engage with online popular culture and the digital world. Such studies provide powerful glimpses into multimodal and emergent literacy and textual forms, and into the power and significance of such sites and literacies in many young people's lives. Seeing literacy first and foremost as socially situated cultural practice, they provide insights into new and emergent forms of literacy and literate practice (e-literacies; multiliteracies; literacy conceptualized as 'design,' etc.). They raise questions about the kinds of expectations about texts, participation, and literacy that characterize students' experience of online digital culture and communication, and about what might be their expectations and understanding of working with texts and utilizing literacies. Also significant are questions about the nature of meaning-making which draws on a mix of on- and offline texts, media and forms of knowledge, along with issues of authority, identity, and relationships, and the ways these are configured across and between participation in on- and offline worlds.

Yet there are still signs of conflict, contradiction, and confusion in this regard. Various commentators have observed that, notwithstanding widespread endorsement of the need for change, education systems and bureaucracies remain somewhat schizophrenic and otherwise ambivalent in their attitude to such technocultural challenges, particularly in assessment policies and practices (e.g., Luke and Woods, 2009; Tan and McWilliam, 2009). This can only create ongoing difficulties for teachers and their students, as well as for teacher education and curriculum development. In this chapter, we have sought to highlight a distinctive trajectory in scholarly inquiry from the early 1990s onwards, over three decades, from arguments initially presented in Green (1993) through those mounted by Kress a decade later (Kress, 2003a), and then on yet a further decade to the present moment, in 2013 and beyond. This line of inquiry has consistently pointed to the profound changes underway in what has been called here the new media age – indeed, a veritable 'intensity of change' (Lister *et al.*, 2009, p. 10), embracing postmodernity, globalization, new forms of postindustrial economy and technocapitalism, and the emergence of a new geopolitical order. The question is what is emerging now as the necessary next phase in literacy education, or is there rather something quite different hovering just beyond the horizon? Is there indeed an imminent successor-project for those forms of curriculum and cultural practice that we have known historically, first as English teaching and then as literacy education? Is literacy now better formulated as learning new media? Is that the future? Whatever the case, a significant challenge remains to understand and engage what is happening all around us with regard to changing forms of textuality and technology, and the ever-complex relationships among culture and history, pedagogy and generation.

Notes

1. It is worth noting here the emphasis on history in Lister *et al.*'s (2009) account of 'new media': 'Paradoxically . . . it is precisely our sense of the "new" in new media which makes history so important – in the way that something so current, rapidly changing and running toward the future also calls us back to the past' (p. 65).
2. Mills (2010) provides a similar list in her review of the 'digital turn' in the New Literacy Studies: 'The literacies are digital, pluralized, hybridized, intertextual, immediate, spontaneous, abbreviated, informal, collaborative, productive, interactive, hyperlinked, dialogic (between author and reader), and linguistically diverse' (p. 255).

3. Worth considering, however, is the possibility that the notion of 'text' has its own limits, a point made very strongly by Robert Morgan (1996) some time ago now, in his account of 'pan textualism,' affective performativity and media education.

References

Alvermann, D. (2008) Why bother theorizing adolescents' online literacies for classroom practice and research? *Journal of Adult and Adolescent Literature*, 52(1): 8–19.

Alvermann, D. (ed.) (2010) *Adolescent Online Literacies: Connecting Classrooms, Digital Media, and Popular Culture*. New York: Peter Lang.

Apperley, T., and Beavis, C. (2011) Literacy into action: Digital games as action and text in the English and literacy classroom. *Pedagogies: An International Journal*, 6(2): 130–143.

Barton, D., and Hamilton, M. (1998) *Local Literacies: Reading and Writing in One Community*. London: Routledge.

Beavis, C. (2006) English at a time of change: Where do we go with text? *English in Australia*, 41(2): 61–68.

Beavis, C., O'Mara, J., and McNeice, L. (eds) (2012) *Digital Games: Literacy in Action*. Adelaide: Wakefield Press.

Black, R. (2007) Fanfiction writing and the construction of space. *E–Learning*, 4(4): 384–397.

Buckingham, D. (2003) *Media Education: Literacy, Learning and Contemporary Culture*. Cambridge: Polity Press.

Burnett, C., and Merchant, G. (2011) Is there a space for critical literacy in the context of new media? *English Teaching: Practice and Critique*, 10(1): 41–57.

Cope, B., and Kalanztis, M. (eds) (2000) *Multiliteracies: Literacy Learning and the Design of Social Futures*. South Yarra, Victoria: Macmillan.

Corio, J., Knobel, M., Lankshear, C., and Leu, D. (eds) (2008) *Handbook of Research on New Literacies*. New York: Routledge.

Cowan, J. (2010) Webkinz, Blogs, and avatars: Lessons learned from young adolescents. In D. Alvermann (ed.) *Adolescent Online Literacies: Connecting Classrooms, Digital Media, and Popular Culture*. New York: Peter Lang, pp. 27–50.

Davies, J., and Merchant, G. (2009) *Web 2.0 for Schools: Learning and Social Participation*. New York: Peter Lang.

Dezuanni, M. (2010) Digital media literacy: Connecting young people's identities, creative production and learning about video games. In D. Alvermann, (ed.) *Adolescent Online Literacies: Connecting Classrooms, Digital Media, and Popular Culture*. New York: Peter Lang, pp. 125–144.

Dovey, J., and Kennedy, H.W. (2006) *Game Cultures: Computer Games as New Media*. Maidenhead: Open University Press.

Du Gay, P., Hall, S., Janes, L., *et al.* (1997) *Doing Cultural Studies: The Story of the Sony Walkman*. London: Sage Publications in association with the Open University.

Facer, K. (2011) What futures for digital literacy in the 21st century?. In L. K. Stergioulas and H. Drenoyianni (eds) *Pursuing Digital Literacy in Compulsory Education*. New York: Peter Lang, pp. 223–240.

Gee, J. (2007) *What Video Games have to Teach us About Learning and Literacy*, 2nd edn. New York: Palgrave Macmillan.

Green, B. (1993) Literacy studies and curriculum theorizing; or Insisting on the letter. In B. Green (ed.) *The Insistence of the Letter: Literacy Studies and Curriculum Theorizing*. London and Philadelphia: The Falmer Press, pp. 195–225.

Green, B., and Beavis, C. (eds) (2012) *Literacy in 3D: An Integrated Perspective in Theory and Practice*. Camberwell, Victoria: ACER Press.

Gutierrez, A., and Beavis, C. (2010) 'Experts on the field': Redefining literacy boundaries. In D. Alvermann (ed.) *Adolescent Online Literacies: Connecting Classrooms, Digital Media, and Popular Culture*: Peter Lang, pp. 145–162.

Jewitt, C. (ed.) (2009) *The Routledge Book of Multimodal Analysis.* London: Routledge.

Kress, G. (2003a) *Literacy in the New Media Age.* New York and London: Routledge.

Kress, G. (2003b) Interpretation or design? From the world told to the world seen. In M. Styles and E. Bearne (eds) *Art, Narrative and Childhood,* Stoke on Trent: Trentham Books, pp. 137–153.

Kress, G., Jewitt, C., Ogborn, J., and Tsatsarelis, C. (2001) *Multimodal Teaching and Learning: The Rhetorics of the Science Classroom.* London and New York: Continuum.

Lankshear, C., and Knobel, M. (2006) *New Literacies: Everyday Practices and Classroom Learning,* 2nd edn. Maidenhead: Open University Press.

Leander, K. (2010) Afterword. In D. Alvermann (ed.) *Adolescent Online Literacies: Connecting Classrooms, Digital Media, and Popular Culture.* New York: Peter Lang, pp. 202–208.

Levinson, P. (2009) *New New Media.* Boston: Pearson.

Lister, M., Dovey, J., Giddings, S., *et al.* (2009) *New Media. A Critical Introduction,* 2nd edn. London and New York: Routledge.

Luke, A., and Woods, A. (2009) Policy and adolescent literacy. In L. Christenbury, R. Bomer and P. Smagorinsky (eds) *Handbook of Adolescent Literacy.* New York: Guildford Press, pp. 197–219.

Marsh, J. (2008) Out-of-school play in online virtual worlds and the implications for literacy learning, accessed November 9, 2012: http://w3.unisa.edu.au/eds/documents/jackiemarsh.pdf

Merchant, G. (2009) Web 2.0, New literacies and the idea of learning through participation. *English Teaching Practice and Critique,* 8(3): 107–122, accessed November 9, 2012: http://education. waikato.ac.nz/research/files/etpc/files/2009v8n3art7.pdf

Mills, K.A. (2010) A review of the 'digital turn' in the new literacy studies. *Review of Educational Research,* 80(2): 246–271.

Morgan, R. (1996) Pan textualism: Everyday life and media education. *Continuum,* 9(2): 14–34.

Morgan, W. (1998) Old letteracy or new literacy: Reading and writing the wor(l)d online. In F. Christie and R. Misson (eds) *Literacy and Schooling.* London and New York: Routledge, pp. 129–154.

O'Mara, J., and Laidlaw, L. (2011) Living in the iWORLD: Two literacy researchers reflect on the changing texts and literacy practices of childhood. *English Teaching: Practice and Critique,* 10(4): 149–159.

Pahl, K., and Rowsell, J. (2006) *Travel Notes from the New Literacies Studies: Instances of Practice.* Clevedon, UK: Multilingual Matters.

Selwyn, N. (2010) *Schools and Schooling in the Digital Age: A Critical Analysis.* London and New York: Routledge.

Steinkhuehler, C. (2006) Massively multiplayer online video gaming as participation in a discourse. *Mind, Culture and Activity,* 13(1): 38–52.

Steinkhuehler, C. (2007) Massively multiplayer online gaming as a constellation of literacy practices. *E-Learning,* 4(3): 297–318.

Street, B. (1995) *Social Literacies.* London: Longman.

Street, B., Pahl, K., and Rowsell, J. (2009) Multimodality and new literacy studies. In C. Jewitt (ed.) *The Routledge Book of Multimodal Analysis.* London: Routledge, pp. 191–200.

Tan, J.P-L., and McWilliam, E. (2009) From literacy to multiliteracies: Diverse learners and pedagogical practice. *Pedagogies,* 4(3): 213–225.

Walsh, C.S. (2010) Systems-based literacy practices: Digital games research, gameplay and design. *Australian Journal of Language and Literacy,* 33(1): 24–40.

Wikipedia (2012) New literacies, accessed November 28, 2012: http://en.wikipedia.org/wiki/New_ literacies

Willett, R., Robinson, M., and Marsh, J. (eds) (2009) *Play, Creativity and Digital Cultures.* London: Routledge.

Chapter 5

Connecting with Parents and the Community in an Urban Primary School

Creative Partnerships to Build Literacy/ies

Pat Thomson and Johanne Clifton

Introduction

Education policy makers around the world generally agree that schools should foster parental involvement. This is usually taken to mean an active elected school governing body or parent committee, good parent attendance at school events, positive parent satisfaction survey results and – for schools in urban contexts where parents are seen to have significant needs –parent information sessions, parenting workshops, and educationally oriented classes such as computing. Allens Croft Primary School, in the United Kingdom, did all of these things, but wanted to do more. School leaders were not satisfied that they really connected with the majority of parents, and sometimes wondered how much they actually knew about them. Partnership work with creative practitioners and a critical friend offered new possibilities.

In this chapter we describe the steps that the school took. We begin by outlining the theoretical lens we bring to this chapter and then go on to provide some contextual information about Allens Croft School, its community, and its use of creative practitioners. We then address the two stages of the project. We provide a short description of the first phase of the project before analyzing the second, a storytelling project, in more detail. We conclude by considering the contribution made to school–parent connectivities by creative practices.

Johanne (Headteacher) and Pat (a university-based critical friend) worked together on this project. Johanne devised and led both stages of the project and Pat observed the second stage in detail, observing, filming, and interviewing the creative practitioner and the children involved. The chapter thus combines our two perspectives and offers an integrated practitioner and research narrative.

Thinking about Parents and Communities: Our Theoretical Lens

There is a very significant body of literature about schools, parents, families, and communities: it includes policies, professional literatures, social media, and research. It ranges from self-help

International Handbook of Research on Children's Literacy, Learning, and Culture, First Edition.
Edited by Kathy Hall, Teresa Cremin, Barbara Comber, and Luis C. Moll.
© 2013 John Wiley & Sons, Ltd. Published 2013 by John Wiley & Sons, Ltd.

guides for parents to systematic reviews of experimental research. Here we are concerned with literatures addressed to schools and teachers.

There is a large number of guides for schools on how to involve parents and/or families (e.g., Epstein *et al.*, 2008; Henderson, Mapp, and Johnson, 2007; Lucas, 2006) and these generally focus on communication and participation strategies. Drawing on research that details correlations between students' achievement (usually as measured on test results) and parental participation in activities such as homework, reading aloud, visits to museums, and the like (e.g., Christensen, 2003; Deforge and Abouchaar, 2003; Fishel and Ramirez, 2005), these school-focused guides increasingly emphasize the benefits for children's learning of involving parents and families (e.g., Harris, Andrew-Power, and Goodall, 2009; Whalley, 2007). Some of the school guides specifically focus on parents and families whose children do not do well at school, looking at, for example, interagency provision (Dryfoos, 1998; Siraj-Blatchford, Clarke, and Needham, 2007), multicultural communities (Davis, 1995), the 'hard to reach' family (Feller, 2010; Finders and Lewis, 1994) and families in poverty (Payne, 2006).

There is also a body of research that questions the premises on which many of these guides are written. Scholars note that: it is usually mothers who are 'parents' and that schools have highly stereotypical expectations of them (David, 1993; Griffith and Smith, 2005; Reay, 1998); official and school parental policies homogenize class and race differences (McKinley and Else, 2002; Williams, 2009); the ubiquitous term 'partnership' fails to recognize the power differences between schools and parents (Crozier, 2000; Hallgarten and Edwards, 2000; Maclure and Walker, 2000); and welfarist and marketized policies cast parents as clients and consumers rather than as citizens (Fege, 2000; Munn, 1993). This more critical scholarship takes issue with literatures and policies that presume a highly deficit view of working class and racially 'othered' communities (Tatto *et al.*, 2001; Tett, 2001), arguing that they need to be seen as positioned – historically, socially, economically, and politically – as the binary lesser of an advantaged minority whose languages, knowledges, and interests dominate the education system (Anyon, 1997; Apple and Buras, 2006; Connell *et al.*, 1982).

We took up this critical perspective in the work at Allens Croft School. We adopted the view espoused by McKnight (1995; McKnight and Kretzmann, 1996) that all communities possess not only needs, but also a range of assets which consist of, inter alia, institutions such as churches, social and sporting clubs, and people with reservoirs of life/work knowledge and know-how, networks, experiences, and literacies.

Schooling has typically disregarded these assets. Children who do not come to school with the 'right' set of understandings and behaviors are, like their families and neighborhoods, seen as deficient (Comber, 1997). The problem is seen to reside in them, rather than in taken-for-granted educational practices (Comber, 1998). This is not to say that all children do not need to learn how, for example, to speak and write Standard English. It *is* to say that it is important that schools learn how to seek out, value, and use what it is that all children (not just some) bring with them to school. It is also important that schools find ways to make respectful connections with families and the wider community, establishing reciprocity in communication and in learning.

There are multiple ways of understanding this 'assets-based' approach. We read the interconnected ideas of funds of knowledge (Gonzales, Moll, and Amanti, 2005), local literacies (Barton and Hamilton, 1998), place-based education (Gruenewald and Smith, 2008), permeable schools (Dyson, 1997) and students' virtual school-bags (Thomson, 2002); despite their different emphases, trajectories, and places of origin, these concepts share a positive regard for working-class, immigrant and indigenous children and the life experiences and knowledges that they and their families and communities possess. We decided that this was a fruitful basis on which to build an intervention.

In this chapter we want to bring to our situated school narrative the particular notion of 'texts of their lives,' as elaborated by Bob Fecho (2011) in his explication of the dialogical writing classroom. Fecho begins from the claim, with which we agree, that in school many students are given assignments and exercises that have no connection with their own lives. They do these dutifully, reluctantly or not at all, and the learning that results is valuable only in terms of test results. Fecho argues for classrooms that not only allow students to gain the skills and scores that count but which also 'create opportunities for students to use writing to explore who they are becoming and how they relate to the larger culture around them' through the provision of 'systematic and intentional means for reflection and action,' which offer 'a means for making sense of their lives' (pp. 4–5). Such a classroom sees the lives of students and their families and communities as valued, key classroom multimodal texts from which to build and extend learning. This is not the same as an experiential curriculum but is rather, as Fecho puts it, an extended ongoing conversation that brings together the intersections of the personal and academic in ways that help children and young people – and their teachers – build understandings of themselves and their worlds (pp. 7–9).

Fecho proposes that teachers take the idea of 'texts of their lives' as central to their classroom practice. While we agree completely with this, we also know that there is a considerable distance between the dominant literate practices in English classrooms and this ideal. This chapter addresses a strategy adopted by one school in order to move away from narrow policy-approved, target-driven approaches that ignore local literacies and knowledges to include the introduction of creative approaches designed to help teachers to 'see' their children, their families, and their neighborhood. We will suggest the value of such interventions and of involving creative practitioners, whose arts practices rely on critical 'recognition' (Fraser, 1997) of the everyday and the production of counter-narratives and counter-representations of policy-marginalized peoples.

The creative practitioners and approaches described in this chapter were funded by Creative Partnerships (CP), which ran from 2003–2011. CP offered funding to English schools in designated deprived areas for creative practitioners to work with teachers in order to change pedagogies to become more engaging, exploratory, negotiated, and inventive. The programme's goal was not simply to change classrooms but also whole schools (see Bragg and Manchester, 2011; Faultley, Hatcher, and Millard, 2011; Thomson, Jones, and Hall, 2009; Thomson and Sefton Green, 2010). Allens Croft was a designated national school of creativity and Pat was its critical friend.

We now turn to the school and its efforts to get to know its students and community better.

Introducing Allens Croft Primary School

Allens Croft Primary School is a one-form entry primary school in the south of Birmingham. In 1997, it was ranked the third lowest school in the country for attainment. Its official designation is in an area of high deprivation across a range of indices, with at least 90 percent of families being in the highest quintiles for childhood deprivation, access to health and education and poor housing.

Originally a post-war housing estate built for white working-class factory workers it had become, by the 1970s, notorious as a 'sink estate.' This, of course, created a reputation for the area as profoundly unpleasant – not somewhere to go after dark. The area had deep local ties and interfamily connections and disputes that could spill over into the playground and classrooms. The children in the school were often from families who had attended the school themselves in the past and there were deeply entrenched patterns of mistrust in formal education and the staff.

By 2002, work had begun on regeneration of the area and the local population had begun to change as families from a more diverse range of ethnic backgrounds moved in. However, there were still deep-rooted official perceptions of a 'problem community' containing a large number of people with 'anti-social behavior.'

By 2006, when Johanne became the Headteacher at Allens Croft, there were ongoing concerns about children's achievement and engagement in learning and the interaction of the community with the school. Johanne decided that the first priority was to focus on raising attainment and progress swiftly in order to improve the school's test results. Although the school had some success in this, it was clear that formal interventions such as spelling programs were not making a long-term difference to children's learning. Teachers often noted that the children seemed passive and disinterested in lessons and lacked independence.

In early 2007, some children from the school were involved in a film-making project in a local allotment called 'Feed Me TV.' By tracking their attainment, and in particular their writing, the senior management identified that attainment had risen by at least a sub-level beyond that of the rest of their class. This insight marked a turning point for the school and its approach to the curriculum; it became clear that learning had to be relevant, hands-on and based on the children's interests. From Summer Term 2007, the school began a series of projects looking at the impact of creative learning, mostly with a specific focus on progress in writing as well as staff development. Projects included working with boys in Reception on creating open-ended stories using the environment, community stories based on memories of the school, and developing a learning network with other local schools.

By autumn 2009, Allens Croft decided to focus further on working within the local community. A key area for further development was parents' participation in the life of the school and their being able to share in their child's education.

The First Phase of the Project

The project began with a false start. In September 2009, the school established a school Arts Forum and invited a small group of eight parents. The parents decided that they would make a film to promote healthy eating. However, over a four-week period all but two parents began to make excuses not to come. The remaining two made the film and Johanne was left with a strong sense of failure but could not analyze the cause at this point. Together with Pat, Johanne and the management team decided that the issue was that they were still deciding *for* the parents what was 'good for them' and limiting the involvement to a chosen few who then reflected back what they thought the school wanted them to say. A different approach was needed.

This consisted of a number of steps:

1 *A focus on dreams:* In early 2010 Tim Burton's *Alice in Wonderland* film was released. The advertising for the film included an intriguing invitation written on a parcel tag inviting the viewer in to share in a dream world. This prompted Johanne to initiate a discussion with staff – we all have hopes, dreams, and aspirations – what did our families hope for their children? Were they content for their children to remain in Allens Croft or did they hope for more? A trip to a local cinema was organized for the whole school and every parent was sent a parcel tag in an envelope and invited to share their hopes and dreams for their children. The school then held a special 'Dreams Day' when every child was asked to invite

a person who was important to them to come into school and make a special container to hold their dreams inside. The day itself was a very moving occasion. The school was full of families and every child had a dream to share. Staff learned that all of the families had high aspirations for their children, just as much as at any other school.

2   *Using photography to make contact:* The focus for this activity was a Year 4 class, which had had the lowest test results for several years; staff thought at the time that it was due to their passivity and the level of special needs within the pupil group. However, in the previous year, several of the children had been part of a fantasy/drama project and teachers had since seen their attainment rise significantly, particularly in writing (Clifton, Davies, and Higgins, 2011). This group had swiftly developed independence in their personal organization and learning that made them ideal to lead a research project within their own families.

Ming de Nasty, an experienced photographer, was recruited due to her experience in working with children and the accessibility of photography as a medium. A photographic studio was set up in a small room and all Year 4 families were invited to have a free family portrait taken by a professional photographer. There was no issue with encouraging parents to step over the threshold of the school – the queues stretched out of the front door onto Allens Croft Road! Families arrived, some dressed in formal suits, some in cool street gear, with jewelry, prized possessions, and even a dog. While people were waiting in line, staff got talking to them and the ice was broken.

3   *Touring the area to 'find' stories:* The next step saw children taking staff on a guided tour of the area (see Comber, Thomson, and Wells, 2001). At each home, the children introduced their house and told stories about where they lived and what they liked about Allens Croft. Many parents joined in on the doorsteps and staff began to learn about the many layers of history that were right next to the school.

Each child was then given a disposable camera together with a notebook and asked to take photographs during a weekend of whatever they felt was important to them in their home and nearby. Ming then worked with the children to create story maps of their family history using Photoshop Pro. More skills and stories emerged and it became evident that even though many parents may not have engaged in formal education nevertheless often had fascinating life stories.

4   *Listening to elderly residents:* The school purchased small microphones with an internal memory card that the children used to record stories at home and with local elderly residents who met at the Allens Croft Project, a community organization with a specific focus on domestic violence and the elderly. This created a fascinating library of stories from Pakistan, Somalia, Barbados and the estate (see Figure 5.1 for an example).

Johanne recruited a graphic designer to co-interpret the stories with the Year 4 children; these became six sets of class readers to be used as part of the daily Guided Reading.

The Second Phase of the Project 2010–2011

In 2010 the school decided to extend the project to another class and take a different approach. This time, a Year 5 class was to work on stories drawn from the lives of people in their community. Women in Theatre, a Birmingham company, were selected, on the basis of their 23 years of experience in developing scripts and performances from interviews, to work on the project.

Terina, the artist, and the school decided that this time the project would not focus on families but on some community members who worked in the school in nonteaching roles. Many of these people came from the local area and some were, or had been, parents of the

---

All life's a struggle

I was born in a military hospital in Malta. I shouldn't be here. I was meant to travel back to England on an earlier ship. That ship was bombed.

I was very small at school and everyone picked on me. The head bully in the school lived next door to me and one day he came in my house. I locked the door and gave him a good beating. After that he was my best friend and he stopped other people picking on me.

We were very poor and sometimes I used to go on 'the wag' – that means I used to have the day off to go stealing apples or train spotting. If the policeman caught you, he'd give you a clip round the ear. I was caned a lot.

When I grew up, I worked on the steam train, shovelling the coal. I did a lot of shunting work. You get two trains together and you have to push them up an incline. I remember when I first saw a diesel train. That's when we knew steam trains were finished.

There was a lot of ash. The dustmen used to carry tin baths on their heads to collect all the ash from the coal fires.

For a six penny piece, you could catch the bus to Selly Oak, go and see a film, buy a speckled apple and catch the bus back home.

Figure 5.1   Community stories: An interview by Umera

school. Johanne asked the ancillary staff for volunteers and four did: Sharon, the School Cook, Mary, a Higher Level Teaching Assistant, Shirley, a Teaching Assistant, and Angela, a Clerical Assistant.

The story-making program was designed to run over a two-month period:

- Introductory session in which Story Lady was introduced and the project outlined;
- Introductory session for volunteers;
- Teaching about interviews (whole class);
- Four groups of children interview one adult each;
- Groups of children work with Terina to turn the interview into stories;
- One-day workshop to develop the story into a performance piece, which was then shown to classmates, the subject of the story and their invited guests, parents, and other school staff. In total there were four days of workshops and four performances.
- Texts printed and turned into 'Allens Croft Readers.'

We will focus here on two parts of this program in order to give a flavor of what was involved.

Introductory session with children

Creative practitioners typically begin their involvement in schools with an event that will arouse interest, curiosity, and excitement – some kind of provocation (Thomson *et al.*, 2012). In this instance, while the children were sitting in their classroom, they heard someone singing outside the door. At this point they did not know anything about the forthcoming project in which they would be involved. As one of the teaching assistants later noted, singing aloud in the corridor was a highly unusual occurrence. Inside the classroom children speculated about who this might be and what might be happening. When the door was opened, they saw Story Lady, dressed in bright green and holding a bulging bag. The children were then invited to follow her and her trail of green footsteps and leaves to the library where they sat in a circle. Story Lady pulled an apparently aged book from her bag and began to read the story of Gelert, a brave dog who rescues his Master's baby from a vicious wolf. Tragically, when the Master returns, he leaps to the conclusion that the dog has harmed the baby and kills the faithful hound. He then realizes his mistake and his debt to his courageous dog.

This story may seem a long way from the local community and the lives of children in an urban estate. However, throughout the story Terina engaged the children in conversation. What kind of dog was Gelert? What did the dog do as it was guarding the sleeping baby? What did the baby look like as it was sleeping? What color were the curtains and furniture in the room? She invited the children to populate the story with their own knowledges, their own 'pictures in their mind.' At the conclusion of the story, she initiated a discussion about courage and invited the children to provide her with examples of courageous acts. At this point the children drew on examples from television, other literatures, and their own experiences (cf. Marsh, 2000). Terina then introduced the project and outlined what the children would be doing. She told them that bravery and courage were qualities that ordinary people possessed and practiced, it was not just people and animals in stories in places long ago and far away, but people that they knew and encountered everyday also behaved in courageous ways.

The connections Terina made between the legend of Gelert and the everyday worlds of children were thus not simply about immediate engagement with a text, but also formed the basis of the project. Courage was presented in this first session as an asset possessed by ordinary people; their stories were therefore worth finding and worthy of telling.

In the debrief with staff that followed immediately after the session with children, Terina talked about the importance of allowing children time and space to form pictures in their mind, and to share them. 'There are no right pictures,' she said. 'Even if they seem silly to us' (such as Gelert being a sausage dog, one of the imagined pictures offered during the session), 'they're all still valuable and important.' Terina explicitly told teachers that it was important for children to connect their everyday knowledges with a text, and through the process of *imagining* to rewrite it, so that it could become a text that was meaningful to them. When the children could add to the story images that they knew from home, their neighborhood and from the popular texts that they routinely encountered, it became both a listening and rewriting event. Terina repeated several times that all children had pictures in their mind and that teachers could do exactly what she had done.

From story to performance

The stories that were produced from interviews all focused on parents and children – a child with a heart defect who ultimately died as a very young adult, a child with learning difficulties, a child who goes to university in another city, and the reunion of one child with an illegitimate sibling. These are not unusual stories. But they may have been stories that some teachers might have thought that children in Year 5 were too young to hear. Yet of course they were the kinds of experiences with which they lived every day. Terina was able to work with these stories in ways that many teachers may have found difficult.

An edited and anonymized version of one of these stories appears in Figure 5.2.

In order for the children to interview staff about their stories of courage, Terina had to work through how to deal respectfully and sensitively with information that could be distressing or hurtful if presented in the wrong way. The discussion about truth, representation, ethics, and emotions was not dissimilar in content to those held by researchers although, again, it was couched in terms that children understood and was based in children's experiences of playground and neighborhood gossip. Children were asked continually to consider how they would feel if this was their story that was being recounted by someone else.

Once upon a time . . . Twenty eight years ago to a couple named Shirley and Peter a son was born, who they named Michael. Followed two years and three months later, by a beautiful daughter called Kylie. Both had fair hair and blue eyes.

Shirley chose not to go to work while her children were growing up and instead she stayed at home to look after them. Her husband, Gary, went to work every day.

It was hard sometimes (you know how it is running a family).

Everything was going smoothly and calmly . . . When Michael was about two-and-a-half years old Shirley and Peter both started to notice things.

Something was going wrong with Michael. Something wasn't quite right with how he was developing. They felt that Michael was 'different'.

He had been quite slow to start walking and had only really begun to do it at the age of sixteen months. And he still wasn't saying any words at all. They were getting a bit worried.

They were concerned about Michael so they took him to see the doctor. They wanted someone to reassure them.

It was spring time, and the doctor saw Michael and tested his ears. Then he told Shirley to take him to what they called a 'development centre' for tests. They had to go every day for two weeks. They did lots of different tests on him to find out what was wrong.

After that, a psychologist visited them at home and told Shirley and Peter that Michael was two years behind his learning and that's why he wasn't even trying to talk or walk. They were very upset, nobody could tell them why or how it happened. And it was all so unknown.

The doctor suggested that Michael should go to a 'Special School' where children go if they have different needs to other children their age. Shirley wasn't sure he needed to do that. But he settled down at the school. He went every day in a taxi. And there were no problems, apart from his learning.

But sometimes Michael used to come home and get into tempers. Sometimes he got so angry that he would throw his shoes at Shirley. Sometimes he hit her and made her cry. Shirley's husband Peter was at work, so she was on her own with the children and it was hard.

Sometimes when they were at the supermarket Michael would lose his temper. Everyone would look and stare (you know how people do). Shirley could tell they were thinking 'What a naughty child' or 'Keep your child under control.' She got upset and though she didn't mean to she sometimes took it out on her husband Peter when he came home from work.

Over the years Michael had even more tests and when he was fifteen he was diagnosed with a type of Autism.

Now Michael is twenty eight and grown up and his mum Shirley says 'he has a lovely nature and a good sense of humour.' This has helped ease Shirley and Peter's fears and worries. They have learned that there is light at the end of every tunnel and they believe things have happened for a reason.

Figure 5.2 Shirley's story

Each performance was shared by Story Lady and the group of children who had conducted the particular interview and written and edited the story. Children acted out some parts of the story – for example, Michael's birth consisted of two children acting as mother and father, a doctor, nurse, and a doll-baby. The doctor said 'Congratulations, it's a boy' handing the baby to the parents. These scenes were cooperatively developed and rehearsed during the day of the afternoon performance. During these performances various aspects of stage-craft were learned – how to project the voice, how to stand and move so that the audience gets the best view, how to represent an event simply and economically in a few words and gestures, how to present emotions in ways that seem authentic.

For some of the children, acting was a frightening prospect, and they had to overcome this in order to participate. For a couple, this was an experience which opened up drama as a possible extra-curricular and formal curricular pathway that they might explore further in the future.

Affordances from the Story-making Project

A number of important literacy processes were explicitly covered in this story-making project – devising interview questions, conducting an interview, transcribing key pieces of text, and composing and editing a narrative that was not only to be performed but also had to stand alone as a printed text after the event. Writing the stories required attention to syntax, rhythm, word selection, plot development, setting, character development, and dialogue. Children also had to work together in small groups for protracted periods of time, far longer than the usual lesson length. They also had to meet a deadline and produce a real text for a real audience, many of whom were not dispassionate observers but who were intimately involved in the events being narrated (cf. Heath and Wolf, 2005).

It is important, we think, to see what was on offer to children in this project. They were confronted with the responsibilities of representation by being provided with an opportunity where they could allow people to represent themselves rather than simply be spoken about (Janks, 2009). However, these were not just any people, but people who were like them, and who they saw everyday in particular kinds of roles. Here they were presented as people with lives – and lives in which they acted courageously. Courage was no longer seen as the stuff of fictional characters and people in other places, but an everyday practice of 'people like us.' Shirley's story was not simply one in which a parent lives with and through a child who is 'different.' It was this in part, but it was also about the interactions that Shirley had with the medical and school system; the narrative hints at her persistence in pursuing a diagnosis but shies away from a romantic portrayal of heroic struggle. We also see the ways in which these kinds of tensions are played out in families, something with which children are very familiar.

Fecho's (2011) notion of 'texts of our lives' is a very helpful description of this kind of literacy practice. The definition outlined at the beginning of the chapter suggested that this was writing that allowed students to explore their own life-worlds and communities, to reflect on these experiences, and to use the writing as a means of making sense of their own lives and those of people around them. These stories then became reading for other children in the school; local meaning making practices continued after the project had finished (Luke, O'Brien, and Comber, 1994).

The notion of these texts as a counter-narrative (Giroux *et al.*, 1996) is also helpful. Residents of estates in England are typically portrayed in media and policy alike as a majority that lack aspiration for themselves and their children; their neighborhoods are said to be inhabited by large numbers of dysfunctional families in need of welfare and remedial interventions and over-endowed with pregnant teenagers, anti-social youth in 'hoodies,' and feckless unemployed.

This kind of representation legitimates policy focused largely on the diagnosis of individual needs and the provision of early intervention and integrated services. Welfarist, 'therapeutic' approaches (Ecclestone, 2004) for the compliant, with a 'get tough on crime' approach to those who were unruly, have demonstrably not assisted communities to become self-determining and empowered (Lingard, Nixon, and Ranson, 2008), despite rhetoric that espoused these goals. By contrast, the portrayal of ordinary lives as exhibiting honesty, dignity, capability, hope, decency – all positive strong values – stands in direct opposition to discourses of deviance and deficiency. These 'little stories' provide resources for positive individual and social identity formation as well as evidence that confound the taken-for-granted views of many teachers and professionals who work in such locations.

Working with Creative Practitioners

Throughout the two phases of this work at Allens Croft creative practitioners brought with them particular kinds of know-how, habits, values, and dispositions (these are explained in detail in Thomson *et al.*, 2012):

- They were *oriented positively to children*. They approached children not as bundles of needs or as empty vessels to be filled up with the 'stuff' that they knew how to do. Rather, they understood children to have ideas, humor, and interesting and worthwhile perspectives. They also deemed them all equally capable of the kinds of creative activities that were to be on offer.
- They were *positively oriented to the community*. The practitioners chosen had personal artistic practices oriented to the everyday rather than the exotic. Working within the traditions of community and participatory arts, they also had critiques of art practices that were distanced from ordinary people and from children in particular. They also all had a critical view of the kinds of media and policy representations of estates that represented very partial stories and images. Terina for example worked for a feminist theater company that had consistently developed work based in the life experiences of groups designated as deprived – and which, through this designation, were ironically often further marginalized. They saw their practice as a modest 'speaking back to power.'
- The creative practitioners were *able to gently disrupt usual ways of school thinking and doing*. The new affordances the creative practitioners brought into the school setting were not simply from their formal education in photography, design, and theater. It was the way in which these orientations and their training combined as pedagogies that valued conversations, which saw the potential for interesting ideas in the most mundane and most trivial remarks, regardless of who made them, when or where.
- Creative practitioners *offered new resources that the school could use to connect with parents and the wider community*. There is no doubt that the school would have struggled to find something as attractive to children's families as a free family portrait. There is little evidence that teachers would have felt confident in turning interviews with parents into co-designed books that were able to share pride of place on the school library shelves with commercially published materials. It does not seem likely that school staff would have told their stories had it not been part of a project in the capable and experienced hands of Story Lady. And the staff certainly were not initially comfortable with the notion of performing.
- The notion of creativity itself *offered a 'way in.'* The staff were convinced that they needed to do something to make schooling more engaging. They also wanted to do something more about the parent community. Bringing the two together created a space/time pocket in which staff could be guided by creative practitioners into different pedagogical practices. Community stories functioned as a kind of Trojan horse for bringing different ideas, understandings and representations into the school.
- The artistic basis of these creative activities offered *engaging new avenues for meaning-making and communication for students* – they were writing for a purpose and there was an obligation to meet deadlines and to produce a quality performance/product. The photography, tour, and performance also provided a *real reason for parents to come into the school*, an occasion where they could see for themselves, in a 'non-report' evening context, what their school and their children were able to do.

Conclusion

The Allens Croft case suggests that working with creative practitioners opens up new avenues for both parent and student engagement (Burnaford, Aprill, and Weiss, 2001; Wilkinson, 2000) and teacher professional development (Faultley *et al.*, 2011; Galton, 2008). It also supports general understandings of the productive nature of university–school partnerships and the value of critical friends in providing additional intellectual resources. However, there are questions that this case and other research into creativity do not answer.

The importance of students' life-worlds in a literacy-focused curriculum is not new news, but while a considerable amount of research has been conducted into literacy teaching, and there is an emerging body of work around creative practices in the curriculum, there is much less research focusing on creative pedagogies and literacies. There is also insufficient investigation of literacies, cross-curricular activities, including those in the arts – and how these can be and are enacted across early childhood, primary, and secondary sectors. There is undoubtedly still a long way to go in thinking about how the pedagogical principles that underpinned this two-year intervention, and others like it, might inform more widespread curriculum change.

One reason for this relative 'gap' is the sheer time that it takes to undertake such work. The Allens Croft case covers a three-year span and relied on the kind of trusting critical friend relationship that takes time to build. It is still comparatively uncommon for university staff to maintain relationships of this duration with particular schools (but see McLaughlin, Black-Hawkins, Brindley, McIntyre, and Taber, 2006; Nixon, Comber, Grant, and Wells, 2012), although the benefits for both may well be considerable, if anecdotal evidence and that from these and other similar projects is to be believed. The challenge to take up such research/practice partnerships remains significant but, we suggest, may well be a very fruitful venture of benefit to all those involved.

References

Anyon, J. (1997) *Ghetto Schooling. A Political Economy of Urban Educational Reform.* New York, London: Teachers College Press.

Apple, M., and Buras, K. (2006) *The Subaltern Speak. Curriculum, Power and Educational Struggles.* New York: Routledge.

Barton, D., and Hamilton, M. (1998) *Local Literacies. Reading and Writing in one Community.* London and New York: Routledge.

Bragg, S., and Manchester, H. (2011) *Creativity, School Ethos and the Creative Partnerships Programme.* London: Creativity, Culture and Education.

Burnaford, G., Aprill, A., and Weiss, C. (2001) *Renaissance in the Classroom. Arts Integration and Meaningful Learning.* Mahwah, NJ: Lawrence Erlbaum.

Christensen, S.L. (2003) The family-school partnership: An opportunity to promote the learning competence of all students. *School Psychology Quarterly,* 18(4): 454–482.

Clifton, J., Davies, E., and Higgins, A. (2011) Of dreams and curiosity: What works and how do we know? In R. Elkington (ed.) *Turning Pupils Onto Learning: Creative Classrooms in Action.* London: David Fulton.

Comber, B. (1997) Literacy, poverty and schooling: Working against deficit equations. *English in Australia,* 119/20: 22–34.

Comber, B. (1998) The problem of 'background' in researching the student subject. *The Australian Educational Researcher,* 25(3): 1–21.

Comber, B., Thomson, P., and Wells, M. (2001) Critical literacy finds a 'place': writing and social action in a low income Australian grade 2/3 classroom. *Elementary School Journal,* 101(4), 451–464.

Connell, R.W., Ashenden, D., Kessler, S., and Dowsett, G. (1982) *Making the Difference. Schools, Families and Social Divisions.* Sydney: Allen and Unwin.

Crozier, G. (2000) *Parents and Schools. Partners or Protagonists?* Stoke on Trent: Trentham Books.

David, M. (1993) *Parents, Gender and Education Reform.* Cambridge: Polity Press.

Davis, B. (1995) *How to Involve Parents in a Multicultural School,* accessed June 1, 2001: www.ascd.org/readingroom/books/davis95book.html

Deforge, C., and Abouchaar, A. (2003) *The Impact of Parental Involvement, Parental Support and Family Education on Pupil Achievement and Adjustment, A Literature Review.* DfES Research Report 433. Norwich: The Queen's Printer.

Dryfoos, J. (1998) *Safe Passage. Making it Through Adolescence in a Risky Society. What Parents, Schools and Communities Can Do.* New York: Oxford University Press.

Dyson, A.H. (1997) *Writing Superheroes. Contemporary Childhood, Popular Culture, and Classroom Literacy.* New York, London: Teachers College Press.

Ecclestone, K. (2004) Learning or therapy? The demoralisation of education. *British Journal of Educational Studies,* 52(2): 112–137.

Epstein, J., Jansom, N.R., Sheldon, S.B., and Sanders, M.G. (2008) *School, Family and Community Partnerships: Your Handbook for Action.* Thousand Oaks: Corwin Press.

Faultley, M., Hatcher, R., and Millard, E. (2011) *Remaking the Curriculum.* Stoke on Trent: Trentham.

Fecho, B. (2011) *Writing in the Dialogical Classroom. Students and Teachers Responding to the Texts of their Lives.* Urbana, IL: National Council of Teachers of English.

Fege, A. (2000) From fundraising to hell raising: New roles for parents. *Educational Leadership,* 57(7): 39–43.

Feller, A. (2010) *Engaging 'Hard to Reach' Parents: Teacher-Parent Collaboration to Promote Children's Learning.* London: Wiley-Blackwell.

Finders, M., and Lewis, C. (1994) Why some parents don't come to school. *Educational Leadership,* 51(8): 50–54.

Fishel, M., and Ramirez, L. (2005) Evidence based parent involvement interventions with school-aged children. *School Psychology Quarterly,* 20(4): 371–402.

Fraser, N. (1997) *Justice Interruptus. Critical Reflections on the 'Postsocialist' Condition.* London: Routledge.

Galton, M. (2008) *Creative Practitioners in Schools and Classrooms.* London: Arts Council England.

Giroux, H., Lankshear, C., McLaren, P., and Peters, M. (1996) *Counternarratives. Cultural Studies and Critical Pedagogies in Postmodern Spaces.* New York: Routledge.

Gonzales, N., Moll, L., and Amanti, C. (2005) *Funds of Knowledge.* Mahwah, NJ: Lawrence Erlbaum.

Griffith, A., and Smith, D. (2005) *Mothering for Schooling.* New York: RoutledgeFalmer.

Gruenewald, D.A., and Smith, G.A. (eds) (2008) *Place-Based Education in the Global Age. Local Diversity.* New York: Lawrence Erlbaum.

Hallgarten, J., and Edwards, L. (2000) *Parents as Partners. Findings of a Programme of Consultation with Wednesbury Parents.* Wednesbury Education Action Zone. London: Institute for Public Policy Research.

Harris, A., Andrew-Power, K., and Goodall, J. (2009) *Do Parents Know they Matter? Raising Achievement through Parental Engagement.* London: Continuum.

Heath, S.B., and Wolf, S. (2005) Focus in creative learning: drawing on art for language development. *Literacy,* 39(1): 38–45.

Henderson, A.T., Mapp, K., and Johnson, V.R. (2007) *Beyond the Bake Sale: The Essential Guide to Family-School Partnerships.* New York: The New Press.

Janks, H. (2009) *Literacy and Power.* New York: Routledge.

Lingard, B., Nixon, J., and Ranson, S. (eds) (2008) *Transforming Learning in Schools and Communities. The Remaking of Education for a Cosmopolitan Society.* London: Continuum.

Lucas, B. (2006) *Pocket PAL: Involving Parents in School (Teacher's Guide).* London: Continuum.

Luke, A., O'Brien, J., and Comber, B. (1994) Making community texts objects of study. *The Australian Journal of Language and Literacy,* 17(2): 139–149.

Maclure, M., and Walker, B. (2000) Disenchanted evenings: The social organisation of talk in parents-teacher consultation in UK secondary schools. *British Journal of Sociology of Education*, 21(1): 5–21.

Marsh, J. (2000) Teletubby tales: Popular culture in the early years language and literacy curriculum. *Contemporary Issues in Early Childhood*, 1(2): 119–133.

McKinley, S., and Else, A. (2002) *Maori Parents and Education*. Wellington: New Zealand Council for Educational Research.

McKnight, J. (1995) *The Careless Society. Community and its Counterfeits*. New York: Basic Books.

McKnight, J., and Kretzmann, J. (1996) *Mapping Community Capacity*. Evanston, IL: Institute for Policy Research. Northwestern University.

McLaughlin, C., Black-Hawkins, K., Brindley, S., *et al.* (2006) *Researching Schools. Stories from a Schools-University Partnership for Educational Research*. London: Routledge.

Munn, P. (ed.) (1993) *Parents and Schools: Customers, Managers or Partners?* London: Routledge.

Nixon, H., Comber, B., Grant, H., and Wells, M. (2012) Collaborative enquiries into literacy, place and identity in changing policy contexts: Implications for teacher development. In C. Day (ed.) *The Routledge Handbook of Teacher and School Development*. London: Routledge, pp. 175–184.

Payne, R. (2006) *Bridges Out of Poverty: Strategies for Professionals and Communities Workbook*. Highlands, TX: aha! Process.

Reay, D. (1998) *Class Work: Mother's Involvement in their Children's Schooling*. London: University College Press.

Siraj-Blatchford, I., Clarke, K., and Needham, M. (eds) (2007) *The Team Around the Child: Multi-Agency Working in the Early Years*. Stoke on Trent: Trentham.

Tatto, M.T., Rodriguez, A., Gonzalez-Lantz, D., *et al.* (2001) The challenges and tensions in reconstructing teacher-parents relations in the context of reform: A case study. *Teachers and Teaching: Theory and Practice*, 7(3): 315–333.

Tett, L. (2001) Parents as problems or parents as people? Parental involvement programmes, schools and adult educators. *International Journal of Lifelong Education*, 20(3): 188–198.

Thomson, P. (2002) *Schooling the Rustbelt Kids. Making the Difference in Changing Times*. Sydney: Allen and Unwin.

Thomson, P., Hall, C., Jones, K., and Sefton Green, J. (2012) *Signature Pedagogies*. London: Culture, Creativity and Education.

Thomson, P., Jones, K., and Hall, C. (2009) *Creative Whole School Change. Final Report*. London: Creativity, Culture and Education; Arts Council England.

Thomson, P., and Sefton Green, J. (2010) *Researching Creative Learning: Methods and Issues*. London: Routledge.

Whalley, M. (2007) *Involving Parents in their Children's Learning*, 2nd edn. Thousand Oaks: Sage.

Wilkinson, J. (2000) Literacy, education and arts partnership: A community-system programme integrating arts across the curriculum. *Research in Drama Education: The Journal of Applied Theatre and Performance*, 5(2): 175–197.

Williams, T.J. (2009) *Save our Children: The Struggle between Black Parents and Schools*. New York: African American Images.

Chapter 6

At Home and at School

Bridging Literacy for Children from Poor Rural or Marginalized Urban Communities

Celia R. Rosemberg, Alejandra Stein, and Florencia Alam

Introduction

Within the framework of a socio-cultural perspective on human learning and development (Nelson, 1996, 2007, 2010; Vygotsky, 1964, 1978; Werstch, 1988), writing is seen as one of the most powerful instruments of thought mediation (see Olson, 2002). Writing allows for the externalization of personal meanings just like mimesis in play, dance, drawing, and other fine arts, or like oral language in communicative exchanges and narrations. With its external support system, writing, like photography and video, gives meanings stability and durability in space and time. In addition, as a conventional code, writing allows one to publicly and accurately evoke mutually interpretable meanings and state the complex relationships between bits of registered information (Nelson 2007, 2010). In this way, the possibilities of communication and complex cognitive processing are increased.

As a cultural instrument, writing is 'rooted' in systems of joint activity. Along this line, a large number of studies on the processes of family literacy have shown that children begin to learn the writing system earlier when raised in households where they have the opportunity to participate in shared reading and writing situations (Snow, 1983; Sulzby and Teale, 1987; Taylor, 1983). These studies show that the type and frequency of activities that the children participate in, as well as the way that the writing system is used in these activities, varies based on the family's social or cultural group (Leseman and van Tuijl, 2006; Reyes, Alexandra, and Azuara, 2007; Taylor, 1983). Therefore, the above mentioned studies highlight differences in childhood reading and writing experiences.

As Tomasello (2003) and Nelson (2007, 2010) state, writing acquisition, like other forms of socio-cultural learning, involves not just a certain level of development and socio-cognitive preparation on the part of the child, but also the support of cultural partners (peers and adults), who structure the children's learning experience through providing them with learning tools and activities for participation. Children's learning is made possible by their biological inheritance, individual genetic and epigenetic conditions, and by their body and brain, which change their power, size, and abilities over the course of development. Children's learning is also made possible by their previous experiences, their residual memory, and the contributions

International Handbook of Research on Children's Literacy, Learning, and Culture, First Edition.
Edited by Kathy Hall, Teresa Cremin, Barbara Comber, and Luis C. Moll.

and/or constraints derived from their ecological and geographical situation, as well as from their social environment and cultural world (including language). These are, at least initially, external to the child (Nelson, 2007, 2010).

Nelson (2007, 2010) highlights the subjective, experiential component of these individual-world transactions. The children create 'experienced' meaning using objects, knowledge and other instruments that are found in the social and cultural activities in which they participate. A child's experiences also depend on those who provide the verbal and nonverbal interactional opportunities and scaffolding that the child uses in the process of 'collaboratively constructing' the structures of personal meaning (Nelson, 1996; Tomasello, 2003). Additionally, the 'history of their previous experiences' – the experiences that the child has accumulated – will have an influence on the child's future encounters with objects, activities, and unknown people, as well as on the child's ability to collaboratively construct knowledge and meanings associated with such events.

Studies conducted in the past 30 years have shown several important differences between social and cultural groups in terms of the activity systems that shape children's daily lives (e.g., Rogoff, 1993, 2003). Each activity system is comprised of a wide range of knowledge of its resources and on the methods and techniques used as a part of the system. As a result, the child will access the system in a particular way. These 'funds of knowledge' (González, Moll, and Amanti, 2005), are important for the child in three ways: first, they involve an identification with the social environment, as they are practices that have been developed over the course of a historical process. Second, they are transmitted and communicated to the child within the context of the activity system that shapes their lives. Third, the goals of the system are previously known to the child.

Several studies have also shown important cultural and social differences in the social relationship networks that the children have been a part of since birth (Rogoff, 1993; Vélez-Ibáñez and Greenberg, 2005; Volk and de Acosta, 2004). Differences can also be seen in the patterns and forms of the verbal and nonverbal interactions that characterize the children's communicative exchanges, in the linguistic variation and style of discourse in which the children have been socialized (Borzone and Rosemberg, 2000; Simons and Murphy, 1988) and also in their previous writing experiences (Leseman and van Tuijl 2006; Reyes, Alexandra, and Azuara, 2007; Taylor, 1983).

Many studies have indicated that for children coming from cultural and minority group environments, the processes of knowledge elaboration, types of social relationships, linguistic variations and styles of discourse used in their homes differ from those usually emphasized in the school environment (Adger *et al.*, 1992; Borzone and Rosemberg, 2000; Michaels, 1988; Martinez, 2003). With respect to the relative dimensions of the knowledge elaboration process it has been stated that the frameworks, or the 'funds of knowledge' that children learn in rural families and communities or marginalized urban populations are not usually recovered in the school environment (Borzone and Rosemberg, 2000; González, Moll, and Amanti, 2005). Differences in knowledge use strategies have also been found, in terms of comparison and conceptual analysis at school and the holistic approach to real situations at home and in the community (Cole, 1999; Rogoff, 1993).

Among the linguistic issues, it is important to note that discontinuities exist between the phonological, morphological, syntactical, and lexical characteristics of the dialects spoken by the children and by their teacher (Adger *et al.*, 1992; Cazden, 1991; Martinez, 2003). Additionally, differences have been identified between the discursive and contextualized informal register typical to the oral tradition that characterizes communication in families with a low literacy level, whatever their cultural group of origin. Differences have also been found in the 'decontextualized' style of discourse that characterizes writing at school (Collins and Michaels,

1988; Rosemberg and Borzone, 1998; Simons and Murphy 1988). In addition, these children frequently have less pre-school experiences with books and other types of written texts than the school assumes they do (Leseman and van Tuijl, 2006; Reyes, Alexandra, and Azuara, 2007; Taylor, 1983).

Taking into account the cultural matrices of child development, the difficulties that are frequently observed over the course of these children's reading and writing learning process while at school can be understood as the result of these mismatches in the complex interplay between the child's family environment and school environment (Cook-Gumperz, 1988; Rosemberg and Borzone, 1998; Tharp and Gallimore, 1991).

The importance of capitalizing on the funds of knowledge, interaction patterns, and language uses that the children have learned in their family and community environment to promote writing becomes evident when one considers that writing is a form of linguistic representation that complements, with new vicarious experiences, the subject's experience in their immediate environment (Nelson, 1996, 2007). The new experiences mediated by writing can evoke distant places, past and future eras, unknown people and imagined realities for the child. Children can master this instrument and use it to access new knowledge if said knowledge is relevant in the framework of their previous experiences and the meanings that they have constructed based on them. Children must also understand that they themselves can use writing to produce knowledge about their environment.

In line with these statements, this study presents three pedagogical strategies that give a socio-cultural anchor to children's literacy in impoverished rural communities and with marginalized urban populations in Argentina. The design of these strategies is carried out within the framework of projects that combine the study and documentation of funds of knowledge, interaction patterns, dialectical variations, and ways of learning that characterize the activity systems in which children are embedded. The cultural design (Álvarez and del Río, 2001; Cole and Engeström, 2007) of new mediation structures – instruments and interactional situations – that promote the learning of writing, and the study of the impact that these new structures have on participants' learning is also addressed.

Ethnographic Reading Books: Children's Perspective in Books

One of the pedagogical strategies that we devised to capitalize on the knowledge and uses of language that the children have developed in their communities and with their families consists of the elaboration and use of ethnographic reading books. This strategy also aims to promote early childhood literacy learning. These books arose as pedagogical strategies from a series of research studies performed by our research team in collaboration with teachers, community members, and social organizations. Research was conducted in various indigenous communities such as the Collas, Qom, and Mocovíes, and other impoverished rural groups, as well as in marginalized urban communities, all in Argentina (Rosemberg, 1997, 2001).[1]

In these studies we document ethnographically, through audio- and video-recorded observations, the activities, funds of knowledge, linguistic variations, and forms of language from these communities, as well as school-based interaction situations involving children from each one of these socio-cultural groups. The results of the comparative analysis of the recordings in the school setting and in the family and community setting corroborate the results of studies conducted in Hispanic communities in the United States (González, Moll, and Amanti, 2005) and Maya communities in Guatemala (Rogoff, 1993). The funds of knowledge, patterns of interaction, and linguistic variation that these children are socialized into, starting in early life, are usually not incorporated into the school setting, which generally follows classical teaching formats. The way that the linguistic variation is used as an instrument of communication to establish relationships with other people, discover information about the world, imagine other worlds, and tell others about objects, events, and feelings is not incorporated in their school setting either. That the cultural and linguistic capital of poor rural and marginalized urban children are not used to facilitate the learning of writing may account, in some part, for the difficulties that these children face in literacy acquisition and, in consequence, for the instances of 'school failure' that these children often experience (Borzone and Rosemberg, 1999).

In response to this situation, we sought to help overcome these mismatches between the home and the school, to facilitate the children's first experience with teaching in general and with literacy in particular. We tried to develop a strategy to include in the teaching situations the speech, customs, and daily lives of the children who belong to social groups that don't share the linguistic dialect or types of knowledge most frequently valued at school. This was the origin of the book *Ernestina's Adventures* (Rosemberg, Borzone, and Flores, 2002), the first ethnographic reading book that we developed. The book is a direct result of research conducted in the Colla community. Ernestina, like the protagonists of our later ethnographic reading books, is one of the children whose daily activities (at home and in her community) were recorded by our team over the course of many days. These books are based on observations of the children's daily lives, and in this sense, are strictly ethnographic and not just books that refer to local issues, knowledge, and concerns.

The observations on which the book's events are based, allow readers to see the child and the people they interact with not just as mere informants of knowledge and stories, but in the real situation, as actors in their own reality. The books show the children's point of view with respect to their reality, their interests, and their interactions with objects, people, and the problems of their communities.

The books are organized into episodes that represent situations from the children's everyday lives. For example, the book *The Adventures of Huaqajñe* (López *et al.*, 2010), written for the Northern Argentina Qom community with a group of bilingual Spanish– Qom teachers, represents the life experiences of children from this community. The events recorded by teachers and other community members are fictionalized. One of the girls observed, Huaqajñe, is the story's protagonist, and the plot is devised by fictionally reconstructing her participation situations and links to other children (Figure 6.1). These events organize the book from within and not from the imposed perspective of an outside cultural observer. The actors, the situations, the objects and actions are presented from the children's subjective point of view.

One of the events in the book *The Adventures of Huaqajñe*, which can be seen in Figure 6.2, was written based on observations of the children while they picked fruit on a hill near their grandmother's house. The children in these communities start participating in household subsistence activities early on in their lives; they hunt small animals, fish, and collect fruit. Through these activities, they learn which wild fruits are edible and which are not, and when they are ripe enough to be picked. They also learn at an early age the importance of caring for nature. They know that you shouldn't pick more fruit than you can carry and eat, nor should you hunt or fish more animals than you are going to consume.

Through participation in these activities, the children internalize other norms that regulate life in their community. These norms, which emphasize interdependence in children's exchanges and relationships with adults and other children, are evident when observing the way they care for small children and share food with relatives and other members of the community. The children, through performing these activities, highlight this knowledge, the abilities that they have developed, and their interests, feelings, and reactions in relation to the objects, actions, and people with whom they are involved. The book's events aim to reflect the experiences that shape the children's lives (see Figure 6.2).

Figure 6.1 The front cover of *'Huaqajñe's Adventures' (Las Aventuras de Huaqajñe)*, an ethnographic reading book for children from Qom native communities in Chaco, Argentina

Come, Try This Fruit	Vení, probá estas frutas
Huaqajñe and Agustina each carried two big bags to hold the fruit. Noni put Loyin down and he went running off towards the plants.	Huaqajñe y Agustina llevaban dos bolsas grandes para cargar la fruta. Loyin se bajó de los brazos de Noni y se acercó corriendo a las plantas.
Loyin: There are a lot here! They're low to the ground too!	*Loyin:* ¡Acá hay muchos! ¡Acá hay bajitos!
Julián: Huaqajñe, hold the bag open!	*Julián:* ¡Abrí, Huaqajñe, la bolsa!
While Loyin, Avín, and Julián picked the low-hanging fruit, Huaqajñe, Yasmín, Cintia, and Agustina shook the higher branches, which were full of fruit.	Mientras Loyin, Avín y Julián sacaban los frutos de los gajos de abajo, Huaqajñe, Yasmín, Cintia y Agustina sacudían las ramas más altas que estaban llenas de frutos.
Noni couldn't reach the higher branches, so he climbed the tree. He sat on a large branch and shook the branches with lots of fruit very hard. 'Avín, anato. Collect the ones that fall', he cried.	Como Noni no llegaba a las ramas más altas, se trepó al árbol y sentada en una rama grande, sacudía fuerte las ramas que tenían frutos. 'Avín, anato. ¡Juntá vos los que se caen!'.
Illustration of Noni in the tree	*Ilustración de Noni en un árbol*
Yasmín didn't want to waste the fruit, so she told Noni, 'Saishet. Don't shake the branches any more, we have a lot already, any more will go to waste'.	Yasmín no quería que se desperdiciaran los frutos y le dijo a Noni: 'Saishet. No sacudás más, son muchos frutos ya, sino caen de balde'.
From his spot high up in the tree, Noni could see his cousin Dana in the distance. She was busy hunting little birds. 'There's Dana!'	Desde arriba del árbol, Noni vio a lo lejos a su prima Dana que estaba mariscando. Estaba cazando pajaritos con la honda. '¡Ahí está Dana!'
'Dana, Dana, Dana 'ayala!' the children called to their cousin.	'¡Dana, Dana, Dana, 'ayala!', llamaron los chicos a su prima.
Illustration of Dana hunting with a slingshot	*Ilustración de Dana cazando*
Huaqajñe went up and took the fruit. She squeezed it and juice came out.	Huaqajñe se acercó y tomó la fruta. La apretó y salió jugo.
Loyin: It is juice.	*Loyin:* Te' ena jugo.
Yasmin: Be careful, don't squeeze it like that because it will stain your shirt and it won't come out. That's what mommy says.	*Yasmín:* Loyin saishet. No lo aprietes porque mancha tu remera y no sale. Así dice la mami.
Loyin grabbed a very big and long fruit and showed it to the other kids, saying 'this is the daddy fruit, right?'	Loyin agarra un fruto muy grande y alargado y se lo muestra a los otros niños. 'Este es el papá, ¿no es cierto?'.
Illustration of Loyin with the big fruit and another smaller one.	*Ilustración de Loyin con dos frutas, una grande y otra más pequeña.*
Agustina takes the fruit out of Loyin's hand and eats it. 'These ones are tasty. I spit the seeds out'.	Agustina le saca a Loyin el fruto de la mano y se lo come. 'Son ricos estos. Yo escupo las semillas'.
Huaqañe: Güe! Don't eat it all! Not right now. When we get to grandma's house we'll eat them, they're for everyone to share.	*Huaqajñe:* ¡Güe!, no vaya a comer todo. Ahora no, cuando lleguemos a la casa de la abuelita. Son para convidar.
The oldest girls grabbed the bags filled with fruit and everyone started walking.	Las niñas más grandes agarraron las bolsas con frutos y todos empezaron a caminar.

Figure 6.2   Episode from *Las Aventuras de Huaqajñe*

Ethnographic reading books, therefore, try to represent the children's subjective experiences and, in this way, allow them to experience the functionality of writing as an external support system that is used to represent information, ideas, and feelings. However, writing is not only an instrument of externalization that allows for the representation and production of one's own knowledge but it also serves as a means of accessing knowledge produced in other social and cultural groups. Therefore, in the narrative contexts created, the knowledge and objects from the child's culture are interwoven with other knowledge and other cultural norms, trying to account for an intercultural perspective.

Furthermore, the books are bi-dialectical, as the narrator uses a standard dialect, while the book's characters employ their community's linguistic variation in their dialogue. As can be seen in the book episode in Figure 6.2, the dialogues between Huaqajñe and the other children are in the Spanish linguistic variation used by the Qom community. In this way, ethnographic reading books are clearly different from the majority of reading books circulated in schools. Such books only reflect, typically in a stereotyped and timeless fashion, the daily life of a child from an urban area: their dialect, customs, knowledge, and social and family environment.

Ethnographic reading books, on the other hand, contain the words of the dialect of the children for which they are written. In this way, the children can easily understand that writing can be used as a tool to transmit knowledge and feelings. As the majority of the events that appear in the text represent everyday situations in their lives, or their own experiences, reading comprehension difficulties are reduced to a minimum, at least in the first stage of acquisition and the children can focus all their attention on trying to understand the writing system.

Children's spontaneous concepts are reflected in the activities, which are ethnographically recorded and textualized to provide the conceptual fabric through which other scientific concepts, which are introduced over the course of the book, acquire meaning. In this way, knowledge of the local physical, social, and spiritual world is juxtaposed with scientific knowledge and school curriculum. This allows children to learn conventional scholastic information and scientific thinking skills, while also giving greater importance to local society and culture. As the book's characters are real children from the community, the child can identify with them, feel like they themselves are the story's protagonists, and reaffirm their individual and socio-cultural identity.

In this regard, ethnographic reading books are qualitatively different from other reading books. They aim to reposition children in the foreground of the teaching and learning process. They are an instrument to incorporate into 'the heart' of school teaching situations children who often face discrimination, not necessarily explicitly, but usually implicitly, by not including their knowledge, values, and way of speaking in the school environment. Through this instrument, we seek that the children learn to read and write, and learn the standard dialect as well as content from different cultures. These knowledge and abilities will facilitate children's performance in different socio-cultural situations, at school and later in life. In this way, these books serve to increase children's personal growth by capitalizing on, rather than denying, their linguistic and cultural heritage.

At Oscarcito's House: A Program to Promote Family Literacy

The second pedagogical strategy consists of the design and implementation of a family early literacy program for children from urban-marginalized populations.[2] The program is implemented in the homes of children aged 3 to 5. The majority of the participating families are migrants from Northern Argentina or from neighboring countries such as Bolivia, Peru, or Paraguay. The adult members of the family have a low literacy level (they completed 7 or fewer years of schooling) and are unemployed or have low-skilled unstable occupations that offer no social benefits. There are no storybooks for children or books or magazines for adults in these homes.

The program is called '*Oscarcito: Desarrollo lingüístico y cognitivo de niños en contextos de pobreza*' [*The Oscarcito Program: Linguistic and Cognitive Development of Children Living in Poverty*] (Rosemberg and Borzone, 2005), and is implemented through child linguistic development training workshops for families, and through the use of specially designed children's books, the '*En la Casa de Oscarcito*' [*'At Oscarcito's House'*] series (Rosemberg *et al.*, 2008). Each one of these books presents a narrative that was created based on ethnographic recordings. The books' protagonist is Oscarcito, a little boy who lives in an urban-marginalized neighborhood with his family. The ending of this narrative leads to a story that is further from the child's reality. The book also includes games and other learning activities intended to promote the children's literacy skills development. All the activities are designed so that the children can carry them out at home, in the context of the interaction with their mother, father, grandparents, and older siblings.

The child linguistic training workshops for families – 12 per year – are organized in community centers and in pre-schools located in their neighborhoods. The child's mother, father, grandparent or an older sibling participates in the workshops. In each workshop, families are given one book from the '*En la Casa de Oscarcito*' [*'At Oscarcito's House'*] series (Rosemberg and Borzone, 2005). During the meeting, the book is read and the best strategies for promoting a certain aspect of the children's linguistic development are discussed.

In general, intervention programs aimed at promoting early literacy and family literacy in populations with a low socio-economic level focus their intervention strategies on the mother–child dyad. They provide specific training and instructions aimed to modify the ways that mothers collaborate with their children during reading and writing situations (Britto, Fuligni, and Brooks-Gunn, 2006). Our program, on the other hand, provides general orientations on the importance that certain activities have for promoting different aspects of linguistic development and child cognition (narrative discourse, vocabulary, writing), but does not provide strict guidelines. This was done to allow the families to 'assume ownership' of reading and writing activities.

During the program's implementation, a researcher visited the children's families and recorded the literacy situation exactly as it took place in the home. Analysis of these situations revealed that the family's extended composition, as well as the interdependent relationships between family members, shape the literacy situations in particular ways. In many of these families, reading is not done in the context of the dyadic interaction between the mother and the child. Instead, in many urban-marginalized families, reading situations involve multiple and diverse participants. Relationship networks were established between family members depending on the role that each actor assumed in the situation.

In some story reading situations, the adult reads while other older children (brothers, young aunts or uncles, cousins, or neighbors) act out the story. In other situations the comments of the older child contribute to the elaboration of the text information. The adult regulates the activity and focuses the children's attention. For their part, the young child listens and collaborates, to a greater or lesser extent, with the reading.

In the Excerpt 6.1, Candela listens to her mother and older brother Luciano read the story *The Giant Squash*. Then they discuss different types of squash.

In this exchange we can see not only the collaboration between the different situation participants, but the way in which the mother refers to the experiences and knowledge of everyday life to clarify the meaning of the words:- 'They're the trees that look like big trees but that have oranges or apples. Grandma Teresa had one on the corner that had apples, in the field over there. Mommy used to cut up apples from Grandma's tree for you.'

Excerpt 6.1   Reading *The Giant Squash/ El zapallo gigante*

Mother: {Reading} Troncón Robusto was a small and quiet village. The villagers worked in the fields and in the afternoon cared for the gardens in their houses where they grew flowers and vegetables and fruit trees. Do you know what fruit trees are?

Candela: ((Shakes her head no)).

Mother: They're the trees that look like big trees but have oranges or apples.* Grandma Teresa had one on the corner that had apples, in the field over there.

Candela: Oh.

Luciano: And she had figs.

Candela: Did I eat them when I was a baby?

Mother: ((Nods with her head)). You ate the apples. Mommy used to cut up the apples from Grandma's tree for you. There were mandarin trees too. Those are trees that grow fruit, they're called fruit trees. {Continues reading}: 'One day, a small seedling with thick leaves started growing on the Bustos family's patio. Each day it grew bigger and bigger. Many rainy days passed and one clear, sunny morning a little squash appeared on the plant'. {Candela's mother reads the story in which a squash grows and grows until it becomes giant-sized. A stranger who comes to the village says that they should cook it and eat it to verify that it is in fact a squash}.

Mother: Did you see how the naughty man ate the squash?

Candela: Yes.

Mother: And that's why he's happy. You guys also have to learn to eat squash. What type of squash do you like Candela?

Candela: Orange [the orange kind].

Mother: But what is the orange squash called? Bu . . . butternut.

Candela: . . . nut

Luciano: I like green squash.

Candela: I like orange squash.

Luciano: Mommy, I like yellow squash.

Candela: No, there are no yellow squashes.

Mother: That's the squash we use for stew, that we say is half green – it's orange inside.

Madre: {Lee} Troncón Robusto era un pueblo chico y tranquilo. Los vecinos del pueblo trabajaban en el campo y por las tardes cuidaban los patios de sus casa[s] donde crecían flores plantas y verduras y árboles frutales'. ¿Vos sabés qué son árboles frutales?

Candela: ((Niega con la cabeza)).

Madre: Son los árboles esos que parecen árboles grandes, pero que tienen naranja, manzana. La abuela Teresa tenía en la esquina, que tenía manzanas en el campo allá.

Candela: Sí.

Luciano: Y tenía higos.

Candela: ¿Cuándo yo era bebé la comía?

Madre: ((Asiente con la cabeza)). Manzana sí. La mamá te rallaba la manzana de la casa de la abuela. Había mandarinas. Esos son árboles de frutos, se llaman árboles frutales. {Continúa leyendo} 'Un día, en el patio de la familia Bustos nació una plantita de hojas gruesa[s] y tallo finito que con los días se hacía cada vez más larga. Pasaron unas cuantas lluvias y una linda mañana de sol apareció un pequeño zapallo.{La madre de Candela lee el cuento de un zapallo que crece hasta hacerse gigante. Un desconocido que llega al pueblo pide que lo cocinen y probarlo para constatar que se trata de un zapallo}.

Madre: ¿Vieron que el pícaro como come zapallo?

Candela: Sí.

Madre: Y por eso se va contento. Ustedes también tienen que aprender a comer zapallo. ¿Qué zapallo te gusta a vos Candela?

Candela: El naranjado [anaranjado].

Madre: Pero ¿cómo se llama el zapallo anaranjado? Ca . . . calabacín.

Candela: . . . cin.

Luciano: A mí me gusta el zapallo verde.

Candela: A mí me gusta el zapallo naranjado [anaranjado].

Luciano: Mami, a mí me gusta el zapallo amarillo.

Candela: Que no, que no hay zapallos amarillos.

Madre: Este es el zapallo para locro, que es verde digamos y medio naranja adentro.

* In Spanish, the difference between the words for fruit tree and a tree that grows fruits are more differentiated than in English (árboles frutales), so young children would not as easily understand the meaning upon first encountering the word.

Excerpt 6.2　A story reading by an elder sibling

{Jorge listens to a story read by his 11-year-old brother, Israel. In this situation, his mother and 5-year-old sister, Estefany, are also present}.

Mother: {To Israel} Read them the story son. Start here ((points to a page in the book)). The one about the fox and the hen. Listen, because he's gonna tell the story.

Israel: {Reading} 'Rosita was a fat hen that lived in a hen house on a farm. One day, Rosita the hen went out for a walk. A hungry fox saw her go out, and wanted to eat her, so he followed her. The hen was walking by the side of a fence. The fox, which was behind her, jumped to catch her'.

Mother: This is the hen and this is the fox ((points to the illustrations)).

(. . .)

Israel: {Reading} 'Because the fox wanted to catch the little hen, he had to jump over the fence and he fell on an ant hill filled with ants. The ants were very mad and they bit the poor fox very hard. The fox got up and ran away very fast'.

Mother: He got away from the ants that were biting him.

{Jorge escucha un cuento leído por su hermano Israel, de 11 años. En la situación, también están presentes su madre y su hermana Estefany, de 5 años de edad}.

Madre: Leéles el cuento hijo {A Israel}. Ahí comienza ((señala una página del libro)). Del zorro y la gallina. Escuchen que va a contar el cuento.

Israel: {Lee} 'Rosita era una gallina muy gorda que vivía en el gallinero de una granja. Un día, la gallina Rosita salió de paseo. Un zorro hambriento la vio salir, quiso comérsela y la siguió. La gallina se fue caminando por el costado del charco. El zorro, que estaba detrás de ella, dio un salto para atraparla'.

Madre: Esta es la gallina y este es el zorro ((señala los dibujos)).

(. . .)

Israel: {Lee} 'Como el zorro quería atrapar a la gallinita, tuvo que saltar para pasar por encima del cerco y cayó arriba de un hormiguero lleno de hormigas. Las hormigas, muy enojadas, picaron muy fuerte al pobre zorro. El zorro se levantó corriendo y se alejó muy rápido'.

Madre: Se escapó de las hormigas que le picaban.

Sometimes the participation of older children helps literacy situations to develop in homes where the adult has a very low literacy level and cannot fluidly read a text. In these situations the older sibling reads and the adult regulates the task, and gives instructions to both, the older child ('read the story') and the younger one ('listen to your brother'). In these cases, the adult pays close attention to the objects mentioned in the story and provides explanations (Excerpt 6.2).

In the exchange above, one can observe that the mother, while not reading, regulates the reading situation by distributing the children's tasks – 'Read them the story son.' The mother also contributes to the mediation of the written text by pointing out in the illustrations the characters and objects that the text alludes to: 'This is the hen and this is the fox.' She rewords parts of the text that could be confusing to the small child: 'He got away from the ants that were biting him.'

These collaboration networks display similar patterns of interaction to those observed by Volk and de Acosta (2004) in literacy situations that take place in the homes of Puerto Rican families living in the United States. In these networks, the children's siblings, cousins, and mothers assume different roles, which are not interchangeable. In this way, they show the importance of social networks for children's development. This is also concurrent with findings from studies performed in African American communities (Ward, 1971, cited in Rogoff, 1993), indigenous Hawaiian populations (Farran *et al.*, 1993), and Mexican communities (Vélez-Ibáñez and Greenberg, 2005). Although these studies did not focus on the literacy process, they showed how the differentiation and division of roles in shared activities allows for the successful completion of these activities in which the child develops skills and abilities.

The literacy situations observed in urban-marginalized populations capitalize on the opportunities provided by the socio-cultural environment. The introduction of the books generates situations in the homes that make use of certain features of these populations' natural settings, such as the quantity and diversity of interlocutors, and transforms other features, such as the sustaining of interaction over the course of an extended period of time. In this way, children can take advantage of the linguistic and cognitive potential implicated in the interactions with written texts. The activity system (Cole, 1999; Cole and Engeström, 2007) involved in the literacy situations is the result of a co-construction in which the children's books, provided by the program, and the singular characteristics of the community and families are articulated. Thus, we strategically generate 'a socio-cultural anchor to literacy.'

Reading among Children: A Child Literacy Tutors Program

The role that older siblings took on in the homes during the family literacy situations as well as the assistance that they spontaneously offered to the young children during the reading led us to the design of a new pedagogical strategy: a program of child tutors. This program aims to capitalize on the interactions between children of different ages to form a matrix that scaffolds the beginning of the literacy process for the younger children. At the same time, the program aims to generate meaningful reading and writing situations in which the older children develop a deeper understanding of the writing system, improving their abilities as readers and writers.

The program's design is based on findings from previous studies on the relationship between tutor and tutee (Kronqvist, 2008; Pilkington and Parker-Jones, 1996; Roscoe and Chi, 2008), as well as on findings from tutoring programs that focused on reading promotion (Topping and Bryce, 2004; Wright and Cleary, 2006).

Studies on the interactions between tutor and tutee, which were performed with quasi-experimental methodologies, sought to study the impact of tutoring on the child's learning. In many cases, they tend to focus on the development of one of the subjects involved in the dyad: the tutor (e.g., Chi and Roy, 2010; Roscoe and Chi, 2008), or the tutee (e.g., Chi, Roy, and Hausmann, 2008; Cohen, Kulik, and Kulik, 1982).

In the school environment, educational tutoring programs are implemented as part of intervention projects. On the whole, these programs promote the development of both subjects (tutor and tutee) and take the tutor's previous training into account. Our literacy tutoring program incorporates the results from previously implemented programs that emphasize the importance of two factors to the efficiency of the tutoring: having a minimum of a 2-year age difference between the tutor and tutee (Barone and Taylor, 1996; Schrader and Valus, 1990) and the tutor's previous training (Berliner and Casanova, 1998; Palincsar, Brown, and Martin, 1987).

The program implementation was carried out in the schools of children and adolescents from urban-marginalized backgrounds. The older children were trained in weekly workshops led by pedagogical coordinators and members of the research team. They read the stories that they would later read with the younger children, discussed strategies to keep the small child's attention, and worked on formulating different kinds of questions. They also reflected on the vocabulary used in the texts and how to explain the meaning of unknown words to a young child. Tutors were encouraged to retell personal past experiences linked to the texts and to provide decontextualized descriptions of objects and scenes that appear in the book. The children learned to formulate clear and precise instructions for activities and

Excerpt 6.3   Erica helps Mauricio solve a riddle

Participants: Erica (12) and Mauricio (4)	Participantes: Erica (12) y Mauricio (4)
Erica: {Reads the activity instructions} 'Should I tell you some riddles?'	*Erica:* {Lee el enunciado de la actividad} '¿Te digo algunas adivinanzas?'
Mauricio: ((Nods)).	*Mauricio:* ((Asiente)).
Erica: {Reads the riddle} 'She walks in a caravan with her friends, carrying leaves and crumbs'. What do you think she is? They walk in a line. Huh?	*Erica:* {Lee la adivinanza} 'En caravana con sus amigas pasa cargada de hojas y migas'. ¿Qué te parece que es? Que van caminando en fila. ¿Eh?
Mauricio: {Points to a drawing of some ants in the book} Little bugs.	*Mauricio:* {Señala el dibujo de unas hormigas en el libro} Bichitos.
Erica: Right, what are those little bugs called?	*Erica:* Claro, ¿qué son estos bichitos?
Mauricio: Ants.	*Mauricio:* Hormigas.
Erica: Ants. Very good! When ants go to the anthill they walk in a caravan, like this ((moves her fingers on the table as if they were walking)). One behind the other.	*Erica:* Las hormigas. ¡Muy bien! Las hormigas cuando van al hormiguero van en caravana o sea {mueve los dedos sobre la mesa como si caminara}. Una atrás de la otra
Mauricio: ((Nods)).	*Mauricio:* ((Asiente)).
Erica: They walk one behind the other.	*Erica:* Caminando una atrás de la otra.

games, and strategies to help a small child write their name and other simple words. They also learned sound games to promote the development of the young child's phonological awareness.

The tutoring session took place the week after the training. Each older child read one of the books from the '*At Oscarcito's House*' series to a pre-school aged child. They completed the activities and games suggested in the book. The tutoring sessions were audio and video-recorded. Analysis of these situations provided us with the necessary input to be able to design the next set of training workshops for the older children, and also provided data for our research project on the interaction processes that occur in tutoring situations involving children of different ages.

The exchange in Excerpt 6.3 comes from one of the tutoring sessions in which Erica (12) is helping Mauricio (4) solve a riddle included in the book.

The exchange displays the knowledge and abilities that the younger and the older children put to use in the tutoring situation. On the one hand, Mauricio uses Erica's scaffolding to refine his vocabulary, from the generic concept of *little bugs* to the basic-level concept of *ants*. It is important to note the way in which the older girl's scaffolding provides the younger child with the opportunity to understand that when talking about *little bugs*, the precise terminology is *ants*. In effect, Erica does not reject the child's production, but creates her scaffolding on the basis of the child's wording: 'Right, what are those little bugs?'

On the other hand, Mauricio hears a word that is probably quite rare for him: 'caravan.' The appearance of the term entails a series of explanations by the tutor. These explanations, that may facilitate access to meaning, involve the linguistic reformulation of the term; 'The ants go to the anthill in a caravan, or one behind the other; Walking one behind the other' as well as nonverbal resources. Erica moves her fingers on the table as if the ants were walking. The diverse strategies employed by the tutor are consistent with the Rosemberg and Stein's (2009) observations in family literacy situations. When the adults and older children are faced with the need to explain unfamiliar vocabulary to young children, they rely not just on linguistic information but also on other semiotic fields.

In the situation analyzed above Erica must reflect on the term 'caravan' in order to explain its meaning to Mauricio. Therefore, she is acquiring meta-knowledge about the term while she is considering how to make a four-year-old child understand its meaning. As Roscoe and Chi (2004, 2008) state, these exchanges allow tutors, like Erica, to learn through the explanation that they give to the younger child and from the self-monitoring that they perform as a part of the tutoring situation. The tutees, by means of their questions or doubts, lead the tutors to revise their explanations.

Thus, the child tutor literacy program creates a space for nonhabitual interactions in the formal educational institutions, which generate opportunities to promote learning for the older and younger children. Both of them expand their knowledge of the writing system, refine their vocabulary, and develop discursive strategies. This is accomplished within the framework of cooperative relationships, affect and solidarity that may contribute to children's self-esteem.

Some Final Considerations

The three pedagogical strategies presented in this paper draw on an empirical research process that seeks to understand why and how children learn in their home and community environments. The strategies take the children's knowledge, uses of language, and ways of learning and participating in daily activities as the starting point of their design. The intervention strategies seek to promote learning in a particular social group at a particular moment in time (Cole and Engeström, 2007). Thus, they capitalize on the children's primary socialization experiences and weave them into the design of the activities (the tutoring sessions and the family literacy program) and the instruments (the ethnographic reading books), which mediate the child's first experiences with reading and writing. The research project also focuses on how these activities and learning instruments impact on the children's learning and on the activities systems at home and in the school.

The activities and learning instruments are designed to address the bilingual and bidialectical situation, recover community funds of knowledge, and facilitate the child's learning within their own cultural and linguistic universe in a manner that is congruent with historical and cultural educational principles. They generate teaching situations that create a 'zone of proximal development' (Vygotsky, 2007), in which new contents become more proximal to them (del Río, 1994; del Río and Álvarez, 2007). In this way, the children can advance in the literacy acquisition process through experiences in which they 'collaboratively construct' (Nelson, 2007, 2010) knowledge about written texts.

The design of these activities and learning instruments is only possible in the context of intercultural and collaborative work among community members, teachers, and researchers in literacy acquisition (Rosemberg, 2004). This social fabric may be an education-enhancing factor as it bridges the current gap between the school and the community. Therefore, the restructuring of teaching situations can benefit from the instrumental and social fabric of the child's community.

The reciprocal interests of the diverse actors are satisfied in such interactions. The researchers collaborate with the teachers and the members of the community in the creation of educational resources. At the same time, they are able to advance the development of their research. Therefore the 'collaboration' becomes a methodological strategy that does not just imply performing actions together, but mainly thinking collaboratively. The exchange of viewpoints, which implies heterogeneous and alternative systems of thinking, allows for a broader view on the problem. These exchanges also serve to diversify and intensify creativity (Lotman, 1988; Tulviste, 1988) in terms of the design of the resources and activities that address a real crucial issue: children's literacy.

Notes

1. *Las Aventuras de Ernestina* (Rosemberg *et al.*, 2002); *Las Aventuras de Antonio y Romina* (Rosemberg *et al.*, in press) for Mocovi communities, *Las Aventuras de Tomás* for urban marginal populations (Borzone and Rosemberg, 2000); *Las Aventuras de Anita* for children in the rural area of La Rioja (Diuk, Borzone, and Rosemberg, 2004) and *Las Aventuras de Huaqajñe* (Codutti *et al.*, 2010) for Qom communities

2. These populations are called 'villas de emergencia' ['emergency towns' or 'shantytowns'] and are characterized by precarious housing that has mostly been built from wood and salvaged materials, and have insufficient or nonexistent infrastructure services. Although most of the neighborhoods have drinkable water, they all lack sewer and natural gas lines. In many cases, they receive electricity through illegal means, because the inhabitants do not have the resources to pay for the service. The neighborhood is accessed by narrow dirt- or cement-floored alleys. In the city of Buenos Aires, 116,000 people live in '*villas de emergencia*' and in the outskirts of the city, another 1,114,500 people live in these conditions (*source*: Statistics of the City Government of Buenos Aires).

References

Adger, C., Wolfram, W., Detwyler, J., and Harry, B. (1992) Confronting dialect minority issues in special education: Reactive and proactive perspectives. In *Proceeding of the Third National Research Symposium on Limited English Proficient Studies Issues*, United States Department of Education.

Álvarez, A., and del Río, P. (2001) Introducción: Culturas, desarrollo humano y escuela. Hacia el diseño cultural de la educación. *Cultura y Educación*, 13(1): 9–20.

Barone, M.M., and Taylor, L. (1996) Peer tutoring with mathematics manipulatives: A practical guide. *Teaching Children Mathematics*, 3(1): 8–15.

Berliner, D., and Casanova, U. (1998) Peer tutoring: A new look at a popular practice. *Instructor*, 97(5): 14–15.

Borzone, A.M., and Rosemberg, C.R. (1999) Alfabetización y fracaso. Una investigación en las comunidades collas. *Revista Argentina de Educación*, 26: 29–46.

Borzone, A.M., and Rosemberg, C.R. (2000) *Leer y escribir entre dos culturas. El caso de las comunidades collas*. Buenos Aires: Aique.

Britto, P.R., Fuligni, A.S., and Brooks-Gunn, J. (2006) Reading ahead: Effective interventions for young children's early literacy development. In D.K. Dickinson and S.B. Neuman (eds) *Handbook of Early Literacy Research*, Vol. 2. New York: Guilford Press, pp. 311–332.

Cazden, C. (1991) *El discurso en el aula. El lenguaje de la enseñanza y del aprendizaje*. Barcelona: Paidós.

Chi, M.T.H., and Roy, M. (2010) How adaptive is an expert human tutor? In J. Kay and V. Aleven (eds) *International Conference on Intelligent Tutoring Systems* (ITS'10) ITS, pp. 401–412.

Chi, M.T.H, Roy, M., and Hausmann, R.G. (2008) Observing tutorial dialogues collaboratively: Insights about human tutoring effectiveness from vicarious learning. *Cognitive Science*, 32(2): 301–341.

Cohen, P.A., Kulik, J.A., and Kulik, C. (1982) Educational outcomes of tutoring. A meta-analysis of findings. *American Educational Research Journal*, 19: 237–248.

Cole, M. (1999) *Psicología cultural*. Madrid: Morata.

Cole, M., and Engeström, Y. (2007) Cultural-historical approaches to designing for development. In J. Valsiner and A. Rosa (eds) *The Cambridge Handbook of Sociocultural Psychology*. New York: Cambridge University Press, pp. 484–507.

Collins, J., and Michaels, S. (1988) Habla y escritura: estrategias de discurso y adquisición de la alfabetización. In J. Cook-Gumperz (ed.) *La construcción social de la alfabetización*. Barcelona: Paidós.

Cook-Gumperz, J. (1988) *La construcción social de la alfabetización*. Barcelona: Paidos.

del Río, P. (1994) Re-present-acción en contexto: Una alternativa de convergencia para las perspectivas cognitiva e histórico-cultural. In P. del Río, A. Álvarez and J. V. Werstch (eds) *Explorations in Socio-cultural Studies. Vol. I. Historical and Theoretical Discourse*. Madrid: Fundación Infancia y Aprendizaje, pp. 129–146.

del Río, P., and Álvarez, A. (2007) The zone of proximal development: Inside and outside. In H. Daniels, M. Cole and J. V Werstch (eds) *The Cambridge Companion to Vygotsky*. Cambridge, MA: Cambridge University, pp. 276–303.

Diuk, B., Borzone, A.M., and Rosemberg, C. (2004) *Las aventuras de Anita*. La Rioja: Ministerio de Educación de la Provincia de La Rioja.

Farran, D., Mistry, J., Ai-Chang, M., and Herman, H. (1993) The social networks of preschool part-Hawaiian children. In R. Roberts (ed.) *Advances in Applied Developmental Psychology: Vol. 7. Coming Home to Preschool: The Sociocultural Context of Early Education*. New York: Ablex, pp. 42–58.

González, N., Moll, L.C., and Amanti, C. (eds) (2005) *Funds of Knowledge: Theorizing Practices in Households, Communities, and Classrooms*. Mahwah, NJ: Erlbaum.

Kronqvist, E. (2008) Challenges in the qualitative analysis of peer counseling- explorations of young children's learning. In G.L. Huber (ed.) *Qualitative Approaches in the Field of Psychology*. Berlin: Center Qualitative Psychology, pp. 11–31.

Leseman, P.P.M., and van Tuijl, C. (2006) Cultural diversity in early literacy: Findings in Dutch studies. In D.K. Dickinson and S.B. Neuman (ed.) *Handbook of Early Literacy Research*, Vol. 2. New York: Guilford Publications Inc., pp. 211–228.

López, A., Silvestre, A., and Rosemberg, C.R., *et al*. (2010) *Las aventuras de Huaqajñe*. Buenos Aires: CIIPME-CONICET, AECID, Fundación Infancia y Aprendizaje, Save The Children, Finland Embassy, Universidad Carlos III de Madrid.

Lotman, Y.M. (1988) Text within a text. *Soviet Psychology*, 26(3): 32–51.

Martinez, G.A. (2003) Classroom based dialect awareness in heritage language instruction: A critical applied linguistic approach. *Heritage Language Journal*, 1: 1.

Michaels, S. (1988) Presentaciones narrativas: una preparación oral para la alfabetización con alumnos de primer curso. In J. Cook-Gumperz (ed.) *La construcción social de la alfabetización*. Barcelona: Paidos, pp. 109–136.

Nelson, K. (1996) *Language in Cognitive Development*. Cambridge: Cambridge University Press.

Nelson, K. (2007) *Young Minds in Social Worlds. Experience, Meaning and Memory*. Cambridge: Harvard University Press.

Nelson, K. (2010) Developmental Narratives of the Experiencing Child. *Child Developmental Perspectives*, 4(1): 42–47.

Olson, D.R. (2002) What writing does to the mind. In E. Amsel and J.P. Byrnes (eds) *Language, Literacy and Cognitive Development*. The Jean Piaget Symposium Series. New Jersey: Lawrence Erlbaum, pp. 153–165.

Palincsar, A.S., Brown, A.L., and Martin, S. (1987) Peer interaction in reading comprehension instruction. *Educational Psychologist*, 22(3&4): 231–253.

Pilkington, R., and Parker-Jones, C. (1996) Interacting with computer based simulation: The role of dialogue. *Computers and Education*, 27(1): 1–14.

Reyes, A., Alexandra, D., and Azuara, P. (2007) *Las prácticas de lectoescritura en los hogares de inmigrantes mexicanos. Infancia y aprendizaje*, 19(4): 395–407.

Rogoff, B. (1993) *Aprendices del pensamiento*. Barcelona: Paidos.

Rogoff, B. (2003) *The Cultural Nature of Human Development*. New York: Oxford University Press.

Roscoe, R.D., and Chi, M. (2004) The influence of the tutee in learning by peer tutoring. In K. Forbus, D. Gentner, and T. Regier (eds) *Proceedings the 26th Annual Meeting of the Cognitive Science Society*, Chicago, pp. 1179–1184.

Roscoe, R.D., and Chi, M.T.H. (2008) Tutor learning: The role of explaining and responding to questions. *Instructional Science*, 36: 321–350.

Rosemberg, C.R. (1997) *Los libros de lectura etnográficos en el marco de un programa de alfabetización intercultural para plurigrado*. Presentation at the Congreso Internacional de Políticas Lingüísticas. Buenos Aires, May 1997.

Rosemberg, C.R. (2001) *Elaboración de libros de lectura etnográficos.* Panel at the Congreso de promoción de la lectura. Fundación El Libro, Buenos Aires.

Rosemberg, C.R. (2004) *La colaboración entre la investigación y las organizaciones sociales.* Conferencia Internacional de Sociología de la Educación. Buenos Aires, abril de 2004.

Rosemberg, C.R., and Borzone, A.M. (1998) Interacción verbal y cognición: el desarrollo de los niños collas en el entorno familiar y escolar. *Lenguas Modernas*, 25: 95.

Rosemberg, C.R., and Borzone, A.M. (2005) Programa Oscarcito: Promoción del desarrollo lingüístico y cognitivo infantil. Funding: CARE-Germany, CONICET, SECyT.

Rosemberg, C.R., and Borzone, A.M. (2008). En la casa de Oscarcito. Buenos Aires: Fundación Care.

Rosemberg, C.R., Borzone, A.M., and Flores, E. (2002) *Las aventuras de Ernestina.* Buenos Aires: Ministerio de Educación, Ciencia y Tecnología. Programa de Acciones Compensatorias.

Rosemberg, C.R., Ojea, G., Gómez, A., and Sánchez, O. (in press) *Las aventuras de Antonio y Romina.* Buenos Aires: Ministerio Nacional de Educación, Programa Nacional Intercultural Bilingüe.

Rosemberg, C.R., and Stein, A. (2009) Vocabulario y alfabetización temprana. Un estudio del entorno lingüístico en hogares de poblaciones urbano-marginadas. In M.C. Richaud and J.E. Moreno (eds) *Investigación en Ciencias del Comportamiento*, Buenos Aires, Ediciones CIIPME-CONICET, pp. 517–541.

Schrader, B., and Valus, A. (1990) Disabled learners as able teachers: A cross-age tutoring project. *Academic Therapy*, 25: 589–597.

Simons, H.D., and Murphy, S. (1988) Estrategias en el lenguaje hablado y en la aptitud de leer. In J. Cook-Gumperz (ed.) *La construcción social de la alfabetización.* Madrid: Paidós, pp. 213–233.

Snow, C.E. (1983) Literacy and language: Relationships during the preschool years. *Harvard Educational Review*, 53(2): 165–189.

Sulzby, E., and Teale, W.H. (1987) *Young Children's Storybook Reading: longitudinal Study of Parent-Child Interaction and Children's Independent Functioning*, (Final Report for the Spencer Foundation). Ann Arbor: University of Michigan.

Taylor, D. (1983) *Family Literacy.* Portsmouth, NH: Heinemann.

Tharp, R.G., and Gallimore, R. (1991) *The Instructional Conversation: Teaching and Learning in Social Activity.* Washington, DC: National Center for Research on Cultural Diversity and Second Language Learning.

Tomasello, M. (2003) *Constructing a Language: A Usage-Based Theory of Language Acquisition.* Cambridge, MA: Harvard University Press.

Topping, K., and Bryce, A. (2004) Cross-age peer tutoring of reading and thinking: Influence on thinking skills. *Educational Psychology*, 24(5): 595–621.

Tulviste, P. (1988) *Cultural-Historical Development of Verbal Thinking.* Commack, NJ: Nova Sciencia Publishers.

Vélez-Ibáñez, C., and Greenberg, J. (2005) Formation and transformation of funds of knowledge. In N. González., L.C. Moll and C. Amanti (eds) *Funds of Knowledge: Theorizing Practices in Households, Communities, and Classrooms.* Mahwah, NJ: Erlbaum, pp. 47–70.

Volk, D., and de Acosta, M. (2004) Mediating networks for literacy learning: The role of Puerto Rican siblings. In E. Gregory, S. Long and D. Volk (eds) *Many Pathways to Literacy. Young Children Learning with Siblings, Grandparents, Peers and Communities.* New York: Routledge Falmer, pp. 24–38.

Vygotsky, L.S. (1964) *Pensamiento y lenguaje.* Buenos Aires: Lautaro.

Vygotsky, L.S. (1978) *El desarrollo de los procesos psicológicos superiores.* México: Grijalbo.

Vygotsky, L.S. (2007) *El instrumento y el signo en el desarrollo del niño.* Madrid: Fundación Infancia y Aprendizaje.

Ward, M.C. (1971) Them children: A study in language learning. New York: Holt, Rinehart and Winston.

Werstch, I. (1988) *Vigotsky y la formación social de la mente.* Barcelona: Paidós.

Wright, J., and Cleary, K.S. (2006) Kids in the tutor seat: Building schools' capacity to help struggling readers through a cross-age peer tutoring program. *Psychology in the Schools*, 43(1): 99–107.

Chapter 7

Temporality, Trajectory, and Early Literacy Learning

Catherine Compton-Lilly

Introduction

Time for people may be like water for fish. As fish live in water, we live within time without paying much attention to how temporality informs how we grow, develop, and make sense of our worlds. While we fixate on time as we schedule our days, weeks, months, and years, we rarely attend to the ways meanings about ourselves, others, literacy learning, and schooling are constructed within and across time. These invisible aspects of temporality are the focus of this chapter. Specifically, I aim to:

- increase awareness of the multiple dimensions of times that affect schooling and literacy learning;
- contribute to a nuanced understanding of context that entails multiple dimensions of temporality; and
- draw attention to how young children operate and become literate within rich temporal contexts.

The chapter opens by exploring *time as context* – the recognition of time as a constitutive dimension of experience that affects identity, literacy, and meaning construction. Next, I present insights related to temporality from developmental psychology, sociology, and life narrative studies. I then provide a general discussion of time and trajectory in schooling followed by a review of research that attends to various dimensions of time in early childhood literacy research.

While this chapter explores theoretical and methodological issues related to time, time is more than a theoretical and methodological dimension. Temporalities of schooling and literacy learning have serious effects on children and their experiences. To illustrate the significance of time, I introduce Jermaine, a student I followed from my first grade classroom through to age 17. When I last saw Jermaine, he was seventeen and read at the fourth grade level. He had been retained once in second grade and five times in middle school. Jermaine left school when he was again assigned to eighth grade. At our final interview, Jermaine commented

International Handbook of Research on Children's Literacy, Learning, and Culture, First Edition.
Edited by Kathy Hall, Teresa Cremin, Barbara Comber, and Luis C. Moll.
© 2013 John Wiley & Sons, Ltd. Published 2013 by John Wiley & Sons, Ltd.

'I don't like reading. It's not me.' The construction of Jermaine as a poor reader and a struggling student involved a long-term trajectory marked by falling behind in his ability to read grade level texts and being labeled a behavior problem, a student with a 'disorder of written language,' a consistent failure on standardized tests, and as over age for his assigned grade. Jermaine complained about not being able to keep up with the pace of instruction, teachers not spending time with him, and not being in his 'right grade.' As I will discuss in the paper's conclusion, Jermaine's trajectory is not separate from his positioning as an African American male residing in a high poverty community and attending school in a chronically underfunded school district. In this chapter, I explore dimensions of *time as context* to reveal how temporal dimensions of schooling act upon students, like Jermaine, defining them as sub-literate, academic failures.

Time as Context

Time is a dimension of all human experience. However, common descriptions of context often neglect time, focusing on physical settings or the social contexts in which events occur. I argue that time is an inextricable aspect of the contexts in which people exist, operate, and construct understandings of the world and themselves. While earlier conceptualizations drawing on anthropology and sociology (see Thomas, 1927) defined context in terms of both space and time, with the exception of references to participants' background knowledge or prior linguistic experiences, recent discussions of context have generally focused on social, linguistic, interactional, and spatial aspects of context. For example, while typologies constructed by Duranti and Goodwin (1992) and Rex, Green, and Dixon (1998) recognize people's background experiences and past language practices, neither directly names nor addresses time as a contextual dimension of people's experiences nor highlights the range of temporal dimensions that accompany experience.

Adam (2008) maintains that time is multifaceted and 'involves a number of irreducible elements' (p. 7) including time frame, temporality, timing, tempo, duration, sequence, and temporal modalities. She notes that when these dimensions are brought together 'patterns of rhythmicity, periodicity, and cyclicality' (p. 8) become visible. I argue that these patterns inform the ways students make sense of literacy, identity, and schooling framing the trajectories that students both assume and construct. Development occurs, learning takes place, and school trajectories are enacted across time; thus, it is essential that educational researchers attend explicitly to *time as context*. *Time as context*, references time as a constitutive dimension of experience, alongside space, language, texts, artifacts, relationships, values, cultures, policies, traditions, social roles, practices and institutions. I maintain that attention to time has the potential to reveal insights and understandings that can help researchers and educators to understand students' experiences of literacy and schooling.

Conceptualizations of Time

In this section, I explore three conceptualizations of time reflected in developmental psychology, sociology, and research that documents relationships between narratives and time. I argue that each discipline invokes a different conceptualization of time – time as evidenced by a series of developmental levels and stages; temporality as resulting in shared social constructions within groups and societies; and time as a resource for the construction of life narratives.

Conceptualizations of time in developmental psychology

Developmental psychologists focus on time as series of developmental levels and stages. For example, Bronfenbrenner (1976, 1977) identified ecological transitions that involved changes in roles, settings, and maturation that occurred across the life course. Elder (1995) situated development within a set of temporal dimensions that highlight the significance of living during particular historical times, the social ties that temporally link lives, and the historically constructed mechanisms of socialization that surround and define people's experiences.

A related body of developmental research focuses on the architecture of human development. Baltes (1997) developed frameworks to describe general biological and cultural mechanisms that define the life course. Baltes documented patterns of gains and losses that characterize lives as people develop and age. Although Baltes identified patterns across time, he simultaneously highlighted the significance of interindividual differences and plasticity arguing that the same developmental outcomes could be reached through various means. He maintained that research had moved away from 'unilinear, unifunctional, and deterministic models of ontogenesis to a theoretical framework that highlight the contextual, adaptive, probabilistic, and self-organizational dynamics of ontogenesis' (Baltes, Staudinger, and Lindenberger, 1999, p. 499).

A third group of researchers highlighted social expectations associated with age. As Neugarten (1979) argued, 'being on time or off time is a compelling basis for self-assessment' (p. 888). People tend to correlate age-related expectations with expected life course experiences (e.g., education, employment, and retirement). As Settersten (2003) argued, 'The effects of institutionalization presumably trickle down to the minds of individuals as they set and strive for developmental goals' (p. 84). However, these conceptualizations of age-related expectations also entail 'heterogeneity, discontinuity, and contingency' (Settersten and Mayer, 1997, p. 234).

Conceptualizations of time in sociology

Sociologists have attended to time as a shared social construction within groups and societies. Notably, Zerubavel (1981, 2003) attended to the temporal organization of social life and explored the ways people regulated their lives relative to time. Zerubavel examined the ways temporal differentiation contributed to the separation of the holy from the profane, work from pleasure, and public from the private. As he maintained, time constitutes 'one of the major parameters of the context on which the meaning of social acts and situations depends' (Zerubavel, 1981, pp. 101–102). His later work extended this connection between temporality and meaning construction to explore how memory both 'shapes and distorts' (Zerubavel, 2003, p. 11) what we remember. Problematizing linear and cumulative notions of time and history, Zerubavel explored how people 'transform essentially unstructured series of events into seemingly coherent *historical narratives*' (p. 13).

Adam also challenges temporal accounts that present temporality as 'serial, linear, progressive, or cumulative' (Adam, 1990, p. 6). She encourages social scientists to grapple with the full complexity of time arguing that when people focus on minute-to-minute and day-to-day interactions time appears linear, but when the lens is widened cycles of days, weeks, months, semesters, seasons, and years become evident (Adam, 2008). While some social scientists have argued that cyclical and linear conceptions of time distinguish between traditional and modern societies, Adam maintains that cyclical and linear conceptions are complementary ways of considering time. Cycles of making dinner, eating dinner, washing dishes, and putting children to bed operate alongside longitudinal identity construction for women while making sense of individual trajectories often involves nonlinear, selective, and reiterative processes that draw on particular experiences while forgetting others. For Adam, all human action is situated within people's conceptions of past, present, and future. The habits people form, the traditions they honor, the goals they seek, the wishes they make, and the meanings they construct are all constructed within time. Adam reminds us that physical time, biological time, and social, experience-based conceptions of time operate in parallel – each contributing to how people comprehend themselves and the world.

Conceptualizations of time in life narratives

Scholars have also attended to the role time plays in the construction of life narratives. McAdams (2001) argues that identity takes the form of a story complete with plots, characters, settings, scenes, and themes. During late adolescence youth 'begin to reconstruct the personal past, perceive the present, and anticipate the future in terms of an internalized and evolving self-story' (McAdams, 2001, p. 101). Over time these narratives are continuously written and rewritten. McLeod and Yates (2006) argue that the high school students that they worked with looked to both their envisioned futures and their pasts as they constructed identities in the present and that these identities were always complicated by institutional expectations related to schooling.

Lopez-Bonilla (2011) provides a detailed micro-analysis of two students' narratives. Specifically, she reveals how cultural models related to gender and social class operated for Mexican high school students as they recursively reflected on their experiences in high school. Tensions between cultural models of being a 'good student' and the gendered expectations that defined appropriate participation in classrooms were highlighted as Lopez-Bonilla considered how students retrospectively constructed understandings of self. Likewise Nespor (2004) described how one elementary school teacher constructed understandings about teaching and learning by drawing recursively and selectively on her past experiences as mother, student, and teacher. As Nespor argues, 'Teaching and learning play out in complex, layered processes in which actions and events are simultaneously produced and made meaningful at multiple spatio-temporal scales' (p. 309). A related group of scholars have examined relationships between personal stories and larger public collective accounts. Of particular importance is what constitutes a story that is worthy of remembering, telling and retelling (Gerogakopoulou, 2006) and the contributions small stories make to long-term identities.

Conceptualizations of time in psychology, sociology, and life narrative studies highlight multiple dimensions of time – time as evidenced by a series of developmental levels and stages; temporality as resulting in shared social constructions within groups and societies; and time as a resource for the construction of life narratives. Each of these dimensions is relevant to the ways Jermaine operated and constructed meaning as he moved through school. When Jermaine was retained once in second grade and repeatedly in middle school, his developmental trajectory was interrupted leaving him to operate in an eighth grade classroom at age 17. Being out of sync had significant effects on Jermaine that reflected the social meanings reportedly expressed by peers – 'Ah-hah, you're a second grader.' Researchers interested in life narratives might highlight Jermaine's account of self, presented during our final interview, 'If I was reading like when I was with ya'll [in first grade and in Reading Recovery], [if] after I left that school, if I would have kept on reading, I would have been a real good reader.'

Time, Trajectories, and Schooling

Traditionally, time in schools has been treated as a resource. Recent conversations devoted to time on task and extended school days and school years attest to the theory that the more time children spend in school, the more they will learn. This conversation is not new. In the late 1800's, William T. Harris, then the US Commissioner of Education, lamented shortened school days and years (NEC, 1994/2005). Between 1910 and 1930 the efficiency movement focused on producing more learning in less time (Callahan, 1962). More recently in 1994, the National Educational Commission on Time and Learning critiqued how time was allocated in schools. Reprinted over a decade later, *Prisoners of Time* (NEC, 1994/2005) and advocated 'not only more learning time, but for all time to be used in new and better ways' (p. 2).

Classic research by Carroll (1963) complicated theories of time as a resource by identifying student aptitude as a critical consideration noting that more capable students required less time to learn. Berliner (1990) highlighted the degree to which students were focused on learning tasks (e.g., engagement, time on task). He described aptitude, perseverance, and the pace of instruction as relevant temporal dimensions. Anderson (1985) further complicated discussions of instructional time by considering the rate at which topics were introduced. For example, instructional programs designed for special education students often cover material at a slower pace (Arlin, 1984; Hocutt, 1996). Other compensatory programs (Clay, 2005; Renaissance Learning, 2009; Scientific Products Learning, 2009) are designed to accelerate students' learning, enabling them to catch up with their peers. The number of minutes per week students spend in mainstream classrooms, resource rooms, and/or self-contained classrooms is often determined by the diagnosed severity of students' disabilities (Hocutt, 1996).

Trajectories and schooling

Longitudinal notions of time involve trajectories that students assume as they move through school. Gorard and his colleagues (1998) described trajectories as 'characteristic patterns of movement' (p. 401). Dauber, Alexander, and Entwisle (1996) extend this definition arguing that trajectory can act as both a 'guide and restraint on the path to attainment' (p. 302). Researchers have linked early experiences with long-term outcomes including factors that correlate with high school graduation (Dauber, Alexander, and Entwisle, 1996), educational success (Morrison *et al.*, 2006) and employment outcomes (Kerckhoff, 2001). These notions of trajectory attempt to predict outcomes based on early experiences.

In contrast to these conceptualizations of time as a resource and a linear trajectory, other notions of temporality involve negotiations and understandings that challenge linear, causal, and reproductive models. These subjective and personal conceptions of time have a long history and can be traced to the work of Rousseau (1762/2007) who argued that schools must 'lose time' (Ben-Peretz, 1990, p. 212) – allowing growth and development to direct learning rather than the clock. These alternative notions of trajectory recognize people as 'situated participants in structures of social practice' (Dreier, 2009, p. 196). Dreier notes the structural contribution of institutions that offer particular trajectories including 'stations, divisions, tracks, curricula, programmes, and career paths' (p. 198). Wortham (2006) argues that trajectories involve enacted, and represented metapragmatic models of 'recognizable kinds of people . . . operating in a recognizable kind of interaction' (p. 32). He notes that contemporary anthropologists draw attention to events and actions alongside shared metapragmatic models and socio-historical understandings to conceptualize how individuals, including students, are positioned and ultimately treated. Further complicating notions of trajectory, Erickson (2004) argues for a 'more practical theory of practice' (p. 140) that documents 'moment-by-moment action and judgment' (p. 138) allowing analyses at multiple points on a trajectory.

Polman (2006) illustrates how ongoing experiences may or may not affect student trajectories. In particular, Polman considers how trajectories related to learning history and identity construction intersect within a community of learners. Polman (2006) presents the cases of two students and explores how the ways in which their interests and lived histories are taken up and used within an after-school program affect their future academic trajectories. Mercer, Dawes, and Staarman (2009) analyze teachers' use of dialogue to connect present learning with past experiences and to link content to students' past and anticipated experiences.

Trajectories and literacy learning

Literate trajectories have been described in causal terms with early patterns of literacy achievement affecting long-term outcomes. The 'Matthew effect' (Stanovich, 1986) described early high achieving literacy learners as benefiting from ongoing literacy instruction while low achieving early learners fell further behind. Good, Simmons, and Smith (1998) argued that the Matthew effect is based on 'a predictable and consequential series of reading-related activities that begin with difficulty in foundational readings skills' (p. 58) that include phonological awareness, alphabetic knowledge, phonological recording, reading accuracy, and fluency. As they report, '"Catching up" [is] all but impossible for students on a low developmental reading trajectory' (Good, Simmons, and Smith, 1998, p. 60). Linear and sequential conceptions of literacy learning are evident in reading programs that draw upon developmental stages (Chall, 1983), the scope and sequences of basal reading textbooks (Shannon and Goodman, 1994), leveled books that correlate with grade-level benchmarks (Pinnell and Fountas, 1996), and writing rubrics to identify students who have fallen behind.

Linear and sequential notions of literacy learning have been challenged from both qualitative (Bloome and Katz, 1997; Genishi and Dyson, 2009) and quantitative perspectives (Kaplan, 2002; Parrila *et al.*, 2005). Kaplan (2002) argues that linear growth models in reading assume that student growth trajectories represent a 'random sample from a single population' when large populations are more likely composed of 'smaller, finite populations, each with its own unique trajectory' (p. 190). Parrila and colleagues (2005) challenged the Matthew effect (Stanovich, 1986) noting that reading growth appeared to speed up and slow down at various points in time reflecting language differences and cultural and institutional expectations. They maintain that linear models 'may mask important variability in growth over an extended period of time' (p. 301). Mixed methods accounts have also challenged linear and sequential notions of literacy learning. Snow *et al.* (2007) drew upon a longitudinal, mixed methods data set to ask whether successful early literacy learning was sufficient to support academic success for adolescents; their findings challenged the predictive powers of early literacy experiences.

To return to my opening narrative, Jermaine's multiple retentions, lack of school progress, and behavior in school placed him on a problematic school trajectory. However, there were several times when Jermaine, his parents and school personnel made efforts to shift his trajectory. For example, his mother used her limited economic resources to purchase a computer that Jermaine could use for school tasks, sent him to summer school almost every year, and agreed to having him classified as a special education student so that he would receive help. In a particularly poignant effort on the part of his middle school, Jermaine was assigned to spend half of each school day completing phonemic awareness activities on a computer in order to accelerate his reading achievement.

> They let me know they had a program I could join and they could skip me up [to a higher grade]... I was like in 8th grade class. They gave me 8th grade work and everybody else 7th grade work... I'm in the 9th or 10th grade now.

When this intervention ended, Jermaine expected to be promoted to high school. Instead, he was retained again in grade eight. While it could easily be argued that interventions such as computerized reading programs and summer school do not provide sufficient support for children who are significantly behind in school, despite home and school efforts, Jermaine's trajectory proved difficult to disrupt. On a national level, disrupting the negative school trajectories of millions of children from high poverty and culturally diverse communities has proven to be similarly intractable.

Time in Early Literacy Classrooms

On the following pages I examine time in early childhood classrooms: construction and time, cultural historical views of literacy, and longitudinal qualitative literacy research. Although relevant and currently of interest to many early childhood scholars, this chapter does not address issues related to time and technology.

Uses of time in early childhood classrooms

While some scholars (Bloome *et al.*, 2009; Nystrand *et al.*, 2003) have focused on how time operates in secondary literacy classrooms, others have attended specifically to early childhood literacy classrooms. For example, Anderson-Levitt (2002) explored how first grade teachers in the United States and France allocated time for literacy instruction. Her analysis revealed that despite the philosophical differences among teachers who implemented basal programs or 'natural methods' (p. 142), they all adhered to similar self-imposed schedules to guide classroom instruction. While early lessons focused on whole word reading and analysis, later lessons taught children to blend increasingly complex letter patterns and develop reading fluency. In an analysis of how time operated in a First Holy Communion class, Tusting (2000) documented how children's investment of time in completing assignments was interpreted as a measure of their religious commitment. In addition, she explored how the parish newsletter, with its accounts of activities and event calendar, provided a textual reference for synchronizing events in time and contributing to community identity.

Working in five pre-school and early childhood classrooms in South Africa, Dixon (2011) highlighted the ways classroom timetables controlled the schooled bodies of children. The established temporal schedules of the classrooms imposed particular activities on children within particular classroom spaces. Dixon's analysis reveals how time and space operated in the service of literacy learning while documenting the lack of opportunities for children to use reading and writing for their own purposes and engender children's full meaning-making potentials.

Matusov (2009) argued that in traditional monologic classrooms, existing conceptions of time, often dominated by the need to cover material, resulted in missed opportunities for teachers to pursue children's interests and ideas. Children in these classrooms were defined as successful or unsuccessful based on uni-dimensional and 'testable' definitions of success. Erickson (2004) argued that timing is central to the social organization of attention, activity, and interaction. He used descriptions of children in classrooms to illustrate difficulties faced by children who did not share the classroom's temporal expectations.

Genishi and Dyson (2009) described 'child speed,' maintaining that educators must allow young students the time they needed to learn language and literacy and recognize the 'diverse developmental time lines' (p. 35) that students bring to school. They argued that even young children draw on the past as they construct themselves as members of social and historical literate communities. 'Children might play games that their teachers played in their childtimes, recite rhymes that have been passed through generations of students . . . alongside child-created dramas and stories of contemporary superheroes' (Genishi and Dyson, 2009, p. 139).

Meaning construction and timescales

Conversations about time have also involved social semiotics and the ways people construct meanings. Lemke (2000, 2001) has argued that people draw on experiences across multiple scales of time as they make sense of experiences in the present. Specifically, ongoing events are interpreted in reference to multiple timescales including lived past experiences, the past accounts of family members and friends, and historical accounts. Processes that occur slowly over long periods of have constraining effects on the ways people experience and make sense of lived events at shorter timescales. As Lemke (2000) argues, long-term processes, including identity construction and literacy learning,

> cannot take place on short timescales. Even if short-term events *contribute toward* such changes, it is only the fact that they are *not* soon erased, do *not* quickly fade – that subsequent events do not reverse the change – which makes it count. (p. 282)

According to Lemke (2001), meaning construction involves zooming in and out across multiple timescales to interpret experiences and construct meaning. Thus, timescales analysis acknowledges both micro and macro influences. Some researchers have applied timescales to the learning experiences of high school students and adults to explore identity construction (Wortham, 2006), analyze classroom dialogue (Mercer, Dawes, and Staarman, 2009), and to explore the methodological and theoretical affordances of time for making sense of ethnographic and linguistic data (Burgess and Ivanic, 2010). Others have focused on how timescales inform meaning construction for young children.

Pahl (2007) explored the way a young immigrant Turkish boy in London repeatedly drew on the motif of a bird in drawings he completed at the family literacy centre, comments he made about stories read in his classroom, memories of his grandmother's home in Turkey, and in his family nickname (which meant 'little bird' in Turkish). Pahl argued that more nuanced understandings of home meanings could inform school literacy practices that would build on the multiple temporalized meanings that children bring. Specifically, she highlighted the 'tapestry of meanings attached to the bird theme' (p. 187) that involved macro accounts of family immigration, meso experiences of institutions including family, school, and the family literacy centre, alongside the micro events of daily life.

As timescales involve multiple scales of time, the experiences of children in early childhood have contributed to longitudinal analyses of children across time. Compton-Lilly (2011) drew on the construct of timescales to explore how ongoing, familial, and historical events were accessed by one student, Alicia, as she moved from first grade through middle school. In particular, Compton-Lilly documented the circulation of repeated discourses related to literacy and schooling within this family. For example, accounts of Alicia mother's school experiences were used to make sense of Alicia's experiences (e.g., 'teachers seemed like they cared' [when Alicia's mom was in school]). Some past events were repeatedly invoked while others were forgotten highlighting the selective and recursive sense-making processes across multiple and nonlinear timescales.

Cultural historical views of literacy

Researchers have also attended to the ways children are contextualized within particular social histories. In these accounts, time is treated as historical context that informs the ways various cultural groups are positioned.

Gregory and Williams (2000) conducted multiple studies occurring across over a decade within the same East London community. Their work references not only the current residents of this community, but also its former residents whose past presence is inscribed on buildings and embodied in the spaces in which the current residents reside. Findings from Gregory and Williams' studies (2000) highlight various socio-historically based myths about poor linguistically diverse communities – in particular, the 'myth that linguistic minority children's reading success depends upon experience with "authorised" reading experiences at home' (p. 11). Specifically, they argued that the students' experiences with texts were grounded in social histories. Their work is explicitly situated within the history of the local community and in the 'contrasting literacies' (p. 203) that are embodied in the generations of people who constitute that community. In a similar vein, Valenzuela (1999) situated her ethnographic study with immigrant Mexican American students in Houston. Compton-Lilly (2007) noted the role of her school community in the race riots of the 1960s.

Longitudinal qualitative literacy research

Longitudinal qualitative research studies that focus on students have been conducted in a variety of disciplines (e.g., sociology, education, life study) and in countries around the world including Australia (McLeod and Yates, 2006), Finland (Lahelma, 2009), India (Lacey, Copper, and Torrance, 1993), Italy (Cosaro and Molinari, 2000), Serbia (Tomanovic, 2004), the United Kingdom (Henderson *et al.*, 2007), and the United States (Reese, Kroesen, and Gallimore, 2000; Rogers, 2011).

Shirley Brice Heath (1983) conducted a quintessential long-term qualitative research study between the years 1969 and 1978 to examine oral language and literacy events in two North Carolina communities. Her focus was on the language and literacy practices that children brought to school and the efforts of teachers to build on those practices. More recently, Heath (2010) returned to the same research site to document changes that had occurred over the past 40 years. This longitudinal work treats time as a methodological resource that can be used to acquire rich insights into particular communities and to document changes that occur in those communities over time.

Similarly, Denny Taylor (1983) observed the literacy practices of families over a five-year period. Not only did her work contribute to a methodological depth and knowledge about families, but it also revealed how time operated as parents interpreted their children's literacy development over time through the lens of their own memories of learning to read.

Comber and her colleagues (2002) conducted a series of qualitative case studies following children from their entry into school through their first four years of formal schooling. As they reported, these case studies 'take us inside individual children's literacy development' (2002, p. 10). The case studies involved observations of children in classrooms, literacy assessment data, and interviews with some parents to explore the 'kinds of literacies and pedagogies made available to students in very different contexts over a period of time' (p. 4). Findings indicate that while there was a 'relationship between early literacy predictors and later school success' (p. 4), all children did not follow predictable trajectories. Specifically, Comber and her colleagues maintained that, for students who had fallen behind in literacy, ' "catching up" was possible when teachers, parents, and students made it a priority' (p. 5). They highlighted the significance of the 'recognition factor' – 'the extent to which what children can do *counts*, and they can see that it counts' (p. 6; italics in the original). These longitudinal accounts provide a depth of information about students' lives and reveal patterns that are invisible in shorter term studies.

Conclusions

The first goal of this chapter was to raise the awareness of scholars, researchers, and educators of the many ways in which time operates in people's lives. While we are continuously acting and interacting within time, we seldom give thought to how literacies are learned, identities are constructed, and meanings are made and remade within and across time. While educators have tended to highlight time as a resource that can be exchanged for learning, more complicated accounts have been offered. Some studies of young children's learning literacy have focused on how early literacy experiences contribute to later school achievement. Others have highlighted the unique rates at which children learn, and the ways elementary literacy teachers use and allocate time. These varied accounts support my assertion that time is a dimension of context within which people experience literacy, construct school trajectories, and craft visions of themselves as readers and writers. Time is both an arbitrator of student success and a tool for making sense of ourselves and our literate abilities.

I maintain that attention to time can contribute to a more nuanced understanding of literacy learning for students, like Jermaine, who attend underfunded schools and live in high poverty communities. Jermaine's trajectory represents one story among millions. While low socio-economic status children generally encounter well-intentioned and capable teachers, these professionals often lack the time, space, and resources needed to change trajectories for students. In first grade, Jermaine received Reading Recovery services that enabled him to read at the level of the average readers in his class; however, over the next 11 years, he fell behind and was never provided with instruction that addressed his difficulties.

Based on the findings of this review, I suggest that:

- Alternative temporal conceptions of early childhood must be developed. While many accounts of young children's literacy learning focus on correlations between early literacy experiences and long-term student achievement, more work is needed to explore how children position themselves within time and how literate identities are constructed.
- More longitudinal accounts of literate trajectories are needed. While Jermaine's story is uniquely his own, insights related to Jermaine's case invite us to ask related questions about the long-term trajectories of other students.
- Researchers must explore opportunities for disrupting and rewriting established school trajectories. Once young children, like Jermaine find themselves on problematic paths, new actions must be taken.

This review of research related to time, alongside the case study of Jermaine, invites us to consider the temporal dimensions of our own work and to consider how time operates as context. It is my hope that each reader envisions a set of temporal possibilities that provides a useful lens for thinking about literacy learning for young children.

References

Adam, B. (1990) *Time and Social Theory*. Cambridge, UK: Polity Press.

Adam, B. (2008) Researching lives through time: Time, generation and life stories. *Timescapes Working Paper Series No. 1*. Leeds, UK: University of Leeds.

Anderson, L.M. (1985) What are students doing when they do all that seatwork? In C.W. Fisher and D.C. Berliner (eds) *Perspectives on Instructional Time*. New York: Longman, pp. 189–202.

Anderson-Levitt, K.M. (2002) *Teaching Cultures: Knowledge for Teaching First Grade in France and the United States*. Cresskill, NJ: Hampton Press.

Arlin, M. (1984) Time, equity, and mastery learning. *Review of Educational Research*, 54(1): 65–86.

Baltes, P.B. (1997) On the incomplete architecture of human ontology: Selection, optimization, and the compensation as foundation of developmental theory. *American Psychologist*, 52(4): 366–380.

Baltes, P.B., Staudinger, U.M., and Lindenberger, U. (1999) Lifespan psychology: Theory and application to intellectual functioning. *Annual Review of Psychology*, 50: 471–507.

Ben-Peretz, M. (1990) Perspectives in time in education. In M. Ben-Peretz and R. Bromme (eds) *The Nature of Time in Schools: Theoretical Concepts, Practitioner Perceptions*. New York: Teachers College Press, pp. 64–77.

Berliner, D. (1990) What's all the fuss about instructional time? In Ben-Peretz, M., and Bromme, R. (eds) (1990) *The Nature of Time in Schools: Theoretical Concepts, Practitioner Perceptions*. New York: Teachers College Press, pp. 3–35.

Bloome, D., Beierle, M., Grigorenko, M., and Goldman, S. (2009) Learning over time: Uses of intercontextuality, collective memories, and classroom chronotopes in the construction of learning opportunities in a ninth-grade language arts classroom. *Language and Education*, 23(4): 313–334.

Bloome, D., and Katz, L. (1997) Literacy as a social practice and classroom chronotopes. *Reading and Writing Quarterly*, 13(3): 205–225.

Bronfenbrenner, U. (1976) The experimental ecology of education. *Educational Researcher*, 5(9): 5–15.

Bronfenbrenner, U. (1977) Toward an experimental ecology of human development. *American Psychologist*, 32(7): 513–531.

Burgess, A., and Ivanic, R. (2010) Writing and being written: Issues of identity across timescales. *Written Communication*, 27(2): 228–255.

Callahan, R.E. (1962) *Education and the Cult of Efficiency*. Chicago, IL: University of Chicago Press.

Carroll, J.B. (1963) A Model of School Learning. *Teachers College Record*, 64(8): 723–733.

Chall, J. (1983) *Stages of Reading Development*. New York: McGraw-Hill.

Clay, M.M. (2005) *Literacy Lessons: Designed for Individuals, Parts I and II*. Portsmouth, NH: Heinemann.

Comber, B., Badger, L., Barnett, J., *et al.* (2002) *Literacy after the Early Years: A Longitudinal Study*. My read: Strategies for teaching reading in the middle school years, accessed November 12, 2012: www.myread.org/readings_literacy.htm.

Compton-Lilly, C. (2011) Time and reading: Negotiations and affiliations of a reader, grades one through eight. *Research in the Teaching of English*, 45(3): 224–252.

Compton-Lilly, C. (2007) *Re-Reading Families: The Literate Lives of Urban Children, Four Years Later*. New York: Teachers College Press.

Cosaro, W., and Molinari, L. (2000) Entering and observing in children's worlds: A reflection on a longitudinal ethnography of early education in Italy. In P. Christensen and A. James (eds) *Research with Children: Perspectives and Practices*. London: Falmer Press.

Dauber, S.L., Alexander, K.L., and Entwisle, D.R. (1996) Tracking and transitions through the middle grades: Channeling educational trajectories. *Sociology of Education*, 69(4): 290–307.

Dixon, K. (2011) *Literacy, Power, and the Schooled Body: Learning in Time and Space*. New York: Routledge.

Dreier, O. (2009) Persons in structures of social practice. *Theory and Practice*, 19(2): 193–212.

Duranti, A., and Goodwin, C. (eds) (1992) Rethinking context: Language as an interactive phenomenon. *Studies in the Social and Cultural Foundations of Language, No 11*. Cambridge: Cambridge University Press.

Elder, G.H. (1995) The life course paradigm: Social change and individual development. In P. Moen, G.H. Elder, K. Lüscher (eds) *Examining Lives in Context: Perspectives in the Ecology of Human Development*, Washington, DC: American Psychological Association, pp. 101–139.

Erickson, F. (2004) *Talk and Social Theory: Ecologies of Speaking and Listening in Everyday Life*. New York: Polity Press.

Genishi, C., and Dyson, A.H. (2009) *Students, Language and Literacy: Diverse Learners in Diverse Times*. New York: Teachers College press.

Gerogakopoulou, A. (2006) Thinking big with small stories in narrative and identity analysis. *Narrative Inquiry*, 16(1): 122–130.

Good, R.H., Simmons, D.C., and Smith, S.B. (1998) Effective academic interventions in the United States: Evaluating and enhancing the acquisition of early reading skills. *Educational and Child Psychology*, 15(1): 56–70.

Gorard, S., Rees, G., Fevre, R., and Furlong, J. (1998) Learning trajectories: Traveling towards a learning society. *International Journal of Lifelong Education*, 17, 400–414.

Gregory, E., and Williams, A. (2000) *City Literacies: Learning to Read across Generations and Cultures*. London: Routledge.

Heath, S.B. (1983) *Ways with Words: Language, Life, and Work in Communities and Classrooms*. Cambridge, MA: Cambridge University Press.

Heath, S.B. (2010) Family literacy or community learning? Some critical questions on perspective. In K. Dunsmore and D. Fisher (eds) *Bringing Literacy Home*. Newark, DE: IRA, pp. 15–41.

Henderson, S., Holland, J., McGrellis, S., *et al.* (2007) *Inventing Adulthoods: A Biographical Approach to Youth Transitions*. Thousand Oaks, CA: Sage.

Hocutt, A.M. (1996) Effectiveness of special education: Is placement the critical factor? *The Future of Students*, 6(1): 77–102.

Kaplan, D. (2002) Methodological advances of individual growth with relevance to educational policy. *Peabody Journal of Education*, 77(4): 189–215.

Kerckhoff, A.C. (2001) Education and social stratification processes in comparative perspective. *Sociology of Education*, 74: 3–18.

Lacey, C., Copper, B., and Torrance, H. (1993) Evaluating the Andhra Pradesh Primary Education Project: Problems of design and analysis. *British Education Research Journal*, 19(5): 535–554.

Lahelma, E. (2009) Dichotomized metaphors and young people's educational routes. *European Educational Research Journal*, 8(4): 497–507.

Lemke, J. (2000) Across the scales of time: Artifacts, activities, and meanings in ecosocial systems. *Mind, Culture, and Activity*, 7(4): 273–290.

Lemke, J. (2001) The long and short of it: Comments on multiple timescale studies of human activity. *The Journal of the Learning Sciences*, 10(1&2): 17–26.

Lopez-Bonilla, G. (2011) 'Teamwork': Conflicting cultural models of gender, class, school, and family among high school students. In G. Lopez-Bonilla and K. Englander (eds) *Discourses and Identities in Contexts of Educational Change: Contributions from the United States and Mexico*. New York: Peter Lang, pp. 75–98.

Matusov, E. (2009) *Journey into Dialogic Pedagogy*. Hauppauge, NY: Nova Science Publishers.

McAdams, D.P. (2001) The psychology of life stories. *Review of General Psychology*, 5(2): 100–122.

McLeod, J., and Yates, L. (2006) *Making Modern Lives: Subjectivity, Schooling and Social Change*. Albany: State University of New York.

Mercer, N., Dawes, L., and Staarman, K. (2009) Dialogic teaching in the primary science classroom. *Language and Education*, 23(4): 353–369.

Morrison, G.M., Brown, M., D'Incau, B., *et al.* (2006) Understanding resilience in educational trajectories: Implications for practice possibilities. *Psychology in Schools*, 43(1): 19–31.

NEC (National Education Commission of the States Education Reform) (2005/1994) *Prisoners of time, Reprint of the National Education Commission on Time and Learning*. Denver, CO: ECS Education Reform Reprint Series.

Nespor, J. (2004) Educational scale-making. *Pedagogy, Culture, and Society*, 112(3): 309–326.

Neugarten, B.L. (1979) Time, age, and the life cycle. *American Journal of Psychiatry*, 136(7): 887–894.

Nystrand, M., Wu, L.I., Gamoran, A., *et al.* (2003) Questions in time: Investigating the structure and dynamics of unfolding classroom discourse. *Discourse Processes*, 35(2): 135–198.

Pahl, K. (2007) Timescales and ethnography: Understanding a child's meaning-making across three sites, a home, a classroom, and a family literacy class. *Ethnography and Education*, 2(2): 175–190.

Parrila, R., Aunola, A.K., Leskinen, E., *et al.* (2005) Development of individual differences in reading: Results from longitudinal studies in English and Finnish. *Journal of Educational Psychology*, 97(3): 299–319.

Pinnell, G.S., and Fountas, I. (1996) *Guided Reading: Good First Teaching for all Children*. Portsmouth, NH: Heinemann.

Polman, J.L. (2006) Mastery and appropriation as a means to understand the interplay of history learning and identity trajectories. *The Journal of the Learning Sciences*, 15(2): 221–259.

Reese, L., Kroesen, K., and Gallimore, R. (2000) Agency in school performance among urban Latino youth. In R.D. Taylor and M.C. Wang (eds) *Resilience across Contexts: Family, Work, Culture, and Community*. Mahwah, NJ: Lawrence Erlbaum, pp. 295–332.

Renaissance Learning (2009) Inspire and enthrall students' imaginations with the power of Accelerated Reader, accessed November 12, 2012: www.renlearn.com/ar/

Rex, L., Green, J., and Dixon, C. (1998) What counts when context counts?: The uncommon 'common' language of literacy research. *Journal of Literacy Research*, 30(3): 405–433.

Rogers, R. (2011) The sounds of silence in educational tracking: A longitudinal ethnographic case study. *Critical Discourse Studies*, 8(4): 1–14.

Rousseau, J. (1762/2007) *Emile*. New York: Brownell Press.

Scientific Products Learning (2009) Fast ForWord®, accessed November 12, 2012: www.scilearn.com/products/index.php.

Settersten, R.A. (2003) Age structuring and the rhythm of the life course. In J.T. Mortimer and M.J. Shanahan (eds) *The Handbook of the Life Course*. New York: Kluwer Academic /Plenum Publisher, pp. 81–98.

Settersten, R.A., and Mayer, K.U. (1997) The measurement of age, age structuring, and the life course. *Annual Review of Sociology*, 23: 233–261.

Shannon, P., and Goodman, K. (1994) *Basal Readers: A Second Look*. Katonah, NY: Richard C. Owen Publisher.

Snow, C., Porche, M., Tabors, P., and Harris, S.R. (2007) *Is Literacy Enough? Pathways to Academic Success for Adolescents*. New York: Brookes Publishing.

Stanovich, K.E. (1986) Matthew effects in reading: Some consequences of individual differences in the acquisition of literacy. *Reading Research Quarterly*, Fall: 360–407.

Taylor, D. (1983) *Family Literacy*. Portsmouth, NJ: Heinemann.

Thomas, W.I. (1927) Situational analysis: The behavior pattern and the situation. Papers and Proceedings from the Twenty-Second Annual Meeting of the American Sociological Society, 1–13.

Tomanovic, S. (2004) Family habitus as the cultural context for childhood. *Childhood*, 11: 339–360.

Tusting, K. (2000) The new literacy studies and time. In D. Barton, M. Hamilton, and R. Ivanic (eds) *Situated Literacies: Reading and Writing in Context*. New York: Routledge.

Valenzuela, A. (1999) *Subtractive Schooling: U.S.- Mexican Youth and the Politics of Caring*. Albany: State University of New York Press.

Wortham, S. (2006) *Learning Identity: The Joint Emergence of Social Identification and Academic Learning*. Cambridge, UK: Cambridge University Press.

Zerubavel, E. (1981) *Hidden Rhythms: Schedules and Calendars in Social Life*. Chicago: University of Chicago Press.

Zerubavel, E. (2003) *Time Maps: Collective Memory and the Social Shape of the Past*. Chicago: University of Chicago Press.

Chapter 8

'This is a Job for Hazmat Guy!'

Global Media Cultures and Children's Everyday Lives

Victoria Carrington and Clare Dowdall

Introduction

In a middle-class semi-detached house, nestled behind flowering shrubs in a quiet street in the suburbs of an English city, live two young children. Boys. Energetic, playful and just entering the first years of formal school. It is the weekend. The lounge room is strewn with newspapers, toy catalogues, cat toys and handheld video game consoles, but the middle of the room has been cleared. In this clearing is a vast array of LEGO® blocks. There are hundreds of brightly colored, plastic engineered blocks and wheels, minifigures, and miniature windscreens. Some of the blocks are hand-me-downs, some came in complete kits and one set is featured in the toy catalogue lying on the floor open at the LEGO® page. Both boys have been to the online LEGO® games site to play Indiana Jones and Star Wars games and have used LEGO® Creator to design bespoke sets. Both parents have been, with the boys, to the main LEGO® website, spent time discussing the LEGO® kits displayed in the various toy catalogues that appear in the mail, bought LEGO® kits as gifts for their children, and have worked on building (and later photographing) magnificent LEGO® structures with their sons. For the boys in this family, LEGO® exists as an online destination, as a creative and often social activity, as a consumer item, and as an artifact.

In this chapter, we are interested in media culture and spaces as important contexts for early literacy development. The things we each do with and understand about text and its uses find their initial impetus in socially relevant communities and sites: homes, bedrooms, virtual worlds, affinity groups, shopping malls, schools, workplaces (Carrington, 2008). Focusing on the LEGO activities of these boys reminds us that young children, such as these two boys, build literate identities and early repertoires of practice in relation to valued artifacts and within the material culture of their everyday lives. At the same time, children's early literacy practices and identities are crosscut by the power and reach of global and local media forms. These media impact on children's developing literate selves as they shape the contexts in which young people build repertoires of practice and a sense of themselves as particular kinds of literates. As Marsh (2006, p. 35) notes, 'for many children in contemporary societies, communicative practices in

International Handbook of Research on Children's Literacy, Learning, and Culture, First Edition.
Edited by Kathy Hall, Teresa Cremin, Barbara Comber, and Luis C. Moll.
© 2013 John Wiley & Sons, Ltd. Published 2013 by John Wiley & Sons, Ltd.

the home focus on popular culture, media and new technologies. No longer is it possible to explore the literacy practices of young children as an isolated set of social practices.' We wish to add an additional element to this theoretical frame. Drawing from the new material studies (Miller, 1987, 2008, 2009) we wish to acknowledge the key role of children's artifacts in the constructions of life worlds and dispositions. This is the key focus of this chapter.

We have chosen to focus on LEGO® to show the connection between media and literacy in young children's lives because frankly, LEGO® is an excellent example of the ideas we wish to think through. We take the view that the world in which children learn about literacy practices and begin to deploy them is constructed out of these broader cultural influences around media alongside the artifacts and practices of everyday life. In this sense, LEGO® is a tool for our thinking. In its contemporary form, LEGO® is multiplatform and transmedia: it traverses a diverse range of media forms accessed across and by multiple technologies (Jenkins, 2006). The media of LEGO® include, for instance, virtual worlds and online movies, television advertising, magazines, online advertising and build-it locations; the technologies include laptops, mobile phones, DVD/televisions and games consoles. In this, it reflects the current state of media: No longer stand alone; always enmeshed in an endlessly growing net of connections both on and offline, becoming an 'inter-media textual web' (Kinder, 1991, cited in Marsh, 2006, p. 35). However, LEGO® is also an iconic piece of material culture. Each LEGO® piece is one of the two million produced each hour in factories around the world and one of the more than 400 billion blocks estimated to be in circulation in homes, shops, and institutions. Consequently, we consider LEGO® to be simultaneously a media form and an everyday artifact. From our position as educators and researchers, we believe LEGO® to be a particularly appropriate vehicle for our analysis because of its strongly articulated links to learning and creativity (Ackermann *et al.*, 2009) and to the everyday worlds of childhood.

Constructing an Object Ethnography

In order to engage the complex influence of LEGO® we have chosen to undertake a modest and exploratory object ethnography of LEGO®. This approach is adapted from the 'thing theory' seminar programs held at Columbia University in Spring 2006–2008. The seminar program located itself theoretically in the New Material Studies with its interest in the mediation of the social and the agency of objects. Object ethnographies begin with the object. These artifactual analyses are then used as 'platforms for commentary on issues of identity, meaning, structure, social critique, materiality' (Columbia University, 2006). In this, they provide the starting point for broader, situated explorations.

Our examination of LEGO® therefore takes place across three levels. It starts from the material. We examine the blocks as artifacts in the daily life of these two young boys. Here we are particularly interested in the design affordances of LEGO®; what characterizes them as objects and what can be 'read' in relation to the intentions and expectations of the designers of these objects. The second level focuses on the social life of objects, taking up Appadurai's point that objects have a social biography. From Verbeek (2005, 2006) we understand this to mean that artifacts such as LEGO® have an agency or intentionality, but also that they have an individual history that is significant for the people that make use of them. The intentionality, or agency, of each artifact becomes entwined overtime with its social history. The final level draws from Barthe's view of objects as players in the building and maintenance of social and cultural myth (Barthes, 1972). Undertaking the object ethnography positions LEGO® as a material artifact, an agent in the construction of everyday social worlds, and a contributor to the larger cultural and political narratives that shape the world in which we live. We believe this to be an appropriate and potentially fruitful way of conceptualizing LEGO®'s dual existence as material everyday artifact and global media conglomerate. We believe that we are then in a position to comment on the complexities of children's life worlds and the social contexts of their engagements with text and early literacy practices.

LEGO® as an Artifact

The LEGO® universe provides us with an array of material artifacts, built up over successive production and distribution cycles and spread across homes the world over. Across more than 130 countries, seven LEGO® sets are sold every second and the children (and adults) in receipt of these sets spend 5 billion hours each year playing with them (Meet the Boss, n.d.). There are thought to be around 400 billion bricks in circulation around the world.

LEGO® is both a single block and a system of blocks that, in total, number in the hundreds of billions. This means that any single block found in any house around the world can potentially connect to any other block from any other home. LEGO® exists therefore as single, individual artifacts in separate homes, but also as the component parts of larger networks. Each studded and colored molded plastic LEGO® block and accessory is a mass-produced work of glossy plastic industrial art. LEGO® components are created from acrylonitrile butadiene styrene (ABS) granules, turned into recognizable blocks and minifigures via a high temperature automated molding system. Changing production technologies over time have impacted on the shape and design flexibility of the blocks. Early blocks were based around an interlocking mechanism that destined most constructions to be architectural. However, from the late 1950s improved manufacturing technologies allowed the development of increasingly interchangeable and flexible systems. Each individual block is glossy and brightly colored; the tubular formation working to lock bricks from any source together.

We turn now to examples of the specific blocks in use in the home described earlier. This handful of blocks (Figure 8.1) and the minifigure Hazmat Guy (Figure 8.2) are artifacts of significance to the two young boys as they play in the living room of their home. The shape

Figure 8.1 An example of LEGO® blocks

Figure 8.2   Minifigure Hazmat Guy

and styling of each artifact, the characteristics of the material from which they are fashioned, the ways in which each object can be coupled with others, customized and shared impact on how and where they are used. In design terms, these features are the 'script' of the artifact, that is, the particular affordances and design features that tend to direct or influence what is done with the object by its user. Miller (1987, 2009) argues that material objects such as these have significance in the construction and experience of everyday life and in the types of identities available to each of us to craft. Verbeek (2005, 2006) would go further, arguing that these artifacts are actively engaged in the co-construction of everyday lifeworlds, experiences and perceptions. These views give these everyday artifacts and the values attached to them particular importance to the ways in which these two young boys construct their identities and life worlds.

Figure 8.1 shows the basic block shapes and the interlocking system of round studs on the top of each block and tubes on the inside. Each brick is intricately tooled with 'LEGO' stamped on each individual stud. On each brick, the studs are slightly larger than the tube spaces into which they are pushed. As the studs are pressed into the tubes, the tendency of the plastic to hold its original shape, along with the friction created by the slight difference in size, locks the bricks together securely. The 'script' (Latour 2007; Verbeek 2005) embedded in the artifacts encourages joining the sections together. The stud system ensures that intricate structures will maintain structural integrity. The blocks are glossy and sturdy, inviting connection in particular ways. The boys use them to construct spaceships, boats, houses, vehicles, and a range of other items. They push them together, pull them apart, think through and experiment with the various design options available to them. On occasion, they also throw the sharp little blocks at each other or wince when they accidentally walk on individual pieces.

Figure 8.2 shows Hazmat Guy, one of the minifigures in the Series 4 collection of LEGO® owned by our two young boys. Minifigures are used to populate the LEGO® worlds constructed in homes across the world. They are also collector's items; base figures for bespoke customization and lead actors in stop motion animations. Minifigures series figures are purchased in generic packaging. It is not until the package is opened that the identity of the particular minifigure is revealed.

This is a sophisticated artifact. Hazmat Guy has a stocky body, seemingly encased in a yellow hazard suit. His little claw hands – shaped that way to enable it to hold various accessories – are black, potentially gloved. The hazard suit has an oxygen pipe and controls carved into the chest plate, indicating that the suit is airtight. Although engineered from hard plastic, Hazmat Guy can be posed. Featuring the six-part construction characteristic of contemporary minifigures, his arms and legs are moveable, his hips and body can tilt, and his head can be turned. In concert with his expressive face, the options for creating a visual narrative are virtually endless. When purchased, Hazmat Guy carries a rubber nozzle gun attached to a rubber hose attachment that hooks into the back of the helmet for spraying away toxic hazards. The little face inside the removable helmet – that looks very much like a deep sea diving helmet – with its clear plastic faceplate appears to be at best stressed, and at worst fearful. For a miniature plastic block figure it is surprisingly emotive/expressive and, slightly humorous. The plastic is glossy and sturdy and the detailing gives the little figure a great deal of character. Hazmat Guy, along with all the LEGO® minifigures, has his own bio information on the LEGO® home site:

> When you've got a bad case of mysterious glowing goo in your city, the hard-working Hazmat Guy is just the fellow to call. Whether the job involves searching the sewers for mutant sludge or cleaning up after giant radioactive chickens from outer space, he's always ready to put on his airtight protective suit, grab his hi-tech equipment, and make the streets safe and tidy once more. Of course, when you get sent into dangerous situations to handle hazardous materials every day, you're bound to get a bit jittery. Although he never backs away from an emergency, the Hazmat Guy is always nervous that this is the one time his gear won't work. After all, with all the crazy substances he's exposed to, it's a wonder he hasn't grown an extra face on the other side of his head! (LEGO® minifigures, n.d.)

The humorous back narrative involves a postapocalyptic world in which 'giant radioactive chickens,' aliens and 'mutant sludge' form everyday hazards. In a world where ecocrises have become commonplace, the choice of narrative and construction of an everyday hero is telling.

His emotive face, capacity to remove/replace accessories and poseable body make Hazmat Guy a regular player in the LEGO® constructions and games created by the two small boys in their English suburban home. Hazmat Guy has fought wars, saved lives, looked out of windows, fallen out of windows, jumped from moving trucks, and interacted with other minifigures. The design features or 'script' (Akrich, 1992; Akrich and Latour, 1992) of this minifigure encourages some practices and not others. Akrich (1992) argues that every artifact contains a message or instructional manual from its maker that outlines the artifacts intended use and meaning (see also Fallan, 2008). The boys for instance have not altered Hazmat Guy's clothing. His outfit is imprinted permanently onto the molded plastic chest piece. He has however, had his accessories removed and reattached, been posed and angled and has been thrown and dropped endlessly, a testament to his durable material qualities.

The design of the minifigures means that the individual body parts are interchangeable. This encourages remixing of the various parts. Heads, legs, arms, torso and hands can be mixed and matched to reassemble bespoke minifigures. In Figure 8.3, Buzz Light Year's wings have been added to Harry Potter's chest and an anonymous grimacing, bespectacled yellow head. This redesigned minifigure carries Mace Windu's lightsabre. Within the larger 'script' carried in the materiality of the various pieces, the boys have redesigned and redeployed parts and narratives.

As artifacts, Hazmat Guy, individual blocks, and 'bespectacled yellow head' are present in the lounge room of this house, contributing to the design and implementation of the play and construction activities of these two boys. The blocks and minifigures come with a narrative that is both local and global, that is taken up and played out in the local space of the family home and yet it sits within a global media franchise.

Figure 8.3   An altered minifigure

The Social Life of LEGO®

LEGO® has both an official and an unofficial biography. Officially, LEGO® is a dynamic, global manufacturer that has changed its production values in the last decade to include users in the development process. It has, for instance, LEGO® 'ambassadors' in 27 countries who provide input into the development of new ranges and act as communication channels to the massive LEGO® fan base. Unofficially, the growth of new technologies has enabled a large and growing participatory fan culture that includes young people and adults to develop and flourish. There are flickr.com sites, LEGO® online auction sites, LEGO® focused blogs, youtube.com videos, discussion threads and offline, LEGO® conventions and exhibitions around the world.

In homes, LEGO® pieces and sets also have unofficial, individual biographies that weave in and out of the larger cultural narratives. As Figures 8.1 and 8.2 show, LEGO® pieces are used to design, redesign, and build in the everyday spaces and lives of young and old. The constructions are displayed with pride, sometimes photographed, and then often disassembled. For some LEGO® users, time is spent researching and planning construction ideas as a key part of the building process. In these homes and other sites, the initial sets of individual blocks have been supplemented with staged set piece constructions that come with a back narrative. While initially critiqued as single purpose constructions the more recent iterations of branded sets have interchangeable and multipurposed parts. The range of *Star Wars* kits, for example, draw from the cultural positioning of the now classic George Lucas *Star Wars* series of movies as well as the parodies, merchandizing, and intertextual references across a range of media (who can forget the ongoing *Star Wars* references that have colored the *The Simpsons* over the years?).

In this suburban English family, each LEGO® block and kit has its own biography. Some were bought as special occasion gifts; some were hand-me-downs from neighbors and friends. Each child has favorite sets and minifigures. Hazmat Guy is one of these minifigures. He arrived in the family home in generic packaging and therefore unknown before unwrapping. He has been used as part of the larger set but also as an individual toy in play across a range of scenarios. His helmet and other accessories have been removed and reattached depending on the play context, and his anxious facial expression has been the source of many imagined dialogues. Hazmat Guy has lain on the floor under the sofa – lost – for days, has been through the washing machine hidden in pockets, spent time playing outside in the garden, and has been a key player in elegant family constructions, duly posing for photographs. He has lost and then been reunited with his hose. He has become a much-loved and used artifact in this family, central to many LEGO® play moments and discussions.

Yet, while a key LEGO® piece in this family's collection, Hazmat Guy has a biography that extends beyond this particular suburban lounge room, connecting with children and adults around the world. There are numerous websites dedicated to analyzing and reviewing each minifigure series and individual piece. On other fan sites, the minifigures are used to stage scenes and videos that are then photographed or filmed and posted online. On one such site, four Hazmat Guy minifigures are assembled, hoses poised, around melted blocks and a half-melted LEGO® figure with a caption that says 'The M.A.N. (Minifigures Against Nuclear) say NO to Nuclear!!!' (Kenny, 2011).

Myth Making with a Global Media Brand

LEGO®, an abbreviation from the two Danish words 'leg godt,' means literally 'play well' first launched in its current molded plastic form in Denmark in 1958. This new shape featured the now iconic hollow tubes in the underside of each block that allowed more flexibility in design and a stronger locking base providing support for more complex constructions. By the early 1960s, the company had introduced wheels (and is now the world's largest manufacturer of tires), effectively expanding exponentially the creative potential of the blocks. By 1963 the company was improving the quality of the plastic used in the production of the blocks, moving from cellulose acetate to the more durable acrylonitrile butadiene styrene that is characteristic of the blocks today. In 1966, LEGO® released its first train sets. These sets included a 4.5-volt motor and rails, which again provided further opportunity for innovation and experimentation.

From its beginnings in Denmark in 1932, the LEGO® Group has grown in influence to the point where it now has a global presence. The name and incumbent meaning have become the LEGO® brand's ideal. The LEGO® brand recognized by the two young boys as they play in their lounge room now encompasses a diverse and ever-increasing range of products that have their origins in the manufacture of the traditional LEGO® brick. According to company information listed on the LEGO®.com website, the LEGO® Group is now the world's fourth largest manufacturer of toys, with LEGO® products being sold in more than 130 countries, stretching from Europe through Asia to Australia. Reflecting this reach, the LEGO® brand defines itself as a modern global enterprise.

As a 'global' enterprise, LEGO® is focused on growth and diversification. Within the LEGO® brand's 'Future Direction' statement, a strategy of diversifying product activity as well as increasing market share is articulated. This diversification includes not only the development of new LEGO® toy products and four theme parks in four countries, but also the expansion of the role of the LEGO® brand and its accompanying practices. These plans for expansion include continued development of the brand in existing markets as well as new development in previously untapped markets, such as China, Brazil, Mexico, and India. The growth of LEGO® Education, LEGO® electronic activities, such as MMOGs and video games, and LEGO® 'direct to consumer' activities such as the LEGO® club magazines and sales channels form part of this plan (LEGO®, n.d.).

Whether officially, as part of the ongoing LEGO® brand marketing policy, or unofficially, via the consumer-generated construction of LEGO® brand spin-offs, the concept of the LEGO®

brand has evolved significantly from the original plastic molded brick to a plethora of products realized in online and material forms. It is possible to buy LEGO® photo frames, money boxes, clocks, book ends, watches, cake moulds, salt and pepper shakers, clothing, chess sets, party packs, advent calendars, and Christmas tree decorations to name but a selection. There are LEGO® theme parks in Denmark, the United Kingdom, Germany, and California, each park receiving around 1.4 million visitors each year. These offline artifacts and destinations are accompanied by video and handheld games, online worlds, online and offline magazines, DVD movies, online movie-making competitions, amateur fan movies posted online, and online auction and sale sites.

The plastic bricks and minifigures, however, remain central to LEGO®'s global media and franchising activities. Children and adults have enjoyed classic sets such as LEGO® and DUPLO bricks and more for the past 50 years. In recent decades, these sets have been very effectively marketed on the premise that the builder develops skills of creativity and strategic thinking, using his/her imagination while being engaged in the act of construction. These classic construction sets are positioned alongside long-running *Play Themes* products such as the LEGO® fire station, and LEGO® knights and castles. The *Play Theme* products are designed to encourage the builder to build and play within a themed story world. While originally these story worlds were generic in design, allowing children to play 'pirates' or 'fire fighters,' more recently, the LEGO® brand has launched additional themed story world sets, where the sets are part of a specific LEGO® story with characters, plot, setting, and back story, extended across the LEGO®.com website, LEGO® club, and junior club magazines.

Supplementing the various themed sets, including Power Miners, LEGO® minifigures such as Hazmat Guy began to appear in 1978, and while initially created to people the various sets, are now also sold separately. The minifigures are designed either as generic characters (such as fireman, policeman, pirate, knight, or astronaut) or specific characters licensed from film franchises (for example, Hans Solo from the *Star Wars* film franchise, Indiana Jones from the *Indiana Jones* series, and Lucius Malfoy from the *Harry Potter* franchise). In their original design, the minifigures were yellow, faceless, undifferentiated figures without arms or legs. However, ongoing design evolution and customer feedback have moved the minifigures to the point where they come with character idiosyncrasies such as peg legs and hook hands, and the skin coloring has been shifted away from yellow towards more natural and racially representative shades. The contemporary minifigure is generally built around six body parts: head, torso, hips, arms, legs and hands. These parts allow the minifigures articulated movement and the ability to swivel and pose. Minifigures also feature a hole in the head to ensure that if one becomes lodged in the throat, a child can continue to breathe. A large range of minifigure accessories has grown up around the increasingly differentiated characterizations. These include hats, guns, shields, lightsabers, hoses, hair, and helmets. In addition to the official accessories it is possible to buy bespoke accessories such as retro space guns to customize minifigures. The figures have become so popular that they are considered collectables by adults and children, were featured in the Pixar-Disney movie *Toy Story 3* (2010), and appear across a variety of media content both professional and amateur.

A purchase of LEGO® does not necessarily end the interaction at the store counter. Alongside the release of new toy lines, online worlds and websites, magazines and merchandising, in 2006 LEGO® launched the 'Builders of Tomorrow' initiative. According to the LEGO® CEO, this was specifically aimed at 'reminding' parents 'to actually take out an hour every week to spend creative time with their children. We believe that's a time that is not being spent enough in today's society' (LEGO® Corporation, 2006). This is a very strong signal about the type of family and child–parent relationship considered beneficial to children and foregrounds the company's discourse of creativity and learning. Since then, the company has also produced an education manifesto, *A System for Learning*, and an aligned publication that looks specifically at the possibilities and challenges of digital and online environments for systematized creativity learning (Ackermann *et al.*, 2009). Together, these documents build a powerful statement about the possibilities of developing a 'systemic creativity.' This LEGO® learning and education documentation pivots around a model of child as creative potential. In the LEGO® model, children have endless potential to learn creativity, to plan, collaborate and solve problems. In order to fulfill this creative potential, children need to be nurtured along their individual and developmental pathways. LEGO®'s learning and developmental manifesto makes an explicit connection to play, learning, creativity, and imagination across each and every media platform (Ackermann *et al.*, 2009).

This model of systemic creativity is particularly well suited to the knowledge economies in which we now operate. It supports the notion of lifelong learning, flexibility and adaptability, and the importance of open-ended explorations. Notions of community, sharing, and engagement are also promoted strongly. LEGO®'s shift from a philosophy of 'assembly' to 'creativity' (Lauwaert, 2008) coincided with moves by governments, corporations, and educational authorities to extol the virtues of the 'creativity agenda.' Florida (2005, p. 3) argued that:

> Globally, a third of the workers in advanced industrial nations are employed in the creative sector, engaged in science and engineering, research and development, and the technology-based industries, in arts, music, culture, and aesthetic and design work, or in the knowledge-based professions of health care, finance, and law.

The creative class narrative (Florida 2002, 2005) and the 'creativity agenda' began to influence government planning and development and the ways in which individuals and groups working in particular fields articulated their identities and ambitions. In 1998, for instance, Tony Blair established the Creative Industries Task Force (CITF) to harness the power of this new cultural economy and by 2008 the UK had established the £70 million Creative Britain Strategy designed to 'move the creative industries from the margins in the mainstream of the UK economy' (Creative Britain, 2008). The strong belief that creativity is crucial to a modern economy and that it can be systematically learned has grown over the past 20 years. This has become a powerful political and cultural narrative within which LEGO®'s education and learning manifesto can be positioned. The artifacts and multiple media associated with LEGO® have become linked to the same notions of creativity and active learning. According to LEGO® (Ackermann *et al.*, 2009, p. 28) creativity 'is the ability to generate ideas and artifacts that are new, surprising and valuable.' Three types of creativity are identified: combining artifacts or ideas in surprising or innovative ways; exploring new ways of making something that leads to new, valuable understanding; and using these new ideas or constructions to transform the ways in which we view the world.

Conclusion: LEGO® and the Mythology of Creativity, Learning, and Literacy

Undertaking an object ethnography is possibly an unusual entry point to a discussion of global media and children's everyday literacies. However, taking this approach has required us to consider the intersections between everyday artifacts and global media discourses, and simultaneously to acknowledge the centrality of these same artifacts in the construction of the very worlds in which children are developing beliefs and practices. These are the everyday worlds in which dispositions to text and literacy practices are developed. With this in mind, we believe that the object ethnography foregrounds a number of important points.

The object ethnography reminds us that the material matters. In fact, it matters a lot. Children live and learn in spaces made possible and populated by artifacts. New work in the fields of anthropology and material culture (Miller, 2009) and postphenomenology (Verbeek, 2005, 2006; Ihde, 2009) clearly articulates the crucial role of artifacts in the construction of lives and identities. In this view, artifacts work to co-construct our perception and experience of the worlds around us. For young children, those worlds are constructed out of the artifacts of the home. As we have described here, the artifacts we share our space with are not neutral. They come with intentionality (Verbeek, 2005), they are taken up differentially by children and often repurposed, and as the case of LEGO® shows, often they are linked to the particular ideologies of global media franchises. The artifacts co-construct the lived worlds and experiences of these boys and link directly back to a global media enterprise with quite specific views about learning, childhood, family, and creativity.

Early literacy practices and skills are built around material cultures (Pahl and Rowsell, 2010) that include global media artifacts. As a result, children are engaging, from a very early age, in a globalized literacy and media world. In terms of young children's literacies in a media saturated world, we are attempting to tease out how deeply embedded identity, practice, and even the construction of everyday life is bound up with mass media texts and artifacts, and their underpinning ideological stances. The two children described in this paper could be any two children with access to LEGO® blocks and some engagement with the global merchandizing and media activities of the brand. Their interactions with the blocks as artifacts impacts on how they believe the world works and in effect, constructs that world around them. The types of texts that are disseminated via the brand, from the character narratives displayed on packaging to the magazines to the activity instructions, across all of the various media platforms influence what kinds of literate identities these young boys construct for themselves.

At a different level, the object ethnography suggests that for contemporary children living in relatively affluent parts of the world, everyday practices are increasingly carried out both on and offline. While this is not a breathtakingly new observation, the example of LEGO® illustrates how seamless this movement between domains is, foregrounding the ways in which global media franchises conceptualize and operationalize this movement. Young children are being mentored and scaffolded into what we might describe as an integrated social, cultural, and textual space that draws equally from both online and offline. An examination of LEGO® also sharpens our understanding of how embedded this hybridity or integration has become in the media landscapes and popular cultural forms of childhood. The texts and textual practices made accessible via LEGO® are extensive and are spread across a range of media that include printed artifacts, online sites, and other digital mass media. LEGO® demonstrates the now mainstream expectation that children will proficiently traverse these varied domains and modes, developing the capacity to mix and match domains and modes according to their own needs and purposes.

The object ethnography also allows us to situate artifacts and engagements with them in broader cultural, economic, and political narratives. Myths operate to naturalize the cultural and the political, making particular beliefs and practices seen entirely normal, natural, and self-evident (Allen 2003). In *Mythologies*, Barthes (1972, p. 59) describes the connection of French identity with the drinking of wine, describing how an object such as wine can be turned into the sign of a universal value or identity. For Barthes, rather than stories of long-dead heroes and gods, myths are the dominant ideologies and narratives of our time. As we argued above, the power of creativity has become one of the key myths of contemporary economic and educational landscapes. The different layers of the object ethnography have, together, mapped the ways in which global media franchises are connected to the dominant myths. This is seen in the depictions of childhood and family life embedded in LEGO®'s media discourses as much as in relation to creativity. LEGO®, as a media and artifact powerfully promotes a particular idealized childhood as well as a cultural narrative around creativity and developmental play. These beliefs are embedded in the artifacts themselves but they are also in evidence across each of the media platforms in which LEGO® operates. This examination of LEGO® in the everyday lives of these children shows clearly that while discourses of childhood are linked to modern cultural myths around creativity, they also reflect acknowledgement of a sense of hybridity around the cultural and social spaces in which children develop a range of early literacy and learning dispositions and skills.

We believe that the three levels of the object ethnography, separately and together, have something to offer in relation to the early literacy practices of contemporary children immersed in global media cultures. In brief, artifacts matter beyond their role as cherished toys. On one level, they embody the values and worldviews of their designers; on the other they are taken up and redesigned in-use by the children who use them. The New Material Studies and emerging work in postphenomenology tells us that these engagements are the material from which everyday realities, perceptions, values, and practices are made. These are the life worlds in which dispositions towards text and repertoires of literate practices are constructed. These artifacts also serve as entry points to other engagements.

What we have described in this chapter is one part of the lifeworlds of the two young boys described earlier. The LEGO® described here links these children to the texts created and disseminated by a global media corporation as they read, recreate, and reshape the narratives that accompany the various sets and characters; as they move into online games and communities to share their interest in all things LEGO®; and as they engage in print based books, magazines, and activities that revolve around the world of LEGO®. This object ethnography has allowed us to begin to map some of the complex intersections between global media franchises and the lived worlds of these young children. Their early literacy practices and dispositions are formed and take place in these worlds and more than that they are the stuff of which these worlds are made.

References

Ackermann, E, Gauntlett, D., Wolbers, T., and Weckström, C. (2009) Defining systematic creativity in the digital realm. LEGO® Learning Institute 2009, accessed November 12, 2012: http://parents.lego.com/en-gb/childdevelopment/systematic%20creativity%20in%20the%20digital%20realm.aspx

Akrich, M. (1992) The de-scription of technological objects. In W. Bijker and J. Law (eds) *Shaping Technology/Building Society: Studies in Socio-technical Change*. Cambridge, MA: MIT Press, pp. 205–225.

Akrich, M., and Latour, B. (1992) A summary of a convenient vocabulary for the semiotics of human and nonhuman assemblies. In W. Bijker and J. Law (eds) *Shaping Technology /Building Society: Studies in Sociotechnical Change*. Cambridge, MA: MIT Press, pp. 259–262.

Allen, G. (2003) *Roland Barthes*. New York: Routledge.

Barthes, R. (1972) *Mythologies*. New York: Hill and Wang.

Carrington, V. (2008) From blog to Bebo and beyond: Text, risk, participation. *Journal of Research in Reading*, 32(1): 6–21.

Columbia University (2006) Thing theory, accessed November 12, 2012: www.columbia.edu/~sf2220/Thing/web-content/Pages/Syllabus.html

Creative Britain (2008) Accessed January 6, 2010: www.culture.gov.uk/what_we_do/creative_industries/6089.aspx

Fallan, K. (2008) De-scribing design: Appropriating script analysis to design history. *Design Issues*, 24(4): 61–75.

Florida, R. (2002) *The Rise of the Creative Class: And How It's Transforming Work, Leisure, Community and Everyday.* New York: Basic Books.

Florida, R. (2005) *The Rise of the Creative Class.* New York: Routledge.

Ihde, D. (2009) *Postphenenonology and Technoscience: The Peking University Lectures.* New York: SUNY Press.

Jenkins, H. (2006) *Convergence Culture: Where Old and New Media Collide.* New York: New York University Press.

Kenny, S. (2011) MOCpages: Share your LEGO® creations, accessed November 12, 2012: www.mocpages.com/moc.php/261998

Latour, B. (2007) *Reassembling the Social: An Introduction to Actor-Network-Theory.* Oxford: Oxford University Press.

Lauwaert, M. (2008) Playing outside the box– on LEGO® toys and the changing world of construction play. *History and Technology*, 24(3): 221–237.

LEGO® (n.d.) About us, accessed 3 December, 2012 http://aboutus.lego.com

LEGO® Corporation (2006) *Builders of Tomorrow*: LEGO Builders of Tomorrow Creativity Panel Discussion Transcript, April 6, 2006. Accessed 1 Novermber 12, 2012: www.legobuildersoftomorrow.com/news_panel.html

LEGO® minifigures (n.d.) Hazmat Guy accessed November 12, 2012: http://minifigures.lego.com/en-us/Bios/Default.aspx#Hazmat Guy

Marsh, J. (2006) Global local/public, private: Young children's engagement in digital literacy practices in the home. In K. Pahl and J. Rowsell (eds) *Travel Notes from the New Literacy Studies*, London: Multilingual Matters, pp. 19–38.

Meet the Boss (n.d.) http://www.meettheboss.tv/Broadcast/CEO/96/The-Man-Who-Rescued-Lego, accessed 3 December, 2012.

Miller, D. (1987) *Material Culture and Mass Consumption.* Oxford: Blackwell.

Miller, D. (2008) *The Comfort of Things.* Cambridge, UK: Polity Press.

Miller, D. (2009) *Stuff.* London: Polity Press.

Pahl, K., and Rowsell, J. (2010) *Artifactual Literacies: Every Object Tells a Story.* New York: Teachers College Press.

Verbeek, P. (2005) *What Things Do: Philosophical Reflections on Technology, Agency, and Design*, trans. R. Crease. University Park: Pennsylvania State University Press.

Verbeek, P. (2006) Materializing morality: Design ethics and technological mediation. *Science, Technology and Human Values*, 31(3): 361–380.

Chapter 9

Literacy as Shared Consciousness

A Neurocultural Analysis

Alicia Curtin and Kathy Hall

Introduction

This chapter critically links socio-cultural and neuroscientific perspectives on literacy and learning in a way that confirms the significance of culture, experience, and opportunity to participate in the practices of literacy. It highlights the varied ways in which these practices are pertinent in different social contexts. This integration of socio-cultural and neuroscientific research also points to the importance of individual agency and how the uniqueness of each brain, as a result of biology, experience, and culture, implies and confirms the intentional, meaning-making, and negotiating potential of humans. Our neurocultural analysis of learning and language suggests that mind and body are inextricably linked through neural, cultural, and social networks that become apparent in a study of brain development, everyday experiences, and social interaction.

An understanding of brain plasticity, the ability of the brain to change as a result of experience and social interaction, unites socio-cultural and neuroscientific perspectives and is the basic premise of this chapter. Although we do not come from a neuroscientific background we have studied neuroscientific literature pertaining to learning and development. We conclude that the insights gleaned from neuroscientific research, when synthesized with socio-cultural understandings of learning and literacy, show strong parallels regarding implications for pedagogy. These parallels point education and literacy research forward in new, diverse, and exciting directions. We illustrate this claim, prioritizing depth rather than breadth by looking closely at one very small circuit in the vast neurocultural network of learning – the emerging relationship between social interaction and mirror neurons. We begin with an analysis of relevant neuroscientific and socio-cultural research in the area of social interaction, moving towards the recent discovery of the importance of mirror neurons in this process. Since language and literacy are basic tools of social interaction, attention to social interaction, in the broadest sense, from the twin perspectives of socio-culture and neuroscience, is highly pertinent in the context of possible new directions for future research on learning and literacy.

International Handbook of Research on Children's Literacy, Learning, and Culture, First Edition.
Edited by Kathy Hall, Teresa Cremin, Barbara Comber, and Luis C. Moll.
© 2013 John Wiley & Sons, Ltd. Published 2013 by John Wiley & Sons, Ltd.

Consciousness as the Appearance of a World

Consciousness has been described in neurological terms as the appearance of a world (Metzinger, 2010a. p. 15). We suggest that, from a neurocultural perspective, literacy itself becomes the appearance of a world. This world is culturally, socially, and biologically dependent, where the social ability to recognize signs and symbols that are shared and recognized by others in the culture and the biological capacity to respond to these add up to a functioning and literate individual. However, this literacy means something far more than the ability to read and write.

Neuroscientific studies often use the metaphor of the sleepwalker to illustrate the existence and importance of consciousness. A sleepwalker, in many ways an unconscious human being, is not aware of the world around them. They walk straight ahead and do not interact in any literate way with the objects they encounter. Comparing this experience to the experience of a conscious and awake individual reveals exactly what a difference consciousness makes. It is

> a certain fluidity, a flexibility, a context sensitivity . . . We have the feeling of being present in the real world . . . You could describe it as a specific illusion, but it is a major neurocomputational achievement of the human brain – the sense of presence as a self in a conscious scene. (Metzinger, 2010b, pp. 12–14)

What much neuroscientific research fails to acknowledge however, is that this task, the task of consciousness, is *biologically and culturally* based. This context sensitivity, this major neuro-computational achievement, is based on social interaction and occurs through the recognition of social symbols. In essence, it presents literacy as a social construct and a social process. If consciousness can be described as the appearance of a world, then literacy, and the ability to interact with this world, can be described as the appearance of a self within this shared world. In this sense literacy is not just an extension of the self, it is part and parcel of the self; it constitutes the self.

Some neuroscientific research such as the work undertaken by Professor V.S. Ramachandran (Oberman, Pineda, and Ramachandran, 2007) dubbed the modern Paul Broca by Eric Kandel, has begun to explore the relationships between mirror neurons and human culture. His work aims to understand the neurological basis of human self-awareness. At its most basic neuro-logical level acquiring literacy skills impacts the functional organization of the brain (Petersson *et al.*, 2001). Immordino-Yang and Fischer (2009, p. 2) define learning as:

> the construction of distributed neural networks to support skills such as for reading, math, or managing social relationships. General brain processes including emotion, attention, and social processing modulate and facilitate the development and recruitment of these neural networks.

Their article, 'Neuroscience Bases of Learning' reveals that current research in neuroscience reinforces the idea that children's experience and social interaction shape their biology and their biology shapes their experiences:

> All human behavior and learning, including feeling, thinking, creating, remembering and deciding, originate in the brain. Rather than a hardwired biological system, the brain develops through an active, dynamic process in which a child's social, emotional and cognitive experiences organize his or her brain over time, in accordance with biological constraints and principles (National Research Council, 1999; Immordino-Yang, and Damasio, 2007). In the other direction, a child's particular neuropsychological strengths and weaknesses shape the way he or she perceives and interacts with the world. Like the weaving of an intricate and delicate web (Fischer and Bidell, 2006),

physiological and cultural processes interact to produce learning and behavior in highly nuanced and complex patterns of human development. (Immordino-Yang and Fischer, 2009. p. 2)

The idea that experience shapes brain networks (as well as the latter shaping the former) is an important point. It confirms socio-cultural research on learning and literacy (Bussis *et al.*, 1985; McDermott, 1993) that endorses the significance of environment, of experience, of the opportunity to learn, of the chance to 'catch up', of the time to practice, and of access to the valued language and literacy practices in communities. Though coming from a different epistemological stable, neuroscience also confirms socio-cultural perspectives on learning that challenge deficit models of learning and development. Worth remembering is that according to the theorizing of Lev Vygotsky, the original and classical socio-culturalist, individual mental processes have their origin in social interaction. Vygotsky's general genetic law of cultural development lies behind the advocacy of social interaction, the mediation of language, and the role of the more accomplished other in supporting learning. His words are reproduced here because of their fit with the second part of the above quotation on the significance of experience:

> Any function in the child's cultural development appears twice, or on two planes. First it appears on the social plane, and then on the psychological plane. First it appears between people as an interpsychological category, and then within the child as an intrapsychological category (Vygotsky, 1981, p. 163).

For Vygotsky, higher-order mental functions such as thinking and memory are processes that exist between people, they are *inter*mental. In other words the cultural, social, and relational aspect is inescapable. Decety and Lamm's (2006) 'Human Empathy Through the Lens of Neuroscience' reviews neuroscientific studies in this area and reveals that neuroscientific research aligns with the socio-cultural, where learning occurs in social interaction and the meanings of everything we do are always social. Here neuroscientific and socio-cultural understandings of learning come together to elucidate how and what is learned through experiences and social interactions influencing brain development. Becoming literate socially as well as neurologically suddenly brings a world that we are a part of and have helped create. Being present in this world means being literate in its structures, signs, and symbols – this is a social as much as it is a biological process.

The Genetics of Culture – Agents, Activities, and Worlds

Reading and writing are cognitive abilities that depend on human cultural evolution (Vygotsky, 1962). If becoming literate is the appearance of a present self in a shared world, then this world must first be communally constituted, reconstituted, and shared through histories of social interactions. Neuroscientific research reveals massive interconnections between different areas of the brain suggesting that learning can never be separate from emotions, meanings, and experience (Fuster, 2003). Akin to a kind of shared consciousness, in this understanding literacy becomes not only the ability to be a part of present experience but is also dependent on past agents, activities, and worlds. As we go about our day-to-day experiences we engage in conversations and social interactions in our negotiation of identity and purpose. Socio-cultural research argues that it is through these meaningful social experiences, and not committing information to memory in isolation, that we learn (Rogoff, 1991; Wenger 1998). Learning, doing, being, and our very existence itself as individuals, are entirely social phenomena as the meanings of our actions are always social.

From the smoke signals of American Indians to our instant SMS, humans have always expressed a keen need and desire to share, to communicate, to learn and, what we are sharing, communicating, and learning is only meaningful and important when it is considered in a social context. Taking, for example, the ancient smoke signals of the American Indians, one of the oldest recorded methods of social interaction in history, these mighty feats are meaningless if not experienced, read, and understood in their social context, as well as having more than one person involved to bring meaning to the process. Recent neuroscientific research is beginning to tell a similar story. Kenji Hakuta's (2008) neuroscientific study of bilingualism holds many important implications for our understandings of literacy and learning. Hakuta's research into language acquisition by bilingual individuals reveals that while language acquisition has a biological basis in terms of age and other biological factors, it is not something we do in our heads – it is a shared process rather than an achievable product. As Hakuta explains, bilingualism is an individual condition nested within a distribution of broader societal circumstances that cause language contact (Hakuta, 2008. p. 1). While neuroscientific aspects such as the age of the learner influence language acquisition, so too societal characteristics such as the social status of the language, the compartmentalization or representation of different aspects of different languages, the literacy history of the individual, participation in a bilingual speech community, and historical circumstance have a large role to play in how well an individual learns a language. It is of note that the majority of present and future generations of children will be exposed to two or more languages and will attempt to attain literacy in more than one language. This makes our understanding of literacy today all the more critical.

In his comparison of Canadian English speaking and immigrant communities Hakuta (2008) reveals that bilingualism is usually attained by the English speakers trying to learn French to gain access to the privileges of bilingualism. For the immigrant communities however, who go to school and learn and live using the English language there is no societal value associated with their native language and as a result, for most of these bilinguals their native language will have a limited range of use. It is also unlikely to survive in future generations. The differing social status of each language influences the strength and stability of an individual's bilingualism. The work of Marshall *et al.* (2008) with Romanian orphans also dramatically reveals that cognitive, social, and physical growth was delayed in institutionalized children, relative to their peers raised in foster or biological families. Marshall *et al.* (2008) state that although the institutionalized children's basic physical needs were met, the lack of high-quality social interaction and cognitive stimulation was instrumental in the children's failure to thrive. This research has many implications for how we should position our studies of literacy within social, emotional, and cultural spheres.

Mapping the social brain

Recent neuroscientific research using fMRI (functional magnetic resonance imaging) techniques has begun to map the circuitry of the *social brain*, identifying specialized neural pathways and mechanisms that have evolved to process social information. Such specialized mechanisms include the perception of social signs and symbols in the vomeronasal system, the formation of social memory through social recognition (in terms of gender, kin, status, and individual), filial imprinting (by defining species and parental phenotypes), sexual imprinting (defining future potential sexual partners), and the broader identification of the neural consequences of social experience. Interestingly, unlike other social mechanisms in the brain, filial and sexual imprinting does not change easily through experience and social interaction. Again, current neuroscientific research confirms and extends the main concepts of socio-cultural theory. Now it is scientific fact that not only does the brain influence behavior, but behavior, experience, and social interaction influence brain development and learning on evolutionary, life time, and real time levels. From birth, humans seek social interaction as an integral part of their day-to-day lives. Thus knowledge of others, as well as knowledge of self, becomes central to our everyday experiences in our navigation of the social world in which we live.

Socio-cultural theory explains that this knowledge cannot be acquired and stored in the brain, rather it is socially constructed between people in their everyday interactions and experiences. Patricia Kuhl's (Kuhl, Tsao, and Liu, 2003) neuroscientific study exemplifies this socio-cultural concept as does a study conducted in southern Portugal on 'illiterates' and 'literates' by Petersson, Ingvar, and Reis (2009). Kuhl's presentation of Mandarin Chinese to a group of nine-month-old babies either through a television set or through interaction with real life Mandarin speakers revealed that the babies who experienced Mandarin through the television set showed no more ability to discriminate Mandarin speech sounds than the control group. The group of babies introduced to the language through social interaction displayed, after twelve sessions, an enhanced ability to discriminate certain Mandarin speech sounds. A more recent study (Christakis *et al.*, 2009) reveals that the effect of conversations and social interaction on language competence is almost six times greater for children than just listening to adults talk. What such research from neuroscience affirms is the socio-cultural evidence that meaning, participation, negotiation, and intersubjectivity are all fundamental to a full understanding of the learning process.

A bird on the wire and broken mirrors

Studies such as those by Martin and Weisberg (2003) who showed participants basic geometric shapes interacting in a number of different ways (social, mechanical, or random) have tentatively identified the specific 'social circuit' of the brain to comprise of the lateral segment of the fusiform gyrus, the superior temporal sulcus, the amygdala, and the ventromedial prefrontal cortex. This study understands these mechanisms for social learning to be built on the previously researched, generic neural systems for learning. Gopnik, Meltzoff, and Kuhl (1999) have likened the neural functioning of these systems to ever expanding telephone wires that communicate with each other. From infancy these telephone wires crisscross as experiences and social interaction send messages that must find their way to the corresponding area of the brain. Neural pathways are created through this process just as telephone poles and wires are strategically placed to provide contact to each house from the network.

These advances in neuroscientific research now allow researchers to investigate in much greater detail how brain functioning and physical development correspond to experience and social interaction. The main function of the brain is to employ sensory representations to achieve desired future actions. However, the synthesis of neuroscientific and socio-cultural research as outlined in this chapter reveals that this process is not a straightforward one and occurs in a number of different ways. It appears that there are many different ways to effectively develop literacy or other skills such as reading (Fischer, Bernstein, and Immordino-Yang, 2007) or math (Singer, 2007).

Research into disorders such as autism, suggesting that individuals with autism may be unable to successfully imitate the actions of others, have allowed some theorists to hypothesize that social learning requires the use of a brain mechanism that allows individuals to automatically detect and attribute the mental states of self and others. Daniel Goleman (2006) writes about the brain to brain hook-ups we experience as we go about our day-to-day lives and social interactions, automatically identifying and reacting to the expressions of others as a sort of neural Wi-Fi. Moving from interaction to interaction, we automatically initiate certain social conventions and neural link ups depending on the social situation.

Neurons that fire together wire together[1]

Recent neuroscientific research has revealed that these processes of social interaction or 'spontaneous synchrony' as we have outlined thus far occurs neurologically through the activation of mirror neurons in the brain that allow individuals to recognize and engage in meaningful social interaction and interpret the emotions and intentions of others. Studies such as that of Rizzolatti and Craighero (2004) show that children continuously and unconsciously learn from what is modeled by others in their experiences – from what is available to be learned. The same cortical circuits involved in executing an action are also stimulated when individuals see others complete an action.

In their groundbreaking book *Mirrors in the Brain*, Rizzolatti and Sinigaglia (2008) state that mirror neurons are essential to the sharing of experience that is at the root of our capacity to act both as individuals and as members of society. Rizzolatti moves this idea forward by stating that as previously discussed mirror neurons are also responsible for our ability to understand the emotions of others. In this way, mirror neurons become essential to understanding the bonds we share with other people and ultimately, what it is that makes us human. What is also important here is that the research suggests that at this cortical level the system is not concerned with single movements, but with actions. Actions, rather than simple movements, have meaning for the watcher and it is the meaning behind these actions that causes the activation of these cortical circuits. Thus, aligning with socio-cultural research and Patricia Kuhl and colleagues' study (2003), this research reveals that in order to be conscious and literate in our shared world, one thing is very important – meaning. According to socio-cultural theory as social beings the meanings of what we do must also always be social. As if waking from a very beautiful dream the mirror system in the brain mirrors both consciousness and literacy and controls an individual's ability to relate to others and take part in social interaction. It is also interesting to note that the mirror neuron system is also triggered when individuals listen to sentences that describe another human being completing an action (Tettamanti *et al.*, 2005).

At the physiological level the brain learns by looking for consistencies in what we experience, learning to attend to and map those patterns and events that repeat themselves frequently. The brain's job is to code neutrally based on its experiences, what's going to matter and what's not going to matter, and also to predict what is going to happen next (Miller and Tallal, 2006, p. 2). Mirror neurons become extremely important when it comes to the social act of trying to understand the meaning of our own and another's actions. However, it is important to note that a significant amount of mirror neuron research has been undertaken with primates and animals other than humans. Despite this, understanding the activity of mirror neurons offers a neuroscientific explanation for the pain or sympathy felt for a friend who suddenly stubs their toe on the ground, or the feelings of adrenalin, excitement and shouting when watching a football match. Similarly, a punch on the arm can be interpreted as friendly or intimidating depending on the perceived intentions of the puncher.

The emergence of mirror neurons and their relationship to social interaction and learning opens up the possibility of the investigation of the neurological underpinnings of social interaction and provide an important mechanism through which social and cultural literacy practices can be better understood. Previous to this development, social interaction was understood as an engagement in logical thought that individuals undertook to understand and predict the behavior of others. Understanding the neural process of social interaction, however, in terms of the firing of mirror neurons in the brain, allows us to understand social interaction and other people not only by thinking, but also by feeling as anticipated by a socio-cultural perspective. Moreover, the socio-cultural notion of intersubjectivity (Bruner, 1996; Rogoff, 1990) involving shared thinking is further confirmed by the line of inquiry prompted by the study of mirror neurons. The goal of intersubjectivity is to develop a common frame of mind. It seems this is immensely enabled through the working of mirror neurons. The activation of mirror neurons in the brain allows us to simulate and experience not only the actions of others, but the feelings and emotions behind those actions. In this way mirror neurons also mediate our understanding of our emotions again through imitation and translation of observed expressions and experiences. When you meet an old friend in the street, for example, and they smile at you, your mirror neurons for smiling fire up too and you return the action according to social convention, accompanied by the feeling associated with smiling in your brain. There is no need to ponder what is intended by your friend, the meaning of the interaction is experienced socially and neurologically. In our early experiences we learn that a smile is, more often than not, met with another as our parents and caregivers become ecstatically happy when we curl our lips upward. Encouragement, care, and happiness are all presented as linked to a smiling face and we quickly adopt these social meanings to this neural action. Thus, seeing a frown on the face of a friend or teacher causes a certain worry and a sense of foreboding that all is not well.

Literacy as the appearance of a self

This understanding of early learning as occurring through the recognition of social signals and facial expressions begs the question of how we, as individuals, develop very early in our lives such an important and social skill. An understanding of this process also develops our awareness of learning as neurocultural. A large part of our learning in early life occurs through the perception and imitation of the social behavior of others. This is most evident in infants as their experience is limited and much research has been completed on early learning. Imitation allows infants and also individuals through social interaction to internalize both the actions of others and larger cultural values of the sociological group. Infants begin by imitating the facial expressions of those around them, and later move to imitate their carer's actions and speech as they experience them.

This ability to read facial expressions learnt and developed in our early social interactions shapes the neurology of our brains in specific and identifiable ways, and is essential to how we learn and experience the world in later life. Our first experiences of learning are, as all our others, entirely social processes occurring through social recognition, negotiation, interaction, and imitation. Throughout our lives our brain reads facial expressions at an extremely fast speed. It is through this social and neural process and processes similar to these that our brain develops neurologically and our experience is changed in future social interactions.

Our early experiences shape our future literacy development in many ways. The current neuroscientific research reviewed in this chapter reveals that reading and wider literacies are not innate skills, but must be performed and shared to become a part of our everyday experience. In 2003 Elise Temple and colleagues at Cornell University published the first fMRI study claiming that brain differences in dyslexic children aged between eight and twelve can be addressed by neuroplasticity-based teaching and that this adjustment is accompanied by significant increases in reading scores on standardized testing. Similarly in 2007 Byrne *et al.*'s longitudinal twin study of early literacy development in Australia and the United States revealed that because of a more intensive kindergarten curriculum in Australia more genes are *online* earlier because of overall accelerated learning development. These studies highlight the importance of social interaction and intervention in literacy and learning and are supported by other neuroscientific studies (Begley, 2007; Doige, 2007) that show that many areas of the cortex are literally shaped by experience and particularly shaped by literacy experiences (Dehaene *et al.*, 2010).

In their neuroscientific study of language and literacy, Petersson, Ingvar, and Reis (2009) suggest that literacy influences important aspects of cognition – most particularly, the processing of phonological structure, verbal working memory, and object-recognition/naming. Literacy, they suggest, also influences corresponding structural and functional properties of the brain. Their analysis leads them to hypothesize that certain structural and functional properties of the brain are changed by literacy and schooling.

Research by Goswami (2004) showing that the phonological system in a dyslexic child is immature rather than deviant, would suggest a distinctly different approach to meeting their needs in learning environments – one that would challenge assumptions based entirely on deficit. Time and opportunity to learn and to participate in an enriched, interactional environment now become important. A review by McChandliss and Noble (2003) of the neuroscientific evidence pertaining to developmental dyslexia consistently points to two cortical areas that exhibit dysfunction. They conclude that there is a reduced tendency in dyslexic individuals to draw on left perisylvian regions when faced with a phonologically challenging task. This common finding in the research literature has been proposed as a hallmark neurophysiological phenotype of developmental dyslexia. However, their review also shows how pedagogic studies have provided strong support for the claim that children with mild to severe reading impairments can benefit significantly from intervention techniques that involve explicit training and support in phonological awareness and alphabetic decoding skills. With this kind of remediation, activity in the left temporal and parietal areas appears to align with that of nondyslexic learners (see also Temple *et al.*, 2003).

Once again, the brain is malleable or plastic and thus capable of adapting neurologically to an appropriate pedagogic environment and meaningful experience of literacy learning. Noninvasive neuroimaging methods can examine the impact of such intervention techniques on functional neural activity, through measures collected over the course of the intervention and can show how the intervention achieves its effects neurologically, for example, whether by correcting deficits or by recruiting and developing compensatory mechanisms or by some combination of these two. While the knowledge base is as yet in its infancy the advancing techniques of neuroscience have the potential to shed light on the many controversies and complexities in the study of dyslexia and how to support learners with this label (see Eden and Moats, 2002; Katzir and Paré-Blagoev, 2006).

In our everyday learning experiences, and in the research, socio-cultural understandings and neurobiology form a chain of development that ties together brain development, everyday experience, social interaction, and learning. During this process it is again the activation of our mirror neurons that serve to decompose observed biological actions in the brain into motor acts that themselves activate the corresponding motor representations in the brain itself, specifically in the parietal and ventral pre-motor cortices and the inferior frontal gyrus. These representations are then activated in the brain and recombined by the pre-frontal cortex according to neuroscientists such as Buccino *et al.* (2004), revealing learning to be dependent on brain plasticity *and* social interaction as the brain reorganizes what we have experienced in our social interactions, changing its own physical shape and the shape of our future experiences and social interactions. This is how we learn.

However, it is important to remember that the facial expressions observed in infancy, which apprentice us in this process, are themselves also always a result of emotions such as fear, jealousy, anger, lust, embarrassment, and are therefore always caused by social interaction and a social awareness of the consequences of an individual's actions. Thus, an investigation of neurology and brain development returns us again and again to the experiences and social interactions which, through brain plasticity, form the shape and design of our brains – the organ of the mind, and necessitate a neurocultural perspective on learning. Susan Greenfield

(2000) explains how brain cells involved in activities that occur most frequently have the most extensive connections in the brain, while those with fewer connections atrophy and their targets are taken over by others. This is what is at the core of neuronal plasticity:

> Certain configurations of neuronal connections, then, imperceptibly personalize the brain, and it is this personalized aspect of the physical brain that actually is the mind. The individual mind continues to respond to and react by shifting neuronal allegiances as we live out our lives. (Greenfield, 2000, p. 64)

During this process of learning through neural activity stimulated by social interaction it becomes essential to develop agency in experience, defined according to socio-cultural theory as the strategic making and remaking of the selves within structures of power (Lewis, Enciso, and Moje, 2007. p. 4). This is a way of positioning oneself within a group so as to allow for new identity development. In neuroscientific terms, this process occurs through a mechanism in the brain outside the mirror system, the right inferior parietal cortex, through the active process of intermodal perception and exploration (Neisser, 1991). Developing agency is essential if we are to distinguish between participation and observation and is again dependent on neurological and social factors. To perceive ourselves as agentic we are dependent on our brain neurology, however, this perception at a neural level is aided by our social interactions and experience, where our in life experiences influence our brain neurology at a real-time level.

Caine *et al.* (2005) based on extensive research, meta analyses and syntheses of this research, formulated twelve brain/mind learning principles that encapsulate the emerging findings of much of the current research on learning and the learning of literacy in particular. They are summarized below and are very useful in recapping much of our discussion.

1 All learning engages the physiology.
2 The brain/mind is social.
3 The search for meaning is innate.
4 The search for meaning occurs through patterning.
5 Emotions are critical to patterning.
6 The brain/mind processes parts and wholes simultaneously.
7 Learning involves both focused attention and peripheral perception.
8 Learning is both conscious and unconscious.
9 There are at least two approaches to memory.
10 Learning is developmental.
11 Complex learning is enhanced by challenge and inhibited by threat associated with helplessness and/or fatigue.
12 Each brain is uniquely organized.

Behind the Smoke and Mirrors

If we understand agency, imitation, recognition, literacy, and ultimately learning as the firing of certain neurons in the brain and the building of neural pathways, then the smoke that emerges from this fire emerges in experience and social interaction and tints these experiences and interactions with their own particular colors, smells, and tastes. The smoke and mirrors at the heart of the trick that is literacy and learning are unveiled for all to see and the true mechanisms of learning are brought into full view. Looking at the role of social interaction and experience in learning returns us again and again to the necessity of a socio-cultural and a neurological understanding of brain plasticity.

If, according to socio-cultural understandings experience and social interaction are essential to learning and these experiences and social interactions fundamentally change the form and structure of the brain, then from a neurological perspective the most important prerequisite for learning and literacy development is this idea of brain plasticity. Having discussed thus far the role social interaction, mirror neurons, and experience play in learning from both a socio-cultural and a neuroscientific perspective, our next task is to explore the other side of the coin. Having looked at how these experiences affect and activate certain areas of the brain, the next question must be what exactly changes in the brain as a result of these interactions and experiences to learn.

Brain plasticity is essential for learning. From a neurological perspective it is through the reorganization of the neural pathways of the brain that occurs when we experience something new that we learn. From a socio-cultural perspective if neural networks are changed through experience and social interaction then there must be some changes in the corresponding behaviors and social interaction. These changes in the brain and social interaction occur at both functional and physical levels across real time, life time, and evolutionary scales. These neural changes are dependent on genetic, environmental, and social factors and must be stimulated by activity as previously discussed to function.

The popular metaphor for the process through which the brain utilizes its plasticity to learn what is experienced in social interactions through mirror neurons is that of film photography. Likening the brain to the film in a camera and the camera itself to the human body is indeed a very useful analogy. Using the camera to take a picture of, for example a cascading waterfall, exposes the film to new information. In order to create the photograph certain attributes and features of the scene have to be imprinted on the film to record the image. In the process of taking the photograph both the form and function of the piece of film have changed drastically. In a similar way to learn the brain needs to represent new information through changes in its neurology. In this way reality is never directly perceived from the environment, rather through the employment of patterning the brain guesses, interprets, and expects context.

In neurological terms Drubach (2000) explains that through brain plasticity learning causes, in the brain, a change in the internal structure of the neurons as well as an increase in the number of synapses between neurons. A synapse is a junction that allows neurons to transmit electrical or chemical signals between each other to learn in the everyday. In a similar way our experiences and social interactions in the everyday can be described as synaptic, as these are the junctions or crossroads where brain, mind, and society meet, intersect, and interact. Thus, social interaction and everyday experience perform in a very similar way to the neurons and synapses of the brain as it is through the building and developing of pathways and understandings through these actions, which are then rebuilt in the brain, that we learn.

The neuroscientific concept of brain plasticity elevates the importance of an understanding of socio-cultural theory in learning as it reveals without doubt that it is our everyday experiences and social interactions that cause learning as our experiences change us socially and neurobiologically as we learn. The nature of these experiences and the opportunity to engage in the practices valued by the society in which we live, in other words, the opportunity and time to learn, then become key for the educator. The idea of brain plasticity also calls into question what we prioritize as learning in schools and institutions, and how different this may be to how we learn in the everyday. School learning is often more a test of memory than it is of learning and uses entirely different brain areas and functions to 'learn'. Such a mismatch of learning is problematic experientially but also neurologically as we engage in very different activities across both sites and for some learners the discontinuity is immense (Moje and Lewis,

2007). In our everyday experience we do not often have to learn by rote. Instead we learn in social interaction and imitation, firing mirror neurons and engaging in social interaction that is shared meaningfully and results in a development of our identity. It is always important to remember however that there is no smoke without fire, or rather learning occurs through a complex web of social and neural networks, whose complementarities and conflicts we are just beginning to unearth.

Literacy: Where Are We Now? – From Synapse to Society

In this chapter we have begun to critically develop one small area of neurocultural research in the hope that the interdisciplinary support between two very different fields of study – the neuroscientific and socio-cultural – will move forward our understanding of literacy learning (developed further in Hall, Curtin, and Rutherford, in preparation). The synthesis of socio-cultural and neuroscientific research such as is presented in this chapter recasts literacy as a social and biological process that is both experience and brain dependant. Moving from synapse to society and back again *literacy* becomes a shared social consciousness framed by biology, neurology, experience, interaction, society, and culture.

Note

1.   Miller and Tallal (2006).

References

Begley, S. (2007) *Train your Mind Change your Brain*. New York: Ballantine Books.

Bruner, J. (1996) *The Culture of Education* London: Harvard University Press.

Buccino, G., Vogt, S., Ritzl, A., *et al.* (2004) Neural circuits underlying imitation learning of hand actions: An event-related fMRI study. *Neuron*, 42(2): 323–334.

Bussis, A., Chittenden, F., Amarel, M., and Klausner, E. (1985) *Inquiry into Meaning: An Investigation of Learning to Read*. Hillsdale, NJ: Lawrence Erlbaum Associates.

Byrne, B., Samuelsson, S., Wadsworth, S., *et al.* (2007) Longitudinal twin study of early literacy development: Preschool through Grade 1. *Reading and Writing: An Interdisciplinary Journal*, 20 (1–2): 77–102.

Caine, R., Caine, G., McClintic, C., and Klimek, K. (2005) *12 Brain/Mind Learning Principles in Action: The Field Book for Making Connections, Teaching, and the Human Brain*. Thousand Oaks, CA: Corwin Press.

Christakis, D.A., Gilkerson, J., Richards, J.A., *et al.* (2009) Audible television and decreased adult words, infant vocalizations, and conversational turns: A population-based study. *Archives of Pediatric and Adolescent Medicine*, 163(6): 554–558.

Decety, J., and Lamm, C. (2006) Human empathy through the lens of social neuroscience. *Scientific World Journal*, 6: 1146–1163.

Dehaene, S., Pegado, F., Braga, L.W., *et al.* (2010) How learning to read changes the cortical networks for vision and language. *Science*, 330(6009): 1359–1364.

Doige, N. (2007) *The Brain that Changes Itself*. New York: Penguin Group.

Drubach, D. (2000) *The Brain Explained*. Upper Saddle River, NJ: Prentice-Hall, Inc.

Eden, G.F., and Moats, L. (2002) The role of neuroscience in the remediation of students with dyslexia. *Nature Neuroscience* 5 Suppl: 1080–1084, accessed November 12, 2012: http://csl.georgetown.edu/publications/edenmoats_NatNeurosci_2002.pdf

Fischer, K.W., Bernstein, J.H., and Immordino-Yang, M.H. (eds) (2007) *Mind, Brain, and Education in Reading Disorders*. Cambridge UK: Cambridge University Press.

Fischer, K.W., and Bidell, T. (2006) Dynamic development of action and thought. In W. Damon and R. Lerner (eds), *Handbook of Child Psychology, Vol. 1: Theoretical Models of Human Development*, 6th ed. Hoboken, NJ: John Wiley, pp. 313–399.

Fuster, J.M. (2003) *Cortex and Mind. Unifying Cognition*. New York: Oxford University Press.

Goleman, D. (2006) *Social Intelligence: The New Science of Human Relationships*. New York: Bantam Books.

Gopnik, A., Meltzoff, A.N., and Kuhl, P.K. (1999) *The Scientist in the Crib: Minds, Brains, and How Children Learn*. New York: Morrow.

Goswami, G. (2004) Neuroscience and education. *British Journal of Educational Psychology*, 74: 1–14.

Greenfield, S. (2000) *The Private Life of the Brain*. London: Penguin.

Hakuta, K. (2008) Bilingualism, accessed November 12, 2012: www.stanford.edu/~hakuta/Publications/%282008%29%20-%20Encyclopedia%20of%20Neuroscience,%20Hakuta.pdf

Hall, K., Curtin, A., and Rutherford, V. (in preparation) *Networks of the Mind: A Critical Neurocultural Perspective on Learning*.

Immordino-Yang, M.H., and Damasio, A.R. (2007) We feel, therefore we learn: The relevance of affective and social neuroscience to education. *Mind, Brain and Education*, 1(1): 3–10.

Immordino-Yang, M.H., and Fischer, K.W. (2009) Neuroscience bases of learning. In V.G. Aukrust (ed.) *International Encyclopedia of Education*, 3rd edn. Oxford: Elsevier.

Katzir, T., and Paré-Blagoev, J. (2006) Applying cognitive neuroscience research to education: The case of literacy. *Educational Psychologist*, 41(1): 53–74.

Kuhl, P.K., Tsao, F.-M., and Liu, H.-M. (2003) Foreign-language experience in infancy: effects of short-term exposure and social interaction on phonetic learning. *Proceedings of the National Academy of Sciences of the United States of America*, 100: 9096–9101.

Lewis, C.J., Enciso, P., and Moje, E.B. (eds) (2007) *Reframing Sociocultural Research on Literacy: Identity, Agency, and Power*. Mahwah, NJ: Lawrence Erlbaum Associates.

Marshall, P., Reeb, B., Fox, N., *et al.* (2008) Effects of early intervention on EEG power and coherence in previously institutionalized children in Romania. *Development and Psychopathology*, 20: 861–880.

Martin, A., and Weisberg, J. (2003) Neural Foundations for understanding social and mechanical concepts. *Cognitive Neuropsychology*, 20: 575–587.

Metzinger, T. (2010a) *The Ego Tunnel: The Science of the Mind and the Myth of the Self*. New York: Basic Books.

Metzinger, T. (2010b) Brain science podcast interview. March 10, 2010, accessed November 12, 2012: http://brainsciencepodcast.squarespace.com/storage/transcripts/bsp-year–4/67-bsp-Metzinger2.pdf

McChandliss, B.D., and Noble, K.G. (2003) The development of reading impairment: a cognitive neuroscience model. *Retardation and Developmental Disabilities: Research Reviews*. 9: 196–205.

McDermott, R. (1993) The acquisition of a child by a learning disability. In S. Chaiklin and J. Lave (eds) *Understanding Practice*. New York: Cambridge University Press, pp. 269–305.

Miller, S., and Tallal, P. (2006) Addressing literacy through neuroscience. *School Administrator*, December: 19–23.

Moje, E.B., and Lewis, C. (2007) Examining opportunities to learn literacy: The role of critical sociocultural literacy research. In C. Lewis, P. Enciso, and E.B. Moje (eds) *Reframing Sociocultural Research on Literacy: Identity, Agency and Power*. LEA: Mahwah, NJ, pp. 15–48.

National Research Council (1999) *How People Learn: Brain, Mind, Experience, and School*. Washington DC: National Academy Press.

Neisser, U. (1991) Two perceptually given aspects of the self and their development. *Developmental Review*, 11: 197–209.

Oberman, L.M., Pineda, J.A., and Ramachandran, V.S. (2007) The human mirror neuron system: A link between action observation and social skills. *Social Cognitive and Affective Neuroscience*, 2(1): 62–66.

Petersson, K.M., Ingvar, M., and Reis, A. (2009) Language and literacy from a cognitive neuroscience perspective. In N. Torrance and D. Olson (eds) *Cambridge Handbook of Literacy*. Cambridge: Cambridge University Press, pp. 152–181.

Petersson, K.M., Reis, A., and Ingvar, M. (2001) Cognitive processing in literate and illiterate subjects: A review of some recent behavioral and functional neuroimaging data. *Scandinavian Journal of Psychology*, 42, 251–267.

Rizzolatti, G., and Craighero, L. (2004) The mirror-neuron system. *Annual Review of Neuroscience*, 27: 169–192.

Rizzolatti, G., and Sinigaglia, C. (2008) *Mirrors In The Brain: How Our Minds Share Actions and Emotions*. New York: Oxford University Press.

Rogoff, B. (1990) *Apprenticeship in Thinking: Cognitive Development in Social Context*. New York, Oxford: Oxford University Press.

Rogoff, B. (1991) Social interaction as apprenticeship in thinking: Guidance and participation inspatial planning. In L.B. Resnick, J.M. Levine, and S.D. Teasley (eds) *Perspectives on Socially Shared Cognition*. Washington, DC: American Psychological Association.

Singer, M. (2007) *Language across the Mathematics Curriculum in Romania*. Strasbourg: Council of Europe.

Temple, E., Deutscgh, G.K., Poldrack, R.A., *et al.* (2003) Neural deficits in children with dyslexia ameliorated by behavioural remediation: evidence from functional fMRI. *Proceedings of the National Academy of Sciences of the United States of America*, 100: 2860–2865.

Tettamanti, M., Buccino, G., Saccuman, M.C., *et al.* (2005) Listening to action-related sentences activates frontoparietal motor circuits. *Journal of Cognitive Neuroscience*, 17: 273–281.

Vygotsky, L. (1962) *Thought and Language*. Cambridge, MA: MIT Press.

Vygotsky, L.S. (1981) The development of higher forms of attention in childhood. In J.V. Wertsch (ed.) *The Concept of Activity in Soviet Psychology*. Armonk, NY: Sharpe.

Wenger, E. (1998) *Communities of Practice: Learning, Meaning and Identity*. Cambridge: Cambridge University Press.

Chapter 10

An Ethnographic Long Look

Language and Literacy Over Time and Space in Alaska Native Communities

Perry Gilmore and Leisy Wyman

Introduction

The authors of this chapter come to the study of literacy from an anthropological and socio-linguistic perspective basing its understandings of literacy on ethnographic fieldwork that seeks to discover the social meanings of literacy in the ever-changing contexts of daily lives of ordinary people. Influenced by linguistic anthropology, particularly the ethnography of communication (Hymes, 1964), the ethnography of literacy has emerged as a significant area of research providing insight into complex conceptions of language and literacy (e.g., see Boyarin, 1993; Collins and Blot, 2003; Finnegan, 1988; Gee, 1996; Gilmore and Glatthorn, 1982; Heath, 1983, 2012; Heath and Street, 2008; McCarty, 2005; McDermott and Gilmore, 2010; Schieffelin and Gilmore, 1986; Scollon and Scollon, 1981; Street, 1984; Wyman, 2012). These studies examine literacy-related communicative competencies (Hymes, 1972) along an oral/written continuum, often documenting students' rich language and literacy abilities. Many of these studies document hidden competencies, what Gilmore (1983, 1986) identifies as 'sub-rosa' literacy skills, and demonstrate that students' sophisticated language, literacy, and multimodal competencies are often ignored, unnoticed, and even rejected in conventional assessments and classroom instruction.

Ethnographic studies of literacy powerfully detail the socio-cultural aspects of literacy that manifest ongoing relations of domination, resistance, and internalized stigma in our society. They shift the interpretive frame of learning to read and write from an individual psychology focused on cognitive skill development, to a cultural view that examines the functions, uses, and meanings of literacy behaviors in context. Ethnographic studies of literacy produce findings that 'underscore the educational reality that literacy has more to do with access than instruction, more to do with power than pedagogy (McDermott and Gilmore, 2010, p. 80). This expanded view of literacy challenges simple definitions and boundaries and demonstrates that what it means to be literate 'varies according to one's time and place in society and history' (Schieffelin, 1986, p. viii).

International Handbook of Research on Children's Literacy, Learning, and Culture, First Edition.
Edited by Kathy Hall, Teresa Cremin, Barbara Comber, and Luis C. Moll.
© 2013 John Wiley & Sons, Ltd. Published 2013 by John Wiley & Sons, Ltd.

Few ethnography of literacy studies, however, carry on inquiry over extended time periods. Ethnography conducted over time and across place allows behaviors and practices to be observed across historical, political, economic, technological, and social situations, providing more accurate understandings of the dynamic relational nature of language and literacy. Longitudinal studies underscore how context can be understood in its most complex, fluid, reflexive, and broadest sense – not simply the immediate set of static surrounding variables but the larger dynamic cycles and fluctuations of context and language change in mutually constructed relationships (e.g., see Duranti and Goodwin, 1992). An ethnographic 'long look' can capture the nature of dramatic and nuanced contextual changes, subtle or abrupt, across shifting time periods; the ways such changes shape particular individual, family, and community literacy practices. What remains constant? What changes? How are identities, ideologies, relationships and power arrangements reconstructed and negotiated as contexts shift? What does 'being literate" actually mean?

In this chapter, we draw on overlapping, complementary, and continuous long-term ethnographic language and literacy research each of us separately conducted in Alaska Native communities. We have continued our work formally and informally, funded and unfunded, over three decades. Each has sustained collaborative research relationships with the populations with whom we worked. We discuss this work collectively to deepen and reinforce the ethnographic gaze of our individual research projects, joining others who seek to find new means of 'putting anthropology to work,' through 'situated comparisons' across individual projects and emerging forms of collaborative Indigenous research (Field and Fox, 2007). We present these studies to both illustrate the kinds of insights that ethnographies of literacy can produce in specific Alaska Native Indigenous communities, and to demonstrate the significant contributions that long, sustained ethnographic collaboration with specific communities over time and across economic, political, linguistic, technological, and social change can provide.

A Brief History

Alaska's 663,268 square mile area maintains a population of only 722,718 people. According to the 2011 census data, 14.8 percent of the state's population is identified as Alaska Native. With only a handful of cities and few major paved roads, there are vast natural uninhabited areas with only a scattering of remote villages, primarily Indigenous communities, dotting the state's rugged, diverse and resource rich landscape. Although seldom mentioned in the classical literature on Native American issues, Alaska with its more than 100,000 Indigenous citizens, represents 21 separate language traditions and boasts its own history of dramatic disruptions and betrayals. The 'Great Death' or combined influenza and measles epidemic of 1900, stemming from contact with early explorers, was a calamitous event in the history of multiple Alaska Native communities, decimating entire villages and causing estimated deaths of 25–60 percent of the Yup'ik people alone (Fortuine, 1989; Napoleon, 1991). Throughout both Russian and US occupations, Alaska Natives have also been targets of official policies of exploitation and assimilation into the most subaltern statuses. Churches and schools have been the major tools for carrying out these policies. (See Barnhardt, 1994; Darnell, 1990; Reder and Green, 1983; Scollon and Scollon, 1981 for a fuller discussion of these policies and their effects on Alaska Natives.)

In 1971, the discovery of oil and the need to build a pipeline to move it to world markets were the impetus for the settlement of the important, yet highly complex and problematic, Alaska Native Claims Settlement Act (ANCSA). The changes wrought by ANCSA forever changed the face of Alaskan racial and cultural politics; the Native community found itself a player with an often-contested voice in state policy and economic decisions (see Berger, 1988 and Ongtooguk, 1986 for details and discussion).

In the 1970s several important developments impacted the educational lives of Alaska Natives. The first was a court decision popularly referred to as the 'Molly Hootch Case' (for fuller history, see Cotton, 1984). In 1972, a lawsuit was filed on behalf of 27 Alaska Native students representing 126 villages covered by the litigation. Molly Hootch, a 16 year old from the Yup'ik village of Emmonak, was the first name on the list. Her name came to be the popular name by which people referred to this landmark case which is actually entitled *Tobeluk v. Lind.* Prior to the 'Molly Hootch' decision, in order to complete their high school education, students in Alaska Native rural communities had to leave their families and villages to attend boarding schools, some as far away as Oregon and Oklahoma, or live in boarding homes in urban areas cut off from their communities. These policies created painful histories of parentless students and childless villages, demoralizing the Alaska Native population and threatening the continuation of Indigenous language and culture in Native communities. In keeping with colonizing assimilationist policies, many of the government and missionary run primary village schools, as well as the Bureau of Indian Affairs (BIA) boarding schools were sites of cultural and linguistic oppression, explicitly forbidding any expressions of traditional Indigenous languages, culture, values and identity – often harshly punishing those who resisted.

Additionally, there were many reports of abuse and neglect in these schools. These stigmatizing and shaming experiences often severely traumatized and still haunt the many Alaska Native students who endured them. Finally, in 1976, after years of discriminatory educational practices and legal and political maneuvering, the 'Molly Hootch Case' was settled. No longer would students be forced to trade their culture for an education. The Alaska Supreme Court ruled that any village with an elementary school and one or more secondary students had the right to a local high school program. Today there are over 120 small rural high schools in Alaska (Barnhardt, 1994).

A second dramatic educational shift resulted from the passing of the federal Bilingual Education Act in 1968, which called for ' "new and imaginative" programs that used children's native language while they used English' (McCarty, in press). In 1971 Alaska passed a law requiring every school, with 15 students or more with a dominant language other than English, to provide a 'bilingual-bicultural education program.' Building on fledgling Indigenous self-determination and bilingual education movements and legislation elsewhere, Alaska Native community members and allies made an historic push to introduce bilingual education into public schools serving Alaska Native students (see Krauss, 1980; Morrow, 1990; Wyman *et al.*, 2010a). In multiple communities and school districts, the bilingual education movement laid the groundwork for dramatic shifts in schools that had for decades meted out punishment for speaking Alaska Native languages, opening spaces for Alaska Native languages as a medium of instruction, and for locally-based curriculum materials.

Gilmore's research focuses on a diverse Alaska Native population widely varied in ethnicity, languages, traditional/modern and urban/rural life ways. They represent all of the ethnic groups and Indigenous languages of Alaska. These languages include Eskimo-Aleut (i.e., Aleut, Alutiiq, Central Yup'ik, Siberian Yup'ik, and Inupiaq), the southeast Alaska languages (i.e., Tsimpshian, Haida, Tlingit), Eyak, and Athabaskan (i.e., Ahtna, Dena'ina, Tanana, Tanacross, Han, Gwich'in, Upper Tanana, Upper Kuskokwim, Lower Tanana, Deg Hit'an, Holikachuk, Koyukon). Gilmore highlights shifting political power arrangements surrounding, and constantly transforming, access to and assessment of the language and literacy skills of her university students as they negotiated an academic terrain, from grade school through college, dominated by continuously circulating deficit discourses and policies – and yet persist to achieve their educational goals.

Wyman's research has primarily focused on the specific Yup'ik region of Southwest Alaska. Over the past two decades, Wyman has longitudinally examined language and literacy practices in a single remote and traditional Yupik community, collaborated with youth and adults on books of elders' narratives in Yup'ik, and conducted action research with a team of Indigenous researchers and non-Indigenous allies in the largest school district serving Yup'ik communities. While Wyman's long-term work as a teacher and as a researcher focuses on one Alaska Native group and small rural villages, her research, as well, highlights the complex flows and diversities of experience that define even seemingly remote, homogeneous, 'small scale' Alaska Native communities today.

Presented in the next two sections of this chapter, the two sets of studies highlight a broader vision of literacy than either study could capture alone. We will illustrate how people in the Alaska Native communities, with whom we have worked, have developed literacy practices in response to historically rooted language uses, ideologies, and circulating authoritative discourses as they also rapidly reshaped channels of communication to support unique ways of life, knowledge systems and, in many cases, endangered languages in new Indigenous networks and spaces.

Achieving Academic Literacy: Overcoming Stigma with Persistence, Activism and Leadership (Gilmore)

Originally brought to the University of Alaska Fairbanks to build a graduate program, Gilmore quickly discovered that the Alaska Native population at the university had a very high attrition rate and that most Native students dropped out within the first or second year. The situation was blamed on a combination of 'academic skill deficiency' and 'homesickness.' Gilmore requested that she be able to teach undergraduate courses so that she could have the opportunity to work with Alaska Native students. The timing was fortuitous. By 1985, when Gilmore arrived at the University of Alaska Fairbanks, the first generation of 'Molly Hootch' high school graduates was arriving on campus.

In the discussion below Gilmore presents her research in an ethnographic chronology across three decades, highlighting major themes in each. One striking change across the decades was that Alaska Native students were *not* dropping out as many had previously and as the university had predicted. Instead they were, often in the face of challenging institutional, political and cultural obstacles, persisting with tenacity, to complete their academic degrees and programs.

Decade of 1980: Narratives of stigma, shame, and persistence

Autobiographical narratives were generated in Gilmore's classes and subsequently analyzed collaboratively and auto-ethnographically with her students (see Gilmore and Smith, 2005). These narratives capture the language and literacy stories of first generation Alaska Native college students recounting the educational experiences of their youth. The population ranged in age from 18 to 53. The educational background of the undergraduates ranged from traditional subsistence life ways in small, isolated, bilingual, rural community 'Molly Hootch' schools to nontraditional, urban, multicultural, monolingual, densely populated stratified educational institutions. Although the community backgrounds and degrees of traditional experiences varied considerably, the narratives demonstrated recurring themes that were pervasive throughout the data regardless of ethnic, linguistic, and regional differences. The texts document a counter narrative that articulates subaltern knowledge and a reality quite separate from the dominant reality captured in the public deficit discourses that surrounded them (see Gilmore, 2001; Gilmore and Smith, 2002). Though no longer attending boarding schools the Molly Hootch school education that allowed students to stay in their home communities still carried with it painful pedagogies of shame and stigma. Most of their teachers and administrators were non-Native outsiders who came to Alaska with negative biases and preconceived deficit notions of Native peoples and oral traditions. These biases were captured repeatedly in the student narratives. (It should be noted that there no doubt were dedicated teachers and positive school experiences, however, such narratives were virtually absent in these data.) Consider some of the following examples.

An Alutiiq student from a small village on Kodiak Island recalled being told by his high school principal that he would grow up to be nothing but a 'dumb drunken Native.' As a sophomore in college reflecting on these experiences, he wrote, 'It has taken me this long to realize that I was ashamed of myself, my skin color and past.'

In small remote Native villages and mixed race communities on the road system, the narratives recounted similar stigmatizing events. An Inupiaq undergraduate sharing her reflections in her rural public school wrote,

> I have experienced what Chester Pierce termed racist 'microaggression' within my school, maybe not intentionally caused but nonetheless very real. For example, the attitude of many teachers portrayed a sense of low expectation; a sense of demeaning spirit to my community and home life, my community, our beliefs, values. High expectations were always there for the non-Native students; many of these being the teachers' offspring. Many students came away 'brain-washed' believing that we could never be as intelligent as the others. I may sound racist; this is not my intention as I am merely sorting out feelings that have lain submerged for a long time.

Urban communities presented a different challenge for many Alaska Native students who were frequently tracked into lower level academic classes. One Inupiaq woman, from a multicultural urban city context, wrote poignantly about her experiences in a low-tracked, all Native classroom. She recalled the harsh corporal punishment inflicted on her and was sure that her teacher would not have hit a white student. She knew she was very good in math but was never recognized for or encouraged to advance her academic competencies. She personally felt vindicated in high school when she won the statewide chess championship – an achievement that surprised and even shocked her teachers and affirmed her tentative and constantly challenged belief in her own intelligence.

Indigenous language use was another site for discrimination in many of the urban and rural schools. A 19-year-old Yup'ik student recalled being pushed and having her hair pulled by her teacher when she couldn't pronounce English words correctly in her second grade monolingual classroom. These memories carry deep scars. Many years later when she experienced racial discrimination at the university, she testified in an open forum that she felt as though her second grade teacher was pulling her hair again. The trauma of the event became a metaphor for discrimination conveying continuing painful language status and stigma messages.

Yet in spite of all of these educational injustices, prejudicial challenges, and predictions of failure, Alaska Native students were achieving academic successes and graduating from high school and college in record numbers. While educational institutions too often held the students in low esteem, they were held in high esteem by their families and communities. These students, nurtured by the Molly Hootch ruling, had arrived on campus, deeply rooted in their own families, languages, traditions and values. They had believed in themselves and in education.

By the end of the decade they were a new and significant presence on the university campus and in the surrounding urban schools as student teachers and newly hired certified teachers. Non-Native university students and community members had even begun to make comments (neutral and negative) about the growing numbers of Natives in the community.

Decade of 1990: Struggles, resistance, and activism

In 1991, just as Alaska Native student successes were defying stereotypes, a major grading controversy erupted demonstrating institutional backlash in full display. The case serves as a lens through which to explore the shifting nature and meaning of language and literacy in the everyday lives of Alaska Native students. (For a full discussion of this case, see Gilmore, Smith, and Kairaiuak, 1996, 2004; Gilmore and Smith, 2002, 2005).

The incident itself was provoked by a professor's alleged comments regarding the preferential grading of Alaska Native students. After the *Anchorage Times* in November 1991 printed the initial headline claiming that the university was graduating 'unqualified Native students', a torrent of statewide headlines and media attention followed for the entire academic year. The headlines continued amid final exams with articles, letters to the editor, and guest editorials, each taking up some position for or against the professor. Accusations of racism, stereotyping and cultural insensitivity, and defenses of academic freedom, university standards and program quality were dominant themes. The incident carried an 'electric' quality and persisted through the spring. It continued to create controversy, stir emotion and argument, and appeared to be not only irrepressible but unresolvable.

In response to concerns voiced by the newly appointed Native Advisory Committee, formed in response to the crisis, the Chancellor finally issued a statement offering a public apology and affirming that the grading practices for Native students had been fair. But the words came too late. The academic year was over and most students were gone. The damage had been done. To Alaska Native students the year's headlines had read like a catechism of hegemony, a litany of shame, a pedagogy for the oppressed (Freire, 1973). Questioning minority credentials and standards is not a new or unfamiliar response to minority achievement. Unfortunately these are common responses to interrupting gate-keeping practices where race, class, and gender lines are crossed.

From a traditional point of view the Native grading controversy looked even more confusing. The students come from communities that nurture, share, assure, and celebrate learning; communities that take great pains to allow for error but arrange for success. One student narrative provided insight into the characteristics of a traditional pedagogy. He recalled an experience when his older brother told him to 'go to the beach and cast the nets.' He explained that he was surprised and anxious when his brother requested this because he had never cast the nets before. But as he thought about it he realized that his brother would never have asked him to do this if he did not fully believe he was ready and able to do the task. He knew also that his brother had been watching him as they worked together over the years and knew better than he did whether he was ready. The trust in his brother's assessment and his own cultural ways assured him that he was ready and he did perform the task successfully.

This example of Native pedagogy dramatically contrasts with white Western schooling practices. In rural subsistence communities, where not knowing can cost you your life, trial and error, premature performances, or competitive teaching strategies are too risky. In traditional pedagogy everyone is clear about what needs to be learned and when someone has learned. Traditional teachers never ask someone to perform a task unless they think they are ready and tasks are always appropriate for the learner's ability. The success of the learner is everyone's goal. Successes are not only nurtured they are shared and celebrated by the whole community.

One student recalled with pride his first kill – a ring neck seal when he was eleven. There was a 'seal party' given for him where all the meat was distributed. He wrote,

> When I was learning all the hunting skills . . . . I learned to be patient with myself and gain self confidence . . . I had to learn by firsthand experience with the help of my older brothers and my father through suggestions and comments.

The repeated stories of low expectations for Native students and the heavy emphasis on failure and attrition stood in striking contrast to the scaffold-like support systems in traditional Native pedagogy which, in the students' views, clearly and effectively maintain high standards, high expectations, and high success. The institution's lack of support for their hard earned accomplishments, as well as its questionable, elusive, and shifting standards for academic accomplishment, felt like a major betrayal.

Given these harsh circumstances, the students demonstrated an unusual and inspiring amount of resilience throughout and after the grading incident. They displayed a remarkable ability to resist the damaging public discourse. They seemed to draw their strength from traditional values, their families, and communities. Because of their roots in the community as a result of the Molly Hootch ruling, the students had a sense of identity and place that was unshakable. When the administration and faculty failed to interrupt the fractured and disturbing public discourse and to affirm their accomplishments, students served as their own spokespersons organizing open forums to voice their counter narratives. They formed an Alaska Native Student Association, helped establish and serve on the new Chancellor's Native Advisory Board, wrote letters to the media and university committees, organized meetings, drafted position papers and articles, sought advice and support from Native Corporations and Native leaders outside the university, and most difficult of all, were called upon to explain what was happening to their families. While these were stressful and time-consuming roles, causing some students to drop classes and even drop out of programs, the net result was transformational. Many students found a 'voice without fear' (Gilmore, 2008) to unveil what for them had been subjugated knowledge (Foucault, 1980). The irony was that their performances of eloquence, activism, and leadership clearly demonstrated their sophisticated academic language and literacy skills, crafted innovatively in hostile environments imbued with doubt in their possession of the very same abilities. Given the stereotype threat (Steele, 1997) surrounding them, the students' ability to persevere and demonstrate an undaunted resilience was profound.

The students pulled together to find the strength to move forward with their education despite the fact that the University had not created a free or safe space for them. They were able to maintain their traditional ties and seize the educational context for themselves. For the most part they were able to transform anger, hurt, and confusion into professionalism, leadership, and academic successes.

Decade of 2000: Advancing Indigenous knowledge, scholars, and scholarship

Currently we are in the United Nations Second International Decade of the World's Indigenous Peoples (2005–2014). Worldwide, there is recognition that Indigenous peoples face problems in such areas as culture, education, health, human rights, and social and economic development. It is also recognized that Indigenous peoples must be actively engaged in finding the solutions to these problems and taking leadership roles in the programs and policies that will address them.

In Alaska these have been years of strengthened Native leadership, privileging of Indigenous knowledge, and the advancement of Indigenous scholars. Newly formed Indigenous conferences, research networks, publications, and associations reflect strong cultural identity and solidarity. The situation at the University has much improved. The two most recent Chancellors have listened to the grievances and concerns expressed by the Alaska Native communities and have demonstrated greater sensitivity and support for Native students and faculty. Many programmatic and structural advances have been made. The university has increased their numbers of Native faculty and administrators through vigorous recruiting, support, and a 'grow your own' strategy, most recently graduating their own Alaska Native PhDs (e.g., Charles, 2011; Leonard, 2007; John, 2010) who have become professors in various programs and departments. Several faculty members have secured substantial career ladder grants that have contributed to the increased support and mentorship of Alaska Native students at the high school, undergraduate, master's, and doctoral levels. Other funds were secured to generate, document, promote, and disseminate Native knowledge, Indigenous languages, K-12 Indigenous curriculum, and Indigenous scholarship (e.g., see The Alaska Native Knowledge Network website at www.ankn.uaf.edu).

The Morgan Project provides one such example. Funded by a grant Gilmore received from the US Department of Education's Office of Bilingual and Multicultural Affairs (1999–2005), Beth Leonard (Athabascan) and Nancy Furlow (Tlingit) worked with Gilmore to coordinate the program. The project targeted three distinct populations for career advancement – high school students, bilingual paraprofessionals, and Alaska Native certified teachers.

A high school population was recruited as 'Alaska Native Language Scholar Interns' receiving scholarships and stipends for advanced placement language courses. The purpose of these language courses was twofold – they offered Indigenous language credits for students interested in careers in language and education, and they contributed to the elevation of status and prestige of the Indigenous languages of Alaska that had been historically suppressed, stigmatized, and neglected in the World Languages curriculum. The languages, Koyukon and Gwich'in, were taught by a team of fluent Native elders, linguists, and certified classroom teachers. Additionally, students worked with elders and linguists in the archives at the Alaska Native Language Center at the university. The students participated in a range of these different offerings over a six-year period embracing their linguistic heritage and cultural identities.

Bilingual paraprofessionals were fully supported to complete their undergraduate degrees and teacher certification credentials. As a result, many of these bilingual graduates were able to secure full-time teaching and administrative positions. The Morgan project also developed a statewide graduate endorsement in Alaska Native Language Education. The courses for the endorsement could be taken alone or as a significant part of a master's degree. Apprenticeships with fluent elders were arranged for graduate credit. The participants were matched with an elder as their mentor and spent time with them in their daily routine activities, learning language in cultural context. Eight certified teachers completed their master's degrees during the grant period. These teachers advanced their credentials and have made a strong and visible impact on the policies and practices in the school district. Several teachers developed Indigenous language and culture curricula for the school district and have led professional development courses helping Native and non-Native teachers infuse Indigenous curriculum content into their classrooms.

The Morgan Project seems to have functioned as a site for resistance to language and culture oppression and a space for identity reconstruction (Gilmore, 2005). So often we think of language revitalization programs in terms of pedagogical activities and linguistic skills and as a result only describe them in terms of their successes or failures in achieving language fluency and reversing language shift. We often ignore the other significant social, political, and pragmatic functions these programs serve including the creation, or recreation of language identities and language communities, a place of pride and possibility, agency, activism, and power. Many of the elders who taught the language classes in the high schools had themselves been severely punished for merely uttering their languages when they were in school. The symbolic capital of having them paid to teach the language in the very schools that condemned them was a public vindication and a personal healing. The Morgan activities were public markers of legitimacy and resilience in the wider community. Through these official documents, programs, pedagogies, and policies, the project helped create new spaces for Native students and teachers to learn and teach their own languages, to become a visible, public, and proud speech community, and reconstruct their identities as Native people.

Linguistic Survivance, Endangerment, Activism and Appropriation (Wyman)

In the following section, using a second longitudinal body of work, we will further explore the ways Alaska Native peoples have negotiated historically rooted inequities and damaging language ideologies, maintaining powerful connections to local pedagogies and lifeways while shaping new literacy practices both in and out of schools. Wyman's ethnographic research has focused on the ways that adults and youth in the Yup'ik region negotiate rapidly changing sociolinguistic practices and increasing language endangerment, and how they interact in contact zones marked by imbalances of power, demonstrating what she calls *linguistic survivance*. Building on Vizenor's (1994, 2008) notion of survivance, Wyman defines linguistic survivance as the use of language to creatively express, adapt, and maintain identities under difficult or hostile circumstances. As Wyman (2012) explores at length elsewhere, forms of linguistic survivance can range from overt attempts to pass on Indigenous language and knowledge to more subtle forms of Indigenous commentary and learning. Acts of linguistic survivance also commonly involve *translanguaging* – the moving across or intermixing of languages and language varieties (García, 2009), and the appropriation of language and literacy. Here, drawing on Wyman's research, we further trace how Alaska Native peoples' emergent literacy practices have related to dynamic and complex needs for new forms of expression and activism over the decades.

Early bilingual brokering, leadership, and linguistic survivance

Looking back in Alaska Native history, as in Gilmore's research, Wyman found many examples of youth who were brought up with a sense of confidence in traditional pedagogies of subsistence who survived damaging experiences in missionary schools. In the early days of schooling in Piniq (pseudonym), the small Yup'ik village where Wyman taught and later conducted long-term ethnographic research, individuals gained some literacy skills through submersion in English-only elementary schools. From the 1950s to the turn of the century, however, the dramatic historical shifts described above brought changing demands for bilingualism, biliteracy, and local literacy practices (Reder and Wikelund, 1993), pushing many of these same youth 'into positions of leadership in unprecedented ways' (Fienup-Riordan, 1990). In many Yup'ik communities, youth played the historical roles of bilingual brokers within new institutional and economic contexts shaped by external relationships of power, negotiating a local pedagogy emphasizing intent observation, listening and silence as a way of showing respect for adults, and performance only upon mastery, with local adults' and outsiders' demands. In interviews, adults remembered how they interpreted for their parents' interactions with local white teachers and doctors. Individuals who later gained recognition as experienced community interpreters also remembered how they, over time, took on very public responsibilities as teenagers performing new roles as educational aides in schools, interpreters for travelling missionaries and government representatives, and as health aides using new radio systems to connect outside doctors to remote health posts.

Society and literacy demands changed dramatically over the course of this generation's lifetimes, and leaders from this group described how they viewed literacy as inherently tied to local struggles for self-determination and legal avenues for addressing outsiders' abuses, as in the following comment:

> We are getting like you, we can read, and we have watched how you do things. Now if we don't like what you are doing we can write it down and take you to court. We have learned your way. Now we are somebody you look in the eyes like equals. We are not like our fathers, who maybe you looked down on, but even then we had our ways of dealing with people. [Name of local white principal] was asking me about how he heard that there was some trouble at the council [with a white outsider] and I said, 'You better be careful, it may be you next.' [laughs] We are educated and we can deal with you legally.

The generation of early bilingual brokers and village leaders came of age around the time of the Molly Hootch decision. Adults remembered how villagers debated whether to send youth to schools, and how most youth were brought home before completing high school by worried parents who witnessed the toxic consequences of family disruptions. In interviews, numerous adults alluded to the 'damaging habits' brought home by youth from the failed experimental boarding schools. Yet others noted how they learned new forms of linguistic survivance in boarding schools, and 'how to stand up to *kass'aq*s [whites]' over educational and societal inequities 'because we know their way' (Wyman, 2012).

Literacy and linguistic survivance in the Yup'ik bilingual education movement: 1970s–1990s

In the early 1970s, bilingual education legislation created opportunities for Yup'ik adults who came of age right before and after the Molly Hootch decisions to spearhead a new movement for educational self-determination in the Yup'ik region; 17 Yup'ik villages had adopted local elementary bilingual programs by 1973. The ongoing work to support and develop these programs brought multiple positive entailments in local schools over the next three decades, including the development of the first generation of Yup'ik teachers in village spaces.

In the 1980s and 1990s Yup'ik educators became increasingly networked across village spaces. A new group of Yup'ik educational leaders designed bilingual programs to develop specific language and literacy skills, and also more broadly tie schooling to locally-valued community members, practices, and perspectives. Through parallel efforts in the Lower Kuskokwim School District (LKSD) – a large school district serving 22 remote Yup'ik villages and the hub town of Bethel – (described in Wyman *et al.*, 2010b) and the Ciulestet Yup'ik teacher-researcher group (described in Lipka, Mohatt, and the Ciulestet Group, 1998), Yup'ik educators and non-Indigenous allies worked to document and recognize *yuuyaraq* – an Indigenous knowledge system. They also created an extensive set of materials reflecting a unique Yup'ik way of life, aligned new materials to state standards, and worked on locally-grounded curricula and assessments. Today in LKSD and some villages elsewhere, the grandchildren of elders who were punished for speaking Yup'ik speak Yup'ik with elementary teachers and read colorful Yup'ik books written by their aunties reflecting wide-ranging local activities.

Wyman first taught in Piniq, one of the villages in LKSD in the early 1990s, the heyday of bilingual education movement and efforts to connect classroom teaching to local language and culture. As a secondary English teacher and a member of the Alaska Teacher-Researcher Network, Wyman worked with Yup'ik educators to explore how language instruction could be used to connect youth to elders and community funds of knowledge (González, Moll, and Amanti, 2005; Moll, 1992) embedded in everyday village life. In what came to be simply referred to as 'the elders project' (described in Wyman, 2012), Wyman and colleagues helped students interview local elders, and document their oral narratives. In her English class, Wyman also connected specific assignments, such as required writing assessment essays in English, to local inquiry projects surrounding tribal jurisdiction, having students read about related issues elsewhere and interview local tribal leaders in Yup'ik.

As Wyman and colleagues learned to 'teach through the community' (Moll, 1992) students developed more confidence in their academic literacy. They successfully completed common-place school assignments such as writing speeches, and opinion and research papers in academic English. They also took on increasingly sophisticated stances towards their own work as learners and researchers, discussing with Wyman and Yup'ik adults the ethical dimensions of the project, deciding the emerging direction of the work, and reflecting on what they had learned. Through the project, a group of Yup'ik community adults and Wyman developed new computer literacy skills and used early word processing and publishing software to publish elders' narratives and students' reflections. One resulting homespun book from the project used a school-based Yup'ik writing system to make the work accessible to younger generations, English for students' reflections on their learning, and a church-based Yup'ik writing system to make the book accessible to the large numbers of elders who shared their stories and reflections. The project temporarily disrupted toxic dynamics of mistrust between the local school and community, transforming students' schooling experiences.

Through the youth-oriented work, and a later, ongoing effort to publish elders' narratives in an ANA-funded project with a local Traditional Council (Fredson *et al.*, 1998; Fredson *et al.*, in press), Wyman became aware of the ways Yup'ik leaders in tribal governments used complex new forms of literacy and translanguaging to negotiate outside regulations and to protect a unique subsistence way of life. In her long-term study of Piniq, Wyman (2012) documented how one village leader used multiple forms of critical literacy to involve elders in tribal government and navigate federal and state legislation affecting village sovereignty, and how another village leader negotiated elders' teachings and outside regulations to develop a local tribal court.

Continuing to explore out-of-school literacy practices, Wyman also followed the youth she had taught, tracking their postsecondary educational and work opportunities, and the kinds of language they were using as young adults in their first five years after high school. In 2000 and 2001, Wyman found that youth with 'decent local jobs' were actively using sophisticated language and literacy to negotiate local socialization processes with bureaucratic regulations as child welfare counselors, early childhood literacy specialists, leaders of educational programs bringing youth together with elders, as scribes in local courts, and, in one case, as a researcher working with scientists and local hunters to track Avian flu in North American migratory bird populations.

In interviews with Wyman in 2000, youth reflected on types of reading and writing they needed in their work, such as grant and report writing. They also reflected more broadly on how their everyday work involved complex forms of literacy and translanguaging, as they interpreted and worked across different types of formal and informal language varieties, documents in English and Yup'ik, and legal, scientific, and local discourses (Wyman, 2012). Over the same time period, Wyman also saw how many other emergent forms of translanguaging among younger groups were related to complex, ongoing processes of language shift/ endangerment, a topic we turn to here.

Language ideologies and endangerment: 1990s–2000

Wyman's long-term work has been carried out against a complicated backdrop of ongoing, uneven processes of language shift/endangerment, and counter-efforts to reclaim Yup'ik for future generations. In language endangerment and reclamation settings, language ideologies often proliferate (Hill, 2006), as community members try to take their own 'long look' and make sense of the ways everyday language and literacy practices are shaped, or might potentially be shaped, 'across the scales of time' (Lemke, 2000). As communities navigate language shift and endangerment, youth also commonly wrestle with language ideologies and express feelings of linguistic loss, guilt and insecurity (McCarty and Wyman, 2009; Wyman, 2012).

In Wyman's long-term ethnographic study of Piniq, young people's and adults' seemingly straightforward discussions of language and literacy often morphed into complex reflections on the reverberating effects of schooling, migration, and concerns about losing language. In interviews with Wyman, for instance, youth pointed to the impact of the school's emphasis on English as a key force in language shift, and expressed yearnings for more Yup'ik teachers so their siblings could learn to speak to their grandparents. Other youth talked about how urban migration and childhood friendships with individuals from shifting families had led to linguistic insecurities, causing them to 'lose' Yup'ik as they grew up (Wyman, 2009, 2012, in press).

Before and during language shift, multiple youth also commented on their challenges writing in Yup'ik, related to the constraints of local bilingual programs. As Wyman and others discuss, historically the bilingual program models in the Yup'ik region only extended to the third grade level. Outsiders who generally stay for short periods of time have continued to have disproportionate influence over village schools, undermining efforts to strengthen locally-responsive forms of pedagogies and programs. Since 2000, new high stakes testing practices in English have also placed further pressures on school-based efforts to develop bilingualism and biliteracy (Wyman, 2012; Wyman *et al.*, 2010a, 2010b).

During language shift, multiple intergenerational community members worried that future generations would lose the ability to access elders' historically accumulated oral teachings, often referred to as traditional Yup'ik literacy. Youth wrestled with the stigma of being the first group to speak mostly English as a peer language in a setting of language endangerment. Yet the study also showed how youth navigated complex language ideologies, changing linguistic resources, and their own divergent language socialization trajectories, using new forms of linguistic survivance to shape and connect to the Indigenous knowledge system of their community. Youth in general, and young hunters, in particular, shared everyday stories with one another about their many experiences participating in subsistence as apprentices alongside adults, and in small groups of peers alone. Their stories, shared in varying mixes of Yup'ik and English, showed how youth were continuing to learn how to carry out complex local work, increasing their understanding of land conditions, animal behavior, and in-the-moment subsistence strategies, and developing strong orientations towards local adults and community knowledge. As youth faced increasing difficulty communicating with Yup'ik-speaking elders, however, community members wrestled with finding new ways to share rich socialization genres and teachings across intergenerational divides.

Appropriating Internet connections and exercising research possibilities: 2000–2010

Between the early 1990s and the turn of the century, students in Yup'ik villages, like youth elsewhere became connected to the Internet and began to form a 'Yup'ik Worldwide Web'

(Fienup-Riordan, 2000). Here, too, we find locally-rooted forms of linguistic survivance, related to, but expanding beyond both traditional conceptions of subsistence as Alaska Native pedagogy, and traditional views of literacy as reading and writing. As in many lower class minority and/or rural communities elsewhere in 2000, early Internet connections in the Yup'ik region were highly constrained by issues of access to computers and Internet. From 2000 to the time of this writing, however, new technologies have continued to change forms of everyday communication. Through the use of new technologies, many Yup'ik adults and most youth now read and write for an expanded range of social purposes, as people in remote villages find new ways to use the Internet to participate in intergenerational networks that extend within and beyond local settings.

Such new connections hold promise for Alaska Native grassroots efforts and new forms of linguistic survivance. As Yup'ik youth have increased their access to outside worlds, they have also increased their access to Yup'ik knowledge and literacy. Since 2009 many Yup'ik households have now connected to the Internet, and many Yup'ik educators, parents, and youth have taken up globally-popular, web-based applications to write to family and friends in local and translocal communities-of-practice. Through Facebook and YouTube, youth are creating new participatory networks and multimodal competencies (e.g., Ito *et al.*, 2009). Importantly, Yup'ik individuals are also using new public Internet spaces to engage in new forms of community-making, while using new literacy forms to discuss topics of local concern.

On one webpage named after a symbolically important Yup'ik subsistence food, for instance, interconnected individuals living in villages, regional hub towns, and the broader Yup'ik diaspora post recaps of hunting stories, stories of subsistence practices, as well as newly-digitized historical photos of elders and friends. Friends and family members share exclamations of joy and pride in one another's pictures of children learning how to collect eggs from the tundra, ice-fish, bird and seal hunt, and participate in related food-processing activities, celebrating a unique and vibrant subsistence lifestyle. On the site, individuals also express multiple identities, at times sharing Christian testimonies, at other times, sharing experiences in urban settings or even war zones elsewhere. Hunters and others additionally share information about subsistence legislation, one of the most controversial topics affecting Alaska Native rights.

On a second public website, another participatory network supports Yup'ik language. On the page individuals crowdsource questions about how to translate English words into Yup'ik and vice-versa. In conversation threads, mostly Yup'ik contributors and a few linguists also discuss the challenges of language shift and reclamation. Individuals share powerful testimonies of personal language loss, individual and family language reclamation, and encouragement for maintaining Yup'ik for the future.

Increasing connection to the Internet and locally affordable computers and mobile phones between 2000 and 2010 have supported rapid changes in intergenerational uses of new media, the development of new everyday forms of community-making, and the emergence of new multimodal literacy practices and spaces. Across the region, virtual spaces provide new possibilities for expanding Yup'ik literacy, with implications for community struggles including Yup'ik language maintenance/revitalization efforts.

Schools have a long way to go, however, to integrate the many forms of complex and powerful forms of literacy and linguistic survivance described above, as historical and contemporary forms of inequity in and out of school shape language and literacy, and increasing language endangerment in the Yup'ik region. Fast-changing technologies raise new challenges, as well, as market-driven companies entice community members to invest in developing language-learning software that remains unproven in endangered language settings. As Indigenous community members consider how new technological possibilities might support local goals, they must now learn to critically weigh the benefits and drawbacks of devoting scarce resources to new media in endangered languages.

In the past decade, however, an increasing numbers of Yup'ik educational leaders have been appropriating research processes to address the challenges existing in bilingual programs and make critical decisions in the complex endangered language settings described above. Yup'ik researchers are studying topics ranging from the multimodal literacy practices found in Yup'ik dance forms (John, 2010) to the use of dynamic assessment in supporting Yup'ik language learners' efforts to develop heritage language skills in university classes (Charles, 2011). Wyman and Patrick Marlow from the University of Alaska Fairbanks have also worked with a team of co-researchers including Gayle Sheppard Miller, LKSD's head of academic instruction, and Yup'ik team members Fannie Cikuyaq Andrew, Rachel Cikigaq Nicholai and Nita Yurrliq Rearden to consider how Yup'ik bilingual programs might be strengthened, and how educators might address some of the damaging language ideologies that continue to circulate in and out of schools (Wyman *et al.*, 2010a, 2010b; Wyman *et al.*, 2011). Meanwhile, a group of Yup'ik educators are working with Sabine Siekmann to create new multimodal curricula and a third research group of Yup'ik educators are working to develop locally-responsive assessments to replace high stakes tests, while the aforementioned Ciulestet group continue their work in this vein.

Taken together, examples from the Yup'ik region underscore how literacy remains deeply related to questions of context, access, culture and power, as new types of outside contact compel Yup'ik adults and youth to combine languages, writing systems, language varieties, pedagogical approaches, and types of knowledge in efforts to sustain Alaska Native lifeways in an interconnected world. Wyman's long-term ethnographically grounded work, along with the work of others highlights how a growing number of Yup'ik role models from multiple generations are now using upper levels of literacy in its broadest sense to support communities and language learners. We also see how specific aspects of literacy can take decades to emerge and unpredictable turns, as communities make and remake themselves over time, developing critical capabilities, appropriating changing technologies, and shaping new social expressions.

Conclusion

In this chapter we have explored an ethnographic 'long look' at specific Alaska Native communities over shifting, often threatening historic time periods, and across politically charged continually reconfigured contextual spaces. Our data, taken together, demonstrate the highly complex, dynamic, ever-changing, and adaptive nature of language and literacy practices of Alaska Native communities struggling for educational equity, privileged linguistic and cultural identities, and institutional recognition of their rich knowledge and striking achievements. Both the Wyman and Gilmore studies affirm the undaunted persistence and academic successes of Alaska Native students across the decades. In spite of the continuous threats to their educational advancement, Alaska Natives have steadily responded to each new assault with remarkable resilience, strategic activism, and creative institutional transformation. Regardless of the many political and educational policies and practices that regularly confronted students, in many cases inflicting shame and stigma, the data from both studies show the many varied ways in which family and community support, cultural strength, and traditional values celebrated and reassured youth, fostering innovation, activism, and academic advancement. Both studies document the powerful initiative of youth to resist suffocating institutional discourses of failure and doubt, and to serve as their own agents in response to pressures on their traditional ways of life. This agency includes pursuing Indigenous scholarship and ways of knowing, developing new forms of linguistic survivance, and exploring multimodal spaces for meaningful literacy engagement and displays of cultural identity. The studies collectively demonstrate that new language and literacy practices provided important access and tools for original forms of community-making and community-defending thus creating potential for sustaining and regenerating unique Indigenous life ways and knowledge systems.

We have presented the examples in this chapter to illustrate the need for researchers to examine literacy and language practices over time in order to recognize the larger shifting power arrangements undergirding limited school-based assessments of literacy and the historical and continuing danger and damage of accepting these narrow, inaccurate, and misguided assumptions. By considering such things as shifting political power arrangements, multimodal transformations, bi/multilingual dynamics of languages and peoples in contact, and rapid technological change, researchers can better understand what 'being literate' actually means. This context focused multilayered exploration has hopefully created for the reader a more textured and nuanced portrait of the complicated and changing meanings over time of language and literacy in the everyday lives of Alaska Native peoples. We hope that it provides food for thought and points of situated comparison, as well, for those who wish to deepen their understanding of Indigenous peoples' literacy practices elsewhere.

References

Barnhardt, C. (1994) Life on the other side: Alaska Native education students and the University of Alaska Fairbanks. Unpublished doctoral dissertation, University of British Columbia.

Berger, T. (1988) *Village Journey: A Report of the Alaska Native Review Commission.* New York: Hill and Wang.

Boyarin, J. (1993) *The Ethnography of Reading.* Berkeley, CA: University of California Press.

Charles, S.W. (2011) Dynamic assessment in a Yugtun second language intermediate adult classroom. Unpublished doctoral dissertation, University of Alaska Fairbanks.

Collins, J., and Blot, R. (2003) *Literacy and Literacies: Texts, Power and Identity.* New York: Cambridge University Press.

Cotton, S. (1984) Alaska's 'Molly Hootch Case': High schools and the village voice. *Educational Research Quarterly*, 8(4): 30–43.

Darnell, F. (1990) Alaska's dual federal-state school system: A history and descriptive analysis. Unpublished doctoral dissertation, University of Alaska Fairbanks.

Duranti, A., and Goodwin, C. (1992) Rethinking context: An introduction. In A. Duranti and C. Goodwin (eds) *Rethinking Context; Language as an Interactive Phenomenon.* New York: Cambridge University Press, pp. 1–42.

Field, L., and Fox, R. (eds) (2007) *Anthropology Put to Work.* New York: Berg Publishers.

Fienup-Riordan, A. (1990) *Eskimo Essays: Yup'ik lives and How We See Them.* London: Rutgers University Press.

Fienup-Riordan, A. (2000) *Hunting Tradition in a Changing World: Yup'ik Lives Today.* New Brunswick, NJ: Rutgers University Press.

Finnegan, R. (1988) *Literacy and Orality.* Oxford and New York: Basil Blackwell.

Fortuine, R. (1989) *Chills and Fever: Health and Disease in the Early History of Alaska.* Anchorage: University of Alaska Press.

Foucault, M. (1980) *Power/Knowledge: Selected Interviews and Other Writings, 1972–77.* New York: Pantheon.

Fredson, A., Mann, M.J., Dock, E., and Wyman, L.T. (1998) *Kipnermiut tiganrita igmirtitlrit: Qipnermiut tegganrita egmirtellrit.* Fairbanks: Alaska Native Language Center.

Fredson, A., Mann, M.J., Dock, E., and Wyman, L.T. (in press) *Kipnermiut tiganrita igmirtitlrit: Qipnermiut tegganrita egmirtellrit*, Vol. 2. Fairbanks: Alaska Native Language Center.

Freire, P. (1973) *Pedagogy of the Oppressed.* New York: Seabury Press.

García, O. (2009) *Bilingual Education in the 21st Century: A Global Perspective.* Chichester, UK: Wiley-Blackwell.

Gee, J. (1996) *Social Linguistics and Literacies.* London: Taylor and Maxwell.

Gilmore, P., and Glatthorn, A.A. (eds) (1982) *Children In and Out of School.* Washington, DC: Center for Applied Linguistics.

Gilmore, P. (1983) Spelling Mississippi: Recontextualizing a literacy related speech event. *Anthropology and Education Quarterly,* 14: 234–255.

Gilmore, P. (1986) Sub-rosa literacy: Peers, play and ownership in literacy acquisition. In B. Schieffelin and P. Gilmore (eds) *The Acquisition of Literacy: Ethnographic Perspectives.* Norwood, NJ: Ablex, pp. 155–168.

Gilmore, P. (2001) Autoethnography on-site and on-line: Creating free spaces for counternarratives and subaltern knowledge. Paper presented at the American Educational Research Association Meeting (April): Seattle, Washington.

Gilmore, P. (2005) The Morgan Project: Language revitalization as a site for identity reconstruction in interior Alaska. *Development of Indigenous Siberian language and cultures in a changing Russia.* Online conference proceeding, accessed September 2005: www.linguapax.org/en/docang.html

Gilmore, P. (2008) Engagement on the backroads: Insights for anthropology and education. *Anthropology and Education Quarterly,* 39(2): 109–116.

Gilmore, P., and Smith, D.M. (2002) Identity, resistance and resilience: Counternarratives and subaltern voices in Alaska higher education in 1991. In D.C.S. Li (ed.) *Discourses in Search of Members: In Honor of Ron Scollon.* Lanham, MD: University Press of America, pp. 104–134.

Gilmore, P., and Smith, D.M. (2005) Seizing academic power: Indigenous subaltern voices, metaliteracy, and counternarratives in higher education. In T.L. McCarty (ed.) *Language, Literacy and Power in Schooling.* Mahwah, NJ: Lawrence Erlbaum, pp. 67–88.

Gilmore, P., Smith, D., and Kairaiuak, L. (1996) Resisting diversity: An Alaskan case of institutional struggle. In M. Fine, L. Weis, L. Powell, and L. Mun (eds) *Off White: Readings on Race, Power, and Society.* New York: Routledge, pp. 90–99.

Gilmore, P., Smith, D., and Kairaiuak, L. (2004) Resisting Diversity: An Alaskan case of institutional struggle. In M. Fine, L. Weis, L. Powell Pruitt, and A. Burns (eds) *Off White: Readings on Power Privilege, and Resistance.* New York: Routledge, pp. 273–283.

González, N., Moll, L., and Amanti, C. (2005) *Funds of Knowledge: Theorizing Practices in Households, Communities and Classrooms.* Mahwah, NJ: Lawrence Erlbaum.

Heath, S.B. (1983) *Ways with Words: Language, Life and Work in Communities and Classrooms.* New York: Cambridge.

Heath, S.B. (2012) *Words at Work and Play: Three Decades in Family and Community Life.* Cambridge: Cambridge University Press.

Heath, S.B., and Street, B. (2008) *Ethnography: Approaches to Language and Literacy Research.* New York: Teachers College Press.

Hill, J. (2006) The ethnography of language and language documentation. In J. Gippert, N. Himmelmann and U. Mosel (eds) *Essentials of Language Documentation.* Berlin: Mouton de Gruyter, pp. 113–128.

Hymes, D. (1964) Introduction: Toward ethnographies of communication. *American Anthropologist,* 66(6): 1–34.

Hymes, D. (1972) On communicative competence. In J.B. Pride and J. Holmes (eds) *Sociolinguistics: Selected Readings.* Harmondsworth: Penguin, pp. 269–293.

Ito, M., Baumer, S., Bittanti, M., *et al.* (2009) *Hanging Out, Messing Around, Geeking Out: Living and Learning with New Media.* Cambridge: MIT Press.

John, T.A. (2010) Yuraryararput kangiit-llu: Our ways of dance and their meanings. Unpublished doctoral dissertation, University of Alaska Fairbanks.

Krauss, M. (1980) *Alaska Native Languages, Past, Present and Future.* Fairbanks, AK: Alaska Native Language Center.

Lemke, J.L. (2000) Across the scales of time: Artifacts, activities, and meanings in ecosocial systems. *Mind, Culture, and Activity*, 7(4): 273–290.

Leonard, B. (2007) Deg Xinag oral traditions – Reconnecting Indigenous language and education through traditional narratives. Unpublished doctoral dissertation, University of Alaska Fairbanks.

Lipka, J., Mohatt, G., and the Ciulestet Group (1998) *Transforming the Culture of Schools: Yup'ik Eskimo examples*. Mahwah, NJ: Lawrence Erlbaum.

McCarty, T.L. (ed.) (2005) *Language, Literacy, and Power in Schooling*. Mahwah, NJ: Lawrence Erlbaum.

McCarty, T.L. (in press) *Language Planning and Policy in Native America: History, Theory, Praxis*. Bristol: Multilingual Matters.

McCarty, T.L., and Wyman, L. (2009) Indigenous youth and bilingualism – Theory, research, praxis. *Journal of Language, Identity and Education*, 8(5): 279–290.

McDermott, R., and Gilmore, P. (2010) Reading and reigning: The anthropology of literacy and the politics of learning. In P.L. Anders (ed.) *Defying Convention, Inventing the Future in Literacy Research and Practice: A Tribute to Ken and Yetta Goodman*. New York: Taylor and Francis, pp. 76–95.

Moll, L. (1992) Bilingual classroom studies and community analysis: Some recent trends. *Educational Researcher*, 21(2): 20–24.

Morrow, P. (1990) They just want everything: Results of a bilingual education needs assessment in southwestern Alaska. In *Proceedings of the Symposium Languages in Contact/12th Annual Congress of Anthropology of Ethnological Sciences*. Institute of Linguistics, University of Zagreb. Electronic version available: http://www.eric.ed.gov/ERICWebPortal/search/detailmini.jsp?_nfpb=true&_&ERICExtSearch_SearchValue_0=ED320725&ERICExtSearch_SearchType_0=no&accno=ED320725

Napoleon, H. (1991) *Yuuyaraq: The Way of the Human Being*. Fairbanks: Center for Cross-Cultural Studies, University of Alaska.

Ongtooguk, P. (1986) The annotated ANCSA. In P. Ongtooguk (ed.) *The Alaska Native Claims Settlement Act: Selected Student Readings*. Kotzebue: Northwest Arctic Borough School District. Retrieved October 18, 2012, from http://www.alaskool.org/projects/ancsa/annancsa.htm

Reder, S., and Green, K.R. (1983) Contrasting patterns of literacy in an Alaska fishing village. *International Journal of the Sociology of Language*, 42: 9–39.

Reder, S., and Wikelund, K. (1993) Literacy development and ethnicity: An Alaskan example. In B. Street (ed.) *Cross-Cultural Approaches to Literacy*. Cambridge: Cambridge University Press, pp. 176–197.

Schieffelin, B. (1986) Introduction. In B. Schieffelin and P. Gilmore (eds) *The Acquisition of Literacy: Ethnographic Perspectives*. Norwood, NJ: Ablex, pp. viii–xiii.

Schieffelin, B., and Gilmore, P. (eds) (1986) *The Acquisition of Literacy: Ethnographic Perspectives*. Norwood, NJ: Ablex.

Scollon, R., and Scollon, S. (1981) *Narrative, Literacy and Face in Interethnic Communication*. Norwood, NJ: Ablex.

Steele, C. (1997) *A Threat in the Air: How Stereotypes Shape Intellectual Identity and Performance*. *American Psychologist*, 52(6): 613–629.

Street, B. (1984) *Literacy in Theory and Practice*. New York: Cambridge University Press.

Vizenor, G. (1994) *Manifest Manners: Post-indian Warriors of Survivance*. Hanover, NH: Wesleyan University Press of New England.

Vizenor, G. (2008) Aesthetics of survivance: Literary theory and practice. In G. Vizenor (ed.) *Survivance: Narratives of Native Presence*, Lincoln, NE: University of Nebraska Press, pp. 1–23.

Wyman, L. (2009) Youth, linguistic ecology, and language endangerment: A Yup'ik example. *Journal of Language, Identity and Education*, 8(5): 335–349.

Wyman, L. (2012) *Youth Culture, Language Endangerment and Linguistic Survivance*. Bristol, UK: Multilingual Matters.

Wyman, L. (in press) Indigenous youth migration and language contact. *International Multilingual Research Journal*.

Wyman, L., Marlow, P., Andrew, C.F., *et al.* (2010a) Focusing on long-term language goals in challenging times: Yup'ik examples. *Journal of American Indian Education*, 49(1&2): 22–43.

Wyman, L., Marlow, P., Andrew, C.F., *et al.* (2010b) High stakes testing, bilingual education and language endangerment: a Yup'ik example. *International Journal of Bilingual Education and Bilingualism*, 13(6): 701–721.

Wyman, L., Marlow, P., Miller, G., *et al.* (2011) Using collaborative research to negotiate policy disjunctures in school systems and Indigenous endangered language settings: Lessons from a longitudinal Yup'ik project. Documenting Constraints and Imagining Opportunities: The Effects of Federal Policy in Alaska and Arizona. Paper presented at the American Educational Research Association Meeting (April); New Orleans, Louisiana.

Chapter 11

Understanding English Language Learners' Literacy from a Cultural Lens

An Asian Perspective

Guofang Li

Introduction

Research on English language learners (ELLs) has always pointed to the importance of culture in their literacy learning and development. Literacy as a way of living is part of a culture. Language itself is an individual cognitive as well as a cultural phenomenon: it arises in the life of an individual through ongoing exchanges of meanings with significant others (Gee, 1996; Heath, 1983; Street, 1995; Wagner, 1991). Becoming literate is a matter of becoming enculturated in one's socio-cultural worlds; literacy is seen as a social and cultural continuity, the means by which individuals conduct and construct their lives in the community and the society (Cairney, 2009). Since English language learners often cross between two or more languages and cultures, we must understand how culture plays a role in their literacy and living at home and in school in order to understand their literacy learning and development.

This understanding is especially important given the diversity in the nation's ELL population. The National Center for Education Statistics (NCES) has reported that an estimated 11.2 million students (21 percent) were ELL learners in 2009–2010 compared with 3.7 million in 2000–2001 (NCES, 2012). During the same period, while this ELL subgroup grew more than 50 percent, the total pre-K-12 population increased by only 7.22 percent (NCELA, 2011). Among the ELLs, about 70 percent speak Spanish, 10.2 percent speak Asian languages (Chinese, Tagalog, Vietnamese, Korean, Hmong), 6.0 percent European (French, German, Russian), 1.1 percent French Creole, and 12.8 percent other languages (Batalova, Fix, and Murray, 2007). Of these learners 57 percent were US born second or third generation immigrants. These learners who come from diverse backgrounds also bring a wide variety of educational and cultural experiences to their classrooms and considerable linguistic differences that have significant implications for their literacy learning in school (Short and Fitzsimmons, 2007).

This diverse student body also poses unprecedented challenges to US schools and teachers who often are not prepared to teach ELLs. The persistent low achievement in literacy learning among ELLs has been declared as a national crisis that is 'urgent and overlooked' (Alliance for Excellent Education, 2007). For example, despite the limitation of relying on standardized testing as a sole measure of learning, the analysis by the National Assessment of Educational

International Handbook of Research on Children's Literacy, Learning, and Culture, First Edition.
Edited by Kathy Hall, Teresa Cremin, Barbara Comber, and Luis C. Moll.
© 2013 John Wiley & Sons, Ltd. Published 2013 by John Wiley & Sons, Ltd.

Progress (NAEP) shows that the gap in eighth grade reading achievement (about 46 points) between ELLs and non-ELLs has remained consistent in the past decade. In 2007, about 96 percent of ELLs were found to be at or below the basic level (partial mastery of knowledge and skills) in reading and this number has remained largely unchanged since 1998 (NAEP, 2007). Similar trends can also be observed in eighth grade math and science assessments.

Much of the recent effort to close the achievement gaps between ELL and non-ELL have focused on studies of effective reading instructional strategies, and few have paid attention to the social and cultural issues that surround ELLs' lives outside classrooms (see Faulkner-Bond, Waring, and Forte; 2012; Snow and Biancarosa, 2003). Such a narrow focus will not fully address the increasing demands of the diverse groups of ELL students and communities. Voluminous studies on children from diverse backgrounds have revealed the important role the socio-cultural factors play in children's learning in school and home (Heath, 1983; Lee, 2006; Moje *et al.*, 2004; Moll, 1994; Valdés, 1996). Given the increasing cultural diversity within ELL learners, it is therefore imperative to understand ELLs' literacy learning from an acculturation perspective – the interplay between culture and literacy learning and how culture shapes their literacy learning in and out of schools.

Such exploration from an acculturation perspective will help inform literacy pedagogies in mainstream classrooms with students from multiethnic backgrounds. To this end, in this chapter, I illustrate the interplay between culture and literacy learning by drawing on current research on Asian learners of immigrant backgrounds. Specifically, this chapter is guided by the following three questions:

1 What is the interplay between culture and Asian ELLs' literacy learning?
2 What can a cultural lens contribute to understandings of Asian students' literacy learning?
3 How can a cultural lens inform literacy pedagogies in mainstream classrooms for Asian and other minority learners?

Asian ELL Learners: Straddling Two Literacy Cultures

As of 2010, the United States' Asian American population had surpassed 18.2 million, or 5.8 percent of the total US population (US Census Bureau, 2012). Among this group, nearly three-quarters (74 percent) of the adults were born abroad. Asians, now outpacing Hispanics, have become the largest stream of new immigrants coming to the United States annually (Pew Research Center, 2012). In terms of school age children, in 2006, it was reported that there were 2,282,149 Asian students in US schools, comprising 5 percent of the total school population (Gebeloff, Evans, and Scheinkman, 2012). With the rapid increase in Asian immigrant populations in the country since then, there are likely to be more Asian students in the schools today. Although mass media as well as government statistics usually use the terms Asian Americans and Asian American/Pacific Islanders, there is enormous diversity within the Asian American population. The Asian American population consists of many subgroups with distinctly different ethnic backgrounds (O. Lee, 1997; Min, 2006; Pew Research Center, 2012). The major groups are: (a) East Asians (i.e., Chinese, Japanese, Korean); (b) Pacific Islanders (i.e., Fijian, Guamanian, Hawaiian, Marshall Islander, Melanesian, Samoan, Tahitian, Tongan); (c) Southeast Asians (i.e., Cambodian/Kampuchean, Hmong, Indonesian, Lao, Malayan, Thai, Vietnamese); and (d) South Asians (i.e., Bangladeshi, Filipino, Burmese, Asian Indian, Nepali, Pakistani, Sri Lankan). Each of the above sub-groups has its own cultural and political traditions, and has been in North America for various years ranging from new immigrants to descendants of immigrants over 200 years ago.

In addition to the cultural and linguistic diversity, there also exists a vast gap and inequity in achievement between different Asian subcultures. On the one hand, Asian students as a group have not been considered to be part of the national literacy crisis due to their high achievements in some academic areas such as math and reading. According to NAEP (2007), as a group, Asians have consistently outperformed other minority groups such as Hispanics, Blacks, and American Indians and are on par with the whites in reading achievement. These assessment results again help reinforce Asians as the 'model minority' who can succeed on their own (see Li and Wang, 2008).

On the other hand, there is also evidence of great diversity in academic achievement among different ethnic groups of the Asian American population. This is because a rising number of Southeast Asian (including Vietnamese, Cambodian, Laotian, and Hmong) children and youths are found to struggle academically in school and face multiple risks such as difficulties in acculturation, identity conflicts, and inconsistent parental supervision and discipline (AAPIP, 1997; Gold and Kibria, 1993; Le and Warren, 2006; Lee, 2005; Li, 2005). For example, a breakdown by states in the National Assessment of Educational Progress (NAEP) reading report card (grade 8) for 1998–2003 indicates that in some states Asians did not necessarily have higher achievement levels than Blacks, Hispanics, and American Indians. In states such as Hawaii and Minnesota, the percentage of Asian American/Pacific Islanders at or above basic in reading can be as low as 45–55 percent. According to another nationally representative survey of graduating seniors (Kim, 1997), percentages of Asian American high school seniors who scored above the 50th percentile in reading were found to be as follows: South Asian (79 percent), Korean (69 percent), Filipino (50 percent), Chinese (46 percent), Japanese (43 percent), and Southeast Asian (32 percent). Pairwise comparisons found that the South and East Asians significantly outperformed Southeast Asian Americans (e.g., Vietnamese). Recent analysis of Asian American students' performance in standardized assessment tests also revealed a similar pattern of a wider and more uneven (bimodal) distribution of scores than is the case for other populations such as Hispanics, Blacks and Whites (Teranishi, 2010). According to Teranishi (2010), some Asian American students attained scores in the top percentile, there are also many Asian American students who achieved scores in the bottom percentile. Teranishi (2010) points out that this bimodal distribution in scores for Asian Americans is correlated with a high degree of heterogeneity within the population with regard to ethnicity and immigration histories, educational attainment, and poverty rates, and a wide distribution in language backgrounds.

This bimodal phenomenon has been regarded as 'the other gap' (Little and Ahmed, 2008; Maxwell, 2007) or 'an invisible crisis' that many Asian American children face in today's schools (AAPIP, 1997). It has created 'two literacy cultures and two literacy problems' within the Asian ELLs population (Morrison, Bachman, and Connor, 2005). While high achieving Asian students are reported to resent the model minority image (Lee, 1996; McKay and Wong, 1996), many underachieving Asian students are found to face increasing cultural conflicts and psychosocial stress under the cultural pressure to excel (Kao and Herbert, 2006; Li, 2009a). Many are also reported to experience increasing difficulties in acculturation and identity conflicts and are prone to drop out (AAPIP, 1997; Le and Warren, 2006; Little and Ahmed, 2008; Maxwell, 2007). In a study of gifted Asian American adolescent males, Kao and Herbert (2006) found that the students often experienced intergenerational cultural conflict within their families that involved two concerns: parental expectations for academic performance (e.g., differing views of academic rigor, the value of standardized tests, time spent on the home computer, comparisons with classmates) and acculturation issues (such as value differences, parental expectations regarding obedience and respect, differing views of adolescent autonomy, and the importance of learning the ethnic language). In contrast, research on low achieving

Asian learners (e.g., Lee, 2005) shows that even though many adolescent learners are fluent in spoken English, they struggle with acquiring academic English skills and in response to failing grades, many simply give up, start skipping classes and eventually drop out (AAPIP, 1997; Le and Warren, 2006). These students are also reported to have experienced serious cultural conflicts with their parents and their high achieving peers as well as acculturation issues concerning their cultural and linguistic identity.

In sum, Asian ELLs' divergent literacy problems and their shared consequences resulting from various cultural conflicts suggest that culture plays a central role in their literacy learning and development including aspects such as cultural identity, gender, parental expectations and involvement, and social context of reception.

Culture and Asian ELL Literacy Development

In this section, I explicate the ways culture influences Asian ELLs' literacy learning and development from four perspectives: cultural identity, gender, parental expectations and involvement, and social context of reception.

Culture, literacy, and identity development

Learner identities – how learners see themselves and are seen by others in relation to their ethnic language and culture – have a significant impact on their learning and development (Harklau, 2008). As literacy is defined in part by group boundaries and status, the process of becoming literate as well as the types of literacy activities learners engage in embody one's cultural identity. Literacy is thus viewed as an essential part of adolescents' conception of his/her culture and personhood – appropriate to the members of the community to which they belong. Adolescents' language choice at home with family members and in school with their peers, for example, plays a significant role in shaping their identity development. In her ethnographic study of a Filipino family, Li (2000) found that the children's' language choice at home has created intergenerational conflicts. While their parents and grandparents tried to speak Tagalog to them at home and raise them in Filipino ways, the adolescents (Jessie and Jasmine) and their six-year-old sister Salsha chose to speak English at home and identify themselves as Canadians. Since their parents struggled to speak English and their grandma could not understand any English, their language use has created serious cultural conflicts between them.

To conform or to reject family histories is also a matter of how to deal with cultural conflicts between the heritage culture and the mainstream culture. Cultural clash between the old and the new is believed to be the most important factor that can result in students' psychosocial stress and identity crisis. Researchers have pointed out that the clash of values, behaviors, and attitudes between home and school culture often produces serious internal struggles for Asian ELLs in balancing the two (Lam, 2003; Lee and Wong, 2002; Tran, 2002). For example, Vietnamese culture emphasizes obedience, discipline, and filial piety while mainstream culture values autonomy and independence. For Vietnamese students, searching to assimilate and striving for autonomy similar to that of their American peers often places them at risk of family conflict and internal disharmony (Lam, 2003). Many are pressured to assimilate at the expense of their own cultural heritage or withdraw from and reject interactions with the mainstream or act out and become apathetic to preserve their cultural identity (Zhou and Bankston, 1998).

Conflicts between immigrant parents and their US-born or US-raised children are also an important factor that influences the children's psychosocial well-being (Cheung and Nguyen, 2001). For many Asian immigrant families, different life experiences between children and parents inevitably widen the generation gap, leading to intense bicultural conflicts that push children and parents into separate social worlds (Trueba, Jacobs, and Kirton, 1990; Zhou, 2001). The substantial language gap between parents and children, for example, is the most salient generational dissonance that creates acculturative stress. Children often learn the language more quickly and become acculturated at a faster rate than their parents, increasingly become family spokespersons, and assume the roles of interpreters and translators due to the social isolation and limited language proficiency of the parents. As these children increasingly adopt parental roles, parents gradually lose control and the ability to exercise guidance, which often leads to intensified parent–child conflicts, role reversal, and ultimately loss of parental authority (Portes and Rumbaut, 1996; Zhou, 2001). As Harklau (2008) points out, these cultural conflicts and psychosocial stress can ultimately lead to adverse 'lifestage outcomes' (e.g., poor school achievement) and often result in them having a poorer sense of 'personal efficacy' and a tendency to accept perceptions of limited social access rather than to challenge or circumvent them.

In a study on a high-achieving Vietnamese youth (Hahn), Li examined her identity development and socio-emotional struggle during her acculturation processes (Li, 2009b). Li found that despite Hahn's academic success, several socio-cultural factors have resulted in profound social isolation and psychological stress. These factors included family immigration history and early resettlement experience, Vietnamese cultural traditions, her multiple responsibilities and roles at home, as well as negative social context of reception. Hanh's struggles suggest that for immigrant students, high achieving or not, their identity development and socio-emotional well-being are dependent upon a complex combination of home, school, and societal issues. The multidimensional influences on her development suggest that it is necessary to situate our understanding of Asian ELLs, both high and low achievers, within their specific socio-cultural and socio-historical contexts. The identity development of Asian youth like Hanh, a high achiever, is not a linear process; rather, it involves constant negotiation and renegotiation of conflicts and contradictions as defined by their everyday experiences. These interactive effects require schools and families to forgo the stereotypical image of Asian students as problem-free 'model minorities' and move beyond a narrow focus on their academic achievement to include attention to their identity development, their socio-emotional needs and psychosocial wellbeing.

Culture, gender, and Asian ELLs' literacy engagement

Immigrant students, particularly female students, may also face conflicts in gendered identities (Harklau, 2008; Olsen, 1997). Another aspect of cultural identity significant to Asian ELLs is the creation and re-creation of gender roles in their daily interactions, especially in terms of intergenerational transmission of gendered identities. Consistent with previous studies (e.g., Baluja, 2002; Dion and Dion, 2001; Valenzuela, 1999), the immigrant parent generation tends to reconstruct the traditional gender roles in the host society – the domestic code that defines women's domestic and childcare responsibilities and husbands' responsibility for financial support and decision-making. However, as the family stories in Li (2002, 2008) revealed, the economic demands for surviving in the inner city put much more responsibility on the immigrant women while the immigrant men's roles remained unchanged. The women not only had to follow the domestic code from their countries of origin but also took on part of the men's responsibilities of financial support and decision-making to help the family make it in the United States. They often did so without the social support networks of extended families and friends that they had in their countries of origin. As a result, they were left alone in dealing with the increasing demands on them such as helping with their children's homework, while they themselves struggled with learning a new language and adapting to a new environment.

All the women in Li's studies (Li, 2002, 2008) of Asian families, for example, were responsible for childrearing and housework, working in multiple low-wage occupations such as salon technicians or factory workers. However, their jobs were often unstable, which placed a further stress upon the women. These women's experiences suggest that, like their white working-class counterparts described in Weis (2004), their border-crossing has necessitated them to work side by side with immigrant men in the home/family and public spheres – both to supplement the home income and to raise the next generation. However, unlike their white working-class counterparts, they are still doing the 'hard living' – their low-wages cannot afford them the 'accomplishment of a still potentially stable and relatively affluent' lifestyle (Weis, 2004, p. 140).

The immigrant families' newly constructed gender patterns in the host society have significant impacts on how they raise the next generation. The parents' gender adaptation has shaped the expectations of their sons' and daughters' behavior and academic achievements. The elder daughters are often socialized into the double roles of their mothers while the older sons into those of their fathers. That is, the older daughters in the families are all expected to follow the traditional gender role of their heritage culture: helping with household chores and at the same time doing well in school so that they can get better jobs in the future. It is worth noting here that whether they are the eldest child or not affects the expectation on girls' academic achievements. For example, family aspiration for Hanh's school achievement was very high because she is the eldest child and her brother showed less promise of academic achievement (Li, 2009a). In another Vietnamese teenager Nyen Ton's case, because she was the second child, her parents were ambivalent about their aspiration for her and focused all their expectations on her elder brother Mien (Li, 2008). Similar patterns were also seen in other Asian families in the literature (e.g., Lee, 2005; Qin, 2009; Zhou, 2001).

In addition to high expectations, similar to findings in Mexican immigrant households, the elder daughters in Asian (e.g., Vietnamese and Chinese) families take on various domestic roles such as tutors (when children serve as translators and teachers for their parents and younger siblings), advocates (when children intervene or mediate on behalf of their households during difficult transactions or situations), and surrogate parents (when children undertake nanny or parent-like activities) (Valenzuela, 1999). The two Vietnamese ELLs (Hanh and Nyen) mentioned earlier were expected to excel in school and at the same time help with their younger brothers' school work, in addition to doing household chores. Hanh even played an advocate role for her parents with regard to her brother's schooling through questioning the NCLB policy and demanding more school support. Their brothers, even the older ones, however, were exempt from domestic duties and responsibilities. Although the boys were expected to excel academically, they had fewer behavior restrictions – they could go out and socialize while the girls were not allowed to do so: they were expected to stay home all the time, but the boys, like Nyen's brothers Mien and Owen, were 'always going somewhere.' Similar patterns of differential treatments were also observed among Chinese families (see Qin, 2008).

The double standards placed on second-generation Asian girls have significant implications for their cultural translations between home and school, since the two have different codes for their expected behaviors. Unlike the home milieu, the schools often do not have similar differentiated gendered expectations for boys and girls and the children are exposed to more gender equality. The girls are also exposed to peers who do not have the culturally specific gender expectations imposed on them at home. Whether they are able to negotiate the differences between school and home will have significant influence on their psychosocial wellbeing. Furthermore, as Dion and Dion (2001) note, the difference has potential implications not only for parent–child relations but also for the development of ethno-cultural identity among adolescents and young adults.

Culture, Asian ELLs, and parental expectations

Another factor is family expectations and the pressure to achieve. Although many Asian immigrant parents have gone through tremendous upheaval and changes in their lives, their single most important concern is their children's academic performance (Chuong, 1999; Li, 2006; Louie, 2001). Their dedication to education is attributed to two aspects of the traditional Confucian culture. One is that Confucian culture values education and considers men of learning at the top of the social ladder. The other is that parents expect their children to do well so that they will support them better in their old age. Therefore, many set very high expectations for their children's school achievement and are dedicated to providing family support for their education even in hard circumstances (Chuong, 1999, Li, 2009b). Asian ELL students often feel pressured to meet the high expectations of their parents and teachers in academic achievement, particularly in math and science, which simultaneously creates passive learners who avoid risk-taking or creative process. The academic pressures experienced by Asian ELL students often lead to emotional, mental, and socialization problems; they may also result in nonconfrontational approaches (such as strategy of silence) to prejudice against them (Lee, 1996).

In addition to the high pressure from home, Asian ELLs also face the pressure to live up to the 'model minority' image that casts them as 'whiz kids' devoid of problems (Li, 2005, 2009a; Qin, 2008). Researchers have concluded that the model minority stereotype, true or not, shapes students' intellectual identity and their expected performance (S. Lee, 1996; Li, 2005). As evidenced in several studies on Asian adolescent ELLs' identity formation (e.g., Lee, 1996, 2005; McKay and Wong, 1996), the 'model minority' discourse operates as a very powerful force in their academic and personal lives. For students who are underachieving, trying to live up to the model minority stereotype may result in mental and emotional problems (Li, 2005; Louie, 2004; Qin, 2008). Many Asian students struggle with cultural dictates that motivate them to embrace high academic achievement and are reported to resent the success myth (Lee, 1996, 2005; Li, 2009b). In order to measure up to the expectations, many students have been pressured into assimilation into the mainstream and rejection of their cultural identity. As a result, they are more likely to have serious psychological and emotional issues. In their study of Asian American students' emotional and behavioral problems, Lorenzo *et al.* (1995) revealed that many Asian American students were significantly more isolated, more depressed and anxious, and were more likely to internalize their problems and less apt to be involved in after-school activities or seek help for their problems than those from other ethnic groups. These were due to a variety of socio-cultural factors such as high academic pressure, lack of role models, and social support.

Parental involvement and Asian ELLs' literacy development

It is widely recognized that parental active interest in and continuing support of children's learning have a positive impact on school effectiveness and students' academic achievement. Epstein (1995) theorizes that there are different levels of parental involvement ranging from involvement in the home, to participation in activities and events at school, and to participation in the schools' decision-making process. Parental involvement at home includes attending to children's basic needs, discipline, preparing for school, and supporting school learning and/or engaging actively in homework. However, the degree and the ways of involvement vary from family to family and from culture to culture as families of race, class, and religion have different ways of transmitting and socializing literacy, different perceptions of families' and schools' roles in their children's education, and different ways of involvement in their children's academic learning.

As literacy is a cultural practice, parents from different cultures have different beliefs about what it means to be literate, how to acquire literacy, and the role of schooling in achieving literacy. For example, several studies on Asian families have documented how their ways of learning and familial values are distinctively different from other cultures such as White and Hispanics. Parental involvement in Asian families often includes preference for a direct instructional approach, parental supervision of homework, and provision of private tutoring (Li, 2006; Zhang and Carrasquillo, 1995). These practices are different from the White middle-class families' emphasis on independent learning, and the Hispanic families' preferences for learning through observation or collaboration with adults (Anderson and Gunderson, 1997).

Cultural differences also intersect with class differences to shape how families view their involvement in school settings (Lareau, 2000; Li, 2006). White working-class or poor parents, for example, tend to view education as the school's responsibility and often do not recognize the importance of parental participation in school settings or know how to effectively get involved due to different structural barriers (Demie and Lewis, 2010; Lareau, 2000). Many immigrants from other cultures such as Hispanics and Southeast Asians also share similar perceptions that associate teachers with the authority and professionals and parents are to avoid 'trespassing' on those territories. For example, in Huss-Keeler's (1997) study of the mainstream teachers' perceptions of Pakistani parental involvement, many Pakistani parents demonstrated their interest in their children's education by supporting and assisting their children's studies at home and not by being actively involved at school. Their culturally different expectations, however, were perceived by teachers as 'disinterest' in their children's education, and consequently, their children's learning and achievement were frequently undermined.

These different patterns of parental involvement have a profound influence on family–school relations since they may affect how parents and teachers view each other's roles and hence their attitudes and communication to each other. Schools' communications and actions can convey positive, family-oriented attitudes that show concerns for family needs and perspectives as well as negative attitudes (e.g., view differences as deficiencies or parents' active participation as over-involved or intrusive) (Christenson and Sheridan, 2001; Li, 2006). The latter attitude, which often places families in a powerless position, is detrimental to healthy family–school relationships and might increase the potential for conflict between school and parents (Fine, 1993). As Moles (1993) points out:

> Disadvantaged parents and teachers may be entangled by various psychological obstacles to mutual involvement such as misperceptions and misunderstandings, negative expectations, stereotypes, intimidation, and distrust. They may also be victims of cultural barriers reflecting differences in language, values, goals, methods of education, and definitions of appropriate roles. (p. 33)

The mainstream teachers and the middle- and upper-class Chinese parents in Li's (2006) study had culturally different understandings of parental involvement at home and in school. The Chinese parents considered parental involvement at home as monitoring or supervising homework and investing in their children's learning such as tutoring classes. They also pro-vided direct teaching when they could; however, they expected the children to complete their homework independently and seek help only if they encounter difficulties. In terms of school involvement, the parents seemed to have experienced barriers reflecting differences in language, values, goals, methods of education, and definitions of appropriate roles (Moles, 1993). The teachers, on the other hand, viewed homework as a shared activity, a task that should be completed through parent-child interactions at home. The teachers expected the parents' active involvement at school and considered the Asian 'parenting' roles the parents' brought to school as inappropriate. These cultural and social barriers are important for understanding the cultural conflicts experienced by Asian ELLs between school and home.

Asian ELLs and social context of reception

Asian ELL students' perceptions of the context of reception (e.g., racism and discrimination in the host society) are associated with their identity development and psychosocial distress (Juang and Alvarez, 2010; Lam, 2003; Qin, 2008; Tran, 2002). In her study of Vietnamese students in San Diego, Zhou (2001) reported that the Vietnamese students' overall perceptions of racial discrimination and white superiority were substantial. Almost a third of them held pessimistic views on racial discrimination in economic opportunities in the United States. Vietnamese students were also reported to internalize their perceived racial discrimination and such internalization often influenced their adjustment and coping strategies (Alvarez and Helm, 2001). Lam (2003) found that Vietnamese students who were socialized with messages that emphasized positive images of being Asian American seemed to function better psychosocially. In contrast, students who internalized the negative images of racial discrimination tended to demonstrate more social and psychological struggles. In a review of at-risk Asian students, Siu (1996) found that many Southeast Asian students were reported to have experienced different levels of racial discrimination (e.g., name calling or being insulted or ridiculed) at school and these experiences were often manifested in different forms of emotional casualties such as depressive symptoms, withdrawn or deviant behaviors, and social problems.

Research also shows that newly arrived immigrant students not only face intra-racial tension, but also interracial discrimination by other Asian peers who have arrived early and are more assimilated (Fisher, Wallace, and Fenton, 2000; Juang and Alvarez, 2010; Rosenbloom and Way, 2004). From their survey on 181 Chinese adolescent students in North Carolina, Juang and Alvarez (2010) discovered that interracial peer discrimination was related to their poorer adjustment and resulted in loneness, anxiety and somtization in the host society. In their comparative study that included 177 adolescent students from African American, Hispanic, East Asian (Chinese and Korean), South Asian (Indian) and non-Hispanic White backgrounds in an urban public school, Fisher, Wallace, and Fenton (2000) found that both East and South Asian students reported higher levels of distress from peer discrimination than their African American, Hispanic, and White peers. According to their study, both East and South Asian students reported more instances of being called names, excluded from social activities, and threatened by other peers as a result of their race than their peers from other ethnic backgrounds. Similarly, in their study of peer harassment experienced by Chinese immigrant students in Boston and New York, Qin, Way, and Rana (2008) found that multiple factors including the Chinese youths' immigration status and language issues, their higher levels of academic achievement, the perceived preference for the Chinese students by the teachers in the school, and their different physical size from non-Asian students are cited as reasons for being verbally and physically bullied in school.

The Need for a Culture Pedagogy

It is evident that Asian learners are complex social beings whose success or failure in literacy is dependent upon a complex combination of home and school issues that may vary from child to child, as literacy is deeply embedded in the social practices and relationships of schools and homes. Therefore, an understanding of these learners requires us to move beyond a surface level analysis of learners' literacy abilities (e.g., comparing the underachieving children with the successful 'model minorities'). Instead, we need to look deeper and explore their literacy performances within complex socio-cultural contexts. That is, we need to understand how Asian ELLs learn from an acculturation perspective that examines their interactions with others and the larger context such as the school and the mainstream society (Kim and Chun, 1994). Such an understanding will help mainstream teachers become more responsive to ELLs' needs.

The above analysis suggests that understanding cultural differences between home and school is of great significance to Asian ELLs' literacy and living. Making sense of cultural conflicts between home and school, however, is a highly contested process that often results in various levels of displacement and fractures in their daily experiences – from their language use, gender roles to home literacy practices, school expectations, and parental involvement (Li, 2008, 2011). The displacement and fractures that are often cultured, raced, gendered, and classed have affected the children's learning experiences in and out of school. Therefore, helping minority students (i.e., Asians) gain the abilities and skills that enable them to translate the differences among diverse domains of border-crossing, should take a critical place in minority education.

To this end, I propose a new pedagogical framework which I call *culture pedagogy* to empower educators with the theoretical foundation upon which they can develop new curricula to help students to become successful cultural translators (Li, 2008). This culture pedagogy builds on previous culture work that emphasizes a deep understanding of the cultural practices students engage in outside school (e.g., Lee, 2006; Li, 2006; Moje *et al.*, 2004; Moll, 1994) and Giroux's (2005) border pedagogy that encourages the exploration of people moving in and out of borders constructed around coordinates of difference and power. In this framework, culture is seen as a vital source for reshaping the politics of identity and difference. It draws attention not only to students' competence in knowledge building, but also to their actions or proactive steps taken based on their knowledge acquired about differences. Two steps are central to the culture pedagogy: one is cultural reconciliation (Li, 2008) and the other is cultural translation (Jordan, 2002).

Cultural reconciliation involves helping students recognize the consequences of the cultur-ally different literacies. To help students do so, teachers and educators need to know more about students' lived realities and the socio-cultural contexts of their learning in and out of school through collecting student social and cultural data outside school (Li, 2006, p. 211). This data collection process will not only help teachers reconcile cultural differences between home and school but also enable them to help students understand the discursive cultural dualities surrounding their own lives. Only when teachers come to a deep and comprehensive understanding of the school and home cultural practices can they help minority students come to terms with the cultural differences and dualities. And only by doing so, teachers can establish positive relationships with the students and really care for them (Bartolomé, 2002; Noddings, 2005).

Teachers' understanding of cultural contestations their ELLs experience in school and home will help them redesign school literacy practices and avoid fracturing minority students' literacy experiences. Teachers must abandon the scripted, one-size-fits-all curriculum to address the diverse cultural practices in ELLs' literacy development. First, teachers and schools must value students' first language and culture and treat them as 'funds of knowledge' (González, Moll, and Amanti, 2005). Mercado (2005) believes that, with the cultural knowledge of their minor-ity students, teachers should be able to 'build on and support bilingualism, multidialectalism, biliteracy, and language play for learning in the school' (p. 147).

Another important part of the curriculum redesign is to help students recognize the cultural contestations in their lives and learn how to reconcile with them. González (2005) argues that the school site should provide students with an ideological space not only for the development of bilingualism and biliteracy but also for multidiscursive practices and readings of the world. Teachers can help students to read their own socio-cultural worlds by engaging them in analyzing how ideologies and cultures are actually taken up in the contradictory voices and lived experiences of students in and out of school. To do so, teachers must use students' cultures and literacies as texts in literacy instruction and build on students' histories, languages, memories, and narratives. Further, as Giroux (2005) argues, literacy education must also allow space for cultural remapping. That is, students not only need to learn how to analyze and understand their lived cultural experiences but also need to develop abilities to explore alternatives that may help them resolve the cultural tensions to achieve academic success and psychosocial health.

The process of cultural reconciliation provides teachers and students who are 'linguistically armed and culturally knowledgeable' with a repertoire of knowledge or competence to move across the in-between cultural spaces (Bartlett, 2001, p. 30). In addition to gain this competence, students' performance (i.e., the ability to enact) in cultural translation between school and home is of critical importance – they need to be aware of the concept and consequences of 'oppositional identities' and at the same time to develop strategies that help make choice and decisions that lead to neither ethnic flight (distance from one's own language and culture) nor identification (resistance to mainstream literacy and culture), but a third space that is characterized by aporetic coexistence of different cultural codes at different social contexts (Bhabha, 1994).

Cultural translation is therefore not some happy consensual mix of diverse cultures; it is the strategic, translational transfer of tone, value, signification, and position – a transfer of power – from an authoritative system of cultural hegemony to an emergent process of cultural relocation and reiteration (Seshadri-Crooks, 2000). It involves continual interface and exchange of cultural difference. As Jordan (2002, pp. 99–101) describes:

> Cultural translation is a holistic process of provisional sense making . . . We are constantly involved in translating self to other and other to self . . . It reinforces the importance of starting with the self, making strange of one's own practices and learning to articulate them afresh from another, more reflexive, stance . . . learning to live another form of life and speak another kind of language.

Jordan (2002) further cautions that performing cultural translation is 'not a question of replacing text with text but of co-creating text, of producing a written version of a lived reality, and it is in this sense that it can be powerfully transformative of those who take part' (p. 98). Pedagogically, cultural translation requires teachers to rethink what and how major questions in literacy education are asked and how cultural diversity should be addressed in their classrooms. It means that teachers must teach students to ask questions such as 'Where do I belong presently? In what forms do I identify with or distance from 'we' or my first language and culture? And in what forms do I identify with or distance from 'they' or the 'others'? In addition, they must also engage students in constant inquiry into how their present might interface with their future.

In terms of addressing diversity, the cultural translation requires teachers to abandon the 'hallway multiculturalism' currently practiced in many inner-city schools – the happy mix of different cultures at face value by simply adding ethnic content such as the foods, folkways, and holidays approach (Hoffman, 1996). This popular multiculturalism is for a token effect of including differences, rather than opening up opportunities for negotiating identities and differences discursively constructed in ELLs' literacy learning experiences. As noted above, cultural translation involves developing competence to challenge one's own self and one's own ways of seeing the world; therefore, the popular multiculturalism will not work. Hoffman (1996, p. 555) argues:

> Culture cannot and should not be artificially inserted, bits and pieces, into everything and anything in the guise of multiculturalizing it; indeed, infusing culture in the curriculum in this way is at best futile and at worse damaging, for it encourages us to think of culture as simply something that can be dissected, categorized, and inserted into convenient slots. Rather, it requires a holistic and a comparative perspective that allows students to draw their own conclusions and abstractions from evidence, rather than being [forced] proper attitudes or principles (such as 'All cultures are equal/special'), that in the end mean nothing without a grounding in a knowledge base or context.

Thus, instead of clinging to practices that are futile and damaging, it is necessary to approach minority literacy education from a new perspective – an interstitial perspective that allows teachers of Asian ELLs to move beyond the make-believe curriculum and examine the cultural hybridities – to develop knowledge about different cultural ways of seeing the self-other relationship and to explore new alternative versions of self (Bhabha, 1994). By focusing on the emergence of the interstices – the overlap and displacement of domains of difference, as Bhabha (1994, p. 2) argues, the social articulation of difference, must be seen as 'a complex, on-going negotiation that seeks to authorize cultural hybridities that emerge in moments of historical transformation.'

This perspective is 'not simply a discourse about "diverse others", but rather is a practice that engages both self and other, students and teachers in rethinking constructions of identity, culture, representation, and power' (Asher, 2005, p. 1081). To work from this perspective, as Hoffman (1996) suggests, teachers must approach culture as children do – as genuine and natural explorers who are able to transform and to be transformed by their encounters. Teaching literacy through this interstitial perspective will transform students' lives and help them connect the present with the past and the future. Asher (2005, p. 1083) describes this kind of new social imaginary in education:

> Imagine then a multiculturalism that engages the 'possibility of a cultural hybridity' and recognizes identities and cultures as fluid, dynamic, negotiated at the intersections of race-class-gender-culture. Imagine then students and teachers in teacher education and in K–12 classrooms participating in critical, self-reflexive, pedagogical processes that go beyond essentialized representations of diverse 'others' toward engaging the interstices at which self and other are located.

Finally, curriculum redesign for cultural reconciliation and translation should not be limited to the efforts of individual teachers only. Rather, it should be a school- and district-wide endeavor. In the current educational and economic climate, without institutional supports at local, state, and even federal levels, teachers' abilities to enact these recommendations will be limited. There is a need for a policy of mutual literacy accommodation in which both schools make use of the languages and literacies of immigrant and minority students in teaching and ELL students use the school literacy and culture for learning.

References

AAPIP (1997) *An Invisible Crisis: The Educational Needs of Asian Pacific American Youth.* New York: Asian American/Pacific Islanders in Philanthropy.

Alliance for Excellent Education (2007) Urgent but overlooked: The literacy crisis among adolescent English language learners, accessed November 29, 2012: http://www.all4ed.org/files/UrgentOver.pdf

Alvarez, A., and Helm, J. (2001) Racial identity and reflected appraisals as influences on Asian Americans' racial adjustment. *Cultural Diversity and Ethnic Minority Psychology*, 7(3): 217–231.

Anderson, J., and Gunderson, L. (1997) Literacy learning outside the classroom. *The Reading Teacher*, 50: 514–516.

Asher, N. (2005) At the interstices: Engaging postcolonial and feminist perspectives for a multicultural education pedagogy in the South. *Teachers College Record*, 107(5): 1079–1106.

Baluja, K.F. (2002) *Gender Roles at Home and Abroad: The Adaptation of Bangladeshi Immigrants*. New York: New Americans LFB Scholarly Publishing LLC.

Bartlett, T. (2001) Use the road: The appropriacy of appropriation. *Language and Intercultural Communication*, 1(1): 21–39.

Bartolomé, L.I. (2002) Creating an equal playing field: Teachers as advocates, border crossers, and cultural brokers. In Z.F. Beykont (ed.) *The Power of Culture: Teaching across Language Differences*. Cambridge, MA: Harvard Education Publishing Group, pp. 167–192.

Batalova, J., Fix, M., and Murray, J. (2007) *Measures of Change: The Demography and Literacy of Adolescent English Learners – A Report to Carnegie Corporation of New York*. Washington, DC: Migration Policy Institute, accessed November 13, 2012: www.migrationpolicy.org/pubs/Measures_of_Change.pdf

Bhabha, H.K. (1994) *The Location of Culture*. New York: Routledge.

Cairney, T. (2009) Home literacy practices and mainstream schooling: A theoretical understanding of the field. In G. Li and P.R. Schmidt (eds) *Multicultural Families, Home Literacies, and Mainstream Schooling*. Greenwich, CT: Information Age Publishing, pp. 3–28.

Cheung, M., and Nguyen, S.M.H. (2001) Parent-child relationships in Vietnamese American families. In N.B. Webb (ed.) *Culturally Diverse Parent-Child and Family Relationships: A Guide for Social Workers and Other Practitioners*. New York: Columbia University Press, pp. 261–282.

Christenson, S.L., and Sheridan, S.M. (2001) *School and Families: Creating Essential Connections for Learning*. New York: The Guilford Press.

Chuong, C.H. (1999) Vietnamese American students: Between the pressure to succeed and the pressure to change. In C.C. Park and M.M. Chi (eds) *Asian American Education: Prospects and Challenges*. Westport, CT: Bergin & Garvey, pp. 183–200.

Demie, F., and Lewis, K. (2010) *Raising the Achievement of White Working Class Pupils: School Strategies*. London: Lambeth Council.

Dion, K.K., and Dion, K.L. (2001) Gender and cultural adaptation in immigrant families. *Journal of Social Issues*, 57(3): 511–521.

Epstein, J.L. (1995) School, family, community partnerships: Caring for the children we share. *Phi Delta Kappan*, 76: 701–712.

Faulkner-Bond, M., Waring, S., and Forte, E. (2012) *Language Instruction Educational Programs (LIEPs): A Review of the Foundational Literature*. Washington DC: Office of Planning, Evaluation, and Policy Development, US Department of Education.

Fine, M. (1993) [Ap]parent involvement: Reflections on parents, power, and urban public schools. *Teachers College Record*, 94(4): 682–710.

Fisher, C.B., Wallace, S.A., and Fenton, R.E. (2000) Discrimination distress during adolescence. *Journal of Youth & Adolescence*, 29: 679–695.

Gebeloff, R., Evans, T., and Scheinkman, A. (2012) Diversity in the classroom, accessed November 13, 2012: http://projects.nytimes.com/immigration/enrollment.

Gee, J.P. (1996) *Social Linguistics and Literacies: Ideology in Discourse*. London: Taylor & Francis.

Giroux, H. (2005) *Border Crossing: Cultural Workers and the Politics of Education*, 2nd edn. New York: Routledge.

Gold, S., and Kibria, N. (1993) Vietnamese refugees and blocked mobility. *Asian and Pacific Migration Journal*, 2(1): 27–56.

González, N. (2005) Beyond culture: The hybridity of funds of knowledge. In N. González, L.C. Moll, and C. Amanti (eds) *Funds of Knowledge: Theorizing Practices in Households, Communities, and Classrooms.* Mahwah, NJ: Lawrence Erlbaum, pp. 29–46.

González, N., Moll, L.C., and Amanti, C. (2005) *Funds of Knowledge: Theorizing Practices in Households, Communities, and Classrooms.* Mahwah, NJ: Lawrence Erlbaum.

Harklau, L. (2008) The adolescent English language learner: Identities lost and found. In J. Cummins and C. Davison (eds) *Handbook of English Language Teaching.* New York: Springer, pp. 639–654.

Heath, S.B. (1983) *Ways with Words: Language, Life, and Work in Communities and Classrooms.* New York: Cambridge University Press.

Hoffman, D.M. (1996) Culture and self in multicultural education: Reflections on discourse, text, and practice. *American Educational Research Journal,* 33(3): 545–569.

Huss-Keeler, R.L. (1997) Teacher perception of ethnic and linguistic minority parental involvement and its relationships to children's language and literacy learning: A case study. *Teaching and Teacher Education,* 13(2): 171–182.

Jordan, S.A. (2002) Ethnographic encounters: The processes of cultural translation. *Language and Intercultural Communication,* 2(2): 96–110.

Juang, L.P., and Alvarez, A.A. (2010) Discrimination and adjustment among Chinese American adolescents: Family conflict and family cohesion as vulnerability and protective factors. *American Journal of Public Health,* 100(12): 2403–2409.

Kao, C., and Herbert, T.P. (2006) Gifted Asian American adolescent males: Portraits of cultural dilemmas. *Journal of the Education of the Gifted,* 30(1): 88–117.

Kim, H. (1997) Diversity among Asian American high school students, accessed November 13, 2012: www.eric.ed.gov/PDFS/ED408388.pdf

Kim, U., and Chun, M.B.J. (1994) Educational 'success' of Asian Americans: An indigenous perspective. *Journal of Applied Developmental Psychology,* 15, 329–343.

Lam, B.T. (2003) *The psychological distress among Vietnamese American adolescents: Toward an ecological model.* Unpublished doctoral dissertation, Columbia University, New York.

Lareau, A. (2000) *Home Advantage: Social Class and Parental Intervention in Elementary Education,* 2nd edn. New York: Rowman & Littlefield Publishers.

Le, T.L., and Warren, J.L. (2006) Self-reported rates and risk factors of Cambodian, Chinese, Lao/Mien and Vietnamese Youth. In *Beyond the 'Whiz Kid' Stereotype: New Research on Asian American and Pacific Islander Youth.* Los Angeles, CA: UCLA Asian American Studies Center.

Lee, C.D. (2006) *Culture, Literacy, and Learning: Taking Bloom in the Midst of the Whirlwind.* New York: Teachers College Press.

Lee, O. (1997) Diversity and equity for Asian American students. *Science Education,* 81: 107–122.

Lee, P.W., and Wong, S.L. (2002) At-risk Asian and Pacific American youths: Implications for teachers, psychologists and other providers. In E.H. Tamura, V. Chettergy, and R. Endo (eds) *Asian and Pacific Islander American Education: Social, Cultural, and Historical Contexts.* South EI Monte, CA: Pacific Asia Press, pp. 85–115.

Lee, S. (1996) *Unraveling the 'Model Minority Stereotype': Listening to Asian American Youth.* New York: Teachers College Press.

Lee, S. (2005) *Up against Whiteness: Race, School and Immigrant Youth.* New York: Teachers College Press.

Li, G. (2000) Family literacy and cultural identity: An ethnographic study of a Filipino family in Canada. *McGill Journal of Education,* 35(1): 1–27.

Li, G. (2002) *'East is East, West is West'? Home Literacy, Culture, and Schooling.* New York: Peter Lang.

Li, G. (2005) Other people's success: Impact of the 'model minority' myth on underachieving Asian students in North America. *KEDI Journal of Educational Policy,* 2(1): 69–86.

Li, G. (2006) *Culturally Contested Pedagogy: Battles of Literacy and Schooling between Mainstream Teachers and Asian Immigrant Parents.* Albany, NY: SUNY Press.

Li, G. (2008) *Culturally Contested Literacies: America's 'Rainbow Underclass' and Urban Schools.* New York: Routledge.

Li, G. (2009a) Behind the 'model minority' mask: A cultural ecological perspective on a high achieving Vietnamese youth's identity and socio-emotional struggles. In C. Park, R. Endo, and X.L. Rong (eds) *New Perspectives in Asian American Parents, Students, and Teacher Recruitment*. Greenwich, CT: Information Age Publishing, pp. 165–192.

Li, G. (2009b) *Multicultural Families, Home Literacies, and Mainstream Schooling*. Greenwich, CT: Information Age Publishing.

Li, G. (2011) The role of culture in literacy learning and teaching. In M.L. Kamil, P.D. Pearson, E.B. Moje, and P. Afflerbach (eds) *Handbook of Reading Research*, Vol. IV. Mahwah, NJ: Lawrence Erlbaum, pp. 515–538.

Li, G., and Wang, L. (eds) (2008) *Model Minority Myths Revisited: An Interdisciplinary Approach to Demystifying Asian American Education Experiences*. Charlotte, NC: IAP.

Little, D., and Ahmed, A. (2008) Struggling Asians go unnoticed: Poor grades lumped in with standout students. *Chicago Tribune*, March 30.

Lorenzo, M.K., Pakiz, B., Reinherz, H.Z., and Frost, A. (1995) Emotional and behavioral problems of Asian American adolescents: A comparative study. *Child and Adolescent Social Work Journal*, 12(3): 197–212.

Louie, V. (2001) Parents' aspirations and investment: The role of social class in the educational experiences of 1.5- and second-generation Chinese Americans. *Harvard Educational Review*, 71(3): 438–474.

Louie, V. (2004). *Compelled to Excel: Immigration, Education and Opportunity among Chinese Americans*. Stanford, CA: Stanford University Press.

Maxwell, L.A. (2007) The 'other' gap. *Education Week*, 26(23): 26–29.

McKay, S.L., and Wong, S.C. (1996) Multiple discourse, multiple identities: Investment and agency in second language learning among Chinese adolescent immigrant students. *Harvard Educational Review*, 66(3): 577–608.

Mercado, M. (2005) Seeing what's there: Language and literacy funds of knowledge in New York Puerto Rican homes. In A.C. Zentella (ed.) *Building on Strength: Language and Literacy in Latino Families and Communities*, New York: Teachers College Press, pp. 134–147.

Min, G.P. (2006) *Asian Americans: Contemporary Issues and Trends*. New York: Pine Forge Press.

Moje, E.B., Ciechanowski, K., Kramer, K., *et al.* (2004) Working toward third space in content area literacy: An examination of everyday funds of knowledge and discourse. *Reading Research Quarterly*, 39(1): 38–71.

Moles, O.C. (1993) Collaboration between schools and disadvantaged parents: Obstacles and openings. In N.F. Chavkin (ed.) *Families and Schools in a Pluralistic Society*. Albany, NY: SUNY Press, pp. 2–20.

Moll, L.C. (1994) Literacy research in community and classroom: A sociocultural approach. In R.B. Ruddell, M.R. Ruddell, and H. Singer (eds) *Theoretical Models and Processes of Reading*. Newark, DE: International Reading Association, pp. 179–207.

Morrison, F.J., Bachman, H.J., and Connor, C.M. (2005) *Improving Literacy in America: Guidelines from Research*. New Haven, CT: Yale University Press.

NAEP (National Assessment of Educational Progress) (2007) The nation's report card, accessed November 13, 2012: http://nces.ed.gov/NationsReportCard/

NCELA (National Clearinghouse for English Language Acquisition) (2011) The Growing Numbers of English Learner Students, accessed June 19, 2012: www.ncela.gwu.edu/files/uploads/9/growinglep_0809.pdf

NCES (National Center for Education Statistics) (2012) *English Language Learners in Public Schools (Indicator 8–2012)*, accessed November 13, 2012: http://nces.ed.gov/programs/coe/indicator_ell.asp

Noddings, N. (2005) *The Challenge to Care in Schools: An Alternative Approach to Education*, 2nd edn. New York: Teachers College Press.

Olsen, L. (1997) *An Invisible Crisis: The Educational Needs of Asian Pacific American Youth*. New York: Asian American/Pacific Islanders in Philanthropy.

Pew Research Center (2012) *The Rise of Asian Americans*. Washington DC: Pew Social & Demographic Trends.

Portes, A., and Rumbaut, R. (1996) *Immigrant American: A Portrait*, 2nd edn. Berkeley, CA: University of California Press.

Qin, B. (2008) The other side of the model minority story: Understanding psychological and social adjustment of Chinese American Students. In G. Li and L. Wang (eds) *Model Minority Myths Revisited: An Interdisciplinary Approach to Demystifying Asian American Education Experiences*. Charlotte, NC: IAP, pp. 133–157.

Qin, D.B. (2009) Being 'good' or being 'popular': Gendered and ethnic identity formation of Chinese Immigrant adolescents. *Journal of Adolescent Research*, 24(1): 37–66.

Qin, D.B., Way, N., and Rana, M. (2008) The 'model minority' and their discontent: Examining peer discrimination and harassment of Chinese American immigrant youth. *New Directions for Child and Adolescent Development*, 121, 27–42.

Rosenbloom, S.R., and Way, N. (2004) Experiences of discrimination among African American, Asian American and Latino Adolescents in an urban high school. *Youth and Society*, 35, 420–451.

Seshadri-Crooks, K. (2000) Surviving theory: A conversation with Homi K. Bhabha. In F. Afzal-Khan and K. Seshadri-Crooks (eds) *The Pre-occupation of Postcolonial Studies*. Durham & London: Duke University Press, pp. 369–379.

Short, D., and Fitzsimmons, S. (2007) *Double the Work: Challenges and Solutions to Acquiring Language and Academic Literacy for Adolescent English Language Learners*. New York: Carnegie Corporation of New York and Alliance for Excellent Education.

Siu, S.F. (1996) *Asian American Students at Risk: A Literature Review*. Report No. 8. Baltimore, MD: John Hopkins University.

Snow, C.E., and Biancarosa, G. (2003) *Adolescent Literacy and the Achievement Gap: What Do We Know and Where Do We Go from Here?* New York: Carnegie Corporation.

Street, B. (1995) *Social Literacies: Critical Approaches to Literacy in Development, Ethnography and Education*. London: Longman.

Teranishi, R.T. (2010) *Asians in the Ivory Tower: Dilemmas of Racial Inequality in American Higher Education*. New York: Teachers College Press.

Tran, A.N. (2002) Acculturative stressors affecting Vietnamese American Adolescents and their parents. Unpublished doctoral dissertation. Pacific Graduate School of Psychology, Palo Alto, California.

Trueba, H.T., Jacobs, L., and Kirton, E. (1990) *Cultural Conflict and Adaptation: The Case of Hmong children in American Society*. New York: The Falmer Press.

US Census Bureau (2012) *The Asian Population 2010: 2010 Census Briefs*. Washington DC: US Department of Commerce Economics and Statistics Administration.

Valdés, G. (1996) *Con Respeto: Bridging the Distance between Culturally Diverse Families and Schools: An Ethnographic Portrait*. New York: Teachers College Press.

Valenzuela, Jr., A. (1999) Gender roles and settlement activities among children and their immigrant families. *American Behavioral Scientist*, 42(4): 720–742.

Wagner, D.A. (1991) Literacy as culture: Emic and etic perspective. In E.M. Jennings and A.C. Purves (eds) *Literate Systems and Individual Lives: Perspectives on Literacy and Schooling*. Albany, NY: State University of New York Press, pp. 11–22.

Weis, L. (2004) *Class Reunion: The Remaking of the American White Working-Class*. New York: Routledge.

Zhang, S.Y., and Carrasquillo, A. (1995) Chinese parents' influence on academic performance. *New York State Association for Bilingual Education Journal*, 10, 46–53.

Zhou, M. (2001) Straddling different worlds: The acculturation of Vietnamese refugee children. In R.G. Rumbaut and A. Portes (eds) *Ethnicities: Children of Immigrants in America*. Berkeley, CA: University of California Press, pp. 187–228.

Zhou, M., and Bankston, C.L. III. (1998) *Growing up American: How Vietnamese Children Adapt to Life in the United States*. New York: Russell Sage.

Chapter 12

Exploring Multiple Literacies from Homes and Communities

A Cross-cultural Comparative Analysis

Iliana Reyes and Moisés Esteban-Guitart

Introduction

Across communities, members participate in social practices that influence their ways of speaking and thinking with each other. Each of the various practices highlights particular *knowledge* and *ways* in which community members contribute to young children's literacy development. A socio-cultural approach studies language and literacy as socially constructed, culturally-mediated practices, with the goal of documenting how these play a vital role in children's learning (Scribner and Cole, 1981; Taylor, 1983). Studies under this approach explain how children or adults act as *agents* rather than passive *participants* in co-constructed practices (Freire, 1970; Vygotsky, 1978). In addition, cultural practices among members of the same community determine the 'acceptable' ways of interacting and engaging in literacy practices as part of caregiver and literacy models for the young child and their peers (Rogoff, 2003). Similarly, studies that have taken an ecological approach to the study of language and literacy practices within bilingual contexts reveal that children's and students' use of the dominant and native languages is determined by the functions for which language and literacy are used in specific ecological contexts (e.g., Hornberger, 1989; Hornberger and Skilton-Sylvester, 2000; Reyes, 2009). That is, if adults and peers can and actually do provide these children with the tools and mediations they need to continue developing the minority language, then they have higher chances of developing bilingualism and perhaps also biliteracy (Dworin, 2003).

More recently, another wave of research that addresses the multiple pathways to literacy that children follow is the *syncretic literacy studies*. Gregory, Long, and Volk (2004) describe how children live and develop literacies in their 'simultaneous worlds' (Kenner, 2004). These researchers show how children are able to blend knowledge from these simultaneous worlds, that from which their families originated, and the new multicultural communities to which they along with their families immigrated. Gregory, Long, and Volk (2004) define *syncretic literacies* in multilingual communities not just as a blending of pre-existing cultural, language, and

International Handbook of Research on Children's Literacy, Learning, and Culture, First Edition.
Edited by Kathy Hall, Teresa Cremin, Barbara Comber, and Luis C. Moll.
© 2013 John Wiley & Sons, Ltd. Published 2013 by John Wiley & Sons, Ltd.

literacy forms but a negotiated re-creation of cultural practices in an activity of transformation. In this regard, Syncretic Literacy Studies:

> go beyond issues of methods, materials and parental involvement towards a wider interpretation of literacy, including what children take culturally and linguistically from their families and communities (prolepsis), how they gain access to the existing funds of knowledge in their communities through finely-tuned scaffolding by mediators and syncretism. (Gregory, Long, and Volk, 2004, p. 5)

In the next section we review particular examples from studies undertaken with these theoretical approaches.

Literacy Practices across Cultures and Contexts

Duranti and Ochs (1997), in their study of a Samoan family in California whose literacy practices blended those from the Unites States with their heritage literacy, defined literacy as 'an intermingling of culturally diverse traditions that informs and organizes literacy activities' (p. 172). Along similar lines, the studies reviewed in this chapter move far beyond a limited view of literacy as isolated features of decoding and encoding sound to text to show the intricate ways that literacy can unfold when fostered and used for authentic communicative purposes.

The influence of parental and family beliefs on young children's literacy development: Connections with the home literacy environment and pre-school children's literacy development

Families develop their attitudes and values towards language and literacy through their own personal experiences growing up and through what they absorb and learn in their communities, and how the various languages are valued and used in their children's educational settings (Reyes, 2011). Specifically, the value that people assign to languages and those who use them is key to understanding the ideologies that impact the relationship between participants and how children demonstrate social competence as members of a specific community (Schieffelin, Woolard, and Kroskrity, 1998).

Recent studies with Latino parents in the United States, for example, reveal significant findings about how the value that other members of the community assign to languages and those who use them, impact parents' beliefs regarding supporting bilingual development and literacy in two languages for their children. Relaño Pastor's (2005) study documented Latina mothers' values and beliefs associated with Spanish, English, and raising their children bilingually and biliterately in a border city in Southern California. These mothers transmitted to their children their own beliefs and attitudes about their use of the native language, what Relaño Pastor called the 'moral language order.' These mothers did not define the good child 'based on his or her literacy activities' but instead emphasized *norms of respect* towards adults and children that strengthened relationships between immediate and extended family members. Specifically, home language use for the mothers reflected an effort to maintain the Spanish language, and its use at church, as the language of respect, and related to strengthening their Mexican or Central American identities (see also, Baquedano-López, 1997; Guerra and Farr, 2002). While English, and raising their children bilingual and biliterate, meant connecting these two languages to literacy activities. The privileging of Spanish is thus value laden; the choice of English is instrumental.

Another example of various beliefs by families comes from the work by Li (2006) with Asian immigrant parents and their children's teachers in mainstream classrooms. Her study documented the different beliefs and perspectives white teachers and the case study Chinese families held about literacy education. While the teachers in her study believed and practiced student-centered and meaning-based instruction, White parents, from middle- and upper-class Chinese first generation immigrant families, believed and preferred a teacher-centered and skill-focused instruction for their children. This 'cultural conflict' that Li reports could also be interpreted as a process for these Chinese parents to make sense of their own beliefs along with those they needed to adjust to and learn about in their new communities. Particularly, parents and adult family members continue to rely on their own previous experiences and expected their children to have similar experiences despite the new learning opportunities and experiences in the host community.

Identifying 'successful and/or unsuccessful' literacy practices in households and communities

Generally, research has revealed that when families engage in literacy practices as part of their household's activities, they have greater success in providing their children with literacy support that contributes to early success in school. In other words, it would seem, then, that the presence of 'traditional literacy' in the home always leads to early academic success (Rodgers and Rodgers, 2004). Here, 'literacy' means the ability to read for knowledge, write coherently, and think critically about printed material. It is important for the reader to keep in mind that traditional studies focus on successful literacy practices instead of on the populations most likely to experience difficulties in acquiring basic literacy skills (Rodgers and Rodgers, 2004). In other words, not all literacy practices in households are interpreted as 'successful.' In that sense, Del Valle (2002, 2005) provides examples of the 'successful' and 'unsuccessful' literacies of two Puerto Rican families in Chicago. This contrast between patterns of language, literacy, and learning in the homes of two families allows us to understand why literacy practices in households matter for fostering multiple literacies among young children. Specifically, it could be plausible that particular home literacy practices prepare children for academic success, whereas other home literacy practices do not lead children to academic success. Schooling attitudes, work, literacy as pastime, oral cultural traditions, or religious literacy can be issues that explain differences between contexts for literacy. That is to say, if literacy is a social practice, we need to identify particular uses of literacy in order to understand their efficacy.

According to Del Valle (2005) there are important differences between literacy patterns in the homes he analyzed that explain which kind of literacy environment can be better according to the immediate context. In some fundamental way, these contrasts are based on different economic situations and their relations to mainstream literacy practices. By 'mainstream literacy practices' it is meant the patterns in which 'children and adults are intensely and consistently involved in literacy events involving oral language in connection with learning from and about written texts' (Heath, 1983, p. 256).

In particular, mainstream practices are: 'school-oriented, aspiring to upward mobility through success in formal institutions, and looking beyond the primary networks of family and community for behavioural models and value orientations' (Heath, 1983, p. 392). We could argue that home literacy practices that are close to mainstream literacy practices support each other. It is important to emphasize that the mismatch between children's home cultures and the cultures of schools can play havoc with student achievement. In that sense, building on

Heath's work and Bronfenbrenner's (1979) ecological model, other researchers described the discontinuities that children from diverse backgrounds can experience between the worlds they know at home and the world of school (Ballenger, 1999; Ogbu, 1982). Navigation between two cultures (family and school) is not easy because the expectations that teachers have towards families are not always obvious or explicit, and the other way around as well. For example, immigrant children may find that they do not know how to show the teacher what they know in ways she/he can recognize. School mainstream culture, in contrast to a particular home culture, can be unfamiliar, confusing, chaotic, and strange, in sum: an uncomfortable place and often translates to school referring to these students as 'disadvantaged' children (McIntyre, Rosebery, and González, 2001; Tharp and Gallimore, 1993; Trumbull, Rothstein-Fish, Greenfield, and Quiroz, 2001). In that regard, Delpit (1995), for instance, refers to 'cultural conflict in the classroom' because sometimes children have to negotiate conflicting values in order to respond to family or school scenarios.

One way to organize the literature on discontinuities between literacy practices at home and literacy practices at school is through the way, the usage, the involvement, and the models held in regards to literacy. In that sense, we could distinguish between 'literacy way,' 'literacy usage,' 'literacy involvement,' and 'literacy models.' By 'literacy way' we mean the difference between oral and written literacy. If literacy practices at home are totally oral, or mostly oral, the transition to school will be harder because of the high value placed on written language (Cook-Gumperz and Gumperz, 1981). By 'literacy usage' we mean the kind of 'literacy repertoires' (Shuman, 1986) practiced by the participants. For example, school-related activities, entertainment, or religious activities are particular literacy events documented in children's homes (Reyes, Alexandra, and Azuara, 2007; Reyes and Azuara, 2008). By 'literacy involvement' we mean the frequency of literacy events in a particular home. Literacy involvement is high when families consistently read and discuss some book or paper, for example, the Bible. Finally, 'literacy models' refer to the oral testimonies about the values of reading and models of reading and writing behavior.

The ethnographic study conducted by Del Valle (2005) helps us illustrate these kinds of discontinuities (i.e., in the 'the literacy way,' 'the literacy usage,' 'the literacy involvement,' and the 'literacy models'). The families studied by Del Valle had similar patterns while living in Chicago, but in one family (Ana's) all members were constantly involved in literacy events inside and outside school. Consequently, the literacy way for Ana's family was to combine oral and written language. For instance, Ana receives and reads letters from relatives who live in Puerto Rico, translates documents in English, reads the magazine *Seventeen*, and also reads some of the same texts as her mother (for example, the Bible, a text shared by all her family members). In the same study, Del Valle did not see much evidence of Sandy's (another family he studied) participation in such communal or solitary literacy events. Therefore, the 'literacy involvement' was considered higher in Ana's home ('successful' literacy) than in Sandy's family ('unsuccessful' literacy). 'The consistent presence of recreational, personal, and religious literacy in Cristina's house (Ana's mother) contrasted with the ephemeral nature of literacy in the house of Jackie (Sandy's mother) and later in her own' (Del Valle, 2005, pp. 126–127).

Furthermore, Ana has oral testimonies about the values of reading and different models of reading and writing. For example, literacy models in Ana's family came from her grandfather, who performed a literacy service for the community through 'sung rosaries' and Ana's aunts, who completed college degrees. The value orientation and modeling ('the literacy models') for Sandy, in contrast, came from her older brothers who apparently were heavily involved in some illicit activities related to gangs. In that regard, Gregory, Ruby, and Kenner (2010) pointed out the relevance of 'subconscious modeling' that implicitly teach, when participants are involved in an informal and familiar situation, how to do something. To sum up, the examples described by Del Valle (2005) and others illustrate some 'successful' and 'unsuccessful' literacies. However, we warn researchers to consider carefully the various definitions for 'successful' and 'unsuccessful' and the context and space for meaning found in each community and the ways to distinguish among the four ways to interpret literacy that we have proposed.

Case Studies from Multiple Contexts

Case studies of multilingual communities in the Americas

There is an emergent set of studies focusing on multiple literacies among various diverse communities across Northern and Latin American countries. For example, Schecter and Bayley's (2002) study on bilingual socialization in the United States with Mexican families in Texas and California examined the role of language on different aspects of children's development (10–12 year olds) and the social spaces to which they assigned a symbolic value to the use of Spanish and English during their daily interactions. At home, many of the families used Spanish to discuss the importance of learning about their country of origin because they wanted to transmit to children where they have their family roots and the language that is used there. On the other hand, families use the dominant language, English, at school and in written homework assignments when interacting with their children as another literacy strategy. The reasons for this type of strategy vary, but in general parents decide to maintain the native language as the family language and English as the 'larger' community code. In places, like in Arizona or California, from a young age children identify English as the dominant language in the community and the one that dominates the discourse in the school context (Combs *et al.*, 2005; Tse, 2001).

The study by Faulstich Orellana (2009) reveals how immigrant children or children of immigrants make use of their linguistic 'tool kits' (Gutiérrez, Baquedano-López, and Tejeda, 1999) to assist and support their families to navigate and survive 'the systems' (e.g., educational, medical, financial). As these transactions required linguistic abilities in the dominant language, in this case English, children assist communicating important information on behalf of their parents. Children usually report enjoying this role, describing it almost as part of their regular 'homework'; however, with time, as they grow, they become aware and absorb the dominant perception that what they experienced growing up as part of their routines does not necessarily match the general early childhood experiences of children from non-immigrant families.

Studies also reveal that in some communities parents may not necessarily agree with school literacy practices or feel that their children are benefiting from the school experiences in the *way* they would like to see. The findings presented by Li (2006) on diverse families (including a Vietnamese, Sudanese, and working-class White family) growing up in Buffalo New York describe what she calls '*culturally contested*' literacy practices between home and school. Of particular interest is the apparent 'contrasting' value that families and teachers placed on various literacy practices (e.g., homework). Although both sides agreed that they are looking after the best of interest of the child, the parents, with various levels of English proficiency, are often left out or placed in a limited situation to contribute to their child's literacy activities. Vélez-Ibáñez and Greenberg (2005) have argued that this 'outside' home demand to shift from home languages to English fractures children's literacy development (Li, 2006, p. 164) because 'parents are unable to participate or participate effectively in the children's school work' (p. 165).

Another example reporting challenges in maintaining bilingualism and developing biliteracy comes from a Maya community where Azuara (2009) developed case studies with children and families. The language and literacy practices described by Azuara reflect a command of Spanish as the main language of young children while their parents or primary caregivers still spoke Maya (the local indigenous language) as the native language. One of the main findings that Azuara reports is the decrease in Maya fluency among children; the reason for this decrease was mostly due to pressure from school, peer culture, and the popular media to embrace Spanish and reject their indigenous family language. However, there were a few exceptions where children continue to use Maya to mediate their learning experiences at home, as in the case of Yadira:

(Maya shown in bold; Spanish shown in *italics*; translation in parenthesis):

YADIRA: **Quico je'el a carta'a** (Quico, here is your letter) [she hands her cousin the letter she wrote, the message is inside the envelope]

QUICO: #looks at the envelope confused# t**un** [tu'ux] **yan** [yaan]? (where is it?)

YADIRA: *leelo, leelo* (read it, read it)
          [takes the paper out of the envelope]
          si, jaj- ... *je'ela Quico* (here it is)

QUICO: **taache'** [taase'] (give it to me) #takes the paper #

YADIRA: #starts writing on another piece of paper# **in ka'aj in dzíibt u tia'al Carlitos beora'** (now I will write to César) ... *César ama a sus hermanas* (César loves his sisters)

CESAR: # he sees she is writing a letter to him and becomes curious, she looks at her paper# **ma'a beyo'** (is not like this) ... *y su hermanos* (and his brothers)

QUICO: *una caita* [carta] (a letter) #responds to César, explaining what Yadira is doing#

YADIRA: *Esto es para* ... *como se llama::* ... *después es para, nadien* [nadie] ... (this is for ... what is her name? Then, it is for no one) #gets a piece of paper and folds it to make an envelope # **tu** [tu'ux] **yaan le resistolo'?.. a k'almaj menso le beetik** (where is the glue? It is closed, silly, that is why) [grabs the glue from the table] no lo ha abrido [abierto] (it is not opened)

QUICO: #tries to open the glue# *a que chi* [sí] (it is)

YADIRA: #she commands Quico to read the letter to the researcher# *Leelo y lo oye* (read it and she will hear) #grabs the paper and directs to researcher# *dile a Patricia que lo lea, tú no sabes leer* (ask Patricia to read it because you do not know how to read)

QUICO: *Sí* (yes) #protesting in response to her comment#

YADIRA: **Masa'** [máasima'] **ma' a wojel xooki' Quico?** (you do not know how to read, right, Quico?)
          [she goes back to writing a letter to her other cousin]
          César ama a su papá (César loves his dad)
          [she says this while writing]

QUICO: [he gets frustrated and insulted by Yadira's comment] **Waay** [ba'ax] *cartai* [carta] **le ba'ala' ka'a in jatej?** (what is this letter? I will tear it)

YADIRA: Lee (read it)
          [grabs the paper and models how to read]
          Quico ama a su
          mamá, Quico ama a su papá, Quico ama a su ti prima, Quico ama a su tío ... *listo* (Quico loves his mom, Quico loves his dad, Quico loves his cousin, Quico loves his uncle ... done).

This example reveals Yadira's bilingual strategies and how she draws on her Maya and Spanish linguistic skills, using Maya in her interactions with her cousin Quico. As she writes a letter as part of this literacy event, Yadira is also mediating her sister and cousins' learning. 'She does not learn or use the languages, Spanish and Maya, as two independent identities; instead, each influenced the other' (Azuara and Reyes, 2011, p. 190).

Like other bilingual children and families throughout the Americas, indigenous language speakers find themselves torn between competing language practices at home and in the larger community, including the school (e.g., de la Piedra, 2006). Even though the children in our examples were living in bilingual (Spanish-English and Maya-Spanish, respectively) and bicultural communities, where they used the minority language during their daily life experiences, they had limited opportunities to develop literacy in that language as part of their formal educational and schooling experiences.

In sum, the studies reviewed here report variation in literacy activities, as well as in language socialization practices with respect to parents' cultural background and strategies to foster literacy and biliteracy development with children. Therefore, learning from immigrant parents' perspectives, who often have few economic resources but a wealth of social capital and literacy practices unrecognized outside their homes, is key to bridge knowledge to inform educators and to consider families' linguistic funds of knowledge to support children's learning experiences.

Case studies of multiple literacies in Europe

As in the Americas, diversity of languages and cultural backgrounds is a common reality in European societies – as everywhere else in the world. About one-third of the European population under the age of 35 years has an immigrant background (Gogolin, 2002). Indeed, immigration to Europe increased from the 1980s onward as a result of people's mobility all over the world. For instance, according to the Spanish government, there were 5.7 million foreign residents in Spain in 2011 (12.2 percent of the total population) that contrasts with 1981when there were only 198,042 (0.52 percent of the total population). According to residence permit data for 2011, around 860,000 were Romanians and 770,000 were Moroccan. Other important foreign communities in Spain are the British (around 390,000) and people from Ecuador (above 360, 000) (INE, 2011). According to EUROSTAT (2006), in 2005 Spain had the second highest immigration rates within the European Union, after Cyprus, and the second highest absolute net migration in the World, after the United States.

Immigration is an important cause of linguistic, ethnic, and cultural diversity in Europe, but it is not the only source for expanding the linguistic and cultural complexity within modern European societies. For example, mass and electronic media accelerate the dynamics of linguistic and cultural diversity. Moreover, there is a historical national diversity within countries. In Catalonia (Spain), for instance, non-Spanish immigrants represent an estimated 15 percent in 2011 – in 2000 there were only 181,590 people in Catalonia from other countries. Currently, more than 14 percent of the students have an immigrant origin and 8 percent of them have a mother tongue that is not one of the official languages of the host country, Catalan and Spanish. Moreover, the language of instruction at school is Catalan, but the majority language in the social context is Spanish. This bilingual situation is mixed with the multilingual reality resulting from recent immigration patterns.

Unfortunately, European educational systems, in general, and the Spanish education system in particular, do not adapt very well to the current realities and the immigration changes reflected in classroom communities. Therefore, educators are challenged by similar issues that educators in the United States and Latin American countries face in the school context. It seems that this diversity and national heterogenity serves, not as a means of innovation, but as a means of exclusion and unequal access (Gogolin, 2002). In general, 2009 PISA scores (Program for International Student Assessment) indicate that students from diverse cultural backgrounds (students from migration backgrounds) perform at a lower level than their national counterparts (OECD, 2010). It seems that in diverse European school systems, pupils with immigrant backgrounds are severely disadvantaged. It could be argued that these pupils from diverse cultural backgrounds are illiterate, and they have serious linguistic and cognitive deficits. However, reviews and analyses of student backgrounds all point to 'cultural misunderstandings' and discontinuities between home and school literacy practices (Li, 2006). Fortunately, as we will review next, there are now different examples of how immigrant students develop multiple literacies, and how they draw from the knowledge they bring from their ancestral homeland to adapt to their new host communities.

In Catalonia (Spain), for example, Saubich and Esteban-Guitart (2011) have recently documented several literacy practices and funds of knowledge from a Moroccan immigrant family. These skills and understandings are broad and diverse. Moroccan household knowledge may include information about farming and animal management, associated with the households' rural origins, knowledge about construction and building, related to urban occupations, as well as knowledge about many other matters, such as business, finance, religion, geography, history, politics, or art (for instance, the use of Henna, a plant used in Morocco and many other countries to dye the skin in intricate patterns, sometimes called temporary tattoos). In some ways, each family accumulates diverse bodies of knowledge developed from members' social histories (such as labor occupations) and from their everyday practice (González, Moll, and Amanti, 2005). Moreover, members of these families employ literacy in their daily activities, for example in religious practices. In that regard, the Islamic religion is articulated through the Qur'an, a text considered by its adherents to be the verbatim word of God. Muslim families read and repeat several times the Qur'an text; an important artifact involved in many literacy events. In host countries, parents and children tend to develop Arabic literacy as they participate in different interactions, mediated by religion, an important link to their culture and origins (Saubich and Esteban-Guitart, 2011). In these activities, as well as in community and after-school activities (Islamic religious classes), the native language and literacy are fostered, becoming important strategies for improving learning in the classroom (Reyes and Moll, 2008). Indeed, the community offers several opportunities to engage in literacy events.

For example, Poveda and colleagues examined storytelling and children's literature events in a public library, a park, and a children's bookstore in the city of Madrid (Casla, Poveda, Rujas, and Cuevas, 2008). In these informal educational settings, the storyteller produced multilingual, multimodal, and multimedia narratives, providing opportunities to engage with forms of literary discourse embedded in these specific social events. In contrast to home and school, storytelling events in urban informal settings are based on heterogeneous group interactions through various performers and styles, literary enjoyment being the basic rationale for the event. It is, therefore, not a family routine with a stable parental style and mostly dyadic interactions, nor part of a formal curriculum with a stable teaching style within homogeneous group interactions (Casla *et al.*, 2008). In light of these differences, Poveda *et al.* (2007) pay attention to storytelling and other after-school activities and routines regarding literacy in contexts beyond families and classrooms to examine the specific narrative affordances these contexts may offer children.

For example, in the library there is an interactional strategy the researchers coded as 'cognitively challenging talk,' which is used often in the classroom as well. This point is illustrated by a storyteller, who for this session appears on stage in the library dressed as an 'eggplant.' In this situation, the teacher who role-plays an eggplant (*Berenjena* in Spanish) introduces herself and interacts with the children using indirect and direct challenges, which have cognitive implications because they require children to move beyond common associations in order to make meaning. That is to say, children have to build inferences (to make links) between particular vegetables and traits of the audience. In this case, the library is located in a middle-class residential district, and the storytelling event took place in the library's auditorium, outside school hours (on Saturday morning).

Participants are children and middle-class families from Madrid
(Translation is shown in parenthesis)

1   **Berenjena** (Eggplant): ¡Hola, yo soy Berenjena! ¿qué tal? (Eggplant: Hello, my name is Egg-plant! how are you?)
    [Short silence]
2   **Niño1** (Child1): Bien (fine)
3   **Niños** (Children): Bien (fine) [several children respond at a time]
    [The narrator looks at a child and talks to him]
4   **Berenjena** (Eggplant): Tú tienes toda la cara de llamarte Pepino
    (You look like you're called Cucumber) [group laughter and comments in the audience]
5   **Berenjena** (Eggplant): Pepino eres ¿no? ¡Ah no, perdón! ¡Pepino eres tú! (Ah! Cucumber you are, right? Oh no, sorry! You are Cucumber!)
6   **Niño2** (Child2): ¡No! (No!)
7   **Berenjena** (Eggplant): Tomate eres tú (You are Tomato!)
8   **Niño2** (Child2): No (No!)
9   **Berenjena** (Eggplant): ¿No? No importa ¿Pues cómo os llamáis? (No? It doesn't matter, so what is your name?)
10 **Niño3** (Child3): Yo, Jorge (I'm Jorge)
11 **Niña** (Child): Sandra (Sandra)
12 **Niños** (Children): [Several children shout their names at the same time]
13 **Berenjena** (Eggplant): ¡Hala! (Wow!)
14 **Niños** (Children): [The children continue shouting their names]
15 **Berenjena** (Eggplant): ¡Qué nombres más raros! ¿Cómo? (What strange names! What?)
16 **Niño4** (Child4): XXX
17 **Berenjena** (Eggplant): ¡Ernesto! (Ernesto!)
    [They go on shouting their names and she repeats them]
18 **Berenjena** (Eggplant): Bonitos pero raros ¿Aquí no hay ninguna Lechuga? (Nice [names], but strange, is there a Lettuce in here?)
19 **Niños** (Children): [Some children give different unintelligible answers]
20 **Berenjena** (Eggplant): Ni ningún Tomate, nada (a Tomato neither, nothing)
21 **Niño1** (Child1): ¡No! (No!)

(Casla *et al.*, 2008, p. 49).

Through these kinds of stories, children are exposed to the values, norms, categories, restrictions, and patterns of behavior using specific linguistic patterns and resources that could be distinct from other contexts such as school or daily usages of language. To sum up, storytelling events could be considered organized occasions for socialization into a literacy and literary culture (Casla *et al.*, 2008; Poveda *et al.*, 2007).

Another example of multiple literacies from Europe is provided by Gregory, Kenner and colleagues in the city of London (e.g., Gregory, 2001; Kenner and Gregory, in press). It is important to note that over 300 languages were spoken in London schools in the first decade of the twenty-first century. Specifically, Gregory and colleagues have studied learning processes in the homes of third-generation migrants to the United Kingdom (Gregory, Ruby, and Kenner, 2010). Indeed, these scholars have been studying the literacies of families and communities in East London for over 15 years, from 1994 until the present (e.g., Gregory, 2001; Gregory, Long, and Volk, 2004). The project is based on ethnographic research strategies that provide rich and emic descriptions of literacy activities in homes and communities. These studies, conducted in this multicultural setting of Europe, permit us to illustrate the concept of syncretism that we introduced previously. Specifically, it shows the way in which different cultural belief systems come together. The following excerpt, in Bengali and English, illustrates this point (in italics; translation into English in square brackets):

1   **Maya:** *Er phore... er phorer* letter *khonta nanu?* (next... and next what is the next letter nanu?) [Maya looks to Anayet then to the computer, learning forward and pointing to the keyboard. The toddler also leans forward and looks at the keyboard]

2   **Maya:** *Nanure dekho sain... tomar namor* [show nanu... your name's] (Maya looks to and from Anayet and the computer and the toddler does the same)

3   **Anayet:** 'E'... 'E' (Anayet makes the phonetic sound)

4   **Maya:** 'E'

5   **Anayet:** 'E' *khoi?* [Where is 'E'] (Anayet looks at the screen, both Maya and Anayet look for the letter together, Maya leans towards the keyboard)

6   **Maya:** 'E' *dekho sain... eh... eta khita?* 'E' *nanu dei, nanu dei... ah hoise?* [Look for 'E'... yes... what is that?] (Toddler and Maya look at the keyboard and Anayet looks at the screen. Both Anayet and Maya point to the keyboard, Anayet presses 'E,' Maya leans back satisfied)

7   **Maya:** *eh eta hoise eta* right [yes that is right]

8   **Anayet:** No... (Anayet makes a sound)

9   **Maya:** *er phore khon* letter? [What letter is after that?]

10 **Anayet:** 'A'... (Anayet looks around on the keyboard searching, toddler looks distracted but Maya gently pulls her back while keeping full attention on Anayet)

11 **Maya:** A-N-A-Y-E-T (Anayet says slowly)

12 (Anayet presses some keys on the keyboard looking to and from the keyboard to the screen; his lips shape out the letters he is typing)

13 **Maya:** *er phore khon* letter *nanu?* [What letter is after that *nanu?*]

14 **Maya:** 'T'

15 **Anayet:** (Anayet presses 'T,' smiles and sits back away from the computer) 'T'... I did it (all three are looking at the screen)'

(Excerpt from Gregory, Ruby, and Kenner, 2010, p. 168).

This situation describes a literacy event around a computer, involving the grandmother and her two grandchildren. Anayet is learning to write his name assisted by Maya, his grandmother. Anayet's cousin is sitting on Maya's lap watching closely the interaction between Anayet and Maya. In this example, the grandmother aims to teach the children in a collective way, that is to say, focusing on a socio-affective orientation emphasizing the collective solidarity of traditional societies. However, she focuses on the individual, as well, showing the presence of the academic and cognitive Western way of teaching. In other words, according to Gregory, Ruby and Kenner (2010), this situation illustrates empirically how two belief systems come together. First, the academic and cognitive orientation focusing on the individual (Western way of teaching), Maya, as any teacher would, showing how to succeed in the task, challenging Anayet's performance. Second, the socio-affective orientation emphasizing the collective solidarity of traditional societies (traditional way of teaching) is also present. Maya creates a comfortable space to include the children, both Anayet and her cousin, as active observers of the task, by using Bengali to mediate this learning experience. In summary, the above excerpt informs us about the notion of syncretism because it illustrates how different cultural repertoires from their heritage country (represented by Maya) and strategies borrowed from the host country combine to form mixed literacy ways. Indeed, in their volume about 'Syncretic literacies studies,' referenced above, Gregory, Long and Volk (2004) show how children live and learn actively in 'simultaneous worlds'

(Kenner, 2004), multicultural schools, families and communities, developing syncretic strategies produced by linguistic and cultural diversity rapidly increased along with globalization processes.

Multiple Literacies in Supporting Community Settings

As discussed above, beyond school and family, there are other settings that provide skills connected with literacy. In this section, we move beyond these two settings to understand the broader socio-cultural and historical contexts in which literacies are constructed. Indeed, any community offers activities, as mediators, to teach children the competencies they will need to participate fully in their communities and society. These contexts can complement or extend what people do and learn both at home and at school, and are important because they connect people to their society and culture. For example, religion connects people to a particular cultural heritage. As Farr (2005) pointed out, 'conversion to and membership in these religions (Judaism, Christianity, and Islam) involves literacy abilities... practicing the religions of the book also frequently involves literacy abilities' (pp. 307–308).

Grounded in an ecological perspective (Bronfenbrenner, 1979), Acosta-Iriqui and Esteban-Guitart (2010) delineated four types of nested 'educational resources' that can be considered artifacts involved in teaching-learning activities. Traditionally, educational resources have been reduced to a few instruments such as a manual or textbook, a notebook or black/whiteboard, which can be considered 'micro-educational-resources.' However, a socio-cultural approach suggests that our physical geography (people, objects, and symbols around us) also has psychological and educational value (Esteban-Guitart, 2011). As we described, there is a considerable number of literacy practices evident in homes and communities, consequently the family is a context for critical learning, representing the 'micro-educational-resource' in the interaction between family members. On the other hand, parent and teacher interaction represent the 'meso-educational-resource' that occurs within an institutional space. Moreover, there are external environments, such as parental workplaces, which indirectly influence development for a son or daughter; this is an example, in ecological terms, of an 'exo-educational-resource.' These types of resources often have implications for the adoption of tools that children translate for use, or not, during family literacy practices (Azuara and Reyes, 2011).

Finally, the larger socio-cultural context designs and impacts any teaching and learning context. Religion, ideologies, policies, or laws are examples of 'macro-educational-resources.' It is in the micro systems (such as school, family, workplace) that most direct interactions with social agents take place: parents, peers, teachers, and colleagues. However, we have to take into account connections between contexts, for example, school experiences and church experiences, links between a social setting in which the individual does not have an active role (for example a child's experience at home may be influenced by a mother's experiences at work), and the macro-culture in which individual's live (e.g., socioeconomic status, poverty, educational laws, ethnicity, religion and so on).

Another recent example, provided by Gregory *et al.* (in press), is about the impact of one key sacred text in children's literacy learning in different communities in London (Bangladeshi British Muslim, Tamil Hindu, Ghanaian Pentecostal, and Polish Catholic). We could consider these sacred texts as an example of 'macro-educational-resources' and the interaction between religion and school as a 'meso-educational-resource' (Acosta-Iriqui and Esteban-Guitart, 2010).

Through multiple literacy strategies, such as song, dance, gesture, repetition, recitation, memorization, and echoing, children actively 'gormandize' or consume practices and internalize texts. For example, the Hail Mary Prayer in Polish culture combines biblical, religious, historical, and political aspects. The recitation of this prayer takes place individually, in intimate family groups, with peers and adults. It is an artifact that members use to become a member of a Polish faith community. Another literacy artifact valued, in this instance by the Muslim community, is the Qur'an (Gregory *et al.*, in press; Saubich and Esteban-Guitart, 2011). Children are expected to learn from as young as six or seven to recite excerpts (such as 'Surah Fatihah,' the opening chapter of the Qur'an) several times in a day during prayer time. In order to become a member of a Muslim community, children attend Arabic classes from the age of six. These classes consist of memorizing the text through repetition that is supervised and guided by a Mesab (the Arabic teacher) and Imam (who recite while children are listening). Children read each verse over and over again and listen to the teachers, following and imitating them. In London, children learn the verses in small groups. Teachers correct in English but the recitation and memorization take place in Arabic (Gregory *et al.*, in press).

Clearly, practicing religion involves literacy abilities (Farr, 2005). In another study, Poveda, Cano and Palomares-Valera (2005) analyzed connections between the oral genres displayed by Spanish Gypsy (Gitano) children during religious classes ('*escuela dominical*') organized and developed on Saturday mornings at an Evangelist church, and the writings produced by Gitano children in an after-school computer program organized several evenings a week by a Gitano cultural association. This study also shows how religious practices impact literacy. The researchers analyzed connections between genres of use in the two contexts. Although the content, structure, and topic of the texts written by children varied significantly (for example, personal letters, religious texts, love letters), the most frequent references in these literacy events were to religious themes, which appeared in 37 percent of the texts. These texts are not a simple, transcribed version of oral religion presentations but instructional sessions at an Evangelist church that provided the main generic grid for religious written texts. For instance, religious writings have in common with the oral versions a rhetorical structure based on parallelism and religious openings or the organization of the text divided into lines (verses and stanzas). In these texts, oral and written modes are mixed with each other, creating combinations between both registers.

Another example is provided by McMillon and Edwards (2005). The authors discussed the literacy learning of 4- to 6-year-old children in an African American church, a cultural context within which many literacy skills (emergent reading and reading competencies including print awareness, concepts of print, sightreading, vocabulary building, comprehension and application and oral language development) are acquired and developed through the learning of Bible stories and memorizing of scriptures.

Beyond school and family scenarios, religious settings are an important place and activity through which people acquire literacy, however, it is not the only one. More recently, other modes and contexts such as the Internet and mass media, e-libraries, and bookstores, are other contexts for living that also involve literacy abilities. These contexts represent educational resources that can be used by schools and families, becoming 'meso-educational-resources' and 'meso-intercultural-geographies,' settings in which participants acquire educational artifacts through the synergy of different contexts for learning (Esteban-Guitart, 2011). An example is the project 'Interweaving cultures' conducted in Salt (Girona, Spain) by the 'culture and education' research group at University of Girona, a nonprofit entity GRAMC (action research group for cultural minorities and foreign workers), and the Massagran library (Salt, Girona). The general purpose of this project is to preserve the heritage and culture of immigrant people in Catalonia through recognition of their oral culture. In doing so, a bilingual book is created that compiles several legends and stories from Africa (Oller, 2011). African mothers, with their daughters and sons, attend the Massagran library in order to explain these stories in their mother tongues. Afterwards, these stories are translated into Catalan. It is a significant activity that brings together immigrant families, volunteers from GRAMC entity and the University, and library members in order to extend biliteracy.

Conclusion and Implications for Future Research and Practice

A common finding across studies is that literacy learning is a social process through which meaning is negotiated when learners are engaged with more knowledgeable others in meaningful transactions with texts. (Gregory, Long, and Volk, 2004, p. 14)

Various contexts of children's life such as religious, school, home, and after school settings are spaces for learning and developing literacy. As we have argued, literacy is a socially and culturally co-constructed practice associated with different domains of life, historically situated, and embedded in larger cultural and community practices. People, through daily life and socially mediated and guided processes, participate in these literacy practices that provide resources for their development and for becoming a member of social groups that allow children and their families 'access' to various resources in their communities. We should pay attention to community literacy as sites that contribute to and expand the acquisition of literacy in formal education institutions. In that regard, libraries can support the acquisition of school-like reading and writing. Moreover, multiple forms of literacy coexist and vary within and across naturalistic settings in homes, schools, and communities. Although school-identified literacy is usually privileged, other forms of literacy and mediators, mostly 'invisible' to educators, are relevant and necessary to understand completely the literacy phenomenon (Gregory, Long, and Volk, 2004).

The vast majority of research projects have focused on schools as the site where literacy takes place, on monolingual communities, and on literate societies that privilege written as opposed to oral language. In the present chapter we have moved away from the traditional view of 'literacy' as the development of linguistic strategies in regard to reading and writing. Inspired by socio-cultural and ecological frameworks, we redefine literacy as the linguistic forms and meaning developed through interactions among individuals in several domains of activity, and in different places and situations (Casla *et al.*, 2008; Edwards, McMillion, and Turner, 2010; Farr, Seloni, and Song, 2009; Gregory, Long, and Volk, 2004; Reyes and Moll, 2008). In addition biliteracy and multiple literacies are here taken as the 'normal' practice when communities learn how to effectively translate these 'resources' into tools for children and their families to exchange knowledge and values. It is a move from a singular to multiple pathways to literacy.

According to the syncretic literacy studies reviewed above, children and adults transform culture actively to create new forms of literacies. For example, using a funds of knowledge approach, teachers integrate family resources, such as religion or family labor experiences, into classroom activities (e.g., González, Moll, and Amanti, 2005; Saubich and Esteban-Guitart, 2011). Moreover, rather than viewing children's learning as mostly the result of participation in formal, schooled learning, these studies focus on socio-cultural situations in which children, guided by more experienced others, are introduced into literacy practices, languages and resources. This understanding is crystallized by Street (1995, p. 2):

The concept of 'literacy practice' is pitched at a higher level of abstraction and refers to both behavior and the social and cultural conceptualizations that give meaning to the uses of reading and/or writing. Literacy practices incorporate not only 'literacy events,' as empirical occasions to which literacy is integral, but also folk models of those events and the ideological preconceptions that underpin them.

In that sense, ethnographic research in homes, workplaces, libraries, or religious organizations is needed to understand contemporary pluralingualism and multiple literacies (Baquedano-López, 1997). An important topic is the language ideologies that explain the persistence of a particular literacy practice and the official language policy underlying it. As Farr (2011) argues using the 'linguistic markets' concept, the English language represents the symbolic capital of globalization and it is promoted by public policies, mass media, and particular language ideologies. Further research is needed to illustrate how these macro-cultural factors (Esteban-Guitart and Ratner, 2011; Ratner, 2012) impact human behavior, in general, and literacy practices, in particular. It is important to note here that literacy is embedded in specific social events, associated with different domains of life, and also historically situated and embedded in larger cultural practices dominated by macro-cultural factors such as power relationships and social institutions that privilege certain literacy practices, discourses, and ideologies.

Following a socio-cultural, ecological, and syncretic approach to literacy, we have taken into account multiple sites for literacy practices and multiple paths to literacy learning in bilingual and multicultural settings, privileging both written and oral traditions in several modes: electronic, paper, gestures. The main purpose of this line of research is to show the diversity of ways in which communities organize their daily lives and offer resources to mediate language and literacy learning as dynamic parts of cultural practices.

References

Acosta-Iriqui, J., and Esteban-Guitart, M. (2010) Geografías de los recursos educativos. *Educación y Desarrollo Social*, 2: 119–129.

Azuara, P. (2009) Literacy practices in a changing cultural context: The literacy development of two emergent Mayan-Spanish bilingual children. Unpublished doctoral dissertation, University of Arizona.

Azuara, P., and Reyes, I. (2011) Negotiating worlds: A young Mayan child developing literacy at home and at school in Mexico. *Compare: A Journal of Comparative and International Education*, 41(2): 181–194.

Ballenger, C. (1999) *Teaching Other People's Children: Literacy and Learning in a Bilingual Classroom*. New York: Teachers College Press.

Baquedano-Loópez, P. (1997) Creating social identities through *doctrina* narratives. *Issues in Applied Linguistics*, 8(1): 27–45.

Bronfenbrenner, U. (1979) *The Ecology of Human Development*. Cambridge, MA: Harvard University Press.

Casla, M., Poveda, D., Rujas, I., and Cuevas, I. (2008) Literary voices in interaction in urban storytelling events for children. *Linguistics and Education*, 19: 37–55.

Combs, M., Evans, C., Fletcher, T., *et al.* (2005) Bilingualism for the children: Implementing a dual-language program in an English-only state. *Educational Policy*, 19(5): 701–728.

Cook-Gumperz, J., and Gumperz, J.J. (1981) From oral to written culture: The transition to literacy. In M.F. Whitehead (ed.) *Variation in Writing: Functional and Linguistic-Cultural Differences*. Norwood, NJ: Ablex, pp. 89–109.

de la Piedra, M. (2006) Literacies and Quechua oral language: Connecting sociocultural worlds and linguistic resources for biliteracy development. *Journal of Early Childhood Literacy*, 6(3): 383–306.

Del Valle, T. (2002) *Written Literacy Features of Three Puerto Rican Family Networks in Chicago*. New York: Edwin Mellen.

Del Valle, T. (2005) 'Successful' and 'unsuccessful' literacies of two Puerto Rican families in Chicago. In M. Farr (ed.) *Latino Language and Literacy in Ethnolinguistic Chicago*. Mahwah, NJ: Lawrence Erlbaum, pp. 97–131.

Delpit, L. (1995) *Other People's Children: Cultural Conflict in the Classroom*. New York: New Press.

Duranti, A., and Ochs, E. (1997) Syncretic literacy in a Samoan American family. *NATO ASI Series. Series F, Computer and System Sciences*, 160: 169.

Dworin, J.E. (2003) Insights into biliteracy development: Toward a bidirectional Theory of bilingual pedagogy. *Journal of Hispanic Higher Education*, 2(2): 171–186.

Edwards, P.A., McMillion, G.M., and Turner, J.D. (2010) *Change is Gonna Come: Transforming Literacy Education for African American Students*. New York: Teachers College Press.

Esteban-Guitart, M. (2011) La geografía vital y psicológica de la interculturalidad. *Cuadernos Interculturales*, (9): 33–44.

Esteban-Guitart, M., and Ratner, C. (2011) A macro cultural psychological theory of identity. *Journal of Social Distress*, 20: 1–22.

EUROSTAT (2006) *Population in Europe in* 2005. Luxembourg: European Communities.

Farr, M. (2005) Literacy and religion: Reading, writing, and gender among Mexican women in Chicago. In M. Farr (ed.) *Latino Language and Literacy in Ethnolinguistic Chicago*. Mahwah, NJ: Lawrence Erlbaum Associates, pp. 305–322.

Farr, M. (2011) Urban plurilingualism: Language practices, policies, and ideologies in Chicago. *Journal of Pragmatics*, 43: 1161–1172.

Farr, M., Seloni, L., and Song, J. (2009) *Ethnolinguistic Diversity and Education: Language, Literacy, and Culture*. London: Routledge.

Faulstich Orellana, M. (2009) *Translating Childhoods: Immigrant Youth, Language, and Culture*. New Brunswick, N.J: Rutgers University Press.

Freire, P. (1970) *Pedagogy of the Oppressed*. New York: Herder and Herder.

Gogolin, I. (2002) Linguistic and cultural diversity in Europe: A challenge for educational research and practice. *European Educational Research Journal*, 1: 123–138.

González, N., Moll, L.C., and Amanti, K. (2005) *Funds of Knowledge: Theorizing Practices in Households, Communities, and Classrooms*. Mahwah, NJ: Lawrence Erlbaum Associates.

Gregory, E. (2001) Sisters and brothers as language and literacy teachers: Synergy between siblings playing and working together. *Journal of Early Childhood Literacy*, 13: 301–322.

Gregory, E., Choudhury, H., Ilankuberan, A., *et al.* (in press) Practice, performance and perfection: Learning sacred texts in four faith communities in London. *International Journal of the Sociology of Language*.

Gregory, E., Long, S., and Volk, D. (2004) *Many Pathways to Literacy. Young Children Learning with Siblings, Grandparents, Peers and Communities*. New York and London: Routledge Falmer.

Gregory, E., Ruby, M., and Kenner, C. (2010) Modelling and close observations: Ways of teaching and learning between third generation Bangladeshi British children and their grandparents in London. *Early Years*, 30: 161–173.

Guerra, J.C., and Farr, M. (2002) Writing on the margins: the spiritual and autobiographical discourse of two Mexicanas in Chicago. In G.A. Hulland and K. Schultz (eds) *School's Out: Bridging out-of-school Literacies with Classroom Practice*. New York: Teachers College Press.

Gutiérrez, K., Baquedano-López, P., and Tejeda, C. (1999) Rethinking diversity: Hybridity and hybrid language practices in the third space. *Mind, Culture, and Activity*, 6(4): 286–303.

Heath, S.B. (1983) *Ways with Words: Language, Life, and Work in Communities and Classrooms*. New York: Cambridge University Press.

Hornberger, N.H. (1989) Continua of biliteracy. *Review of Educational Research*, 59(3): 271–296.

Hornberger, N.H., and Skilton-Sylvester, E. (2000) Revisiting the continua of biliteracy: International and Critical Perspectives. *Language and Education*, 14(2): 96–122.

INE (Instituto Nacional de Estadísticas) (2011) *Sondeo de población*. Madrid: Instituto Nacional de Estadística.

Kenner, C. (2004) Living in simultaneous worlds: difference and integration in bilingual script learning. *International Journal of Bilingual Education and Bilingualism*, (7): 43–61.

Kenner, C., and Gregory, E. (in press) Becoming biliterate. In N. Hall, J. Larson, and J. Marsh (eds) *Handbook of Early Childhood Literacy*. London: Sage.

Li, G. (2006) Biliteracy and trilingual practices in the home contexts: Case studies of Chinese-Canadian children. *Journal of Early Childhood Literacy*, 6(3): 355–382.

McIntyre, E., Rosebery, A., and González, N. (2001) *Classroom Diversity. Connecting Curriculum to Students' Lives.* Porstmouth, NH: Heinemann.

McMillon, G.T., and Edwards, P.A. (2005) The African American church. A beacon of light on the pathway to literacy for African American children. In E. Gregory, S. Long, and D. Volk (eds) *Many Pathways to Literacy.* London: Routledge Falmer, pp. 181–194.

OECD (Organization for Economic Co-operation and Development) (2010) *PISA 2009. What Students Know and Can Do: Student Performance in Reading, Mathematics and Science. Compares the Knowledge and Skills of Students across Countries.* Paris: OECD.

Ogbu, J. (1982) Cultural discontinuities and schooling. *Anthropological and Educational Quarterly*, 13: 290–307.

Oller, J. (comp.) (2011) *Teixint cultures: Contes africans per a petits i grans.* Girona: GRAMC.

Poveda, D., Cano, A., and Palomares-Valera, M. (2005) Religious genres, entextualization and literacy in Gitano children. *Language and Society*, 34: 87–115.

Poveda, D., Casla, M., Messina, C., *et al.* (2007) The after school routines of literature-devoted urban children. *Children's Geographies*, 54: 423–441.

Ratner, C. (2012) *Macro Cultural Psychology: A Political Philosophy of Mind.* New York: Oxford University Press.

Relaño Pastor, A.M. (2005) The language socialization experiences of Latina mothers in southern California. In A.C. Zentella (ed.) *Building on Strength: Language and Literacy in Latino Families and Communities.* New York: Teachers College Press.

Reyes, I. (2009) An ecological perspective on minority and majority language and literacy communities in the Americas. *Colombian Linguistic Applied Journal*, 11(1): 106–114.

Reyes, I. (2011) Literacy practices and language ideologies of first generation Mexican immigrant parents. In K. Potowski and J. Rothman (eds) *Bilingual Youth: Spanish in English-Speaking Societies.* Amsterdam: John Benjamins.

Reyes, I., Alexandra, D., and Azuara, P. (2007) Home literacy practices in Mexican households. *Cultura y Educación*, 19(4): 395–407.

Reyes, I., and Azuara, P. (2008) Emergent biliteracy in young Mexican immigrant children. *Reading Research Quarterly*, 43: 374–398.

Reyes, I., and Moll, L.C. (2008) Bilingual and biliterate practices at home and school. In B. Spolsky and F.M. Hult (eds) *The Handbook of Educational Linguistics.* Malden, MA: Blackwell Publishing, pp. 147–160.

Rodgers, A., and Rodgers, E.M. (2004) *Scaffolding Literacy Instruction.* Portsmouth, NH: Heinemann.

Rogoff, B. (2003) *The Cultural Nature of Human Development.* Oxford: Oxford University Press.

Saubich, X., and Esteban-Guitart, M. (2011) Funds of family knowledge go to school: The 'Living Morocco' project (العيش بالمغرب') *REMIE. Multidisciplinary Journal of Educational Research*, 1: 79–103.

Schecter, S.R., and Bayley, R. (2002) *Language as Cultural Practice: Mexicanos en el norte.* Mahwah, NJ: Lawrence Erlbaum.

Schieffelin, B.B., Woolard, K.A., and Kroskrity, P.V. (1998) *Language Ideologies: Practice and Theory.* New York: Oxford University Press.

Scribner, S., and Cole, M. (1981) *The Psychology of Literacy.* Cambridge, MA: Harvard University Press.

Shuman, A. (1986) *Storytelling Rights: The Uses of Oral and Written Texts by Urban Adolescents.* New York: Cambridge University Press.

Street, B.V. (1995) *Social Literacies: Critical Approaches to Literacy in Development, Ethnography and Education.* New York: Longman.

Taylor, D. (1983) *Family Literacy.* Exeter, NH: Heinemann.

Tharp, R., and Gallimore, R. (1993) *Rousing Minds to Life: Teaching, Learning and Schooling in Social Context.* New York: Cambridge University Press.

Trumbull, E., Rothstein-Fish, C., Greenfield, P.M., and Quiroz, B. (2001) *Bridging Cultures. Between Home and School.* Mahwah, NJ: Lawrence Erlbaum.

Tse, L. (2001) *'Why Don't They Learn ENGLISH?': Separating fact from fallacy in the U.S. language debate.* New York: Teachers College Press.

Vélez-Ibáñez, C., and Greenberg, J. (2005) Formation and transformation of funds of knowledge. In N. González, L.C. Moll, and C. Amanti (eds) *Funds of Knowledge: Theorizing Practice in Households, Communities, and Classrooms.* Mahwah, NJ: Lawrence Erlbaum.

Vygotsky, L.S. (1978) *Mind in Society: The Development of Higher Psychological Processes* (M. Cole, V. John-Steiner, S. Scribner, and E. Souberman, eds). Cambridge: Harvard University Press.

Chapter 13

Funds of Knowledge in Changing Communities

Luis C. Moll, Sandra L. Soto-Santiago, and Lisa Schwartz

Introduction

It has been over 20 years since we started research on 'funds of knowledge' in relation to a concern with the literacy education of Latino,[1] mostly Mexican-American, children in the US southwest (e.g., Moll and Greenberg, 1990; Tapia, 1991; Vélez-Ibáñez and Greenberg, 1992). We summarized much of the work of those years in an edited volume by González, Moll, and Amanti (2005), as well as in several other publications (e.g., Moll and González, 2004; González, Wyman, and O'Connor, 2011). The approach we followed, involving close collaboration with teachers as co-researchers and using ethnographic-like household observations and interviews with household members, appears to have been well received in the field. It has become a standard reference to signal a 'socio-cultural' orientation in education that seeks to build strategically on the experiences, resources, and knowledge of families and children, especially those from low-income neighborhoods (e.g., Hogg, 2011). So the work we initiated in Tucson, Arizona, has come to inspire research and practice in many other locations (e.g., Casper, 2011; Cremin *et al.*, 2012; Esteban-Guitart and Vila, 2012; Hedges, 2012).

The central idea, for readers unfamiliar with this work, is that families, especially those in the working-class, who have been our particular focus of study, can be characterized by the practices they have developed and knowledge they have produced and acquired in the living of their lives. The social history of families, and their productive or labor activities in both the primary and secondary sector of the economy, are particularly salient because they reveal experiences (e.g., in farming, construction, gardening, household maintenance, or secretarial work) that generate much of the knowledge household members may possess, display, elaborate, or share with others.

It is also the case that household subsistence may involve establishing and participating in social networks, often with kin, through which such funds of knowledge may be exchanged in addressing some of life's necessities. For example, in a mundane *quid pro quo*, one might help a neighbor fix a car, because one has the required knowledge and experience as an auto mechanic, and the neighbor incurs an obligation to reciprocate and help paint one's house, a task that is within his or her areas of expertise. Notice, then, that the exchange here is not of

International Handbook of Research on Children's Literacy, Learning, and Culture, First Edition.
Edited by Kathy Hall, Teresa Cremin, Barbara Comber, and Luis C. Moll.
© 2013 John Wiley & Sons, Ltd. Published 2013 by John Wiley & Sons, Ltd.

capital for labor, as in commercial transactions; it is an exchange in another currency, that of funds of knowledge, hence the metaphor. One could say, then, that funds of knowledge in a particular household or in a network of households may form part of a broader (non-monetary) household economy.

Thus this type of research, especially if conducted in collaboration with teachers, provides an opportunity to (a) initiate relations of trust with families to enable discussion of their practices and funds of knowledge; (b) document these lived experiences and knowledge that may prove useful in defining households, individually and collectively, as having ample resources or assets that may be valuable for instruction; and (c) establish discursive settings with teachers to prepare them theoretically, methodologically, and analytically to do the research, and to assess the utility of the findings for classroom practice (González, Moll, and Amanti, 2005).

In other words, the knowledge base one can accrue through this approach to households can be treated pedagogically as *bona fide* cultural resources for teaching and learning in schools. It represents, one could say, an opportunity for teachers, as part and parcel of their pedagogy, to identify and establish the 'educational capital' of families often assumed to be lacking any such resources.

The goal of the present chapter, however, is not to recapitulate work previously done, but to offer some reflections on the need to continue elaborating a funds of knowledge approach, or any such approach that depicts students and families, in response to changes in the participants' social conditions for living. We concentrate on two examples; both show different responses to current adverse circumstances and the resilience and resources needed to deal with these adversities. In doing so, we emphasize a 'processual' understanding of funds of knowledge, and of the dynamic, evolving practices that produce such knowledge.

The first involves family strategies for coping with changes in immigration laws that threaten household stability, security, and integrity. These conditions also necessitate that families generate new funds of knowledge for survival and advancement. In this particular case, drawn from the work of Soto-Santiago (Moll and Soto-Santiago, 2010) we highlight the transnational experiences of a young and mobile student trying to cope with going to school, almost simultaneously, in the US and Mexico as a survival strategy to ensure her educational future (c.f., Hamann, Zúñiga, and Sánchez García, 2006).

The second case example, drawn from research by Schwartz (2011), captures the development of students' funds of knowledge in digital spaces. This case, featuring a student also profoundly affected by adverse immigration dynamics, is a clear example of the need to document, not only the adults' experiences but also the knowledge and networks produced by children, in this instance, as they work to innovate with new technologies.

A Changing Understanding of Families: Vulnerability and Livelihood

Although the original research projects on funds of knowledge included mostly (but certainly not exclusively) immigrant and second-generation Mexican households in southern Arizona (e.g., Tapia, 1991), we did not seek to theorize immigrant families per se. However, in many of the households, families were often in close contact with their relatives in Mexico, mostly in Sonora, the state that borders Arizona. Several families certainly lived 'transnationally,' as is common in this borderlands region (Vélez-Ibáñez, 1996; Vélez-Ibáñez and Sampaio, 2002), including frequent trips to towns in Sonora to meet with family members and friends, take or bring goods for sale, or to work, among other purposes. Other families had weaker ties, depending on their social history and legal status, concentrating their activities and social networks on the US side of the border.

Researching the family activities in context, therefore, usually involved some documentation of their moves from one location to another and what they learned in the process. However, forms of transnationalism have changed radically since we undertook our research, mainly in response to severe immigration restrictions, as we shall explain. It is this emphasis on providing an understanding of how families cope with changing social, economic, and political circumstances that we want to highlight here.

González and colleagues (2011) have recently proposed a 'livelihood vulnerability approach,' borrowing from work on food security, and other risks, such as calamities, in developing countries, which examines both the household and its larger social and political context (e.g., von Kotze, 2002). The intent is to couple the ethnographic approach to funds of knowledge with how families respond to 'vulnerabilities,' difficult challenges for living that impact children and their parents. As they explain, 'household vulnerability can be analyzed on various levels and separated into external and internal factors that compromise a household's capacity to absorb and recover from particular risks and shocks. Coping strategies differ from everyday livelihood strategies (although they may become daily livelihood activities) in that they may require substantial trade-offs, increase risk, and constrain long-term responses and adaptation, and are undertaken under duress as short-term responses to a crisis' (p. 6).

From this perspective, attention to such vulnerabilities allows a deeper understanding of how household livelihoods and funds of knowledge may change over time. As von Kotze (2002) suggests, livelihood activities include not only how people make a living economically, but also 'the numerous cultural and aesthetic activities in which individuals and communities engage in order to restore, reproduce and re-invent their identities, a sense of belonging and dignity. As such, the notion of livelihood includes a sense of wellbeing not just of survival.' He continues, 'Livelihood is both a system of activities and a condition of being within the context of particular socio-economic, historical, geographical and political dimensions' (p. 236).

Conducting an investigation of learning in and through livelihood activities, especially in times of crisis, cannot therefore be based solely on general questions such as 'what do you do for a living and how did you learn how to do it?' because each day the activities may vary (González, Wyman, and O'Connor, 2011). Instead, questions must be situated within current conditions for living. One goal is to document not only how people make do under circumstances they cannot control, but also how 'new patterns of migration, and new systems of social control, lead people to fashion new survival strategies, and create their own new forms of social identity, social alliance, and social affiliation' (Lipsitz, 2005, p. x).

The suggestion, then, to combine a funds of knowledge approach with careful attention to household vulnerabilities and livelihood activities is, we believe, compelling given the uncertainness and stress suffered by many immigrant households. Recent developments in Arizona, from where we draw the case examples, are intimately connected to two key societal factors: the changing demographics of the state and the current economic malaise. For example, in the past two decades the state has seen its Latino (mostly Mexican) population grow by 180 percent and the state's racial composition shift from 72 percent to 58 percent white (Frey, 2010). Latinos now represent approximately 30 percent of the total state population; although in the city of Tucson, where the work presented herein is based, they represent about 45 percent of the population (US Census, 2010).

However, as Frey (2010) points out, there is an important demographic nuance to this growth – providing context to what he calls the 'white backlash' in Arizona. The state's swift Latino growth has been concentrated on children and young adults, creating what Frey calls a 'cultural generation gap' with a white and older (age 65+) population. This gap, which may portend the demographic future of the US, represents the disparity between the proportion of white seniors (the elderly) and children. Arizona leads the nation on this gap at 40 percent (the cultural generation gap nationally is 25 percent), where 83 percent of its seniors (65+) are white compared to 43 percent of its child population (under 18), which is a clear minority.

Furthermore, of the country's 100 largest metropolitan areas scoring substantial cultural generation gaps of over 30 percentage points, Phoenix, the capital of and largest city in Arizona, leads the list at 41, and Tucson ranks third at 40. Whites are now a minority of the school-going population, as revealed in the composition of the student population of local school districts, which reflects the shifting demographics. For example, the enrollment of the two largest school districts in Tucson is 61 percent (24 percent white) and 88 percent Mexican/Latino (5 percent white), respectively (TUSD Stats, 2012; SUSD, 2011).

The second factor is the economic depression in the state. The hardest hit industry has been construction, which propels the state economy, and which recruits and depends on immigrant labor. The sales of homes have decreased dramatically while the foreclosure rates of existing homes have increased. Under such circumstances, where the state has lost 53 percent (2007–2011) of its constructions jobs (*Arizona Daily Star*, 2011), immigrants have become, it seems, convenient scapegoats.

In a telling example, in 2010 Arizona legislators passed the most restrictive immigration law (Senate Bill 1070) in the country, authorizing police to determine the immigration status of anyone who might be 'reasonably suspected' of being in the country illegally. Although a federal judge has blocked, at least temporarily, the implementation of the most controversial aspects of the law until a higher court reviews it, the law has reinforced, especially in Phoenix, the state capital, the widespread persecution and harassment of Latinos, actions usually summarized by the term 'racial profiling.' In fact, as of this writing, the primary law enforcement officer in Phoenix, Sherriff Joe Arpaio, is being sued by the US Department of Justice for unlawful and discriminatory police conduct directed at Latino individuals and communities (Santos and Savage, 2012). If confirmed, such law enforcement actions make not only immigrant families but all Latino (and other) families in the state vulnerable to mistreatment by the police.

In addition, Arizona has already denied students who were brought to the country without documents as children the right to in-state college tuition or scholarships. This law requires undocumented students to pay non-resident tuition, prohibiting such students, mostly from low-income families, from receiving any state financial aid, and requiring institutions to report to the legislature the number of undocumented students they enroll. In a related action against the children of immigrants, a new bill would require teachers and administrators to determine and report the legal status of students and their families. Consider the consequence of such a law for student enrollment and parent participation at school. There is also a bill (recently rejected) to deny citizenship to the US-born children of undocumented immigrants. And there is a law that bans ethnic studies in the public schools as seditious, but only if such studies involve Mexican or Mexican-American students. No other groups are singled out, perhaps because Mexican-Americans students, who constitute the overwhelming majority in the schools affected, may represent, to the legislators, the largest threat to the status quo.

None of these immigration rulings were in place when we started the original funds of knowledge research. Neither was the extent of the return migration to Mexico that is currently occurring, motivated in great part by the draconian immigration laws in the United States. The most recent estimates, based in part on the 2010 Mexican census, indicate that since 2005 1.4 million Mexicans have returned to Mexico, including over 300,000 US-born children (thus American citizens), providing a new twist to well-established transnational phenomenon (Passel, Cohn, and González Barrera, 2012).

It is thus important to constantly reassess how the larger social and political context, which is far from monolithic, is shaping household vulnerability and activities, and thus the different kinds of knowledge and strategies households must generate to cope with changing and often hostile circumstances. One such aspect that we addressed but did not elaborate in the original work is the transnational livelihood of the households that we studied. In the borderlands region there is a long tradition of transnational movement and exchange, where one could say that many families live, more or less, simultaneously in both countries. This translocality has also been adapted as a strategy, materially and digitally, as we shall show, to deal with new vulnerabilities present in the Arizona social environment. It is thus an old practice with a new purpose.

The Case Examples

We present two examples of this new transnationalism. In contemporary research, although migration is still generally assumed by many to be unidirectional or a permanent move, return migration is already a well-recognized phenomenon. For example, Dustmann and Weiss (2007), economists from England, claim that temporary, not permanent, migration may be the dominant form of migration to that country. They found that about half of immigrants (40 percent for males; 55 percent for females) to England leave during the first five years. But they also note 'that return propensities differ across different immigrant communities, and between immigrants of different ethnicities' (p. 2), and that the reasons for returning are diverse, ranging from economical to existential ones. Furthermore, in many cases, as in the case of Anaís, the adults may be considered 'return migrants' to their countries of origin, but the children may have never lived or gone to school before in that country. So, in a sense, they are recent arrivals in their country of origin.

In the following example we highlight what Aranda (2007) calls 'the subjectivity of incorporation' (p. 225). That is, a focus of study on how immigrants 'interpret their own experiences of mobility and integration.' This may also include how broader social or institutional structures 'shape experiences of incorporation and immigrants' subjectivity generally' and 'how immigrants view these experiences, and how much importance do they give to their own perceptions when deciding where to permanently settle' (Aranda, 2007, pp. 199–200).

Anaís

The first example focuses on Anaís (a pseudonym), a transnational Mexican student who has experienced schooling both in Sonora, Mexico, and in the State of Arizona. When interviewed she was 16 years old and a high school sophomore. She was born in Mexico and went to school in that country until she was eight years old, then her family moved to Arizona. Anaís is not a US citizen and although she aspires to go to college, she knows that, given current legal restrictions, she will not be able to study in a higher education institution in the United States. As a result, Anaís and her family have developed a strategy that would allow her to obtain a college degree by enrolling in a college in Mexico.

However, in order to go to college in Mexico, she explained, she also needed to attend high school there because if she graduated only from a high school in the United States she would be missing on the academic preparation necessary for college in Mexico. Anaís decided she needed to study in Mexico but also wanted to stay in school in the United States because she felt that she was receiving a good education in Arizona. Hence, she decided to go to school in Mexico and the United States simultaneously in order to benefit from both educational settings.

She had already been successful with this bi-national strategy for middle school by traveling back and forth between the two locations and studying in Mexico for some months and in the United States for the rest of the academic year, so she employed the same methodology in high school. While she was in Mexico, she lived with her older brother and in the United States she lived with her parents. Anaís also had two different lifestyles and social networks in each location.

> I began 10th grade here [in the United States] again in August. When I moved in August I came to tenth grade and like in November I moved back to Mexico and I spent two months or three over there and then when I came back [to the US] in January, this year I lost three credits. I have to make them up and I have to stay for summer school. [I moved] because I want to do my high school over there so I can go to the university over there because I can't come to the university over here. Because I wasn't born here.

Her experiences as a student in both Sonora and Arizona allow Anaís to discuss the differences between the two school systems and the challenges of studying in each.

> The classes are way different from here [the United States]. It's like really hard. Teachers were ok but everyone would understand except me because they knew everything but I had to stay sometimes for a little while during my lunchtime so I could know what to do (learn the content).

As Anaís had lived in Sonora before moving to Arizona, adapting to life in Sonora upon her return was not as challenging as adapting to her classes. Studying in Mexico required more time from her because she had difficulty understanding the curricular materials. She had to dedicate more time to her studies than she was used to in the United States.

In contrast to her experiences in Mexico, when Anaís speaks about her school in the United States it seems as though she feels more comfortable and could understand the materials better when taught at the schools she attended in Arizona.

> [In the United States] there's more fun stuff and it's easier for me. Like in math, it's like easier and I like all the classes. The school is really hard in Mexico, the way they teach it. Math it's like the same way but in Mexico it's harder. I don't know why [In the United States] it's easier.

Although she cannot quite explain what makes the teaching and learning different in both settings, she does know that classes like mathematics are difficult to understand in Mexico whereas in Arizona she can understand everything well. The teaching style and perhaps the academic rigor expected in Mexico and the United States are different and this represents a challenge for students moving from one place to another.

Alongside facing challenges related to her classes while studying in Mexico Anaís had to adapt to other social aspects of the school's policy. Abiding by these new rules and having to modify her personal style were some of the things that Anaís disliked about studying in Sonora.

> They have like a lot of rules, like I have to take off my piercing and I can't wear a lot of makeup and I can't, I'm not supposed to take to school a lot of jewelry and then the uniforms were different. They were ugly.

She did not like having to wear uniforms because she was accustomed to wearing regular clothes to go to school in Arizona. Curtailing the use of makeup and jewelry was also part of her constraints. These changes seemed to have made her feel uneasy because she was being required to adopt an image with which she did not feel comfortable.

Anaís' story provides some insight into the life of transnational students that spend some time in Mexico and some in the United States. She truly lives between two countries, moving back and forth according to her needs. She is currently still trying to finish school in both places, to expand her options, but this also represents challenges of its own. As she explained, upon returning to Arizona she had missed school credits while she was in Sonora and consequently she had to attend summer school in order to make up for these. She also explained that the school in Arizona had warned her that if she left for several months again she would not be allowed to return. Regardless of her efforts, Anaís is aware that she will probably not be able to attend college in the United States, yet the fact that she wants to finish school in Arizona first denotes her appreciation for schools in this country. Going to school in Mexico is perceived as a sacrifice that she must make, given current political circumstances, to complete her secondary education and be able to attend an institution of higher learning.

Melissa

In the second example, we elaborate on the role of new media and digital technologies in establishing networks of communities as a routine part of adolescent life. Youth funds of knowledge with new digital tools are forged through participating in social networks sites, such as YouTube and Facebook, and through messaging practices that span local and transnational connections and communities. However, akin to other lived experiences of Latino families that occur outside classrooms, practices with social media and digital tools are often disallowed or unrecognized as legitimate knowledge in schools.

The case of Melissa (also a pseudonym), a second generation Latina high school student, emerges from research that focused on the possibilities for collaboratively appropriating youth practices and digital tools for school-based teaching and learning (Schwartz, 2011). This example follows the tradition of engaging in funds of knowledge research to reimagine household practices, evolving in networked communities, as pedagogical resources. To initiate the research, students' interests, practices and experiences in multiple domains were included in developing a social network site within an English classroom for 11th and 12th graders. Digital tools are often incorporated into classrooms without allowing students to help determine how they are to be used, resulting in a loss of motivation in the activity. A key component of the approach, then, was for students to have agency in developing the site for their own purposes; this allowed activity in many ways to reflect students' participation in popular social networks. The distributed spaces, networks, and modalities of students' lives and interests became visible as they posted images of places, friends, and family spanning the US Southwest, California and Mexico. Media shared included videos from pop-culture, items on social issues related to Latinos, music, and artwork. Students 'friended' each other and posted comments using English, Spanish, and Internet slang.

Allowing students to participate actively in the classroom social network site invited a view into how students build community ties and identities through social media. In this way students' funds of knowledge derived from their evolving communities and practices emerged as potential resources for learning. We share how these funds of knowledge were extended for personally and academically responsive inquiries through the work of Melissa and other members of her research group.

Like the majority of her classmates, Melissa was a student of Mexican heritage. As a 12th grader who lived with an older sister, because her parents had been deported to Mexico, she was painfully aware of the ever-worsening political climate for Latinos in Arizona, and of the longstanding deficit discourses and challenges facing her within high school and beyond. As part of a project where students were asked to use their social networks to develop research on community and identity, her group, whose interests had surfaced in the classroom social network, developed the overall question: 'Being of Hispanic heritage, how does a country shape your identity?' Comprised of first and second-generation Mexican students, her group chose this question because they felt compelled to share what it was like to experience life in a state consistently moving to curtail opportunities for Latinos.

In addition to her group's questions, Melissa formulated two of her own: (1) Have you lived here all your life? and (2) Have you ever reached the point to where you fear you might be forgetting where you come from? To conduct her research, she used primarily text messaging and instant messaging via the Internet to interview six youths aged 10 to 22. Although this project was not undertaken on a site such as Facebook, the communicative strategies and peer and familial networks accessed for developing the information needed for her research mirrored the daily practices of youth on social networks sites and their uses of cell phones and other mobile tools.

A salient aspect of her interviewees' experiences is that their lives stretched across both sides of the US-Mexico border. Of the six students Melissa interviewed, four had moved back and forth between Mexico and Arizona at least once. Students' answers to the question, 'Have you lived here all your life?' show that in a context where parents and children are often separated as a result of where they were born, questions about origin may elicit a more complicated answer then a simple yes or no. Lupe Martinez, age 14, interviewed through text messaging answered:

> No. Well I currently live in the border town of Nogales, Sonora, Mexico but I go to school in Nogales, Arizona. I lived here in Mexico when I was just a toddler then moved to Tucson. But I recently moved back because of a family matter.

Yet, regardless of where they were born or had lived, all but one student identified as Mexican-American. Additionally, all of the students Melissa interviewed gave answers that confirmed the continuity of their sense of Mexican heritage when asked if they felt they were forgetting where they came from.

For other group questions such as 'Do you feel like you fit in to where your family comes from?' youths' answers spanned from 'yes and no . . . when I visit Mexico they make me feel awkward, because they see me different' and 'I feel like a stranger with in my family' to 'Yes because in [her town] the people love me and I do fit in, no one treats me bad and or looks at me in a bad way.' Answers to the groups' overall question about how a country affects one's identity reflected the promise, 'This country [the United States] made me smarter by giving me education, good jobs etc.' and also the disappointment of life in the United States, 'Racism, la gente [the people], las burlas [the mocking], stereotypes, this is how a country shapes me.' The voices and experiences of the youth Melissa and her peers interviewed demonstrate how youthful funds of knowledge circulate and grow through digital and social networks, and in response to extant political ideologies and discourses.

The students had aimed to show others what it is like to be a young Hispanic (Latino) because 'being a Hispanic in a unknown country is very hard, due to all the racism, but they really don't know what a Hispanic is.' Together they wrote in their self-assessment of their paper, '(this was) more than just a class assignment; this was an eye opener for us that Being of Hispanic heritage a country CAN change your identity.' Highlighting the extension of students' digital practices, one member shared that she 'learned how to work together and use communication such as text messaging, Wiki and MySpace to finish an assignment.' The group's words illustrate how the students used their funds of knowledge, developed through digital spaces and exchanges, for academic learning that became reciprocally related to the multiple social and digital worlds they created and inhabited.

Discussion

In this chapter we have presented two case examples of how students negotiate transnational lives in response to rapidly changing social and political circumstances within their communities. We used these examples, limited as they may be, to illustrate how these circumstances, clearly aversive ones, can influence the nature of the funds of knowledge generated by families and students, and the possibilities they pose for learning in classrooms and other settings. As both examples illustrate, there is a strong sense of vulnerability in these students, as they attempt to decipher their realities or take action in response to the constraints of living and studying in Arizona, with its foreclosed opportunities for higher education.

Anaís is attempting the stressful task of going to school in Mexico after attending US schools for most of her life. She, in a sense, has become, out of necessity not choice, a mobile student, attending schools in both countries in an attempt to keep her options open for higher education. This transnational movement is certainly physically and mentally hazardous (O'Leary, 2008), especially if she is without proper legal documents, but it is also resilient in the face of adversity, as she tries to cope with political edicts in Arizona against students like her. It is, in brief, a remarkable strategy for educational survival. She, along with her family, assumes the risks of bi-national movement anticipating it will benefit her education in the future.

Melissa, about the same age, is a second-generation student, hence a citizen of the United States. However, she is living with a sister because her parents were deported from Arizona. She is, as the example illustrates, well versed in digital tools, having specialized knowledge that, one assumes, exceeds that of her parents, and she developed her expertise primarily through peer relations, not schooling, reminding us of the importance of 'informal' learning. Note also that the same political conditions that motivated Anaís' transnational lifestyle, have motivated Melissa's inquiry about issues of identity with her peers, whom have similar experiences, and with whom she communicates through digital networks. Her interviews reveal the tensions of identity among these students, a dominant issue among second-generation youth (Portes and Rumbaut, 2001). They face the contradictions of acceptance and rejection, including sometimes suffering rejection in both countries, and perhaps fated to be neither from here nor from there. For these youth, then, as for thousands of others similarly situated, living in the borderlands is not merely metaphorical (Boehm, 2012). As Melissa's interviewees reveal, such locality is sometimes a source of frustration and other times a source of inspiration. Notice how digital networks used by youth provide an interstitial space, neither here nor there, where youth can connect and share funds of knowledge.

Consider the directions in which we could take an elaboration of these case examples. As von Kotze (2002) suggests, a key is to analyze learning in daily struggles. We could certainly document, as has been our practice, all the useful funds of knowledge, including bilingual language and literacy practices, involved in Anaís family, and the resources and expertise generated by her translocality (e.g., de la Piedra, 2011). As important, as we have tried to underscore, is accounting not only for the adults' but also their children's activities that may motivate the production of new funds of knowledge. As Jimenez, Smith, and Teague (2009, as cited by de la Piedra, 2011, p. 76) argue, 'it makes pedagogical sense to include transnational and community literacies in the literacy instruction provided to all students, including English language learners, in the United States' (p. 16). In the tradition of the funds of knowledge approach, this strategy: (1) allows teachers to know the lives of their students better and to establish relationships with them; (2) encourages students to learn about diversity in their communities; (3) builds on the student's prior knowledge; and (4) promotes student engagement in learning (p. 18).

We could also consider several other aspects, all also with pedagogical implications, and ripe for critical analysis, we should add, given the political dynamics involved with these issues. These could include the powerful role of emotions in transnational experiences (Zembylas, 2012), the resilience and resources needed to attend school in two countries (Hamann *et al.*, 2006), how one draws nurturance from social relations in both locations (Stodolska and Santos, 2006), the transnational lifeworlds and identities of teachers (Knight and Oesterreich, 2011), and the formation of particular subjectivities in establishing a sense of belonging and well being in either context (Soto-Santiago and Moll, in press).

The goal, ultimately, would be that of understanding, indeed, of theorizing, the production of knowledge and expertise related to coping with the complexities of diverse lifeworlds, be it of families, children, or teachers. The examples featured in this chapter illustrate how funds of knowledge, ways of thinking, values and expectations associated with culturally derived forms of practice are always open to transformation. After all, people always deal actively, each in their own way depending on the resources at hand, with the rapidly changing realities for living.

Note

1. Latino is a generic designation for any population of Latin-American descent; we will use it interchangeably with the term Hispanic throughout this paper.

References

Aranda, E. (2007) Struggles of incorporation among the Puerto Rican middle class. *The Sociological Quarterly*, 48: 199–228.

Arizona Daily Star (2011) AZ has lost 53% of construction jobs, Tucson 48%, March 16, accessed November 28, 2012: http://azstarnet.com/business/local/az-has-lost-of-construction-jobs-tucson/article_a20116e9-b405-5380-a63d-d70641ba1798.html

Boehm, D.A. (2012) *Intimate Migrations: Gender, Family, and Illegality among Transnational Mexicans*. New York: New York University Press.

Casper, V. (2011) Terms of engagement: Preparing pre-service teachers to form authentic partnerships with families and communities. *Education as Change*: S1, S5–S19.

Cremin, T., Mottram, M., Collins, *et al.* (2012) Building communities: Teachers researching literacy lives. *Improving Schools*, 15(2): 101–115.

de la Piedra, M. (2011) 'Tanto necesitamos de aquí, como necesitamos de alla': 'Leer juntas' among Mexican transnational mothers and daughters. *Language and Education*, 25(10): 65–78.

Dustmann, C., and Weiss, Y. (2007) Return migration: Theory and empirical evidence. Centre for Research and Analysis of Migration. Discussion Paper, CDP No. 02-07. Department of Economics, University College London.

Esteban-Guitart, M., and Vila, I. (eds) (2012) Experiencias en educación inclusiva. Vinculación escuela, familia y comunidad [Experiences in inclusive education: Connecting school, family and community]. Barcelona: Horsori Editorial.

Frey, W. (2010) *Will Arizona be America's Future?* Web-ed. The Brookings Institution, April 28, 2010, accessed November 14, 2012: www.frey-demographer.org/briefs.html

González, N., Moll, L.C., and Amanti, C. (eds) (2005) *Funds of Knowledge: Theorizing Practices in Households, Communities, and Classrooms.* Mahwah, NJ: Erlbaum.

González, N., Ríos-Aguilar, C., Reyes, I., *et al.* (2011) Border ecologies and early development: An ecological approach to the early childhood development of English language learners. Unpublished research proposal, University of Arizona.

González, N., Wyman, L., and O'Connor, B.H. (2011) The past, present, and future of 'funds of knowledge.' In B. Levinson and M. Pollock (eds) *A Companion to the Anthropology of Education.* London: Blackwell, pp. 481–494.

Hamann, E.T., Zúñiga, V and Sánchez García, J. (2006) Pensando en Cynthia y su hermana: Educational implications of United States – Mexico transnationalism for children. *Journal of Latinos and Education,* 5(4): 253–274.

Hedges, H. (2012) Teachers' funds of knowledge: A challenge to evidence-based practice. *Teachers and Teaching: Theory and Practice,* 18(1): 7–24.

Hogg, L. (2011) Funds of knowledge: An investigation of coherence within the literature. *Teaching and Teaching Education,* 27: 666–677.

Jimenez, R., Smith, P., and Teague, B. (2009) Transnational and community literacies. *Journal of Adolescent and Adult Literacy,* 53(1): 16–26.

Knight, M.G., and Oesterreich, H.A. (2011) Opening our eyes, changing our practices: Learning through the transnational lifeworlds of teachers. *Intercultural Education,* 22(3): 203–215.

Lipsitz, G. (2005) Foreword: The grounded transnationalism of Robert Alvarez. In R.A. Alvarez, *Mangos, Chiles and Truckers: The Business of Transnationalism.* Minneapolis, MN: The University of Minnesota Press.

Moll, L.C., and González, N. (2004) Engaging life: A funds of knowledge approach to multicultural education. In J. Banks and C. McGee Banks (eds) *Handbook of Research on Multicultural Education,* 2nd edn. New York: Jossey-Bass, pp. 699–715.

Moll, L.C., and Greenberg, J. (1990) Creating zones of possibilities: Combining social contexts for instruction. In L.C. Moll (ed.) *Vygotsky and Education.* Cambridge: Cambridge University Press, pp. 319–348.

Moll, L.C., and Soto-Santiago, S. (2010, October) El vaivén: Return migration and education in Puerto Rico and Mexico. Paper presented at the On New Shores Conference, University of Guelph, Canada.

O'Leary, A.O. (2008) Close encounters of the deadly kind: Gender, migration and border (in)security. *Migration Letters,* 5(2): 111–121.

Passel, J., Cohn, D., and González Barrera, A. (2012) *Net Migration from Mexico Falls to Zero – and Perhaps Less.* Washington, DC: Pew Hispanic Center, accessed November 14, 2012: www.pewhispanic.org/2012/04/23/net-migration-from-mexico-falls-to-zero-and-perhaps-less/

Portes, A., and Rumbaut, R. (2001) *Legacies: The Story of the Immigrant Second Generation.* Berkeley, CA: University of California Press and Russell Sage Foundation.

Santos, F., and Savage, C. (2012) Lawsuit says sheriff discriminated against Latinos. *The New York Times,* May 10, accessed November 14, 2012: www.nytimes.com/2012/05/11/us/justice-department-sues-arizona-sheriff-joe-arpaio.html?_r=2

Schwartz, L. (2011) Forming a collaborative model for appropriating youth practices and digital tools for new literacies development with Latino high school students and teachers. Unpublished doctoral dissertation, University of Arizona.

Soto-Santiago, S., and Moll, L.C. (in press) Transnational mobility, education and subjectivity: Two case examples from Puerto Rico. In P. Portes and S. Salas (eds) *U.S. Latinos in K–12 education: Seminal Research-Based Policy Directions for Change we can Believe.* Charlotte, NC: Information Age Publishing.

Stodolska, M., and Santos, C.A. (2006) 'You must think of familia': The everyday life of Mexican migrants in destination communities. *Social and Cultural Geography,* 7(4): 627–647.

SUSD (Sunnyside Unified School District) (2011): District Vital Statistics, accessed November 14, 2012: www.susd12.org/node/50

Tapia, J. (1991) Cultural reproduction: Funds of knowledge as survival strategies in the Mexican-American community. Unpublished doctoral dissertation, University of Arizona.

TUSD (Tucson Unified School District) Stats (2012), accessed 5 August, 2012: http://tusdstats.tusd.k12.az.us/

US Census Bureau (2010) 2010 Census interactive population search, The city of Tucson, accessed November 14, 2012: http://2010.census.gov/2010census/popmap/ipmtext.php?fl=04

Vélez-Ibáñez, C. (1996) *Border Visions: Mexican Cultures of the Southwest United States.* Tucson, AZ: University of Arizona Press.

Vélez-Ibáñez, C., and Greenberg, J.B. (1992) Formation and transformation of funds of knowledge among U.S.-Mexican households. *Anthropology and Education Quarterly*, 23(4): 313–335.

Vélez-Ibáñez, C., and Sampaio, A. (2002) *Transnational Latina/o Communities.* Lanham, MD: Rowman and Littlefield.

von Kotze, A. (2002) Producing knowledge for living. *Continuing Education*, 24(2): 233–246.

Zembylas, M. (2012) Transnationalism, migration and emotions: Implications for education. *Globalisation, Societies and Education*, 1(1): 1–17.

Chapter 14

The Hand of Play in Literacy Learning

Shirley Brice Heath

Introduction

As modern economies competitively elbow their way into the twenty-first century, monetary goals, economic downturns, and threats of deepening or repeated recessions place primary emphasis on work. Jobs and career development push play and leisure out of consideration. The occasional discussions of play that have appeared in the public media since the turn of the twenty-first century argue the mental and physical health benefits of play as relaxation, exercise, stress alleviation, and as a platform for creative thinking. Advertisements promise the play power of this or that new videogame, mobile phone app, vacation spot, or coming attraction at local theme parks. Play comes in promotions of material acquisition of gadgets and technological advances and selection of destinations, such as entertainment and leisure centers or resorts.

While their elders are urged to play for the sake of their health, the young are cajoled into learning through play. Educators eager to introduce technology into classrooms pump up the attraction of animated films or other video film materials, as well as educational videogames that allow children to play while they gain skills and acquire factual information. Already habituated to forms of technology-delivered distractions, children and teenagers often voluntarily take up videogames, YouTube videos, and DVDs for their entertainment value, competitive action contests, and echoes of favorite television or film action figures. Evidence of what is learned through these video technologies is hotly debated, in spite of evidence from cognitive neuroscience research showing that social interaction pre-empts technological interactions in learning transmission, particularly for young children (Meltzoff *et al.*, 2011).

This chapter looks at contexts of play by and with young children living in families that either aspire to or have achieved mainstream status within modern economies. The summations within this chapter reflect a reluctant acceptance of the projection by economists and political leaders of the modern world that social class disparities will not only continue but accelerate the pace of their spread across the globe in the twenty-first century. Play is highly interdependent with social class and economic access. Children and adults living in poverty without reasonable expectation of wage-earning or salaried employment outside the home

International Handbook of Research on Children's Literacy, Learning, and Culture, First Edition.
Edited by Kathy Hall, Teresa Cremin, Barbara Comber, and Luis C. Moll.
© 2013 John Wiley & Sons, Ltd. Published 2013 by John Wiley & Sons, Ltd.

have resources of space, material, and play partners (adult and peer) that differ in extreme ways from the resources of families who see themselves as middle-class or mainstream. In regions of rural poverty, the play of young children tends to centre in their gradual enlistment into roles within the household, small family business, or farm work (Katz, 2004; Lancy, 2008; Schwartzman, 1978). In contrast, the play of children living in mainstream families will, more than likely, increasingly take place through peer relationships within activities that offer social and technological capital and evidence of interests and talents likely to be interpreted as relevant to successful movement toward further or higher-education institutions, career development, and preparation for lifelong learning through technological innovations.

Within mainstream families, leisure time in homes and communities increasingly turns toward engagement with technologies, often for entertainment. This trend means that adults have little hand in shaping, framing, and extending joint play with children. Moreover, toys created for children have in the past three decades shifted from being objects for free and child-created play (e.g., wooden blocks for building) to programmed plastic items that perform for children (e.g., talking dolls and remote-controlled racing cars). Children now play, more often than not, by pushing buttons, holding control devices, and clicking combinations of keys with symbols and numbers. Interactive talk, making and drawing, socio-dramatic play, joint book reading, and full involvement of the forearm, hand, and digits in these and related activities lose out in households where material objects (especially those involving technology) and entertainment from commercial sources substitute for face-to-face social and imaginative play. This chapter examines processes and implications of changes in the nature of play since the opening of the twenty-first century.

The first section of the chapter gives a backward and forward summation of play within mainstream households of modern economies. A brief look at schooling, the Internet, and entertainment in the twenty-first century follows. The subsequent section lays out findings from cognitive neuroscience relevant to brain development and the neuronal pathways that humans engage through the use of their hands as they produce, interpret, and use structured symbol systems within play. Of special note in this section are five features of play in children's learning environments: time, space, tools, models, and partners. The penultimate section takes a close look at one type of play – the socio-dramatic – to illustrate the cognitive and linguistic consequences of this type of play. The chapter closes with an examination of the integral ties between play and the arts and sciences. Here we reflect on the metaphoric possibilities that speakers of English find within the phrase 'the hand of play.'

The Recent History of Play in Families

Discussions of play during the twentieth century focused on theories that argued the developmental value of play for young children. In large part, this view derived from the notion that as babies become toddlers, and as toddlers move toward entry to formal schooling, their playful explorations of the environment around them provide foundational learning relevant to school (Pellegrini, 1995; Sutton-Smith, 1997). These arguments encouraged kindergartens and other one-year programs of school-before-school to offer not only explorations of the outdoor world around the school, but also involvement in the socio-dramatic play invited by specific spaces within kindergarten classrooms. Here children could dress up, take on kitchen responsibilities, and build with blocks. They could also explore puzzles that represented areas of knowledge (such as colors, shapes, animal names, and numbers) that would prove vital in the first year of *real* school. Throughout their years of primary schooling, the study of academic subjects would be punctuated by times for recess. This free play time brought games of chase, rough-and-tumble challenges, and board games (such as chess and checkers), while after-school time at school meant opportunities for occasional class or school plays, as well as projects in other art forms.

From the 1930s forward, however, consumer culture grew in influence on children's play. Walt Disney films led the way, as did comic books. For boys, futuristic toy guns and other paraphernalia linked with super heroes became favorite accessories in their child re-creations of what they had seen on screen. For girls, films and comic books portraying imitation-worthy role models from Shirley Temple to Wonder Woman pushed choices of dolls as well as gender-based versions of playground dramas (Chudacoff, 2007). These commercially-influenced forms of play took place alongside the imaginative hand work of children who created their own toys from materials found in their natural surroundings or households. In addition, many commercial toys of the early and mid-twentieth century invited creative construction. Lincoln logs, Tinker Toys, and other building sets allowed for handcrafted designs of vehicles, buildings, doll houses, forts, and shopping centers. Paper dolls allowed combinations of wigs and costumes. Tea sets, miniature furnishings, and doll babies with sets of clothing invited socio-dramatic re-enactments of home life (Heath, 1983/1996).

During these decades when commercial supports for play proliferated, children living in rural and suburban areas could become immersed in their surrounding natural world, exploring woods, rivers, and ponds, climbing trees, and building tree houses and lookout posts. City youth explored their environments in similar ways, devising games in backyards, vacant lots, dumps, and rooftops. Renaming as well as reshaping what they found and the spaces in which they played became the very center of much of their play. Numerous testimonies from children of these decades report the improvisational talents of children who could carve and build, literally and figuratively, environments and their physical elements to fit imaginative play schemes (Chudacoff, 2007). Jump-rope games, accompanied by highly inventive rhyming, along with marble and jacks games, were often based on mathematics concepts, folkloric bits, and forms of teasing. Common objects became supports for all types of play from games of war to socio-dramatic re-enactments of school. Their own games and dramas of play provided a key means by which children developed rule structures and worked out problem-solving schemes (Huizinga, 1939/1955; Opie and Opie, 1959; Sylva, Bruner, and Genova, 1976).

The second half of the twentieth century presented a very different scene for the play of children. Television rapidly became part of every household's parlor, living room, or family room. Children watched and imitated characters from shows that featured Walt Disney characters such as Mickey Mouse, as well as programs celebrating learning with puppets (e.g., those from 'Kukla, Fran and Ollie' as well as 'Sesame Street') and friendly adults such as 'Mr Rodgers.' Corporations (e.g., Mattel and Hasbro) moved into advertising on children's television programs as well as onto cereal boxes and other food packaging common in homes where both parents worked and had to make breakfast as brief as possible.

By the end of the twentieth century, the play of children came to be under the supervision of 'intimate strangers,' adults specializing in childcare, sports, arts programming, and guided explorations of the outdoor world (Heath, 2012).[1] Working parents needed childcare during their hours away from home. Children from two-working-parent and single-parent households soon spent more time with these caregiving 'strangers' than with their own parents. While with their intimate stranger caregivers, children played with other children, entered into organized games, and experienced a wide range of commercially-produced toys and riding vehicles, as well as playground equipment that allowed for climbing, hiding, and building muscles and learning eye–hand coordination. Monitored and often guided and instructed by adults, the play of children in their out-of-school settings came to be viewed as essential for instilling collaborative skills, alliance-building, good sportsmanship, and ethical values among children (Edmiston, 2008; Evaldsson, 1993).

Meanwhile, with accelerating force, market forces pushed manufacturers of clothing, toys, and accessories toward remaking children as little adults. They dressed like their parents, had look-alike technologies that mimicked those of the adult world, and were given a wide-ranging choice in entertainment from music to television shows to films. Parents in modern economies were rapidly evolving in response to public media and advertising that promoted the idea that 'good' parents 'gave' their children opportunities – for pleasure-seeking, independent decision-making, and expression of wants, opinions, and objections. A climate of entitlement emerged around childhood and adolescence.

School, the Internet, and Child-selected Entertainment

As the twenty-first century opened, the rapid spread of access to the Internet and technologies of communication matched this climate well. Developments in formal schooling lagged behind the everyday world the public media presented for children. Relevance, personal interests, and individual and group motivation to follow specific issues, activities, and public icons led the young to find numerous ways to choose what they wanted to learn and to find ways of doing so on their own, often applying what they learned in school, while decrying the limited modes through which they could demonstrate in school the knowledge and skills they were acquiring (Heath, 2012).

Meanwhile within formal schooling, standards in curricular selections and forms of assessment were freezing into daily instructional routine what and how children were to learn and to be tested on information acquired. The OECD Programme for International Student Assessment (PISA) began in 2000. Its purpose was to evaluate educational systems in participating countries (70, including all modern economies, in 2012) by testing the knowledge and skills of 15-year-old students. Each year, media coverage within the participating nations accelerated, giving the message to many nations that their educational systems were not producing students with levels of skills and knowledge sufficient for twenty-first century needs in science, mathematics, and literacy.

It took almost no time for the stinging effects of being lower than expected in the PISA rankings to propel key policy changes in education within nations such as the United States and the United Kingdom. Policymakers demanded that education systems intensify study of traditional subjects, such as science, mathematics, and reading, and that teachers of classrooms reflecting low test scores be identified publicly and punished in some way. These moves to what the public and policymakers defined as a 'return to serious attention on the basics' brought significant changes to uses of time and modes of instruction in school. As a consequence, support for any form of play, including creative pursuit of project work, declined sharply. Learning in school came to be tied closely to direct instruction regimented in time and task with an orientation toward raising test scores. All forms of play fell out of favor, and recess and extended lunch breaks were either cut back or eliminated (Meier, Engel, and Taylor, 2010). The same processes applied to arts classes, extracurricular programs, and the in-school time previously provided to enable pupils to take part in theatre, journalism, and other special interest clubs such as chess.

These policy changes for schools came simultaneously with the dropping away of play during the nonschool hours in single-parent households as well as within families where both parents worked full time outside the home. As noted above, families eager to achieve mainstream status for their children and unable to spend after-school hours with their children enrolled them, often as early as the pre-school years, in classes and programs run by intimate strangers to whom they entrusted their children on a daily basis. Sports coaches, karate instructors, directors of museum and parks programs, and teaching artists in community-based organizations became weekly companions for the young. Summer camps, religious programs, and other provisions of childcare during months beyond the school year provided both childcare and 'enhancement' experiences for those parents with the discretionary funds to pay the necessary fees.

When not involved in structured programs during their out-of-school hours, children rarely played either with their parents or outdoors with their friends except under adult supervision. 'Stranger danger,' introduced by the public media as a concept in the late 1990s, led parents to fear for the safety of their children and to prohibit free play in parks, forests, or along river beds (Louv, 2005). In single-parent and two-working-parent families, parents had to find supervision for their children during all their after-school hours. At home, while parents prepared meals and carried out other household tasks, they turned their children over to the baby-sitting powers of commercial entertainment from television and DVDs, videogames, and the social networking offerings of the Internet.

These changes did not escape notice. Simultaneously with the sharp decline in play opportunities for the young, experts from pediatricians to science educators raised cries of alarm. Pediatricians pointed to increased rates of childhood obesity, as well as childhood diabetes and other health-related issues. Children sitting for hours while they watched television, DVDs, and computer screens were not exercising, and often they were consuming packaged snacks, such as crisps and candy, along with high-fructose beverages. Psychologists and child development experts noted troublesome indicators in early child behavior as well as drop-offs in children's perception and understanding of nature. Public intellectuals, hearing political and economic leaders of modern economies proclaim the widening need for creative workers, cautioned against elimination of childhood play. Artists and arts advocates, along with scientists and science educators, spoke out forcefully to remind the public that their creative work came in large measure from a spirit of play, exploration, imagination, and risk-taking. As the next section indicates, the research of ethologists, anthropologists, and cognitive neuroscientists responding to what they viewed as a dangerous loss of play among children gave strong support to the vital role of play by publicizing research on animals from rats to higher-order primates.[2]

Within the latter group, humans, however, have special needs in their play. Central within human play are structured symbol systems. Language, whether signed, spoken, or written, holds central place throughout the natural play that occurs especially for infants and young children. Language itself is a primary source of children's play both when they are alone and with others (Cazden, 1976). Music, dance, socio-dramatics, and the visual arts, especially drawing, hold a close second place to language. The positioning of language in all these forms of representational play calls for other necessities: time, space, tools, models, and partners. Individuals who play must take time from other pursuits to do so, and they often need not only physical space but also mental space, or release from other psychological demands in order to play. Humans who learn to play must do so with partners who include not only peer playmates, but also adults who enjoy building sand castles and towers of wooden blocks; joining in socio-dramatic play to be the witch, monster, or scolding schoolmaster; and spontaneously organizing games in the park with their own children and others. Models matter a great deal to play, even though across the age span, individuals often play on their own initiative.

However, the imitative potential that models provide for novices allows learners to create from what they see others do. This particular capacity – of moving beyond mere imitation to creativity – comes to humans (and several other higher-order primates) as a result of the brain's mirror neurons.[3] While humans observe and see patterns and rules that others enact,

Figure 14.1 Pupil at work with *Thinking hands,* an arts learning project inspired through the Learning Team of Tate Modern. Photo credit and permission: Shelby A. Wolf and Roy Smith.

they have an inner drive to create anew. For centuries, this drive has led children, scientists, and artists to new behaviors, ideas, and inventions (see Figure 14.1). Some would argue that all grasp in their hands 'the physicality and materiality of thought' to 'turn it into a concrete image' (Pallasmaa, 2009, p. 16).

The exploratory nature of play from birth forward enables infants to experience the world through the senses. Smell, sight, touch, taste, smell, and sound bring human infants into being discriminatory individuals. Babies learn to recognize and respond to their mother's face and voice. They learn by taste and touch to know one brand of cereal from another. Often termed 'instinctive' learning, delineating within the environment what is safe, desirable, useful, and meaningful prepares infants for their development into symbol-makers and interpreters. The ability to see similarities and differences among symbols (and for the blind, to do so through touch) emerges early in the play of humans. Size, color, and shape of images enable children to distinguish mature from immature animals, to recognize different phases of the moon, and to know their own doll or truck from that of their playmate. Learning to make distinction in the segments of scenes and sounds surrounding the infant hones skills critical to discernment of the shapes and sounds of symbols, whether auditory or visual. As the child matures, the extent to which children play with adult guides determines in numerous ways the developmental trajectory for later development of language, oral and written.

Contributions from Cognitive Neuroscience

By 2010, play became a focus for cognitive neuroscientists studying the human brain during early child development. At this point, researchers across fields from ethology (the study of animal behavior) to pediatric neurology reached a surprising conclusion that turned around prior theories that argued the primary function of play among mammals (the animals that exhibit play most reliably) contributes primarily to socialization and preparation for adulthood. The twenty-first century breakthrough technologies of fMRI and MEG imaging meant that researchers could now show the role of play in the growth and development of the brain – particularly the cerebellum, the portion of the brain that coordinates movements originating in other parts of the brain. The primary time during which animal's play co-occurs with the time when the cerebellum grows. In essence, there is a sensitive period of brain growth when the brain needs the stimulation of whole-body movement, for this movement helps the brain achieve its ultimate configuration. This research, first set out by an ethologist studying pronghorn antelopes and wild mountain goats, set other neuroscientists to pursue more closely the question of possible effects on the brain of deprivation of play (Byers, 1998a, 1998b, 1999). Research on rats deprived of play during their juvenile period showed an immature pattern of neuronal connections in the medial pre-frontal cortex, part of the cerebrum, the bulk of the brain of mammals. Researchers concluded that a deprivation of play during the critical period before puberty interfered with the pruning of cortical brain cells that goes on during this period as a result of feedback from the environment (Bell, Pellis, and Kolb, 2010; Pellis and Pellis, 2009, 2010; Pellis, Pellis, and Bell, 2010).

During this same period, other researchers turned their attention to the hand and ways in which early use of the hand and forearm for exploring, rearranging, and even creating environments and objects affected the brain. How does the brain respond as young children engage their fingers, hands, and arms during play? These scientists also wanted to know how structured symbol systems, such as language, numbers, visual arts, and music evolved in the course of human history. Evolutionary biologists came to link development of these systems to evolution's remodelling of the hand between the lineage of Homo erectus and Homo sapiens (Donald, 2001; Wilson, 1998). The mechanical capacity of the hand in tool-making and using, manipulation of the environment, and creating art forms as well as gestural sign systems shaped the brain's circuitry across the years. This growing capacity of the hand in harmony with communicational systems enabled humans to live in groups, develop products and trade, and generate ways of moving and exchanging objects as well as recording interactions.

The forms of play made possible through the hand helped shape all these developments in large part because the hand was the primary instrument of representation – presenting in rehearsal and reprisal actions, emotions, and outcomes. Neurologists concluded that language, numeracy, and object combinations develop early linkages among these systems that enable each to develop autonomously as the human matures. However, manipulation of all of these must take place within play, in order for a sense of system to emerge.

By the age of one, infants simultaneously engage in hand-thought-language interactions; all of these have moving parts and include elements for rearrangement and experimentation. 'Playing with anything to make something is always paralleled in cognition by the creation of a story' (Wilson, 1998: 195; see also Galda and Pellegrini, 1985). One goes from beginning to middle to end. Sensorimotor development co-occurs with language, and is moved along through play with the hand. Children learn systems of sign language before they learn to speak, indicating that the hand's symbol-structuring capacity runs along in front of those locomotor operations that support speech.

Moreover, 'the know-how of gesture is not the same as the know-how of instrumental movement' (McNeill, 2005, p. 245). In other words, the production of gesture takes place not entirely through the brain's circuitry that performs instrumental actions, but is instead made possible through linkage to the language centers of the brain. Unlike auditory expression, the communicative power of the hand relates to vision, which is more fundamental for humans than the auditory channel. Well before children speak, their hands can both process and articulate through gestures the shapes and movements of objects as well as features and emotions of fellow humans.

Moreover, from a very young age, children also demonstrate their ability to use their hands to create representations. Every parent in modern economies has winced at the toddler's handfuls of tightly squeezed banana being transformed into thick finger paint on the highchair tray and crayon scribbles on the wall, sidewalk, and books or magazines. At times like this, it is difficult to remember that learning benefits from these early ways of creating representations by scribbles and rudimentary drawings. The haptic feedback gained through direct use of the hand

Figure 14.2 Pupil taking part in *What on Earth is Clay?*, an enquiry project designed to develop haptic skills and heuristic learning through work with clay. Photo credit: Clayground Collective. Photo used by permission of Frith Manor Primary School, London, UK.

and the gripping action that holds the crayon, pencil, or charcoal appears to enhance the act of mentally visualizing (Gilbert, Reiner, and Nakhleh, 2008; Reiner, 2008). The heuristic power of the hand begins early in life and continues into more creative and controlled representations (see Figure 14.2), such as those involved in playing an instrument, sketching architectural designs, and fashioning puppets (Wilson, 1998). Under circumstances when action is relevant to visual imagery, the motor system – particularly that supporting the grasping action of the hand – becomes engaged. Children who use their hands as they play undertake perception, action, and cognition simultaneously when they create representations. Cognition becomes grounded as young children engage in motor-dependent production of visual representations of what they are thinking, imagining, and planning. The hand – as investigator and manipulator of the environment – calls on all the modal systems necessary to produce these representations, especially so when the hand is shaping, grasping, drawing, modeling, or molding materials. Stories and questions that ask 'what if?' and 'what's this about?' result from the 'force patterns' the brain exerts through the fingers, hands, and forearms (Reiner, 2000, 2008).

Enactment and embodiment in gesture, role positioning, agency, and language enable children to play at being and doing. Though they may not yet be able to express verbally the hypothetical or 'what-if?' reasoning behind problems, they can create within their play 'memories of the future' that involve variables, conditions, and possible interactions and consequences (Ingvar, 1998). For example, doing so can take place primarily through monologues that have no known audience. Child language scholars have found that during the moments just before sleep, some children alone in their room replay verbally what they have heard and seen throughout the day. When they do so, they articulate the talk of others with vocabulary and syntactic constructions that exceed the linguistic competency they themselves produce in their everyday reality (Bruner and Lucariello, 1989; Feldman, 1989; Nelson, 1989). Second-language learners achieve the same advantages when they take on roles in dramatic re-enactments. Within the body of another, their language fluency tops that which they portray when they are themselves (Parrish, 2004). Numerous studies examining the effects on both language development and interpretation of scientific concepts have shown that role-playing advances empathy and theory of mind, as well as problem-solving abilities (Fleer, 2009; Heath and Wolf, 2005).

Moreover, the play of hand gestures during such performances before others correlates with the extent to which individuals 'know what they are talking about' (Gentner and Goldin-Meadow, 2003). Thinking through and enlisting 'future memories' in one's embodiment within a performance leads to well-honed and appropriately timed and proportioned deictics, gestures, and schematic demonstrations. These complement verbal explication of what the speaker has in mind. Play using gestures embodies character and ideas and can help clarify thinking processes and offer practice essential to later language development. Meaningful practice across a range of roles (that enlist different amounts of emotional commitment) stimulates fluency in syntax and vocabulary needed to communicate to listeners the components, processes, and meanings that emerge within socio-dramatic play from early childhood through adolescence (Mandel and Wolf, 2003; Wagner, 1999). The reading of children's literature with children often leads them to take part(s) and to interject the voices of characters within the narratives (Wolf and Heath, 1992).

The visual-cognitive enhancement potential that infants hold in the hand and forearm develops into an ability to embody gesture as accompaniment to spoken language, props, and images. Within this capacity to take into the body an 'other' that is not the real person or current scene is the wonder of socio-dramatic play. Across all societies, children acquire the capacity to become someone else through mimicry and imitation in which embodiment of characteristics of personalities and roles can be portrayed. Since the 1960s, scholars have studied the effects of role-playing by young children (Heath and Wolf, 2005; Smilansky, 1968).

The forms of play that involve taking on the role of the other and speaking through that other persona merit particular attention for several reasons. We have noted the importance of gesture as a structured symbol system that undergirds the evolution of speaking. Within the socio-dramatic play of toddlers, gestures carry an extra-dramatic quality, often leading adults to label children (girls, especially) as 'drama queens.' What is often not noted among adults is the extent to which these gestures and the importation into the self of another illustrates the understanding that children of this age have of a theory of mind or recognition of the intentions, plans, and desires that others hold. Children illustrate in maturing ways from about 18 months through their pre-school years their sense of prediction and understanding of the general rules that others use as they interact not only with the child but also with other humans and objects in the environment (Gopnik and Meltzoff, 1998). Children's development of a theory of action, causation, and consequence is often portrayed through their socio-dramatic play.

In the relatively few studies of understanding of visual representations (including socio-dramatic performances) and intuited understanding of their portrayals of meaning that we have, the suggestion is strong that children who see more details and remember them are also likely to reason effectively about the use of certain kinds of evidence to test their beliefs. As children develop their understanding of representation and of themselves as coming to represent (or re-enact) certain actions, they intentionally enter into the cognitive loop of acknowledging as they view a scene that they have certain beliefs about it. Core to such beliefs is expectation of roles as children grow older. They seem to know that they must test their beliefs by sampling the scene or by seeing and integrating more details as they go along. In other words, they internally set out a pace and place toward which their learning moves. Hence they can develop in their mind new representations that may in turn update their beliefs. Moreover, certain kinds of activities (including repetition, decidedly positive emotional responses, etc.) reinforce children's volition (as well as attentiveness) and their willingness to try these actions and to accumulate experiences that lead to more participation and more kinds of activations of learning (Gazzaniga, 2008; Goldman, 2001).

Spokespersons from within professional theatre and education have inspired numerous versions of children's involvement in socio-dramatic play and theatre programs. In the United Kingdom, Dorothy Heathcote led teachers and theatre directors to create and perform plays with children and to follow these productions with the technique of 'hot-seating,' asking an individual who has played a particular character to speak within-character about his or her actions and feelings. This meta-linguistic technique brings into argumentation and deliberation the processes behind interpretation of the minds and emotions of others and inspires creative approaches to problem-solving, development of empathy, and resource-building within communities (Heathcote and Bolton, 1995; Spolin, 1986).[4]

Often the most critical aspect of socio-dramatic play is its multimodal expression of emotion, points of view, and character intentions and desires. The accumulated practice effects on build-up of vocabulary and syntactic structures and effective gesturing for emphasis and punctuation of points has been extensively documented in both educational and health settings of children (see, as examples, Bolton, 1979; Zigmond, 2003). Moreover, similar practice effects from presentation of one's body 'out there' along with one's words and facial expressions provide fundamental grounding for human cognition and later language development. Within embodied activity as performance, individuals build internal mental representations that enable a deep conceptual grasp of adaptive thinking and behavior. This is especially the case when improvisation is called for, as in the case of 'hot-seating' as well as within many types of theatre, such as readers' theater and improvisation workshops (Gibbs, 2006; Johnstone, 1989).

Play in Art and Science

Noted in the first section above was the general view from both scientists and artists that much of what they achieve comes from their sense of play within their work. Art and science are historically and cognitively linked (Edwards, 2008; Stafford, 1999). As children mature, they make projects of their play, and as they do so, they raise hypothetical questions, seek solutions, and search for relevant props, accomplices, and reasons for what they do. Project-based play is not segmented and digested *a priori*. This play results in performance, with individuals playing roles and contributing in improvisational as well as occasional routine ways. Play projects, like those of art and science, exist within the arc that runs from initial planning and preparation through practice and development to completion and meaningful sense of satisfaction (Kelly-Byrne, 1989).

Learning within this kind of play enables children to envision the projected play, undertake it (and perhaps sustain it over several days or more), and determine pace, quality, and ultimate ending point. Projects of play rely to a great extent on one or more child having had at least one human model along with several other sources, such as films, books, situations (e.g., school), and prior projects of play. These resources and models echo those that artists and scientists use as they create their projects.

However, it is perhaps ironic that it is not primarily the creativity that young children exhibit in their play that enables them to be 'scientists in the crib' and beyond. Central within play is making and conforming to routines, rules, and habituated patterns of particular contexts, actors, and, most particularly, of actors in relation to objects and places. Within games of competition, these aspects of play become most evident, but within spontaneous play with others or in monologues and other solitary play episodes, children create and adhere to rules, follow routines, and show their understanding of how others respond to situations and fellow humans. As children mature, they take pleasure in explaining to others a play project, how it originated in their head or evolved within a competitive game or sport, and what its outcome means to participants and onlookers. In doing so, they experience 'the sense of wonder and awe' that scientists and artists report having when they are called upon to explain their work (Gopnik, Meltzoff, and Kuhl, 1999).

Many aspects of play echo projects of art and science through their arousal of peak emotions that stimulate long-term memory and heighten what cognitive psychologists have termed 'executive function.' Children at play, along with artists and scientists, remember the highs and the lows of their imagined, explored, represented, and dramatized worlds. Remembering what they have creatively enacted, they carry forward information and experiences that enable them to think hypothetically, to project a 'what if?' idea into action. They can do this not only because of how they have felt emotionally within their play, art, and science, but also because they must take the fullest possible advantage of their visual powers first and foremost in order to explore, discover, and create 'with the mind's eye.'[5]

Conclusion: Metaphors of the Thinking Hand

The play of young children gives most to their development of productive and receptive abilities with structured symbol systems, including literacies across media, when they engage extensively with interactive partnering adults who explore nature and encourage creative projects of representation. Such play can involve technologies of all types from dolls and scooters to kitchen and garage tools and shovels and rakes. From early childhood through the lifespan, individuals have to play, for only through play do individuals learn to explore the environment, manipulate artifacts and use tools, identify problems and try out solutions, and discover unknowns and new ways of using knowns. As play happens, language learning expands and multiplies uses of images, music, dance, drama, and poetry. Young children whose early lives have been rich with play move into middle childhood and adolescence with a keenness to experiment with and interpret multiple modes of representation that include all those available on the Internet as well as within projects of art and science. Using photographs, charts and graphs, video films, and other modes of representation, they present themselves through the social networking offered by the Internet. They develop self-sustaining interests that often lead them to want to follow these interests toward expertise development. In doing so, they produce and interpret different genres and new media combinations, and they put together for themselves communities of like learners. The Internet and its related technologies generate new and hybrid forms of performance, such as text-messaging, blogging, and tweeting, but they also propel groups and individuals to consider ways to invent new activities as well as to devise innovative combinations of both prior and new components of technology (Barron, 2006).

Reading and writing increase in relation to the number and types of technologies over which maturing young learners seek and gain control. Simply being a spectator of a television program adds little or nothing by way of increased fluency with oral language. However, creating texts of different lengths and being a member of online and face-to-face communities dedicated to particular interests increase a sense of self-as-learner-and-actor. With this developing sense, individuals and small groups of young learners invent, adapt, and revise communication forms and adjust their performances (e.g., as humourist, athlete, videographer, or lyricist) in the hope of positive responses from peer evaluators. A sense of play lies behind the adaptive strategies older children and adolescents develop and practice through the Internet.

But for infants and pre-schoolers, simply pushing buttons, swiping the finger across a screen, hitting keys, and seeing and hearing stories via electronic media do not give children 'the hand of play.' The ultimate craft of the play that children, artists, and scientists naturally take up leads them to create representations of what they and their actions are about. The power of representation lies in the hand that must sketch, draw, model, gesture, and demonstrate what is in the head. The hand leads to represent what is only envisioned. Philosophers recognized the special powers of the hand long before neurologists linked the actions of the hand to the evolutionary course of primates and the language capacities of humans. Martin Heidegger expressed the view that within every motion of the hand at work was an 'element of thinking' (Heidegger, 1977, p. 357). Gaston Bachelard, in his volume on the 'poetics of space' and also in his work on imagination, linked the hand to the human capacity to understand matter (Bachelard, 1969, 1982). Artists, particularly potters and sculptors, but also writers, often express the view that they gain a sense of where their work will take them only when their hands go to work. This play of the hand literally takes the self into the world, crossing the boundary between self as subject and materials and the world as object.

The arguments of artists and scientists join with those of neuroscientists and human developmentalists to underscore the cognitive and linguistic work of the hand. From the forearm through the hand to the digits, infants can touch and come to know those who care for them. As they mature, they reach into the world to explore materials they can mould, objects they can manipulate, and artistic media, including words, with which they can represent their imaginings and tacit knowledge. In a world where economic and political theories and policies promote consumerism, verbal and mathematical knowledge and skills, and greater productivity in work, the processes of envisionment, embodiment, and project embeddedness that play encompasses have been left behind by parents, schools, and society at large. The consequences that medical authorities, learning theorists, and cognitive neuroscientists caution against appear to have little effect on restoring young children's play within families habituated to entertainment and material acquisition. In modern economies where intelligence, good judgment, and accurate assessment of consequences are put forward as the generators of industry and advancement, the interdependence of the hand and brain in children's play cannot, must not, be ignored.[6]

Notes

1. Heath (2012) introduces the concept of 'intimate strangers,' defining these individuals as trustees of children during nonschool hours during both the academic year and summer breaks.
2. The central debates, offered in 'Taking Play Seriously' (Ings, 2002), indicate the extent to which concerns with play have long been interdisciplinary. Ethnologists, such as Robert Fagan and Peter Smith, have led the way in this work, often reaching points of agreement with anthropologists, such as Helen Schwartzman and David Lancy, who study play across cultures. See a collection of works by these authors in Pellegrini (1995).
3. Mirror neurons, discovered in the late 1990s, are aroused as individuals watch another perform. The networks in which they are located draw equivalences between the self-initiated action and those of others. This is possible because the other individual's actions become 'mapped' onto one's own. These neurons occur in other higher-order primates and enable them to imitate. Within humans, these neurons provide partial support for the ability not merely to imitate but also to move from mimesis to creative reconstruction (Rizzolatti, Fogassi, and Gallese, 2001).

4. When Prime Minister Tony Blair came into office in the United Kingdom at the end of the twentieth century, feverish activities promoting and implementing creative partnerships within and beyond schools took place not only within the United Kingdom but also in other parts of the world where creative efforts could be supported through the British Council. Numerous conferences set off rounds of planning, implementing, and assessing. Reports from these conferences portray the conviction that 'creative industry,' craft work with the hands, and the revitalization of creative connections between peoples, across ages, and with the environment, could regenerate areas impoverished by the loss of mining and manufacturing jobs. Creative efforts, often through combinations of several arts, were put forth to help reform medical care, schooling, and community-building. See, for example, Fyfe, 2002; Hoadley, 2003; Jupp, Fairly, and Bentley, 2001; Ings, 2002). Much of the impetus behind these efforts came from the research studies of a team of scholars and practitioners who worked to produce the report that led to Robinson (2001).

5. Human development theorists, along with poets, have written about the parallels of learning through play that children, scientists, and artists share. (See especially Gopnik, Meltzoff, and Kuhl, 1999, pp. 206–211.)

6. With a possible eye toward recognizing the interdependence of hand and brain, some higher education institutions have taken steps to create focused learning of subjects and practices that have the potential to enable recovery of what is increasingly being lost in childhoods deprived of 'the hand of play' and the artistic forms generated within play. For example, as of the opening term of 2013–2014, all Stanford University students, regardless of major or concentration, will be required to take the following set of eight courses in order to receive their college diploma: one course in aesthetic and interpretive inquiry, two courses in social inquiry, two courses in scientific analysis, one course in formal reasoning, one course in quantitative reasoning, one course in engaging difference, one course in moral and ethical reasoning, and one course in creative expression. Of the eight, five seem highly likely to involve elements of play, art, and science, along with opportunities for playful creative expression and aesthetic interpretation.

References

Bachelard, G. (1969) *The Poetics of Space*. Boston: Beacon Press.

Bachelard, G. (1982) *Water and Dreams: An Essay on the Imagination of Matter*. Dallas, TX: The Pegasus Foundation.

Barron, B. (2006) Interest and self-sustained learning as catalysts of development: A learning ecologies perspective. *Human Development*, 49: 193–224.

Bell, H.C., Pellis, S.M., and Kolb, B. (2010) Juvenile peer play experience and development of the orbitofrontal and medial prefrontal cortices. *Behavioural Brain Research*, 207: 7–13.

Bolton, Gavin. (1979) *Toward a Theory of Drama in Education*. London: Longman.

Bruner, J., and Lucariello, J. (1989) Monologue as narrative recreation of the world. In K. Nelson (ed.) *Narratives from the Crib*. Cambridge, MA: Harvard University Press, pp. 73–97.

Byers, J.A. (1998a) The biology of human play. *Child Development* 69: 599–600.

Byers, J.A. (1998b) Biological effects of locomotor play: General or specific? In M. Bekoff and J.A. Byers (eds) *Animal Play: Evolutionary, Comparative, and Ecological Perspectives*. Cambridge: Cambridge University Press.

Byers, J.A. (1999) Play's the thing. *Natural History*, July: 40–45.

Cazden, C. (1976) Play with language and meta-linguistic awareness: One dimension of language experience. In J. Bruner, A. Jolly, and K. Sylva (eds) *Play*. New York: Penguin, pp. 603–608.

Chudacoff, H.P. (2007) *Children at Play: An American History*. New York: New York University Press.

Donald, M. (2001) *A Mind so Rare: The Evolution of Human Consciousness*. New York: Norton.

Edmiston, B. (2008) *Forming Ethical Identities in Early Childhood Play*. London: Routledge.

Edwards, D. (2008) *Artscience: Creativity in the post-Google Generation*. Cambridge, MA: Harvard University Press.

Evaldsson, A. (1993) *Play Disputes and Social Order: Everyday Life in Two Swedish After-school Centers.* Linköping: Department of Communication Studies, Linköping University.

Feldman, C.F. (1989) Monologue as problem-solving narrative. In K. Nelson (ed.) *Narratives from the Crib.* Cambridge, MA: Harvard University Press, pp. 98–122.

Fleer, M. (2009) Supporting scientific conceptual consciousness or learning in 'a roundabout way' in play-based contexts. *International Journal of Science Education*, 31(8): 1069–1089.

Fyfe, H. (2002) *She Danced ... and We Danced: Artists, Creativity and Education.* Belfast, Ireland: Stanmillis Press.

Galda, L., and Pellegrini, A.D. (eds) (1985) *Play, Language, and Stories: The Development of Children's Literate Behavior.* Norwood, NJ: Ablex.

Gazzaniga, M.S. (2008) *Human: The Science Behind what Makes us Unique.* New York: HarperCollins.

Gentner, D., and Goldin-Meadow, S. (eds) (2003) *Language in Mind: Advances in the Study of Language and Thought.* Cambridge, MA: MIT Press.

Gibbs, R.W. (2006) *Embodiment and Cognitive Science.* Cambridge, UK: Cambridge University Press.

Gilbert, J.K., Reiner, M., and Nakhleh, M. (eds) (2008) *Visualization: Theory and Practice in Science Education.* Surrey, UK: Springer.

Goldman, A. (2001) Desire, intention, and the simulation theory. In B.F. Malle, L.J. Moses, and D.A. Baldwin (eds) *Intentions and Intentionality: Foundations of Social Cognition.* Cambridge, MA: MIT Press, pp. 207–224.

Gopnik, A., and Meltzoff, A.N. (1998) *Words, Thoughts, and Theories.* Cambridge, MA: MIT Press.

Gopnik, A., Meltzoff, A.N., and Kuhl, P.K. (1999) *The Scientist in the Crib: What Early Learning Tells us About the Mind.* New York: HarperCollins.

Heath, S.B. (1983/1996) *Ways with Words: Language, Life, and Work in Communities and Classrooms.* Cambridge, UK: Cambridge University Press.

Heath, S.B. (2012) *Words at Work and Play: Three Decades in Family and Community Life.* Cambridge, UK: Cambridge University Press.

Heath, S.B., and Wolf, S.A. (2005) *Dramatic Learning in the Primary School.* London: Creative Partnerships.

Heathcote, D., and Bolton, G. (1995) *Drama for Learning: Dorothy Heathcote's Mantle of the Expert Approach to Education.* Portsmouth, NH: Heinemann.

Heidegger, M. (1977) *Basic Writings.* New York: Harper and Row.

Hoadley, J. (ed.) (2003) *Image and imagination.* Belfast, Ireland: Stanmillis Press.

Huizinga, J. (1939/1955) *Homo Ludens: A Study of the Play Element in Culture.* Boston: Beacon Press.

Ings, R. (2002) *Taking it Seriously: Youth Arts in the Real World.* Leicester, UK: National Youth Agency.

Ingvar, D. (1998) Memory of the future: An essay on the temporal organization of conscious awareness. *Human Neurology*, 4(3): 127–129.

Johnstone, K. (1989) *Impro: Improvisation and the Theatre.* London: Methuen Drama.

Jupp, R., Fairly, C., and Bentley, T. (2001) *What Learning Needs: The Challenge for a Creative Nation.* London: Demos.

Katz, C. (2004) *Growing up Global: Economic Restructuring and Children's Everyday Lives.* Minneapolis, MN: University of Minnesota Press.

Kelly-Byrne, D. (1989) *A Child's Play Life.* New York: Teachers College Press.

Lancy, D.F. (2008) *The Anthropology of Childhood: Cherubs, Chattel, Changelings.* New York: Cambridge University Press.

Louv, R. (2005) *Last Child in the Woods: Saving our Children from Nature Deficit.* Chapel Hill, NC: Algonquin Books.

Mandel, J., and Wolf, J. (2003) *Acting, Learning, and Change: Creating Original Plays with Adolescents.* Portsmouth, NH: Heinemann.

McNeill, D. (2005) *Gesture and Thought.* Chicago: University of Chicago Press.

Meier, D., Engel, B.S., and Taylor, B. (2010) *Playing for Keeps: Life and Learning on a Public (State) School Playground.* New York: Teachers College Press.

Meltzoff, A.N., Kuhl, P.K., Movellan, J., and Sejnowski, T. (2011) Foundations for a new science of learning. *Science*, 325(5938): 284–288.

Nelson, K. (1989) Monologue as representation of real-life experience. In K. Nelson (ed.) *Narratives from the Crib*. Cambridge, MA: Harvard University Press, pp. 27–72.

Opie, I., and Opie, P. (1959) *The Language and Lore of Schoolchildren*. New York: Oxford University Press.

Pallasmaa, J. (2009) *The Thinking Hand: Existential and Embodied Wisdom in Architecture*. Chichester, UK: Wiley.

Parrish, B. (2004) *Teaching Adult ESL: A Practical Introduction*. New York: McGraw Hill.

Pellegrini, A.D. (ed.) (1995) *The Future of Play Theory*. Albany, NY: SUNY Press.

Pellis, S.M., and Pellis, V.C. (2009) Play and the socially competent brain. *PlayRights*, 2: 4–7.

Pellis, S.M., Pellis, V.C., and Bell, H.C. (2010) The function of play in the development of the social brain. *American Journal of Play*, 2: 278–296.

Pellis, S.M., and Pellis, V.C. (2010) *The Playful Brain. Venturing to the Limits of Neuroscience*. Oxford: Oneworld Press.

Reiner, M. (2000) The validity and consistency of force feedback interfaces in telesurgery. *Journal of Computer-aided Surgery*, 9: 69–74.

Reiner, M. (2008) The nature and development of visualization: A review of what is known. In J.K. Gilbert, M. Reiner, and M. Nakhleh (eds) *Visualization: Theory and Practice in Science Education*. New York: Springer, pp. 25–29.

Rizzolatti, G., Fogassi, L., and Gallese, V. (2001) Neurophysiological mechanisms underlying the understanding and imitation of action. *Nature Reviews Neuroscience*, 2: 661–670.

Robinson, K. (2001) *Out of our Minds: Learning to be Creative*. New York: Wiley.

Schwartzman, H.B. (1978) *Transformations: The Anthropology of Children's Play*. New York: Plenum Press.

Smilansky, S. (1968) *The Effects of Sociodramatic Play on Disadvantaged Preschool Children*. New York: Wiley.

Spolin, V. (1986) *Theatre Games for the Classroom*. Chicago: Northwestern University Press.

Stafford, B. (1999) *Artful Science: Enlightenment, Entertainment, and the Eclipse of Visual Education*. Cambridge, MA: MIT Press.

Sutton-Smith, B. (1997) *The Ambiguity of Play*. Cambridge, MA: Harvard University Press.

Sylva, K., Bruner, J.S., and Genova, P. (1976) The role of play in the problem-solving of children 3–5 years old. In J. Bruner, A. Jolly, and K. Sylva (eds) *Play*. New York: Penguin, pp. 244–257.

Wagner, B.J. (ed.) (1999) *Building Moral Communities through Educational Drama*. Stamford, CN: Ablex.

Wilson, F. (1998) *The Hand: How Its Use Shapes the Brain, Language, and Human Culture*. New York: Vintage Books.

Wolf, S.A., and Heath, S.B. (1992) *The Braid of Literature: Children's Worlds of Reading*. Cambridge, MA: Harvard University Press.

Zigmond, H. (2003) Reaching out: Exploring the sensate world through the imagination. In J. Hoadley (ed.) *Image and Imagination*. Belfast: Stanmillis Press, pp. 64–73.

Part II
School, Culture, and Pedagogy

Chapter 15

Building Word and World Knowledge in the Early Years

Susan B. Neuman, Ashley M. Pinkham, and Tanya Kaefer

Introduction

Although educators have made substantial progress in helping children learn how to decode, it is disheartening that we still have not overcome the so-called 'fourth grade slump,' the sudden decline in reading achievement that occurs as children transition from learning to read to reading to learn (Chall, Jacobs, and Baldwin, 1990). Even though the vast majority of students can read simple texts, many students struggle when tackling more complex content texts with academic vocabulary. Children who had previously been average, or even above average, learners begin a steady drop in achievement around age nine that often grows steeper as they move into higher grades.

The decline in achievement may appear sudden. There is increasing evidence, however, that the problems leading to this decline already exist in the early years. Studies have demonstrated that a large language gap exists between advantaged and disadvantaged children by the age of four, if not earlier. Hart and Risley (1995, 2003), for example, have argued that the accumulated experiences with words for children who come from poverty compared with children from professional families may constitute a differential of almost 30 million words. By age seven, middle-class children are likely to have acquired around 6,000 root word meanings, whereas children in the lowest quartile of income know around 4,000 root words. This gap, estimated to equal about two grade levels, may be especially difficult to close (Biemiller, 2006).

Words are conveyors of knowledge and information. Therefore, it is not surprising that studies have reported a strong association between children's vocabulary knowledge and comprehension skills (Verhoeven and van Leeuwe, 2008), with background knowledge as a particularly critical feature of children's developing understanding (Barnes, Dennis, and Haefele-Kalvaitis, 1996; Pinkham and Neuman, 2012). Consequently, in efforts to prepare children for learning to read, it is crucial to recognize the important role of word and world knowledge in early literacy, and to balance children's skill development with their conceptual knowledge development better (Neuman, 2001). To make this argument, we first examine the building blocks necessary for children's word learning and knowledge acquisition. We next review the crucial environmental influences that lead to the vocabulary and knowledge differential, and

International Handbook of Research on Children's Literacy, Learning, and Culture, First Edition.
Edited by Kathy Hall, Teresa Cremin, Barbara Comber, and Luis C. Moll.
© 2013 John Wiley & Sons, Ltd. Published 2013 by John Wiley & Sons, Ltd.

then trace how these differences contribute to a knowledge gap – a gap potentially far more detrimental than achievement score differences. We end by describing a program designed to facilitate low-income children's literacy development through the teaching of word and world knowledge during the early years.

The Building Blocks of Word Learning

On the surface, word learning may look like a simple task. Children listen to their parents and family speaking and, over time, they come to associate individual words with their referents. By this account, word learning can be explained through simple association and imitation. While taking a walk through the park, a young child sees a seagull flying overhead. Noticing her interest, her mother says, 'That is a bird. Do you see the bird flying in the sky?' The child points at the seagull and repeats, 'Bird!' As easy as that, a new word is learned.

In reality, however, word learning appears to be anything but simple. Learning even the simplest words is a complex process requiring rich lexical, social, and conceptual capacities (Bloom, 2000). Consider again the mother telling her child, 'That's a bird.' There could be an infinite number of possible meanings for *bird*. It could refer to birds, but it could also refer to animals in general, or wings, or flying, or things that are white. Furthermore, the child must figure out that the new word is *bird* and not, for example, *abird* or *tisabird*.

Before a new word can be learned, children must solve at least three crucial problems: (1) segmentation, (2) reference, and (3) extension (Quine, 1960). These problems are what make word learning so complex – but the fact that even very young children can solve the problems makes word learning so impressive.

The problem of segmentation

When listening to speech, we hear a sequence of words, yet we do not separate those words with pauses when we speak. For word learning to occur, children must first solve the problem of extracting individual words from continuous speech. The child must figure out that her mother is telling her 'That-is-a-bird' and not 'Thatis-abird.' This is particularly critical because only 9 percent of mother-to-child utterances contain isolated words, such as 'bird' (Brent and Siskind, 2001).

Remarkably, even infants as young as 7.5 months of age are capable of extracting individual words from continuous speech (Jusczyk and Aslin, 1995). How do such young children learn where one word ends and another begins? Children attend to prosody and intonational changes, such as initial stress and pitch movements marking the ends of clauses (Johnson and Seidl, 2009). They listen for familiar carrier phrases, such as 'Look at the __!' or 'Where is the __?' to help identify new words. Children also group together syllables that frequently co-occur (Aslin, Saffran, and Newport, 1998). Given enough experience listening to English, for example, children can establish that in the four-syllable sequence *prettybaby*, the syllables *pre+tty* and *ba+by* are each more likely to co-occur than *tty+ba*. Such statistical learning helps children to correctly identify individual words and word boundaries.

Importantly, children's experience with language helps bootstrap their statistical learning (Lany and Gómez, 2008), which can then bootstrap word learning (Estes *et al.*, 2007). As children gain experience segmenting speech, they construct a lexicon of phonological forms that exemplifies the typical phonological properties of English words. They can then use these properties to segment speech in a usefully biased manner, thereby helping them identify even more new words and facilitating subsequent word learning (Thiessen, Hill, and Saffran, 2005). Language exposure may thus be critical for solving the problem of segmentation but, unfortunately, this is also an area in which profound socio-economic status-related (SES-related) differences exist (Hart and Risley, 2003).

The problem of reference

Once children successfully segment continuous speech into individual words, they must then focus in on the correct meaning of any unfamiliar words. Given the huge number of possibilities, how do children figure out what an unfamiliar word is describing? According to Markman (1990), children may be limited in what they consider as possible word meanings. These lexical constraints include the 'whole object assumption,' which states that children assume new words refer to whole objects (for example, *bird* refers to the bird) rather than parts or properties of the object. They may also make use of words they already know. According to the 'mutual exclusivity assumption,' children expect that each object only has one label. If both a bird and an airplane are flying in the sky and the child already knows the word *airplane,* she may be biased to assume that *bird* refers to the other object – even if she has never heard the word *bird* before.

Lexical constraints, however, are only part of the story. Children must also utilize the social-pragmatic cues provided by the speaker. First, children must figure out the focus of the speaker's attention, determining if it is the same or different than the focus of the child's own attention. In many Western cultures, adults frequently use words to describe what children are attending to at the moment the word is spoken. For infants and toddlers, this may be the case as much as 70 percent of the time (Harris, Jones, and Grant, 1983). That leaves at least 30 percent of cases in which the word learning event is non-ostensive and children must use other cues – such as eye gaze, pointing, and context – to uncover the word's referent. Yet, strikingly, mapping errors are virtually nonexistent under such circumstances (Akhtar, 2005).

In addition to determining the speaker's attention, children must also infer the speaker's referential intention. When hearing a new word, sometimes children are looking at the correct referent, and sometimes they are not. For successful word learning, they must learn that referential intent is more informative than spatial-temporal co-occurrence. In fact, even 18-month-old children appear sensitive to the fact that word-object mappings are established through an intentional process. The child who observes the bird flying in the sky may assume that it is called a *bird* only if the speaker is also attending to the bird. If she just hears a disembodied voice (for example, a voice from across the park shouting 'Check out the bird!') while she is simultaneously looking at the bird, she is unlikely to learn the new word. Similarly, children who hear an unfamiliar verb, such as 'I'm going to stipple,' followed by an intentional behavior, such as a painting demonstration, are more likely to learn the new word-action mapping than if they viewed an accidental one, such as dropping a paintbrush and saying 'Whoops!' However, when interpersonal interaction is lacking and a speaker's referential intention is less clear, children may experience greater difficulty solving the problem of reference and, consequently, their word learning may be limited.

The problem of extension

After children solve the problems of segmentation and reference, one could argue that the only hurdle to word learning is memory: that is, making sure the mapping between the new word and its referent is sufficiently strong to be remembered over time. By this criterion, however, word learning would be extremely limited. If the child only learned that *bird* refers to that particular bird flying over the park and nothing else, she would need to learn a new word for every different bird she encounters. Rather than learning a rich language comprised of count nouns, verbs, and adjectives, she would instead possess a lexicon only filled with proper names. Memory, then, is not the only remaining hurdle; children must also solve the problem of extension. When learning the word *bird*, children must figure out that the word should be extended to other members of the category 'bird', such as seagulls, penguins, flamingos. They need to figure out that *bird* should not be generalized to other white things, other flying things, and so forth. Moreover, children need to recognize, for example, how birds are different from dogs and how seagulls are different from penguins.

Word learning is thus a case of inductive learning, requiring some knowledge of the conditions underlying category membership (Bloom, 2000). Children must understand both the concept of the word, as well as the meaning of the word and its concept. They must then correctly generalize the new word to other members of the category. How do children solve this problem? They may be biased to assume that new words refer to objects of like kind rather than objects that are thematically related (Markman, 1990). Before this can happen, they must first figure out which properties are necessary for category membership. To extend the word *bird* to a penguin she later sees at the zoo, the child in the park must know what properties of seagulls make it a bird (for example, it lays eggs and that it has wings) and what properties are nonessential or irrelevant, such as its color.

Young children are relatively flexible in their categorization and may appropriately consider a range of properties, such as perceptual appearance (Keil, 1989) and shared essences (Gelman, 2003), when determining category membership. However, categorization – and, as a result, the extension of new words – are at least partially dependent upon children's knowledge about the word's underlying concept. Although this knowledge may be introduced at the same time as the new word, children often need to draw upon their pre-existing knowledge. Facilitating children's knowledge acquisition is thus crucial for building their vocabulary knowledge.

The Building Blocks of World Knowledge

Children's knowledge acquisition is vital for successful word learning, but it also influences literacy beyond vocabulary development. In fact, children's world knowledge may be one of the strongest predictors of their literacy development (Neuman, 2011; Pinkham and Neuman, 2012). Consider the following: 'Cut and join enough bias strips for the required length and wide enough to cover the cord plus the seam allowance.' Although each individual word may be familiar, only readers with knowledge of sewing may fully comprehend the sentence's meaning. In this way, background knowledge may be one of the most powerful influences on children's comprehension and may even help compensate for low reading aptitude.

Studies (for example, Shapiro, 2004) have repeatedly demonstrated the importance of background knowledge in reading comprehension. For example, after reading a passage describing a half-inning of a baseball game, children's understanding of the passage depended upon their pre-existing knowledge: poor readers with high knowledge of baseball displayed better comprehension than good readers with low knowledge of baseball (Recht and Leslie, 1988). This process may be further facilitated if children's background knowledge is already organized into a semantic framework that can readily accommodate the new information (Gelman, 2009). When Kendeou and van den Broek (2007), for instance, examined the comprehension of individuals with accurate background knowledge about science as compared to individuals who held misconceptions about science, they found that readers holding misconceptions misunderstood the text more frequently than readers possessing accurate knowledge. In fact, interventions that give attention to the structure and function of children's knowledge base appear particularly beneficial for comprehension outcomes (Taconis, Ferguson-Hessler, and Broekkamp, 2001)

Given the impact of children's knowledge on their literacy development, how can we best facilitate their knowledge acquisition? Children may acquire background knowledge and information through a variety of experiences. In particular, children may draw upon three important resources: their firsthand experiences, interactions with other people, and interactions with materials.

First-hand experience

Children frequently acquire information about the world through firsthand experience. Under some circumstances, young children may even privilege what they have directly perceived or experienced over what trusted adults tell or show them (Ma and Ganea, 2010; Pinkham and Jaswal, 2011). Everyday play activities, for example, may provide children with the experiences necessary for knowledge-building. During object play, children may explore objects, learn about their properties, and consider their possible functions. Accordingly, object play is positively associated with problem-solving skills and literacy development, especially when children are provided with literacy-related materials such as paper, crayons, and plastic letters.

Interactions with other people

Although children can acquire a great deal of information through direct experience, much of the knowledge children need to acquire is difficult or impossible to directly observe. To discover the dietary habits of lions, for example, one is much more likely to ask a zoologist than travel to the savannah to observe the behavior directly. Under these circumstances, learning from others is essential.

Explicit instruction may be a particularly valuable means of transmitting knowledge, especially when information is conceptually challenging or children lack sufficient prior knowledge to guide implicit learning. In a recent meta-analysis of vocabulary interventions, Marulis and Neuman (2010) found that children benefit more from explicit instruction than implicit exposure to unfamiliar words. Similarly, Klahr and Nigam (2004) have reported that children who receive explicit instruction are more able to acquire and transfer new science-related knowledge than children engaged in discovery learning. Moreover, children who receive explicit instruction have been shown to demonstrate superior conceptual understanding as much as five months after the initial lesson (Matlen and Klahr, 2010).

Another important way in which children may gain knowledge is through everyday conversations with adults. The quantity (Hart and Risley, 1995), variety (Weizman and Snow, 2001), and syntactic complexity (Huttenlocher *et al.*, 2002) of these conversations strongly and consistently predict children's language development. Such lexical features, however, essentially transmit code-based information. For these conversations to facilitate children's knowledge acquisition, parents and teachers who *talk* more must also *say* more. Recent research from our lab at the University of Michigan suggests that the content may also matter, particularly when transmitted through talk that is removed from the immediate time and place (Pinkham, Kaefer, and Neuman, 2011a). We asked mothers and their kindergarten-aged children to complete two literacy-related activities: playing a matching game and 'reading' a wordless picture-book. Subsequent factor analyses revealed two distinct constructs related to mothers' talk. The first construct, dubbed 'lexical richness,' included features such as the quantity and variety of maternal language. This construct significantly predicted children's vocabulary knowledge and oral language comprehension, thereby replicating previous research. More interesting was the second construct, which included conceptually demanding elements such as decontextualization, categorization, and symbolic representation. This construct, dubbed 'representational demand,' predicted child outcomes above and beyond lexical richness. These results suggest that while the amount of lexical input may be necessary for children's knowledge development, the conceptually demanding content of that input may also be crucial.

Interactions with materials

Materials can also be important sources of knowledge, and may convey information above and beyond what is learned through interactions with other people. Books, for instance, are valuable sources of rich language and information about the world, and children who read more experience greater opportunities to develop their knowledge (Cunningham and Stanovich, 1998). In recent work (Kaefer, Pinkham, and Neuman, 2011; Pinkham, Kaefer, and Neuman, 2011b), we hypothesized that storybook texts could build knowledge more effectively if they were structured in a manner that would scaffold children's learning. Specifically, we examined whether taxonomically organized storybooks could provide children with a general conceptual framework through which information could be readily encoded and subsequently remembered. We found that children learned significantly more words and content knowledge from taxonomically organized storybooks than traditional storybooks. Although book reading may be an important context for building knowledge, our findings suggest that books also must be selected carefully to provide children with every opportunity to acquire that knowledge.

Screen media, such as television and film, may also build children's knowledge (Neuman, 2008). In fact, children may use the same cognitive resources to comprehend televised messages as they use to comprehend printed text (Kendeou *et al.*, 2005). Although younger children may not learn information as readily from televised content as from firsthand experience (i.e., 'video deficit;' Anderson and Pempek, 2005), screen media can nonetheless be a valuable resource, particularly when information is difficult or impossible for children to directly experience. However, the benefits of screen media may depend upon what is viewed and how it is viewed. Pre-schoolers and elementary school students tend to devote greater attention to screen content that is both cognitively challenging and informative (Lorch and Castle, 1997), and their recall and comprehension of content may be related to the amount of mental effort invested during viewing (Salomon, 1984). But since fewer than 10 percent of the scenes in most child-directed educational programs contain the cognitively demanding language and content that best promote literacy development, screen media may be most beneficial in shared viewing contexts akin to shared book reading experiences.

Summary

In sum, the depth and breadth of children's knowledge base are crucial for their successful literacy development. Vocabulary and background knowledge may be acquired from a variety of sources, and the appropriateness and reliability of the source may depend on the type of knowledge being sought. Although some knowledge may be acquired through firsthand observation and direct experience, other types of knowledge must be gathered from external sources and may require additional guidance. Children need access to a variety of resources that guide and support their content learning, both within the classroom and at home.

Environmental Influences on Literacy Development

There are profound differences in word and world knowledge among learners from different socio-economic groups. Consider, for example, the number of studies showing that six-year-olds from higher-SES backgrounds know at least twice as many words as lower-SES children (Graves, 2006). Furthermore, higher-SES children tend to possess greater world knowledge than their lower-SES peers (Kaefer, Pinkham, and Neuman, 2011). Familial processes for why poverty takes such a toll on children's knowledge and general cognitive processes, in particular, have been explained through two major pathways (Neuman, 2008). By the first pathway, poverty affects families' ability to invest in resources related to children's cognitive development. Income enables families to purchase materials, lessons, summer camps, stimulating learning materials and activities, in addition to better quality early childhood care. Entwisle, Alexander, and Olson (1997) have suggested that these out-of-school experiences are key factors that differentiate low-income from middle-income achievement and perpetuate, rather than reduce, the achievement gap. By the second pathway, poverty affects parents' emotional resources, including their personal well-being and interactions with their children, which, in turn, affects child outcomes. McLoyd (1998), for example, has argued that economic hardship may significantly impact parents' ability to interact and provide warmth and responsive parenting.

Given few material resources and few emotional resources, it is hardly surprising that hundreds of studies have documented dramatic, linear, negative relationships between poverty and children's cognitive developmental outcomes (see Grissmer and Eiseman, 2008, for review). In one large-scale study of children entering kindergarten (Lee and Burkham, 2002), high-status children scored, on average, 60 percent better than low-status children on cognitive skills assessments. These findings were replicated in a recent analysis by Halle and colleagues (2009), who reported disparities across multiple domains of development, including cognitive development, social-emotional development, and general health. In fact, they found that evidence of a SES-related gap emerged as early as 9 months of age.

To develop the comprehension skills essential for reading achievement, children need both vocabulary and background knowledge. Although the presence of these two skills does not necessarily guarantee reading achievement, children will not be successful in reading comprehension in the absence of either skill. However, relatively little research has addressed the differences among children in word and world knowledge, and how these differences may impact literacy development. Left unaddressed, the knowledge gap between socio-economic status groups may widen with each successive age level, becoming insurmountable after just a few years of schooling. The early childhood years are thus crucial for providing children with the foundational knowledge and skills necessary for lifelong reading achievement.

Enhancing Word and World Knowledge for Low-income Pre-schoolers: The World of Words

Given the importance of building children's word and world knowledge during the early childhood years, we developed a supplementary curriculum aimed at enhancing these critical skills. The World of Words (WOW) vocabulary program (Neuman *et al.*, 2007) is designed to maximize children's opportunities to learn words and concepts that target science, math, and health content standards early on in pre-school. Two key principles underlie its design. First, content-related vocabulary is taught through rich concepts structured as taxonomies. Taxonomies are hierarchical groupings based upon shared essential properties; for example, katydid and grasshopper are both members of the taxonomic category 'insects.' As they are hierarchically-nested, children's familiarity with a taxonomic category may allow inferences to be drawn that go beyond firsthand knowledge or experience (Gelman, 2003). If children know that animals need food to survive, for example, they may make inferences about category members at increasingly specific levels: insects are animals, therefore insects need food to survive; grasshoppers are insects, insects are animals, therefore grasshoppers need food to survive; and so forth. By learning words through this categorization process, WOW is intended to help children develop an efficient method for organizing newly acquired knowledge.

The second principle is that WOW uses embedded multimedia strategies in which animations and other videos are woven into teachers' lessons. The use of embedded multimedia is based on two related theoretical models. First, Neuman (2009) proposed that multimedia can support word learning and knowledge development through a synergistic relationship. Second, in his dual-coding theory, Paivio (1990) posited that visual and verbal sources of information are processed by distinct neural channels. As a result, separate mental representations are created of the information processed in each channel; together, these representations are used to organize new knowledge, which can then be stored and retrieved for subsequent use.

Structurally, the curriculum is organized across three units: healthy habits, living things, and mathematical concepts. There are four topics in each unit, and each topic is taught over an 8-day period. Consider, for example, the topic 'insects.' Each day begins with a 1- to 2-minute *tuning-in* (such as a relevant rhyme, song or word-play video clip) to bring children together to the circle and engage them in playing with language. The tuning-in is followed by a *content* video that introduces children to the taxonomic category. After children have viewed the video, the teacher discusses the taxonomic category with the children, particularly focusing on *wh-* questions. For example, she might ask, 'What is an insect?' or 'Where does a katydid live?' Vocabulary is then reinforced through reading an informational book specially designed to review the words and taxonomic category just learned (for example, antennae, wings, camouflage), as well as reinforce information in a different medium. On subsequent days, the teacher provides increasing supports to develop vocabulary and conceptual knowledge, including using additional videos that introduce words and properties that are both in and outside the taxonomic category (for example, insects have six legs and three body segments) and review previously learned information. The teacher then reads a section from a specially-designed information book in which the target vocabulary words are presented in a new context. Picture cards are also used as a strategy for reviewing information; children can also sort these cards by taxonomic category membership. Last, children's learning is reviewed through journal writing activities that involve developmental writing. In this review, they engage in expressing their ideas through pictures and print, providing an opportunity to extend what they have learned about the topic (Dyson, 1993). All topics follow a similar instructional design format.

Study findings

Two recent studies from our lab have demonstrated the potential of WOW to improve children's word and world knowledge. The first study, a quasi-experimental study with 322 children in treatment and control groups, provided initial evidence that children could learn content-rich words and could retain word knowledge over time (Neuman and Dwyer, 2011). The second study (Neuman, Newman, and Dwyer, 2011) was far more ambitious. We conducted a randomized control trial of 28 Head Start classrooms in a high-poverty urban area with the goal of determining how WOW might increase vocabulary and conceptual knowledge tied to pre-kindergarten content standards. Classrooms in the treatment condition participated in the 12-minute, 4-day per week WOW program in addition to their traditional curriculum. Classrooms in the control group, by contrast, used an alternative early literacy curriculum (i.e., High/Scope Growing Readers) in addition to their traditional curriculum. In total, the sample included 1,284 3- and 4-year-old children.

Pre-test and post-test measures to assess children's expressive vocabulary, rhyming, and alliteration skills included the *Woodcock Picture Vocabulary Test* (Woodcock and Mather, 2001), *Peabody Picture Vocabulary Test-III* (Dunn and Dunn, 1998) and *Get It, Got It, Go!* (Missall and McConnell, 2004). Children also completed researcher-designed labeling and categorization assessments. Curriculum-based vocabulary and concept-based properties were assessed pre- and post-units. For each unit of instruction, 40 words were randomly selected and assessed using a receptive task before and after instruction. In addition, 32 items measured children's knowledge of the conceptual properties of the target vocabulary words; four conceptual properties were selected from each topic. Assessment questions used a target vocabulary word in a sentence that was either related (for example, 'Does a *katydid*'s body have three segments?') or unrelated to the target concept (for example, 'Does a *snail*'s body have three segments?'). As a stringent test of children's conceptual knowledge, each taxonomic property was assessed using both in-category and out-of-category target words. Furthermore, inference and generalization tasks were conducted at the end of the intervention.

Given the multilevel nature of the data, we analyzed the data using hierarchical linear modeling. Our results, replicated for each unit of instruction, demonstrated significant effects on children's vocabulary and conceptual development (effect sizes ranged from .80 to 1.16). Children in the Head Start treatment group consistently demonstrated significantly greater word and world knowledge than children in the control group. These findings were educationally significant, as indicated by the substantial sizes of the effects. Because WOW specifically targeted Head Start and pre-K content standards, our results are also important for content learning in science, math, and health. Given that the control group also used a supplemental curriculum, our findings suggest that WOW is especially effective at promoting low-income children's word knowledge in these critical content areas (see Figures 15.1, 15.2, and 15.3).

To further assess children's learning, we also measured their ability to extend their knowledge about recently learned concepts (i.e., tools) to unfamiliar words and exemplars (such as backhoe). In particular, we were interested in whether WOW supported children's self-learning. In this extension task, children were introduced to six unfamiliar objects, half of which were tested with a category-related property (for example, 'Can you use a backhoe to make things?'); the remaining objects were tested using an unrelated property (e.g., 'Can you use a backhoe to count?'). Children completed three steps for each of the six unfamiliar objects. First, they were asked to identify the target object from a set of three pictures; this step helped

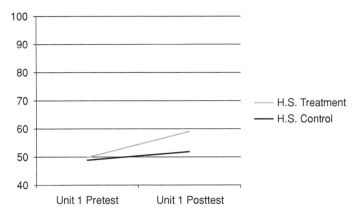

Figure 15.1 Comparisons of Head Start treatment and control groups on concepts: Unit 1

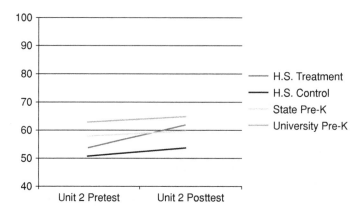

Figure 15.2 Comparisons of all groups on concepts: Unit 2

ensure that the object was, in fact, unfamiliar. Children were next told the name of the target object and its category membership (for example, 'This is a vice. It's a tool.'). Third, children were asked whether the object possessed certain category properties (for example, 'Can you use a vice to make things?').

Our results demonstrated that the Head Start treatment children were significantly more likely to correctly extend taxonomic category properties (and not extend unrelated properties) than children who did not receive the WOW curriculum (Cohen's $d = .46$). Children's extant taxonomic category knowledge appeared to bootstrap their ability to (1) determine the meaning of unfamiliar words and (2) figure out the key properties of unfamiliar objects (see Figure 15.4).

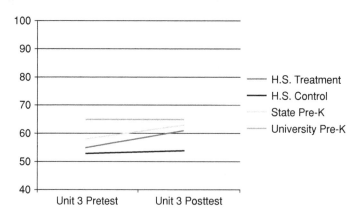

Figure 15.3 Comparisons of all groups on concepts: Unit 3

Conclusion

Many children from low-income circumstances have had little opportunities to engage in knowledge-rich activities and experiences prior to schooling. The lesson of our experience with WOW is that young children's acquisition of word and world knowledge is highly malleable and

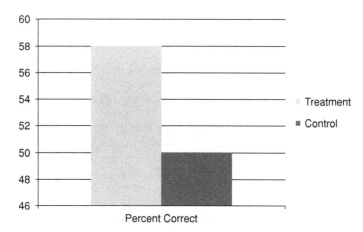

Figure 15.4 Comparison of treatment and control groups: Extension to new words

sensitive to instruction. Their knowledge development should not be limited by their socio-economic circumstances. Instead, children's knowledge development should be a matter of planned, sequenced, and systematic instruction. It should also be a matter of selecting the vocabulary words, concepts, and information that matter most to children and will provide them with the knowledge necessary when they enter formal schooling. Children who enter school in these situations will need skillfully developed instruction that not only improves their word knowledge, but also the world knowledge necessary for language comprehension and literacy development.

Word and world knowledge are foundational for learning to read. They are the entry to comprehension, and they are crucial for later reading success. Consequently, we must engage in substantially greater teacher development efforts to ensure that young children are given opportunities to discuss, describe, and develop the word and world knowledge they will need for reading achievement and content learning throughout the school years. Engaging children's minds early on will not only ensure their success in reading, but also maintain their desire to learn throughout their lifetime.

References

Akhtar, N. (2005) The robustness of learning through overhearing. *Developmental Science*, 8(2): 199–209.

Anderson, D.R., and Pempek, T.A. (2005) Television and very young children. *American Behavioral Scientist*, 48(5): 505–522.

Aslin, R.N., Saffran, J.R., and Newport, E.L. (1998) Computation of conditional probability statistics by 8-month-old infants. *Psychological Science*, 9(4): 321–324.

Barnes, M.A., Dennis, M., and Haefele-Kalvaitis, J. (1996) The effects of knowledge availability and knowledge accessibility on coherence and elaborative inferencing in children from six to fifteen years of age. *Journal of Experimental Child Psychology*, 61(3): 216–241.

Biemiller, A. (2006) Vocabulary development and instruction: A prerequisite for school learning. In D. Dickinson and S. B. Neuman (eds), *Handbook of early literacy research*, Vol. II. New York: Guilford Press, pp. 41–51.

Bloom, P. (2000) *How Children Learn the Meanings of Words*. Cambridge, MA: MIT Press.

Brent, M.R., and Siskind, J.M. (2001) The role of exposure to isolated words in early vocabulary development. *Cognition*, 81(2): B33–B44.

Chall, J., Jacobs, V., and Baldwin, L. (1990) *The Reading Crisis: Why Poor Children Fall Behind*. Cambridge, MA: Harvard University Press.

Cunningham, A.E., and Stanovich, K.E. (1998) What reading does for the mind. *American Educator*, 22(1–2): 8–15.

Dunn, L., and Dunn, L. (1998) *Peabody Picture Vocabulary Test-III*. Circle Pines, MN: American Guidance Services.

Dyson, A.H. (1993) *Social Worlds for Children Learning to Write*. New York: Teachers College Press.

Entwisle, D., Alexander, K., and Olson, L. (1997) *Children, Schools, and Inequality*. Boulder, CO: Westview.

Estes, K.G., Evans, J.L., Alibali, M.W., and Saffran, J.R. (2007) Can infants map meaning to newly segmented words? Statistical segmentation and word learning. *Psychological Science*, 18(3): 254–260.

Gelman, S.A. (2003) *The Essential Child: Origins of Essentialism in Everyday Thought*. New York: Oxford University Press.

Gelman, S.A. (2009) Learning from others: Children's construction of concepts. *Annual Review of Psychology*, 60: 115–140.

Graves, M. (2006) *The Vocabulary Book*. New York: Teachers College Press.

Grissmer, D., and Eiseman, E. (2008) Can gaps in the quality of early environments and noncognitive skills help explain persisting black-white achievement gaps? In K. Magnuson and J. Waldfogel (eds) *Steady Gains and Stalled Progress*. New York: Russell Sage Foundation, pp. 139–180.

Halle, T., Forry, N., Hair, E., *et al.* (2009) *Disparities in Early Learning and Development: Lessons from the Early Childhood Longitudinal Study – Birth Cohort (ECLS-B)* Washington, DC: Council of Chief State School Officers and Child Trends.

Harris, M., Jones, D., and Grant, J. (1983) The nonverbal content of mothers' speech to infants. *First Language*, 4(10): 21–31.

Hart, B., and Risley, T. (1995) *Meaningful Differences in the Everyday Experience of Young American Children*. Baltimore, MD: P.H. Brookes.

Hart, B., and Risley, T. (2003) The early catastrophe: The 30 million word gap by age 3. *American Educator*, 27(1): 4–9.

Huttenlocher, J., Vasilyeva, M., Cymerman, E., and Levine, S. (2002) Language input and child syntax. *Cognitive Psychology*, 45(3): 337–374.

Johnson, E.K., and Seidl, A.H. (2009) At 11 months, prosody still outranks statistics. *Developmental Science*, 12(1): 131–141.

Jusczyk, P.W., and Aslin, R.N. (1995) Infants' detection of the sound patterns of words in fluent speech. *Cognitive Psychology*, 29(1): 1–23.

Kaefer, T., Pinkham, A.M., and Neuman, S.B. (2011) Taxonomic organization scaffolds young children's learning from storybooks: A design experiment. Paper presented at the semiannual meeting of the Society for Research on Educational Effectiveness, Washington, DC.

Keil, F.C. (1989) *Concepts, Kinds, and Cognitive Development*. Cambridge, MA: MIT Press.

Kendeou, P., and van den Broek, P. (2007) The effects of prior knowledge and text structure on comprehension processes during reading of scientific texts. *Memory & Cognition*, 35(7): 1567–1577.

Kendeou, P., Lynch, J.S., van den Broek, P., *et al.* (2005) Developing successful readers: Building early comprehension skills through television viewing and listening. *Early Childhood Education Journal*, 33(2): 91–98.

Klahr, D., and Nigam, M. (2004) The equivalence of learning paths in early science instruction. *Psychological Science*, 15(10): 661–667.

Lany, J., and Gómez, R.L. (2008) Twelve-month-old infants benefit from prior experience in statistical learning. *Psychological Science*, 19(12): 1247–1252.

Lee, V., and Burkham, D. (2002) *Inequality at the Starting Gate: Social Background Differences in Achievement as Children Begin School*. Washington, DC: Economic Policy Institute.

Lorch, E.P., and Castle, V.J. (1997) Preschool children's attention to television: Visual attention and probe response times. *Journal of Experimental Child Psychology*, 66(1): 111–127.

Ma, L., and Ganea, P.A. (2010) Dealing with conflicting information: Young children's reliance on what they see versus what they are told. *Developmental Science*, 13(1): 151–160.

Markman, E.M. (1990) Constraints children place on word meanings. *Cognitive Science*, 14(1): 57–77.

Marulis, L.M., and Neuman, S.B. (2010) The effects of vocabulary intervention on young children's word learning. *Review of Educational Research*, 80(3): 300–335.

Matlen, B.J., and Klahr, D. (2010) Sequential effects of high and low guidance on children's early science learning. Paper presented at the 9th International Conference of the Learning Sciences, Chicago, IL.

McLoyd, V. (1998) Social disadvantage and child development. *American Psychologist*, 53(2): 185–204.

Missall, K., and McConnell, S. (2004) *Psychometric Characteristics of Individual Growth and Development Indicators: Picture Naming, Rhyming and Alliteration.* Minneapolis, MN: Center for Early Education and Development, University of Minnesota.

Neuman, S.B. (2001) The role of knowledge in early literacy. *Reading Research Quarterly*, 36: 468–475.

Neuman, S.B. (ed.) (2008) *Educating the other America.* Baltimore, MD: Brookes.

Neuman, S.B. (2009) The case for multimedia presentations in learning. In A. Bus and S.B. Neuman (eds) *Multimedia and Literacy Development: Improving Achievement for Young Learners.* New York: Taylor and Francis, pp. 44–56.

Neuman, S.B. (2011) The challenge of teaching vocabulary in early education. In S.B. Neuman and D. Dickinson (eds) *Handbook of Early Literacy Research.* New York: Guilford, pp. 358–372.

Neuman, S.B., and Dwyer, J. (2011) Developing vocabulary and conceptual knowledge for low-income preschoolers: A design experiment. *Journal of Literacy Research*, 43: 103–129.

Neuman, S.B., Dwyer, J., Koh, S., and Wright, T. (2007) *The World of Words: A Vocabulary Intervention for Preschool Children.* Ann Arbor, MI: University of Michigan Press.

Neuman, S.B., Newman, E., and Dwyer, J. (2011) Educational effects of a vocabulary intervention on preschoolers' word knowledge and conceptual development: A cluster randomized trial. *Reading Research Quarterly*, 46(3): 249–272.

Paivio, A. (1990) *Mental Representations: A Dual Coding Approach.* New York: Oxford University Press.

Pinkham, A.M., and Jaswal, V.K. (2011) Watch and learn? Infants privilege efficiency over pedagogy during imitative learning. *Infancy*, 16(5): 535–544.

Pinkham, A.M., Kaefer, T., and Neuman, S.B. (2011a) Representational demand positively influences kindergartners' language development. In N. Danis, K. Mesh, and H. Sung (eds) *BUCLD 35: Proceedings of the 35th Annual Boston University Conference on Language Development*, Vol. 2. Somerville, MA: Cascadilla Press, pp. 488–499.

Pinkham, A.M., Kaefer, T., and Neuman, S.B. (2011b) Taxonomic organization scaffolds preschoolers' implicit word learning from storybooks. Poster presented at the biennial meeting of the Society for Research in Child Development, Montreal, QC.

Pinkham, A.M., and Neuman, S.B. (2012) Early literacy development. In B.H. Wasik and B. Van Horn (eds) *Handbook on Family Literacy*, Vol. 2. New York: Routledge, pp. 23–37.

Quine, W.V.O. (1960) *Word and Object.* Cambridge, MA: MIT Press.

Recht, D.R., and Leslie, L. (1988) Effect of prior knowledge on good and poor readers' memory of text. *Journal of Educational Psychology*, 80(1): 16–20.

Salomon, G. (1984) Television is 'easy' and print is 'tough': The differential investment of mental effort in learning as a function of perceptions and attributions. *Journal of Educational Psychology*, 76, 647–658.

Shapiro, A. (2004) How including prior knowledge as a subject variable may change outcomes of learning research. *American Educational Research Journal*, 41: 159–189.

Taconis, R., Ferguson-Hessler, M.G.M., and Broekkamp, H. (2001) Teaching science problem solving: An overview of experimental work. *Journal of Research in Science Teaching*, 38(4): 442–468.

Thiessen, E.D., Hill, E.A., and Saffran, J.R. (2005) Infant-directed speech facilitates word segmentation. *Infancy*, 7(1): 53–71.

Verhoeven, L.T.W., and van Leeuwe, J.F.J. (2008) Prediction of the development of reading comprehension: A longitudinal study. *Applied Cognitive Psychology*, 22(3): 407–424.

Weizman, Z.O., and Snow, C.E. (2001) Lexical input as related to children's vocabulary acquisition: Effects of sophisticated exposure and support for meaning. *Developmental Psychology*, 37(2): 265–279.

Woodcock, R.W., and Mather, N. (2001) *Woodcock Johnson III Tests of Achievement*. Itasca, IL: Riverside.

Chapter 16

The Unfulfilled Pedagogical Promise of the Dialogic in Writing

Intertextual Writing Instruction for Diverse Settings

Rebecca Jesson, Judy Parr, and Stuart McNaughton

Introduction

In this chapter, we use writing as a site to consider the intersection between culture and effective pedagogy. We identify the general principles surrounding pedagogy, which is considered to be culturally responsive, and then examine the research to consider these principles specifically with regard to the teaching of writing in linguistically and culturally diverse contexts. Finally, we seek ways to incorporate deliberately the general principles of culturally responsive pedagogy in the teaching of writing. We offer a view of writing and writing instruction as dialogic, with the aim of incorporating students' existing knowledge and practices. By considering students' intertextual histories as a key resource for writing, we consider that there is potential to develop instruction that is contingent upon and responsive to students' various experiences with texts.

Culture and Effective Pedagogy

What counts as being culturally responsive depends on how culture is conceived. We conceive culture from a socio-cultural perspective; it references the ongoing practices of groups of people (McNaughton, 1996; Rogoff, 2003). Cultural groups may differ from each other in terms of the characteristics of their language and literacy practices (Greenfield, 1995). Cultural groups are internally heterogeneous so that the practices in which children engage are variable; within any given group, families or children can differ one from another in the type and occurrence of specific activities and over time (McNaughton, 1996). For example, parents might vary the ways in which they promote emergent writing with a pre-school child depending on such things as the type of medium and the ideas they hold about the purposes of literacy activities (Heath and Branscombe, 1985). Or, individuals might shift practices as they access new information, for example, about school related practices (Whitehurst and Lonigan, 2001).

The reason for this variability is that development is co-constructed and socialization processes are structured, but are also dynamic. On the one hand, parents' ideas and actions in guiding children create 'channels' of development for children, which increase the likelihood

International Handbook of Research on Children's Literacy, Learning, and Culture, First Edition.
Edited by Kathy Hall, Teresa Cremin, Barbara Comber, and Luis C. Moll.
© 2013 John Wiley & Sons, Ltd. Published 2013 by John Wiley & Sons, Ltd.

of some activity settings for children occurring and decrease the probability of others (Valsiner, 1988). Within these channels development is coconstructed by the children as active learners engaging in these settings with family members, with peers and teachers, and by themselves. Children develop expertise situated in the recurring activity settings that involves coming to know the goals, the actions, and the conditions relevant to those activities (Gee, 2001; Rogoff, 1990).

However, children are not passive and their ideas and actions change. New ideas and ways of acting are constructed from messages available from family, community, and other social sites. Both the commonalities and the diversity of practices within cultural groups can be attributed to the dynamic nature of the ideas and actions of socialization agents and children (McNaughton, 1996).

From this socio-cultural perspective, learning occurs through participation in social practices across varied contexts. Theoretically, then, learning might be constrained by settings where students' existing expertise is left at the door. Conversely, learning might be enhanced when people's repertoires of practice are built upon and then extended in educational settings. There is evidence supporting this disconnection hypothesis; that standard practices of schooling can preclude some students' knowledge and ways of participating. Bloome, Katz, and Champion (2003) described children's styles of narrative and suggested that US schools that emphasize narrative as text diminished the importance of narrative as performance, as valued in some cultural practices. Other studies show that classroom practices of literacy may not explicitly recognize or build on the facility some children have in recitation, developed from religious practices of accurately memorizing and performing texts (McNaughton, 1995). Without knowledge of the array of literacy knowledge children may have, teachers may not recognize literacy resources; for example, observational studies have highlighted negative assessments of African American students' performance based on their linguistic diversity (Dyson and Smitherman, 2009).

Explanations

A number of theoretical constructs can be used to explain why encountering disconnections between practices might make learning difficult. From the perspective of transfer and generalization in learning, a child's capability to draw on language and literacy resources will be enhanced to the degree that the value and use of prior learning are appreciated. The ability to draw on prior knowledge will depend upon the degree to which the learner sees the affordances of an unfamiliar task (Greeno, Smith, and Moore, 1993). Preparation for future learning depends on developing frames of reference to enable the learner to use existing knowledge for future application (Bransford and Schwartz, 1999). It seems reasonable to suppose then, that disconnections operate as constraints on students' ability to see the relevance of their prior knowledge and apply it. Indeed, Rueda (2011) identifies the ways that attempting to learn in an unfamiliar cultural context will make a task more difficult by increasing the cognitive load of the task, making it harder for students to learn.

There are also potential mismatches in engagement in and motivation for classroom practices derived from family, community, and school socialization practices. The corollary of this is that culturally familiar materials can have positive impacts on students' motivation and achievement. Ball and Ellis (2008), for example, propose that linguistically and culturally diverse students may not identify with a vision of themselves as academically successful. They describe an intervention in which students 'came to know themselves and other students of color as writers and producers of knowledge' (p. 509). Their evidence suggests that allowing students to develop hybrid forms of writing that incorporated their community-based literacy skills resulted in students' positive identities as successful and agentive writers.

Moreover, students' identities as learners will be affected by and contribute to the construction of the relationships and expectations they encounter in school settings. In the United States, most black students have more negative interactions with teachers than do white students (Irvine, 1990). In New Zealand, investigation into the experiences of (indigenous) Māori students in school has also illuminated the importance of the quality of interactions that students had with their teachers, and the relationships that were formed (Bishop, O'Sullivan, and Berryman, 2010). The intervention work in this setting focused on supporting teachers to overcome deficit theorizing about their students and to develop contexts for learning that acknowledged students as culturally centered and to promote positive interactions with Māori students as Māori.

There is a two-fold implication of this approach to culture and schooling for effective instructional practices (McNaughton, 2002). There is on the one hand an imperative early on in instructional sequences to find ways to mobilize students' resources through incorporation of what they already know or have experience in doing. On the other hand there is a need to create instructional bridges from those practices and their associated funds of knowledge to what is unfamiliar but highly valued in the curriculum to guarantee productive progress through schooling.

Evidence

Evidence that enhancing these twin processes underlines more effective teaching comes from several sources as we have noted above. A number of studies have used the idea of incorporation by tapping into students' repertoires to enhance what Rueda (2011) has termed 'facilitative encoding' or using students' relevant schemas. To do this teachers need to be well informed about the cultural knowledge that their students bring to school to facilitate the emergence of a third space more effectively (Gutiérrez, Morales, and Martinez, 2009; Moje *et al.*, 2004) and cultural referents (Ladson-Billings, 1995).

One of the few systematic large scale intervention programs has been the KEEP (Au, 2000), which demonstrated positive results in reading comprehension when teachers built on home language, structured interaction in ways consistent with home experiences, focused on meaning making (rather than low-level skills), recognized different forms of storytelling and question answering, and capitalized on students' ability to learn from peers. Another systematic intervention focused on incorporation is the Funds of Knowledge Project (González, Moll, and Amanti, 2005) wherein teachers participate as researchers in a joint inquiry with community members and facilitators to build knowledge of students' cultural context and ways of including these 'funds of knowledge' in the classroom context.

One of the most theoretically developed analyses of the use of funds of knowledge and the implications for effective instruction comes from Lee's (2009) theory of Cultural Modeling. The essential concept is that culturally responsive teaching involves well-planned and deliberate instruction, focusing on the intertextual work needed to move from the cultural repertoires of students to using similar practices on unknown and canonical texts. Within well-designed instructional formats, teachers need to 'see' and perhaps be guided by students' existing repertoires that can be connected to academic disciplines. The use of 'cultural data sets' provides familiar models on which new learning can be based. The challenge is to select highly generative cultural models and not trivialize making connections between everyday knowledge and school-based knowledge. Using this model Lee has shown instructional effects with secondary school students, 'Before instruction, students saw the figuration in signifying dialogues as a practice of the streets, bearing no relation to the problems of figuration they met in the literature they read at school. After instruction, students attended to the nuances of language play in canonical texts with levels of engagement and attention to details found in the practice of signifying outside school' (Lee, 2009, p. 23).

The Teaching of Writing

The two-fold implication of the principles of incorporation of students' resources and teaching using instructional bridges has a parallel in the history of writing instruction. In various ways the models solve a conundrum where teachers are faced with two important and sometimes competing aims. Somehow, teachers need to provide opportunity for the central purpose for writing; that writers achieve their own rhetorical aims. At the same time, teachers are rightly concerned that their students do so in ways that are valued by the academy. Thus, there arises a tension: between the roles that writing has in identity construction, voice, performativity, and dialogue on the one hand, and academic achievement, perceived quality, convention and form on the other. While these two aims need not necessarily be in opposition, the relative importance of each of these foci has played out somewhat differently in writing pedagogy. However in general, the theoretical traditions in writing pedagogy have added to the tensions rather than resolving them.

Models of writing and pedagogy

Three theoretical perspectives, the textual, the individual, and the social, have influenced the research in writing (Faigley, 1986). The 1950s were a period of formalism and writing instruction focused on the features of good texts; learning to write meant understanding how parts of a text worked with all others (exemplified in the teaching of the five paragraph essay) and of learning to avoid errors. By the 1970s, writing was viewed not in terms of texts but rather the cognitive processes involved. Janet Emig (1971) in her 'Composing processes of 12th graders' argued that the central concern of writing teachers should be composing processes rather than texts. Then, by the 1980s, writing was seen as a dynamic, social meaning making process. There was a general orientation of linguistic analyses from syntax (form) to discourse (function). Writing in the models of Flower and Hayes (1980, 1981) was conceived of as a set of distinctive thinking processes that writers orchestrate or organize during the act of composing. Writing involved making choices about a given rhetorical problem, audience, and possible constraints that could influence the shape and direction of one's argument. A later model (Hayes, 1996) emphasized the interaction between the task environment and the capabilities of the individual writer; Hayes called it a person-environment model.

Increasingly, the cognitive emphasis became socialized. Socio-cultural theory viewed meaning as negotiated at the intersection of individuals, culture, and activity. Writers were viewed as members of a community whose discursive practices constrained the way they structured meaning. Learning to write was seen as a case of socialization into a community – like the academic community. Poststructuralists like Bakhtin (1986) saw meaning as residing not in an individual consciousness but as dialogic, determined by the context of use, the interaction of different voices.

Each of these theoretical perspectives has informed pedagogical practice. Arguably, the best known and widespread of pedagogies drawing on theoretical models is the writing process instructional model. The idea was to plan instruction in a way that paralleled how real writers write and the cognitive models of Flower and Hayes (1980, 1981) and of Bereiter and Scardamalia (1987) showed the recursive and problem-solving nature of writing. The process-oriented approach initially involved little teacher direction or explicit instruction; it was a natural process approach where the teacher aimed to act as facilitator (and model) of the writing process for students (Hillocks, 1984); to help them practice the actual craft and find their voice as writers (Graves, 1983).

Such pedagogy has been criticized for favoring students belonging to the literate culture of power (Cope and Kalantzis, 1993). With regard to culturally and linguistically diverse writers, the extent to which voice is culturally determined and associated with identity is significant in thinking about the degree to which students should acquire a mainstream voice; whether teachers take into account motivation and attitude and are tolerant of individual and cultural expression (Albertini, 2008). For Gee (1989) learning the mainstream voice would lead to a conflict in identity and worldview. Others (e.g., Delpit, 1987, 1995) considered that programs that focused on fluency did not meet the needs of culturally diverse students. Placing less emphasis on features of mainstream discourse like grammar and style and focusing on developing the student's writing within the language and style of the home language was, for Delpit, a decision not to teach. Research shows that there are often unintended problematic outcomes when the voice the student is drawing on does not fit the expected discourse (see Dyson, 2009). Additionally, the efforts of some teachers to deal with Delpit's dilemma has led to classroom writing activities for additional language writers that focus on grammatical accuracy, do not emphasize the communicative social aspect of writing, and do not relate to authentic communicative uses of writing outside the classroom.

There has been, however, large variability in process-based instruction in classrooms; there is a lack of agreement among researchers as to what the process approach at its core entails (Pritchard and Honeycutt, 2006). Arguably, the process model itself evolved and integrated a new cognitive approach to writing instruction, specifically the idea that strategies can be directly taught and nurtured like activating schemata to access prior knowledge; teaching self-regulation strategies or developing audience awareness (see Graham, 2006). The self-regulated strategy development approach (Harris and Graham, 1996) is described as a paradigmatic example of the integration of different theoretical perspectives that characterize the new cognitive approach to writing instruction (Boscolo, 2008).

Ideas from socio-cognitive, socio-cultural, and socio-linguistic theories have also informed writing pedagogy. The idea of the social nature of learning is applied to writing instruction. There is evidence that teachers can promote more sophisticated levels of meta-cognition and writing performance with interactive text construction than with solitary work (Mariage, 2001); peer collaboration and interaction fosters rehearsal and reflection. Co-participation and guided practice are key tenets of socio-cultural theory (Rogoff, 1990). Applied to writing, there are examples of instruction structured as participatory apprenticeship where the teacher's moment-to-moment instructional moves, a combination of step-in and step-back, parallel the roles of teachers in an apprenticeship relationship (Englert and Dunsmore, 2001).

Recent theorizing concerning the teaching of culturally diverse students has emphasized the role of the social context in writing. In her review of teaching writing in culturally diverse classrooms in North America, Ball (2006) groups the questions researchers have asked in this regard as concerning the influences of teachers and classroom context; the influence of students' culture and home discourse styles, and the effects of teaching strategies and pedagogical approaches, including how we can develop practices and policies to build on the resources that diverse students bring to scaffold their learning. Some studies are relational, examining selected pedagogical variables (like the degree of emphasis on teaching components skills in context; the connection between writing and students' backgrounds; frequency of student interaction and opportunity to write extended texts) and writing outcomes (e.g., Needels and Knapp, 1994). For example, Langer (2001) found that schools performing highly in literacy with students from diverse cultural backgrounds, displayed particular characteristics, including: integrating skills instruction in purposeful contexts; connecting instructional content across subject areas and to students' out-of-school lives; teachers being explicit with expectations and assessment procedures; and allowing students to work together to challenge and critique. Other studies consider the efficacy of specific pedagogical approaches including explicit instruction in, for example, argumentative structures (Yeh and Stuart, 1998); ensuring the opportunity for extended writing (which benefited all students) (Davis, Clarke, and Rhodes, 1994), or using book clubs to engage culturally and linguistically diverse learners in reading, writing, and talking about books, coupled with explicit instruction (Kong and Fitch, 2002).

As noted in the previous section, research has examined the influence of students' culture and home discourse on their writing (e.g. Ball, 1992, 1999; Fecho, 2000; Rosaen, 2003). From a socio-cultural perspective, the idea of writing as a social and cultural practice, where the term 'genre' refers to the processes involved in 'getting things done' through language (Kress, 1993) has had significance for writing instruction, particularly in efforts to make *how texts work to achieve their purpose* explicit for writers. A text can be seen from two perspectives: 'a thing in itself that can be recorded, analysed and discussed, and also a process that is the outcome of a socially produced occasion' (Knapp and Watkins, 2005, p. 13). Forms of text produced (i.e., genres) in and by specific social institutions (like within schooling) are seen to have some stability, to the extent that there is relative stability of the social structures (Kress, 1993). Likewise, others see genre as a typified rhetorical action based in response to recurrent situations (Bakhtin, 1986; Bazerman, 1988; Freedman, 1995).

Given these notions, the work of the functional genre theorists who identified common genres or patterned responses (e.g., Martin, Christie, and Rothery, 1987) has also impacted writing instruction. The theory of genre has been translated through various instructional models (e.g., Allal, 2004; Bazerman, 2004; Chapman, 1995; Christie, 1993) with varying degrees of prescription. While descriptions from genre analysis or corpus descriptions (Hyland and Tse, 2007) help describe the registers, text structures and discourse conventions for diverse writers and provide a useful starting point, writers need to negotiate the genre or discourse in specific contexts. Multilingual writers need to find the balance between resistance to the dominant discourse and accommodation to it, in order that they become genre-aware but critical writers (Canagarajah and Jerskey, 2009). The preferred approaches are those that genuinely attempt to illustrate the set of rhetorical choices and the complex contextual constraints influencing them (Boscolo, 2008; Myhill, 2009).

Intertextuality/Writing as Dialogue

Observational studies provide evidence for how writers work within a specific context to find such a balance. Consistent with the view of culture at an individual level as co-constructed and active they show that writers negotiate roles and positions for themselves. They do this through appropriation and use of the textual resources available to them via their participation in various social worlds. Ivanic (1998) for example, analyzed the ways in which adult writers positioned themselves from within the possibilities afforded by the context in which they operated. The work of Dyson, in a similar vein, highlights the ways very young writers necessarily draw on the world of their childhoods, and the associated ideologies and symbols, in ways that make school related activities 'relevant to life' (e.g., Dyson, 2001). Both Dyson and Ivanic draw on the work of Bakhtin (e.g., 1981), and theories of writing as a dialogic response, a process of negotiating one's own voice within 'a voice-filled social landscape, differentiating, appropriating, and remixing available symbolic material' (Dyson, 2010, pp. 308–309).

Individuals draw on this voice-filled landscape when they use intertextual links to make meaning by relating the foregrounded text to a background of known texts (Cairney, 1992;

Harris, Trezise, and Winser, 2002; Hartman, 1995). The cognitive and social processes by which this happens in classes have been documented by many descriptive studies of both readers and writers. Harris and Trezise (1999), for example, document the intertextual links made by one learner, who responded to the word 'nephew' by making an intertextual link. His condensed utterance, 'Duckville,' referenced his experience of reading comic books about Donald Duck and his nephews. The intertextual work of writers has also been acknowledged, for example, Jenkins and Earle (1999) trace the intertextual web across a class of student writers, documenting the way the writers 'lean on the texts of others' and then extend these by making their own contribution (p. 8). For the writer, the voices of others are represented by the texts that the writer has experience with and 'these voices create the background necessary for his own voice' (Bakhtin, 1981, p. 278). In linguistically and culturally diverse settings, the links that students make will depend not only on their individual intertextual histories but also their perception of possibilities within the classroom setting for incorporation of differing discourses in that academic setting. The role of instruction then, in supporting intertextual links, is to create possibilities for incorporation by framing intertextual links as powerful ways to make meaning and gather resources for writing.

Thus texts operate as voices with which writers participate through their intertextual histories. However, Bakhtinian theories are also reflected in the understanding that learners participate in literacy practices with coconstructors of knowledge, thus developing 'multivoiced' understandings with multiple layers (Li, 2011). 'The role of the other is critical to our development; in essence, the more choice we have of words to assimilate, the more opportunity we have to learn. In a Bakhtinian sense, with whom, in what ways, and in what contexts we interact will determine what we stand to learn' (Freedman and Ball, 2004, p. 6). In culturally and linguistically diverse writing settings, such interactions occur around texts in home, school, and social settings. The possibilities of interaction with classmates, community members, family, and teachers offer another layer of dialogue and intertextual links via these co-constructors of knowledge.

These researchers argue that writing is dialogic. That is, it is a process of building on the voices of others to position oneself within an ongoing dialogue. Given this there is potential in this conception for refining current teaching practices in ways that explicitly reference this ongoing dialogue. The suggestion here is to consider ways that an understanding of the dialogic nature of writing might be harnessed in instruction, especially for culturally diverse learners. As students learn to write by appropriating textual resources to position themselves within a dialogue, pedagogy might be fashioned that explicitly builds resources for appropriation and supports students to negotiate powerful positions as writers. Like Boscolo (2008) and Myhill (2009), we argue for building textual knowledge so that students might make powerful rhetorical or design choices. However, in order to accentuate the potential for cultural responsiveness within the dialogic conception of writing, we would also highlight the importance of students' various intertextual histories in shaping and framing their design choices. Additionally, we would argue that teachers need to design instruction so that they may better appreciate and incorporate those histories in ongoing dialogue. A further implication is the need for teachers to have knowledge at least at a generic level of the potential features of those histories. That is what the evidence for culturally responsive teaching shows.

Such theorizing is supported by empirical studies which describe the way intertextuality can be capitalized upon for instruction. Varelas and Pappas (2006), used 'dialogically oriented read alouds' as part of a science unit, where teachers encouraged students' comments, and responded contingently to extend students' thinking. They offer evidence of intertextuality as a 'major intellectual scaffold' (p. 252), as children appropriated the language of texts so that they could discuss their emerging scientific understandings. Additionally, they noted that the use of a dialogic approach meant that over time teachers' meanings became less important to the classroom discourse, and students' emerging understandings became central, 'teachers undergo a form of ideational displacement by which ideas and meanings that students bring up displace the teachers' instructional agendas and become anchors of discussion for the class, and, thus, important elements in the instructional ebb and flow' (p. 253).

There is also some evidence that making intertextual links can be a learned, social activity, which can be responsive to instruction. In their studies, Beach, Appleman, and Dorsey (1990) used mapping as an instructional technique to invoke intertextual links across texts to interpret literature. Students differed in the elaboration, abstraction, and flexibility of their intertextual links based on their differing strategies for defining links and on experience making such links. It seems that effective teachers support students to develop these strategies. Pressley and colleagues (2001) describe classrooms of effective teachers, where teachers and students were more likely to make such connections across texts and across conversations. Similarly Parr and Limbrick (2010) identified one of the hallmarks of effective teachers of writing as their strength in making links to what students know and in making connections for students across curriculum areas. Although each of these sources offers only partial evidence, it seems likely that there is potential in developing and refining pedagogy for writing that situates such links as a central resource for students by designing instruction purposefully to be contingent upon students' intertextual histories.

Conclusion: Intertextual Promises and Future Directions

Potentially, the notion of writing as dialogic, backgrounded by the multivoiced intertextual history of the writer, across school, home and social settings, reframes writing instruction to make it more responsive to students' resources. In our context, there is some evidence that professional development based around explicit intertextual links has the potential to result in improved outcomes for students (Jesson, 2010). In this study, when teachers purposefully drew on the notion of intertextuality as a resource for meaning making for writing they made revisions to their instructional routines both to incorporate students' resources and build instructional bridges to new knowledge. To make their writing instruction explicitly intertextual, teachers sought to find out about students' intertextual histories and the sources for their ideas. They gave students explicit permission to 'borrow' from texts that they met in the home and provided more texts as resources at school. Moreover, these teachers supported students' borrowing by devoting portions of writing lessons to reading texts with an evaluative purpose, comparing and contrasting texts with respect to their purposes and effects on the reader. The students then recorded these understandings by co-constructing intertextual supports in the form of charts, signs, or 'tools,' which were then used to support writing. Students' displays, charts, and written work then served as an intermediary links to source texts (Jesson, McNaughton, and Parr, 2011).

Importantly, encouraging students to make diverse intertextual links requires contingent response. Such ideas surrounding responsive teaching in diverse settings are not new. Tharp and Gallimore (1988) highlighted the role of instructional conversations to support students to weave new information with old information. Similarly, Nystrand (1997) offered the notion of teaching as a responsive dialogue with students. In writing pedagogy, contingent response often occurs in the form of feedback to writing, through conferencing, however the possibilities and opportunities within this format are shaped by the teaching and the associated intertextual agenda that has come before. Thus, the intertextual links available to writers are framed by instruction. We would contend that they therefore deserve deliberate forethought.

In general, instructional formats that explicitly invoke intertextual links as a basis for building generative textual knowledge are yet to be developed. Those pedagogies traditionally thought of as more contingent, such as process approaches, have traditionally not explicitly referenced appropriation and revoicing of textual knowledge as a core feature. Conversely, pedagogies that focus on textual knowledge employ apprenticeship models of teaching, offering graduated levels of support for creating a text; from the initial phases, where the teacher takes responsibility, to final stages where the learner moves to independence. The intertextual agenda in such a format is explicitly planned and controlled by the teacher, for example in cycles of modeling, joint construction through to independent construction. Theoretically, teaching from a basis of modeling locates the intertextual agenda with the teacher. Moreover, there is some evidence to suggest that the teacher-led instructional formats result in intertextual conflicts as students and the teacher negotiate divergent intertextual histories and assumptions (Harris *et al.*, 2002).

In seeking to find an example of explicitly intertextual instruction that situates itself as a dialogue with existing expertise, Lee's (2009) description of pedagogy building from cultural data sets stands out as an illustration of a deliberate application of the generative principle inherent in intertextuality, which we argue might also be widely employed for writing. This approach, which relies entirely on links between texts, used oral texts with which students were familiar as a basis for building expertise. In that context the students' expertise with metaphor that was a feature of the practices surrounding 'signifying' (ritual insult) as a cultural practice was the basis for expertise with metaphor more generally. Thus, the pedagogy was explicitly responsive, using students' intertextual histories as a basis for building knowledge valued in school contexts. In this pedagogy, the teacher's role is to 'revoice' contextualized knowledge by renaming it as a resource that can be applied in academic situations. In this way, students were able to see the relevance and potential of their existing expertise.

To allow teachers to do this revoicing, provision must be made as part of the instructional routine for teachers and students to identify existing expertise from which to build. While we agree that teachers need to know about the cultural and textual backgrounds of their students, we see little value in then working within instructional formats that may constrain the possibilities of links to backgrounded texts. There is, therefore, a role for research in developing pedagogy that is more responsive to students' intertextual histories. We see a need to develop a systematic approach to instruction that builds on students' expertise in generative ways.

Lee's cultural modeling approach appears to have some synergies with the Language Experience lesson format as practiced in New Zealand early primary school classrooms (described in Parr, Jesson, and McNaughton, 2009). Both formats begin with dialogic activity, the starting point for which is the learners' experiences, and upon which the teacher bases instruction. Both formats have a distinctive lesson shape that can be contrasted with a traditional 'book end' structure (lessons where the teacher begins and ends the instruction). In both Cultural Modeling and Language Experience the explicit teaching occurs as a result of the dialogic. Rather than at the beginning, the teaching occurs in the middle of the lesson (or lesson series), based on expertise demonstrated during dialogic sequences. Explicit teaching, in this sense, involves developing this existing expertise, demonstrating the generalizability and application to academic settings. Application, in this case in the form of writing, follows the explicit teaching portion. The value of such a lesson shape, which looks less like bookends and more like a fulcrum, has intuitive appeal through its potential to necessitate contingent teaching and generativity. We feel it warrants further research and development.

Currently, writing instruction struggles with the competing aims of building writers' voice and agency while at the same time arming students with expertise that is valued in academic settings. For students in culturally and linguistically diverse settings, the aim of making textual knowledge explicit has been critiqued for devaluing the voice and therefore power available to these writers. Similarly, a focus on voice and creativity may devalue the power of explicitly building textual knowledge. Possibly, the notion of writing as dialogue offers an alternative potential for instruction, reshaping it in ways that make it more responsive to students' various experiences with texts to support the aim of building on the voices of others. Like González, Moll, and Amanti (2005) we agree that the cultural and linguistic resources of students should be used advantageously and we apply this to writing linking students' resources to their intertextual histories. We see potential in refining instruction to highlight the dialogic in order to make use of these resources for ongoing learning.

References

Albertini, J. (2008) Teaching of writing and diversity: Access, identity and achievement. In C. Bazerman (ed.) *Handbook of Research on Writing: History, Society, School, Individual, Text*. New York: Lawrence Erlbaum Associates, pp. 387–397.

Allal, L. (2004) Integrated writing instruction and the development of revision skills. In L. Allal, L. Chanquoy, and P. Largy (eds) *Revision: Cognitive and Instructional Process*. Dordrecht, The Netherlands: Kluwer, pp. 139–155.

Au, K. (2000) A multicultural perspective on policies for improving literacy achievement: Equity and excellence. In M.L. Kamil, P.B. Mosenthal, P.D. Pearson, and R. Barr (eds) *Handbook of Reading Research: Vol III*. New York: Erlbaum, pp. 835–852.

Bakhtin, M.M. (1981) *The Dialogic Imagination: Four Essays*, trans. C. Emerson and M. Holquist. Austin, TX: University of Texas Press.

Bakhtin, M.M. (1986) *Speech Genres and Other Late Essays*, trans. V.W. McGee. Austin, TX: University of Texas Press.

Ball, A.F. (1992) Cultural preferences and the expository writing of African American adolescents. *Written Communication*, 9: 510–532.

Ball, A.F. (1999) Evaluating the writing of culturally and linguistically diverse students: The case of the African American vernacular English speaker. In C. R. Cooper and L. Odell (eds) *Evaluating Writing*. Urbana, IL: National Council of Teachers of English, pp. 225–248.

Ball, A.F. (2006) Teaching writing in culturally diverse classrooms. In C.A. MacArthur, S. Graham and J. Fitzgerald (eds) *Handbook of Writing Research*. New York: Guilford, pp. 293–310.

Ball, A.F., and Ellis, P. (2008) Identity and the writing of culturally and linguistically diverse students. In C. Bazerman (ed.) *Handbook of Research on Writing: History, Society, School, Individual, Text*. New York: Lawrence Erlbaum, pp. 499–514.

Bazerman, C. (1988) *Shaping Written Knowledge. The Genre and Activity of the Experimental Article in Science*. Madison, WI: University of Wisconsin Press.

Bazerman, C. (2004) Speech acts, genres, and activity systems: How texts organize activity and people. In C. Bazerman and P. Prior (eds) *What Writing Does and How It Does It*. Mahwah, NJ: Lawrence Erlbaum, pp. 309–339.

Beach, R.W., Appleman, D., and Dorsey, S. (1990) Adolescents' use of intertextual links to understand literature. In R. Beach and S. Hynds (eds) *Developing Discourse Practices in Adolescence and Adulthood*. Norwood, NJ: Albex, pp. 224–245.

Bereiter, C., and Scardamalia, M. (1987) *The Psychology of Written Composition*. Hillsdale, NJ: Erlbaum.

Bishop, R., O'Sullivan, D., and Berryman, M. (2010) *Scaling up Education Reform: Addressing the Politics of Disparity*. Wellington, NZ: NZCER Press.

Bloome, D., Katz, L., and Champion, T. (2003) Young children's narratives and ideologies of language in classrooms. *Reading and Writing Quarterly*, 19(3): 205–223.

Boscolo, P. (2008) Writing in primary school. In C. Bazerman (ed.) *Handbook of Research on Writing. History, Society, School, Individual, Text*. New York: Lawrence Erlbaum, pp. 293–309.

Bransford, J.D., and Schwartz, D.L. (1999) Rethinking transfer: A simple proposal with multiple implications. *Review of Research in Education*, 24: 61–100.

Cairney, T. (1992) Fostering and building students' intertextual histories. *Language Arts*, 69(7): 502–507.

Canagarajah, S., and Jerskey, M. (2009) Meeting the needs of advanced multilingual writers. In R. Beard, D. Myhill, J. Riley, and M. Nystrand (eds) *The SAGE Handbook of Writing Development*. London: Sage, pp. 472–488.

Chapman, M.L. (1995) The sociocognitive construction of written genres in first grade. *Research in the Teaching of English*, 29: 164–192.

Christie, F. (1993) Curriculum genres: Planning for effective teaching. In B. Cope and M. Kalantzis (eds) *The Powers of Literacy*. London: Falmer, pp. 154–178.

Cope, B., and Kalantzis, M. (1993) *The Powers of Literacy: A Genre Approach to Teaching Writing*. London: Falmer.

Davis, A., Clarke, M.A., and Rhodes, L.K. (1994) Extended text and the writing proficiency of students in urban elementary schools. *Journal of Educational Psychology*, 86: 556–566.

Delpit, L. (1987) Skills and other dilemmas of a progressive Black educator. *Equity and Choice*, 3(20): 9–14.

Delpit, L. (1995) *Other People's Children*. New York: Norton.

Dyson, A.H. (2001) Donkey Kong in Little Bear country: A first grader's composing development in the media spotlight. *Elementary School Journal*, 101(4): 417–433.

Dyson, A.H. (2009) Writing in childhood worlds. In R. Beard, D. Myhill, J. Riley, and M. Nystrand (eds) *The Sage Handbook of Writing Development*. London: Sage, pp. 232–245.

Dyson, A.H. (2010) Opening curricular closets in regulated times: Finding pedagogical keys. *English Education*, 42(3): 307–319.

Dyson, A.H., and Smitherman, G. (2009) The right (write) start: African American language and the discourse of sounding right. *Teachers College Record*, 111(4): 973–998.

Emig, J. (1971) *The Composing Process of Twelfth Graders*. Urbana, IL: National Council of Teachers of English.

Englert, C.S., and Dunsmore, K. (2001) A case study of the apprenticeship process: Another perspective on the apprentice and the scaffolding metaphor. *Journal of Learning Disabilities*, 34, 152–171.

Faigley, L. (1986) Competing theories of process: A critique and a proposal. *College English*, 48, 527–542.

Fecho, B. (2000) Critical inquiries into language in an urban classroom. *Research in the Teaching of English*, 34(3): 368–395.

Flower, L., and Hayes, J.R. (1980) The cognition of discovery: Defining a rhetorical problem. *College Composition and Communication*, 31(1): 21–32.

Flower, L., and Hayes, J.R. (1981) A cognitive process theory of writing. *College Composition and Communication*, 32: 365–387.

Freedman, A. (1995) The what, where, when, why, and how of classroom genres. In J. Petraglia (ed.) *Reconceiving Writing, Rethinking Writing Instruction*. Hillsdale, NJ: Lawrence Erlbaum, pp. 121–144.

Freedman, S.W., and Ball, A.F. (2004) How ideological becoming relates to language literacy and learning. In A.F. Ball, and S.W. Freedman (eds) *Bakhtinian Perspectives on Language, Literacy and Learning*. New York: Cambridge University Press, pp. 3–33.

Gee, J.P. (1989) What is literacy? *Journal of Education*, 171(1): 18–25.

Gee, J.P. (2001) Reading as situated language: A sociocognitive perspective. *Journal of Adolescent and Adult Literacy*, 44(8): 714–725.

González, N., Moll, L.C., and Amanti, C. (eds) (2005) *Funds of Knowledge: Theorizing Practices in Households, Communities and Classrooms*. Mahwah, NJ: Erlbaum.

Graham, S. (2006) Strategy instruction and the teaching of writing: A meta-analysis. In C.A. MacArthur, S. Graham, and J. Fitzgerald (eds) *Handbook of Writing Research*. New York: Guilford Press, pp. 187–207.

Graves, D.H. (1983) *Writing: Teachers and Children at Work*. Portsmouth, NH: Heinemann.

Greenfield, P. (1995) Culture, ethnicity, race, and development: Implications for teaching, theory, and research. *Society for Research in Child Development Newsletter*, Winter: 3–4.

Greeno, J.G., Smith, D.R., and Moore, J.L. (1993) Transfer of situated learning. In D.K. Detterman and R.J. Sternberg (eds) *Transfer on Trial: Intelligence Cognition and Instruction*. Norwood, NJ: Ablex, pp. 99–167.

Gutiérrez, K.D., Morales, P.Z., and Martinez, D.C. (2009) Re-mediating literacy: Culture, difference, and learning for students from nondominant communities. *Review of Research in Education*, 33(1): 212–245.

Harris, K.R., and Graham, S. (1996) *Making the Writing Process Work: Strategies for Composition and Self-regulation*, 2nd edn. Cambridge, MA: Brookline Books.

Harris, P., and Trezise, J. (1999) Duckville and other tales. *Language Arts*, 76: 371–376.

Harris, P., Trezise, J., and Winser, W. N. (2002) 'Is the story on my face?': Intertextual conflicts during teacher-class interactions around texts in early grade classrooms. *Research in the Teaching of English*, 37(1): 9–54.

Hartman, D.K. (1995) Eight readers reading: The intertextual links of proficient readers reading multiple passages. *Reading Research Quarterly*, 30(3): 520–561.

Hayes, J. (1996) A new framework for understanding cognition and affect in writing. In M. Levy and S. Ransdell (eds) *The Science of Writing: Theories, Methods, Individual Differences, and Applications*. Mahwah, NJ: Erbaum, pp. 1–27.

Heath, S.B., and Branscombe, A. (1985) Intelligent writing in an audience community: Teacher, students, and researcher. In S.W. Freedman (ed.) *The Acquisition of Written Language: Revision and Response*. Norwood, NJ: Ablex Publishing, pp. 3–32.

Hillocks, G. (1984) What works in teaching composition: A meta-analysis of experimental treatment studies. *American Journal of Education*, 93: 133–170.

Hyland, K., and Tse, L. (2007) Is there an 'academic vocabulary'? *TESOL Quarterly*, 41(2): 235–254.

Irvine, J.J. (1990) *Black Students and School Failure: Policies, Practices, and Prescriptions*. Westport, CT: Greenwood Press.

Ivanic, R. (1998) *Writing and Identity: The Discoursal Construction of Identity in Academic Writing*. Amsterdam: John Benjamins.

Jenkins, C.B., and Earle, A.A. (1999) When third graders write letters to college penpals: An analysis of genre and intertextual understandings. (ERIC Document Reproduction Service No: ED432013).

Jesson, R. (2010) Intertextuality as a conceptual tool for the teaching of writing: Designing professional development that will transfer. Unpublished doctoral dissertation, University of Auckland, New Zealand.

Jesson, R., McNaughton, S., and Parr, J.M. (2011) Drawing on intertextuality in culturally diverse classrooms: Implications for transfer of literacy knowledge. *English Teaching: Practice and Critique*, 10(2): 65–77.

Knapp, P., and Watkins, M. (2005) *Genre, Text, Grammar: Technologies for Teaching and Assessing Writing*. Sydney, Australia: University of New South Wales Press.

Kong, A., and Fitch, E. (2002) Using a book club to engage culturally and linguistically diverse learners in reading, writing, and talking about books. *The Reading Teacher*, 56(4): 352–362.

Kress, G. (1993) Genre as a social process. In B. Cope and M. Kalantzis (eds) *The Powers of Literacy: A Genre Approach to Teaching Writing*. Pittsburg, PA: University of Pittsburg Press, pp. 22–37.

Ladson-Billings, G. (1995) Toward a theory of culturally relevant pedagogy. *American Educational Research Journal*, 32(3): 465–491.

Langer, J.A. (2001) Beating the odds: Teaching middle and high school students to read and write well. *American Educational Research Journal*, 38: 837–880.

Lee, C. (2009) *Culture, Literacy, and Learning: Taking Bloom in the Midst of the Whirlwind*. New York: Teachers College Press.

Li, G. (2011) The role of culture in literacy, learning, and teaching. In M.L. Kamil, P.D. Pearson, E.B. Moje, and P.P. Afflerbach (eds) *Handbook of Reading Research*, New York: Routledge, pp. 515–538.

Mariage, T.V. (2001) Features of an interactive writing discourse: Conversational involvement, conventional knowledge, and internalization in 'Morning Message.' *Journal of Learning Disabilities*, 34(2): 172–196.

Martin, J.R., Christie, F., and Rothery, J. (1987) Social processes in education: A reply to Sawyer and Watson (and others). In I. Reid (ed.) *The Place of Genre in Learning: Current Debates*. Geelong, Australia: Typereader Publications, pp. 55–58.

McNaughton, S. (1995) *Patterns of Emergent Literacy: Processes of Development and Transition*. Melbourne, Australia: Oxford University Press.

McNaughton, S. (1996) *Cultural Contexts for Schooling Improvement*. Keynote address to Redesigning pedagogy: Culture, knowledge and understanding, National Institute of Education, Singapore.

McNaughton, S. (2002) *Meeting of Minds*. Wellington, New Zealand: Learning Media.

Moje, E.B., Ciechanowski, K.M., Kramer, K., *et al.* (2004) Working toward third space in content area literacy: An examination of everyday funds of knowledge and discourse. *Reading Research Quarterly*, 39(1): 38–70.

Myhill, D. (2009) Becoming a designer: Trajectories of linguistic development. In R. Beard, D. Myhill, M. Nystrand, and J. Riley (eds) *Handbook of Writing Development*. London, UK: Sage, pp. 402–414.

Needels, M.C., and Knapp, M.S. (1994) Teaching writing to children who are underserved. *Journal of Educational Psychology*, 86: 339–349.

Nystrand, M. (with Gamoran, A., Kachur, R., and Prendergast, C.) (1997) *Opening Dialogue: Understanding the Dynamics of Language and Learning in the English Classroom*. New York: Teachers College Press.

Parr, J.M., Jesson, R., and McNaughton, S. (2009) Agency and platform: The relationships between talk and writing. In R. Beard, D. Myhill, J. Riley, and M. Nystrand (eds) *Sage Handbook of Writing Development*. London: Sage, pp. 246–259.

Parr, J.M., and Limbrick, L. (2010) Contextualising practice: Hallmarks of effective teachers of writing. *Teaching and Teacher Education*, 26(3): 583–590.

Pressley, M., Wharton-McDonald, R., Allington, R., *et al.* (2001) A study of effective first-grade literacy instruction. *Scientific Studies of Reading*, 5(1): 35–58.

Pritchard, R.J., and Honeycutt, R.L. (2006) The process approach to writing instruction. In C.A. MacArthur, S. Graham, and J. Fitzgerald (eds) *Handbook of Writing Research*. New York: Guilford Press, pp. 275–290.

Rogoff, B. (1990) *Apprenticeship in Thinking: Cognitive Development in Social Context*. New York: Oxford University Press.

Rogoff, B. (2003) *The Cultural Nature of Human Development*. Oxford: Oxford University Press.

Rosaen, C. (2003) Preparing teachers for diverse classrooms: Creating public and private spaces to explore culture through poetry writing. *Teachers College Record*, 105(8): 1437–1485.

Rueda, R. (2011) Cultural perspectives in reading: Theory and research. In M.L. Kamil, P.D. Pearson, E.B. Moje, and P.P. Afflerbach (eds) *Handbook of Reading Research*. New York: Routledge, pp. 84–103.

Tharp, R.G., and Gallimore, R. (1988) *Rousing Minds to Life: Teaching, Learning, and Schooling in Social Context*. Cambridge, MA: Cambridge University Press.

Valsiner, J. (1988) *Developmental Psychology in the Soviet Union*. Bloomington, IN: Indiana University Press.

Varelas, M., and Pappas, C.C. (2006) Intertextuality in read-alouds of integrated science-literacy units in primary classrooms: Opportunities for the development of thought and language. *Cognition and Instruction*, 24: 211–259.

Whitehurst, G.J., and Lonigan, C.J. (2001) Emergent literacy: Development from prereaders to readers. In S.B. Neuman and D.K. Dickinson (eds) *Handbook of Early Literacy Research*. New York: Guilford Press, pp. 11–29.

Yeh, S.S., and Stuart, S. (1998) Empowering education: Teaching argumentative writing to cultural minority middle-school students. *Research in the Teaching of English*, 33: 49–83.

Chapter 17

Reading Engagement Research

Issues and Challenges

Sue Ellis and Cassandra S. Coddington

Introduction

This chapter gives an overview of reading engagement research, drawing on cognitive and socio-cognitive, sociological, ethnographic, historical-and-educational survey, curriculum, pedagogy, and economic research perspectives. This multidisciplinary approach enlightens many issues central to reading engagement, but also many that are central to wider educational research including the social context of learning, the nature of reading instruction in schools, and the extent to which researchers, and the research knowledge they generate, might be able to prevent policy makers opting for narrow, technocratic pedagogies and frameworks for curriculum design and assessment.

Engaged readers are people who want to read, who make time to read, and who read widely, with intrinsic purpose, thought, and enjoyment. Engagement is the product of readers' individual skills and dispositions, their interactions with the social environment, their physical and economic resource, and their cultural legacy. Reading engagement is therefore a meta-construct that crosses research disciplines and is studied in the context of schools and schooling but also in out-of-school contexts such as families and the workplace. It is linked to what researchers in German-speaking countries refer to as *Literarische sozialisation*, which translates as 'reading / literary socialization,' a term that encompasses the totality of a reader's encounters with literacy, whether fleeting or sustained and 'both the intentional influence of parents, schools, libraries, and other forms of directed reading development *and* unintended or even negative effects of school literary teaching, the media environment, and the home reading climate' (Garbe, 2004, p. 232).

There is considerable agreement among researchers that reading engagement has a long-term impact on language and literacy attainment and offers a wide range of desirable outcomes for individuals, schooling, and society. Longitudinal studies indicate that high reading engagement in pre-school children can mitigate the impact of receptive language disorders (Schoon *et al.*, 2010) and also that adults who report reading in their mid-teenage years are more likely to be engaged in civic activities and to hold liberal views two and three decades later, even after allowing for other variables such as course-taking, educational attainment, gender, and

International Handbook of Research on Children's Literacy, Learning, and Culture, First Edition.
Edited by Kathy Hall, Teresa Cremin, Barbara Comber, and Luis C. Moll.
© 2013 John Wiley & Sons, Ltd. Published 2013 by John Wiley & Sons, Ltd.

socio-economic status (Paterson, 2009). International surveys indicate a strong connection between reading engagement and attainment: PIRLS linked frequent reading for fun, positive attitudes, and self-concepts with higher attainment (Mullis *et al.*, 2007), and analysis of PISA 2009 data indicates that that almost 70 percent of the gender gap and 30 percent of the socio-economic gap in reading attainment can be linked to disparities in the breadth and depth of reading (OECD, 2010a). Some researchers suggest that a stronger focus on increasing reading engagement could narrow these socio-economic and gender effects (Brozo *et al.*, 2007; Guthrie, Schafer, and Huang, 2001). European analyses of international PISA survey results however, indicate that the trend in reading engagement over the past decade is actually moving in the opposite direction; there has been a small general decline in reading engagement, from 68 percent of students in 2000 to 63 percent in 2009 (Eurydice, 2011).

Measures of Literacy Engagement

Measuring engagement can be challenging and researchers have adopted several methodological, conceptual, and theoretical strategies for capturing student engagement in the classroom. One measure of reading engagement that has gained a high profile is that used by the PISA international survey. It uses measures similar to those used in the United States' *National Assessment of Educational Progress* (Campbell *et al.*, 1997) and takes engagement as a composite measure based on variables such as the diversity of reading, the frequency of leisure reading, students' attitudes to, and interest in, reading and the 'depth' of their reading, which is measured by the comprehension strategies that readers report using. While the PISA international survey and other researchers (Marks, 2000) combine subscale variables into a composite engagement score, other researchers maintain separate subscales, choosing to measure engagement using unique subscales (Lutz, Guthrie, and Davis, 2006; Skinner and Belmont, 1993). The difficulties with current research efforts to measure academic engagement are discussed by Fredricks, Blumenfeld, and Paris (2004). They identify three overarching aspects of research definitions of engagement and how they are operationalized in the research literature: behavioral engagement, emotional engagement, and cognitive engagement. Traditionally, researchers have used self-report surveys to capture all three of these aspects of student engagement, although fewer self-report measures of cognitive engagement are discussed in the literature. Observational reports by teachers or researchers are an alternative or, more successfully, a complement to self-report surveys of student engagement. Lutz, Guthrie, and Davis (2006) used observational and self-report measures to capture student reading engagement in the three categories outlined by Fredricks *et al.* (2004). By videotaping small-group and whole-class interactions between teachers and students, Lutz *et al.* (2006) were able to code and analyze very small units of student engagement during a reading lesson, including high and low points of total engagement (behavioral, affective, and cognitive engagement). Their analysis revealed that individual teacher attention within any given observation time span increased the probability that the student was highly engaged, while teacher time spent not giving students individual attention increased the probability that the student was disengaged (Lutz *et al.*, 2006).

Cognitive and Socio-cognitive Perspectives on Reading Engagement

Much socio-cognitive research has explored the relationship between reading engagement and reading attainment, motivation, and comprehension. Experimental, cohort and case study methodologies, as well as analysis-by-synthesis approaches have been applied in understanding how schools and educators can foster engaged readers who 'coordinate their strategies and knowledge (cognition) within a community of literacy (social) in order to fulfill their personal goals, desires, and intentions (motivation)' (Guthrie and Wigfield, 2000, p. 404).

There is a reciprocal relationship between reading engagement and reading achievement. Stanovich (1986) adopted the sociological concept of *Matthew Effects* to explain why the gap between successful and struggling readers widens as children progress through school. He suggested that young readers who experience early success in decoding print accumulate positive emotional/social experiences of literacy. They internalize literacy as a part of their identity and look for, and are given, additional reading experiences, which provide further practice opportunities. They enter an upward spiral of success and make rapid progress. However, those who make a marginally slower start to decoding words have a different trajectory. They do not feel as capable or confident and tend to read less, which means they get less practice. They do not develop a positive personal or social identity as a reader and, as they fall further behind their more successful peers, begin to actively avoid reading. They enter a downward learning spiral in which low reading engagement means they get less and less practice, which leads to them making slower progress.

Other empirical studies have confirmed these links between reading attainment and reading engagement. Engaged readers in fifth grade have been shown to read more books and to spend more time reading (Cipielewski and Stanovich, 1992). A national survey of students aged 9, 13 and 17 in the United States showed that engaged readers have more growth in their reading achievement trajectories (measured by narrative and expository text comprehension) than their peers who were less engaged, and that 13 year olds with high reading engagement achieved at a higher level than 17 year olds with less engagement (Campbell, Voelkl, and Donahue, 1997). Successful encounters with reading also increase readers' self-confidence in their own reading ability (Guthrie *et al.*, 1999) and highly engaged readers who are interested in the text and who believe that they are capable of reading the text are more likely to persist when faced with more challenging and difficult texts (Schunk, 2003).

Studies of reading motivation focus on the personal values and beliefs that energize and direct the behavior of individuals. Intrinsic motivation (where individuals are driven by their interest and enjoyment to master a particular task or skill) and social motivation (where individuals are driven by the desire to take part in a community of learners) have the strongest associations with reading achievement because they influence the decisions students make about how often they read, the kind of books they read, and their willingness to persist in the activity should it become challenging (Baker and Wigfield, 1999; Guthrie and Coddington, 2009; Wigfield and Guthrie, 1997, 2010). Guthrie and Wigfield (2000) suggest that improving the intrinsic and social reading motivations of students may help to curtail *Matthew Effects* because of the role these motivations play in increasing the amount of reading and the reading competence of readers. Extrinsic motivation is sometimes researched and discussed as an antithesis for intrinsic motivation, but the research on extrinsic motivators is more subtle and complex (Gambrell, 2011). Some extrinsic motivators, such as constructive teacher feedback for example, have been found to motivate students to read (Wang and Holcombe, 2010). In particular, teacher feedback that builds capacity for learning by scaffolding, focusing, or directing effort is highly motivating (Lepper and Cordova, 1992). However, other incentives and extrinsic motivators, such as prizes and money, which are used in many reading classrooms, have been found in replicable studies to undermine intrinsic motivation (Deci and Ryan, 1992). Self-efficacy is another motivation that may play a crucial role in the development and sustainment of engaged reading. While intrinsic motivation and social motivation have been shown to be strong contributors to reading engagement, research has also demonstrated that struggling readers are particularly susceptible to low self-efficacy in reading (they do not believe they are capable of completing the reading task) and this can lead to avoidance of reading and disengagement (Ivey and Guthrie, 2008; Kamil *et al.*, 2008).

Without intrinsic and social motivation, increased reading competence may not prompt strong increases in reading engagement. With high intrinsic and social motivation however, increases in reading competence lead to a self-sustaining cycle of improvement whereby readers engage in reading activities more frequently and become more practiced, which further increase their proficiency and attainment. Wigfield and Guthrie (1997) report that highly motivated readers read three times the material that less motivated readers read and that reading motivation at the beginning of the school year, particularly intrinsic motivation, predicts the amount students read. Those who are more motivated to read experience a much faster rate of growth in their reading ability than less motivated readers.

Reading provides access to many curricular areas but it also paves the way for academic success in other ways. Highly engaged readers read more texts, but they also read a more diverse and challenging range of texts (Guthrie and Cox, 2001). Avid readers develop wider vocabularies, better verbal reasoning powers, and a wider general knowledge and understanding of the world. This gives them a cognitive advantage that benefits their learning in every curricular area (Cunningham and Stanovich, 1998). High reading engagement thus has long-term and compounding effects on academic achievement.

Engaged readers are motivated to comprehend and use their knowledge and comprehension strategies to actively question and make meaning from the texts they read. High reading engagement affords practice opportunities that contribute to gains in reading comprehension skills but the social motivation associated with reading engagement further increases these skills. Comprehension involves internal effort and questioning to construct meaning but it is also developed by external, social interactions. Unique experiences and knowledge shape and filter each reader's individual interpretation of what a text means, and when these are shared in discussion with others, it enables everyone to construct more complex, jointly negotiated understandings of what the text means. Readers learn from their own struggles and questions about the author's intentions, but also from the struggles and questions of others to develop richer, broader frameworks for interpretation. Such discussions also strengthen the social bonds between readers and reinforce collective understandings of the value and purposes of reading, and of ways of talking about reading (Snow, 2002; Sweet and Snow, 2003).

Reading Engagement in the School Curriculum

The 2002 RAND report sets out an agenda for reading research in the United States that positions knowledge, application, and engagement as crucial consequences of reading comprehension (Snow, 2002, p. 54). It calls for researchers to develop reading assessments that reflect these three aspects and argues that if reading engagement were to be factored into the assessment agenda of schools, it would considerably empower effective comprehension teaching and learning. The report identifies three elements to be considered in the teaching of reading comprehension, the reader, the text, and the activity, situated within the wider socio-cultural context, and suggests that researchers focus on understanding how these elements interact and influence the level of engagement a student experiences with a reading task (Snow, 2002).

In a meta-analysis and synthesis of reading engagement research, Guthrie and Humenick (2004) identify several important aspects of curriculum design and pedagogy that can promote engagement. These include: purposeful tasks that foster intrinsic, rather than extrinsic motivation and create mastery-orientated (rather than performance-orientated) conditions for learning; opportunities for students to exercise choice and to read interesting, relevant, and stimulating texts; collaborative tasks, which promote self-efficacy and social motivation, improve students' willingness to 'have a go' at complex tasks, and encourage them to persist with difficult tasks; and finally, teaching pedagogies that focus on teaching comprehension strategies and on promoting their use across the curriculum.

The engagement research challenges any curriculum debate focused entirely on curriculum programs or teaching content by suggesting that *how* tasks and content are presented to students may be as important as the *content* presented. It shows that the context and coherence that skilled classroom teachers create for literacy is of central importance, not an add-on or a frippery. Teaching approaches that ensure purposeful tasks, in which (for example) young writers actually *see* their writing being enjoyed or used by others, and get a genuine response to *what* they have communicated (rather than simply grades to show how their writing is rated against pre-determined criteria) make a difference to the students' engagement. Equally, reading tasks need to be designed and contextualized to ensure that readers *use* their reading. Asking readers to teach or explain knowledge gained from their reading to people who need to know and understand it (i.e., not in a test) or to discuss and share their thoughts and reactions with others will create more highly engaged readers than asking them to read the same text to answer comprehension questions about it, or some other performative task. The engagement research also indicates that teachers should not minutely prescribe everything for their students; opportunities for students to read and write for their own purposes are important, but may sit poorly alongside narrow teacher-accountability agendas that exclude roles such as increasing interest and enjoyment of books. It also requires good resourcing in the form of a rich variety of reading materials likely to appeal to different individual tastes, and available for students to read at school and at home (Allington and McGill-Franzen, 1993; Kim 2004; Neuman and Celano, 2001). Teaching that focuses on students applying comprehension strategies across the curriculum creates a curricular coherence that exists at the level of the students' learning but may require quiet but important shifts in current pedagogies. For example, in the United Kingdom and elsewhere, formative assessment strategies suggest that teachers ask students to identify what they have learned after a particular lesson. However, to emphasize curricular coherence they perhaps should also ask students to identify when else they might apply and use the strategies they have just been taught.

Cultural and Socio-cultural Perspectives on Reading Engagement

The 2009 PISA report on reading engagement indicates large gender differences in reading engagement (OECD, 2010b): 73 percent of girls compared with only 54 percent of boys reported reading for enjoyment outside school. Boys were less likely to enjoy reading, to read on a daily basis or to read widely, and they also reported making less use of comprehension strategies to summarize and understand texts. In general, reading fiction had the strongest association with reading performance and boys reported reading less fiction than girls (OECD, 2010a, p. 97). Comparison of the reading engagement data from the PIRLS and the PISA studies indicate that reading engagement in boys decreases more rapidly between the ages of 10 and 15 years than it does for girls, and also that the general decline in reading for enjoyment between 2000–2009 has been more pronounced among 15-year-old boys than among 15-year-old girls (OECD, 2010b).

A number of explanations for the gender-based differences in reading engagement have been suggested. Among these, evidence for the impact of any differences in brain structure/function or differences in the supposed 'learning styles' of boys and girls are most strongly contested

(Baron-Cohen, 2004; Coffield *et al.*, 2004; Younger *et al.*, 2005). Research perspectives that position reading as a profoundly social act, tied to social purposes and understandings have gained wider acceptance and suggest explanations that focus on the ways that boys and girls are socialized to become literate. Some research indicates that the differences are rooted in gendered attitudes and beliefs about self-identity (Garbe, 2007) or that they result from the strong peer pressure on boys to conform to masculine identities, coupled with stereotyped views of reading as a 'female' activity (Brozo, 2010; Smith and Wilhelm, 2009). Such research has led to practical campaigns in which, for example, sports stars promote reading specifically to boys (Dungy, 2011; NLT, 2011b). Others argue that the problem lies with the 'feminization' of literacy and identify the influence of mothers and the impact of a largely female teaching workforce in primary schools as particularly problematic. This view suggests that women bring female assumptions about the contexts and purposes for literacy, choice of texts, ways of responding to texts and choices of assessment and teaching methods that deter boys (Brozo, 2010; Millard, 1997).

Whereas sociological researchers have focused on the impact of social mores to explain gendered patterns of literacy engagement, ethnographic studies have focused on literacy use within and across communities to understand what it *means* to be a reader or a writer within a particular community. Such studies attend to how

> the social world in its many facets is continuously remade in particular encounters which are both shaped by the past but also have the potential to transform how things stand. Change and continuities are equally important with an accent on individual agency, tempered by an understanding of the social history which structures how any social interaction takes place and the resources which constrain as well as enable the choices individuals can make. (Moss, 2010, p. 127)

Clearly, 'what counts' as literacy in school and other communities may be different, and some people have more power than others to define what counts in any particular situation (Janks, 2009). However, by focusing on how and why literacy events, texts, and interactions are woven into the social fabric of particular groups, ethnographic research can also reveal the impact that fleeting interactions and unacknowledged organizational structures have on the reading engagement of different groups.

For example, Moss (2003) explored why some 10–11-year-old boys choose to read nonfiction books. Her observations indicated that their preference for nonfiction had little to do with the content of the books. Instead, nonfiction books allowed low-attaining boys to preserve their social status in classroom contexts that placed a strong emphasis on reading proficiency. Whereas fiction books signal the competence of the reader through the number of illustrations and the size and quantity of print on a page, nonfiction books do not. The nonfiction books had illustrations regardless of text difficulty and these allowed struggling readers to share their expertise on the topic and participate in the social networks around reading without necessarily reading the book. For readers in the 'can read but don't' category, the nonsequential structure of nonfiction books such as *Dorling Kindersley Eyewitness Guides*, and the 'linear dip' structures of, for example, the *Horrible Histories* series, allow the reader to commit to reading small chunks of text. Whereas the narrative structure of fiction meant committing oneself to reading the whole text from start to finish, the nonfiction texts, because they are not designed to be read in this linear fashion, were more appealing. Moss showed that although status-conscious boys are drawn to nonfiction, promoting such books may not produce a lasting and positive impact on reading engagement or on attainment. Her research reveals the complexity of the literacy landscape in schools and indicates why some 'solutions' to reading engagement may ultimately prove unsuccessful.

Moss' research may in part also explain the links that PISA 2009 (OECD, 2010a) found between high reading engagement and fiction but does not preclude teachers from using nonfiction texts as a practical 'way in' to address reading engagement in particular groups (see for example Dreher, 2003). Understanding the social context of literacy and how, through their response to reading and writing in the classroom and at home, students create their social identity and align themselves to particular social groups and power structures is a rich and complex strand of literacy engagement research. Dyson (1997) describes how children network around literacy tasks in school, using apparently off-task, social talk 'below the teacher's radar' to negotiate the meaning of the task and cement social relationships by writing each other into their stories. Ito (2010) describes how children use literacy in social media and networks, pointing out that the role digital literacies play in stimulating reading and writing engagement is a rich and developing strand of research. The dynamics of how engagement in both old and new literacies actually operates on the ground, and of the social context and consequences of being female or male, being a good or a struggling reader and of a home culture that supports agency in, and dispositions towards, different types of literacy networks and leisure reading are of huge significance (Love and Hamston, 2004; Smith and Wilhelm, 2002).

A later study (Moss and McDonald, 2004) combined statistical analysis and qualitative methodology. Statistical analysis of school library borrowing records allowed them to investigate the influence of social networks on the children's book choice. This showed that reading networks, indicated by friends borrowing the same titles either simultaneously or in close sequence, flourished in one class but not in others. Interviews indicated that in the class where reading networks flourished, the teacher was interested in the children as readers, and knew what they were reading, but didn't have strong rules about what they should read or how many books they should get through in a month. She allowed the children freedom and social space to negotiate their own consensus about what was and was not worth reading. The children internalized literacy as part of their social identity. The other classes, despite access to the same library, showed little evidence of any reading networks operating. Their teachers monitored closely the quantity of books and ensured the children read a range of genres, which seemed to result in children who tended to view all books as of equal merit. The library visits in these classes did not function to allow the children to define themselves as readers within their own social space; children read because it was a school requirement. Thus seemingly small differences in context, setting, and implementation led to radically different outcomes.

It can be difficult to protect 'social spaces' in the curriculum for children to create their own identities as readers. The challenge is to foster contexts that help young people create the social networks that are advantageous to their learning and enable them to forge positive personal identities in relation to literacy. Accountability agendas have tended to result in crowded, over-directed curricula in which any learning that is better nudged than taught tends to be sidelined or re-cast as a teacher-led activity. For example, some iterations of literature circles (Daniels, 1994; Harste *et al.*, 1988; Short and Kauffman, 1995) emphasize their power to make reading part of the social context of the classroom. Without a teacher present, the pupil discussions are wide-ranging, unfocused and anecdotal, but they do allow young readers to argue, share opinions, and personalize texts in ways that both bring the texts to life and bring them into their lives (Pearson, 2010; Allan *et al.*, 2005). However, literature circles can easily become colonized by the school system into more teacher-centric reading groups in which, as Daniels (2002) complains: 'It doesn't matter if the teacher has picked the story, if the book is a basal (or a science textbook), if the teacher is running the discussion, if the kids have no voice – it's just cool to call it a literature circle' (Daniels, 2002, p. 2).

If creating the conditions that promote reading in schools requires context-sensitive intervention, ensuring the right teaching input, the right starting points, the right activities, and the right champions are all crucial. This requires respecting a pedagogy that aligns teaching with, among other things, 'nudging,' 'facilitating,' and 'inspiring.' Current monitoring systems may encourage teachers in many countries to attend instead to measuring, telling, delivering, and controlling which, as the reading engagement research shows, are important but not sufficient for efficient learning. In this context, teachers' own attitudes to children's literature and to becoming literate are most important. Studies show that teachers often rely on a narrow repertoire of authors, poets, and picture fiction creators (Cremin *et al.*, 2008). Cunningham (2005) outlines the implications of this for vocabulary growth. Computer software programs designed to encourage reading by creating personalized 'reading pathways' are the obvious technocratic answer to teachers' limited knowledge of children's books, but they don't foster the networks or the social spaces that appear to be so important in creating truly engaged readers and the benefits that accrue from that. Moreover, the affordance of the technology, which allows teachers to track the number of books, the time taken to read them, the text difficulty and the comprehension scores for each pupil, risks diverting teachers attention further away from fostering reading engagement and instead could encourage them to measure and control reading. Teaching children to celebrate the stories, friendships, and insights into life that result from sharing a good book should be an important goal for education.

Reading Engagement beyond Schools: Families and Homes

Reading engagement can mitigate some of the impact of socio-economic status on reading attainment. We know that literacy, far from being a neutral 'skill,' is socially constructed and that different social groups see different purpose in it and develop different practices around it (Gee, 2004). Researchers describe a cycle of disadvantage that associates low literacy skills with socio-economic status and low literacy engagement. This matters because early and positive literacy engagement has long-term effects on both language acquisition and literacy development (High *et al.*, 1999; Raikes *et al.*, 2006). While parents with low literacy are no more or less likely to teach their children the alphabet, they are much less likely to read to their children, or to read with them. They tend to have fewer books in the home and their children, by age ten plus, are less likely to report reading for enjoyment (Parsons and Bynner, 2008).

For this reason, policy efforts to improve reading engagement are targeted at a wide range of social and literacy environments and not limited to schools and schooling, or introduced only after children have become independent readers. Family-based interventions to engage young children with books now exist in Japan; Korea, Thailand, the Falkland Islands, Germany, Ireland, Portugal, Malta, the Netherlands, and Belgium (O'Hare and Connolly, 2010) as well as in the United States (Klass, 2002), the United Kingdom (Brooks *et al.*, 2008) and Canada (Thomas, 1998). Carpentieri *et al.*'s (2011) review of family literacy programs throughout Europe indicates that, although complex to develop, administer, and transfer, they impact successfully on attainment. It also notes some of the different ways they foster engagement in childhood and instill a lifelong, intergenerational culture of reading.

National and local projects to promote reading engagement in wider society are run by a variety of agencies and target a range of social groups (Eurydice, 2011). Campaigns that are broadly focused and are run by literacy professionals such as teachers and librarians tend not to impact on lower income groups, nonprofessional households, and those on unemployment benefits because schools and libraries often lack strong and positive relationships with these hard-to-reach groups, which means that they are not best-placed to influence their behavior. Social marketing campaigns that tap into the strong existing relationships between these groups and, for example, major food manufacturers, supermarkets, and newspapers may be more successful, but are hard to evaluate (e.g., NLT, 2010a, 2010b, 2011a; Reading Agency, 2009). Reaching into families and homes is important. A UK survey of 18,141 young people mostly aged between 11 and 13 found that children were more likely to own a mobile phone than a book. While accepting that mobile phones do represent a form of literacy use, it is still shocking that 27.4 percent owned no books at home (Clark and Poulton, 2011). Allington *et al.* (2010) show that owning books makes a difference to children's experience of reading, their expectations of reading, and their willingness to engage in it, and that making chosen books available at home can significantly reduce the 'summer attainment drop' in vulnerable groups.

There is certainly much work to be done to promote reading in wider society and foster a lifelong culture of reading. A marketing study for the Arts Council for England (BML, 2005) indicated that 47 percent of adults had not bought a book in the past year, 13 percent had not opened at a book, and 40 percent did not know how to find a book they would enjoy. Some respondents, mostly men, felt unable to judge from the book cover and description, whether they would enjoy a book and, in general men were less likely than women to take a chance on reading a book they might not like. Reading has few role models in the media and many respondents felt guilty about 'wasting time' reading. The survey advocates active campaigns to emphasize reading as a good-value, long-lasting, portable entertainment that promotes relaxation and imagination.

The research on reading engagement in adult populations is limited and tends to indicate beneficial outcomes – it is, for example, a protective factor against dementia and cognitive deterioration (Verghese *et al.*, 2003). However, adult reading engagement forms the family backdrop for children's reading engagement at home, and for reading in society. A deeper understanding of the development of reading engagement across the lifespan and of how adult readers' motivations and goals are different from children's would help policy makers, educators, and publishers to understand how to create and support a self-sustaining lifelong culture of reading. Schutte and Malouff (2007) found that adult readers' motivations for reading were rooted in their identity in the larger world rather than their self-identity or the social factors found in children's motivations. While most current research assumes that creating engaged readers during childhood is the pivotal predictor of engaged reading as an adult, the existing research on adult readers indicates that maintaining adults' reading engagement to create a self-sustaining intergenerational culture of reading, may require a different set of motivations, environments, and materials.

Reading Engagement Research: A Final Question

Much of the current policy dialogue about reading engagement links it to reading attainment and is rooted in a paradigm of economic rationalism that positions literacy as a key element of human capital within the knowledge economy of high-income countries (see for example, Sum *et al.*, 2004; High *et al.*, 1999). The rationale is that reading engagement can help raise attainment in literacy and, by doing so, will improve human capital and contribute to the wider economic well-being and growth of society. This may be one reason why reading engagement has recently captured such fierce attention from policy bodies. However, there are ideological objections to education being seen in this way (Gillies, 2010). There are also concerns that harnessing reading engagement, even in part, to a discourse of economic rationalism may result in narrow, technocratic solutions to problems of pedagogy and curriculum design being imposed on schools, teachers, and students (Luke, 2003).

Narrow technocratic solutions do not chime with much of the research evidence presented in this chapter. It is clear that reading engagement is a complex construct and requires pedagogies and interventions that are tailored, nuanced, integrated, and intrinsic. A great strength of reading engagement research is the use of multidiscipline and cross-discipline approaches to provide insight into literacy learning. If the research knowledge this generates can be used to scaffold more effective frameworks for curriculum design, teaching and assessment, it is possible that a stronger focus on reading engagement could challenge fundamentally the primacy of skills-based, narrowly technocratic educational agendas. This raises the prospect that, rather than complex, multilayered research understandings being subverted by narrow technocratic solutions, reading engagement research could actually be a central driving force in promoting creative, developmental, and constructivist literacy curricula across the world.

The impact reading engagement research has on the global education discourse will depend in no small part on how effectively and widely the knowledge that has been generated is mobilized and made accessible to educational policy makers, managers, and teachers across the globe, as well as on how this knowledge chimes with broader social and political messages. The question of how reading engagement research will shape and be shaped by the wider educational discourses has still to be answered.

References

Allan, J., Ellis, S., and Pearson, C. (2005) *Literature Circles, Gender and Reading for Enjoyment: Report to The Scottish Executive Education Department*, accessed November 15, 2012: www.scotland.gov.uk/Publications/2005/11/SRLitCir

Allington, R.L., and McGill-Franzen, A. (1993) What are they to read? Not all children, Mr. Riley, have easy access to books. *Education Week*, 42(10): 26.

Allington, R.L., McGill-Frazen, A., Camilli, G., *et al.* (2010) Addressing summer reading setback among economically disadvantaged elementary students. *Reading Psychology*, 31(5): 411–427.

Baker, L., and Wigfield, A. (1999) Dimensions of children's reading motivation for reading and their relations to reading activity and reading achievement. *Reading Research Quarterly*, 34: 452–477.

Baron-Cohen, S. (2004) *The Essential Difference*. London: Penguin.

BML (2005) *Expanding the Book Market: A Study of Reading and Buying Habits in GB*. London: BML/Arts Council England.

Brooks, G., Pahl, K., Pollard, A., and Rees, F. (2008) *Effective and Inclusive Practices in Family Literacy, Language and Numeracy: A Review of Programmes and Practice in the UK and Internationally*. Reading: CFBT/NRDC.

Brozo, W.G. (2010) *To Be a Boy, To Be a Reader: Engaging Teen and Preteen Boys in Active Literacy*, 2nd edn. Newark, DE: IRA.

Brozo, W.G., Shiel, G., and Topping, K. (2007) Lessons learned from three PISA countries. *Journal of Adolescent and Adult Literacy*, 51(4): 304–315.

Campbell, J.R., Voelkl, K.E., and Donahue, P.L. (1997) *NAEP 1996 Trends in Academic Progress* (NCES Publication No. 97–985). Washington DC: US Department of Education.

Carpentieri, J., Fairfax-Cholmeley, K., Litster, J., and Vorhaus, J. (2011) *Family Literacy in Europe: Using Parental Support Initiatives to Enhance Early Literacy Development*. London: NRDC, Institute of Education.

Cipielewski, J., and Stanovich, K.E. (1992) Predicting growth in reading ability from children's exposure to print. *Journal of Experimental Child Psychology*, 54: 74–89.

Clark, C., and Poulton, L. (2011) *Book Ownership and its Relation to Reading Enjoyment, Attitudes, Behaviour and Attainment*. London: NLT.

Coffield, F., Moseley, D., Hall, E., and Ecclestone, K. (2004) *Should We Be Using Learning Styles? What Research Has to Say to Practice*. London: Learning and Skills Research Centre.

Cremin, T., Mottram, M., Bearne, E., and Goodwin, P. (2008) Exploring teachers' knowledge of children's literature. *Cambridge Journal of Education*, 38(4): 449–464.

Cunningham, A.E. (2005) Vocabulary growth through independent reading and reading aloud to children. In Elfrieda H. Hiebert and Michael L. Kamil (eds) *Teaching and Learning Vocabulary: Bringing Research to Practice*. Mahwah, NJ: Lawrence Erlbaum, pp. 45–68.

Cunningham, A.E., and Stanovich, K.E. (1998) What reading does for the mind, *American Educator*, 22(1&2): 8–15.

Daniels, H. (1994) *Literature Circles: Voice and Choice in the Student-Centered Classroom*. Markham: Pembroke Publishers Ltd.

Daniels, H. (2002) *Literature Circles: Voice and Choice in Book Clubs and Reading Groups*. Portland, ME: Stenhouse.

Deci, E.L., and Ryan, R.M. (1992) The initiation and regulation of intrinsically motivated learning and achievement. In A.K. Boggiano and T.S. Pittman (eds) *Achievement and Motivation: A Social Developmental Perspective*. Toronto: Cambridge University Press, pp. 3–36.

Dreher, M.J. (2003) Motivating struggling readers by tapping the potential of information books. *Reading and Writing Quarterly*, 19: 25–38.

Dungy, T. (2011) Keynote Address: The Power of Literacy. 56th Annual Convention of the International Reading Association, May 8–11, 2011, Orange County Convention Centre, Florida.

Dyson, A.H. (1997) *Writing Superheroes: Contemporary Childhood, Popular Culture, and Classroom Literacy*. New York: Teachers College Press.

Eurydice (2011) *Teaching Reading in Europe: Contexts, Policies and Practices*. Brussels: European Commission.

Fredricks, J., Blumenfeld, P., and Paris, A. (2004) School engagement: Potential of the concept, state of the evidence. *Review of Educational Research*, 74: 59–109.

Gambrell, L.B. (2011) Seven Rules of Engagement: What's most important to know about motivation to read? *The Reading Teacher*, 65(3): 172–178.

Garbe, C. (2004) International research: Report from Germany *Reading Research Quarterly*, 39(2): 232–233.

Garbe, C. (2007) ADORE: Teaching struggling adolescent readers: a comparative study of good practices in European Countries. Study supported by the Lifelong Learning Programme of the European Commission. University of Luneburg: Germany.

Gee, J. (2004) *Situated Language and Learning*. London: Routledge.

Gillies, D. (2010) Economic goals, quality discourse and the narrowing of European state education. *Education, Knowledge and Economy*, 4(2): 103–118.

Guthrie, J.T., and Coddington, C.S. (2009) Reading motivation. In K. Wentzel and A. Wigfield (eds) *Handbook of Motivation at School*. New York: Routledge, pp. 503–525.

Guthrie, J.T., and Cox, K.E. (2001) Classroom Conditions for Motivation and Engagement in Reading. *Educational Psychology Review*, 13(3): 283–302.

Guthrie, J.T., and Humenick, N.M. (2004) Motivating students to read: Evidence for classroom practices that increase motivation and achievement. In P. McCardle and V. Chhabra (eds) *The Voice of Evidence in Reading Research*. Baltimore, MD: Paul Brookes Publishing, pp. 329–354.

Guthrie, J.T., Schafer, W.D., and Huang, C. (2001) Benefits of opportunity to read and balanced reading instruction for reading achievement and engagement: A policy analysis of state NAEP in Maryland. *Journal of Educational Research*, 94(3): 145–162.

Guthrie, J.T., and Wigfield, A. (2000) Engagement and motivation in reading. In M.L. Kamil, P.B. Mosenthal, P.D. Pearson, and R. Barr (eds) *Handbook of Reading Research*, 3rd edn. New York: Longman, pp. 403–422.

Guthrie, J.T., Wigfield, A., Metsala, J.L., and Cox, K.E. (1999) Motivational and cognitive predictors of text comprehension and reading amount. *Scientific Studies of Reading*, 3(3): 231–356.

Harste, J., Short, K., and Burke, C. (1988) *Creating Classrooms for Authors: The Reading-Writing Connection*. Portsmouth, NH: Heinemann Educational.

High, P., Hopmann, M., LaGasse, L., *et al.* (1999) Child centered literacy orientation: a form of social capital? *Pediatrics*, 103(4):e55, accessed November 15, 2012: http://pediatrics.aappublications.org/content/103/4/e55.full.pdf+html

Ito, M. (2010) *Hanging Out, Messing around, and Geeking Out: Kids Living and Learning with New Media*. Cambridge, MA: Massachusetts Institute of Technology.

Ivey, S.J., and Guthrie, J.T. (2008) Struggling readers: Boosting motivation in low achievers. In J.T. Guthrie (ed.) *Engaging Adolescents in Reading*. Thousand Oaks, CA : Corwin Press, pp. 115–129.

Janks, H. (2009) *Literacy and Power*. London: Routledge.

Kamil, M.L., Borman, G.D., Dole, J., *et al*. (2008) Improving adolescent literacy: Effective classroom and intervention practices. A Practice Guide (NCEE #2008-4027). Washington, DC: National Center for Education Evaluation and Regional Assistance, Institute of Education Sciences, U.S. Department of Education.

Kim, J.S. (2004) Summer reading and the ethnic achievement gap. *Journal of Education for Students Placed at Risk*, 9(2): 169–189.

Klass, P. (2002) Pediatrics by the book: pediatricians and literacy promotion. *Pediatrics*, 110(5): 989–995.

Lepper, M.R., and Cordova, D.I. (1992) A desire to be taught: Instructional consequence of intrinsic motivation. *Motivation and Emotion*, 16(3): 187–208.

Love, K., and Hamston, J. (2004) Committed and reluctant male teenage readers: Beyond bedtime stories. *Journal of Literacy Research*, 36: 335–400.

Luke, A. (2003) After the marketplace: Evidence, social science and educational research. *The Australian Educational Researcher*, 30(2): 89–109.

Lutz, S.L., Guthrie, J.T., and Davis, M.H. (2006) Scaffolding for engagement in learning: An observational study of elementary school reading instruction. *Journal of Educational Research*, 100: 3–30.

Marks, H.M. (2000) Student engagement in instructional activity: patterns in the elementary, middle and high school years. *American Educational Research Journal*, 37(1): 153–184.

Millard, E. (1997) Differently literate: Gender identity and the construction of the developing reader. *Gender and Education*, 9(1): 31–48.

Moss, G. (2003) Analyzing literacy events; mapping gendered configurations of readers, texts and contexts. In S. Goodman, T. Lillis, J. Maybin, and N. Mercer (eds) *Language, Literacy and Education: A Reader*. Stoke on Trent: Trentham Books, pp. 123–137.

Moss, G., and McDonald, J.W. (2004) The borrowers: library records as unobtrusive measures of children's reading preferences. *Journal of Research in Reading*, 27: 401–412.

Moss, G. (2010) Talk about text; the discursive construction of what it means to be a reader. In S. Ellis and E. McCartney (eds) *Applied Linguistics and Primary School Teaching*. Cambridge: Cambridge University Press, pp. 127–139.

Mullis, I.V.S., Martin, M.O., Kennedy, A.M., and Foy, P. (2007) *PIRLS 2006 International Report*. Chestnut Hill, MA: TIMSS and PIRLS International Study Center, Boston College.

Neuman, S.B., and Celano, D. (2001) Access to print in low-income and middle-income communities: An ecological study in four neighborhoods. *Reading Research Quarterly*, 36(1): 8–26.

NLT (2010a) *Reading for Life: Marmite Campaign*, accessed November 15, 2012: www.literacytrust. org.uk/news/2068_reading_for_life_marmite_promotion_wins_gold_award

NLT (2010b) *Reading for Life: TV Promotion*, accessed November 15, 2012: www.literacytrust. org.uk/resources/videos/3437_reading_for_life_tv_advert

NLT (2011a) *Reading for Life*: Campaigns Policy, accessed September 13, 2012: www.literacytrust. org.uk/campaigns-policy/media/2942

NLT (2011b) *Premier League Reading Stars*, accessed November 15, 2012: www.literacytrust. org.uk/premier_league_reading_stars

OECD (2010a) *PISA 2009: Overcoming Social Background: Equity in Learning and Outcomes*, Vol. III. Paris: OECD.

OECD (2010b) *PISA 2009. Results: Learning to Learn – Student Engagement: Strategies and Practices*, vol. III. Paris: OECD.

O'Hare, L., and Connolly, P. (2010) *A Randomised Controlled Trial Evaluation of Bookstart+: A Book Gifting Intervention for Two-Year-Old Children*. Belfast: Centre for Effective Education, Queen's University Belfast.

Parsons, S., and Bynner, J. (2008) Illuminating disadvantage: Profiling the experiences of adults with entry level literacy or numeracy over the lifecourse: Summary report. National Research and Development Centre for Adult Literacy and Numeracy.

Paterson, L. (2009) Civic Values and the Subject Matter of Educational Courses. *Oxford Review of Education*, 35(1): 81–98.

Pearson, C. (2010), Acting up or acting out? Unlocking children's talk in literature circles. *Literacy*, 44(1): 3–11.

Raikes, H., Pan, B.A., Luze, G., et al. (2006) Mother-child book reading in low-income families: Correlates and outcomes during the first 3 years of life. *Child Development*, 77: 924–953.

Reading Agency (2009) *Reading for Life: Campaigns*, accessed November 15, 2012: www.readingagency.org.uk/about/reading-for-life/

Schoon, I., Parsons, S., Rush, R., and Law, J.L. (2010) Childhood Language Skills and Adult Literacy: A 29-Year Follow-up Study. *Pediatrics*, 125(3): 459–466.

Schunk, D.H. (2003) Self-efficacy for reading and writing: Influence of modeling, goal setting, and self-evaluation. *Reading and Writing Quarterly: Overcoming Learning Difficulties*, 19: 159–172.

Schutte, N.S., and Malouff, J.M. (2007) Dimensions of reading motivation: Development of an adult reading motivation scale. *Reading Psychology*, 28: 469–489.

Short, K., and Kauffman, G. (1995) So what do I do? The role of the teacher in literature circles. In N. Roser and M. Martinez (eds) *Book Talk and Beyond: Children and Teachers Respond to Literature*. Newark, NJ: International Reading Association, pp. 140–149.

Skinner, E.A., and Belmont, M.J. (1993) Motivation in the classroom: Reciprocal effects of teacher behaviour and student engagement across the school year. *Journal of Educational Psychology*, 85(4): 571–581.

Smith, M.W., and Wilhelm, J. (2002): '*Reading Don't Fix No Chevys': Literacy in the Lives of Young Men*. Portsmouth, NH: Heinemann.

Smith, M.W., and Wilhelm, J. (2009), Boys and Literacy: Complexity and Multiplicity. In L. Christenbury, R. Bomer, and P. Smagorinsky (eds) *Handbook of Adolescent Literacy Research*. New York: Guildford Press, pp. 360–371.

Snow, C. (2002) *Reading For Understanding: Toward a Research and Development Program in Reading Comprehension*. Santa Monica: RAND, accessed November 15, 2012: www.rand.org/pubs/monograph_reports/2005/MR1465.pdf

Stanovich, K.E. (1986) Matthew Effects in Reading: Some Consequences of Individual Differences in the Acquisition of Literacy. *Reading Research Quarterly*, 21: 360–406.

Sum, A., Kirsch, I., and Yamamoto, K. (2004) *A Human Capital Concern: The Literacy Proficiency of U.S. Immigrants*. Princeton, NJ: Policy Information Center, Center for Global Assessment, Educational Testing Service.

Sweet, A.P., and Snow, C.E. (2003) *Rethinking Reading Comprehension*. New York: Guildford Press.

Thomas, A. (ed.) (1998) *Family Literacy in Canada: Profiles of Effective Practices*. Ontario: Soleil Publishing Inc.

Verghese, J., Lipton, R.B., Katz, M.J., et al. (2003) Leisure activities and the risk of dementia in the elderly. *The New England Journal of Medicine*, 348: 2508–3516.

Wang, M., and Holcombe, R. (2010) Adolescents' perceptions of school environment, engagement, and academic achievement in middle school. *American Educational Research Journal*, 47(4): 633–662.

Wigfield, A., and Guthrie, J.T. (1997) Relations of children's motivation for reading to the amount and breadth of their reading. *Journal of Educational Psychology*, 89: 420–432.

Wigfield, A., and Guthrie, J.T. (2010) The Impact of CORI on Students' Reading Motivation, Reading Engagement and Reading Comprehension. In J.L. Meece and J.L. Eccles (eds) *Handbook of Schools, Schooling and Human Development*. New York: Routledge.

Younger, M., and Warrington, M. with Gray, J., Rudduck, J., McLellan, R., et al. (2005) *Raising Boys' Achievement*. London: DfE.

Chapter 18

Opening the Classroom Door to Children's Literature

A Review of Research

Evelyn Arizpe, Maureen Farrell, and Julie McAdam

Introduction: Mapping the Research Field

In recent years children's literature (CL) has flourished throughout the world and, particularly since the 1980s, research has provided evidence for the potential it offers learners in the classroom even in the face of radical changes in policies, technologies, and school curricula. This potential is based on the results of national and international studies that show that growing up with books and being a reader continues to be one of the biggest indicators of future success (Clark, Woodley, and Lewis, 2011; Evans, Kelley, Sikora, and Tremain, 2010; OECD, 2002). However, these results also means that CL has found itself embroiled in distracting debates about the teaching of reading as well as about its role as a tool for introducing other curriculum topics.

A useful way of introducing our review of research about the ways CL is used in contemporary literacy classrooms is Serafini's distinction:

> it can be conceptualised in different ways: as an 'add-on' or treat available when children finish exercises in commercial workbooks, a pedagogical balancing device, a way of knowing the world, or a space for critical conversations, used to explore the systems of power that affect the ways that students are positioned as readers and the meanings available to them. (Serafini, 2003, section 6, para. 1)

This chapter will show how theory, practice, and research have shifted the perspective on the role of CL from 'treat' to a resource that aids in the exploration of self, others and knowledge of the world and, more recently, to a core cultural artifact that can enable transformative practices.

Throughout this review we build on the various metaphors that have been used to describe the role of CL expanding these by considering not only how the 'classroom door' has been 'opened' to CL but also 'the road ahead' for teachers and teacher educators. The first section begins with a brief history of CL in the classroom and the influence of theoretical and political narratives that have caused shifts at different times and in different places. In the second section we discuss the research that refers to using CL as a pedagogical and ontological tool in the

International Handbook of Research on Children's Literacy, Learning, and Culture, First Edition.
Edited by Kathy Hall, Teresa Cremin, Barbara Comber, and Luis C. Moll.
© 2013 John Wiley & Sons, Ltd. Published 2013 by John Wiley & Sons, Ltd.

classroom. The third and fourth sections deal with research on the three participants that are key in opening the door: the text, the reader, and the teacher. We have endeavored to cover as much ground and as many international references as possible in a chapter of this length in order to provide the basis for the directions for further research suggested by this review.

The Evolving Role of Children's Literature in the Classroom: A Brief History

At the heart of the historical evolution of the role of CL in the classroom is the tension between literature and pedagogy, 'a couple . . . for better or for worse' as Butlen (2008–2009, p. 29) describes it: inseparable but with a 'troubled' history. Contemporary trends and issues around this role, not only in English speaking countries but in Europe and beyond, find their roots in the history of this relationship. Added to this is the complex distinction between definitions of what is and what is not CL; a distinction that implies beliefs about childhood and therefore beliefs about instruction and entertainment. As Hunt points out, behind this debate is usually the 'suspicion that children's literature is not actually "work"' (1994, p. 175). Before the eighteenth century, in most European countries books for children were written in response to particular religious, moral, or educational requirements and were therefore designed with a distinct instructional purpose that implied 'work' for the reader, usually through rote learning. Gradually, the trend of incorporating some material designed to amuse readers became more common, partly in response to recommendations of educationalists like John Locke and, towards the nineteenth century, a more defined line was drawn between texts designed for teaching reading in the schoolroom and 'children's literature'.

Despite the increasing availability of children's books and the growing recognition of CL as a distinct form of literature, battles between the reading methodologies accompanied the spread of literacy education and the curriculum continued to be dominated by instructional reading material, in the form of primers, basal readers, and textbooks until well into the middle of the twentieth century (and indeed beyond, as reflected in the debates about the merits of reading schemes versus 'authentic' texts for teaching reading; c.f. Solity and Vousden, 2009). However, the potential of CL was highlighted by the coming together of a series of new ideas about reading. These new ideas began to be taken more seriously around the 1950s as traditional reading pedagogies were questioned as a result of a number of related factors in the wider areas of literacy, education, and literature.

Initiatives outside the classroom for promoting reading in the United States, the United Kingdom and around Europe were led by librarians, authors, and others; one seminal event, for example, was the creation of the International Youth Library in Munich in 1949 and the International Board of Books for Young People (IBBY). Other centers such as the Library of Congress Children's Literature Center in the United States and the *La Joie par les livres* library in France followed and extended the drive to engage children with books, building on the realization that children will read what is of interest to them. International prizes and children's book fairs raised the profile of CL among a wider public. Another influence on the reception of CL in schools was the development of CL studies in academic institutions and increasing scholarship in the field from historical, literary, and cultural perspectives.

Influential theories

One of the main factors, however, was the influence of new theoretical understandings of the reading process that led to a more reader-based approach to literature teaching. In the

1960s, in the United States and the United Kingdom, arguments against the skills-based teaching models and for 'whole language' approaches were based on the psycholinguistic work of Kenneth Goodman and Frank Smith who provided evidence for reading as a process of constructing meaning, involving purpose, choice, and pleasure, rather than simply decoding. Published in 1961, Huck and Young's textbook, *Children's Literature in the Elementary School*, was the first of many to put forward a literature-based approach. In the United Kingdom, the 'London School' educators, in particular James Britton, John Dixon, Margaret Meek, and Harold Rosen, raised the profile of meaningful language experiences, including interaction with texts which supported the reading of 'whole' children's books and collaborative classroom discussion (i.e., Meek, Warlow, and Barton, 1978). Meek stressed the power of the text to 'teach reading' (1988) a seminal notion behind the use of CL in the classroom.

Reader-centered literary criticism also made an impression on changing ideas about reading and about what theories teachers ought to know (Beach, 1993). Despite differences in the control allotted to the reader and the text, Reception and Reader response theories, particularly those from Wolfgang Iser, Stanley Fish, and David Bleich also placed interaction at the heart of the act of reading. Ignored by literary critics at the time, the influence of Louise Rosenblatt's transactional reader response theory steadily increased to become one of the most significant reading theories in the field of literacy and in the use of CL. In different ways all the reading theories mentioned above led to more flexible ideas about comprehension, interpretation, and the value of children's responses as well as about the role of CL as a vehicle for both enrichment and learning.

Alongside these theories, several distinctive social and linguistic theories were also beginning to have an impact on understandings of literacy. Social-constructivist learning theories, particularly those of Lev Vygotsky and Jerome Bruner, stressed the social formation of meaning and the importance of reading and narrative for human development and higher order thinking skills. The recognition of reading as a social practice raised issues about what is meant by literacy (Gee, 2004; Street, 1984) and alerted educators to the discourses that select and value particular texts and language practices (Heath, 1983) and thus determine what counts as reading as well as what counts as success in reading.

Many of these theories – literary, social, and linguistic – found their way into the classroom in the 1980s and influenced the shift to literature-based approaches and the validation of the role of CL either as the central basis or as a supplementary part of the curriculum (in the United States this was observed in a series of articles towards the end of the 1990s by influential members of the International Reading Association, for example, Cullinan, 1987; Galda, Ash, and Cullinan, 2000; Morrow and Gambrell, 2000). However, most practitioners continued to use a combination of approaches to teaching early reading and did not abandon more formal methods of instruction (Hall, 2010, p. 7). Serafini (2003) argues that the lack of in-depth knowledge and reflection meant that CL simply became another tool for teaching decoding and other skills for assessment as many approaches were still based on 'outdated' modernist theories and even 'transactional' theories that remain within local contexts, rather than 'critical theories' that take account of wider historical, socio-political, and cultural contexts.

Politics into policy

From the middle of the 1990s the new conservative political climates in the United States and the United Kingdom resulted in educational policies that narrowed the curriculum and focused on 'basic' skills and text-driven approaches with CL being placed on the sidelines. The unprecedented explosion of publications and media coverage of children's books in the past two decades has not been mirrored in worldwide curricular reforms during the same period and the term 'Children's Literature' appears in few policy documents, with Canada, Ireland and Australia being among the exceptions in English speaking countries (ACARA 2012; Government of Ireland 1999; Ministry of Education 2007). In her overview of literature in the elementary classroom, Kathy Short makes clear the socio-political contexts behind the shifts in reading instruction policies and stresses that despite these constraints, 'children's literature as a field of study can be opened up through a focus on literature as inquiry into life' and that 'teachers can and do create conditions for critical literary study through strategic reading, personal reading and transformative reading' (Short, 2011, p. 50). Much of the research reviewed in this chapter supports her argument. It also supports Serafini's (2003) view that a stronger grasp of theory will allow teachers to defend their choices in the face of the demands of policy.

International perspectives

Although some of these theoretical perspectives on reading and literacy began to be taken into account in educational settings and integrated into practice in countries other than the United States and the United Kingdom, official guidelines as to the role of CL in the classroom were (and still are) hard to find. There continue to be tensions, particularly, as in the case of Spain, between a 'formative reading guided by the teacher and the fostering of personal reading habits' (Colomer, 1999, p. 1991) and between instrumental and literary approaches, for example in the Netherlands, despite the fact that CL has a daily presence in early years education (Van der Pol, 2012). Fierce competition for the schools' market has also emerged between educational publishers and publishers of CL, such as in Germany where children's reading in the primary school consists mainly of CL (Ewers, 2009), while in South Africa the English curriculum advocates a text-based approach to a variety of genres but the suggested titles tend to be class readers rather than CL (Hatton and van der Walt, 2011). In the past ten years, even though contemporary children's texts continue to be a part of the reading program and are still considered to bring a wide range of benefits to readers in terms of developing literary competence and culture, fostering core democratic values and citizenship, in some countries such as France (Butlen, 2008–2009) and Sweden (Ewald, 2007) there has also been a return to the 'skills-based' model.

The international PIRLS survey from 2006 (Twist, Schagen, and Hodgson, 2007) reported an international average of 55 percent of pupils whose teacher used, at least weekly, a variety of children's books for the teaching of reading (with England being the highest in Europe) yet a recent study on CL in learning and teaching (LTCLE) in four European countries – the United Kingdom, Turkey, Spain, and Iceland – found that there were wide variations in teachers' understanding of literature and theory leading to wide variations in pedagogy (Aðalsteinsdóttir, 2011). This study also revealed that although the quality of teachers' commitment to using CL was generally high, they held very different perspectives on the role of CL. Although it is impossible to generalize, the situation is similar in countries outside Europe where although the offer of children's books has grown in quantity and quality along with high quality scholarship in the area of CL and there has been an enormous drive to promote reading across all sectors of society, there is still a perception of children's books mainly as didactic tools because the teaching of reading has predominantly utilitarian aims (Short, 2011, p. 53).

The theoretical and political narratives discussed lead to an enhanced understanding of the ways CL has been positioned and subsequently used over time and place. The next section pinpoints the pedagogical and ontological implications of using CL in the classroom, clearly showing that despite global variations in its use, the potential of CL needs to be carefully considered.

Crossing the Threshold

The benefits of early encounters with children's books for the development of language and emerging literacy skills are well documented (i.e., Teale and Sulzby 1986; Wells 1986). Other studies have indicated that, once in school, these encounters lead to positive attitudes to reading, improved literacy skills, and general success in literacy attainment (Krashen, 2004; McKenna, 2001; OECD, 2002). While the pleasure and enjoyment that comes from reading CL may be less documented in the classroom, the development of literary appreciation and competences such as analyzing and interpreting the language and structures of literature in order to understand how texts work have been the subject of academic discussion for some time (Hade, 1991; Hickman and Cullinan, 1989; Meek, 1992; Nodelman and Reimer, 2003; Purves and Monson, 1984; Sipe, 2008; Spencer, 1982 among others). Other uses of CL in the classroom have been explored in a variety of studies, from being used as a resource for gifted readers (Collins and Aiex, 1995) or disabled students (Smith-D'Arezzo, 2003; Williams and McLean, 1997) to being used to promote critical thinking (Sprod, 1995), address equity issues (Sulzby, Brantz, and Buhle, 1993) or explore philosophy with children (Haynes and Murris, 2012). Teachers are not averse to making use of CL to provide access and stimuli to curriculum subjects such as math (Ward, 2005), science (Sackes *et al.*, 2009), and geography (Lintner, 2010).

However, CL has the potential to become not only a means through which to learn key skills but also a vehicle for developing understanding and wisdom about the human condition. Polkinghorne (1988) and Bruner (1990) have documented the value of narrative as a fundamental human activity, an endeavor that allows humankind to make sense of individual and collective experience and construct knowledge through storytelling. Smith (1990) describes the human brain as a story seeking, story creating instrument; St Amour adds to this concept by stating 'stories are the foundations of our identity' and that they 'teach, nourish and inspire' (2003, p. 47). Nilsen and Donelson build on these ideas when they say that 'books are one of the main items that the community provides to young people in the hope of helping them in their journeys into adulthood' (1993, p. 3). Clearly CL as a cultural object contributes to the ongoing identity constructions of children (Sumara, 1998, p. 206) and if we accept poststructuralist definitions of identity as being dynamic and shaped by the environment and socio-political contexts of our time (Britzman, 1994) then CL provides a means of helping children construct and interpret not only who they are but what they do. An analysis of why educators use CL in the classroom keeps coming back to the metaphor of CL as a mirror, window, and door. The mirror suggests that through the reading process, children are able to see new representations of themselves and thus explore new understandings of self (Cullingford, 1998; Ee Loh, 2009; Langer, 1995) through an analysis of one's own life circumstances (Gopalakrishnan, 2011; Sleeter and Grant, 2002). It can lead to a changed sense of self and a greater understanding of one's own culture (Gopalakrishnan, 2011). Meek highlights the sense of 'belonging' brought about by readers thinking themselves into the book as they explore the value systems revealed in the text so that the texts begin to 'reveal what we think we have concealed from ourselves' (1988, p. 35). Children are able to make sense of their own life experiences (Kornfeld and Prothro, 2005) and connect the present to the past (Gough, 1998).

The metaphor continues with the concept of the window echoing all the reasons above, CL allows the reader to see alternative and possible worlds (Kornfeld and Prothro, 2005) and form new understandings of others (Ee Loh, 2009) as the text poses options and alternatives (Gough, 1998) and the idea of living in a complex culturally diverse world (Gopalakrishnan and Ulanoff, 2003). Readers begin to compare what they see out of the window with what they see in the mirror, contrasting their own value systems with those portrayed in the literature

(Meek, 1988). Sleeter and Grant (2002) would argue that this ability to see beyond themselves is the beginning of practicing democracy.

The metaphor moves towards a threshold that needs to be crossed, symbolized by the door, and the choice to resist moving through the door or relocate to new landscapes (Ee Loh, 2009). Sumara (1998) affirms the vocabulary of movement talking about reframing, recasting, shifting, and repositioning of the reader. Story allows children to play with boundaries between the real and the imagined, and take the step from moving through an imaginary door into crossing borders in real life (St Amour, 2003). Meek (1988, p. 29) believes that readers are involved in Mikhail Bakhtin's 'dialogic process of reading' allowing a 'confrontation of truth and falsehood, trust and betrayal' and may choose to take social action (Sleeter and Grant, 2002) and become active citizens in the world (Nieto, 2009, p. xi). While we may consider that books have the potential to break down borders, what remains clear is that books cannot do this by themselves (Hope, 2008); it is only by embracing reading pedagogies that allow a critical analysis of text that the door can be opened and then the threshold crossed.

Before discussing current pedagogical trends and ways forward it is necessary to examine the participants involved in crossing the threshold: the readers and the texts.

Continuing the Dialogue between Readers and Texts

This section combines research on child or young adult as readers and their response to different forms of CL with issues related to the selection of texts. Interest in the centrality of the role of readers to the production of meaning has led to research on the knowledge, experience, and processes involved in the act of reading as well as studies that explore the best ways of obtaining and enhancing their responses. These enquiries are closely linked to the research on the texts that readers are expected to respond to in the classroom and therefore issues of definition, 'quality', tradition, values, authenticity, and censorship. Given that all the research into these issues cannot be covered here, we have highlighted some of the more pertinent.

Literacy practices and choice inside and outside school

Research in the United Kingdom, the United States, and Australia on the literacy experiences that readers bring to their reading continues to show the extent to which out-of-school and home literacy practices tend to be ignored in school (Comber and Hill, 2000; Dyson, 2003; Gee, 2004; Hull and Schultz, 2002). The issue of student enjoyment and choice and how this fits with the 'authorized' school selection is highlighted by a range of surveys, for example, researchers found that pupils in English schools believed there was a discrepancy between the materials they read outside school and those they were encouraged to read by adults in school (Clark, Osborne, and Akerman, 2008). This echoed a United Kingdom government report from 2004 that noted that schools rarely built on pupils' reading interests and on the range of materials they read outside school (Ofsted, 2004) even though children and young people generally have positive attitudes towards reading and it is the opportunity to choose books that are of interest that leads to enjoyment of reading (Clark, 2011; Clark and Foster, 2005; Hall and Coles, 1999; Maynard, 2008). The LTCLE project revealed that teachers do feel responsible for promoting reading for pleasure (Aðalsteinsdóttir, 2011, p. 72), however, less than 50 percent of the children in all participating countries thought that reading in school helped them make choices about what to read (Aðalsteinsdóttir, 2011, p. 51) and even fewer read books recommended by teachers (Aðalsteinsdóttir, 2011, p. 38). Cremin (2007) summarizes other surveys, research, and practice on reading for pleasure and concludes that home, school, and community partnerships must be strengthened in order to enable the creation of a 'reading culture' (p. 10).

Choice and out-of-school literacy practices have been well researched in the context of the primary school in comparison to the context for secondary school. Although 'young adult' (YA) literature now has a strong presence in the book market, it is rarely present in the curriculum where it is usually assumed readers will be 'moving into' the adult literary world. Surveys have noted a decline in reading at this stage (OECD, 2002) suggesting a gulf between adolescent interests and educational objectives: reading and analyzing become 'work', closely monitored and assessed by the system. In the United Kingdom and the United States, the instructional approach to English as a subject persists and centers on a canon that has seen few changes in the past 50 years (Lewis and Dockter, 2011). In Australia, a 2005 review of 30 years of the teaching of literature in secondary schools in that country does not mention the term 'teenage' or 'YA' literature (Watson, 2005). There have been attempts to show how much young people's knowledge of popular literature can enrich their literary learning (i.e., Sarland, 1991) and to adopt new strategies for exploring texts (Karolides, 2000; Crumpler and Wedwick, 2011) but more research is needed to show how the use of YA in the upper levels of schooling can encourage engagement and motivation.

The implications of diversity for readers and texts

An increasing variety of genres and themes are appearing in classrooms, many of them reflecting current interest in diverse experiences and global realities (Hope, 2008; Rutter, 2006). In parallel, the increase in pupils from different cultural backgrounds in some countries has led to a large body of research that looks at home and community literacy practices and 'funds of knowledge' (c.f. the work of Jim Cummins, Eve Gregory, and Luis Moll). The use of 'multicultural' texts to engage readers in responding with a more reflective view on themselves and others has become one the main areas for current research but has also raised concerns about what is meant by this term and issues of authenticity. The debate about 'authentic' texts and who is entitled to write them is crucial when considering the use of CL for promoting cultural diversity and many scholars now present definitions and criteria (i.e., Fox and Short, 2003; Gopalakrishnan, 2011; Maddy and MacCann, 2009) for helping teachers select and evaluate multicultural texts (Botelho and Rudman, 2009; Kornfeld and Prothro, 2005) and how stories can work in diverse classrooms (Sleeter and Grant, 2002). Research on this particular theme is reviewed in more detail in the final section of this chapter.

Modes of response and evolving genres

While a wide range of research in the 1990s provided evidence for the importance of opening flexible spaces for critical conversations and reading communities around CL in the classroom (Short and Pierce, 1990; Chambers, 1993; Roser and Martinez, 1995) studies have also shown that written responses continue to be valued over others (Millard and Marsh 2001). The mismatch between response and text is more evident when multimodal CL is used in the classroom and Millard and Marsh (2001) argue that 'teachers need to be more understanding of different modes in which pupils choose to make sense of social and cultural contexts and to express themselves' (p. 60). Similarly, Bearne (2004) has argued that multimodal texts imply a new way of talking about and working with texts in the classroom to respond to new demands of logic of writing and logic of image. Wolf (2004, chapter 7) reports on the powerful artwork of students responding to texts and on the development of critique of their own and others' images. An overview of studies on response to visual texts can be found in Arizpe and Styles

(2008) who also conclude that there is a need for more in-depth research on new ways of responding to these texts.

Pupils' multiliteracy experiences come into play in their reading (Carrington and Luke, 2002) and at the same time, CL has become part of a multimedia world that has reshaped it into various digital forms. Research that considers the multimodal affordances of all these new texts as well as children's responses to them reveals new possibilities and points to the new directions for using CL in the classroom (Bearne *et al.*, 2004; Gee, 2003; Mackey, 2002). Unsworth *et al.* (2005), for example, summarize research on CD-ROM and online versions of CL and consider response through 'on-line multi-modal social contexts' (p. 126) in order to help teachers and pupils critically understand how stories are constructed in both traditional and digital formats.

A large number of studies on more mainstream CL focus on picture books perhaps because it reveals the complex strategies of interpretation that readers employ to make sense of both text and image. Children's responses have been explored from various perspectives: art and aesthetics (Kiefer, 1995); visual literacy (Arizpe and Styles, 2003); literary understanding (Sipe, 2008); postmodern features (Serafini, 2005; Pantaleo, 2008) and multimodality (Hassett and Curwood, 2009). Some studies explore visual responses, from drawing (i.e., Pantaleo, 2005; Evans, 2009) to photography (Arizpe and McAdam, 2011).

Although poetry has been used in teaching for centuries and publications for practitioners with ideas for using poetry in the classroom have been around for a number of years (i.e., Koch, 1974; Lambirth, 2007; Stibbs, 1981) the general consensus is that poetry does not have a strong presence in the classroom; that teachers tend to avoid it and that it is often poorly taught, not only in the United Kingdom (Walter, 1986; Ofsted, 2007) but also in other countries, for example, New Zealand (O'Neill, 2008) or Germany (Jansen, 2011). Yet in the past few years the profile of poetry for children has been raised, in the United Kingdom, mainly through the efforts of Michael Rosen and Morag Styles (Styles, Joy, and Whitley, 2010) and there seems to be a renewed interest from the perspective of both research and practice which is providing new perspectives for understanding how children understand poetry (Certo, 2004; Chatton, 2010; Gordon, 2010; Tiedt, 2002).

In sum, research on readers and texts seems to be advocating a more critical and reflective approach not only to reader's multicultural and multiliteracy experiences but also to the multiplicity of texts in the classroom. An increasing variety of case studies illustrate response strategies that can support the written word or can lead to more reflective and critical opinions not only on literary aspects of CL but also on issues to do with culture (Jewett, 2011; Short, 2009); gender (Greever, Austin, and Welhousen, 2000), or censorship (Karolides, 2000) among others. These include discussion groups, journal writing, drama, or art. There are a plethora of recommended CL lists for teaching one theme or another as well as recommended strategies for engaging readers with them. Most of the time, however, it is left to teachers to determine each book's appropriateness/relevance to his/her children and curriculum. It is important to take into consideration Serafini's point that a change in texts does not automatically ensure better practice (2003, section 6 para 1). This brings us to the central role of teachers and what they need to know in order to select and approach texts in ways that will allow readers to expand their responses to CL.

The Road Ahead: Consolidating Pedagogy and Practice

Teachers: reading and learning

The importance of teaching based on a theory of learning and pedagogy that includes an understanding of the theories of reading has been highlighted. It follows that teachers also need to have an understanding of theories of CL and knowledge of a wide range of children and young adult texts. This understanding on its own, however, will not transfer to the classroom or motivate their pupils to read if teachers are not keen readers themselves. Nathanson, Pruslow, and Levitt (2008) cite research going back to the 1970s but particularly in the 1990s, that highlight the importance of teachers in affecting student motivation for reading but that also provide evidence that many teachers and student teachers are 'alliterate' and only a minority are enthusiastic readers. These researchers replicated Applegate and Applegate's (2004) survey on literary attitudes which found that teachers 'did not tend to have firmly engrained reading habits' (p. 318).

These attitudes towards reading are also relevant to teachers' enthusiasm and knowledge of CL texts. The most recent and comprehensive study in the United Kingdom, *Teachers as Readers*, has revealed that many teachers are acquainted with only a narrow range of literature for children (Cremin *et al.*, 2008a; Cremin *et al.*, 2008b). The lack of knowledge of CL is not helped by the fact that CL in teacher education is normally optional –if indeed it has a place at all in the programs – and this has been noted not only in the United Kingdom and the United States but also in Europe, Australia, and other countries (Aðalsteinsdóttir, 2011; Croker, 2002; Hoewisch, 2000). The source of a teacher's beliefs in reading and using CL result from their own 'apprenticeship of observation' (Lortie, 2002:61); their own past experiences as readers (Cremin *et al.*, 2009) and their ongoing teacher education and professional development (Aðalsteinsdóttir, 2011; Brindley and Laframboise, 2002). Studies from Brindley and Laframboise (2002) and Gopalakrishnan and Ulanoff (2003) reported that CL provides a tool for student teachers to increase their own powers of reflection and sensitivity towards diversity; to engage in self-examination and experience discomfort with emotions; promote a re-examination of how history has been portrayed in CL and allow pre-service teachers to reflect on their own identities and therefore by consequence on the identities of the children they teach.

Research suggests that teachers' investment in personal reading does have an impact on practice, not only because of the enthusiasm that is reflected in practice but also because of the reading behaviors modeled in the classroom (Manna and Misheff, 1987; Morrison, Jacobs, and Swinyard, 1999). That teachers who were keen readers are more likely to use pedagogic strategies that encourage engagement with text is confirmed in a study by McKool and Gespass (2009) where teachers who valued reading and regularly read for pleasure were aware 'that reading is a socially constructed activity and plan opportunities for students to talk about the books that they are reading in a variety of ways' (p. 271). They allowed students to self-select books and also provided intrinsic motivation for reading in the form of discussions and recommendations.

Findings also suggest that intervention at both teacher education and professional levels can have an impact on both knowledge and enthusiasm for reading in general and CL in particular. Applegate and Applegate (2004) concluded that well-designed courses could be successful in changing the reading attitudes of student teachers. The results of a research study by Thraves (2010) tracing the effects of a CL intervention on first year education students' reading habits and attitudes is also encouraging: findings showed movement from apathy to engagement even at the lowest levels of change and most significantly, the intervention modified students' perceptions of themselves as readers.

At professional development level, the evaluation of the project The Power of Reading (CLPE) in the United Kingdom proved that these kinds of projects can have an effect not only on more creative approaches to teaching but also on the children becoming aware of teachers as readers. Teachers referred to the transformational role of texts in changing the children's attitudes and attainment as readers and in literacy more generally (O'Sullivan and McGonigle, 2010). In the United States, the successful Master Class in CL sponsored by the Children's Literature Assembly had experts and teachers sharing strategies in response to Hade's challenge in 1997 'to develop our own theories about the central importance of literature in the classroom rather than relying on policymakers, school administrators, textbook publishers, or other constituencies to make these decisions for us' (Pierce, 1998, p. 103).

The evidence on the potential of texts and teachers to transform classroom practice leads into our final section which reviews research that shows how enquiry can have a defining role in this transformation.

Teachers: enquiring and transforming

Gay (2005) points to a gap between the theoretical perspectives behind multicultural education and its practice in pedagogical settings; this can be extended to the ways CL is used in classrooms. Banks (2001) makes the link between CL and multiculturalism, believing that to understand one is to understand the other. Children can be introduced to the concept of otherness and cultural difference, perhaps challenging inequalities at a personal or cultural level, but they do not always challenge the structural and institutional forces that bring about inequality and prejudice in the first place (Short, 2009). In order to challenge at a structural level, Sumara (1998), Serafini (2003), and Botelho and Rudman (2009) all argue for the use of critical reading practices.

Souto-Manning (2009) argues that critical literacy needs to be at the core of the curriculum in order for transformative or social action to be possible. Botelho and Rudman (2009, p. 268) argue that for critical analysis to take place we need a paradigm shift in our thinking about the teaching of reading leading to a shift in classroom pedagogy (Short, 2011). The pedagogies used will always depend on the value systems of the teacher and how they interpret the act, purpose, and function of reading (Anstey and Bull, 1996; Smith-D'Arezzo, 2003). It becomes clear that if teachers wish to use CL as a means of practicing democracy and seeking social justice then texts need to be viewed as ideological constructions (Souto-Manning, 2009) and teaching as being about the deconstruction of ideological content (Larson and Marsh, 2005, p. 131).

Anstey and Bull argue that teachers should develop a clear theory of reading (1996), one that incorporates operational, critical, and cultural dimensions of learning and classroom practice (2004). Peer-reviewed literature that emphasizes the use of critical and cultural approaches to CL in the classroom illuminates two clear trends in its usage. The first trend is that teachers should use multiple texts on linked themes, juxtaposing the texts (Butlen, 2008-2009; Hope, 2008; Kornfeld and Prothro, 2005; Smith-D'Arezzo, 2003; Souto-Manning, 2009) and exemplifying Sumara's (1998, p. 207) idea of 'horizontal and multiple readings' of one text. Classroom-based examples include work from Hope (2008) who used a range of texts on the theme of migration and found that these texts validated the refugees' life experiences; increased understanding of migration and what it is like to be a refugee as well as challenging stereotypes and racism. Souto-Manning (2009) reported on using multiple versions of a story to examine perspectives of knowledge and eventually bring about social change to the school curriculum, ending withdrawal programs in her Early Years class.

The second trend clearly echoes the points made that teachers should carefully select from a range of strategies that allow the children to respond to the texts in meaningful ways so that transformation of knowledge becomes a possibility. Responses that favor the use of alternative modes of representation, such as annotating, illustrating, or discussing the book (Botelho and Rudman, 2009; Sumara, 1998) have grown in use. The recent work of Short (2009); Farrell, Arizpe, and McAdam (2010); McAdam and Arizpe (2011), and Charlton *et al.* (2011) on intercultural awareness all promote the use of multimodal responses to texts.

The LTCLE project indicated that CL used in school taught children about new ideas, new words, and something about the world, but that the children were unlikely to say that the literature taught them something about self and others. This is in contrast to the teachers reporting that 'making connections between what is read and children's own lives and experiences' was an area of confidence in their teaching (Aðalsteinsdóttir, 2011, p. 83). This variance points towards a need for further research into pupils' understanding of the purpose of reading CL as well as further practitioner research on using CL in the classroom. Initiatives that build partnerships between teachers in schools and researchers in universities (Cremin *et al.*, 2009; O'Sullivan and McGonigle, 2010) enabling teachers to become enquirers into their own practice (Hope, 2008; Smith-D'Arezzo, 2003; Souto-Manning, 2009; Unsworth *et al.*, 2005; Wolf, 2004) could provide a practical way forward in the present economic research climate.

Concluding Comments

From the introduction of literature into the classroom and in different countries around the globe, CL has had very varied roles in classrooms based on a range of beliefs and attitudes about the potential of these texts and the research in this field has been just as varied. This review has highlighted several areas where research gaps are noticeable:

- Literature charting the history of CL in the classroom is piecemeal, there is no definitive study that has traced this history up to the twenty-first century, in English or in other languages (as far as we could ascertain).
- International comparative studies such as LTCLE (Aðalsteinsdóttir, 2011) are rare, making it a challenge to build a global picture of CL classroom use.

The review also pinpoints three further directions for enquiry:

- Research at secondary school level and with YA literature.
- Research on multimodal forms struggles to keep up with changes in technology and the potential of the Internet to lead to engagement with CL via the classroom has not yet been fully explored.
- Research on theory and practice that considers diversity in keeping with global trends.

Overall, the main argument emerging from this review is that the potential of CL as a heuristic tool in a diverse world can only be fully realized alongside the use of critical literacy practices. For this to take place teachers need a clear grasp of theory and a sense of the grand narratives that shape society. For such a paradigm shift in practice to take place, researchers need to continue to work collaboratively with teachers, communities, and children to chart and disseminate the transformational possibilities of children's literature, ensuring the classroom door is wide open.

References

ACARA (2012) *The Australian Curriculum: English*, Version 3, accessed November 15, 2012: www.australiancurriculum.edu.au/English/

Aðalsteinsdóttir, K. (ed.) (2011) *Learning and Teaching Children's Literature in Europe- Final Report*, October, accessed February 1, 2012: www.um.es/childrensliterature/site/file.php/1/Deliverables/LTCL_final_Report.pdf

Applegate, A., and Applegate, M. (2004) The Peter effect: Reading habits and attitudes of preservice teachers. *The Reading Teacher*, 57: 554–563.

Anstey, M., and Bull, G. (1996) *The Literacy Labyrinth*. Sydney: Prentice Hall.

Anstey, M. and Bull, G. (2004) *The Literacy Labyrinth*, 2nd edn. Sydney: Prentice Hall.

Arizpe, E., and McAdam, J. (2011) Crossing visual borders and connecting cultures: Children's responses to the photographic theme in David Wiesner's *Flotsam*, *New Review of Children's Literature and Librarianship*, 17(2): 227–243.

Arizpe, E., and Styles, M. (2003) *Children Reading Pictures*. London: Routledge.

Arizpe, E., and Styles, M. (2008) A critical review of research into children's responses to visual texts. In J. Flood, S.B. Heath, and D. Lapp (eds) *Handbook on Research in Teaching Literacy through the Communicative and Visual Arts*. London: Lawrence Erlbaum, pp. 363–374.

Banks, J.A. (2001) Multicultural education: Historical development, dimensions and practice. In J.A. Banks and C.A.M. Banks, (eds) *Handbook of Research on Multicultural Education*. San Francisco: Jossey-Bass, pp. 3–29.

Beach, R. (1993) *A Teacher's Introduction to Reader-Response Theories*. Urbana, IL: NCTE.

Bearne, E. (2004) Multimodal texts. What they are and how children use them. In J. Evans (ed.) *Literacy Moves On*. London: David Fulton, pp. 16–30.

Bearne, E., Ellis, S., Graham, L., *et al.* (2004) *More than Words: Multimodal Texts in the Classroom*. London: QCA/UKLA.

Botelho, M.J., and Rudman, M.K. (2009) *Critical Multicultural Analysis of Children's Literature: Mirrors, Windows and Doors*. London: Routledge.

Brindley, R., and Laframboise, K.L. (2002) The need to do more: Promoting multiple perspectives in pre-service teacher education through children's literature. *Teaching and Teacher Education*, 18: 405–420.

Britzman, D. (1994) Is there a problem with knowing thyself? Toward a poststructuralist view of teacher identity. In T. Shanahan (ed.) *Teachers Thinking, Teachers Knowing*. Urbana: NCTE, pp. 53–75.

Bruner, J. (1990) *Actual Minds, Possible Worlds*. Cambridge, MA: Harvard University Press.

Butlen, M. (2008–2009) La littérature de jeunesse à l'école, trente années d'évolution. *L'Ecole des letters*, 4: 29–49.

Carrington, V., and Luke, A. (2002) Reading, homes and families: From postmodern to modern. In A. van Kleeck, S. Stahl, and E. Bauer (eds) *On Reading Books to Children: Parents and Teachers*. Mahwah, NJ: Lawrence Erlbaum Associates, pp. 231–252.

Certo, J.L. (2004) Cold plums and the old men in the water: Let children read and write 'great' poetry. *The Reading Teacher*, 58(3): 266–271.

Charlton, E., Wyse, D., Cliff Hodges, G., *et al.* (2011) Place-related identities through texts: From interdisciplinary theory to research agenda. *British Journal of Educational Studies*, 59(1): 63–74.

Chambers, A. (1993) *Tell Me: Children, Reading and Talk*. Stroud: Thimble Press.

Chatton, B. (2010) *Using Poetry across the Curriculum: Learning to Love Language*. Santa Barbara, CA: Greenwood.

Clark, C. (2011) Setting the Baseline. The National Literacy Trust's first annual survey into young people's reading – 2010. National Literacy Trust, accessed November 15, 2012: www.literacytrust.org.uk/assets/0001/1393/Omnibus_reading_2010.pdf

Clark, C., and Foster, A. (2005) *Children's and Young People's Reading Habits and Preferences: The Who, What, Why, Where and When*. London: National Literacy Trust.

Clark, C., Osborne, S., and Akerman, R. (2008) *Young People's Self-Perception as Readers*. London: National Literacy Trust.

Collins, N.D., and Aiex, N.K. (1995) Gifted readers and reading instruction. Bloomington, IN: ERIC Clearinghouse on Reading, English, and Communication. (ERIC Document Reproduction service No. ED379637), accessed March 9, 2012: www.eric.ed.gov/ERICDocs/data/ericdocs2sql/content_storage_01/0000019b/80/13/ab/7c.pdf

Colomer, T. (1999) *Introducción a la literatura infantil y juvenil* (in text trans. Evelyn Arizpe). Madrid: Síntesis.

Comber, B., and Hill, S. (2000) Socio-economic disadvantage, literacy and social justice; Learning from longitudinal case study research. *The Australian Educational Researcher*, 27(9): 79–97.

Cremin, T. (2007) Revisiting reading for pleasure: Diversity, delight and desire. In K. Goouch and A. Lambirth (eds) *Understanding Phonics and the Teaching of Reading*. Milton Keynes: Open University, pp. 166–190.

Cremin, T., Bearne, E., Goodwin, P., and Mottram, M. (2008a) Primary teachers as readers. *English in Education*, 42(1): 1–16.

Cremin, T., Mottram, M., Bearne, E., and Goodwin, P. (2008b) Exploring teachers' knowledge of children's literature. *Cambridge Journal of Education*, 38(4): 449–464.

Cremin, T., Mottram, M., Collins, F., *et al.* (2009) Teachers as readers: Building communities of readers. *Literacy*, 43(1): 11–19.

Croker, B. (2002) Re-viewing the place of children's literature in teacher education programmes. Challenging Futures conference: Changing Agendas in Teaching Education, February 3–7.

Crumpler, T.P., and Wedwick, L. (2011) Readers, texts and contexts in the middle: Re-imagining literature education for young adults. In S.A. Wolf, K. Coats, P. Enciso, and C.A. Jenkins (eds) *Handbook of Research on Children's and Young Adult Literature*. New York: Routledge, pp. 63–75.

Cullinan, B. (1987) *Children's Literature in the Reading Program*. Newark, DE: International Reading Association.

Cullingford, C. (1998) *How Children Learn to Read and How to Help Them*. London: Kogan Page.

Dyson, A.H. (2003) Popular literacies and the 'all' children: Rethinking literacy development for contemporary childhoods. *Language Arts*, 81(2): 100–109.

Ee Loh, C. (2009) Reading the world: Reconceptualising reading multicultural literature in the English language arts classroom in a global world. *Changing English: Studies in Culture and Education*, 16(3): 287–299.

Evans, J. (2009) Reading the Visual: Creative and aesthetic responses to picturebooks and fine art. In J. Evans (ed.) *Talking Beyond the Page: Reading and Responding to Picturebooks*. London: Routledge, pp. 99–117.

Evans, M.D.R., Kelley, J., Sikora, J., and Tremain, D. (2010) Family scholarly culture and educational success: Books and schooling in 27 nations. *Research in Social Stratification and Mobility*, 28: 171–197.

Ewald, A. (2007) Reading cultures. Teachers, pupils and reading literature in upper elementary school (English summary). Unpublished PhD thesis, Malmö Högskola.

Ewers, H.H. (2009) *Fundamental Concepts of Children's Literature Research: Literary and Sociological Approaches*, trans. W.J. McCann. London: Routledge.

Farrell, M., Arizpe, E., and McAdam, J. (2010) Journeys across visual borders: Annotated spreads of 'The Arrival' by Shaun Tan as a method of understanding pupils' creation of meaning through visual images. *Australian Journal of Language and Literacy*, 33(3): 198–210.

Fox, D., and Short, K. (eds) (2003) *Stories Matter: The Complexity of Cultural Authenticity in Children's Literature*. Urbana, IL: National Council of Teachers of English.

Galda, L., Ash, G.E., and Cullinan, B.E. (2000) Research on children's literature. In R. Barr, P. Michael, P.B. Kamil, and P. Mosenthal (eds) *Handbook of Reading Research*, Vol. III. Mahwah, NJ: Erlbaum.

Gay, G. (2005) Politics of multicultural teacher education. *Journal of Teacher Education*, 56(3): 221–228.

Gee, J.P. (2003) *What Video Games have to Teach us about Learning Literacy*. New York: Palgrave Macmillan.

Gee, J.P. (2004) *Situated Language and Learning: A Critique of Traditional Schooling*. London: Routledge.

Gopalakrishnan, A. (2011) *Multicultural Children's Literature: A Critical Issues Approach*. London: Sage.

Gopalakrishnan, A., and Ulanoff, S. (2003) Making Connections to Cultural Identity: Using multicultural children's literature and storytelling to explore personal narrative. Paper presented at the Hawaii International Conference on Education, Honolulu.

Gordon, J. (2010) What is not said on hearing poetry in the classroom. *English Teaching: Practice and Critique*, 9(3): 40–52.

Gough, N. (1998) Reflections and diffractions: Functions of fiction in curriculum inquiry. In W. Pinar (ed.) *Curriculum: Toward New Identities*. New York: Garland Publishing.

Government of Ireland (1999) *Primary School Curriculum: English*. Dublin: The Stationary Office.

Greever, E.A., Austin, P., and Welhousen, K. (2000) William's Doll revisited. *Language Arts*, 77(4): 324–330.

Hade, D. (1991) Being literary in a literature classroom. *Children's Literature in Education*, 22(1): 1–17.

Hall, K. (2010) Significant lines of research in reading pedagogy. In K. Hall, U. Goswami, C. Harrison, *et al.* (eds) *Interdisciplinary Perspectives on Learning to Read*. London: Routledge, pp. 3–16.

Hall, K., and Coles, M. (1999) *Children's Reading Choices*. London: Routledge.

Hassett, D.D., and Curwood, J.S. (2009) Theories and practices of multimodal education: The Instructional dynamics of picture books and primary classrooms. *The Reading Teacher*, 63(4): 270–282.

Hatton, J., and van der Walt, T. (2011) The use of South African works of fiction as class readers in Grades 7–9. *Teaching English Today*, II(Jan.), accessed March 3, 2012: www.teachenglishtoday.org/index.php/2011/01/the-useof-south-african-works-of-fiction-as-class-readers-grades-7/

Haynes, J., and Murris, K. (2012) *Picturebooks, Pedagogy and Philosophy*. Abingdon: Routledge.

Heath, S.B. (1983) *Ways with Words*. Cambridge: Cambridge University Press.

Hickman, J., and Cullinan, B.E. (1989) A point of view on literature and learning. In J. Hickman and B.E. Cullinan (eds) *Children's Literature in the Classroom* Norwood, MA: Christopher-Gordon, pp. 3–12.

Hoewisch, A.K. (2000) Children's literature in teacher-preparation programs. *Reading Online*, accessed March 9, 2012: www.readingonline.org/critical/hoewisch/childrenlit.html

Hope, J. (2008) 'One day we had to run': The development of the refugee identity in children's literature and its function in education. *Children's Literature in Education*, 39: 295–304.

Huck, C.S., and Young, D.A. (1961) *Children's Literature in the Elementary School*. New York: Holt, Rinehard and Winston.

Hull, G., and Schultz, K. (eds) (2002) *School's Out: Bridging Out-of-school Literacies with Classroom Practice*. New York: Teachers College Press.

Hunt, P. (1994) *An Introduction to Children's Literature*. Oxford: Oxford University Press.

Jansen, A. (2011) *Poetry in the Classroom*. Munich: GRIN Publishing GmbH.

Jewett, P. (2011) 'Some people do things different from us': Exploring personal and global cultures in a first grade classroom. *Journal of Children's Literature*, 37(1): 20–29.

Karolides, N. (ed.) (2000) *Reader Response in Secondary and College Classrooms*, 2nd edn. Mahwah, NJ: Lawrence Erlbaum Associates.

Kiefer, B. (1995) *The Potential of Picture Books: From Visual Literacy to Aesthetic Understanding*. Englewood Cliff, NJ: Merrill.

Koch, K. (1974) *Rose, Where Did You Get That Red?* New York: Vintage Books.

Kornfeld, J., and Prothro, L. (2005) Envisioning possibility: Schooling and students agency in children's and young adult literature. *Children's Literature and Education*, 36(3): 217–239.

Krashen, S. (2004) *The Power of Reading: Insights from the Research*. Portsmouth, NH: Heinemann.

Lambirth, A. (2007) *Poetry Matters*. UKLA: Leicester.

Langer, J.A. (1995) *Envisioning Literature: Literary Understanding and Literature Instruction*. New York: Teachers College, Columbia University.

Larson, J. and Marsh, J. (2005) *Making Literacy Real: Theories and Practices for Learning and Teaching*. Thousand Oaks, CA: Sage.

Lewis, C., and Dockter, J. (2011) Reading literature in secondary school: Disciplinary discourses in global times. In S.A. Wolf, K. Coats, P. Enciso, and C. Jenkins (eds) *Handbook of Research on Children's and Young Adult Literature*. New York: Abingdon.

Lintner, T. (2010) Using children's literature to promote critical geographic awareness in elementary classrooms. *The Social Studies*, 101: 17–21.

Lortie, D.C. (2002) *Schoolteacher: A Sociological Study*, 2nd edn. Chicago: University of Chicago Press.

Mackey, M. (2002) *Literacies across Media: Playing the Text*. London: Routledge/Falmer.

Maddy, Y.A., and MacCann, D. (2009) *Neo-imperialism in Children's Literature about Africa: A Study of Contemporary Fiction*. New York: Taylor and Francis.

Manna, A.L., and Misheff, S. (1987) What teachers say about their own reading development. *Journal of Reading*, 31(2): 160–168.

Maynard, S. (2008) A survey of young people's reading in England: Borrowing and Choosing Books. *Journal of Librarianship and Information Science*, 40(4): 239–253.

McAdam, J., and Arizpe, E. (2011) Journeys into culturally responsive teaching. *Journal of Teacher Education and Teachers' Work*, 2(1): 18–27.

McKenna, M. (2001) Development of reading attitudes. In L. Verhoeven and C. Snow (eds) *Literacy and Motivation*. Mahwah, NJ: Lawrence Erlbaum, pp. 135–158.

McKool, S.S., and Gespass, S. (2009) Does Johnny's reading teacher love to read? How Teachers' personal reading habits affect instructional practices. *Literacy Research and Instruction*, 48 (3): 264–276.

Meek, M. (1988) *How Texts Teach What Readers Learn*. Stroud: Thimble Press.

Meek, M. (1992) *On Being Literate*. London: Heinemann.

Meek, M., Warlow, A., and Barton, G. (eds) (1978) *The Cool Web: The Pattern of Children's Reading*. New York: Atheneum.

Millard, E., and Marsh, J. (2001) Words with pictures: the role of visual literacy in writing and its implication for schooling. *Reading, Language and Literacy*, 35(2): 54–61.

Ministry of Education (2007) *The Ontario Curriculum Grades 9 and 10: English*, accessed November 15, 2012: www.edu.gov.on.ca/eng/curriculum/secondary/english910currb.pdf

Morrison, T.G., Jacobs, J., and Swinyard, W.R. (1999) Do teachers who read personally use recommended practices in their classrooms? *Reading Research and Instruction*, 38: 81–100.

Morrow, L.M., and Gambrell, L. (2000) Literature-based reading instruction. In R. Barr, P.B. Kamil, P. Mosenthal, and P.D. Pearson (eds) *Handbook of Reading Research*, Vol. III. Mahwah, NJ: Erlbaum, pp. 563–586.

Nathanson, S., Pruslow, J., and Levitt, R. (2008) The reading habits and literacy attitudes of inservice and prospective teachers. *Journal of Teacher Education*, 59(4): 313–321.

Nieto, S. (2009) Foreword. In M.J. Botelho and M.K. Rudman (eds) *Critical Multicultural Analysis of Children's Literature: Mirrors, Windows and Doors*. London: Routledge, pp. ix–xii.

Nilsen, A.P., and Donelson, K. (1993) *Literature for Today's Young Adults*. New York: HarperCollins.

Nodelman, P., and Reimer, M. (2003) *The Pleasures of Children's Literature*, 3rd edn. Boston, MA: Allyn and Bacon.

OECD (2002) *Reading for Change: Performance and Engagement across Countries. Results from PISA 2000*. New York: Organisation for Economic Cooperation and Development.

Ofsted (2004) *Reading for Purpose and Pleasure: An Evaluation of the Teaching of Reading in Primary Schools*. London: HMI.

Ofsted (2007) *Poetry in Schools: A Survey of Practice*. London: HMI.

O'Neill, H.J. (2008) *Poetry and Pedagogy*. Frankfurt: VDM Verlag.

O'Sullivan, O., and McGonigle, S. (2010) Transforming readers: Teachers and children in the *Centre for Literacy in Primary Education Power of Reading* project. *Literacy*, 44(2): 51–59.

Pantaleo, S. (2005) 'Reading' young children's visual texts. *Early Childhood Research and Practice*, 7(1), accessed November 15, 2012: http://ecrp.uiuc.edu/v7n1/pantaleo.html

Pantaleo, S. (2008) *Exploring Student's Response to Contemporary Picturebooks*. Toronto: University of Toronto Press.

Pierce, K.M. (1998) Uses and abuses of children's literature in the classroom: Masterclass for teaching college level children's literature courses. *Journal of Children's Literature*, 24(1): 103–105.

Polkinghorne, D. (1988) *Narrative Knowing and the Human Sciences*, New York: State University of New York Press.

Purves, A.C., and Monson, D.L. (1984) *Experiencing Children's Literature*. New York: Scott Foresman.

Rutter, J. (2006) *Refugee Children in the UK*. Maidenhead: Open University Press.

Roser, N., and Martinez, M. (1995) *Book Talk and Beyond: Children and Teachers Respond to Literature*. Newark, DL: International Reading Association.

Sackes, M., Trundle, K.C., and Flevares, L.M. (2009) Using children's literature to teach standard based science concepts in early years. *Early Childhood Education Journal*, 36: 415–422.

Sarland, C. (1991) *Young People Reading: Culture and Response*. Milton Keynes: Open University Press.

Serafini, F. (2003) Informing our practice: Modernist, transactional, and critical perspectives on children's literature and reading instruction. *Reading Online*, accessed November 15, 2012: www.readingonline.org/articles/art_index.asp?HREF=serafini/index.html

Serafini, F. (2005) Voices in the park, voices in the classroom: Readers responding to postmodern picture books. *Reading Research and Instruction*, 44(3): 47–64.

Short, K.G. (2009) Critically reading the word and the world. *Bookbird*, 2: 1–10.

Short, K.G. (2011) Reading literature in elementary classrooms. In S.A. Wolf, K. Coats, P. Enciso, and C.A. Jenkins (eds) *Handbook of Research on Children's and Young Adult Literature*. Abingdon: Routledge.

Short, K.G., and Pierce, K.M. (1990) *Talking about Books: Creating Literate Communities*. Portsmouth, NH: Heinemann.

Sipe, L. (2008) *Storytime: Young Children's Literary Understanding in the Classroom*. New York: Teachers College Press.

Sleeter, C.E., and Grant, C.A. (2002) *Making Choices for Multicultural Education: Five Approaches to Race, Class and Gender*. Upper Saddle River, NJ: Prentice-Hall.

Smith, F. (1990) *To Think*. New York: Teachers College Press.

Smith-D'Arezzo, W.M. (2003) Diversity in children's literature: Not just a black and white issue. *Children's Literature in Education*, 34(1): 75–94.

Solity, J., and Vousden, J. (2009) Real books vs. reading schemes: A new perspective from instructional psychology. *Educational Psychology*, 29(4): 469–511.

Souto-Manning, M. (2009) Negotiating culturally responsive pedagogy through multicultural children's literature: Towards critical democratic literacy practices in a first grade classroom, *Journal of Early Childhood Literacy*, 9(1): 50–74.

Spencer, M. (1982) Children's literature: Mainstream text or optional extra? In R.D. Eagleson (ed.) *English in the Eighties*. Adelaide: Australian Association for the Teaching of English, pp. 114–127.

Sprod, T. (1995) Cognitive development, philosophy and children's literature. *Early Child Development and Care*, 107: 23–33.

St Amour, M. (2003) Connecting children's stories to children's literature: Meeting diversity needs. *Early Childhood Education Journal*, 31(1): 47–51.

Stibbs, A. (1981) Poetry in the classroom. *Children's Literature in Education*, 12(1): 39–50.

Street, B. (1984) *Literacy in Theory and Practice*. Cambridge: Cambridge University Press.

Styles, M., Joy, L., and Whitley, D. (eds) (2010) *Poetry and Childhood*. Stoke on Trent: Trentham.

Sulzby, E., Brantz, C., and Buhle, R. (1993) Repeated readings of literature and low socioeconomic status black kindergartners and first graders. *Reading and Writing Difficulties*, 9(2): 183–196.

Sumara, D.J. (1998) Fictionalizing acts: Reading and the making of identity. *Theory into Practice*, 37(3): 203–210.

Teale, W.H., and Sulzby, E. (1986) *Emergent Literacy: Writing and Reading*. Norwood, NY: Ablex.

Thraves, P. (2010) An investigation into students' reading attitudes and habits using a children's literature intervention programme. CPUT Theses and Dissertations Paper 296, Cape Peninsula University of Technology.

Tiedt, I.M. (2002) *Tiger Lilies, Toadstools, and Thunderbolts: Engaging K–8 Students with Poetry*. Newark, DE: International Reading Association.

Twist, L., Schagen, I., and Hodgson, C. (2007) *Readers and Reading: The National Report for England 2006*. Slough: PIRLS: Progress in International Reading Literacy Study.

Unsworth, L., Thomas, A., Simpson, A., and Asha, J. (2005) *Children's Literature and Computer-based Teaching*. Maidenhead: Open University Press.

Van der Pol, C. (2012) Reading picturebooks as literature: Four-to-six-year-old children and the development of literary competence. *Children's Literature in Education*, 43(1): 93–106.

Walter, C. (1986) The many years of telling: A tradition of failed practice of teaching poetry in the primary school. *English in Education*, 20(3): 31–38.

Ward, R. (2005) Using children's literature to inspire K–8 preservice teachers' future mathematics pedagogy. *The Reading Teacher*, 59(2): 132–153.

Watson, K. (2005) Research and Innovation in the teaching of literature in Australian secondary schools: The last thirty years. *Educational Studies in Language and Literature* 5: 95–103.

Wells, G. (1986) *The Meaning Makers: Children Learning Language and Using Language to Learn.* Portsmouth, NH: Heinemann.

Williams, C., and McLean, M. (1997) Young deaf children's responses to picture book reading in a pre-school setting. *Research in the Teaching of English*, 31: 337–366.

Wolf, S. (2004) *Interpreting Literature with Children*. Mahwah, NJ: Lawrence Erlbaum.

Chapter 19

Writing in Childhood Cultures

Anne Haas Dyson and Sophie Dewayani

Introduction

[I]n the beginning, writing, like reading, was less a solitary pursuit than an attempt to connect with others . . . We would sit together, this friend and I, dreaming up characters and plots (Lahiri, 2011, p. 79).

When the Pulitzer-prize winning author, Jumpa Lahiri, was a child, her interest in writing was tied to a local child practice. In that practice, a small group of children gathered together during recess to sit under a tree or on the edge of the sandbox. There, they would play on paper, jointly authoring a world tied to their reading, a world of orphaned girls with austere governesses or brave children who slipped through a closet into alternative worlds.

In this chapter, we are interested in the potential role of composing as a mediator of childhood practices, indeed, of childhood cultures, as they unfold in school settings for young children. Such a view of composing is hardly a dominant one. Throughout the world, learning to write is most often a matter of learning the conventions of letter form, spelling, and sentence structure. As a result of local educational traditions, testing regimes, and economic circumstances, including a paucity of teachers, space, and supplies (e.g., Lisanza, 2011; Sahni, 1994), learning to write may not entail composition at all; rather, children may copy, fill-in-the-blank, and write teacher-dictated text. Even in situations where progressive writing pedagogies ostensibly occur, uniformity of mandated lessons and testing regimes may squeeze children's intentions out of the official world (Dyson, 2008; Salvio and Boldt, 2009).

Yet, ethnographic work in pre-schools and elementary schools has documented the existence of unofficial or peer-defined cultures (e.g. Corsaro, 1985, 2011; Thorne, 1993). Such cultures require some time and space for decision-making (e.g., opportunity to talk and share with peers). Such times and spaces can give rise to places for textual playgrounds; they may be found in children's reinterpretations of official school composing practices (e.g., Dyson, 2003, 2007): in child-initiated activity in unstructured breaks in the school day (Lisanza, 2011): or even in 'permeable' official activities free from the regulatory expectations – the benchmarks of required progress – of designated literacy lessons (Dyson, 1993; Dewayani, 2011).

International Handbook of Research on Children's Literacy, Learning, and Culture, First Edition.
Edited by Kathy Hall, Teresa Cremin, Barbara Comber, and Luis C. Moll.

Consider, for example, two six-year-olds we met in our respective projects; both projects were ethnographic in nature, but they unfolded in very different geographic, cultural, and institutional spaces. Ezekial, who identified as Mexican American, attended first grade in a US public school in an economically-distressed neighborhood, marked both by lush green trees and boarded up businesses. His school was in a financially-strapped, moderate-sized city in the upper Midwest of the country. Abi was Indonesian and attended a primarily NGO-funded early childhood centre for 4- to 7-year-old children who work in the streets. His school was located amid dusty, unpaved streets and open sewers in a poor section of his large city. The boys differed in language, culture, religion, and in the curricula of their respective schools. And yet, behind their compositions – deceptively static artifacts (Pahl and Rowsell, 2005) – we see images of children at play:

Imagine, first, Ezekial, sitting beside his best friend, Joshua, during the daily writing period in his first grade classroom. On this day, like most, each child is to write a personal narrative, a bit of their 'life story,' as their teacher Mrs. Kay says. Ezekial seems to be doing just that: He has drawn his house and written of an upcoming event in which his best friend Joshua is going to come to his house to play video games with him. Joshua is writing about this same anticipated event. But Joshua, who is homeless, is not going to go to Ezekial's house to play games and, anyway, Ezekial's older brothers control the video console. The boys' composing of an official 'life story' is a form of play and, more particularly, of participating in an unofficial practice of planning never-to-be out-of-school get-togethers. This practice has spread throughout the boys' classroom. It is but one of a complex of childhood practices built in the space between children's material realities and their shared desires to control their world, to imagine possibilities, and, perhaps most importantly, to belong, that is, to have companions. (Based on Dyson, in press)

Now imagine 6-year old Abi sitting by his friend Sandi. The writing lesson is over for the day; it typically consists of copying words or trying to spell the teacher's dictations. It is drawing time, a much more relaxed, less regulated time and space when textual playgrounds may appear. Abi and Sandi are drawing similar pictures, in their case, houses that look a lot like Ezekial's drawn house. The houses have windows and triangular roofs; Abi's has a long twisting pathway leading to his houses. Like Ezekial's text, Abi's piece is misleadingly straightforward. He does not live in such a house. Rather, what Abi's neighbors call 'a house' is actually a rented room with no windows and a sturdy roof. Unlike in Ezekial's writing period, where the literal truth is valued, in Abi's less-regulated drawing period, his teacher is quite willing to join in the play. 'I will come to your house,' she says when she comes by the boys. 'Draw me coming to your house,' and so the play continues. (Based on Dewayani, 2011.)

Official school curricula provided Ezekial, Abi, and their friends with graphic tools, organizational structures, and social companions, all of which contributed to children's construction of imagined worlds. Such forms of joint world-making can give rise to configurations of social practices that help form and sustain childhood cultures themselves.

Some kind of graphic symbol-making is an aspect of children's pretend play throughout the world, whether children are creating images and words using sticks in the mud, No. 2 pencils on primary grade paper, or a mouse and a screen. Children respond to their worlds, appropriate voices and images from human and technological sources, and imagine other lives. There is variation, though, in the cultural material they play with, the nature of their interaction, and how that play is viewed by others, including teachers in the times and spaces of schools (Konner, 1991; Montgomery, 2009). In this chapter, we aim to provide a kind of conceptual scheme for considering writing within the social relations and cultures of childhoods themselves. We are interested in cross-cultural processes and conditions that further writing as play *and* in localized cases that illustrate the embedding of graphic symbolism in particular childhoods. The interrelated topics through which we present this scheme are:

a Children's appropriation of 'textual toys' (Dyson, 2003): that is, their use of cultural texts from their everyday lives as play material for composing, including texts from commercial media, local folk traditions, and religious practices; therefore, all children, not just the economically privileged, have experienced resources for composing;

b The social and textual processes of childhood literacy practices form within, and contribute to, social relations and childhood cultures: thus, these processes are not neutral but are infused with the complexities of social identities, like gender, ethnicity, religion, and economic class; and

c There are variations in the relationship between writing in childhood cultures and writing in official classroom cultures; these variations have consequences for children's opportunities to become both critical and playful composers in social worlds.

Throughout we will use examples from our own studies to illustrate key points. Dyson's was a study of the ideologies about language and childhood that undergirded the perceived literacy 'basics' in two urban US schools serving 'at risk' students. She focused on official writing curricula, highlighting how first graders and kindergarteners interpreted those curricula. Dewayni's was a study of the ideologies of childhood, labor, and schooling undergirding the societal issue of Indonesian children who work in the streets (i.e., 'street children') and children's own narrative representations of their lives as children.

We begin, though, by constructing a theoretical stage, discussing our stance on the chapter's key conceptual tools. To this end, we draw on the new interdisciplinary field of childhood studies, the shifting anthropological discussion of culture, and a situated perspective on literacy itself.

A Theoretical Stage for 'Children Who Compose' versus 'Child Composers'

> Writing should be meaningful to children ... an intrinsic need should be aroused in them, and ... writing should be incorporated into a task that is necessary and relevant for life. Only then can we be certain that it will develop not as a matter of hand and finger habits but as a really new and complex form of speech. (Vygotsky, 1978, p. 118)

In many sites across the globe, writing is indeed taught as a matter of 'hand and finger habits,' along with an association of letters and sounds. One pedagogical approach that does allow for child composition is referred to as a 'writing workshop' approach (Graves, 1983). Still, the approach emphasizes children adopting an identity as a writer, along with the values, goals, and processes associated with adult experts who define themselves primarily as 'writers' (Calkins and Mermelstein, 2003). In this chapter, we are interested in children's identities as children.

We recognize that the concept of childhood is a social one. Children need to be provided food, shelter, and clothing; they need care and guidance. But beyond those basic needs, childhoods vary historically, culturally, and geographically (James and James, 2008). How should we understand those childhoods? In what sense can writing be 'relevant' to children as children and, more particularly, as children who share experiences, values, and practices with other children?

Constructed childhoods

Children do not come into the world 'as naked socially as the bare body of a newborn suggests,' writes Daniel Cook (2002, p. 3). Indeed, they may be literally dressed in particular ways – even in certain gendered colors, provided with gender and class-identifying toys, and laid down in culturally and 'age-appropriate' sleeping arrangements. Childhood is a social institution, and, as such, it is situated within certain societal conditions, informed by certain ideological beliefs, and organized within everyday practices governed by adults. From their caregivers and teachers, children learn what it means to be a good boy or a good girl, a properly progressing child, and one who makes their elders proud. And yet, children do not always do as they are told (Dyson and Genishi, in press).

Although children learn through participating in activities with guiding adults (Vygotsky, 1978): this is not their only way of learning. Children have agency – constrained, embedded in a world in which they are relatively powerless, but agency nonetheless (James, Jenks, and Prout, 1998). Cross-culturally, children observe the world around them, listen to stories about how it works, and they play (Rogoff, 2003). Through that play, children assume control over what can be a confusing world; they examine the workings of the world around them, assuming roles, appropriating the language of those roles, negotiating actions, and facing the consequences of their actions as, for example, pretend parents and children, superheroes and victims, performers and audience members, and, as with Ezekial and Abi, hosts and visitors. Such play is central to childhood cultures evolving within societal institutions like schools.

Childhood cultures in classroom places

We do not take culture to be a static category – a determiner of child behaviors. Rather, we understand culture as actively produced as participants negotiate the local practices of everyday life (Gonzalez, Moll, and Amanti, 2005; Ortner, 2006; Rosaldo, 1993). Those practices, infused with shared values and beliefs, are situated within historical, political, and socio-economic circumstances. And yet, they are always enacted anew, as participants respond to the particular contingences of the moment.

In schools, children are responding to each other within the organizational structure and societal ideologies of school. Their school lives take shape within their cohort. Batches of children are kept in close quarters in confined spaces and, moreover, outnumber adults, sometimes overwhelmingly so (e.g., Lisanza, 2011). As human beings do when they are in close proximity, children share concerns and pleasures, including their knowledge of and play with the public texts – those of commercial media – that saturate many contemporary childhoods (e.g., Dyson, 1997; Marsh, 2003; Newkirk, 2009; Prinsloo, 2004). Moreover, they initiate activities (however subtly) and play out their desires for agency and companionship. Through that interaction, an unofficial or peer culture evolves (Corsaro, 2011; Kalliala, 2006; Thorne, 1993).

Like any culture, unofficial childhood cultures are not homogeneous, nor uniformly experienced; they are formed in response to, and therefore not isolated from, official school worlds and their values and practices; and they are a part of the larger society and thus shaped by relevant structures like race, gender, and class (Christianakis, 2010; Dyson, 1997, 2003; Thorne, 2005). In this chapter, the cases we discuss will illustrate the dialogic quality of childhood cultures in relation to dominant cultures, especially the official school world. The chapter as a whole stresses the performative quality of childhood cultures – that is, children acting together as participants in their worlds. In considering that action, we foreground written language.

Writing as communicative practice

Throughout this chapter, we are taking a 'situated' view of composing. As Ezekial and Abi illustrated, children use their communicative resources (e.g. talking, drawing, writing) to participate in a local instance of a valued practice (Street, 2001). For example, Ezekial's graphic production mediated his friendship with Joshua. The boys enacted and shaped their relationship, as each child took their complementary role as guest or host. Writing and drawing were both graphic tools that mediated participation in a social 'event' (Hymes, 1972); that event was unique instance of a common unofficial practice, that of planning never-to-be get-togethers. Still, the boys infused that practice with their own everyday worlds; that is, they gave it their own 'accent' (Bahtkin, 1981, p. 423). Their unofficial event unfolded along with the official 'life story' event.

Further, considered together, Ezekial's and Abi's vignettes suggest variations in how children's unofficial events figure into official school worlds; they may be unrecognized, actively discouraged, or appreciated and, indeed, furthered. We will consider the contextual and ideological conditions that matter in this differential response. This response merits our attention because it influences the school's ability to recognize and build on child resources and, potentially, children's own view of official schooling as relevant to their lives as children.

With these key concepts of childhoods, cultures, and communicative practices now defined, we take a closer look below at the processes and conditions by which writing practices figure into the construction of experienced childhoods and evolving childhood cultures.

Writing Childhoods: Processes and Conditions

> When Hobbes is a stuffed toy in one [comic] panel and alive in the next, I'm juxtaposing the 'grown-up' version of reality and [six-year-old] Calvin's version, and inviting the reader to decide which is truer. (Watterson, in Christie, 1987)

For 10 years, from 1985–1995, Bill Watterson, the creator of the comic strip *Calvin and Hobbes*, brought readers into the world of perpetually 6-year-old Calvin and his stuffed tiger Hobbes. No matter where Calvin was literally in time and space, he could infuse his material and social constraints into opportunities for agency, for becoming, say, courageous Spaceman Spiff, faced with some evil transformation of poor Mrs. Wormwood, his teacher. In their play, children transform everyday spaces into meaning-infused places with at least some elbow room for child agency (Holloway and Valentine, 2000; cf., Gupta and Ferguson, 1997). Those material spaces might be, for example, an abandoned lot or crowded sidewalk in New York City (Dargan and Zeitlin, 2006); a busy intersection in Bandung (Dewayani, 2011); or, our particular interest here, a variant of the traditional classroom – with its regulated curriculum, its behavioral monitoring, and its literacy lessons for the proper learning child.

Everyday classroom spaces are interesting from the perspective of child transformation. They are not like spaces designed for child play, like city parks, school playgrounds (Beresin, 2010): or open-ended virtual worlds (Marsh, 2011). Ezekial's classroom was more spacious than many; still, children's tables were pushed together so closely that average-sized adults had to elongate their bodies – breathing in deeply, tip toeing – to move between them. In Lisanza's (2011) Kenyan village, there were 89 first graders all tightly packed in a single classroom with a single teacher. In Sahni's (1994) rural Indian school, children sat cross-legged on mats under the trees, slates on their laps. These were not spaces where children could move their bodies with ease or get another's attention by shouting a greeting.

Nonetheless, in a classroom, children spend a great deal of time sitting side by side, attending to each other's efforts, interacting, however surreptitiously. Thus, relations are built, practices are formed, and a culture develops. Writing lessons may be particularly amenable to children's transformative play, given the provision of graphic tools, the presence of social companions, and potentially ample interactive space, as teachers circulate or work in one-to-one conferences with children.

Below we consider, first, the symbolic material children appropriate in order to represent, communicate about, and play out and with their wishes and worries, their values and beliefs, and their understandings of their world. Then we consider the textual and social processes through which composing events become integral to developing child cultures.

Making the World Anew: Children Appropriating and Recontextualizing Cultural Texts

Communities provide children with abundant varieties of cultural texts that children can appropriate and recontextualize in their own meaning-making. These texts come from varied institutional and technological sources. Indeed, across borders of nations and continents, children experience media productions marketed specifically to them (Hengst, 2005). These productions include cultural texts in the format of popular television shows, movies, and music. These texts are said to have governed children worldwide through the drive of consumerism and the reproduction of stereotyped discourses of beauty, gender roles and relations, and so forth.

Cross-culturally, however, children's composing processes have indicated that popular discourses are not necessarily taken as given by children. From their participation in popular culture, children may find appealing figures, powerful storylines, visual icons, and even genres, like cinematic horror stories, the interactive narratives of video games, or the aggressively discursive television sports reports (Dyson, 1997, 2003; Newkirk, 2009; Ranker, 2006; Wohlwend, 2010). Moreover, like all participants in popular culture, they play with, parody, and remix such symbolic stuff (Peters, 1997).

As we will illustrate, this repertoire may include material from religious traditions, like songs and narratives, from childhood folklore, like clapping games or birthday party rituals, or from societal traditions, embedded with such ideologies as gender, power, and race.

To use this material in composing, children must appropriate meanings from their original sources, translate them across semiotic forms and social situations, and, in the process, reproduce, remix, or even challenge ideologies implicit in traditions (Dyson, 2003; Pahl and Rowsell, 2005). Their efforts will be met by diverse responses by the adults in their worlds – cultivated or curtailed, acknowledged or dismissed, encouraged or devalued. The cultural materials children manage to select reflect the ways children negotiate their agency in responding to adults' and society's evaluative responses. Below, we offer examples from our respective projects.

Textual play with folk material in an Indonesian 'street children's' class

To begin, we offer the following vignette:

MRS. YUMA:	Hey Riga, do you remember what to do if you're yawning? You have to cover your mouth! You don't want a fly to get in [your opened mouth]. What if a ghost gets in?
CLASSMATES [TO RIGA]:	Yeah! A ghost may get in!
MRS. YUMA:	And then you will have a stomach-ache.
RIMA:	And it's a disease nobody can cure!

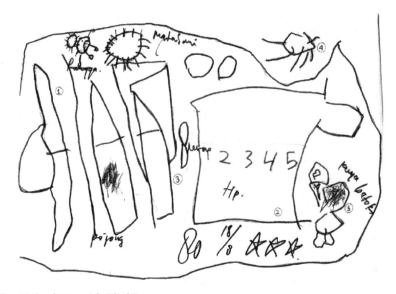

Figure 19.1   Rio's ghosts with BlackBerry
Note: The cursive writing was done by Rio's teacher. The circled numbers were written by Dewayani to indicate the drawn figures. Number (1) on the drawing refers to the first two ghosts or, more culturally accurate, *pocong*. Number (3) is the smallest *pocong*, drawn after the others. Number (2) refers to the BlackBerry, while (4) is the sun and (5) a ladybug.

In the above exchange, teacher and children bring up an example of a cultural narrative from the slum area where Abi and his peers live. This narrative portrays ghosts and supernatural creatures as driving human beings' misbehaviors. Such stories were viewed as superstitions by the middle-class Muslim society and as inappropriate for children, since they could distract them from fear of God (Fatimah, 2009). Children, though, interpreted ghosts differently. In addition to being main characters in children's oral stories, ghosts were invited into their composed narratives and tended to be treated as 'buddies.'

Figure 19.1 presents a drawing by Rio (a seven-year-old peer of Abi). It depicts three ghosts with one of them holding a BlackBerry cell phone, the way a popular character is portrayed in Indonesian soap operas. In Rio's production traditional folk material mixes with contemporary technology as portrayed on the television to capture a child's experience in contemporary times.

Textual play with cultural material in a Midwestern US class

An adult entering Ezekial's first grade classroom might notice the birthday chart on the wall and, if the visitor came on the right date, there might be a cupcake to be had in a classroom celebration for the 'birthday boy' or 'girl.'

Birthday celebrations of ordinary folks (i.e., not political leaders or children of the elite) did not become widespread until the beginning of the twentieth century in the United States (Chudacoff, 1989). In the early twenty-first century, when Ezekial and his friends attended school, the birthday party had become a major ritual for consumption, particularly among the more privileged (McKendrick, Bradford, and Fielder, 2000); in the local scene, commercial establishments enticed young children with happy images of pizza, balloons, and music, or special treatment at an ice skating rink or bowling alley. These, of course, were all quite expensive. The children's actual reported parties involved family occasions, with a special cake and a wrapped gift. However, formal parties, including ones located at commercial sites, became accessible to children in textual playgrounds.

The children's imagined birthday parties were linked to the official curriculum in two ways. First, the children's teacher, Mrs. Kay, often wrote plans for upcoming special occasions in her daily modeling of the writing process. She was going to a movie, on a trip out of town, or maybe to a special restaurant. The children themselves began writing their own special plans, as Ezekial and Joshua did, even though those plans were imaginary (Dyson, 2007). Among planned but invented birthday parties, those at Chuck E. Cheese's (a fast food establishment catering for children), at the ice skating rink, or at the bowling alley were common, but there were also unusual but enticing plans, like Elly's planned parties involving trips to California and Disneyland.

Second, there were official parties for children; the 'Happy Birthday' song was sung, and cupcakes were passed out (if they, or some other baked treat, were brought from home). Official parties were inclusive, but planned private parties were not. Children selectively invited each other–and were earnestly upset not to have their name written in the planned party text, even though the party was never to be.

As an illustration of these textual parties, consider the plans of Ezekial's peer Elly. Her birthday plans (for her July party) began in November. The plans continually changed, as did the invitees. The following is but one illustration of her many efforts (see Figure 19.2); it involves the appropriation of a local resort with kid appeal:

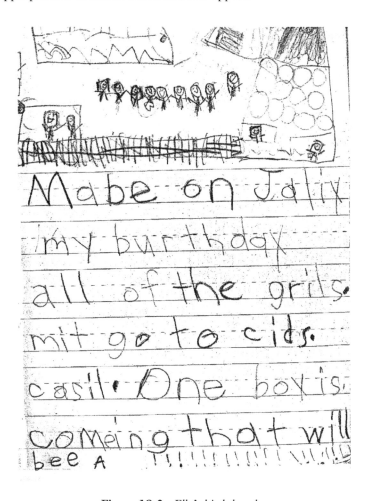

Figure 19.2   Elly's birthday plan

Mabe on Jaliy [July]/ My birthday/ All of the grils.
Mit go to cids./ Casil. One boy is./ Comeing that will
Bee Aaron!!!!!!!!!!!!!!!!!!!!!!

The picture appropriates aspects of the establishment, but it also reflects the social jockeying that sometimes accompanied birthday play. (Was everyone invited? Just 'friends'? Just boys? Just girls? Just children who shared ethnic identity with the party giver?) Note the line of children holding hands, which includes just one figure with short hair and pants – Aaron! Elly's selection of particular children for her very appealing parties set off indignant responses from boys seated nearby. Thus, like Rio, Elly too mixed her cultural material; she combined appealing commercial venues and gendered bodies separate and together to make meaning in and of her world.

In sum, our examples have illustrated children appropriating and remixing cultural material. Additional such examples can be constructed from the literature. For example, in an earlier project (Dyson, 2003), the popular song "I Believe I can Fly," by R. Kelly, was frequently intoned by young African American children in a classroom in the East San Francisco Bay in California. Across the continent and over the ocean, Prinsloo (2004) documented South African girls singing the same song, remixed with a local rap a playful tour-de-force in English and Xhosa.

In Prinsloo's case, as in many schooling contexts for children, there was no official outlet for the children's capacity for multilingual and multimodal manipulation of symbolic stuff – this despite the fact that such collective inventiveness is critical to higher level academic achievement in contemporary times (Jenkins, 2009).

In the next section, we focus on collectivity itself. That is, we ask, what the conditions and processes are that allow children's remixes and plays to spread throughout a group of children and become part of their jointly constructed childhoods.

Composing Child Cultures: The Formation of Unofficial Literary Practices

Abi, Ezekial, and their respective peers were attentive to each other and each other's use of symbolic tools and discursive material. Moreover, those peers shared knowledge of appropriated folk and media resources and of their communities. Given some time and space for individual agency, such common knowledge of resources, community contexts, and playful practices can lead to children *reframing* the official school world within their own relations and practices. In this way, their textual actions gain new social meaning. Moreover, if two or more children's interactions are appealing, others may copy them, adding new variations to a basic schematic routine (Hanks, 2000). In this way a practice can solidify and spread, becoming part of how children compose a local childhood culture. Thus, a mutually beneficial relationship might unfold: children's resources and relations can energize their learning of official composing, just as official composing can support an evolving child culture (Dyson, 2007). To illustrate such conditions and processes, we return to Abi's Center and Ezekial's first grade.

Reframing official activity within a clapping game

In Abi's neighborhood, where the unpaved alleys served as the children's playground, televisions constituted a significant means of children's social life. It was here, in an alley, that the children created a clap play adapted from the globally known television character 'Dora the Explorer,' which the children watched every morning before leaving for school. This, then, became a language practice in the local childhood culture. One of the participants was Abi's peer Danti, a seven-year-old, and eventually so too was her teacher Mrs. Sri, the teacher of the Center who also happened to live in one of the alleys. Danti used that Dora practice to reframe a classroom composing activity. Indeed, she accompanied her drawing of Dora with the clapping game:

DANTI: Dora clap [Clap three times]. Funny Face [Clap three times]. Carry a backpack [Clap three times]. We did it, we did it. Yes! [Danti pumps her fist].

The children's clapping games were dialectically related to the construction of 'fun learning' by teachers in order to promote the learning of their students, children who worked in the street. For example, there was an 'official' clap play called the Ablution Clap, which Mrs. Sri used to teach the ablution ritual in Islamic Study.

Say *Bismillah*, wash your arms [Clap three times]. Rinse your mouth, clean your nose [Clap three times]. Arm to elbow, head and ears, feet is the last one, and then say a prayer, amen! [Clap three times].

Danti's drawing itself, which mediated the performance of the Dora Clap, presented Dora going to sleep in a house with a pillow and a body pillow (a familiar cultural practice): as depicted in Figure 19.3. Danti's multimodal performance, involving singing, clapping, and drawing, illustrated the complex web constructed from the selective use of available cultural texts. Known as a 'reluctant writer' in the official copying/writing school activity, Danti, a

Figure 19.3   Danti's sleepy Dora
Notes: Danti had begun by drawing the clouds and 'tik tik tik,' the sound of raindrops on her house. After the rainbow, she drew the figure of Dora, with her bangs on her forehead. Dora is by her rectangular house and a cozy bed with a head and body pillow and a blanket.

young street musician, demonstrated her engagement in composing when given a space to contribute her expertise as a Dora fan.

In this example, we have seen a child reframe a school practice within an unofficial one from local child culture. In the next example, we return to Ezekial's class and birthday party play to consider the spread of an unofficial composing practice in school.

The spreading of the pretend-party practice

In Ezekial's classroom, Elly was the first to plan a birthday party. Like most young children, she orally monitored her writing of each word in her text, so the children around her knew who was included; and, in any case, during the classroom sharing time, the text was presented in the classroom public.

The writing of birthday plans offered the author social power and peer engagement; the children never failed to be interested in a birthday party. Indeed, in US society generally, children commonly use even pretend parties to mediate relationships (e.g., imagine some version of 'you are not nice and you are not coming to my birthday,' or, more positively, 'if you let me play you can come to my birthday'). Like the clapping game that reframed Danti's piece, in this classroom, the negotiating of party inclusion reframed the official writing activity.

Given the familiarity of party negotiations, the power of authorship, and children's desires for inclusion, party planning was copied by other children; that is, it solidified as a practice. No matter who the author was, written birthday plans included certain schematic elements: a naming of the party, a naming of the invitees, and an indication that fun would be had. Other possible textual items were indications of the party's site and activities.

Moreover, a dialogic dynamic unfolded among the children engaged in the birthday play. For example, if one child wrote that another was coming to the child's party, the designated child would write with some pleasure that they were going! Here, for example, is Ezekial's response to inclusion in Jon's birthday party plan:

> I'm in vited to
> Jon's birday.
> Jon likes Joshua
> and I for
> friends. We got
> fiend sip.

Further, given that the teacher Mrs. Kay allowed a daily free choice activity period, the children had time and space for related practices to evolve, contributing to a configuration of birthday practices. Located outside the official writing time, these practices did not have to conform to the form (if not the actual truth quality) of expected personal narratives. For example, one day Ezekial spent his free choice period making a list of invitees and securing phone numbers. Joshua responded with great enthusiasm:

EZEKIAL: Joshua, do you want to come to my party?
JOSHUA: Party?
EZEKIAL: Yep.
JOSHUA: Yippee! I'll be there.
EZEKIAL: 'Cause I'm going to [a fast food place catering to children] so we can play basketball there.

Elly, witnessing the action, offers Ezekial a written invitation – and a polite request – to the current form of her anticipated party (a trip to California):

Ezekial Plese
    come
        to
        Califony

Ezekial's big grin suggested that he was enormously pleased to be invited.

In Abi's classroom, children did engage in imagined birthday play, but it did not become a literacy practice. There was not a regular celebration of children's birthdays; indeed, children themselves might not remember their date of birth. Yet, in oral storytelling, children imagined having birthday cakes, getting presents, or inviting a birthday clown. This birthday play did not reframe writing activity, however. This would have been difficult, as the official writing time involved little space for child voice, stressing, as it did, copying and, also, spelling teacher dictations. Some time and space for agency is necessary for the evolution of childhood writing practices that reframe official school ones.

Indeed, as we comment below, the literature suggests that such space is found mainly outside school. In the following and final section, we consider the variable relationships between official and unofficial worlds, the conditions that promote an explicit interplay, and, moreover, why these relationships matter for children who compose.

Making Connections:
The Interplay between Unofficial and Official School Worlds

There is no child, we boldly claim, who enters school without resources for representing stories through graphic media, for reaching out to peers, and for collaboratively participating in practices controlled by children themselves. When interests are shared among children, when time and space in school is at least partially open to child agency, when children are socially attuned to each other as companions, playmates, and peers, then writing may become a generative tool mediating childhood cultures themselves.

What is the role of the school and, more particularly, the teacher in the evolution of these childhood cultures? What is, or should be, the relationship of these unofficial worlds to official school writing curricula?

Our position in this chapter is *not* that the official world should colonize the unofficial one. As Goffman (1961) noted, in any regulated institution, there is always an underlife. In schools, children exercise agency and seek out control and companionship among their peers; moreover, their interests and tastes are not synchronistic with those of official worlds. However, we do argue herein for the usefulness of interplay between official and unofficial worlds and, moreover, for the value of that interplay for teachers' own agency. We begin by underscoring the importance of time and space for child agency.

Children have used writing activities as occasions for childhood play and the evolution of peer practices primarily outside school. Many of the descriptions of these practices have featured children slightly older than those of our projects. For example, in her study of literacy across generations of Wisconsinites, Brandt (2001, 2009) describes one participant's, Sam May's, childhood between the World Wars. His outdoor play was filled with literacy. Most relevant for our chapter is his description of how he and his playmates collaboratively wrote and performed shows to coincide with their town's weekly outdoor movie nights in the summer. Inspired by film and by radio theatre (like that of the actor, director, and screen writer Orson Welles) children directed their efforts to the new public audience and even charged admission. The production of shows was a practice that was sustained by neighborhood children. They recontextualized cultural material from varied sources within their own relations and material locations, that is, their times and spaces.

In contemporary times, children may have diverse experiences and a plethora of social, semiotic, and textual resources that could help them generate contexts for and pathways to school literacy. These resources may be rooted in experiences with digital media, like the British children playing in virtual worlds studied by Marsh (2011): with the more globally widespread television media, like Rio's familiarity with soap operas, and with folk material, like Danti's clapping games and Ezekial's birthday rituals. Cultural experiences represented in any medium can be recontextualized yet again in multimodal literacy, as in Pahl and Rowsell's (2005) description of the Turkish child, Faith, whose cultural valuing of birds was transformed into crafted birds, dramatic play, and brief texts.

Moreover, if there is to be a pedagogically useful interplay between official and unofficial worlds, the children's resources must be officially recognized as just that, which brings us to another key classroom condition beyond that of time and space.

Variation in official respect for unofficial composing

We cannot teach young children if we cannot find common ground with them in a communicative space, so that we can go forward together (Rogoff, 2003; Vygotsky, 1978). In composing times, when children have space and time for controlling their own graphic actions and interacting with peers, teachers can learn a great deal about how children are attending to their world, including their interests, their pleasures, and their dreams; and they can learn too about their familiar communicative practices, existent symbolic repertoire, and important social relations.

However, to envision such child resources requires some rethinking about what is relevant to school literacy. For example, too often, children's agency in playing creatively with media texts is curtailed by the marginalization of such texts in a school's literacy practices. This was true in Ezekial's school, where popular conceptions of writing workshop pedagogy viewed such play as reductionist and unoriginal (Dyson, forthcoming; see also Newkirk, 2009). It is also true more generally in Indonesia, where popular television shows and video games are seen as counterproductive to academic performance (Tjahjono, 2004), child behavior (Martani and Adijanto, 1992), and even children's eyesight (Rosmaida, 1993).

Rio's teacher, Mrs. Sri, did actively acknowledge her children's play with the possible and even sensitively entered into scenarios to extend their language and stories. However, Mrs. Sri's curriculum did not view drawing and talking as potential contexts for venturing into writing, as narrative additions or translations are made in written language. So we also suggest a view of composing as multimodal practices – that is, as the purposeful use of differentiated symbolic tools to design a message (Kress, 2010).

Nixon and Comber (2008) provide a powerful example of children's use of textual resources and multimodal imagining to redesign an unattractive outdoor space at their school. Most relevant for our purposes were the efforts of two boys who envisioned a gold-colored concrete maze, full of tricks and challenges. The appealing space they imagined had clear links to their experiences with electronic games and fantasy fictions. Their playful design required serious written exposition to the local powers that be.

Toward a productive interplay of official and unofficial worlds: needed forums

Despite the preceeding discussion, we are not arguing that children's interests and pleasures should simply be built upon. Rather, we envision a kind of classroom cultural 'forum,' to borrow from Bruner (1996), would allow children's represented pleasures to be situated in critical dialogue among children and teachers. For example, in Ezekial's classroom, the birthday party play was enormously involving and popular; yet, when children read about private parties in public sharing time, some classmates looked uncomfortable – they were not included. The concept of private parties, their differentiation from classroom public ones, and the public nature of sharing time were all topics worth exploring in the interest of an inclusive classroom culture.

Finally, there is also a need for researchers to contribute to a forum about childhoods and written language. There is much emphasis now on how new media, particularly through the Internet, are furthering participatory cultures, where students learn to pool their knowledge and to act together collaboratively and playfully to design cultural productions (Jenkins, 2009). The children in our chapter did not attend schools with ready access to new technologies; while Ezekial and his peers lived in a more affluent country, they did not report nor evidence any access to computers at home. However, participatory cultures were in evidence – children cross culturally sing, engage in clapping games and rhymes, narrate stories, and, given time and space, interlink practices to make rich cultural worlds about, say, birthdays or a media figure, like Dora. As a field, we need ethnographic research that describes such localized practices and, moreover, critical participatory research with teachers (like that of Comber and Nixon) to analytically document how such practices might function as resources.

In these ways, researchers and educators can contribute to the productive interplay of official and unofficial worlds. If we teach them that literacy can be a means for playful encounters with friends, we may do much to further the qualities that will bring pleasure to their presents and possibilities to their futures. This is our hope.

References

Bakhtin, M. (1981) *The Dialogic Imagination*. Austin: University of Texas.

Beresin, A.R. (2010) *Recess Battles: Playing, Fighting, and Storytelling*. Jackson: University of Mississippi.

Brandt, D. (2001) *Literacy in American Lives*. Cambridge: University Press.

Brandt, D. (2009) *Literacy and Learning: Reflections on Writing, Reading, and Society*. San Francisco: Jossey-Bass.

Bruner, J. (1996) *The Culture of Education*. Cambridge, MA: Harvard University Press.

Calkins, L., and Mermelstein, L. (2003) *Launching the Writing Workshop*. Portsmouth, NH: Heinemann.

Christianakis, M. (2010) 'I don't need your help!': Peer status, race, and gender during peer writing interactions. *Journal of Literacy Research*, 42: 418–458.

Christie, A. (1987) An interview with Bill Watterson. *Honk Magazine*, accessed November 19, 2012: http://ignatz.brinkster.net/chonk.html

Chudacoff, H.P. (1989) *How Old are You? Age Consciousness in American Culture*. Princeton, NJ: Princeton University Press.

Corsaro, W. (1985) *Friendship and Peer Culture in the Early Years*. Norwood, NJ: Ablex.

Corsaro, W. (2011) *The Sociology of Childhood*, 3rd edn. Thousand Oaks: Pine Forge Press.

Cook, D.T. (2002) Interrogating symbolic childhood. In D.T. Cook (ed.) *Symbolic Childhood*. New York: Peter Lang, pp. 1–14.

Dargan, A., and Zeitlin, S. (2006) City play. In D.P. Fromberg and D. Bergen (eds) *Play from Birth to Twelve: Contexts, Perspectives, and Meanings*. New York: Routledge, pp. 315–322.

Dewayani, S. (2011) Stories of the intersection: Indonesian 'Street Children' negotiating narratives at the intersection of society, childhood, and work. Unpublished doctoral dissertation, University of Illinois at Urbana-Champaign, IL.

Dyson, A.H. (1993) *Social Worlds of Children Learning to Write in an Urban Primary School*. Columbia, NY: Teachers College.

Dyson, A.H. (1997) *Writing Superheroes: Contemporary Childhood, Popular Culture, and Classroom Literacy*. New York: Teachers College Press.

Dyson, A.H. (2003) *The Brothers and Sisters Learn to Write*. Columbia, NY: Teachers College.

Dyson, A.H. (2007) School literacy and the development of a child culture: Written remnants of the 'gusto of life.' In D. Thiessen and A. Cook-Sather (eds) *International Handbook of Student Experience in Elementary and Secondary School*. Dordrecht, The Netherlands: Kluwer Academic Publishers, pp. 115–142.

Dyson, A.H. (2008) Staying in the (curricular) lines: Practice constraints and possibilities in childhood writing. *Written Communication*, 25: 119–157.

Dyson, A.H. (in press) *Writing 'Basics'?: Views from Children's Worlds*. New York: Teachers College Press.

Dyson, A.H., and Genishi, C. (in press) Social talk and imaginative play: Curricular basics for young children's language and literacy. In N. Unrau and D. Alvermann (eds) *Theoretical Models and Processes of Reading*, 6th edn. Newark, DE: International Reading Association.

Fatimah, S. (2009) The influence of watching television intensity toward student learning achievement at SD Negeri Sidorejo Kecamatan Kalasan Kabupaten Sleman, undergraduate's thesis, Islamic University of Indonesia.

Goffman, E. (1961) *Asylums*. Garden City: Anchor Books.

Gonzalez, N., Moll, L.C., and Amanti, C. (2005) *Funds of Knowledge: Theorizing Practices in Households, Communities, and Classrooms*. New York: Routledge.

Graves, D. (1983) *Writing: Teachers and Children at Work*. Exeter, NH: Heinemann.

Griffiths, M., and Machin, D. (2003) Television and playground games as part of children's symbolic culture. *Social Semiotics*, 13: 147–160.

Gupta, A., and Ferguson, J. (1997) Beyond 'culture': Space, identity, and the politics of difference. In A. Gupta and J. Ferguson (eds) *Culture, Power, Place: Explorations in Critical Anthropology*. Durham, NC: Duke University Press, pp. 33–51.

Hanks, W.F. (2000) *Intertexts: Writings on Language, Utterance, and Context*. Lanham, MD: Rowman and Littlefield.

Hengst, H. (2005) Complex interconnections: The global and the local in children's minds and everyday worlds. In J. Qvortrup (ed.) *Studies in Modern Childhood*. New York: Palgrave Macmillan, pp. 21–38.

Hymes, D. (1972) Introduction. In C. Cazden, V.P. John, and D.H. Hymes (eds) *Functions of Language in the Classroom*. Columbia: NY: Teachers College, pp. vi–lvii.

James, A., and James, A. (2008) *Key Concepts in Childhood Studies*. Los Angeles: Sage.

James, A., Jenks, C., and Prout, A. (1998) *Theorizing Childhood*. Columbia, NY: Teachers College.

Jenkins, H. (2009) *Confronting the Challenges of Participatory Culture: Media Education for the 21st Century*. Cambridge, MA: MIT Press.

Kalliala, M. (2006) *Play Culture in a Changing World*. London: Open University Press.

Konner, M. (1991) *Childhood*. Boston, MA: Little Brown and Company.

Kress, G. (2010) *Multimodality: A Social Semiotic Approach to Contemporary Communication*. London: Routledge.

Lahiri, J. (2011) Trading stories: Notes from an apprenticeship. *New Yorker*, June 13 and 20: 78–85.

Lisanza, E. (2011) What does it mean to learn oral and written English language?: A case study of a rural Kenyan classroom. Unpublished doctoral dissertation, University of Illinois at Urbana-Champaign.

Marsh, J. (2003) Early childhood literacy and popular culture. In N. Hall, J. Larson and J. Marsh (eds) *Handbook of Early Childhood Literacy*. Los Angeles: Sage, pp. 112–125.

Marsh, J. (2011) Young children's literacy practices in a virtual world: Establishing an online interaction order. *Reading Research Quarterly*, 46: 101–118.

Martani, W., and Adijanto, M. G. (1992) Pengaruh film televisi terhadap tingkahlaku agresi anak [The impact of television movies on children's aggressivity]. *Jurnal Psikologi*, 1: 1–4.

McKendrick, J.H., Bradford, M.G., and Fielder, A.V. (2000) Time for a party!: Making sense of the commercialization of leisure space for children. In S.L. Holloway and G. Valentine (eds) *Children's Geographies: Playing, Living, Learning*. London: Routledge, pp. 100–118.

Montgomery, H. (2009) *An Introduction to Childhood: Anthropological Perspectives on Children's Lives*. Malden, MA: Wiley-Blackwell.

Newkirk, T. (2009) *Holding on to Good Ideas in a Time of Bad Ones: Six Literacy Principles Worth Fighting For*. Portsmouth, NH: Heinemann.

Nixon, H., and Comber, B. (2008) Redesigning school spaces: Creating possibilities for learning. In J. Sefton-Green, P. Thomson, K. Jones, and L. Bresler (eds) *The Routledge International Handbook of Creative Learning*. London: Routledge, pp. 249–259.

Ortner, S. (2006) *Anthropology and Social Theory: Culture, Power, and the Acting Subject*. Durham: Duke University Press.

Pahl, K., and Rowsell, J. (2005) *Literacy and Education*. London: Paul Chapman.

Peters, J.D. (1997) Seeing bifocally: Media, place, culture. In F.A. Gupta (ed.) *Culture, Power, Place: Explorations in Critical Anthropology*. Durham: Duke, pp. 75–92.

Prinsloo, M. (2004) Literacy is child's play: Making sense in Khwezi Park. *Language and Education*, 18: 291–314.

Ranker, J. (2006) 'There's fire magic, electric magic, ice magic, or poison magic': The world of video games and Adrian's compositions about Gauntlet legends. *Language Arts*, 84: 21–33.

Rogoff, B. (2003) *The Cultural Nature of Human Development*. Oxford: University Press.

Rosaldo, R. (1989/1993) *Culture and Truth: The Remaking of Social Analysis*. New York: Beacon Press.

Rosmaida (2009) Bahaya radiasi televisi terhadap kesehatan mata anak [The danger of television radiation toward children's vision health], accessed November 19, 2012: http://repository.unikom.ac.id/

Sahni, M.U. (1994) Building circles of mutuality: A socio-cultural analysis of literacy in a rural classroom in India. Unpublished doctoral dissertation, University of California at Berkeley.

Salvio, P.M., and Boldt, G.M. (2009) 'A democracy tempered by the rate of exchange': Audit culture and the sell-out of progressive writing pedagogy. *English in Education*, 43: 113–128.

Street, B. (2000) Literacy events and literacy practices: theory and practice in the New Literacy Studies. In M. Martin-Jones and K. Jones (eds) *Multilingual Literacies*. Philadelphia, PA: John Benjamins, pp. 17–29.

Thorne, B. (1993) *Gender Play: Girls and Boys in School*. New Brunswick, NJ: Rutgers University Press.

Thorne, B. (2005) Unpacking school lunchtime: Structure, practice, and the negotiation of differences. In C.R. Cooper, C.T.G. Coll, W.T. Bartko, *et al.* (eds) *Developmental Pathways through Middle Childhood: Rethinking Contexts and Diversity as Resources*. Mahwah, NJ: Erlbaum, pp. 63–88.

Tjahjono, I.I. (2004) Perancangan kampanye sosial pentingnya peran orangtua dalam menyembuhkan sikap 'Kritis TV' pada anak [Designing social campaign regarding parental roles in developing children's critical stance to television], accessed November 19, 2012: www.getcited.org/pub/103458224

Vygotsky, L.S. (1978) *Mind in Society: The Development of Higher Psychological Process*. Harvard, MA: University Press.

Wohlwend, K. (2010) A is for Avatar: Young children in literacy 2.0 worlds and literacy 1.0 schools. *Language Arts*, 88: 144–152.

Chapter 20

Children's and Teachers' Creativity In and Through Language

Teresa Cremin and Janet Maybin

Introduction

Recent work in the arts and social sciences has challenged the idea that language creativity resides in timeless works of great literature, produced by exceptional individuals. While the growing popularity of generic hybridity and play across modes has challenged the boundaries of literary language, there is also increasing interest in the everyday spoken language creativity of ordinary people. This more vernacular creativity appears to be collaboratively constructed, responsive to previous texts and practices and bound up with the construction of relationships and identity (Swann, Pope and Carter, 2011). Foreshadowed by the Czech structuralist Mukarovsky's argument (1970) that many linguistic items lie on the border between art and communication, this more plural, democratic conception of aesthetics foregrounds poetic, narrative, and performative uses of language for a range of everyday functions, and highlights ongoing processes of improvisation, adaptation, and transformation. The focus has thus been switched from creative products to creativity as process, where the roles of performer and audience, or creator and critic, are dynamically interdependent.

Similarly, in the field of anthropology, Hallam and Ingold (2007) challenge the boundary between innovation and tradition, and the image of an exceptional creative individual who stands out against conventional society. They replace 'innovation' that they suggest is associated with a backwards-looking post hoc definition of creativity as product, with a forwards-looking concept of 'improvisation,' arguing that people are constantly having to improvise as part of their ongoing engagement in social and cultural processes. They link this notion of creativity as processual and unfinished with medieval understandings of wonder and novelty as involving the combination and fusing of disparate elements, in contrast to the modernist concepts of unique great works. It is within this context of changing ideas about creativity that we present the following thematic review. While recognizing the interest and importance of analyzing specific instances of language creativity, we would argue that it is the use of this creativity for specific purposes in particular contexts, its cultural valuing and its potential connections with learning, which generate meaning and significance in the lives of children and teachers.

International Handbook of Research on Children's Literacy, Learning, and Culture, First Edition.
Edited by Kathy Hall, Teresa Cremin, Barbara Comber, and Luis C. Moll.
© 2013 John Wiley & Sons, Ltd. Published 2013 by John Wiley & Sons, Ltd.

Language creativity, or the artful use of language, is central to children's emotional, cognitive, and social development and education, as well as to communication in general. Linguists and psychologists have shown that children naturally play and experiment with language sounds, structures and meanings, and it has been argued that this kind of spontaneous, often playful, creativity *in* language contains the seeds of more prestigious poetic, literary, and dramatic cultural forms (Cook, 2000; Tannen, 2007). Children also pursue creative activity *through* language, using it for practicing social roles, speculative thinking, intellectual exploration, and the creation of alternative worlds, as we explore in this chapter. We also consider how older children and teenagers continue to use language creatively in their engagement with peer group culture and popular media, and for questioning social norms as they pursue relationships and reflect on identity. Significantly however, in drawing on a substantial synthesis of research, we reveal that while there is rich evidence of children's spontaneous language creativity, there is little research on it being explicitly fostered in the classroom context. Furthermore, in relation to adults, while analyses of large corpora of naturally occurring language suggest that adults also use language creatively (Carter, 2004), this review reveals that teachers' creativity in and through language is a notably under-researched area. We do however examine the available research documenting teachers moving beyond a recitation script, engaging playfully and multimodally and their use of language and identity work in 'collective third spaces' (Gutierrez, 2008), and in professional collaborations with writers and other artists.

In terms of the review methods and criteria, we chose to undertake a thematic review to address the issue of children's and teachers' creativity in and through language in order to ascertain theoretical and pedagogical insights afforded by research in these areas. In reviewing existing work from the point of view of both children *and* teachers the review encompasses a number of methodological approaches, with the main focus on qualitative studies that have influenced current research in this area. We draw on multiple perspectives from anthropology, psychology, sociology, and linguistics and in particular connect to Bakhtin's (1981) emphasis on the social origins and workings of language creativity. In order to develop a thorough understanding of the field and to identify tensions, gaps, and recommendations, the close collaboration of the authors was essential, this also enhanced the quality of the review; the topics and dimensions selected were debated and discussed at length. The time frame of the mid 1990s onwards was agreed upon and we read and reread research across this period, while also deciding to draw upon a few seminal studies from decades before, such as the work of Opie and Opie (1959/2001) and Chukovsky (1928/1963) who documented and revealed the verbal creativity of the young, as well as the ethnographic work of Heath (1983) who showed that children's culturally different ways with words are not necessarily built upon in education. There are parallels here with our argument, we reveal that children's vernacular and popular playful practices are not fully harnessed in school (while acknowledging this can be problematic), and argue that the interplay between teachers' and students' creative language use warrants investigation.

The chapter commences with an examination of research that documents children and young people's spontaneous language, and then we examine studies that focus on the relatively untapped potential for creativity within the official language and literacy curriculum. Next, we review empirical work that connects to teachers' creativity in and through language in the classroom, noting the limited research-base in this area. Our analysis and synthesis led us to identify several themes and issues across these topics that we discuss, these include: play and playfulness, narrative and collaboration, and resistance and risk, as well as identity, and the potency of 'what if' language – the language of possibility. The challenges involved in educators' building on the creative language resources that students bring to school and the consequences for curriculum and pedagogy are also debated and new research directions outlined. Finally, we close by recommending that the research community affords increased attention to the creative language capacity of both the young and of those who teach them.

Children's Naturally Occurring Language Creativity

In this section we not only discuss evidence of children and young people's naturally occurring creativity *in* language, for instance through rhythm, rhyme, and play with meaning, but also consider their spontaneous creativity *through* language in the construction of identity and relationship, and their creative use of language for subversion, resistance, and critique. To some extent this is a developmental story as children progressively extend their forms and uses of language, but linguists have also stressed the sophistication and complexity of young children's spontaneous language creativity, right from the early years (Cook, 2000; Crystal, 1998) Often, creativity is multifunctional, for instance language play may be aesthetically appealing and cognitively enhancing while simultaneously accomplishing important identity and relationship work.

The importance of play

In the early stages the musicality of language is particularly important and many games with babies, before they understand grammar or meaning, involve rhythm, intonation, and touch (Cook, 2000; Trevarthen and Aitken, 2001). In proto-language behavior, babies actively manipulate the forms and interactive patterns of talk; in their earliest 'conversations,' infants as young as a few months old have been recorded playing face-to-face games, repeating and creatively embroidering a 'text' offered by someone else, for example the word 'boo' with accompanying body movement (Murray and Andrews, 2000). Researchers have suggested that this natural propensity for language play and creativity has important educational implications. For instance, young children's enjoyment of rhythm and rhyme in linguistic routines and nursery rhymes stimulates their phonological awareness, which can assist early literacy development (Goswami, 2002). Children learning a second language have been found to spontaneously play with sounds and grammar to produce nonsense forms, alliteration, onomatopoeia, playful rhymes and humorous mislabeling (Broner and Tarone, 2001; Cekaite and Aronsson, 2005). Cekaite and Aronsson (2005) argue that language play among the seven to ten year olds they studied made second language use more memorable, it enabled pupils to experiment and take risks while saving face and it stimulated further exploration of language form.

In addition to this kind of creativity *in* language, linguists and psychologists have also documented how, from the early stages, children also use language for imaginative reflection. In her classic study of a young child's recorded pre-sleep monologues, Nelson (1989) found that, between the ages of 21 and 36 months, her daughter reproduced fragments of talk and narratives that played out past and future events and routines. Nelson suggests that these narratives involved understanding and imagining experience, making inferences and solving problems and she suggests that the monologues contributed to her daughter's self-regulation and self-development. The importance of young children's narratives for social, cognitive, and identity work is picked up by a number of researchers. Engel (2005) argues that when children around three years old use language to weave their symbolic play into a narrative, for example, using a wooden spoon to brush their hair and saying 'I have to get ready for the ball,' this opens up an alternative symbolic world in which the child can explore and embellish different kinds of scenarios, reality, and spheres of experience. Their manipulation of perspective, imagery, and form facilitates experimentation with speculative thinking and the rearrangement of the real world. Engel suggests that children's stories, which become quite complex by their fourth year, enable them to slip easily between play simulating everyday life ('what is' narratives), and a pretend world of fantastic possibilities ('what if' narratives). Engel's suggestion that children's stories stimulate their thinking echoes earlier findings by Fox (1993), who studied the oral narratives told by four and five year olds with extensive experience of stories being read and told to them. These children put together the structure and content of the story texts they had heard with stories about their own lives, to produce complex narrative and linguistic structures that stimulated exploration of physical laws and logical thought, as well as of their social world.

In Vygotskian theory, imagination and play are seen as leading children's emotional, social, and cognitive development, creating zones of proximal development where they can temporarily fulfill desires tempered by the social rules they rehearse alongside roles and values in re-enactments of remembered experience. These re-enactments are transformed by the child's imaginative activity where meaning takes precedence over objective reality, enabling the child to practice elementary abstract thought (Vygotsky, 1978). The kind of imaginative activity described by Vygotsky has also been associated with the reading and experience of fiction, which Meek (2002) suggests is, like play, a dialogue with a child's future and has the capacity to enrich their realist thinking as well as stretch the bounds of their imagination. While language creativity opens up alternative worlds, Chukovsky (1928/1963) also suggests that children's use of language to experiment with the impossible and nonsensical enables them to gain a stronger sense of reality. Thus, creativity confirms and enhances 'what is' as well as providing a window into 'what if.'

It is important to recognize that these early creative practices are clearly culturally shaped and some verbal dexterity and imaginative activity may not translate easily into schooled practices. In her classic monograph the anthropologist Heath (1983) described how pre-school age children in the highly oral environment of the Trackton community learnt to 'talk junk,' creating stories that used fictionalizations, metaphoric connections and imaginative exaggeration of real events. Young children learnt to capture and hold an audience in the sociable, outdoor family and neighborhood life on the plaza. However, Heath found that this emphasis on oral culture and on the skills of imaginative embellishment of reality, and performing and interacting with an audience, were not transferable into the school classroom. Here, children were asked questions about labels, attributes, and discrete features of objects and events. By the time they had reached a stage of schooling where their creative and imaginative use of language would have been valued, many of the children had already been alienated through the initial emphasis on skilling and drilling (Heath, 1983). Heath's work underlines the important anthropological point that cultures vary both in terms of the amount and type of creativity that are acceptable in different social contexts, and in relation to what is seen as appropriate in terms of the aesthetics and ethics of creative activity. Verbal creativity is not simply innovation, but a recognizable variation, guided by culturally specific aesthetic, practical and moral values, from an expected pattern (Duranti and Black, 2011). In this respect, children are socialized into specific forms of creativity that are valorized by their society, and innovation that cannot be linked to existing cultural patterns is seen as inappropriate, or remains unrecognized.

Poetic and narrative creativity in older children and teenagers

Linguistic ethnographic research has emphasized the socio-cultural functions of young people's creativity in and through language. Both poetic and narrative languages are used spontaneously and extensively by older children. Rampton (2006) provides an account of students' use of exaggerated posh and Cockney accents, associated respectively with social distance, superiority and constraint and with solidarity, vigor, and passion. Teenagers strategically manipulated these accents and their associated imagery to, for example, negotiate the reception of a personal story, keep down powerful girls and juggle between school and peer values. At the same time, they played with the sounds of the German they were being taught, restyling words and phrases in talk among themselves.

In terms of narrative, Maybin (2006) studied stories about personal experience exchanged among ten to twelve year olds, where she found children tried out and conveyed judgments about people, relationships, and events through the ways in which they rephrased and reframed reported speech and through their orchestration of dialogues. This revoicing enabled them to reflect jointly on social events and to challenge and sometimes subvert adult positions. Georgakopoulou (2007), who researched the 'small stories' exchanged among a small group of teenage girls with a long shared history of friendship and shared experience, noted that they imagined future encounters with men and told 'breaking news' stories of currently unfolding events, as well as tales from their past experience. The girls recorded their favorite stories, some of which were recast as rhyming poems, in a carefully guarded 'Book of Minutes.' Georgakopoulou argues that the social construction of each girl's individual identity through their dual roles as both storyteller and character within the stories was bound up with the 'we' of their shared interactional history. In Engel's (2005) terms, their narratives included both 'what is' stories about the girls' personal experience and also 'what if' fantasies of imagined future encounters.

Resistance, subversion, and reappropriation

Language creativity thus plays an important simultaneous role in linguistic dexterity, sociability, and socialization. It can also provide a space for subversion, resistance, and critique, for instance through breaking social taboos, or providing radical commentary. Folklorists have found that rhythmic and rhyming scatological humor and taunts are ubiquitous in older children's riddles, playground games, and rhymes (Bishop and Curtis, 2001; Opie and Opie, 2001/1959). Ackerley (2002) recorded playground taunts in New Zealand: 'I am the ghost of a place named Venus / Come near me and I'll bite your penis' and 'I'm an Australian / Born and bred / Long in the legs /And thick in the head.' Grugeon (2001) has documented how, through a further layer of subversion, girls parody media texts and use rhymes to resist masculine as well as adult authority. In addition, longstanding research by linguists on African American oral artistry (see Morgan, 2002) includes accounts of the repetitive language play and scatological themes that run through verbal dueling among adolescents for example in the parallel grammar and lexical oppositions of 'A: Your momma drink pee B: Your father eat shit' (quoted from Sherzer, 1992 in Cook, 2000). The rapid improvisation of playful rhyming, sound symbolism and jokes in these ritual insult exchanges involves complex inferential processes (Duranti and Black, 2011).

Inventive verbal combat is also important within hip hop artistry, which combines music sampling and mixing by DJs, breakdancing and graffiti and MCing or rapping, where lyrics, often improvised, are chanted against a rhythmic background. Often anti-establishment and highlighting injustice and social issues, hip hop's celebration of American speech styles has been appropriated by youth internationally, and reinvented in terms of local issues and cultures (Alim, Ibrahim, and Pennycook, 2009). In addition to oral practices, including the reproduction of hip hop lyrics where linguistic innovation can provide a resource for developing literacy skills (Smitherman, 2007), Androutsopoulos (2007) documents the multimodal creativity of hip-hop web homepages designed by young people who experiment with styles and language crossing in visual symbols, nicknames, and appropriated conversational routines. However, while hip hop can be studied for its use of rhyme, rhythm, imagery, dialect, and performance, translating popular verbal art forms into curriculum activities is not straightforward. For instance, Newman (2009) found that in a college hip-hop project where teachers' focused on progressive politics, this focus was rejected by the teenage students, who preferred artists with violent and sexist themes.

In sum, children and young people are frequently creative both in play within language, and in using it creatively to pursue particular purposes, which may or may not align with the purposes of teachers and other adults. Research in this area, and particularly on hip hop, has also been used to raise questions about how creativity itself is conceptualized (Pennycook, 2007), and has contributed to the conceptual and aesthetic shifts discussed at the beginning of the chapter. For instance, hip hop practices of remixing and recontextualizing the music and lyrics of others have contributed to fresh ways of defining authorship and originality in terms that acknowledge their social and responsive nature. Creativity in remixing and recontextualization emerges through a response to a previous text or performance, which produces aesthetically pleasing forms of reordering, recombining and reimagining. This kind of intertextual, dialogic creativity invokes Bakhtin's (1981) vision of language as an ongoing struggle within heteroglot genres and registers between canonical forms and authoritative voices on the one side and inwardly persuasive voices, 'oversaturated' as he puts it, with other people's meanings, on the other. Speakers or writers are never the first to use language in a particular way, but they wrest meaning and artistry through the way in which they recast and recontextualize a previous utterance, 'reaccenting' it (Vološinov, 1973) with new meanings and significance. Thus adaptation involves creative appropriation, transposition, and translation (Hutcheon, 2006), students may engage creatively with texts using interplay, answering back, and reproduction (Pope, 2005) and children combine playground folklore and popular culture to create new hybrid forms (Marsh and Willett, 2010).

The Creative Potentialities of the Official Language and Literacy Curriculum

In the context of schooling, the extent to which the spontaneous language creativity of the young is acknowledged, valued, or built upon depends in part on professional recognition of this playful capacity and its role in the social and cognitive development of the young. Additionally, professional understanding of the creative potential inherent in the official language and literacy curriculum is likely to influence classroom practice, alongside teachers' own stance towards creativity and literacy teaching. We discuss these and other factors more fully in the following sections. Here, in order to highlight research that directly or indirectly, reveals the creative scope of the curriculum, we have confined ourselves to reviewing studies of arguably open-ended language and literacy practices such as storytelling and drama, poetic play, online creativity and those that highlight the contribution of spoken language.

Oral Narratives: Storytelling and Drama

Analyses of children's storytelling in the early years of schooling reveal its generative nature, the fluid interplay between oral and written language, and the scope for play and enactment (Gupta, 2009; Paley, 1981). The storytelling competence of young adolescents adept at employing satire, word play, humor and hyperbole, and prompting audience participation has also been documented in school contexts (Heath, 1994; Rosen, 1988), although the teenagers in these studies were not perceived to be particularly literate in their respective UK and US education systems. Their social and cultural capital as informal story performers and artful language users was not only underestimated, but remained under-developed. In a similar manner when the pre-schoolers that Fox (1993) studied entered formal education, their narrative capacity remained unrecognized; one was never invited to tell a story and another was 'tested on suspicion of "language retardness" during the period when he was recording 29,000 words of narrative at home' (Fox, 2004, p. 193). As multimodal storytellers, young people are likely to employ prosodic features such as intonation and volume, poetic features such as rhyme, repetition, and metaphor and paralinguistic features such as gesture, movement, and facial expression, though school students' aesthetic use of such verbal, visual, textual, gestural, and dramatic elements has not been widely researched. Furthermore, within the curriculum the retelling of autobiographical and traditional tales is arguably often marginalized, confined to festivals, or tightly framed within functionalist drives towards raising attainment in writing. Yet, as we discussed in the previous section, retellings are not simply imitations; each is a unique example of reaccenting (Vološinov, 1973) likely to involve 'ventriloquation' (Bakhtin, 1986) as tellers appropriate and transform texts, making them their own in interaction with their audience.

Drama, also a visual, verbal, and embodied art form is indivisibly linked to creativity and language. Like storytelling, improvisational drama proceeds without a script and is a prime example of Sawyer's (2004) 'performance creativity' in which the creative process and the resulting product are co-occurring. However, while cultivating creativity and enriching language are commonly referred to as core aims in drama, few studies explicitly examine students' language creativity or the collaborative construction of new meanings through imagined experience. School-based studies suggest that vocabulary can be enhanced through combining storytelling and enactment (Gupta, 2009), that role-play encourages 'creative jumps and seeking reconciliation among disjuncture and disparities' (Heath and Wollach, 2008, p. 7) and that students' engagement with fictional problems in drama nurtures their possibility thinking (Lin, 2010). Drawing on a cross-case analysis of five studies, Crumpler and Schneider (2002) found that writing composed in drama had more depth and detail, and Cremin *et al.* (2006) argue that it can make a significant contribution to students' ideational fluency and creative language use. In this work, the presence of creative tension, the strength of imaginative engagement and the multiple role perspectives voiced and heard, appeared to combine to enrich children's writing in-role. The students' compositions, originating from moments of broken play appeared to resonate with the 'what if' world that they were inhabiting, though more research is needed to explore how the outer play and discourse of drama fosters the inner play of the imagination and flexibility with language and ideas.

Digital technologies and poetic play

As noted in the previous section, young people's creativity is often evidenced in their playful engagement with contemporary textual forms outside school. Recent classroom studies also demonstrate that through drawing on students' technoliteracy practices outside school and engaging them in authentic multimodal and multidimensional activities in school, teachers not only motivate students but also develop their capacity to work imaginatively as designers, collaboratively creating websites, podcasts, and wikis for example (Edwards-Groves, 2011; Goodson and Skillen, 2010; Walsh, 2007). Productive design-based pedagogies (Marsh, 2008) afford significant opportunities for the collaborative exploration of ideas, recontextualization and joint text construction, and are likely to be highly intertextual 'as traditional and con-temporary texts are "reaccented" by teacher and students alike and meaning making ensues' (Brooks, 2011, p. 75). For instance, Lotherington (2011) describes how elementary school students used digital technologies to design new multimodal versions of traditional tales, infus-ing these with their own cultural associations and linguistic resources. However challenges exist for teachers in reconceptualizing writing as a multimodal design process, recognizing the role of collaboration and tapping into students' digital literacies and design repertoires.

In relation to poetry, despite its rich oral and aural heritage, it could be argued that inter-nationally most curricula frame it as a print-based medium, somewhat detached from the playful language of youth. Attention to the auditory imagination (Eliot, 1933/1981) and spoken word poetry in school both in research and practice appears limited, although work with young bilingual learners posits the benefits of exploring rhythm across cultures (Datta, 2000) and work with older students claims to demonstrate their understanding of the audi-tory affordance of heard poems (Gordon, 2010). Furthermore, teacher research studies posit that through extended immersion in reading, writing, and performing poetry, risk taking and experimentation are fostered (Schillinger, Meyer, and Vinz, 2010), and that political perfor-mance poetry can be a useful teaching tool, creating student centered, critical discursive spaces in classrooms (Camangian, 2008). This work, building on students' spoken word practices, also reveals the difficulties involved: many teachers view expressive popular literacy practices such as hip-hop for example as inferior to academic literacy (Delpit and Dowdy, 2003) and in addition, they may not know enough about the everyday language practices of the children they teach in order to create responsively aligned curricula (though see Moll *et al.*, 1992).

Playful on and 'off-task' talk

In Mercer's (2000) seminal studies of small group discussion in the classroom, children's playful talk was widely recorded, however, as one of his team noted years later, this aspect of the dataset was initially neglected, viewed as 'apparently off-task nonsense talk or banter' of little educational value (Wegerif, 2005, p. 227). Through revisiting the transcripts and reanalyzing the abundance of word-play, humor, punning and intertextuality, Wegerif suggests that such verbal creativity serves to open a resonant space for reflection; a dialogic space in which children's ideas and images surface and reverberate, fostering the collaborative construction of new meanings. To some extent this is also evidenced in the work of Rojas-Drummond, Albarrán and Littleton (2008, p. 187), who claim that in collaborative writing the creative 'ideas that "germinate" in the previous oral discussion "ripen" in the written production,' though in this context the talk is more likely to be deemed on task. In relation to classroom talk about literature there is relatively little research that explicitly analyses the creative nature of students' responses. Though the UK-based Philosophy for Children program foregrounds students' roles as question posers and recognizes the potential for critical and creative thinking (Trickey and Topping, 2004). Additionally, Arizpe and Styles (2004) demonstrate the scope of picture fiction in fostering children's informal and often creative conversational engagement.

In relation to written text production, there are several studies that document the potential for creativity in and through apparently 'off task' talk. Dyson for example (1993, 1997, 2009), highlights how children use the language practices of childhood as they write and recontextualize familiar cultural material in the world of school. Her work suggests that even in highly structured writing activities, writing is socially embedded in playful peer dialogues often of an unofficial nature. Drawing on Bakhtin's theory of voice, Dyson demonstrates that as the young writers sing, dance, tell tales, and inhabit the situated voices of others (appropriated from home, school, the community, and the media), they reorganize and rearticulate their own resources and expand their knowledge about social practices, symbolic systems and their social world. This textual play, Dyson argues, 'potentially promotes communicative flexibility and adaptability, not to mention language learning itself' (2009, p. 243). Pahl's (2007) work too demonstrates how children playfully draw upon multiple events and practices at home and school to convey their meanings, which, she suggests, reveals the creativity and intertextuality involved. Vass (2007), in her empirical research examining collaborative composition, also documents students engaging in playful dialogues, which she claims help to inspire and channel the creative flow of ideas. The key features of the students' affect-driven discourse include musing, acting out, singing, and considerable humor. Vass posits that her work 'illustrates how emotions serve both as the generator and moderator of creative thought' (2007, p. 113), though as she acknowledges some of the children's playfulness with language may not entirely satisfy the constraints of the task and may not therefore be deemed creative in the strictest sense.

The fine line between off-task playfulness and task-oriented uses of language play as evidenced in several of the studies noted above may create challenges for practitioners, particularly regarding the presence and value of such talk in the classroom. Teachers may also be challenged by the specification of literacy curricula, particularly in countries where assessment and accountability hold sway and the written word is foregrounded the expense of the spoken. Yet it is evident that some pedagogic practices within language and literacy curricula afford opportunities for fostering children's creative capacity to play with language, interpretation and meaning and that there is a pressing need for empirical research that documents in more detail the nature and significance of such language creativity in children's learning and development.

Teachers' Creativity In and Through Language

Although adult oral creativity is extensively evidenced through anecdote, word play, and the use of metaphor and reported dialogue in playful everyday conversations (Carter, 2004; Coates, 2007; Tannen, 2007), scant attention has been paid to teachers' creativity in language in classrooms. The extent to which teachers conceive of themselves as creative language artists within and beyond school is not known and no studies were found exploring teachers' sense of themselves as oral language artists – tale tellers, performance poets or role players, for example. In contrast, there is considerable research exploring teachers' identities as readers and writers (Brooks, 2007; Cremin and Baker, 2010; Gennrich and Janks, Chapter 33 this volume; McKinney and Giorgis, 2009) and their digital practices (Burnett, 2011; McDougall, 2009). Debates about teachers' literate identities and the extent to which they draw upon their life practices and creative engagement as readers and writers mainly focus on the value of practitioners' apprenticing learners and modeling possibilities through participation. Advocates claim students benefit when teachers share their aesthetic and affective responses as readers (Commeyras, Bisplinghoff, and Olson, 2003) or demonstrate their creative thinking as writers (Pritchard and Honeycutt, 2008), though others observe that if practitioners voice their personal responses to texts or emotional and cognitive challenges during writing this may result in exposure, ambiguity, and discomfort (Cremin, 2006; Gleeson and Prain, 1996). Modeling the imaginative use of spoken language, through oral storytelling, discussion, teacher in-role work, or in the context of an improvised poetry performance, for example, also involves taking risks, tolerating uncertainty, and the adoption of a playful, improvisational, and arguably artistic stance.

Moving beyond a recitation script

To work artistically it is suggested that teachers need to move beyond a recitation script that demonstrates the certain and 'authoritative voice' of the teacher (Bakhtin, 1981), be able and willing to express themselves creatively, and need to respond creatively to students. Such risk taking is noted as a common characteristic of successful literacy teachers, not merely in relation to their artistic engagement, but also in their capacity for improvisation and willingness to experiment and remain open to new ideas and strategies that may benefit learners (Wilson and Ball, 1997). Research into creative teaching and learning also suggests it involves taking risks and is a fundamentally collaborative form of 'disciplined improvisation' (Sawyer, 2004). In describing teachers who position themselves as risk takers and 'meddlers in the middle,' McWilliam argues that such practitioners engage in shared endeavors with students as codesigners, coeditors, co-constructors of meaning and 'collaborative critics' (2008, p. 265). However, no studies were found offering an analysis of the discursive processes at play when teachers position themselves as fellow artists or 'meddlers,' though work in England suggests that teachers' overarching questions for classroom enquiry play a crucial role in nurturing children's 'what if' thinking – their possibility thinking (Chappell *et al.*, 2008). Additionally, the value of teachers' modeling ambiguity, employing creative juxtapositions and hedging comments to denote provisionality is noted by Heath and Wolf (2004), whose work suggests that children's creative responses to text are fostered by such language, in particular their teachers' use of metaphorical comparisons to create novel meanings.

Exploring 'collective third spaces'

Other empirical work indicates that the likelihood of student innovation increases when teaching is relevant to their lives, enabling the young to capitalize upon the cultural, linguistic, and social assets they bring to school (Jeffrey and Woods, 2009). This is borne out in the work of Gutierrez (2008) who seeks to transform students' home practices and classroom activities into 'collective third spaces'; spaces where the potential conflict between the teacher's language and knowledge (formal, academic, mainstream) and the student's (vernacular) is translated into a site of collaboration and learning. In summer schools with high school students, Gutierrez argues that the intersection of official and unofficial spaces and teacher scripts and students' counter scripts become a source of innovation, with students able to use their own language and everyday knowledge to engage with curriculum material. The learning activities, in which both teachers and students engage, tend to privilege dialogue, conversation, and critique as well as the exploration of contradictions, and include *testimonio*, *teatro*, comprehension circles, and writing conferences, for example.

In analyzing the language and grammar of these third spaces, Gutierrez found that instead of traditional classroom directives and rhetorical question and answer sequences, instructors used 'imagine' 'try,' 'let's,' and questions with rising intonation to confirm and build shared understanding. She also found a lot of code-switching, metaphorical language, modals, questions, and volitional directives (want/wanna). Additionally auxiliary modal verbs such as 'may,' 'will,' 'could,' and 'should' were used in offering advice and suggestions. 'May,' 'might,' 'can,' and 'could' also denoted possibility, particularly when combined with questions. Furthermore the word 'hope' was regularly used. All this suggests that learning in these third spaces was mediated by a language of future possibility, arguably a language of creativity, which she terms 'social dreaming – a collective dream for a better world' (Gutierrez, 2008, p. 158).

Drawing on oral histories and professional collaborations

In a not dissimilar manner, Stein's practitioner work with South African teachers included an autobiographical element in order both to validate the practitioners' histories and 'permit the invention of a future' (Stein, 2004, p. 518). Her courses sought to integrate teachers' cross-cultural perspectives and multiliteracies and culminated in collaborative dramatic performances in which they represented their own and each others' literacy histories. Stein shows that these intertextual and often emotional performances drew upon the oral traditions of their communities, and foregrounded gestural forms of communication rather than print-based literacy, incorporating dance, costume, props, and visual design as well as considerable storytelling, praising, and singing. Through working playfully and multimodally, Stein claims that the teachers were able to reframe and transform their literacy histories. She also suggests that the role adoption and multivocality involved enabled them to inhabit others' worlds and perspectives and explore cultural diversity. Aligned to the act of remembering, this ensemble performance approach to pedagogy appears to afford opportunities to develop teachers' personal and professional awareness of language, literacy, and difference.

Working in partnership with professional artists may also offer practitioners support for increasing understanding and development of their own and their students' language creativity, yet studies suggest that in UK-based partnership work there is a tendency to dichotomize artists' and teachers' roles (Galton, 2008; Pringle, 2008). In one study, a playscript about the local community, composed by a class of primary children working with a writer (in the teacher's absence), was effectively censored due to staff concerns about the language used, in particular the children's playful pleasure in the grotesque and their inclusion of challenging social issues such as teenage pregnancy, alcohol, and drugs (Thomson, Hall, and Russell, 2006). As the researchers highlight this demonstrates the controversial potential of language creativity and the difficulties of competing professional agendas; the writer saw the work as blurring home-school knowledge boundaries and building on the children's vernacular, the teachers classified the work as Literacy/English framed by national requirements.

In sum, while there are examples of practitioners adopting arguably more creative positions and some evidence of the use of open, futures-oriented language, the posing of questions, use of metaphors and code-switching, overall very little attention has been paid to teachers using language creatively. The area is ripe for research. Potential studies might build on Gutierrez's conceptualization of collective third spaces as a source of innovation, investigate the latent scope of practitioners' use of intonation and humor, examine the modeling of texture and musicality in language (through oral storytelling for example), or investigate the relationship between teachers' and children's creative use of language in particular pedagogic contexts.

Conclusions and Implications

This thematic review has been compiled in the context of changing conceptions of creativity and an increasing interest in its dynamic, processual, relational, and culturally contingent dimensions. Creativity in and through language is not only evident right from the beginning of life, but is also clearly important for aesthetic, developmental, educational, and wider social functions. It appears that children's creativity *in* language through rhyme, rhythm, imagery, and play with meaning is a driving force that continues across the life-span, from nonsense words, riddles, jokes, made-up languages and scatological playground rhymes through verbal insult dueling and hip-hop raps. It has been argued that similar forms of language creativity are found in magical and religious ritual, prayer, and literature, and that the narrative forms underpinning children and young people's play, imaginative speculations, and collaborative identity work are reworked in popular and canonical fiction (Cook, 2000; Tannen, 2007). Children's creativity *through* language to construct identity and relationship, and to generate alternative realities allowing innovative thinking and experimentation, also appears to be crucial for their emotional and social development, and for intellectual innovation.

Despite the rich evidence of children's naturally occurring language creativity, a 'ludic gap' appears to exists between students' verbal creativity and teachers' recognition and explicit development of this in classroom practice. Crystal (1998) first noted the existence of such a gap between the linguistic worlds of young children and the lack of playful uses of language in educational materials such as reading schemes. It appears this gap persists, albeit in a different form. However, while drama, storytelling, poetic play, composition (on- and offline), and text discussion afford opportunities to nurture creativity in and through language, it is not simply a question of advocating the pedagogic appropriation of children's vernacular and popular creative practices. These may cut across a nationally imposed pedagogy or introduce controversial anti-establishment positions and values that are difficult to renegotiate within the curriculum. Alternatively, these practices may simply lose their original raison d'être when transposed into the classroom context.

Additionally, the framing of literacy and language and the varied conceptualizations and values afforded creativity internationally, both in policy and practice, create challenges for the profession. In many countries, high stakes assessment has arguably led to an instrumental approach to teaching and learning literacy. Such an approach views literacy as a body of skills to be taught and tested, and fails to recognize it as highly complex, socio-cultural practice. This not only sidelines the open-ended, playful, and generative nature of language, but also reinforces the place of English at the margins of debates about arts education, despite the perception that language creativity is positioned at the intersection of play and art. Furthermore, underpinned by play and experimentation, the assessment of children's creativity and language and the social and collaborative processes involved present problems for the profession that may construe language creativity as potentially subversive and anarchic. There are implications for classroom management and discipline too, since playing with language, acting out, singing, telling jokes, and so forth do not conform to the behavioral norms typically expected from students in school. In this sense, language creativity in education remains controversial, although as Vass (2007, p. 115) observes such 'playfulness needs to be recognised and embraced as necessary for creative purposes, despite the reluctance to do so in educational settings.'

Notwithstanding these challenges, on the basis of this original review that unusually drew upon literature to examine both children's *and* teachers' creativity in and through language, we argue that the playful and improvisational nature of teaching (Sawyer, 2004) also needs to be recognized and fostered; that the positioning and creative language use of student teachers and practitioners deserves to be more seriously considered and researched and its relationship to students' language explored. Further we argue that the social and educational salience of language creativity needs to be acknowledged in education and that the distinctive features of children's (and adults') spontaneous language creativity could be harnessed more effectively in school. In particular, we recommend the broadening of conceptions of language creativity in education to include remixing, recontextualization, interplay, translation and adaptation, and argue that future research should recognize that creativity, embedded within communicative activity, often involves a range of other modes as well as language. Accordingly, the social, dialogic and intertextual dimensions of language creativity deserve further exploration and connection to the classroom, as do the connections between spoken and written text, visual, and kinesthetic modes.

In the wider context of global economic uncertainty and social and technological change, Cook suggests that the human propensity for complex language creativity has key evolutionary functions. Indeed he asserts that the most important function language has may be 'the creation of imaginative worlds: whether lies, games, fictions or fantasies' (Cook, 2000, p. 47). Such future possibilities and 'social dreaming' (Gutierrez, 2008, p. 158), may be crucial as we move further into the twenty-first century, though much will depend upon the extent to which children, young people, and their teachers, who already demonstrate considerable capacities for creativity in and through language, are enabled to exploit this in education and to utilize the metaphoric language of 'what if' in the context of the curriculum and beyond.

References

Ackerley, J. (2002) Playground rhymes keep up with the times. *Play and Folklore*, 42: 4–8.

Alim, S.H., Ibrahim, A., and Pennycook, A. (eds) (2009) *Global Linguistic Flows: Hip Hop Cultures, Youth Identities and the Politics of Language*. London, Routledge.

Androutsopoulos, J. (2007) Style online: Doing hip-hop on the German-speaking web. In P. Auer (ed.) *Style and Social Identities: Alternative Approaches to Linguistic Heterogeneity*. New York: de Gruyter, pp. 271–317.

Arizpe, E., and Styles, M. (2004) *Children Reading Pictures: Interpreting Visual Texts*. London: Routledge Falmer.

Bakhtin, M. (1981/1935) Discourse in the novel. In M. Holquist (ed.) *The Dialogic Imagination: Four Essays by M.M. Bakhtin*, trans. C. Emerson and M. Holquist. Austin: University of Texas Press, pp. 259–422.

Bakhtin, M. (1986/1953) The problem of speech genres. In C. Emerson and M. Holquist (eds) *Speech Genres and Other Late Essays*, trans. V.W. Mc Gee. Austin, TX: University of Texas Press, p. 60ff.

Bishop, J.C., and Curtis, M. (2001) *Play Today in the Primary School Playground*. Buckingham: Open University Press.

Broner, M., and Tarone, E (2001) Is it fun? Language play in a fifth-grade Spanish immersion classroom. *The Modern Language Journal*, 85(3): 363–379.

Brooks, G.W. (2007) Teachers as readers and writers and teachers of reading and writing. *The Journal of Educational Research*, 100(3): 177–191.

Brooks, K. (2011) Resistance is futile: 'Reaccenting' the present to create classroom dialogues. *Pedagogies: An International Journal*, 6(1): 66–80.

Burnett, C. (2011) Pre-service teachers' digital literacy practices: exploring contingency in identity and digital literacy in and out of educational contexts. *Language and Education*, 25(5): 433–449.

Camangian, P (2008) Untempered tongues: Teaching performance poetry for social justice. *English Teaching: Practice and Critique*, 7(2): 35–55.

Carter, R. (2004) *Language and Creativity: The Art of Common Talk*. London/New York: Routledge.

Cekaite, A., and Aronsson, K. (2005) Language play: A collaborative resource in children's L2 learning. *Applied Linguistics*, 26(2): 169–191.

Chappell, K., Craft, A., Burnard, P., and Cremin, T. (2008) Question-posing and Question-responding: at the heart of possibility thinking in the early years. *Early Years*, 28(3): 267–286.

Chukovsky, K. (1928/1963) *From Two to Five*, trans., and ed. Miriam Morton. Berkeley: University of California Press.

Coates, J. (2007) Talk in a play frame: More on laughter and intimacy. *Journal of Pragmatics*, 39: 29–49.

Commeyras, M., Bisplinghoff, B.S., and Olson, J. (2003) *Teachers as Readers: Perspectives on the Importance of Reading in Teachers' Classrooms and Lives*. Newark: IRA.

Cook, G. (2000) *Language Play, Language Learning*. Oxford: Oxford University Press.

Cremin, T. (2006) Creativity, uncertainty and discomfort: Teachers as writers. *Cambridge Journal of Education*, 36(3): 415–433.

Cremin, T., and Baker, S. (2010) Exploring teacher-writer identities in the classroom: Conceptualising the struggle. *English Teaching: Practice and Critique*, 9(3): 8–25.

Cremin, T., Goouch, K., Blakemore, L., *et al.* (2006) Connecting drama and writing: Seizing the moment to write. *Research in Drama in Education*, 11(3): 273–291.

Crumpler, T., and Schneider, J. (2002) Writing with their whole being: A cross study analysis of children's writing from five classrooms using process drama. *Research in Drama Education*, 7(2): 61–79.

Crystal, D. (1998) *Language Play*. Harmondsworth: Penguin.

Datta, M. (2000) *Bilinguality and Literacy*. London: Continuum.

Delpit, L., and Dowdy, J. (eds) (2003) *The Skin that We Speak: Thoughts on Language and Culture in the Classroom*. New York: The New Press.

Duranti, A., and Black, S. (2011) Language socialisation and verbal improvisation. In A. Duranti, E. Ochs, and B. Schieffelin (eds) *The Handbook of Language Socialization*. Oxford: Blackwell, pp. 443–463.

Dyson, A.H. (1993) *Social Worlds of Children's Learning to Write in an Urban Primary School*. New York: Teachers' College Press.

Dyson, A.H. (1997) *Writing Superheroes: Contemporary Childhood, Popular Culture and Classroom Literacy*. New York: Teachers' College Press.

Dyson, A.H. (2009) Writing in childhood worlds. In R. Beard, D. Myhill, J. Riley and M. Nystrand *The Sage Handbook of Writing Development*. London: Sage, pp. 232–245.

Edwards-Groves, C.J. (2011) The multimodal writing process: Changing practices in contemporary classrooms. *Language and Education*, 25(1): 49–64.

Eliot, T.S. (1933/1981) *The Use of Poetry and the Use of Fiction*. London: Faber and Faber.

Engel, S. (2005) The narrative worlds of *what is* and *what if*. *Cognitive Development*, 20: 514–525.

Fox, C. (1993) *At the Very Edge of the Forest: The Influence of Literature on Storytelling by Children*. London: Continuum.

Fox, C. (2004) Playing the storyteller. In N. Hall, J. Larson, and J. Marsh (eds) *Handbook of Early Childhood Literacy*. London: Sage, pp. 189–198.

Galton, M. (2008) *Creative Practitioners in Schools and Classrooms. Final Report of the Project: The Pedagogy of Creative Practitioners in Schools*. Cambridge: University of Cambridge.

Georgakopoulou, A. (2007) *Small Stories, Interaction and Identities*. Amsterdam: John Benjamins.

Gleeson, A., and Prain, V. (1996) Should teachers of writing themselves? An Australian contribution to the debate. *English Journal*, 5: 42–49.

Goodson, L.A., and Skillen, M. (2010) Small town perspectives, big-time motivation: Composing and producing place-based podcasts. *English Journal*, 100(1): 53–57.

Gordon, J. (2010) Articulating the auditory imagination. In M. Styles, L. Joy, and D. Whitley (eds) *Poetry and Childhood*. Stoke on Trent: Trentham, pp. 203–210.

Goswami, U. (2002) Early phonological development and the acquisition of literacy. In S.B. Neuman and D.K. Dickinson (eds) *Handbook of Early Literacy Research*. New York: Guildford Press, pp. 111–124.

Grugeon, E. (2001) 'We like singing the Spice Girls songs . . . and we like Tig and Stuck in the Mud': Girls' traditional games on two playgrounds. In J.C. Bishop and M. Curtis (eds) *Play Today in the Primary School Playground*. Buckingham: Open University Press, pp. 98–114.

Gupta, A. (2009) Vygotskian perspectives on using dramatic play to enhance children's development and balance creativity with structure in the early childhood classroom. *Early Child Development and Care*, 179(8): 1041–1054.

Gutierrez, K.D. (2008) Developing a sociocritical literacy in the third space. *Reading Research Quarterly*, 43(2): 148–164.

Hallam, E., and Ingold, T. (eds) (2007) Creativity and cultural improvisation. *ASA Monograph 44*. Oxford: Berg.

Heath, S.B. (1983) *Ways with Words: Language, Life and Work in Communities and Classrooms*. Cambridge: Cambridge University Press.

Heath, S.B (1994) Stories as ways of acting together. In A.H. Dyson and C. Genishi (eds) *The Need for Space*, Urbana: NCTE, pp. 206–220.

Heath, S.B., and Wolf, S. (2004) *It Looks To Me As If: Talking about Picture Books*. London: Creative Partnerships.

Heath, S.B., and Wollach, R. (2008) Vision for learning: History, theory and affirmation. In J. Flood, S.B. Heath, and D. Lapp (eds) *Handbook of Research on Literacy through the Communicative Arts*, Vol. III. Mahwah, NJ: Lawrence Erlbaum, pp. 3–11.

Hutcheon, L. (2006) *A Theory of Adaptation*. New York and London: Routledge.

Jeffrey, B., and Woods, P. (2009) *Creative Learning in the Primary School*. London: Routledge.

Lin, Y.S. (2010) Drama and possibility thinking – Taiwanese pupils' perspectives regarding creative pedagogy in drama. *Thinking Skills and Creativity*, 5: 108–119.

Lotherington, H. (2011) *Pedagogy of Multiliteracies: Rewriting Goldilocks*. London: Routledge.

Marsh, J. (2008) Productive pedagogies: Play creativity and digital cultures in the classroom. In R. Willet, M. Robinson, and J. Marsh (eds) *Play, Creativity and Digital Cultures*. NewYork/Oxford: Routledge Falmer, pp. 200–218.

Marsh, J., and Willett, R. (2010) Mega mash-ups and remixes in the cultural borderlands: Emergent findings from the ethnographic studies of playground games and rhymes in two primary schools. Paper presented at 'Children's Playground Games and Songs in the New Media Age,' February 25, 2010, London Knowledge Lab, London.

Maybin (2006) *Children's Voices: Talk, Knowledge and Identity*. Basingstoke: Palgrave Macmillan.

McDougall, J. (2009) A crisis of professional identity: How primary teachers are coming to terms with changing views of literacy. *Teaching and Teacher Education*, 24: 1–9.

McKinney, M., and Giorgis, C. (2009) Narrating and performing identity: Literacy specialists' writing identities. *Journal of Literacy Research*, 41(1): 104–149.

McWilliam, E. (2008) Unlearning how to teach. *Innovations in Education and Teaching International*, 45(3): 263–269.

Meek, M. (2002) 'What more needs saying about imagination?' Address at the 19th International Reading Association World Congress on Reading, Edinburgh, Scotland.

Mercer, N. (2000) *Words and Minds, How We Use Language to Think Together*. London: Routledge.

Moll, L., Amanti, C., Neff, D., and Gonzalez, N. (1992) Funds of knowledge for teaching: Using a qualitative approach to connect homes and classrooms. *Theory into Practice*, 31: 132–141.

Morgan, M. (2002) *Language, Discourse and Power in African American Culture*. Cambridge: Cambridge University Press.

Mukarovsky, J. ([1936] 1970) *Aesthetic Function, Norm, and Value as Social Facts*, trans. M.E. Suino. Ann Arbor: University of Michigan.

Murray, L., and Andrews, L. (2000) *The Social Baby*. Richmond, UK: CP Publishing.

Nelson, K. (1989) *Narratives from the Crib*. Harvard, MA: Harvard University Press.

Newman, M. (2009) 'That's all concept: it's nothing real': Reality and lyrical meaning in rap. In S. Alim, A. Ibrahim, and A. Pennycook (eds) *Global Linguistic Flows: Hip Hop Cultures, Youth Identities and the Politics of Language*. London: Routledge, pp. 195–214.

Opie, I., and Opie, P. (2001/1959) *The Language and Lore of Schoolchildren*. New York: Review Books.

Pahl, K. (2007) Creativity in events and practices: A lens for understanding children's multimodal texts. *Literacy*, 41(2): 81–87.

Paley, V.G. (1981) *Wally's Stories*. Cambridge, MA: Harvard University Press.

Pennycook, A.D. (2007) 'The rotation gets thick. The constraints get thin': Creativity, recontextualization, and difference. *Applied Linguistics*, 28(4): 579–596.

Pope, R. (2005) *Creativity: Theory, History, Practice*. London: Routledge.

Pringle, E. (2008) Artists' perspectives on art practice and pedagogy. In J. Sefton-Green (ed.) *Creative Learning*. London: Creative Partnerships, pp. 41–50.

Pritchard, R., and Honeycutt, R. (2008) The process approach to writing instruction. In C. MacArthur, S. Graham, and J. Fitzgerald (eds) *Handbook of Writing Research*. New York: Guildford, pp. 275–290.

Rampton, B. (2006) *Language in Late Modernity: Interaction in an Urban School*. Cambridge: Cambridge University Press.

Rojas-Drummond, S.M., Albarrán, C.D., and Littleton, K.S. (2008) Collaboration, creativity and the co-construction of oral and written text. *Thinking Skills and Creativity*, 3: 177–191.

Rosen, B. (1988) *And None of it was Nonsense: The Power of Storytelling in School*. London: Mary Glasgow.

Sawyer, K.R. (2004) Creative teaching: Collaborative discussion as disciplined improvisation. *Educational Researcher*, 33(3): 12–20.

Schillinger, T., Meyer, T., and Vinz, R. (2010) Poetry immersion. *English in Education*, 44(2): 110–125.

Smitherman, G. (2007) The power of rap: The black idiom and the new black poetry. In S.H. Alim and J. Baugh, *Talking Black Talk: Language, Education and Social Change*. New York: Teachers' College.

Stein, P. (2004) Reconfiguring the past and the present: Performing literacy histories in a Johannesburg classroom. *TESOL Quarterly*. 517–528.

Swann, J., Pope, R., and Carter, R. (eds) (2011) *Creativity in Language and Literature: The State of the Art*. Basingstoke: Palgrave Macmillan.

Tannen, D. (1989/2007) *Talking Voices: Repetition, Dialogue and Imagery in Conversational Discourse*. Cambridge: Cambridge University Press.

Thomson, P., Hall, C., and Russell, L. (2006) An arts project failed, censored *or*...? A critical incident approach to artist-school partnerships. *Changing English*, 13(1): 29–44.

Trevarthen, C., and Aitken, K. (2001) Infant intersubjectivity: Research, theory, and clinical applications. *Journal of Child Psychology and Psychiatry*, 42(1): 3–48.

Trickey, S., and Topping, K. (2004) Philosophy for children: A systematic review. *Research Papers in Education*, 19(3): 365–380.

Vass, E. (2007) Exploring processes of collaborative creativity: The role of emotions in children's joint creative writing. *Thinking Skills and Creativity*, 2: 107–117.

Vološinov, V.N. (1929/1973) *Marxism and the Philosophy of Language*, trans. L. Matejka and I.R. Titunik. Cambridge, MA: Harvard University Press.

Vygotsky, L. (1978) *Mind in Society: The Development of Higher Psychological Processes*. M. Cole, V. John-Steiner, S. Scribner, and E. Souberman (eds). Cambridge, MA: Harvard University Press.

Walsh, C. (2007) Creativity as capital in the literacy classroom: Youth as multimodal designers. *Literacy*, 41(2): 74–80.

Wegerif, R. (2005) Reason and creativity in classroom dialogues. *Language and Education*, 19(3): 223–237.

Wilson, S., and Ball, D. (1997) Helping teachers meet the standards: new challenges for teacher educators. *The Elementary School Journal*, 97(2): 121–138.

Chapter 21
Educational Dialogues

Karen Littleton and Neil Mercer

Introduction

In this chapter we will consider the significance of talk and social interaction for classroom-based learning. We will discuss what research tells us about the educational role of spoken language in classroom settings and how its effective use might be promoted. Our discussion will encompass both a consideration of how teachers can use talk to help children learn and how knowledge and understanding can be jointly constructed by pupils talking and working together relatively autonomously in the classroom. In recent decades, classroom talk has been the subject of research in an increasing number of countries; we will draw on that international research in our discussion. Diverse research methods have been used, but methodology is outside the scope of our discussion here (see Kumpulainen, Hmelo-Silver, and Cesar, 2009; Mercer, 2009; Mercer, Littleton, and Wegerif, 2009; Rex, Steadman, and Graciano, 2006 for relevant methodological reviews). As we will explain, the focus on the significance of social interaction for learning, and language as one of the principal tools for constructing knowledge and understanding, derives from socio-cultural theory and has its roots in the seminal work of Lev Vygotsky. Although the theoretical base for socio-cultural research has been developed considerably since his original specifications, and is still developing (see for example, Daniels, 2001), we would argue that language should still be accorded prime place as a cognitive and cultural tool for the pursuit of education. We draw on psychological and linguistic research to highlight characteristic patterns and functions of talk in the classroom, and argue that it is vital to distinguish linguistic form from language function. From our review of relevant research, we also conclude that improvements to the quality of education in the classroom can be achieved by focusing on the effectiveness of strategies for engaging students in spoken dialogue.

Socio-cultural Theory and the Functions of Language

Detailed explanations of the socio-cultural approach to education can be found elsewhere (see for example, Daniels, 2001 and Wells and Claxton, 2002). In summary, however, socio-cultural

International Handbook of Research on Children's Literacy, Learning, and Culture, First Edition.
Edited by Kathy Hall, Teresa Cremin, Barbara Comber, and Luis C. Moll.
© 2013 John Wiley & Sons, Ltd. Published 2013 by John Wiley & Sons, Ltd.

theory suggests that if we are to understand the nature of thinking, learning, and development we need to understand the fundamentally social and communicative nature of human life. While not denying the significance of individual capabilities and activities in processes of learning and cognitive development, socio-cultural theorists argue that intellectual growth is an interactional accomplishment realized largely through dialogue and that the quality of education is crucially dependent upon the nature and quality of talk between students and teachers. Classroom interactions both instantiate and constitute the historical development, cultural values, and social practices of the societies and communities in which educational institutions are situated (see Mercer and Littleton, 2007, 2010; Rojas-Drummond *et al.*, 2010). Seen from a socio-cultural perspective, then, education is a cultural process, shaped by the history of a community, which enables each new generation to develop knowledge and understanding. Spoken language plays a key role as a mediator of that development, on both the social and psychological planes.

Language was characterized by Vygotsky (1978 [1934]) as being both a cultural tool (for the construction and sharing of knowledge among members of a community or society on the social plane) and a psychological tool (for structuring the processes and content of individual thought on the psychological plane). He proposed that there is an inextricable interrelationship between these two kinds of use, which can be summarized in the claim that 'intermental' (social, interactional) activity forges 'intramental' (individual) cognitive functioning. The creation of meaning is thus both an interpersonal and intrapersonal process, with ways of thinking and learning being embedded in ways of using language. As we have explained elsewhere (Littleton and Mercer, 2010), the implication of this is that educational success, and failure, may be explained partly by the quality of educational dialogues rather than being just the result of: 'the intrinsic capability of individual students or the didactic presentational skills of individual teachers, or the quality of the educational methods and materials being used' (p. 272) (see also Mercer 1995, 2000; Mercer and Littleton, 2007, 2010; Rojas-Drummond, 2000). This gives the study of talk in educational settings a special significance, and implies that its effective use in classrooms is crucial.

While Vygotsky's seminal ideas have informed, and continue to inform, educational research it is evident that in his writings the significance of language is characterized in very general terms – as a single homogeneous mediating tool. However, contemporary scholars are emphasizing the need to move beyond a conception of language as a unitary tool. Taking a socio-cultural perspective, Wells (1999), describes language as a 'toolkit' rather than a single tool. The tools within it can be identified with specialized ways of using language, such as those used in academic subjects, professional spheres, and technical work. Following Halliday (1993) systemic functional linguists call these 'genres'; but as Martin (1993) makes clear, they are not using this term to refer merely to varieties of text, but to distinguish the ways that members of communities use language to pursue collective goals. Vygotsky's conception of the educational functions of language has been elaborated by those linguists, such as Christie and Martin (1997) and Gibbons (2002). They have shown how the educational process must involve children being inducted into the use of particular ways with words. From a psychological perspective, Littleton and Howe (2010, p. 5) have suggested that what is needed are: 'research-based accounts of educational dialogues, and productive interaction, that are sensitive to the variety of forms and functions of language as used in pursuit of teaching and learning in classroom settings.' Their assertion is that plurality and complexity are ignored at our peril. This is because: 'if we are to be able to conceptualize, resource and promote productive educational dialogues, then we need a secure research evidence base from which to develop practical theories of educational dialogues rooted in classroom realities' (Littleton and Howe, 2010, p. 5). Recognizing this, in this chapter we highlight the research evidence base that underscores the variety of forms and functions of language use in classroom settings. As much of the research in this area has focused on understanding the nature and significance of teacher-led whole class interaction – a form of interaction that has been said to be ubiquitous across cultures, teachers and school subjects (see for example, Alexander 2001) – we begin our discussion with this body of work.

Teacher-led Whole Class Interaction

The linguists Sinclair and Coulthard (1975), in their classic work, suggested that the basic unit of most whole class interaction is a three-turn *IRF exchange*, as exemplified below:

TEACHER: So what is the capital of Sweden? (I)
PUPIL: Is it Stockholm? (R)
TEACHER: That's right, very good, Stockholm, remember we talked about this yesterday (F)

This is a pattern of interaction in which a teacher will initiate (I) a topic or issue for discussion, typically through posing a question or questions to which pupils usually provide responses (R) on which the teacher offers feedback (F). Once one is aware of the existence of IRF exchanges, they become strikingly apparent in any transcription of classroom talk. The IRF exchange is now considered to be such a well-established feature of classroom interaction that it has often been referred to as a 'traditional' structure (e.g., Cazden, 2001) and a high frequency of occurrence continues (e.g., Hardman, 2008). While they can have a variety of functions (Wells, 1999) as typically used, IRF exchanges are often found to result in dialogue of a limited kind – largely because teachers use 'closed' questions as initiations (e.g., Alexander 2004, 2008; Galton *et al.*, 1999; Mercer and Littleton 2007). Of course, closed questions can have a very useful function, such as enabling a teacher to assess what relevant factual knowledge students have already gained – and few educational researchers today would argue that teachers should not use them. However, closed questions do not usually permit a range of contributions from students, nor do they typically support cumulative knowledge building or the gradual development of a coherent, progressive intellectual 'journey' (Littleton and Howe, 2010). The concern is that if they are the only kind of questions teachers ask, potentially valuable opportunities for productive dialogue can be lost or squandered (Littleton and Howe, 2010, p. 4). This is because, as Hardman (2008, p. 133) explains, the: ' "recitation script" of closed teacher questions, brief student answers and minimal feedback . . . requires students to report someone else's thinking rather than think for themselves, and to be evaluated on their compliance for doing so.' Through the use of IRFs, much of the talk teachers invite from pupils is what Douglas Barnes has termed 'presentational,' being proffered for knowledge display and teacher evaluation rather than for knowledge building, engagement, and onward progressive dialogue (Barnes, 2008). Reviewing international studies of teaching reading, Wolf, Crosson, and Resnick (2006) concluded that when teachers merely check and evaluate students' comprehension by seeking yes-no answers to a 'closed' question, this does not help develop students' high-level reading skills. From this point of view, it might be thought that the very frequent use of IRF exchanges by teachers should be discouraged. However, Wolf, Crosson, and Resnick (2006) also concluded that when teachers use questions to encourage students to express and elaborate their ideas (for example by asking 'How did you know that?' 'Why?'), this does develop students' comprehension skills. Teachers can also ask not just one, but several students for reasons and justifications for their views before going into a topic, or ask students to comment on each other's views (Dawes, 2008). So, as Wells (1999), has also argued, teachers' questions can sometimes serve very useful functions in the development of children's learning, and help to develop their own use of language as a tool for thinking. In analyzing classroom talk, one must avoid confusing language forms with their functions and recognize that the skilful use of questions and the 'spiraling' of IRFs can enable a teacher to lead a class through a complex sequence of ideas (Rojas-Drummond and Mercer, 2004) which can result in useful discussion (Alexander, 2004; Cazden, 2001; Wells 1999). That said, the restricted and linear usage of IRF exchanges to elicit only a series of brief pupil responses has resulted in calls for teacher talk to be more 'dialogic.'

Dialogic teaching (Alexander, 2004) is that in which both teachers and pupils make significant and sustained contributions to classroom talk – contributions which enable children to articulate their ideas and reflect upon them such that that their thinking on a given idea progresses. It is a concept that is specifically intended to emphasize how teachers can foster and encourage students' active participation in extended dialogues and is indicated by certain features of classroom interaction:

- questions are structured so as to provoke thoughtful answers;
- answers provoke further questions and are seen as the building blocks of dialogue rather than its terminal point; and
- individual teacher-pupil and pupil-pupil exchanges are chained into coherent lines of enquiry rather than left stranded and disconnected. (Alexander, 2004, p. 32.)

Our own characterization of dialogic teaching (Mercer and Littleton, 2007, p. 42) is that in which:

- students are given opportunities and encouragement to question, state points of view, and comment on ideas and issues that arise in lessons;
- the teacher engages in discussions with students that explore and support the development of their understanding of content;
- the teacher takes students' contributions into account in developing the subject theme of the lesson and in devising activities that enable students to pursue their understanding themselves, through talk and other activity;
- the teacher uses talk to provide a cumulative, continuing, contextual frame to enable students' involvement with the new knowledge they are encountering.

Mortimer and Scott have also examined the nature and functions of classroom-dialogue (Scott, 1998; Mortimer and Scott, 2003) focusing specifically on the nature and significance of dialogic teaching in secondary science classrooms. Their research has drawn attention to ways in which dialogue with a teacher can enable students to adopt a scientific perspective on natural phenomena and the systematic study of them. Crucially, however, their work has indicated that effective dialogic teaching uses a judicious combination of authoritative talk and dialogue. Different types of teacher talk vary in the extent to which they position the teacher as 'expert' (through the use of authoritative talk involving the use of closed questions, informing, and instructing) and the extent to which they offer possibilities for substantial contributions by students (through the use of dialogue characterized by the use of open questions, listening, and the discussion of problems/misunderstandings). Mortimer and Scott insist that these different types of talk do not constitute 'better' or 'worse' teaching strategies in any absolute sense. The implication of this is that even in the classrooms of 'dialogic teachers' classroom talk need not always be 'dialogic.' There will be occasions when the teacher justifiably feels that it is not appropriate to explore pupils' ideas and encourage an extended discussion of them. The teacher may instead decide that the time is right to focus on new curriculum content or instruct students in a procedure. The key, then, is in the teacher's application of a varied repertoire of ways of using the diversity of language as a toolkit for teaching and learning. It is the strategic balance and interplay of authoritative and dialogic discourse that matters.

Before leaving our consideration of teacher-led whole class interaction it is salient to note that the metaphors of 'orchestration' and 'improvisation' are relevant to the conduct of successful dialogic teaching. The notion of orchestration is relevant as it draws attention to the ways in which a teacher makes moment-by-moment shifts between what is foregrounded and what is backgrounded, taking into consideration the contributions of students while doing so (Littleton *et al.*, 2010, p. 131). Such responsive creativity on the part of the teacher is also encapsulated by the idea that teaching can be construed as a form of disciplined improvisation – a process which enables the emergent exploration of students' ideas within a supportive structure or frame:

> Conceiving of teaching as improvisation emphasizes the interactional and responsive creativity of a teacher working together with a unique group of students. In particular, effective classroom discussion is improvisational, because the flow of the class is unpredictable and emerges from the actions of all participants, both teachers and students. Several studies have found that as teachers become more experienced, they improvise more ... Creative teaching is disciplined improvisation because it always occurs within broad structures and frameworks. Expert teachers use routines and activity structures more than novice teachers; but they are able to invoke and apply these routines in a creative, improvisational fashion ... Several researchers have noted that the most effective classroom interaction balances structure and script with flexibility and improvisation (Sawyer, 2004, pp. 12–13).

Dialogic teaching thus involves helping students to improvise and to find their own voice and way of seeing things. It enables them to share their ideas, methods, and ways of thinking and to formulate and ask their own questions. The world of pupils' improvisations is inevitably unpredictable, and thus if they are to feel comfortable with dialogic teaching, teachers need to have secure disciplinary knowledge and also to be enabled to talk and work in this way (Sawyer, 2004). However, while researchers can characterize and identify dialogic teaching, it may be a challenge for teachers to transform its characterization into practice (Scott *et al.*, 2010). In this respect teachers may learn much from exploring each others' practice. Scott and his collaborators (2010), for example, suggest that 'dialogic teaching routines' surrounding the teaching of key concepts and ideas should be opened up for appraisal by practitioners and then put to use by these teachers with their classes with some awareness and foresight of the questions and issues that may arise. Of course, providing examples of dialogic teaching by one teacher does not straightforwardly enable another to engage in dialogic practice, and: 'there are a multitude of challenges to be faced – not least those that are involved in getting to know the discipline-specific, intellectual terrain for a particular piece of teaching' (Littleton and Howe, 2010, p. 268). A process for pedagogic development used by Japanese teachers, known as 'lesson study,' could provide a suitable framework for the development of dialogic teaching. This process has recently been adapted for use by British teachers (Dudley, 2011). In a lesson study process, groups of teachers identify an area of need in pupil learning and progress in their classes that is need of improvement. They then inquire into developments in teaching that are likely to have an impact on this aspect of pupil learning. The teachers next plan a 'research' or 'study' lesson together, aimed specifically at addressing the problem they have identified. Having jointly planned the research lesson in detail, one person teaches the lesson and the others observe. They then critically discuss what happens, and build plans accordingly. In the British project led by Dudley (2011), teachers also prepared for these joint sessions by setting appropriate 'ground rules' for discussion (as discussed in relation to small group activity below).

Small Group Work

Given the calls for more 'dialogic' approaches to teaching that have arisen in part from the reservations that have been expressed in relation to the restrictiveness of teacher-led whole class interaction, is it the case that pupils engage in open, extended discussion and debate when they are working with their peers? As we will see, the findings of research on group-work in classrooms represent something of a paradox. This is because, on the one hand, research has shown that collaborative learning is potentially beneficial for the development of children's skills and understanding; but on the other hand it also has shown that in the majority of classrooms, most of time, group-work is of little educational value. To resolve this paradox, we need to consider what factors are involved in making collaborative activity productive.

The classic investigations undertaken by Galton and colleagues (Galton *et al.*, 1980, 1999) have highlighted the paradox of children working everywhere *in* groups but rarely *as* groups (see also Alexander, 2001, 2004). This meant that while children could often be observed seated in close proximity at a table in a group this did not mean that they were necessarily collaborating or talking and working effectively together. Typically they were observed working in parallel on individual tasks or informally chatting about out of school activities. A notable specific example of the problem was reported in the Spoken Language and New Technology (SLANT) project (see Wegerif and Scrimshaw, 1997). Detailed analysis of UK-based primary school children working in small groups at a computer suggested that the activity was not typically task-focused or productive. The interaction between peers was often inequitable and in some cases the groups of children seemed to ignore each other altogether. They were frequently observed taking turns at the computer, each pursuing their own ideas when it was 'their turn.' Many groups' talk involved them in fiercely disputational encounters and interpersonal conflict. So while there was certainly a lot of talk in evidence, it was seemingly to little educational effect.

Research has shown that one of the strongest influences on how children talk during group-work is the way their teacher talks with them (Webb, Nemer, and Ing, 2006). Yet it seems that teachers give little priority to their role for guiding and modeling children's effective use of talk (Fisher and Larkin, 2008). Some studies have indicated that the quality of collaboration between children can be enhanced if teachers foster an atmosphere of trust and mutual respect in the classroom (Kutnick and Colwell, 2010). The starting point for the research on classroom talk by ourselves and colleagues (see for example Wegerif and Dawes, 2004), however, has been a Vygotskian concern with enabling children to use language as a tool for reasoning, and with helping teachers use the best strategies for enabling that development. From our perspective, while developing such a relational climate in the classroom is of course desirable, children need to be enabled to do more than engage with each other in a positive and supportive way. Rather, they should also be enabled to use educationally efficacious forms of language as tools to collectively build knowledge and understanding together. Our view is that children need to be inducted into ways of using language to 'interthink,' so that they learn to use talk to reason together and build constructively and critically on each other's ideas. As this cannot be expected to happen 'naturally,' through simply participating and being immersed in the ongoing life and work of the classroom, our argument is that children need to be explicitly inducted into ways of talking and working together. In other words forms of educationally effective talk and the 'ground rules' implicated in them need to become familiar and accessible to pupils.

Exploratory Talk

A particularly educationally effective type, or genre, of talk is a form of talk called 'exploratory talk' (a term taken from the pioneering work on classroom talk by Barnes, 1969). This is talk in which partners engage critically but constructively with each other's ideas. Statements and suggestions are offered for joint consideration. These may be challenged and counter-challenged, but challenges are justified and alternative hypotheses are offered. Partners all actively participate, and opinions are sought and considered before decisions are jointly made. Compared with cumulative talk (in which speakers build positively but uncritically on what the others have said) and disputational talk (which is characterized by disagreement and individualized decision making), in exploratory talk knowledge is made more publicly accountable and reasoning is more visible in the talk (Wegerif, Mercer and Dawes, 1999; Mercer and Littleton, 2007, pp. 58–59).

There are some obvious synergies between the concept of exploratory talk and what some educational researchers have described as 'accountable talk' (Resnick, 1999; Michaels and O'Connor, 2002):

> Talking with others about ideas and work is fundamental to learning. But not all talk sustains learning or creates intelligence. For classroom talk to promote learning, it must have certain characteristics that make it *accountable*. Accountable talk seriously responds to and further develops what others in the group have said. It puts forth and demands knowledge that is accurate and relevant to the issue under discussion. Accountable talk uses evidence in ways appropriate to the discipline (for example, proofs in mathematics, data from investigations in science, textual details in literature, documentary sources in history). Finally, it follows established norms of good reasoning. Accountable talk sharpens students' thinking by reinforcing their ability to use knowledge appropriately. As such, it helps develop the skills and the habits of mind that constitute intelligence-in-practice. Teachers can intentionally create the norms and skills of accountable talk in their classrooms. (Resnick, 1999, p. 5.)

'Exploratory talk,' or 'accountable' talk, thus constitutes a *distinctive social mode of thinking* – a very particular way of using the tool of language, which is not only the embodiment of critical thinking, but which is also essential for successful participation in 'educated' communities of discourse (Mercer and Littleton, 2007). It was the dual recognition of both the potential and the relative scarcity of exploratory talk in classrooms that led us to explore how its use might be promoted. This concern to promote productive educational dialogues reflects a belief, shared by other researchers that talk in educational contexts is profoundly important and yet is commonly not of the right quality (Alexander 2004; see also various contributions to Mercer and Hodgkinson 2008).

Promoting Effective Educational Dialogues

The *Thinking Together* classroom-based intervention program was designed to transform the character and context of talk in educational settings, by inducting children into using exploratory talk (for a fuller account see Mercer and Littleton 2007). Children aged between 6 and 13 have been involved in the program of work, together with their teachers, but research with the age group 8 to 11, has been the most sustained. The *Thinking Together* program focuses on the use of talk that integrates teacher-led whole class dialogue and group activity. Its primary aim is to ensure that children and teachers construct and work according to a set of collectively generated ground rules for exploratory talk, such that they enter collaborative activities with a shared conception of how they can talk and reason together effectively. The program comprises an initial set of *Thinking Together* lessons created by researchers working collectively with teachers (as included in Dawes 2008, 2012; Dawes, Mercer, and Wegerif, 2003; Dawes and Sams, 2004). The initial sequence of core lessons constitute activities for jointly negotiating and establishing a set of class 'ground rules' that embody the essential qualities of exploratory talk (serving to open up and maintain a 'dialogic space' (Wegerif, 2010) in which alternative solutions to problems are generated and allowed to develop and compete as ideas without threatening either group solidarity or individual identity). That is, these lessons are mainly aimed at developing children's understanding and use of exploratory talk. The complete program includes lessons that relate to specific curriculum subjects and consists of both teacher-led sessions and group activities (some of which use specially designed computer-based tasks based on curriculum topics). School-based evaluations of the program for enhancing the quality of children's talk and educational achievement have been positive and have evidenced the positive effects of the program for increasing children's use of exploratory talk and their collective and individual performance on non-verbal reasoning tests (see Mercer and Littleton, 2007).

Although the *Thinking Together* evaluation work was initially focused on examining whether there were changes in children's talk and reasoning as a consequence of involvement in the program, this research has also demonstrated how teachers make a powerful contribution to the creation of contexts for learning in their classrooms. Teachers should be seen as powerful models for their pupils – this is because how they talk, act, and structure classroom activities afford significant exemplars of how learning and talking together are to be done. Research suggests that where *Thinking Together* is most efficacious the teacher models and exemplifies exploratory ways of talking during whole class sessions – for example, asking 'Why?' at appropriate times, giving examples of reasons for opinions and checking that a range of views is heard. Also, in plenary sessions at the end of the lessons the teacher reviews with the whole class what has been done and what they might have learned from it. The organized continuity of this experience helps children to consolidate learning and gain educational benefits from their activity. It is by using and modeling exploratory ways of talking that the teacher acts as the children's 'discourse guide,' showing them how to use talk to address problems and solve them. In these ways, the *Thinking Together* research integrates well with research on effective whole class teaching discussed earlier (e.g., Alexander 2004; Mortimer and Scott 2003; Wells, 1999). Information Communications Technology (ICT) also has a distinctive role to play in integrating peer group dialogue with teacher-student interaction (Wegerif and Dawes, 2004). This is exemplified well by research involving a technique called *prescriptive tutoring* (Soong, Mercer, and Siew, 2010). Used in secondary science education, its aim is to reveal students' misconceptions and misunderstandings in their pre-examination study of the physics curriculum by getting them to solve physics problems with a partner. Although both in the same classroom, the partners use computer-mediated communication to solve the problems, and their dialogue is saved as text. Students are encouraged by their teacher to agree on a set of 'ground rules' for making their discussions suitably explicit and equitable (as described in relation to the *Thinking Together* research earlier). By agreement with the students, their teacher is allowed to read their online dialogues and use them as a basis for subsequent whole class instruction and discussion. A study of this approach in a Singapore secondary school showed that students in the experimental group significantly outperformed students in a matched control class on postintervention tests of understanding of physics concepts (Soong and Mercer, 2011).

Recent research also indicates that use of the interactive whiteboard can provide both a tool and an environment that can encourage the creation of a shared dialogic space within which children's peer-based co-constructed knowledge building can take place (Mercer *et al.*, 2010). A teacher can provide a very effective 'scaffolding' for children who are working together on a problem-solving activity through the combined use of the whiteboard and contingent, supportive talk (Warwick *et al.*, 2010). However, this only occurs where there is active support from the teacher for fostering collaborative, dialogic activity in the classroom and where the teacher is able to devise tasks that use board affordances to promote active collaborative learning and pupil agency (Hennessy *et al.*, 2011).

Beneficial changes in the nature of pupils' talk and their learning outcomes suggest that we should be supporting children to appropriate new norms ('ground rules') for their classroom discussions. This notion is, however, resisted by some commentators, such as Lambirth (2006), who reject the idea that the ground rules for exploratory talk constitute a productive basis for joint activity. Rather, it is claimed that the linguistic identities and communicative self-confidence of children may be compromised if they are expected to shift from established sets of ground rules that operate in their out-of-school experience. Such a critique appears to be predicated on a 'subtraction' model of language learning, whereby the addition of any new language genre to a child's language repertoire is assumed to involve the deletion of some existing genre. While such a model of language learning has no secure scientific foundation, it signals: 'that for some educators there are ideological reasons why they would not advocate adopting a "ground rules" approach to the promotion of productive educational dialogues' (Littleton and Howe, 2010, p. 268). There is also a concern that teaching interventions, such as *Thinking Together*, that focus on the efficacy of establishing inclusive ground rules for educational dialogues neglect some of the harsher social realities of the classroom. Lefstein (2010) for instance suggests that an emphasis on plurality, openness, and equality that inheres in the commitment to promoting pupil questioning, answering, and the exchange of ideas may be in conflict with some social goals that are often pursued by students in classroom contexts. Such goals can include establishing their dominance and self-promotion. Clearly, social goals could in principle be considered within a ground rules approach, although research to date has not addressed this issue. The key issue is that in most classrooms, the dominant ground-rules are left tacit and implicit and thus remain unexamined and unquestioned. It is hard to see how encouraging pupils (and their teachers) to consider language itself as one vital aspect of the world about which they can gain metacognitive awareness and understanding, and develop a broader expressive repertoire, can be regarded as undermining their educational progress and social empowerment.

Onward Research: Developing Situationally Sensitive Accounts of Productive Educational Dialogues

While we have advocated the value of exploratory talk as a particularly effective genre of educational dialogue, it is important to acknowledge that what constitutes educationally efficacious dialogue is inextricably linked to the nature of the task in hand. For example, recent work analyzing children's creative story writing suggests that for open-ended, divergent tasks where there is no 'right' answer, 'co-constructive talk' (in which children integrate, elaborate and/or reformulate each other's contributions to negotiate meaning without necessarily engaging in explicit, reasoned argument) can be very effective (Rojas-Drummond, Albarrán, and Littleton, 2008; Rojas-Drummond *et al.*, 2010). While this does not negate the educational importance of children being able to use exploratory talk, it illustrates the need to avoid the over-simplification of how talk is involved in different kinds of collaborative intellectual tasks: different genres of talk will have different functionalities. This is well illustrated by Vass's work on children's joint creative writing (2004; Vass and Littleton, 2010). Vass's functional analyses of children's collective writing suggest that the shared processes of content generation were typically supported by the uncritical accumulation and sharing of ideas. More reflective phases of work involving, for example, the evaluation of the 'appropriateness' of a suggestion, were resourced by detached perspective-taking and explicit argumentation. So here a characterization of productive educational dialogue emerges in the movements across and the interplay between these different forms of talk – rather the privileging of a particular form. This draws attention to the significance of the patterning of dialogue over time and the relationship between time, talk, and learning that is important to classroom education (Mercer and Littleton, 2007; Mercer, 2008). It could be both theoretically and practically useful to investigate further how classroom talk is used by teachers and learners to represent past shared experience, carry ideas forward from one occasion to another, approach future activities, and achieve learning outcomes.

Concluding Remarks

Research has shown clearly that the ways children learn from talk in the classroom, and the impact of social interaction upon their psychological development and educational progress, depend a great deal on the range and quality of the talk in which they are engaged. Our current understanding of the nature and functions of spoken language in the classroom provides a strong basis for the development of more effective pedagogy. Socio-cultural theory provides a good explanatory framework for understanding the educational functions of language, and of its relationship to the development of reasoning and the 'ways with words' that are associated with effective collaborative learning and the content matter of particular curriculum subjects. This is therefore a field of study in which theoretical development, empirical research, and practical application can be very effectively combined.

References

Alexander, R. (2001) *Culture and Pedagogy: International Comparisons in Primary Education*. Oxford: Blackwell.

Alexander, R. (2004) *Towards Dialogic Teaching: Rethinking Classroom Talk*. Cambridge: Dialogos.

Alexander, R. (2008) Culture, dialogue and learning: Notes on an emerging pedagogy. In N. Mercer and S. Hodgkinson (eds) *Exploring Talk in Schools*. London: Sage, pp. 91–114.

Barnes, D. (1969) The language of the secondary classroom. In D. Barnes, J.N. Britton, and H. Rosen (eds) *Language, the Learner and the School*. Harmondsworth: Penguin, pp. 21–38.

Barnes, D. (2008) Exploratory talk for learning. In N. Mercer and S. Hodgkinson (eds) *Exploring Talk in School*. London: Sage, pp. 1–16.

Cazden, C. (2001) *Classroom Discourse: The Language of Teaching and Learning*. Portsmouth, NH: Heinemann.

Christie, F., and Martin, J. (1997) *Genre and Institutions: Social Processes in the Workplace and School*. London: Cassell.

Daniels, H. (2001) *Vygotsky and Pedagogy*. London: Routledge.

Dawes, L. (2008) Encouraging students' contribution to dialogue during science. *School Science Review*, 90(3): 101–107.

Dawes, L. (2012) *Talking Points: Discussion Activities in the Primary Classroom*. London: David Fulton.

Dawes, L., Mercer, N., and Wegerif, R. (2003) *Thinking Together: A Programme of Activities for Developing Thinking Skills at KS2*. Birmingham: Questions.

Dawes, L., and Sams, C. (2004) *Talk Box: Speaking and Listening Activities for Learning at Key Stage 1*. London: David Fulton.

Dudley, P. (2011) Lesson Study Development in England: From school networks to national policy. *International Journal for Lesson and Learning Studies*, 1(1): 85–100.

Fisher, R., and Larkin, S. (2008) Pedagogy or ideological struggle? An examination of pupils' and teachers' expectations for talk in the classroom. *Language and Education*, 22(1): 1–16.

Galton, M., Hargreaves, L., Comber, C., *et al.* (1999) Changes in patterns of teacher interaction in primary classrooms: 1976–96. *British Educational Research Journal*, 25(1): 23–38.

Galton, M, Simon, B., and Croll, P. (1980) *Inside the Primary Classroom*. London: Routledge and Kegan Paul.

Gibbons, P. (2002) *Scaffolding Language, Scaffolding Learning: Teaching Second Language Learners in the Mainstream Classroom*. Portsmouth, NH: Heinemann.

Halliday, M.A.K. (1993) Towards a language-based theory of learning. *Linguistics and Education*, 5(2): 93–116.

Hardman, F. (2008) Opening-up classroom discourse: The importance of teacher feedback. In N. Mercer and S. Hodgkinson (eds) *Exploring Talk in School*. London: Sage (pp. 131–150).

Hennessy, S., Warwick, P., and Mercer, N. (2011) A dialogic inquiry approach to working with teachers in developing classroom dialogue. *Teachers College Record*, 113(9): 1906–1959.

Kumpulainen, K., Hmelo-Silver, C.E., and Cesar, M. (eds) (2009) *Investigating Classroom Interaction: Methodologies in Action*. Rotterdam: Sense Publishers.

Kutnick, P., and Colwell, J. (2010) Dialogue enhancement in classrooms: towards a relational approach for group working. In K. Littleton and C. Howe (eds) *Educational Dialogues, Understanding and Promoting Productive Interaction*. London: Routledge, pp. 192–215.

Lambirth, A. (2006) Challenging the laws of talk: Ground rules, social reproduction and the curriculum. *The Curriculum Journal*, 17(1): 59–71.

Lefstein, A. (2010) More helpful as problem than solution: some implications of situating dialogue in classrooms. In K. Littleton and C. Howe (eds) *Educational Dialogues, Understanding and Promoting Productive Interaction*. London: Routledge, pp. 170–191.

Littleton, K., and Howe, C. (2010) *Educational Dialogues: Understanding and Promoting Productive Interaction*. London: Routledge.

Littleton, K., Twiner, A., and Gillen, J. (2010) Instruction as orchestration: Multimodal connection building with the interactive whiteboard. *Pedagogies: An International Journal*, 5(2): 130–141.

Martin, J. (1993) Genre and literacy: Modeling context in educational linguistics. *Annual Review of Applied Linguistics*, 13: 141–172.

Mercer, N. (1995) *The Guided Construction of Knowledge: Talk amongst Teachers and Learners*. Clevedon: Multilingual Matters.

Mercer, N. (2000) *Words and Minds: How We Use Language to Think Together*. London: Routledge.

Mercer, N. (2008) The seeds of time: Why classroom dialogue needs a temporal analysis. *Journal of the Learning Sciences*, 17(1): 33–59.

Mercer, N. (2009) The analysis of classroom talk: Methods and methodologies. *British Journal of Educational Psychology*, 80: 1–14.

Mercer, N., and Hodgkinson, S. (eds) (2008) *Exploring Talk in School*. London: Sage.

Mercer, N., and Littleton, K. (2007) *Dialogue and the Development of Children's Thinking*. London: Routledge.

Mercer, N., and Littleton, K. (2010) The significance of educational dialogues between primary school children. In K. Littleton and C. Howe (eds) *Educational Dialogues: Understanding and Promoting Productive Interaction*. London: Routledge, pp. 271–288.

Mercer, N., Littleton, K., and Wegerif, R. (2009) Methods for studying the processes of interaction and collaborative activity in computer-based educational activities. In K. Kumpulainen, C. Hmelo-Silver, and M. César (eds) *Investigating Classroom Interaction: Methodologies in Action*. Rotterdam: Sense Publishers, pp. 27–42.

Mercer, N., Warwick, P., Kershner, R., and Kleine Staarman, J. (2010) Can the interactive whiteboard provide 'dialogic space' for children's collaborative activity? *Language and Education*, 24(4): 1–18.

Michaels, S., and O'Connor, M.C. (2002) *Accountable Talk: Classroom Conversation that Works*, CD-ROM, University of Pittsburgh.

Mortimer, E.F., and Scott, P.H. (2003) *Meaning Making in Science Classrooms*. Milton Keynes: Open University Press.

Resnick, L.B. (1999) Making America smarter. *Education Week Century Series*, 18(40): 38–40.

Rex, L., Steadman, S.C., and Graciano, M.K. (2006) Researching the complexity of classroom interaction. In L.J. Green, G. Camilli, and P.B. Elmore (eds) *Handbook of Complementary Methods in Education Research*. Mahwah, NJ: Lawrence Erlbaum, pp. 727–771.

Rojas-Drummond, S.M. (2000) Guided participation, discourse and the construction of knowledge in Mexican classrooms. In H. Cowie and D. van der Aalsvoort (eds) *Social Interaction in Learning and Instruction: The Meaning of Discourse for the Construction of Knowledge*. Exeter: Pergamon Press, pp. 193–213.

Rojas-Drummond, S., Albarrán, D., and Littleton, K. (2008) Collaboration, creativity and the construction of oral and written texts. *Thinking Skills and Creativity*, 3(3): 177–191.

Rojas-Drummond, S., Littleton, K., Hernández, F., and Zuniga, M. (2010) Dialogical interactions among peers in collaborative writing contexts. In K. Littleton and C. Howe (eds) *Educational Dialogues, Understanding and Promoting Productive Interaction*. London: Routledge, pp. 128–148.

Rojas-Drummond, S., and Mercer, N. (2004) Scaffolding the development of effective collaboration and learning, *International Journal of Educational Research*, 39: 99–111.

Sawyer, R.K. (2004) Creative teaching: Collaborative discussion as disciplined improvisation. *Educational Researcher*, 33(2): 12–20.

Scott, P. (1998) Teacher talk and meaning making in science classrooms: A Vygotskian analysis and review. *Studies in Science Education*, 32: 45–80.

Scott, P., Ametller, J., Mortimer, E., and Emberton, J. (2010) Teaching and learning disciplinary knowledge: developing the dialogic space for an answer when there isn't even a question. In K. Littleton and C. Howe (eds) *Educational Dialogues, Understanding and Promoting Productive Interaction*, London: Routledge, pp. 298–303.

Sinclair, J., and Coulthard, M. (1975) *Towards an Analysis of Discourse: The English Used by Teachers and Pupils*. London: Oxford University Press.

Soong, B., and Mercer, N. (2011) Improving students' revision of physics concepts through ICT-based co-construction and prescriptive tutoring. *International Journal of Science Education*, 33: 1055–1078.

Soong, B., Mercer, N., and Siew, S.E. (2010) Revision by means of computer-mediated peer discussions. *Physics Education*, 45: 264–269.

Vass, E. (2004) Understanding collaborative creativity: Young children's classroom-based shared creative writing. In D. Miell and K. Littleton (eds) *Collaborative Creativity*. London: Free Association Books, pp. 79–85.

Vass, E., and Littleton, K. (2010) Peer collaboration and learning in the classroom. In K. Littleton, C. Wood, and J. Kleine Staarman (eds) *International Handbook of Psychology in Education*. Leeds: Emerald, pp. 105–136.

Vygotsky, L.S. (1934/1978) *Mind in Society: The Development of Higher Psychological Processes*. Cambridge, MA: Harvard University Press.

Warwick, P., Mercer, N., Kershner, R., and Kleine Staarman, J. (2010) In the mind and in the technology: The vicarious presence of the teacher in pupils' learning of science in collaborative group activity at the interactive whiteboard. *Computers and Education*, 55: 350–362.

Webb, N., Nemer, K., and Ing, M. (2006) Small-group reflections: parallels between teacher discourse and student behavior in peer-directed groups. *Journal of the Learning Sciences*, 15(1): 63–119.

Wegerif, R. (2010) Dialogue and teaching thinking with technology: opening, expanding and deepening the 'inter-face'. In K. Littleton and C. Howe (eds) *Educational Dialogues, Understanding and Promoting Productive Interaction*. London: Routledge, pp. 304–323.

Wegerif, R., and Dawes, L. (2004) *Thinking and Learning with ICT: Raising Achievement in Primary Classrooms*. London: Routledge.

Wegerif, N., Mercer, N., and Dawes, L. (1999) From social interaction to individual reasoning: an empirical investigation of a possible socio-cultural model of cognitive development. *Learning and Instruction*, 9(6): 493–516.

Wegerif, R., and Scrimshaw, P. (eds) (1997) *Computers and Talk in the Primary Classroom*. Clevedon, UK: Multilingual Matters.

Wells, G. (1999) *Dialogic Inquiry: Towards a Sociocultural Practice and Theory of Education*. Cambridge: Cambridge University Press.

Wells, G., and Claxton, G. (eds) (2002) *Learning for Life in the 21st Century*. Oxford: Blackwell.

Wolf, M., Crosson, A., and Resnick, L. (2006) Accountable Talk in Rading Comprehension Instruction. *CSE Technical Report 670*. Learning and Research Development Center: University of Pittsburgh.

Chapter 22

Literacy and Curriculum

Language and Knowledge in the Classroom

Peter Freebody, Eveline Chan, and Georgina Barton

Introduction: Literacy In and For School

In contemporary schooling, students' learning is comprehensively and unrelievedly dependent on the development of their literacy capabilities. So mapping the relationship between literacy and curriculum would mean navigating through almost the entire corpus of educational research and theory. However, we can inquire into a more modest, but nonetheless disconcertingly large question: How are students' literacy resources worked up, worked on, put to work day to day – across the school years and across the curriculum areas? In this chapter, we outline two distinct approaches to questions of literacy development and differentiation, one from the linguistic study of language features and the other from the sociological analysis of naturally occurring interactions.

We draw attention both to the foundational, stable literacy resources that are recognizable across the curriculum areas, and to those resources that are specific to each curriculum domain. We argue that these curriculum-specific resources, while deeply consequential for pedagogy, assessment, and curriculum organization, are under-represented as focal points for theory, research, policy, and practice. It is their growing specificity, we claim, that is central to the literacy–curriculum relationship, and therefore to our understanding of students' emerging use of language to understand experience and develop school knowledge. The bulk of the chapter is concerned with introducing interactional and linguistic approaches, summarizing some conceptual and empirical works in each, and illustrating key points with exhibits from classrooms. We conclude by drawing out some directions for further research.

Literacy in the Curriculum, Across and Within

'Literacy' is a term covering a range of technologies and practices. In minimalist definitions, it refers to the use of symbols to represent language. In more expansive definitions, it incorporates the individual and social accommodations occasioned by those technologies and practices: intellectual practices, forms of debate, beliefs, relationships, community membership, modes of governance, and so on (Johnson, 2010; McKitterick, 1990; Smith, 1987; Street, 1984).

International Handbook of Research on Children's Literacy, Learning, and Culture, First Edition.
Edited by Kathy Hall, Teresa Cremin, Barbara Comber, and Luis C. Moll.
© 2013 John Wiley & Sons, Ltd. Published 2013 by John Wiley & Sons, Ltd.

Historians generally use 'literacy' as an open-textured concept (Graff, 1995) referring to 'the sequencing of standardized symbols (characters, signs or sign components) in order to graphically reproduce human speech, thought and other things in part or whole' (Fischer, 2001, p. 12), whose particular forms are shaped by the diverse uses to which literacy is put in any given setting. In the setting of twenty-first century schooling, these definitions direct our attention to the evolution of literate forms into distinct branches as the school years progress, forms that represent different kinds of 'speech, thought and other things.'

Literacy testing programs and research studies have long labeled as a fiction the belief that significant literacy learning is generally over and done with by the middle years of primary schooling. So it is puzzling to observe what is and is not attended to in the daily activities in many educational settings in the middle and secondary school years, in the preparation of middle- and secondary-years teachers, and in the lean body of literacy scholarship on those years compared to the early years of schooling (Pressley, 2004). This fiction – that 'basic' literacy learning in the first four years of formal schooling is an educational-inoculation-for-life – seems to be treated as a fiction everywhere except in actual institutional practice. The separation of literacy development and curricular learning is in fact one of the bedrocks on which is built the organizational foundation of many educational systems and programs, providing a key rationale and organizational basis for curriculum, pedagogy, and assessment.

It seems, therefore, more than just useful to insist on distinguishing two kinds of literacy demands facing students progressing through school. On the one hand, foundational capabilities underlie literacy in and for school and are called upon as resources across the school's various curriculum areas (the 'traditional basics' or 'constrained skills') (Paris, 2005). Crucially, there are, on the other hand, literacy demands that are the distinctive expression of each curriculum domain (e.g., Christie and Derewianka, 2008; Deng and Luke, 2008; Freebody and Muspratt, 2007; MacDonald, 1994; Shanahan and Shanahan, 2008). It is this latter aspect of literacy development, and significantly the institutional and pedagogical silences around it, that put teachers and students to the test daily, and that locate literacy research and theory squarely within the topic of curriculum and knowledge building.

Here we approach these issues through an examination of the details of the often-unremarked classroom activities through which students are to access classroom participation, literacy, and curricular knowledge. We do this to exemplify how the literacy–curriculum relationship is done, rather than beginning with speculations about how it could or should be done. Our examples in later sections are taken from senior secondary classrooms where the stakes are high around this relationship, even though the various pathways to these senior classrooms begin much earlier.

As an introduction, consider Exhibit 1, a two-minute excerpt from a Year 5 lesson. It shows a teacher (T) focusing students (Ss) on how to read and write about their curricular knowledge. Before reading the source text to Ss, a text about a migrant ship's voyage to Australia, T talks about previous work and about the meaning of key terms. (See the Appendix at the end of the chapter for transcription markups.) It is useful to consider this transcript as representing both interactional activities and learning activities.

We see this as a highly familiar piece of classroom talk. Considering it first as talk, in terms of the speech exchange systems (Schegloff, 2007) in which these Ss took part, we see features that are unlike ordinary conversation:

- one party takes every second turn at talk and asks all the questions;
- there is a recognizable three-part cycle whereby
  - T provides places for Ss to come in with responses, (called 'transition-relevant places'), usually by asking a question (e.g., turns 1, 3, 5) or by leaving a sentence unfinished with an upward inflection (1, 11);

Exhibit 1

1.	T	Do you remember that we had a problem with some of the things that people were saying? Who remembers what I kept saying last time? I kept commenting about^ (.) do you remember^ Ryan?
2.	S1	There was no proof about diseases^
3.	T	Good boy (.) What was the word I used? It started with 'e'
4.	S2	Evidence
5.	T	Yes (.) the <u>evidence</u>. There were a couple things you people said that we didn't have evidence for and remember I said you can't write those unless you have evidence that had something to do with disease . . . and I found a couple of things so I'll read them to you. The first one is about <u>typhus</u>. Does anyone know what typhus is?
6.	S3	A disease
7.	T	Yes it's a disease. Do you know what it causes? (1) Is it different to typhoid?
8.	Ss	((some nodding))
9.	T	Yes. Well if you get this disease you get very severe headache, rash and become very ill and it's transmitted by little mites, little insects, so when people were on the ship that's where it spread very rapidly. Now this is an article written on the 22nd Dec 1852 about typhus hitting the ship. ((reading)) THE CLIPPER ARRIVED TODAY AFTER A DISASTROUS VOYAGE FROM ENGLAND WITH 96 OF ITS 646 MIGRANT PASSENGERS DYING OF TYPHUS. THE SHIP'S COMPANY AND PASSENGERS HAVE BEEN TAKEN TO THE NEW QUARANTINE STATION AT POINT NEPEAN. MANY ARE ILL AND SCORES OF THEM APPEAR TO BE IN A TERMINAL STATE. What does that mean^ terminal state?
10.	S4	Very bad
11.	T	Very <u>very</u> bad (.) and they look like they will^ (2)
12.	S4	Die
13.	T	Will die.

- ◦ an S provides some response; and
- ◦ T provides some feedback on that response (e.g., turns 1–3, 5–7);

- T's feedback can include repeats of S's answer (4–5, 6–7, 10–11), new questions (3, 7), reminders (5), or new information (9);
- if a transition-relevant place is not accepted by the students within a certain time, T will offer a hint (3) or new invitation (7).

Many of these features have been summarized under the heading of the long-documented three-part cycle, Initiation-Response-Feedback (IRF) (Mehan, 1978; Sinclair and Coulthard, 1975) that is a marker of pedagogical exchanges.

Considering this as a learning event, we can make at least three observations:

- T locates this interaction within the flow of Ss' previous and prospective work (1, 5);
- Ss' contributions are repeated by T (4–5, 6–7) or reworked into new words (2–5); words from the text are also reworked (9–13); and
- this reworking may involve common or formal vocabulary (2–5) or specific textual conventions (5).

Much of T's work takes place in the third part of the cycle, which has been described as 'particularly important because its relevance and influence take shape across the contingencies generated by the students' second turn,' and it does its work of 'steering the discourse in particular directions and exploring alternative interactional trajectories in the course of action' (Lee, 2007, p. 203).

Finally, this talk is simultaneously a lesson on disease and on how to talk, read, and write about disease in Social Studies. It is not a lesson to professional historians on the disease or on the voyage of this ship, nor is it a chat about these topics with children out of school. Its features show that it is a lesson to novices a little way along in their understanding of both the topics and the ways in which 'you people' should talk, read, and write about them in this school subject.

We expand on the exchange and lesson structures (what we term the 'first curriculum' and the 'formal curriculum' respectively) in sections below. Our interest is in how teachers and students confront and manage changing, curriculum-specific literacy practices in text and talk. We take it as profitable to see this ongoing process, the way teachers and students see it: as facing an increasingly distinctive set of materials, language, images, and interpretive practices that in turn present them with an increasingly distinctive set of demands, demands that relate directly to how well they can 'create, communicate, and evaluate knowledge' in different curricular settings (Shanahan and Shanahan, 2008, p. 54). We turn to our two illustrative approaches to these issues to develop these points.

Interaction Analysis

Social science approaches to literacy and curriculum include sociology, anthropology, ethnography, and ethnomethodology. These focus on the patterns in, and the meanings drawn from everyday practice. Their interests include documenting how categories of practice (e.g., 'learning,' 'literacy,' 'knowledge') are variously defined, built, and oriented to in formal and informal settings, and the consequences of these categories of practice for the structuring of experience and practice.

Such approaches explore the relation of literacy to curriculum via the notion of participation in the activities of communities of practice, shown to develop specialized ways of using language in particular social and cultural contexts – homes, schools, worksites, churches, and so on (Barton *et al.*, 2007). These communities and their practices are also understood in their historical, political and economic contexts (Gee, 2004; Luke, 1988; Luke, 1989).

Social science approaches have consistently acknowledged the distinctiveness of literate practices associated with different curriculum domains: the texts students read, the knowledge they bring to content, and the relationships between teachers and learners (Comber *et al.*, 2002; Jacobs, 2008; Lee and Spratley, 2010; Moje *et al.*, 2011).

Within this category we find the ethnomethodological tradition, which we draw on by way of illustration. A point of departure for ethnomethodologists is that mundane social activities involve the coordination, largely through talk-in-interaction, of particular, generally unremarked methods that the members of a society engage in to accomplish the activity at hand. Simultaneously, and by the same methods, members make their activities visibly recognizable and rational (e.g., 'dinner-party chats,' 'science lessons'). Ethnomethodologists do not evaluate the activities under scrutiny against some external criteria, but rather document the details of how these particular people interacted to make sense, then and there, visibly, reportably, and adequately as part of the practical purposes at hand. Thus, social and/or institutional order is built through practice rather than being determined by, or reflected from outside the everyday, unremarked sites of social life (Garfinkel, 1967; Heritage and Clayman, 2010; Hester and Francis, 2007; McHoul and Rapley, 2001).

Ethnomethodologists have built a long, distinctive tradition of scholarship based on documentations of many interactional settings, schools and classrooms included (Austin, Dwyer, and Freebody, 2003; Francis and Hester, 2004; Freebody and Freiberg, 2011; Heap, 1997; Lee, 2010; McHoul and Watson, 1984; Mehan, 1978). Macbeth's sustained programmatic research (e.g., 2003, 2011) is exemplary in demonstrating the level and intensity of ethnomethodology's interest in settings that are as mundane but as puzzling as classrooms:

> Novices do not know their curriculum, yet must in some way join in co-producing their lessons about it. It is this 'some way' that holds interest. Notice how the curriculum cannot then be a resource to its own instruction. One cannot use math to teach math to those who do not know it. . . . We must make of their instruction a practicum of the most practical sort. We must teach them how to *do* this knowledge, without requiring that they 'know' it already. In some sense, they must produce their lessons *before* they know them. (Macbeth, 2011, p. 449, emphases in original)

The methods that participants use to co-produce lessons, Macbeth observed, are 'everywhere underfoot' – primordial, organizational processes he termed 'the first work of common-understanding and the organizations that ensure its recurrent achievement,' the 'first curriculum.' This work, he noted, is generally unnoticed by researchers whose educational interests remain firmly fixed on 'something more formal, credentialed, or genuflectional' (2011, p. 440), the knowledge enshrined in the curriculum domains.

Macbeth's primordial 'first curriculum' includes the basic definitions of classroom activities themselves ('reading,' 'revising,' 'summarizing' etc.). Teachers and students coordinate activities that produce the procedural definitions, which, in turn, provide descriptions of, and warrants for, the work at hand (Heap, 1985). The reversal of commonsense logic here is critical: Definitions of activities are not seen as production-sites of organized social practices; it is the other way around. Below we provide a closer view of the workings of the 'first curriculum' and how particular literacy resources are worked on, worked up, and put to work in senior classrooms.

The 'first curriculum' in senior music

Of primary emphasis in this section are the interactional-analytic features of a Year 11 music classroom. We can note that this music lesson comprises a complex ensemble of aural and visual modalities (Barton, 2005; Kress, 2003) – recordings, teacher performances, annotated scores, and so on.

In Exhibit 2, we see an excerpt from this lesson, in which T has asked Ss to compare two early dance genres, a Pavane and an Estampie. Once Ss had written comparative responses, T led a discussion focusing on the music scores. During this discussion, T oriented to sensory and theoretical knowledge to describe what was heard-and-read by Ss. Ss contributed by recognizing musical elements using both everyday vernacular and specialized terms. As in Exhibit 1, T highlighted this distinction by continually shuffling between vernacular and specialized discipline-specific descriptions (Gibbons, 2006; Hammond, 1990; Luke, 2008).

Exhibit 2

1	T	So we are talking//
2	S1	//it has a limited range (.) like it stays on the same notes for a few bars and then changes one or two notes
3	T	OK so what element are we talking about? (.) What are you describing?
4	S1	Pitch
5	T	Melody or pitch (1) yeah so you said something about the melody seems to have a lot of repeated notes and it's a smaller range (2) Yep. Something else?
6	S1	Um the texture (.) the textures are different (1) there's more in the <u>five</u> melodies in the Pavane and there's only <u>one</u> in the Estampie
7	T	OK (.) good (.) Who had something like what he just said? Something about texture (.) or the amount of melodies or the amount of layers? Yeah and is there a drone, was there a drone in this? (1) No. So there's no drone (.) now (1) texture (.) so if you said something like (.) it had a thicker texture or it had more layers of melodies you're on the right track. Once we start to get into the realm of ((higher voice pitch)) is it homophonic? polyphonic? did anyone dare to go there?
8	S2	I had polyphonic
9	S3	Yeah, polyphonic
10	T	It's it's difficult (.) essentially it's a homophonic texture. You've got some kind of tune at the top and what are the other five parts doing?
11	S2	Harmonising
12	T	They're just filling out the notes from theˆ (1)
13	S2	Chords^V
14	T	Chords^V

We note similarities and differences between this and the interactional patterns shown in Exhibit 1 from Year 5, some of which we may read as the older Ss' mastery of the IRF cycle. We see this cycle throughout the transcript; but

- Ss interrupt T's apparently vernacular Initiation and cut straight to a technical response (1–2);
- as 1–2 shows, S's response can sound like a feedback component – a technical term is elaborated in everyday language, and confirmed in T's feedback turn (3);
- T's initiation turn can comprise straightforward questions, or questions that are:
  - specified or replaced by new versions of the question (3, 7);
  - self-answered (7); or
  - unfinished sentences with upward inflections (12-14);
- T's Feedback turn can be made up of:
  - a straight confirmation (3, 7);
  - a confirming repeat (14);
  - an elaboration containing a repeat (5); or
  - an acknowledgement with the provision of a more acceptable answer (10).

As a lesson, we note the continual mixture of everyday and technical terms, a feature of this classroom more generally. In an interview with T, he described the Ss in this class as a mix between 'Music Extension' Ss and 'Popular Music' Ss:

> the music extension kids are very serious then you've got a group of boys who drive me *nuts* because their approach to music is not structured (.) their brain doesn't cope with me trying to

give them structures for the learning (.) the whole idea of getting them to move beyond what they can already do (1) I think it is hard (2) I would say all these boys are *passionate* about guitar and they are really quite gifted on it (.) but they don't have that *cognitive* understanding

The regular interplay of technical and vernacular musical language is what allows such lessons, for this T, to go on; they are an element of Macbeth's 'practicum' that affords the accomplishment of a recognizable 'Year 11 lesson' for both apparent groups of Ss – all can actively continue with this, here and now, as a lesson. Reflexively, this pattern of interactional activity again confirmed for both T and Ss the categories T used to understand the different kinds of Ss in the room. The talk patterns build, organize, and confirm two definitions of 'musical knowledge for Year 11.'

The 'first curriculum' in Exhibit 2 is procedurally similar in many respects to that in Exhibit 1 from Year 5. In both, the interactional rights and responsibilities of participants in categories T and S are re-established and reaffirmed, even though in Exhibit 2, we can note more range in what can count as Ss' responses, and more extensive instructional insertions in T's feedback.

Summary

The IRF cycle has been found to be an enduring and widespread feature of the 'first curriculum' of the classroom. However, it has also been criticized often by educationists, particularly on the grounds that teachers' Initiation components are usually questions with known answers. An interaction analysis of this perennial feature provides us with another, 'first curriculum' perspective. Macbeth (2003), for instance, has shown how questions with known answers are used as, and thus can be analytically seen as, interactional organizations whose importance lies in their role as a resource for the public display and installation of knowledge in the ongoing talk of classrooms:

> The power and utility of the three-turn sequence lies in how it writes filaments of understanding into public, witnessable organizations of interactional regularity and coherence. Like an apparatus in a gymnasium, the sequence organizes the novice's tasks of understanding within sequential-organizational fields that can be seen and grasped in ways that permit the novice to 'go on.' It renders the tasks of understanding a curriculum that is beyond what they know, a curriculum they nonetheless can do. (Macbeth, 2011, p. 446)

Interaction analysis helps maintain attention on the interactive demands that students and teachers face as they try to participate in the institutional exchanges foundational to their work. It can thus offer an important antidote to the powerful judgmental intuitions experienced.

The distinctive research interests raised by interaction-analytic approaches include how textual and other semiotic materials are brought into classroom activities, how they are made practical objects of inquiry when students are or are not already familiar with their content. They also include how perceptions of differing levels of students' lesson-relevant knowledge have consequences for the organization of interactions, and the variations in local speech exchange systems, activities, and the evident rationales for these from one curriculum domain to another (Koole, 2010).

A Linguistic Approach

Linguists have made significant contributions to the study of the literacy–curriculum relationship via their interest in disciplinary practices and how these are translated into the language of classrooms. We outline illustrations from the Systemic Functional Linguistics (SFL) tradition (Halliday and Hasan, 1985) aimed at providing social-semiotic descriptions of school texts, within and between curriculum domains.

Early SFL studies of the literacy–curriculum relationship identified the genres students need to learn in a range of curriculum areas, such as history, English, and science (Martin, 1986). Further analyses provided accounts of the specific language features that constitute these specialized discourses, including the vocabulary, grammatical, and textual patterns characterizing texts in the social and physical sciences and humanities (e.g., Halliday and Martin, 1993; Martin and Veel, 1998; Rothery and Stenglin, 2000; Wignell, 2007).

As an instance, SFL researchers have drawn attention to the educational role of grammatical metaphor, whereby 'processes (congruently worded as verbs) and properties (congruently worded as adjectives) . . . [are] reworded metaphorically as nouns' (Halliday and Matthiessen, 2004, p. 656). 'Protons decay into neutrons' can be re-represented in the nominalized form: 'The decay of protons into neutrons,' allowing it to be readily named ('beta decay') and thus used in more complex formations with other processes and objects in the discourse. Grammatical metaphor objectifies experience, grammatically representing processes and properties as things; experience is now readily categorizable 'into classes and hierarchies of classes' (Halliday and Matthiessen, 1999, p. 548), providing a distinctive, second-order reality that is semiotically construed.

Grammatical metaphor is thus significant in the shift from the 'commonsense' of everyday discourse to the 'uncommonsense' of schooled literacy (Derewianka, 2003). Noncongruent grammar is increasingly implicated in the expanding intellectual and procedural distinctiveness of knowledge domains across the school years, presenting an often-underestimated challenge for teachers and students:

> one of the major barriers to the technical, discipline-based knowledge of secondary education . . . (is that) . . . the nominalising grammar of scientific discourse demands a massive act of reconstruction. (Halliday, 1998, p. 223)

Christie and Derewianka (2008) demonstrated how students' writing in history, English, and science develops across schooling into forms beyond what can be accomplished in the primary years. In describing major linguistic developments called upon as curriculum literacy demands become more specialized, these researchers mapped students' writing trajectories into four stages:

1 Early childhood (6–8 years): 'commonsense' knowledge expressed in everyday language through a grammar matched to generalized categories of experience and simple attitudinal expressions.
2 Late childhood to adolescence (9–12 years): 'commonsense' knowledge reshaped into the 'schooled' knowledge as grammatical resources expand, and grammatical metaphor emerging to express knowledge and attitude.
3 Mid-adolescence (13–15 years): school knowledge increasingly differentiated into curriculum areas, becoming more 'un-commonsense-ical' as demands on grammatical resources are amplified and attitudinal expression expands.
4 Late adolescence (16–18+ years): curriculum-specific knowledge characterized by non-congruent grammar expressing abstraction, generalization, value judgment, and opinion. (adapted from Christie and Derewianka, 2008, p. 218.)

It is around the shift from stages 2 to 3 that students' writing can show, and is expected to show, a major shift toward grammatical metaphor. It is also, not coincidentally, at this juncture that Christie and Derewianka found many students failing to progress, still 'writing like they talk' in the senior years.

SFL researchers have also attended to the recent proliferation of multimedia and digital objects in both school and out-of school texts (Bezemer and Kress, 2008; Jewitt, 2006; Kress, 2003; New London Group, 1996). They have examined how multimodal semiotic resources interact with the language of various disciplines in constructing knowledge (e.g., Coffin, 2006; Lemke, 2002; Love, 2008; Macken-Horarik, 2009; O'Halloran, 2007; Unsworth, 2001). Emphasis has been on visual representations (Kress and van Leeuwen, 2006), and how images interact with language in the multimodal texts and talk of schooling (e.g., Chan and Unsworth, 2011; Jewitt, 2008). The following section briefly illustrates some of these issues through analyses of snippets from a Year 11 physics lesson.

Cumulative knowledge building in physics

What counts as being 'literate' in Year 11 physics? Here we exemplify SFL's approach by singling out the features of technicality, abstraction, and multimodality. Figure 22.1 and Exhibit 3 are excerpts from a lesson introducing medical physics. Figure 22.1 shows the PowerPoint slide that T reads, as in Exhibit 3. Note that the transcript is presented in sections for ease of discussion.

There are no contributions from Ss here because T did not provide any transition-relevant places. He nonetheless established the relative importance of ideas in the talk in various ways: selective extended vowels for emphasis (Section 3), upward and downward inflections (Section 4), and pausing (middle Section 1). Also, as in other exhibits, we find the interspersing of reading materials with talk that, among other things, distinguished what Ss were taken to know already from new knowledge: 'we have a new word pop-up here[V] (.) that I need you to know about[V]' (Section 2). As in the Exhibit 1 from Year 5, we see the current activity located in a sequence of previous and projected learning.

The Building Blocks of a Dew Drop

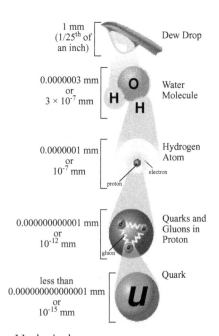

A dew drop is made up of many molecules of water (10^{21} or a billion trillion). Each molecule is made of an oxygen atom and two hydrogen atoms (H_2O). At the start of the 20th century, atoms were the smallest known building blocks of matter.

Each atom consists of a nucleus surrounded by electrons. Electrons are leptons that are bound to the nucleus by photons, which are bosons. The nucleus of a hydrogen atom is just a single proton. Protons consists of three quarks. In the proton, gluons hold the quarks together just as photons hold the electron to the nucleus in the atom.

1 mm
(1/25th of an inch) — Dew Drop

0.0000003 mm or 3×10^{-7} mm — Water Molecule

0.0000001 mm or 10^{-7} mm — Hydrogen Atom

0.000000000001 mm or 10^{-12} mm — Quarks and Gluons in Proton

less than 0.000000000000001 mm or 10^{-15} mm — Quark

Figure 22.1 PowerPoint slide for Year 11 physics lesson

Exhibit 3 (transcript)

1	T	A DEW DROP IS MADE UP OF MANY MOLECULES OF WATER^ (.) ABOUT TEN TO THE TWENTY-ONE which is about^ (.) a billion trillion^V (1) a dew drop (1) about a billion trillion (2) Um (.) EACH MOLECULE IS MADE OF AN OXYGEN^ ATOM AND TWO HYDROGEN ATOMS (1) AND AT THE START OF THE TWENTIETH CENTURY (1) ATOMS^V WERE THE SMALLEST KNOWN BUILDING BLOCKS OF MATTER and that's what you guys have been up to so far in your studies.
2	T	OK^ So you understand about the structure of the atom (1) a:ah molecules (.1) that they make up other things^V (.) EACH ATOM CONSISTS OF A NUCLEUS SURROUNDED BY ELECTRONS we know that^ (1) and then^ we have a new word pop-up here^V (.) that I need you to know about^V. It says ELECTRONS ARE^ LE:EPTONS (1) THAT ARE BOUND TO THE NUCLEUS (1) BY PHO::OTONS^V and these words are going to be popping up now we gotta be (.) start exploring those ones (.) um (1) and PHOTONS ARE BO:OSONS^ and a:ah (.)
3	T	it gets a bit weird from there but (1) we'll take that slowly (.) if^ you have a look at this^ (2) a dew drop it says here (.) about^ a millimeter is what we're talking about for a tiny dew drop THE WATER MO:OLECULE^ IS ABOUT THREE BY TEN TO THE MINUS SE:EVEN (1) MILLIMETERS (1) so three by (.) ten to the minus nine (.) metres^ (1) three nano-metres^ ... QUARKS^ GLUE-ONS ARE PROTONS THAT MAKE UP AN ATOM (.) ((30 seconds talk omitted))
4	T	So when I asked you befo::ore^ (.) what's the universe made of and we got those excellent answers of space (.) of-ah (.) matter energy and (.) and space (1) and ah (.) we then looked at particles^ (.) particles protons and neutrons (.) and today^ (.) we're gonna hear^ (1) that um (.) quarks make up what we think of as protons and neutrons^ (2) le:eptons make up ele:ectrons and a few other types^ (.) which we'll look at (.) and then we have these^ guys here called bosons^V (1) which a:are kind of weird a:and they're responsible for the forces (.) of nature^v

In this lesson, knowledge was introduced by way of formal definitions from the printed and graphic texts. There was little of the staged movement between everyday language and technicality seen in the previous exhibits. Rather, new knowledge was encoded in lexically dense, technical language, with abstract grammatical patterns in which processes were embedded within nominal groups:

a nucleus [[*surrounded* by electrons]]
leptons [[that *are bound* to the nucleus by photons]]
protons [[that *make up* an atom]][1]

In this excerpt and the longer lesson, classifications and taxonomies of physical phenomena (e.g., types of molecules) were combined with abstractions (e.g., scale, force). These combinations were interpretable only with prior knowledge of physics, mathematics, and chemistry. T's explanations relied on multiple modalities (e.g., diagrams, animations, talk, gesture), these being the 'practicum' aimed at giving access to these understandings.

SFL analyses lead us to attend to the demands made on both teachers and students as they try to access meanings embedded in often abstract, multimodal representations, across semiotic systems, and as they try to integrate the complex concepts and relationships central to these curriculum-specific resources. In spite of the 'practicum' work in T's commentaries on the reading, access here relied largely on sophisticated understandings of technical content knowledge and specialized literate practices. The prior knowledge that underlies parts of the senior physics classroom includes accumulating understandings from several disciplines as well as semiotic conventions that are distinctive and fundamental to the ways in which physics builds knowledge. Clearly, Exhibit 3 shows us a point well into students' long interactional and linguistic journeys.

Summary

Linguistic approaches of the sort sketched above connect directly to the interests of curriculum theorists through their preoccupation with knowledge as an object of study and the ways in which the systems of talk and writing have developed particular affordances to know and re-know the world. Linguists view the disciplines and their reflections in school curriculums as having evolved purpose-built textual formations that allow the pursuit of focused inquiry, the conduct of debate among practitioners, and the building and storing of knowledge. Most accounts of acquiring, storing, and retrieving knowledge systematically ignore this ongoing respecification of commonsense forms of understanding into more broadly applicable, and theoretically coherent configurations. The literacy–curriculum connection is thus precisely the focal inquiry of this work.

The conclusions emanating from the SFL body of work have at least three kinds of implications for pedagogy and research (illustrated and outlined in Christie and Maton, 2011). The first set of implications relates to the critical shifts in children's literacy development; the second to the mediating role of teacher's language in 'translating' disciplinary knowledge to subject area knowledge; and the third to the evolving nature of disciplinary knowledge and the technologies that accompany knowledge production, representation, and communication, not least the way these are recast for use in classrooms.

Conclusions: 'A Curriculum for the Adults in the Room'

Of the disciplines contributing to the study of literacy, of curriculum and, more sparsely, of their relationship, we chose two that we believe promise clearer views of that relationship and potentially richer and more effective research programs than most. We briefly illustrated our main points with examples from actual classroom settings. We see the beginnings of particular forms of literacy being worked up in the late primary years. By Year 11 the compounding effects of students' diverse learning histories and the contrasting consequences of long-term success and failure in dealing with the literacy demands of chosen curriculum areas are in stark relief.

The strong form of our argument is that at the heart of the schooling project is the increasing differentiation among the curriculum areas in literacy demands. This differentiation is taken to signal growth and specialization in knowledge and expertise. But any difficulties students present as they face both increasing and increasingly complex literacy demands, increasingly dense and abstract curriculums, and, in a second-order acceleration, increasingly differentiated literacy–curriculum relationships, are commonly accounted for in terms of individual students' shortfalls in aptitude or effort. Not being implicated, the pedagogical silences in the earlier years around the literacy–curriculum relationship are often not highlighted, and thus even more rarely addressed. What this means for researchers and educational policy-makers, (and parents, university, college and workplace teachers, employers, and the rest) is that in the school setting the uncoupling of literacy and curriculum into distinct objects of study allows the crucial, defining phenomena of teaching and learning to escape, the phenomena associated with the myriad ways 'literacy–curriculum' looms larger every day for teachers and students.

A number of under-researched lines of inquiry arise. Principal among these is documenting how each domain of school knowledge uses a diverse array of communicational and knowledge-accessing technologies to put semiotic systems to work in its own way. Of particular interest are changing interactional patterns and activity structures, and changing resources of technicality, abstraction, and grammatical metaphor in knowledge representation. Specifically called for are ongoing pictures of how the relationships among differing semiotic systems diversify over the course of 'apprenticeship' in curriculum-specific ways – how participating in multisemiotic textual interpretation and knowledge building in this curriculum domain at this year level looks increasingly distinctive as the school years advance. Such documentation can never reach closure because of the rapidly changing backgrounds and learning histories of students attending schools in most countries. The 'new mainstream' classroom (Enright, 2010) comprises teachers and students who are more diverse, hybrid in their cultural backgrounds, and mobile physically, culturally, and digitally. What they bring to the literacy–curriculum relationship at different moments in the school program will evolve into a continuously new set of 'first' and 'formal' curriculum experiences.

A second under-researched area concerns how practicing and prospective teachers might learn from research and theory on literacy teaching and learning in both the 'first' and the 'formal' curriculum (May and Wright, 2007). As Macbeth commented, studies of classrooms from these perspectives 'offer a curriculum for the adults in the room. In matters of educational study, it is our instruction that may be the most neglected' (Macbeth, 2011, p. 450). Most educational researchers and most teachers – the adults in the room – have spent many years in school classrooms at some point in their lives. Their immense sense of familiarity with such settings, with the interactional features they no longer need to see or evaluate, can prematurely constrict a sense of the empirical and conceptual aspects of studying the shifting intricacies of the literacy–curriculum relationship.

Finally, we can note that inquiring into these issues calls for research methodologies that are sensitive enough to map the features of talk and texts in pedagogically productive ways, and in ways that retain fidelity to the experienced realities of teachers and learners (Freebody, Maton, and Martin, 2008). Bringing coherence out of the raft of linguistic, sociological and epistemological interests that the literacy–curriculum relationship demands calls for interests traditionally separated in research institutions. While trying to resist the naïve yearning for 'amalgamating' neighboring research methodologies, an urge that understandably surfaces in complex applied research areas, we nonetheless think it worth suggesting that research teams using a variety of approaches could advance, at the least, a more compelling sense of the complexity of the relationship between literacy and curriculum. We submit this suggestion with caution, conscious of the hint of irony that accompanies its appearance in a chapter whose weight has been largely behind the idea that disciplines are constituted by what are at least distinctive, and at most incommensurate, forms of talk and text.

A curriculum is a program via which educational suppositions, some of which are organized into theories, are made consequential for youngsters and for societies. Failing to participate in the practicums of the 'first' or the 'formal' curriculum, or failing to keep up, or getting good at things in the wrong order, are taken to reflect poorly on individuals and institutions. They can also be taken to indicate broader negative social, economic, and cultural outcomes. The long-standing suppositions that hold literacy somehow apart from curriculum in practice, including the Early Inoculation Fiction, seem so shared as to be commonsensical, and so commonsensical as to be translatable into bureaucratic imperatives for youngsters and the educators with whom they work. These imperatives, and the programs of research, teacher preparation, and assessment that both are supported by, and support them have all contributed to the processes by which material, socio-economic, linguistic, and cultural differences continue to be silently but systematically converted into educational disadvantage, amplifying and consolidating inequalities in life trajectories.

Appendix: Transcription conventions used in this chapter

^ v	respectively noticeable upward and downward inflection
(n)	pause of about n seconds
(.)	brief but noticeable pause
Underline	emphasis ((transcriber comment))
UPPER CASE	words being read
//	interruption
Sn	distinguishing student ID

References

Austin, H., Dwyer, B., and Freebody, P. (2003) *Schooling the Child: The Making of Students in Classrooms*. London: Routledge.

Barton, D., Ivanic, R., Appleby, Y., *et al.* (2007) *Literacy, Lives and Learning*. London: Routledge.

Barton, G.M. (2005) Looking forward: An investigation into how music teachers perceive their practice. In P. de Vries (ed.) *Proceedings of the XXVIIth Annual Conference*. Melbourne: Australian Association for Research in Music Education, pp. 15–24.

Bezemer, J., and Kress, G. (2008) Writing in multimodal texts: A social semiotic account of designs for learning. *Written Communication*, 25: 166–195.

Chan, E., and Unsworth, L. (2011) Image-language interaction in online reading environments: Challenges for students' reading comprehension. *Australian Educational Researcher*, 38: 181–202.

Christie, F., and Derewianka, B. (2008) *School Discourse*. London: Continuum.

Christie, F., and Maton, K. (2011) *Disciplinarity: Functional Linguistic and Sociological Perspectives*. New York: Continuum.

Coffin, C. (2006) *Historical Discourse: The Language of Time, Cause, and Evaluation*. London: Continuum.

Comber, B., Badger, L., Barnett, L., *et al.* (2002) Literacy after the early years. *Australian Journal of Language and Literacy*, 25: 9–23.

Deng, Z., and Luke, A. (2008) Subject matter: Defining and theorizing school subjects. In F.M. Connelly, M.F. He, and J. Phillion (eds) *The SAGE Handbook of Curriculum and Instruction*. Thousand Oaks, CA: Sage, pp. 66–87.

Derewianka, B. (2003) *Grammatical Metaphor in the Transition to Adolescence*. In A. Simon-Vandenbergen, M. Taverniers, and L. Ravelli (eds) *Grammatical Metaphor: Views from Systemic Functional Linguistics*. Amsterdam: John Benjamins, pp. 185–220.

Enright, K. (2010) Language and literacy for a new mainstream. *American Educational Research Journal*, 48: 80–118.

Fischer, S.R. (2001) *A History of Writing*. London: Reaktion.

Francis, D., and Hester, S. (2004) *An Invitation to Ethnomethodology: Language, Society and Interaction*. London: Sage.

Freebody, P., and Freiberg, J. (2011) Ethnomethodological research in education and the social sciences: studying 'the business, identities and cultures' of classrooms. In L. Markauskaite, P. Freebody, and J. Irwin (eds) *Methodological Choice and Design*. Dordrecht, Netherlands: Springer Science, pp. 79–92.

Freebody, P., Maton, K., and Martin, J.R. (2008) Talk, text and knowledge in cumulative, integrated learning. *Australian Journal of Language and Literacy*, 31: 188–201.

Freebody, P., and Muspratt, S. (2007) Beyond generic knowledge in pedagogy and disciplinarity: The case of science textbooks. *Pedagogies: An International Journal*, 2: 35–48.

Garfinkel, H. (1967) *Studies in Ethnomethodology*. Englewood Cliffs, NJ: Prentice-Hall.

Gee, J.P. (2004) *Situated Language and Learning: A Critique of Traditional Schooling*. New York: Routledge.

Gibbons, P. (2006) *Bridging Discourses in the ESL Classroom*. London: Continuum.

Graff, H.J. (1995) *The Labyrinths of Literacy: Reflections on Literacy Past and Present*. Pittsburgh, PN: University of Pittsburgh Press.

Halliday, M.A.K. (1998) Things and relations: Regrammaticalising experience as technical knowledge – stratification and metaphor, semogenic power of nominalisation, types of grammatical metaphor. In J.R. Martin and R. Veel (eds) *Reading Science: Critical and Functional Perspectives on Discourses of Science*. London: Routledge, pp. 185–235.

Halliday, M.A.K., and Hasan, R. (1985) *Language, Context and Text: Aspects of Language in a Social-semiotic Perspective*. Victoria: Deakin University Press.

Halliday, M.A.K., and Martin, J.R. (1993) *Writing Science: Literacy and Discursive Power*. London; Washington DC: Falmer.

Halliday, M.A.K., and Matthiessen, C.M.I.M. (1999) *Construing Experience Through Meaning*. London: Cassell.

Halliday, M.A.K., and Matthiessen, C.M.I.M. (2004) *An Introduction to Functional Grammar*, 3rd edn. London: Arnold.

Hammond, J. (1990) Is learning to read and write the same as learning to speak? In F. Christie (ed.) *Literacy for a Changing World*. Victoria: ACER Press, pp. 26–35.

Heap, J. (1985) Discourse in the production of classroom knowledge: Reading lessons. *Curriculum Inquiry*, 15: 245–279.

Heap, J. (1997) Conversation analysis methods in researching language and education. In N.H. Hornberger and D. Corson (eds) *Encyclopedia of Language and Education*. Amsterdam: Kluwer, pp. 217–226.

Heritage, J., and Clayman, S. (2010) *Talk in Action: Interactions, Identities and Institutions*. London: Wiley-Blackwell.

Hester, S., and Francis, D. (2007) Analysing orders of ordinary action. In S. Hester and D. Francis (eds) *Orders of Ordinary Action: Re-specifying Sociological Knowledge*. Aldershot, UK: Ashgate, pp. 3–12.

Jacobs, V. (2008) Adolescent literacy: Putting the crisis in context. *Harvard Educational Review*, 78: 7–39.

Jewitt, C. (2006) *Technology, Literacy and Learning*. London: Routledge.

Jewitt, C. (2008) Multimodality and literacy in school classrooms. *Review of Research in Education*, 32: 241–267.

Johnson, W.A. (2010) *Readers and Reading Culture in the High Roman Empire: A Study of Elite Communities*. New York: Oxford University Press.

Koole, T. (2010) Displays of epistemic access: Student responses to teacher explanations. *Research on Language and Social Interaction*, 43: 183–209.

Kress, G. (2003) *Literacy in the New Media Age*. London: Routledge.

Kress, G., and van Leeuwen, T. (2006) *Reading Images: The Grammar of Visual Design*, 2nd edn. London: Routledge.

Lee, C.D., and Spratley, A. (2010) *Reading in the Disciplines: The Challenges of Adolescent Literacy*. New York: Carnegie Corporation.

Lee, Y.-A. (2007) Third-turn position in teacher talk: Contingency and the work of teaching. *Journal of Pragmatics*, 39: 180–206.

Lee, Y.-A. (2010) Learning in the contingency of talk-in-interaction. *Text and Talk*, 30: 403–422.

Lemke, J. (2002) Multimedia semiotics: Genres for science education and scientific literacy. In M. Schleppegrell and M.C. Colombi (eds) *Developing Advanced Literacy in First and Second Languages*. Mahwah, NJ: Erlbaum, pp. 21–44.

Love, K. (2008) Literacy across the school subjects: A multimodal approach. In L. Unsworth (ed.) *Multimodal Semiotics: Functional Analysis in Contexts of Education*. London: Continuum pp. 173–186.

Luke, A. (1988) *Literacy, Textbooks, and Ideology*. London: Falmer Press.

Luke, A. (2008) Pedagogy as gift. In J. Albright and A. Luke (eds) *Pierre Bourdieu and Literacy Education*. London: Routledge, pp. 68–91.

Luke, C. (1989) *Pedagogy, Printing, and Protestantism: The Discourse on Childhood*. Albany, NY: SUNY Press.

Macbeth, D. (2003) Hugh Mehan's *Learning Lessons* reconsidered: On the difference between the naturalistic and critical analysis of classroom discourse. *American Educational Research Journal*, 40: 239–280.

Macbeth, D. (2011) Understanding understanding as an instructional matter. *Journal of Pragmatics*, 43: 438–451.

MacDonald, S.P. (1994) *Professional Academic Writing in the Humanities and Social Sciences*. Carbondale, IL: Southern Illinois University Press.

Macken-Horarik, M. (2009) Multiliteracies, metalanguage and the protean mind: Navigating school English in a sea of change. *English in Australia*, 44: 33–43.

Martin, J.R. (1986) *Writing to Mean: Teaching Genres across the Curriculum*. Bundoora, Victoria: Applied Linguistics Association of Australia.

Martin, J.R., and Veel, R. (eds) (1998) *Reading Science: Critical and Functional Perspectives on Discourses of Science*. London: Routledge.

May, S., and Wright, N. (2007) Secondary literacy across the curriculum: Challenges and possibilities. *Language and Education*, 21: 370–376.

McHoul, A., and Rapley, M. (eds) (2001) *How to Analyse Talk in Institutional Settings*. London: Continuum.

McHoul, A., and Watson, D.R. (1984) Two axes for the analysis of 'commonsense' and 'formal' geographical knowledge in classroom talk. *British Journal of the Sociology of Education*, 5: 281–302.

McKitterick, R. (1990) *The Uses of Literacy in Medieval Europe*. Cambridge: Cambridge University Press.

Mehan, H. (1978) *Learning Lessons: Social Organization in the Classroom*. Cambridge, MA: Harvard University Press.

Moje, E.B., Stockdill, D., Kim, K., and Kim, H.-J. (2011) The role of text in disciplinary learning. In M.L. Kamil, P.D. Pearson, E.B. Moje, and P.P. Afflerbach (eds) *Handbook of Reading Research Volume IV*. New York: Routledge, pp. 453–486.

New London Group (1996) A pedagogy of multiliteracies: Designing social futures. *Harvard Educational Review*, 66: 60–92.

O'Halloran, K. (2007) Mathematical and scientific forms of knowledge: A systemic functional multimodal grammatical approach. In F. Christie and J. Martin (eds) *Language, Knowledge and Pedagogy. Functional Linguistic and Sociological Perspectives*. London: Continuum, pp. 205–138.

Paris, S. (2005) Reinterpreting the development of reading skills. *Reading Research Quarterly*, 40: 184–202.

Pressley, M. (2004) The need for research on secondary literacy education. In T.L. Jetton, and J.A. Dole (eds) *Adolescent Literacy Research and Practice*. New York: Guilford Press, pp. 415–432.

Rothery, J., and Stenglin, M. (2000) Interpreting literature: The role of appraisal. In L. Unsworth (ed.) *Researching Language in Schools and Communities: Functional Linguistic Perspectives*, London: Cassell, pp. 222–244.

Schegloff, E. (2007) *Sequential Organization in Interaction*. Cambridge: Cambridge University Press.

Shanahan, T., and Shanahan, C. (2008) Teaching disciplinary literacy to adolescents: Rethinking content-area literacy. *Harvard Educational Review*, 78: 40–59.

Sinclair, J., and Coulthard, M. (1975) *Towards an Analysis of Discourse*. Oxford: Oxford University Press.

Smith, D.E. (1987) *The Everyday World as Problematic: A Feminist Sociology*. Boston, MA: Northeastern University Press.

Street, B.V. (1984) *Literacy in Theory and Practice*. Cambridge: Cambridge University Press.

Unsworth, L. (2001) *Teaching Multiliteracies across the Curriculum: Changing Contexts of Text and Image in Classroom Practice*. Buckingham, UK: Open University Press.

Wignell, P. (2007) Vertical and horizontal discourse and the social sciences. In F. Christie and J.R. Martin (eds) *Language Knowledge and Pedagogy: Functional Linguistic and Sociological Perspectives*, London: Continuum, pp. 184–204.

Chapter 23

The Digital Challenge

Sandra Schamroth Abrams and Guy Merchant

Introduction

Over a decade into the twenty-first century, researchers, practitioners, administrators, and policy makers alike continue to grapple with classroom integration of technology. Calls continue to circulate among literacy educators and policy makers for a more concerted drive to develop 'twenty-first century skills,' to respond to the evolution of what has been described as 'participatory culture,' and to make education more relevant to the everyday lives of children. Despite the resultant sense of urgency, there is little consensus or consistency of response within and between education systems nationally and internationally. Educational standards set by government and private organizations acknowledge the general inclusion of technology (Alliance for Excellent Education, 2012; DCMS and BIS, 2009; ICTC, 2011; IRA, 2009; NCTE Position Statement, 2008), and broad criteria enable educators some interpretive room, but questions abound concerning the integration of technology, its position in the curriculum, and its impact on student learning. A systematic review of literature is needed to begin to answer these questions and to uncover what this century's research has revealed about technology *within* the classroom.

In this chapter, we present a review of research of technology integration in elementary and middle school classrooms undertaken between 2000 and 2011, highlighting the affordances and limitations of attempts to contemporize practice across the grade levels. As noted in greater depth throughout the chapter, the review of research suggests that technology in education continues to be considered through traditional lenses primarily because 'we do not yet have a theory which allows us to understand and account for the world of communication as it is now' (Kress, 2010, p. 7). As a result, the effective use of digital resources remains in question. In the United States, national reports indicate that public school students' use of technology in school 'for higher-order skill development' remains below the 50 percent mark, with under 20 percent of students 'developing demonstrations or simulations' or 'designing and producing products' (Alliance for Excellent Education, 2012, p. 8). Likewise, in the United Kingdom, students are not using technology for higher-order thinking; rather, 'children are being forced to learn how to use applications, rather than to make them. They are becoming slaves to the user interface

International Handbook of Research on Children's Literacy, Learning, and Culture, First Edition.
Edited by Kathy Hall, Teresa Cremin, Barbara Comber, and Luis C. Moll.
© 2013 John Wiley & Sons, Ltd. Published 2013 by John Wiley & Sons, Ltd.

and are totally bored by it' (Burns, 2012, para. 15). Thus, echoing Kress's sentiments, we see a digital challenge – that is the integration of technology within the classroom. Educators face financial, environmental/spatial and curricular constraints, and researchers are challenged to find evaluative means to measure the effective use of technology in the classroom. Just as Kress (2010) asserts that 'adequate theoretical tools are needed to deal both with the present social, economic, political and cultural situation and the resultant conditions for semiosis,' (p. 7), so too, we recognize that a framework is needed to evaluate the adoption of contemporary tools in the educational system more effectively.

To this end, this chapter will explore some of the more influential theoretical frames that have shaped the ways in which we understand and describe digital texts and twenty-first century learning, and it will provide a synthesis of studies that have drawn attention to students' involvement in new literacy practices in both their elementary and middle school years. Focusing on the application of technology in the classroom, the chapter offers a new perspective on the digital challenge: what the literature reveals about educators' uses of technology, the relationship between technology and curricula, and the issues facing researchers of digital literacy. These seminal classroom studies raise key issues for digital practices vis-à-vis curricula and pedagogy; our analysis provides a framework for systemizing current knowledge and contributes to setting the agenda for new research in the field. We begin by looking at the ways in which digital technology has begun to unsettle conceptions of literacy and learning. After this, we explore what current research reveals about technology in the classroom, following with a discussion of the key methodological dilemmas and an agenda for future research.

Literacy and Digital Learning: An Evolution

As the impact of new technology on literacy practices has become better understood, practitioners have begun to see how these new practices may destabilize the dominant narratives of literacy and learning (Lankshear and Knobel, 2006). At the same time, teachers are facing the educational charge to help students to develop twenty-first century skills, which has instrumental value for policy makers with an interest in educating a workforce for new kinds of labor (Livingstone and Hope, 2011). In digital spaces, 'knowledge is socially constructed and mediated by the learners rather than simply absorbed unchanged from the expert' (Carrington and Robinson, 2010, p. 5), and schools are now faced with the challenge of accommodating 'the new' in a system that is predicated on a set of assumptions about literacy and learning that pre-date current understandings about meaning-making.

Tracing conceptual shifts

Although educational reform and the proliferation of digital resources may have prompted a focus on what has been referred to as twenty-first century learning (Leadbetter, 2008), the increasing interest in nonformal learning has also helped to validate the new kinds of meaning-making that are associated with digital media. Ethnographic studies from Heath (1983) through to Barton and Hamilton (1998) have led to a fundamental reconceptualization of literacy, showing that literacy is not only multiple and complex, but also that meaning-making itself is socially and culturally situated (Street, 1995). This conceptual shift, together with the emergence of a literature on multiliteracies (Cope and Kalantzis, 2000, 2009) and multimodality (Kress, 2003, 2010), has offered an even more nuanced view of literacy, one that extends the concept of 'text' to include any mode or combination of modes. This has led to various reconceptualized notions of literacy and learning.

In addition to this shift, those with an interest in the role of popular culture and new technologies in the lives of children and young people have continued to emphasize the importance of including performance-based or media-based texts, such as television, websites, street rap, and popular music, as part of literacy education for 'New Times' (Goodson and Norton-Meier, 2003; Hull, 2003; Luke and Elkins, 1998). This expanded understanding of meaning-making has challenged the traditional view of literacy as an autonomous typographic practice – a view that still lies at the heart of curriculum design. It is perhaps unsurprising then that, as literacy educators have grappled with the diversity of practices associated with popular culture and new technology, they also have highlighted the gap between in-school and out-of-school literacy (cf. Alvermann, 2002; Lacasa, Méndez, and Martínez, 2008 for example). 'There are deep incompatibilities between the demands of the new technologies and the traditional school' (Collins and Halverson, 2009, p. 6), and all too often, the school system tends to position students as the passive recipients of a narrow range of meaning-making practices rather than the engaged producers of meaning that they often are outside of school (Abrams, 2009; Alvermann *et al.*, 2006; Carrington and Robinson, 2010; Solomon, 2009).

Innovations in pedagogy and practice based on the use of twenty-first century texts in classrooms have led to a range of new approaches to teaching across grade levels and content areas (Beach and O'Brien, 2009; Coiro, 2003; Larson, 2008; Merchant, 2009; O'Brien and Scharber, 2008; Wagner and Dobbin, 2009), and in turn these have raised concerns regarding curricula and implementation. For instance, educators' use of technology may depend on previous experience (Casey, 2011; Goodson *et al.*, 2002), proficiency (Labbo *et al.*, 2003; Marsh, 2004; Millard, 2003), and technological resources and time limitations (Baek, 2008; Kirriemuir and McFarlane, 2003). Furthermore, teachers may experience conflict and constraint as a result of curricular expectations and school culture (Goodson *et al.*, 2002; Hawisher and Selfe, 2004; King and O'Brien, 2002; Van Eck, 2006).

Further, a new impetus has been added to the debate by Jenkins, who has argued that new technologies foster new kinds of participation. Jenkins uses the term 'participatory culture' to capture this theme, and highlights the significance of active participation and collective intelligence in youth engagement with popular media. In an influential White Paper, written for the MacArthur Foundation, Jenkins *et al.* (2006) describe this participatory culture as one in which members 'believe their contributions matter, and feel some degree of social connection with one another' (p. 3). The White Paper suggests that technology has transformed the lives of many (but not all), and that new skills and understandings are necessary for full participation in the digital world. The authors argue that, because of 'the participation gap,' which is characterized by different levels of access and engagement, these skills should be incorporated in the school curriculum.

Tracing digital implementation: Establishing a systematic review

Put together, there is a sense of a gathering momentum for change – a change in which new ideas about learning (cf. Gee, 2008) and new ways of making meaning combine with a policy imperative to make classrooms places in which children and young people's diverse literacy resources are recognized and developed in ways that will be advantageous to them (cf. Burnett and Merchant, 2011). In what follows, we trace the shape of recent research and innovation in order to identify what we already know about changing textual practices in school settings. An exhaustive search of studies of technology used in content area elementary and middle school classrooms yielded fewer reports than initially anticipated; there appears to be a dearth of research on how educators are adopting digital resources during class time in elementary and middle schools. Thus, based on a review of 29 studies published between 2000 and 2011 we begin with a critique of how these play out across the 5–13 age range before moving on to look at how they are framed in terms of the curriculum. When a study also involved older students, we only included the study if we could distinguish the data for the 5–13 year olds. In the course of our review, we read studies that focused on the integration of technology into mainstream content-area classrooms (e.g., no after school programs, special provision, or at-home uses of digital texts); further, we defined technology as computer- or video-related resources, including, but not limited to computers (hardware, software), interactive white boards, video/digital cameras, videogames, Internet sites, and mobile technology. This framework facilitated a focused examination of how technology has been utilized in classroom contexts.

We did not restrict our review to particular methodological approaches, but, nonetheless, the framework we adopted imposed certain constraints. As we examined studies on classroom-based work, this selection favored naturalistic inquiries most of which fell in the qualitative paradigm. Of the 29 studies we found that fitted our criteria, only six of the studies, had a quasi-experimental design. Further, because our criteria included technology use within the classroom, many studies could be classed as practitioner-based action research, and the majority, including those conducted by outside researchers, focused on specific segments of technology integration, such as time-limited digital story projects. In most studies then, the timescales were short and, of the research studies that reported their duration, only one that sustained inquiry of a total of 13 months (Barfurth and Michaud, 2008) seemed to record technology use throughout the majority of the school year instead of semester-bound or shorter increments of time. However, over the course of Barfurth and Michaud's study of the 'Canadian Digital Video in the Classroom project,' which included 13 and 14 year olds, 'teachers opted for more specific projects and limited the scope of video digital activities,' and 70 percent of students only completed one or two digital video projects within the year (2008, p. 306). In other words, for the majority of students, there was no continual and prolonged use of technology within the classroom over the school year, an inconsistency and sporadicity noted in other studies across the globe (Henderson and Honan, 2008). Overall, the rather piecemeal data from all the studies we reviewed suggest that, although the uses of digital resources are widely advocated, research and the documentation of sustained implementation are still limited.

Furthermore, given the increased usage of mobile technology, there is surprisingly little research about its educational use in this age range. University classrooms appear to be the primary space for such research, and, although there are some reports on mobile learning with older students, such as the MoLeNET's work in 14 plus provision (Attewell *et al.*, 2010), we found few studies that reported on work with younger students. Hartnell-Young (2007) provides a snapshot of three primary school classes' use of mobile technology in England, though implementation sometimes included out-of-school activities. In general, the majority of discussions about mobile devices in schools can be found in blogs and school- or publisher-sponsored websites that feature how-to instructions and lesson plan ideas (cf., Rimes, 2007). When websites included data, they surfaced in the form of vignettes, sound bites, or personal testimonies, as evidenced on Wolverhampton City Council's website that showcases how a class of 9–10 year olds in the United Kingdom was involved in producing animations and information texts using PDAs (personal digital/data assistant) (Wolverhampton Engage, 2011). Nonetheless, data that reveal what actually happens in the classroom appears to be missing. Even articles published in academic journals (cf. Norris and Soloway, 2004; Soloway *et al.*, 2001) or practice-based journals (cf. Waller, 2010) primarily rely upon anecdotal accounts to illustrate the affordances of mobile technology in the classroom.

The overall picture suggests that there is growing recognition of how literacies are evolving in an era that is marked by widespread digital communication. It is clear that the changing ways of producing and distributing texts and the forms associated with new media are having some impact on classroom practice. Although the research base is limited, it does suggest that new pedagogies and new approaches to learning are needed. In all, the aggregation of what are mostly practitioner-focused qualitative studies highlights some significant promises and challenges in the uses of digital literacy.

Technology inside the classroom walls: Promises and challenges

A cross-section of the research reveals that the use of digital texts inside the classroom is primarily computer-based, which seems logical given that such activities as digital storytelling, interactive white board presentations, Internet use, and the integration of video or music require a software program and/or hardware to host and display the information. Handheld devices ranging from laptop computers to digital cameras and mobile phones appear to add the dimension of mobility to learning, and many studies reveal that the integration of technology also extends into spaces outside the confines of the classroom and the school day. To capitalize on the affordances of technology (e.g., mobility, asynchronous learning scenarios, virtual collaboration) often involves moving beyond curricular requirements and may include activities that hinge on the confluence of in- and out-of-school learning. It is possible, but as yet unproven, that this connection could promote learner engagement. Nevertheless, across the majority of the studies (approximately 75 percent), there was an acknowledged increase in student motivation and interaction through the use of digital resources; only one (Hartnell-Young, 2007) acknowledged that, in addition to providing support, the technology had an associated 'novelty factor' that was motivating (p. 92). Those studies that did not address motivation focused either on academic gains, curricular constraints, and/or teacher education.

Though it seems that assignments that included technology (e.g., digital stories, podcasts, web page construction) often required collaboration, research reveals how a digital medium, itself, seems to promote student-centered learning and inspires the inclusion of students' out-of-school literacy practices. So for example, in one instance, the creation of podcasts enabled students in a Midwestern US rural high school to hear and share their stories (Goodson and Skillen, 2010). The podcasts helped the students to establish connections between their literacy practices, a finding that is echoed in other research that included elementary, middle, and high school students sharing a digital text with an audience (Bledsoe, 2009; Hodgson, 2009; Honan, 2008). Further, as studies suggest, digital media production is an iterative process that requires collaborative exploration and analysis (Erstad, 2002; Rantala and Korhonen, 2008; Serrier, 2010). Although an emphasis on collaborative learning has a long and respectable history in the literature and one that certainly pre-dates digital technology, it has frequently taken the shape of formal and informal group activity that functions as a precursor to individual outputs. Many digital texts are, by contrast, dependent upon joint construction. So for example, building a wiki is in essence a participatory practice and one in which collaboration is embedded in the technology and the task. We, therefore, argue that collaboration in joint textual production is a key twenty-first century skill and one that warrants closer examination.

Measuring learning gains

In addition to collectively engaging students, the integration of technology appears to have had academic implications. The six quantitative or mixed method studies we examined (Din and Calao, 2001; Folkesson and Swalander, 2006; Ke and Grabowski, 2006; Metcalf and Tinker, 2004; Valkanova and Watts, 2007; Rosas *et al.*, 2003) all suggest that the use of specific software or computer/videogames impacted elementary or middle school students' literacy or numeracy skills. The studies, which ranged from 4 to 20 weeks in length at sites as diverse as the United Kingdom, Sweden, Australia, United States, and Chile, not only reveal an international interest in classroom digital literacies, but also suggest that more quantitative, global research is needed. Of the six, three studies from the earlier part of the decade (Din and Calao, 2001; Ke and Grabowski, 2006; Rosas *et al.*, 2003) addressed video/computer gaming and learning, and three (Folkesson and Swalander, 2006; Metcalf and Tinker, 2004; Valkanova and Watts, 2007) focused on software program-based learning. All but one study (Din and Calao, 2001) explicitly indicated curricular or national standard measures that guided the use, implementation, and/or assessment of technology. It is unclear whether the focus on curricular alignment was a result of quantitative sensitivities to statistical assessment or if the temporal climate of educational reform – that is the increased attention to test-driven standards and curricula – narrowed the researchers' focus to primarily addressing academic gains in 'the basics.' Whatever the cause, the outcome is an under-valuing of students' historical knowledge, critical thought, and application, as well as their personal understanding of material. The conscious discussion of curricular measures and mandates reveals the researchers' attention to, what appears to be, a growing force shaping the face of technology in education.

Further, the three studies of gaming referred to above suggest academic improvement in elementary students' spelling, reading and/or math. Each of the gaming studies addressed math achievement, but only two (Ke and Grabowski, 2006; Rosas *et al.*, 2003) found the experimental group performing significantly better than the control group in math. In the two studies that addressed literacy skills (Din and Calao, 2001; Rosas *et al.*, 2003), the experimental group had shown gains in spelling and reading; however, the research by Rosas *et al.* (2003) indicated that the improvement in reading scores was not as significant as that for spelling. Though the data across the studies suggest a relationship between video/computer game play and improved academic performance, the data remain inconclusive at best, and it is unclear how the implementation of technology or the type of technology used may have impacted student achievement both across content areas and throughout the school year. Further, the paucity of quantitative research on gaming in the mainstream classroom suggests that there may be limited instances of its use, and there is a need for research that evaluates the long-term impact of in-class gaming. Curricular frameworks or infrastructure constraints (Baek, 2008) may well limit mainstream implementation of games. Additional investigations into gaming in the classroom might help to reveal how educators are successfully utilizing them in the classroom and introduce suggestions for implementation. Just as there is a framework for organizing videogame play in public libraries in the United States (Neiburger, 2007), so, too, can there be suggested structures for classroom gaming. The caveat, however, would be to resist absolutes, restrictive approaches, sanctioned pedagogies, and attitudes that stem from the 'institutionalization of critique' (Burnett and Merchant, 2011) that could limit educator and student creativity and reduce students' pleasures to sterile assessments (Alvermann and Heron, 2001; Burnett and Merchant, 2011).

Of the other three quantitative or mixed methods research studies, which focused on computer-based learning (e.g., use of a specific program), only one (Metcalf and Tinker, 2004) extended beyond the elementary level to include middle school classrooms. One study (Folkesson and Swalander, 2006) focused on reading comprehension and found that the experimental group outperformed the control group. Findings may have been impacted by the motivation, collaboration, and information sharing the researchers observed in relation to the second graders' computer use. The other two studies (Metcalf and Tinker, 2004; Valkanova and Watts, 2007), specific to science education, suggest that the computer software helped to strengthen students' concept and/or vocabulary knowledge, with immediate data and visuals helping students grasp material. Overall, the literature reveals a dearth of quantitative research and a need for future studies to address the integration of technology in and across all content area classrooms.

Implementation of technology: A challenge for educators

Unlike the quantitative research, the 23 qualitative studies made fewer references to gains in students' academic performance (though they did report increased motivation and interest as noted above). However, the studies canvassed the implementation of technology in the classroom and the need for curricular reform. Of particular interest to us is the impact curricular standards may have had on educators' use and/or discussion of technology. In just about half of the studies we examined, there was an overt recognition and adherence to specific national or state standards. However, in the other half of the studies, there was no specific alignment of technology use with the standards. Nonetheless, the ways the educators applied technology in the classroom suggest that they privileged traditional literacy and perceived technology as a supplement. Digital technology appeared to be utilized for production purposes – 'to share their students' work and to display final products' (Honan, 2008, p. 41), which satisfied curricular demands. Visual texts were used primarily for modeling instruction, prompting pre-writing, or scaffolding tasks (Frye, Trathen, and Koppenhaver, 2010; Henderson and Honan, 2008), displaying short films (Graham, 2009), and focusing on content knowledge (Manfra and Hammond, 2006). Given the studies' sketches of technology in the classroom, it is difficult to discern the level of integration and the frequency of technology use. Even though Graham (2009) asserts that 'digital technologies are used only when they enhance the learning; there is no evidence of "technology for technology's sake"' (p. 111), her one-day study of the Greater London primary classroom provides only a limited view of technology integration throughout the year. Nonetheless, Graham raises an important point necessary to distinguish in the digital challenge – technology does not need to be the sole medium for teaching and learning. In most cases, the literature identified technology use that was project-bound, with many studies featuring students' creation of a digital text, and teachers who viewed the 'digital texts as the final outcome of a unit of work, rather than texts to be used in their daily teaching' (Honan, 2008, p. 42). Technology, therefore, did not help to extend instruction beyond curricular limits, and the rather limited implementation of technology did not always capitalize on its affordances.

In a few instances, educators employed technology in dynamic ways – ways that enabled students to explore and collaborate beyond the scope of curricular or standardized structures. Technology aided unique extensions of classroom material and meaningful experiences that hinged on applications beyond the classroom walls. Some educators utilized software as a means to achieve multifaceted learning rather than confining student activities to the directives of an 'educational' program; more specifically, in three instances technology facilitated students' real-time interaction with real-world events and exploration – be it communicating via satellite telephone with an American and Norwegian explorer (Erstad, 2002), following a teacher's daily online, real-time chronicles of his Mt. Kilimanjaro climb (Moos and Honkomp, 2011), or using the GPS, camera, and text message features on mobile phones to learn about coordinates and mapping (Hartnell-Young, 2007). These dynamic instances, however, were extensions of in-class work that took place outside the classroom, either after school or at home. When work took place during class time (Hartnell-Young, 2007), students were separated into two groups – one that explored spaces outside the school building and one that remained in the classroom and relied upon computer mapping and text messages to help guide their colleagues' exploration. This suggests that the affordances of technology – mobility, immediacy, and synchrony/asynchrony – automatically move students away from the confines of traditional pen, paper, and desk-driven work; to use technology in ways that do not replicate traditional assignments or literacy practices requires an epistemological and pedagogical shift and the ability to connect learning inside the classroom to learning outside the classroom. Further, these examples suggest that time and space for classroom activity (be it 45 minutes or larger blocks) may not be sufficient for students and educators to look beyond the confines of a computer program and benefit from the level of extended iteration, engagement, and exploration that occurs outside the time restrictions of class schedules (cf. Merchant, 2010). When students, educators, and researchers have 'sufficient time' to utilize technology, greater academic gains are realized (Metcalf and Tinker, 2004).

As with class time restricting production or exploration, and infrastructure limitations that required printers to be stationed at the end of a school hallway (Garthwait and Weller, 2005), curricular requirements also infringed upon the integration of technology in the classroom. Inconsistencies between district policies and school needs (Garthwait and Weller, 2005), time constraints imposed by standardized test preparation (Manfra and Hammond, 2006), and concerns about teacher comfort with and/or implementation of technology (Barfurth and Michaud, 2008; Henderson and Honan, 2008; Hofer and Swan, 2006; Sylvester and Greenidge, 2009) are issues arising across the literature. Educator autonomy appears to be limited, as utilizing technology in a classroom cannot be divorced from an assessment culture and school structure. The call for educational reform may extend across the globe, but education is so heavily enmeshed with national policies that the dynamic integration of technology and a reconstruction of educational cultures will need to be supported by thorough and repeated investigations of educator and student in-class uses of technology.

Examining the Data through Our Framework: Issues that Arise

The framework used to identify literature for this review – studies written in English that focused on technology in mainstream classrooms – precluded the examination of after school programs or at-home literacies that may inform in-class technology use. In some ways this is a limitation. Given the significance of the learning ecology of children and young people (Barron, 2006), we are aware that literacies are repeatedly recontextualized across different domains (Dyson, 2006). However, the narrow focus allows us to see the strengths and the weaknesses of school-based provisions. Similarly our review has excluded countries in which English is not the main language of instruction, such as those from Europe or Asia, where technology use is prevalent. However, the specific focus has enabled us to review extant literature and identify areas for future research and consideration in settings in which English is dominant.

With an 11-year scope (2000–2011), we are forced to acknowledge the impact of technological development and obsolescence. Early twenty-first century (2000–2005) research is limited by the scope and availability of technology and academic insights at that point in time. Further, regardless of chronology, the introduction of new technologies to the marketplace does not necessarily mean there will be an automatic educational endorsement; not all commercial technologies are perceived as educationally appropriate or relevant. In addition, the lag time between general availability of technology to consumers and its integration into schools can be constrained by institutional finances, administrator/educator interest, and professional training.

In addition, we found methodological issues arose because we solely examined instances of technology use inside the classroom. As noted earlier, the majority of the studies we found were qualitative in nature, and 12 out of the 29 (roughly 41 percent) were published in journals that feature practice-based articles. In seven instances, the focus on reporting classwork or best practices superseded an explicit acknowledgement of methodology, and the discussion of data seemed to stem from action research. The presence of practitioner voices provides an authenticity to the discussion of curricular constraints and teacher frustrations. However, the selectivity of data also calls into question the variables that may not have been accounted for in the literature and that may have impacted educator and/or student use of technology in the classroom. Finally, the inconsistent reporting of data makes it difficult to discern the frequency and extent to which technology was integrated into classroom instruction and the extent to which students and educators were involved in the meaningful consumption and/or production of digital texts.

Of the work published in research-based academic journals, the overwhelming majority only provide a window into explicit digital practices in the classroom. In order to more fully understand how technology is utilized in the classroom and how it may be integrated into the literacy curriculum, researchers need to extend the length of their studies and immerse themselves more thoroughly in the setting. Further, though more quantitative data are needed, the presence of an outside researcher for a discrete period of time, as well as the imposition of surveys and additional tests, may impact student and educator behavior and, thus, affect the data. Naturalistic inquiry helps to capture an authentic view of phenomena *in situ* (Lichtman, 2010), but the findings cannot be generalized. More longitudinal, mixed-method studies that include the researcher as a participant observer may present a methodological middle ground that provides statistical assessments of student learning and higher-order thinking while featuring thick, rich description and participant testimony. With greater time invested in the field, researchers also may be able to work alongside educators to help provide an added depth to action research.

Finally, our framework for examining research also included a broad understanding of the terms, 'technology' and 'digital,' in a purposeful attempt to widen our search. The literature included computer- or game-based hardware or software, and, though the terms, 'technology' and 'digital,' did not seem problematic, the concept of integration appeared too broad. The literature suggests that there is a spectrum of technology implementation, with most educators appropriating digital practices only to privilege and/or replicate aspects of traditional literacy, such as basing audio or video recordings on written scripts or research (Frye, Trathen, and Koppenhaver, 2010; Goodson and Skillen, 2010; Hofer and Swan, 2006; Manfra and Hammond, 2006), producing slide show presentations (Henderson and Honan, 2008; Honan, 2008), or using the interactive whiteboard as a projection screen or writing surface (Graham, 2009; Manfra and Hammond, 2006). Such findings are important to note; however, if we are going to explore technology in the classroom, we need to consider *why* educators are making the decisions they do and if we should count all forms of technology use – including digital visuals as writing prompts – when we examine how educators utilize twenty-first century tools with their classes.

Gaps in the Data: Recommendations for Future Research

In order to understand better how technology is being utilized in classrooms across continents, content areas, and socio-cultural contexts, it is important that future research adopts a systematic approach to addressing the extent to which technology integration is impacted (for better or for worse) by curricula and national policies, teacher training and educator interest, and time constraints and financial resources. There needs to be a better categorization of technology in the classroom to distinguish student-driven capacities, higher-order thinking, and dynamic integration of digital resources from extensions of 'drill-and-skill' activities. Further, we need to examine to what extent the technology, itself, is responsible for increasing student motivation and/or interaction. How much of the student engagement is due to the teaching or learning style, the change in classroom practice, or the requirement to collaborate with others?

The digital challenge, therefore, is for research to be more comprehensive and longitudinal, include teacher-researcher partnerships, and explore issues of time, space, and motivation as they relate to the teacher, the student, and the administrator. Equally important are the notion of social justice and the exploration of the types of technology integration in schools located across socio-economic domains. Not only would it be essential to examine technology use according to demographic data, but also it would be crucial to acknowledge how technology works to replicate and reinforce established positions of power on curricular, academic, and social levels. Likewise, we question to what extent does the 'productive power' of design (Cope and Kalantzis, 2000) provide students the opportunity to challenge existing power structures and recreate meaning through autonomous reconstruction of text.

Inherent in the discussion of digital texts is the participatory culture and empowerment that seem to be important elements in the development of student interaction and social identities across virtual and real contexts. The data we reviewed highlight student collaboration and engagement, and it is necessary to consider how situated identities may exist across plural media, how digital practices may help reveal student agency, and how technology may expose collective and individual ways of being (Burnett and Merchant, 2011). Students' inhabitation of their virtual and real literate spaces may signal the dispositions and assumptions they may relegate to or carry across specific contexts, restricting or advancing their meaning making experiences. Further, digital practices may reinforce or mitigate existing perceptions of self in relation to academic achievement. Identity may complicate the discussion of digital practices and curricular measures (McDougall, 2010), but it cannot be ignored if we are going to consider criticality and ownership in the production and consumption of digital texts.

In terms of curricula, national and international core and content-area standards are written with general language that leaves room for educators to rationalize the use of technology. However, it is unclear what will be the main impetus for technology integration, and, based on the inconclusive data we have reviewed, it is difficult to ascertain the extent to which curriculum drives technology-inclusive instruction. The digital challenge, therefore, extends into the academic realm and provokes researchers to examine and report more thoroughly, and perhaps collaboratively, on the ways technologies are integrated into instruction, are enhanced or restricted by curricula, and are empowering students to be critical, twenty-first century thinkers.

References

Abrams, S.S. (2009) A gaming frame of mind: Digital contexts and academic implications. *Educational Media International*, 46(4): 335–347.

Alliance for Excellent Education (2012) The digital learning imperative: How technology and teaching meet today's education challenges, accessed November 20, 2012: www.all4ed.org/files/DigitalLearningImperative.pdf

Alvermann, D.E. (2002) Effective literacy instruction for adolescents. *Journal of Literacy Research*, 34(2): 189–208.

Alvermann, D.E., and Heron, A. (2001) Literacy identity work: Playing to learn with popular media. *Journal of Adolescent and Adult Literacy*, 45: 118–122.

Alvermann, D.E., Jonas, S., Steele, A., and Washington, E. (2006) Introduction. In. D.E. Alvermann, K.A. Hinchmann, D.W. Moore, *et al.* (eds) *Reconceptualizing the Literacies in Adolescents Lives.* Mahwah, NJ; Lawrence Erlbaum, pp. xxi ff.

Attewell, J., Savil-Smith, C., Douch, R., and Parker, G. (2010) *Modernising Education and Training: Mobilising Technology for Learning*. London: LSN, accessed May 26, 2011: www.moleshare. org.uk/molehole/7032BFB756/100103.pdf

Baek, K.Y. (2008) What hinders teachers in using computer and video games in the classroom? Exploring factors inhibiting the uptake of computer and video games. *CyberPsychology and Behavior*, 11(6): 665–671.

Barfurth, M.A., and Michaud, P. (2008) Digital video technologies and classroom practices. *International Journal of Instructional Media*, 35(3): 301–315.

Barron, B. (2006) Interest and self-sustained learning as catalysts for development: A learning ecology perspective. *Human Development*, 49: 193–224.

Barton, D., and Hamilton, M. (1998) *Local Literacies: Reading and Writing in One Community*. New York: Routledge.

Beach, R., and O'Brien, D. (2009) Teaching popular-culture texts in the classroom. In J. Coiro, M. Knobel, C. Lankshear, and D. Leu (eds) *Handbook of Research in New Literacies*. New York: Lawrence Erlbaum, pp. 775–804.

Bledsoe, G.L. (2009) Collaborative digital writing: The art of writing together using technology. In A. Herrington, K. Hodgson, and C. Moran (eds) *Teaching the New Writing: Technology, Change, and Assessment in the 21st-Century Classroom*. New York: Teachers College Press, pp. 39–54.

Burnett, C., and Merchant, G. (2011) 'Is there a space for critical literacy in the context of new media?' *English, Practice and Critique*, 10, 1: 41–57.

Burns, J. (2012) School ICT to be replaced by computer science programme. *BBC News*, accessed January 11, 2012: www.bbc.co.uk/news/education–16493929

Carrington, V., and Robinson, M. (2010) Introduction: Contentious technologies. In V. Carrington and M. Robinson (eds) *Digital Literacies: Social Learning and Classroom Practices*. London: Sage, pp. 1–10.

Casey, H. (2011) Virtual constructions: Developing a teacher voice in the 21st century. In S.S. Abrams and J. Rowsell (eds) *Rethinking Identity and Literacy Education in the 21st century. National Society for the Study of Education Yearbook*, 110(1).

Coiro, J. (2003) Reading comprehension on the Internet: Expanding our understanding of reading comprehension to encompass new literacies. *The Reading Teacher*, 56(5): 458–464.

Collins, A., and Halverson, R. (2009) *Rethinking Education in the Age of Technology: The Digital Revolution and Schooling in America*. New York: Teachers College Press.

Cope, B., and Kalantzis, M. (2000) *Multiliteracies: Literacy, Learning, and the Design of Social Futures*. London: Routledge.

Cope, B., and Kalantzis, M. (2009) 'Multiliteracies': New literacies, new learning. *Pedagogies: An International Journal*, 4(3): 164–195.

DCMS and BIS (Department for Culture, Sport and the Media and Department for Business Information and Skills) (2009) *Digital Britain – The Final Report*. Norwich: The Stationery Office, accessed November 20, 2012: www.official-documents.gov.uk/document/cm76/7650/7650.pdf

Din, F.S., and Calao, J. (2001) The effects of playing educational video games on kindergarten achievement. *Child Study Journal*, 31(2): 95–102.

Dyson, A.H. (2006) Why popular literacies matter. In J. Marsh and E. Millard (eds) *Popular Literacies, Childhood and Schooling*. London: Routledge, pp. xvii–xxii.

Erstad, O. (2002) Norwegian students using digital artifacts in project-based learning. *Journal of Computer Assisted Learning*, 18: 427–437.

Folkesson, A., and Swalander, L. (2006) Self-regulated learning through writing on computers: Consequences for reading comprehension. *Computers in Human Behavior*, 23: 2488–2508.

Frye, E.M., Trathen, W., and Koppenhaver, D.A. (2010) Internet workshop and blog publishing: Meeting student (and teacher) learning needs to achieve best practice in the twenty-first-century social studies classroom. *The Social Studies*, 101: 46–53.

Garthwait, A., and Weller, H.G. (2005) A year in the life: Two seventh grade teachers implement one-to-one computing. *Journal of Research on Technology in Education*, 37(4): 361–377.

Gee, J.P. (2008) A sociocultural perspective on opportunity to learn. In P. Moss, D. Pullin, J.P. Gee, and E. Haertel (eds) *Assessment, Equity, and Opportunity to Learn*. New York: Cambridge University Press, pp. 76–108.

Goodson, I.F., Knobel, M., Lankshear, C., and Mangan, J.M. (2002) *Cyber Spaces/Social Spaces: Culture Clash in Computerized Classrooms*. New York: Palgrave Macmillan.

Goodson, F.T., and Norton-Meier, L. (2003) Motor oil, civil disobedience, and media literacy. *Journal of Adolescent and Adult Literacy*, 47(3): 258–262.

Goodson, L.A., and Skillen, M. (2010) Small town perspectives, big-time motivation: Composing and producing place-based podcasts. *English Journal*, 100(1): 53–57.

Graham, L. (2009) It was a challenge but we did it! Digital worlds in a primary classroom. *Literacy*, 43(2): 107–114.

Hartnell-Young, E. (2007) Making the connections: Theory and practice of mobile learning in schools. In J. Pearce and A. Norman (eds) *Proceedings of mLearn International Conference*. Melbourne: The University of Melbourne, pp. 86–95, accessed November 20, 2012: http://repository. unimelb.edu.au/pid/61794

Hawisher, G.E., and Selfe, C.L. (2004) Becoming literate in the information age: Cultural ecologies and literacies of technology. *College Composition and Communication*, 55(4): 642–692.

Heath, S.B. (1983) *Ways with Words: Language, Life, and Work in Communities and Classrooms*. Cambridge: Cambridge University Press.

Henderson, R., and Honan, E. (2008) Digital literacies in two low socioeconomic classrooms: Snapshots of practice. *English Teaching: Practice and Critique*, 7(2): 85–98.

Hodgson, K. (2009) Digital picture books. In A. Herrington, K. Hodgson, and C. Moran (eds) *Teaching the New Writing: Technology, Change, and Assessment in the 21st Century Classroom*. New York: Teachers College Press, pp. 55–72.

Hofer, M., and Swan, K.O. (2006) Technological pedagogical content knowledge in action: A case study of middle school digital documentary project. *Journal of Research on Technology in Education*, 41(2): 179–200.

Honan, E. (2008) Barriers to teachers using digital texts in literacy classrooms. *Literacy*, 42(1): 36–43.

Hull, G.A. (2003) Youth culture and digital media: New literacies for new times. *Research in the Teaching of English*, 38(2): 229–233.

ICTC (2011) *Digital Literacy: Canada's Productivity Opportunity*, accessed October 6, 2011: www.ictcctic.ca/uploadedFiles/About_Us/ICTC_News/News_Items/ICTC_DL_E%20print.pdf

IRA (International Reading Association) (2009) *New Literacies and 21st Century Technologies: A Position Statement of the International Reading Association*, accessed November 20, 2012: www.reading.org/General/AboutIRA/PositionStatements/21stCenturyLiteracies.aspx

Jenkins, H. with Purushota, R., Clinton, K., *et al.* (2006) *Confronting the Challenges of Participatory Culture: Media Education for the 21st Century*. Chicago: MacArthur Foundation, accessed May 7, 2011: http://mitpress.mit.edu/books/full_pdfs/confronting_the_challenges.pdf

Ke, F., and Grabowski, B. (2006) Gameplaying for maths learning: Cooperative or not? *British Journal of Education Technology*, 38(2): 249–259.

King, J.R., and O'Brien, D.G. (2002) Adolescents' multiliteracies and their teachers' needs to know: Toward a digital détente. In D.E. Alvermann (ed.) *Adolescents and Literacies in a Digital World*. New York: Peter Lan, pp. 40–50.

Kirriemuir, J., and McFarlane, A. (2003) Use of computer and video games in the classroom. *Proceedings of the Level up Digital Games Research Conference*, Universiteit Utrecht, Netherlands, accessed November 20, 2012: www.digra.org/dl/order_by_author?publication=Level%20Up%20Conference%20Proceedings

Kress, G. (2003) *Literacy in the New Media Age*. London: Routledge.

Kress, G. (2010) *Multimodality: A Social Semiotic Approach to Contemporary Communication*. London: Routledge.

Labbo, L., Leu, D. Jr., Kinzer, C., *et al.* (2003) Teacher wisdom stories: Cautions and recommendations for using computer-related technologies for literacy instruction. *The Reading Teacher*, 57(3): 300–304.

Lacasa, P., Méndez, L., and Martínez, R. (2008) Bringing commercial games into the classroom. *Computers and Composition*, 25: 341–358.

Lankshear, C., and Knobel, M. (eds) (2006) *New Literacies: Everyday Practices and Classroom Learning*, 2nd edn. Maidenhead: Open University Press.

Larson, L.C. (2008) Electronic reading workshop: Beyond books with new literacies and instructional technologies. *Journal of Adolescent and Adult Literacy*, 52(2): 121–133.

Leadbetter, C. (2008) *What's Next? 21 Ideas for 21st Century Learning*. London, DCFS: Innovations Unit.

Lichtman, M. (2010) *Qualitative Research in Education: A User's Guide*. Thousand Oaks, CA: Sage Publications.

Livingstone, I., and Hope, A. (2011) Next Gen.: Transforming the UK into the world's leading talent hub for the video games and visual effects industries. *NESTA*, accessed November 15, 2012: www.nesta.org.uk/library/documents/NextGenv32.pdf

Luke, A., and Elkins, J. (1998) Reinventing literacy in 'New Times.' *Journal of Adolescent and Adult Literacy*, 42(1): 4–7.

Manfra, M.M., and Hammond, T.C. (2006) Teachers' instructional choices with student-created digital documentaries: Case studies. *Journal of Research on Technology in Education*, 41(2): 223–245.

Marsh, J. (2004) The techno-literacy practices of young children. *Journal of Early Childhood Research*, 2(1): 51–66.

McDougall, J. (2010) A crisis of professional identity: How primary teachers are coming to terms with changing views of literacy. *Teaching and Teacher Education*, 26(3): 679–687.

Merchant, G. (2009) Digital writing in the early years. In J. Coiro, M. Knobel, C. Lankshear, and D. Leu (eds) *Handbook of Research in New Literacies*. New York: Lawrence Erlbaum, pp. 751–774.

Merchant, G. (2010) 3D Virtual worlds as environments for literacy teaching. *Education Research*, 52(2): 135–150.

Metcalf, S.J., and Tinker, R.F. (2004) Probeware and handhelds in Elementary and middle school science. *Journal of Science Education and Technology*, 13(1): 43–49.

Millard, E. (2003) Towards a literacy of fusion: New times, new teaching and learning? *Reading*, 37(1): 3–8.

Moos, D.C., and Honkomp, B. (2011) Adventure learning: Motivating students in a Minnesota Middle School. *Journal of Research on Technology in Education*, 43(3): 231–252.

NCTE (National Council of Teachers of English) (2008) *NCTE Position Statement: 21st Century Curriculum and Assessment Framework*, accessed November 20, 2012: www.ncte.org/positions/statements/21stcentframework

Neiburger, E. (2007) *Gamers . . . in the Library?! The Why, What, and How of Videogame Tournaments for All Ages*. Chicago: American Library Association.

Norris, C., and Soloway, E. (2004) Envisioning the handheld-centric classroom. *Journal of Educational Computing Research*, 30(4): 281–294.

O'Brien, D., and Scharber, C. (2008) Digital literacies go to school: Potholes and possibilities. *Journal of Adolescent and Adult Literacy*, 52(1): 66–68.

Rantala, L., and Korhonen, V. (2008) New literacies as a challenge for traditional knowledge conceptions in school: A case study from fifth graders' digital media production. *Studies in Media and Information Literacy Education*, 8(2): 1–15.

Rimes, B. (2007) Cell phones in math class. *The Tech Savvy Educator*, accessed November 20, 2012: www.techsavvyed.net/?p=200

Rosas, R., Nussbaum, M., Cumsille, P., *et al.* (2003) Beyond Nintendo: Design and assessment of educational video games for first and second grade students. *Computers and Education*, 40: 71–94.

Serrier, S.C. (2010) Carpet-time democracy: Digital photography and social consciousness in the early childhood classroom. *The Social Studies*, 101: 60–68.

Solomon, P.G. (2009) *The Curriculum Bridge: From Standards to Actual Classroom Practice*, 3rd edn. Thousand Oaks, CA: Corwin Press.

Soloway, E., Norris, C., Blumenfeld, P., *et al.* (2001) Handheld devices are ready-at-hand. *Communications of the ACM*, 44(6): 15–20.

Street, B.V. (1995) *Social Literacies: Critical Approaches to Literacy in Development, Ethnography, and Education.* New York: Longman.

Sylvester, R., and Greenidge, W. (2009) Digital storytelling: Extending the potential for struggling writers. *The Reading Teacher*, 63(4): 284–295.

Valkanova, Y., and Watts, M. (2007) Digital story telling in a science classroom: Reflective self-learning (RSL) in action. *Early Child Development and Care*, 117(6): 793–807.

Van Eck, R. (2006) Digital game-based learning: It's not just the natives who are restless. *EDUCAUSE*, 41: 16–30, accessed November 20, 2012: www.educause.edu/EDUCAUSE+Review/EDUCAUSEReviewMagazineVolume41/DigitalGameBasedLearningItsNot/158041

Wagner, T., EduServe, and Dobbin, G. (2009) Learning environments: Where space, technology, and culture converge. *EDUCAUSE Quarterly*, 32(4): 1–14.

Waller, M. (2010) 'It's very very fun and ecsiting' – using Twitter in the primary classroom. *English Four to Eleven*, 39: 14–16, accessed November 20, 2012: www.changinghorizons.net/2010/08/using-twitter-in-the-primary-classroom/

Wolverhampton Engage (2011) Mobile Learning at Dunstall Hill Primary School, accessed November 2012: www.wolverhampton-engage.net/sites/anonymous/Documents%20for%20Public%20Page/Mobile%20Learning%20at%20Dunstall%20Hill%20Primary%20School.aspx

Chapter 24

Digital Literacies in the Primary Classroom

Rachael Levy, Dylan Yamada-Rice, and Jackie Marsh

Introduction

In this chapter, we review literature that has outlined how many teachers in primary classrooms are using new technologies in innovative ways to develop children's digital literacy skills, knowledge, and understanding. There is now much evidence to suggest that young children enter primary schools having accrued a range of competencies in relation to digital technologies (Blanchard and Moore, 2010; Marsh *et al.*, 2005). This impacts upon their school lives, even when technological hardware and software is hard to access in the classroom. As an informative illustration of this point, Wohlwend (2009) observed children aged from five to seven, who were based in a classroom that did not have extensive ICT facilities, making artifacts from paper and pencil resources to enact mobile phone conversations and video game play. Wohlwend argues that this demonstrates how children's literacy-based play is now heavily influenced by their use of technology texts in the home. While it is undoubtedly the case that in some classrooms, children do not have sufficient opportunities to build on their out-of-school technological competencies (O'Hara, 2008), there is an increasing number of teachers who are developing innovative curricula and pedagogy that enable pupils to access, respond to, and create multimodal, multimedia texts. This chapter identifies some of these practices in order to develop a body of evidence that can inform future developments in this field.

In a chapter focusing on digital literacies, it is important to begin with an attempt to define that term, given in its varied use across a wide range of contexts. For some, 'digital literacy' signals a focus on the development of skills and competences related to a general use of technology, such as the ability to access and manage digital data, although Bawden (2008) argues that the phrase should signal attitudes and mindsets in addition to skills, such as the ability to learn independently. Here, we use the term much more narrowly to refer to reading, writing, and meaning-making mediated through new technologies.

Issues connected to the ways in which children make meaning from and produce texts are complex and this is partly due to the fact that definitions of the term 'text' are no longer straightforward (Bearne, 2009). In a recent review of research into technology and early childhood settings, Burnett (2009) concluded that it is now clear that 'complex interactions . . .

International Handbook of Research on Children's Literacy, Learning, and Culture, First Edition.
Edited by Kathy Hall, Teresa Cremin, Barbara Comber, and Luis C. Moll.
© 2013 John Wiley & Sons, Ltd. Published 2013 by John Wiley & Sons, Ltd.

occur between children, technology, and their wide-ranging experiences of literacy' (p. 260). This is a particularly important issue for all teachers working with children in schools today. There is much to suggest that young children entering the formal education system today are already proficient in handling a variety of digital media and multimodal texts (Marsh *et al.*, 2005, p. 5). Indeed, young children are demonstrating that they have developed skills in analyzing and creating multimodal texts, even before entry to the formal education system. For example, Levy (2009) discovered that children as young as four were drawing upon their interactions with digital texts in order to develop strategies to make sense of a whole variety of symbolic representations, including print. This work indicates that digital literacy skills have not replaced traditional constructions of reading and writing. Rather, it is being suggested that part of the complexity surrounding the issue of children's interactions with text is that traditional constructions of literacy now merge with new literacy practices, in ways that are, perhaps, not yet fully understood.

There are many aspects of digital literacy that could be addressed in a chapter such as this. We have focused on three main areas that emerged as dominant in the field from a review of the literature: Web 2.0 applications, film and television, and computer games. Inevitably, there are areas that we have not considered, such as the use of mobile technologies and GPS systems. Further, the studies reviewed were undertaken primarily in Europe and Australia. While there are accounts of digital literacy practices in primary classrooms emerging in other areas of the world, such as the United States (Razfar and Yang, 2010) and Asia (Churchill *et al.*, 2008), these studies are at present more limited in number.

In the first section of the chapter, we outline the way in which Web 2.0 applications have been used to enable young children to engage with audiences outside the classroom. Given the centrality of film and television in young children's lives, it is important to consider ways in which teachers have attempted to build on these interests and further children's understanding of moving image media. The second section of the chapter therefore considers research on young children's engagement with film and television. These moving image media are very important in the development of pupils' understanding of narrative, setting, and character; this is also the case in relation to computer games (Beavis and O'Mara, 2010). In the third section of the chapter, we outline research that has considered the use of computer games in the primary curriculum. We conclude by identifying the main features of classroom practice that foster the development of children's digital literacy skills knowledge and understanding and outline key areas of research that are required in the decades ahead. The overarching aim of the chapter, therefore, is to consider research that has identified how the teaching and learning of digital literacy in primary classrooms can be approached in order to inform an understanding of the key principles that should underpin such work in the future. We begin with a review of research that has focused on the use of Web 2.0, outlining recent developments in this area.

Use of Web 2.0 in Primary Classrooms

Web 2.0 programs and tools have become used increasingly in primary classrooms in recent years. Drawing on O'Reilly (2005) and Lankshear and Knobel (2011), Davies and Merchant (2009) describe Web 2.0 as having four characteristics: presence, modification, user-generated content, and social participation. The term 'Web 2.0' is generally used to describe certain types of web applications, for example, blogs, wikis, and other social networking sites, that have these four characteristics embedded within them. The value of these types of applications for primary schools is that they enable engagement with others outside the classroom. This, of course, has always been a possibility with the use of the Internet. For example, Maher (2010) reports on the ways in which email was used within a suburban Australian primary school class, in order for pupils to interact with children in a rural Australian setting and a rural class in the United States. However, the use of Web 2.0 tools means that pupils can now interact with both known and unknown interlocutors.

The practice of blogging is increasing in educational settings, offering chances for children to engage with these external, 'real-world' audiences (Bazalgette, 2010; Marsh, 2009; Merchant 2009a; Walsh, 2011), as readers can offer comments on pupils' blogs. This engagement with unknown others has become even more possible through the use of sites such as Twitter, which provide an immediate and, potentially, very wide audience through written communications. Twitter is a micro-blogging site which combines social networking with Tweets-messages of up to 140 characters and the possibility of sending images, which can be posted through Twitpics. The service has become widely popular outside educational establishments. Waller (2010a) described how he embedded Twitter into the 'everyday life' of his Year 2 (children aged 6 and 7) classroom in the north of England to 'develop competencies with literacy and digital technologies within a meaningful and enriching context' (p. 14). He asks pupils, 'What are you doing?' as the starting point for postings, which he sees as a question that 'embodies literacy in the reflections and interactions of users of the site' (p. 14) and he allows children to respond by sharing their learning to gain a better understanding of literacy as a 'real world' practice. Waller (2010a) has observed how Twitter use in his class has prompted pupils to take increasing pride in their work. He also believes that its incorporation has increased the pupils' (who include a group of struggling writers) engagement and interest in writing. Perhaps the 140 character limit imposed is ideally suited to younger learners' growing writing abilities. Marwick and Boyd's (2010) study into Twitter users' 'imagined audience' suggests people present themselves differently based on who they believe they are interacting with, regardless of whether this corresponds to an actual audience, and they state that this audience is often 'constructed by an individual in order to present themselves appropriately' (p. 2). On the other hand, Marwick and Boyd (2010) also found a significant number of participants' 'imagined audience' included the writer, causing them to perceive their interactions to be with someone with similar interests. This might play a role in young children's interactions if they likewise presume the audience will 'appreciate their work' (p. 8).

The use of these social networking sites not only promotes communication with unknown others, it also provides other valuable learning opportunities. Walsh (2011) describes how the online diary VoiceThread, blogs, and wikis have been used in Australia. While she notes that these applications allow pupils to interact with what she calls 'authentic' audiences, she emphasizes how they additionally encourage increased interaction within the class through peer engagement and critique. This was also the case in an English teacher's account of the use of wikis and word clouds in her classroom (Stone, 2011). Such tools can also promote oracy. Vardy, Kervin, and Reid (2007) explain how one teacher successfully integrated podcasts (played on iPods) into the primary school literacy syllabus, in order to support the teaching of literacy and to help develop speaking and listening in particular.

More recent developments in Web 2.0 include young children's increasing use of virtual worlds (Marsh, 2011). There is, as yet, little research which has identified how teachers might utilize children's interest in virtual worlds in the classroom. Merchant's (2009b) work on 'Barnesborough' is an exception. Merchant demonstrates how, when primary teachers in the north of England set up a range of literacy practices that are embedded in the virtual world, children responded with enthusiasm and interest. What is important in the success of such activities, however, is that teachers are prepared to forfeit their power in the teacher–pupil relationship and let the pupils lead the learning. The work in this virtual world enabled children to engage in the navigation and analysis of online, multimodal texts, but it also led to a rich range of activities that could be classified as 'traditional' literacy practices, focused on print. This fluid movement suggests that we need to move away from terminology such as 'old' and 'new' literacy practices, as suggested in the introduction to this chapter, and instead view children's engagement in reading and writing as a continuum that involves analysis, meaning-making, and creation of a broad range of texts that can be constructed in numerous modes and disseminated through a variety of media.

The examples offered by these classrooms demonstrate how teachers can provide children with varying degrees of freedom in interactions beyond school boundaries and respond to the fact that 'representation and communication are motivated by the social' (Kress, 2005, p. 6). These practices also take account of the wider social spheres in which children currently make meaning through digital technologies out-of-school (see for example Levy and Marsh, 2010). Bringing such Web 2.0 practices into schools may help to bridge home and school practices and prevent children losing confidence in their literacy abilities, which Levy's (2008) study found to be a problem when there were significant differences between school and home definitions of literacy. This premise was supported by Waller's (2010b) findings from a small-scale study in England, which indicated that children's views of literacy once they started school were consistent with the narrowly conceived 'common language' of the National Literacy Strategy (in place in the UK from 1998–2011), despite the fact that research on home literacy practices sees young children using a wide range of modes (image, writing, music, gesture, and speech) and media (Marsh *et al.*, 2005; Yamada-Rice, 2010). Feedback from pupils partaking in the Web 2.0 based learning projects described in Walsh (2011) suggests that they enjoyed opportunities for ongoing communication and interaction with their peers and wider audiences, being able to exchange ideas and express personal opinions, and they liked the fact that learning in this way can be open-ended. Teachers involved in the projects discussed here also noticed the benefits of a more engaged class, particularly among pupils who are normally disengaged, in addition to overall increased levels of participation in literacy (Waller, 2010b; Walsh, 2011).

Use of Film, Television, and Animation in Classrooms

Television, film and animation have long been found to be a favored daily activity among young children, with strong implications for emerging communication practices (Alburquerque *et al.*, 2003; Marsh *et al.*, 2005). Recent research on four-year-olds' home engagement with predominantly visually-based media confirms the primary importance of television in young children's home lives, despite the influx of newer screen-based technologies, and indicates that they continue to talk more enthusiastically about television and animation than other digital media (Yamada-Rice, 2010). Although television is not new, the consumption of it now takes place alongside the use of more recent digital screen-based technologies that introduce new means of learning and communication, such as the Web 2.0 sites mentioned previously. As such, it is now commonly accepted that wider digital media have helped to foreground the screen as the main site for communication and meaning-making (Kress, 2010), creating a shift from a primarily fixed period of monomodal focus on the written to one which preferences multimodal representations. These changes also allow young children to be producers, not only consumers, of texts which include television, film, and animation. As a result, a new consideration for the way in which television, film, and animation can be included into classrooms to support children's multimodal learning is emerging, with a particular emphasis on children as creators as well as consumers of such texts. This section focuses on some exemplary ways in which this is being achieved and the implication for young children's learning.

Marsh's (2006) one-year study of a project in which three and four year olds used imovie2 editing software to create short animated films from still images found that the majority were able to complete most of the activities independently, indicating that the children already had a degree of technical ability. Perhaps more importantly, the data pointed to the children's emergent ability to comprehend differences in modal affordances, which was displayed in the way they were able to select and utilize modes for different purposes. The emphasis on extending young children's knowledge of how to create multimodal texts was also the backbone to Waller's (2010b) four-week film-making project with his primary classroom, in which children altered and recreated a piece of animation to include references to their own cultural backgrounds. In so doing, the children drew story backdrops and then used 'green-screen' techniques to enable them to appear in front of the drawings on screen, thus becoming part of the final animation. In a different project, the same skills were explored when children made modern versions of the Brer Rabbit stories. Again, his class painted backgrounds for the settings, but this time animated the characters using stop-motion techniques similar to those used in Marsh (2006). Waller's (2010b) aim for these projects was 'the development of critical literacy skills achieved through the embedded and meaningful use of technology' (Waller, 2010b, p. 2). Thus, the digital media were not the focus of learning (although of course learning took place), but rather animation was included to extend young children's understanding of the transduction that occurs in translating knowledge from one mode to another, an important skill in work on film (Marsh, 2006). Similarly, in a study of 11-year-old pupils' film-making skills in Australia, Mills (2011) suggests that children need to develop 'a flexible multimodal metalanguage for work in kineikonic design' (p. 26), which are the skills required to work with moving image, such as an understanding of the value of camera angles or transitions.

This work, inevitably, normally focuses on the needs of a specific audience. Walsh (2011) describes how video recordings and photography were used in the Australian classrooms in her study to investigate learning topics and illustrates how the material gathered was developed into story boards and digital texts using 2create a story or Photostory 3. Some settings chose to produce a final DVD version for an audience or to be archived for future learning or assessment. In this way 'video was used as both a process for learning and a final product' (Walsh, 2011, p. 49). The final production of a DVD was not necessarily the main focus, but pupils were highly motivated to demonstrate their work for a specific audience (Walsh, 2011, p. 51).

This was also the case in the schools involved in the work of Bhojwani, Lord, and Wilkes (2008), who outline a range of case studies of the use of film in primary classrooms in the United Kingdom to promote writing and multimodal authoring. They suggest that an important aspect of this work is that it should offer opportunities to produce work for an intended audience who are able to view/read the texts. Such ideas appear to take advantage of an audience for children's learning beyond the classroom. It is this final point, Walsh (2011) asserts, that particularly distinguishes new uses of film and photography in the classroom from old; that the means of production and distribution have become a larger focus of contemporary communication practices. In addition to extending learning of multimodal practices, such projects can also be used to create stronger links between home and school literacy practices. Research by Parry (2010) illustrates how this relationship can be successfully extended. For example, Parry's (2010) film-making project in a primary classroom strengthened the connection between home and school by asking children to draw on their experience of films viewed at home. This work requires teachers to be comfortable about the potential for pupils to be more knowledgeable about the texts that are the focus of classroom study (Nixon and Comber, 2005).

The examples provided in this section show how the inclusion of film and animation in young children's educational settings can provide ways for them to extend their skills and knowledge with regard to multimodal design and, further, demonstrates the interrelationship between digital and nondigital texts. Kervin (2009) reports findings from a case study in Australia in which primary school aged children created and filmed short commercials on a social justice issue. Kervin (2009, p. 35) concludes that access to ICT meant that the texts these children created displayed a 'blurring' between the boundaries of text medium and genre. Moreover, she also suggests that by observing the process the children engaged with, she could identify a complex relationship between 'the language modes and use of "old" technology with the new,' which facilitated a powerful learning experience for the children. Kervin thus reiterates that children's interactions with text (both reading and producing texts), is very often dependent on a complex relationship between traditional constructions of literacy and the affordances of 'new' literacies.

The work reviewed in this section has outlined how educators have demonstrated 'increased recognition of the significance of children and young people's engagements with popular children's films as integral to their development as readers and creators of narrative texts' (Parry, 2009, p. 148); in light of the fact that these are 'complex texts, which offer opportunities for engagement, creativity and emotional response' (p. 169). This is also the case with computer games.

Use of Computer Games in the Classroom

There is a range of types of computer games, from games which are primarily educational in purpose and focus on developing specific skills, to games which aim to amuse and entertain – and of course, many games do both. Computer games can also differ according to whether they are played online or offline, or played using a computer, handheld computer, games console, and so on. Whatever their provenance, computer games are now an inherent feature in the social lives of many children. Studies suggests that computer and videogames are 'integral parts of family life' (Aarsand and Aronsson, 2009, p. 513), with further research indicating that even the youngest children are regularly playing games within virtual world contexts such as Club Penguin and Barbie Girls (Marsh, 2010). Yet it is becoming increasingly recognized that computer games have a significant role to play within the context of the classroom, as well as featuring within children's social lives (Devai, 2007). In a recent wide-scale project, 528 teachers, from a variety of European countries, were surveyed about their use of electronic games in school (Wastiau, Kearney, and Van den Berghe, 2009). It was reported that 70 percent of these teachers said that they already used digital games in the classroom, while 80 percent also stated that they believed digital games have a place in schools. What exactly do computer games offer in terms of supporting pedagogy in the primary classroom?

The first point to make is that there is much continuity in relation to the structures of narrative across media, including computer games (Mackey, 2005). There is work to suggest that children's understanding of narrative is developed through their engagement with computer games (Bearne and Wolstencroft, 2005). A further issue that appears to continually resurface in the literature on children's interactions with computer games in school is the concept of motivation for learning. Researchers have claimed that using computer games in the classroom is motivating for children for all ages (Barab *et al.*, 2005; Dalgarno and Lee, 2010; Robertson and Miller, 2009). For example, Tuzun *et al.* (2008) examined the effects of using a computer game with primary school age children (4th and 5th grades) in order to support their understanding of geographical features such as world continents and countries. They concluded that pre- and post-achievement tests revealed that as well as making 'significant learning gains'

(p. 68), their motivations for learning in the games-based environment showed statistically significant gains in comparison with those recorded in their traditional learning environment.

However, Sandford and colleagues (2006) challenge the view that simply introducing computer games into the classroom environment is motivating for children. Even though they argue that their own work has revealed that teachers and pupils report high levels of motivation and engagement when using computer games in school, they argue that it was not simply the presence of the games that initiated such engagement, but the 'specific features of games' (p. 50) and game-play that encouraged motivation and engagement. As a consequence, Sandford *et al.* stress that we need to move beyond the belief that children are motivated by playing computer games, and understand 'exactly what in games play is motivating' (p. 50) in order to be able to capitalize on the use of such resources in the classroom.

Indeed, it has been suggested that computer and video games are compelling for a number of reasons, but Gee (2003) argues that issues of user-identity may be central to this discussion. Gee explains that many games encourage the player to construct some element of the virtual world within which the player will become immersed; this can include creating a character, designing a car, making a home, and so on. Moreover, Gee argues that 'good' computer games continue to invite a high level of engagement by involving 'the player in a compelling world of action and interaction, a world to which the learner has made an identity commitment' (Gee, 2003, p. 68). As a consequence, the medium of the computer game encourages various skills to be practiced repeatedly, even though the player may not realize that such practice is taking place.

This is a particularly important issue when considering the ways in which teachers can use computer games effectively in the classroom to support their practice. As Sandford *et al.* (2006) state, the factors that shape various approaches to games-based learning are not, therefore, connected solely to the fact that computer games are being used for learning, but 'reflect a broader set of issues around both the use of digital technologies more generally and, arguably, the processes which serve to shape any form of educational innovation' (p. 48). This point is taken further in the work of Compton-Lilly (2007). In her exploration of the links between computer/video games and the teaching of reading, she argued that this immersion in a text 'is precisely what good readers do' (p. 722). She stresses that 'avid' readers do not read in order to improve their ability to decode print or extend their sight vocabulary, but they read a lot because 'they are engaged in an activity that is not boring' (p. 722).

Recent work has begun to explore the value of games across platforms, including games which draw on social networking features of Web 2.0. Colvert's (2009, 2010) study of a year-long Alternate Reality Gaming (ARG) literacy project outlines a multimedia, cross-curricular literacy project for a Year 6 (children aged 10 and 11) class in London in which she instigated an ARG where the children had to convince a Year 5 (children aged 9 and 10) class that the fictional characters in a novel were real. Web 2.0 and other digital media brought about an alternate reality in which the characters were made to seem real through, for example, creating character web pages and writing in role on message boards. The key to the success of this project seems to be that a reality of some kind was achieved through the children's use of technologies which have 'real-world,' nonfictional contexts and applications. Thus, although the activity was fictional, it still allowed the children to lock into the benefits of Web 2.0 described earlier in the chapter.

Clearly, there is much we can learn from observing and understanding children's engagement with computer games. The literature discussed in this section suggests that it is naïve to assume that using computer games in the primary classroom will automatically facilitate children's learning; however, there is an urgent need to continue to develop understanding of the ways in which digital media, such as computer games, promote desirable aspects of pedagogy and encourage children to learn.

Conclusion

The work reviewed in this chapter indicates that there is a range of good practice being undertaken in primary classrooms that offers young children opportunities to become competent and creative users and creators of digital texts. In concluding, we would like to suggest that there are a few underlying principles of such work that could inform future policy and practice. The first is that the primary objectives of the teachers' practice as highlighted focused on the development of children's skills, understanding and knowledge in relation to digital literacy; the technologies are used in support of these objectives. In other words, the technologies are not the starting point. Second, this work uses as its foundation the out-of-school experiences and interests of children. This is not to suggest that all children have equal access to new technologies outside school, but the majority will have developed some competencies in relation to ubiquitous technologies such as television and mobile phones (Blanchard and Moore, 2010; Marsh *et al.*, 2005). Using these experiences as a building block for work on digital literacies means that children can bring some level of understanding and confidence to the task at hand. Third, the approaches outlined in this chapter embed within them an acknowledgement that teachers may not always be the ones in any teaching context with the most expertise and knowledge; pupils themselves may have more advanced knowledge and expertise in the area of digital literacies and can guide the learning of others. Fourth, a key feature of many of the examples discussed here is that they offer pupils opportunities for engaging in literacy practices that have a 'real-world' purpose and in some cases, such as in the use of 'Blogger' and 'Twitter,' involve exchanges with audiences outside the classroom. Finally, a key principle underpinning all of this work is that motivation and engagement are key to learning; work using new technologies has the potential to interest pupils and enable them to adopt creative approaches to learning in the classroom context.

There are challenges to this work. The key challenge relates to assessment. There are, as yet, few models of progression in relation to the analysis and creation of multimodal, multimedia texts that can be used by teachers to assess where pupils are and where they need to go next. Bearne (2010) has developed a model of progression in relation to the analysis of multimodal texts that offers a very useful starting point for this work, but there needs to be further research in this area in the years ahead in order to extend understanding of assessment for learning in relation to the creation as well as analysis of digital texts. A further area of work that needs urgent research is the relationship between the development of skills and understanding in one mode as opposed to others. For example, is there a positive relationship between the development of competence in alphabetic literacy and skills in relation to the visual mode? How can teachers support the development of skills and understanding across the modes? There are also questions to be explored regarding the extent to which pupils bring their experiences of digital literacies gained outside the classroom to bear on their in-school activities without direct intervention by the teacher, and how far these experiences can support the development of further understanding.

The research outlined in this chapter indicates that, in the first decade of the twenty-first century, some primary teachers have grasped the significance of the technological changes taking place beyond the school gates and have undertaken work that has enabled their pupils to develop digital literacy skills, knowledge, and understanding that will be important for future employment and leisure activities. Given the conservative pace of change in education systems across the world, it may be some years before these kinds of practices are widespread. Nevertheless, it is important to document and celebrate ways in which individual educators can contribute to the development of practice and policy in an incremental manner. Until policy makers fully embrace the implications of the advancement of the digital age and create the conditions in which appropriate and relevant curriculum pedagogy can be developed, it is up to inspired and inspiring teachers and those who research alongside them to illustrate what can be done and to highlight the significance of this work.

References

Aarsand, P.A., and Aronsson, K. (2009) Gaming and territorial negotiations in family life. *Childhood*, 16: 497–517.

Alburquerque, M., Lacasa, P., Reina, A., and Cruz, C. (2003) Working on media literacy: 'Sharing problems in the classroom as a way to generate critical discussion.' AERA, Annual Meeting Chicago, 21–25 April.

Barab, S., Thomas, M., Dodge, T., Carteaux, R., and Tuzun, H. (2005) Making learning fun: Quest Atlantis, a game without guns. *Educational Technology Research and Development*, 53(1): 86–107.

Bawden, D. (2008) Origins and concepts of digital literacy. In C. Lankshear and M. Knobel (eds) *Digital Literacies: Concepts, Policies and Practices*. New York: Peter Lang, pp. 17–32.

Bazalgette, C. (ed.) (2010) *Teaching Media in Primary Schools*. London: Sage.

Bearne, E. (2009) Multimodality, literacy and text: developing a discourse. *Journal of Early Childhood Literacy*, 9(2): 156–187.

Bearne, E. with Bazalgette, C. (2010) *Beyond Words: Developing Children's Understanding of Multimodal Texts*. Leicester: United Kingdom Literacy Association.

Bearne, E., and Wolstencroft, H. (2005) Playing with texts: The contribution of children's knowledge of computer narratives to their story writing. In J. Marsh and E. Millard (eds) *Popular Literacies, Childhood and Schooling*. London: RoutledgeFalmer, pp. 72–92.

Beavis, C., and O'Mara, J. (2010) Computer games: Pushing at the boundaries of literacy. *Australian Journal of Language and Literacy*, 33(1): 65–76.

Bhojwani, P., Lord, B., and Wilkes, C. (2008) *'I Know What to Write Now!': Engaging Boys (and Girls) through a Multimodal Approach*. Leicester: UKLA.

Blanchard, J., and Moore, T. (2010) *The Digital World of Young Children: Impact on Emergent Literacy*. Pearson foundation White Paper, accessed November 20, 2012: www.pearsonfoundation. org/downloads/EmergentLiteracy-WhitePaper.pdf

Burnett, C. (2009) Technology and literacy in early childhood educational settings: A review of research. *Journal of Early Childhood Literacy*, 10(3): 247–270.

Churchill, N., Ping, L.C., Oakley, G., and Churchill, D. (2008) Digital storytelling and digital literacy learning. Proceedings of ICICTE: Readings in Education and Technology, Corfu, pp. 418–430.

Colvert, A. (2009) Peer puppeteers: Alternate reality gaming in primary school settings. In Proceedings of DIGRA, Breaking New Ground: Innovation in Games, Play, Practice and Theory, accessed November 20, 2012: www.digra.org/dl/db/09287.19018.pdf

Colvert, A. (2010) Alternate reality gaming: Writing just over the non-fiction line in the twenty first century. Paper presented at the United Kingdom Literacy Association 46th International Conference, Winchester, UK, July 10.

Compton-Lilly, C. (2007) What can video games teach us about teaching reading?, *The Reading Teacher*, 60(8): 718–728.

Dalgarno, B., and Lee, M. (2010) What are the learning affordances of 3-D virtual environments? *British Journal of Educational Technology*, 41(1): 10–32.

Davies, J., and Merchant, G. (2009) *Web 2.0 for Schools: Learning and Social Participation*. New York: Peter Lang Publishing Inc.

Devai, V. (2007) Risk-taking principals influence students' study. *Education Review*, 17(3): 14–15.

Gee, J.P. (2003) *What Video Games have to Teach us about Learning and Literacy*. New York: Palgrave Macmillan.

Kervin, L. (2009) 'GetReel': Engaging Year 6 students in planning, scripting, actualising and evaluating media text. *Literacy*, 43(1): 29–35.

Kress, G. (2005) Gains and losses: New forms of texts, knowledge, and learning. *Computers and Composition*, 22: 5–22.

Kress, G. (2010) *Multimodality: A Social Semiotic Approach to Contemporary Communication*. London and New York: Routledge.

Lankshear, C., and Knobel, M. (2011) *New Literacies: Everyday Practices and Classroom Learning*. 3rd edn. Maidenhead: Open University Press.

Levy, R. (2008) Third spaces are interesting places; applying 'third space theory' to nursery-aged children's constructions of themselves as readers. *Journal of Early Childhood Literacy*, 8(1): 43–66.

Levy, R. (2009) 'You have to understand words . . . but not read them'; young children becoming readers in a digital age.' *Journal of Research in Reading*, 32(1): 75–91.

Levy, R., and Marsh, J. (2010) Literacy and ICT in the early years. In D. Lapp and D. Fisher (eds) *The Handbook of Research on Teaching the English Language Arts*, 3rd edn. Mahwah, NJ: Lawrence Erlbaum, pp. 168–174.

Mackey, M. (2005) Children reading and interpreting stories in print, film and computer games. In J. Evans (ed.) *Literacy Moves On: Using Popular Culture, New Technologies and Critical Literacy in the Primary Classroom*. London: David Fulton, pp. 50–62.

Maher, D. (2010) Using the Internet as a communication tool to develop primary school students' cultural awareness. *Social Educator*, 28(2): 12–19.

Marsh, J. (2006) Emergent media literacy: Digital animation in early childhood. *Language and Education*, 20(6): 493–506.

Marsh, J. (2009) Productive pedagogies: Play, creativity and digital cultures in the classroom. In R. Willett, M. Robinson, and J. Marsh (eds) *Play, Creativity and Digital Cultures*. New York: Routledge, pp. 200–218.

Marsh, J. (2010) Young children's play in online virtual worlds. *Journal of Early Childhood Research*, 8(1): 23–39.

Marsh, J. (2011) Young children's literacy practices in a virtual world: Establishing an online interaction order. *Reading Research Quarterly*, 46(2): 101–118.

Marsh, J., Brooks, G., Hughes, J., *et al.* (2005) *Digital Beginnings: Young Children's use of Popular Culture, Media and New Technologies*. Sheffield, U.K: University of Sheffield, accessed November 20, 2012: www.digitalbeginnings.shef.ac.uk/

Marwick, A.E., and Boyd, D. (2010) I tweet honestly, I tweet passionately: Twitter users context collapse, and the imagined audience. *New Media and Society*, 13(1): 1–21.

Merchant, G. (2009a) Web 2.0, new literacies, and the idea of learning through participation. *English Teaching: Practice and Critique*, 8(3): 107–122.

Merchant, G. (2009b) Literacy in virtual worlds. *Journal of Research in Reading*, 32(1): 38–56.

Mills, K. (2011) 'Now I know their secrets': Kineikonic texts in the literacy classroom. *Australian Journal of Language and Literacy*, 34(1): 24–37.

Nixon. H., and Comber, B. (2005) Behind the scenes: making movies in early years classrooms. In J. Marsh (ed.) *Popular Culture, New Media and Digital Literacy in Early Childhood*. London: RoutledgeFalmer, pp. 219–236.

O'Hara, M. (2008) Young children, learning and ICT: A case study in the UK maintained sector. *Technology, Pedagogy and Education*, 17(1): 29–40.

O'Reilly, T. (2005) What is Web 2.0: Design patterns and business models for the next generation of software, accessed November 20, 2012: http://mpra.ub.uni-muenchen.de/4580/1/MPRA_paper_4580.pdf

Parry, B. (2009) Reading and rereading 'Shrek.' *English in Education*, 43(2): 148–161.

Parry, B. (2010) Helping children tell the stories in their heads. In C. Bazalgette (ed.) *Teaching Media in Primary Schools*. London: Sage, pp. 89–101.

Razfar, A., and Yang, E. (2010) Sociocultural theory and early literacy development: Hybrid language practices in the digital age. *Language Arts*, 88(2): 114–124.

Sandford, R., Ulicsak, M., Facer, K., and Rudd, T. (2006) *Teaching with Games: Using Commercial Off-the-shelf Computer Games in Formal Education*. Futurelab, accessed November 26, 2012: www2.futurelab.org.uk/resources/documents/project_reports/teaching_with_games/TWG_report.pdf

Stone, G. (2011) Webs, wikis, word clouds and web collaboration to support primary literacy. *English 4–11*. Spring: 8–11.

Tuzun, H., Yilmaz-Soylu, M., Karakus, T., *et al.* (2008) The effects of computer games on primary school students' achievement and motivation in geography learning,' *Computers and Education*, 52(1): 68–77.

Vardy, J., Kervin, L., and Reid, D. (2007) iPods and podcasting technologies to support talking and listening experiences of Grade 4 students. *Literacy Learning: The Middle Years*, 15(3): 57–70.

Waller, M. (2010a) Its's very very fun and ecsiting' – Using Twitter in the primary classroom. *English 4–11*, 39 (Summer): 14–16.

Waller, M. (2010b) A fixed point in time and pedagogy: Bringing the 'new' into the primary classroom. Proceedings of the ESRC Seminar series: *Children's and Young People's Digital Literacies in Virtual Online Spaces*: Seminar 5–Virtual Literacies in Schools, May 28, Sheffield Hallam University.

Walsh, M. (2011) *Multimodal Literacy: Researching Classroom Practice*. Newtown, Australia: Primary English Teaching Association:

Wastiau, P., Kearney, C., and Van den Berghe, W. (2009) *How are Digital Games Used in Schools? Main Results of Study*, European Schoolnet, accessed November 20, 2012: http://games.eun.org/upload/gis-synthesis_report_en.pdf

Wohlwend, K. (2009) Early adopters: Playing new literacies and pretending new technologies in print-centric classrooms. *Journal of Early Childhood Literacy*, 9(2): 117–140.

Yamada-Rice, D. (2010) New media, evolving multimodal literacy practices and the potential impact of increased use of the visual mode in the urban environment on young children's learning. *Literacy*, 45(1): 32–43.

Chapter 25

Developing Online Reading Comprehension

Changes, Challenges, and Consequences

Bernadette Dwyer

Introduction

The emergence of the Internet as a powerful communication, literacy, and learning tool has led to calls in the literature for a reconceptualization of what literacy entails in the twenty-first century (Flood and Lapp, 1995; International Reading Association (IRA), 2009; Reinking, 1998). One's ability to access, critically evaluate, synthesize, and communicate information quickly, efficiently, and effectively are key components to active and full participation in a global world (Leu and Kinzer, 2000). While online reading skills are built on foundational print-based skills, online reading comprehension is not isomorphic with print-based literacies and additional skills and strategies may be required to fully exploit the potential of the Internet as a site for learning (Leu *et al.*, 2004).

This chapter explores how the changing nature of literacy in an online environment impacts on the development of students' online reading comprehension and information-seeking skills and strategies. It seeks to address the challenges presented for students when conducting information searches online. Further, it explores the challenges for classroom teachers in adopting new pedagogies to accommodate a new literacies curriculum. Finally, it considers the consequences that these changes and challenges have on pedagogy, the development of a classroom curriculum, and the creation of learning communities within classrooms.

Changes Brought About to Literacy with the Advent of the Internet and other ICTs

The Internet is an n-dimensional (Harrison, 2008), nonlinear (Bolter, 1998), multimodal (Kress, 2003, 2010), post-textualist (Purves, 1998) environment. Afflerbach and Cho (2009a) note that Internet reading embodies a 'fundamental change in the architecture of acts of reading' (p. 81). Emerging research suggests that online reading skills are built on related processing and cognitive print-based skills, such as automaticity in decoding, word recognition, and reading fluency. However, online reading introduces additional complexities to the *acts of*

International Handbook of Research on Children's Literacy, Learning, and Culture, First Edition.
Edited by Kathy Hall, Teresa Cremin, Barbara Comber, and Luis C. Moll.
© 2013 John Wiley & Sons, Ltd. Published 2013 by John Wiley & Sons, Ltd.

reading and higher levels of strategic processing, cognitive skills and strategies, and affective dimensions may be required to fully exploit the Internet's potential as a tool for literacy and learning (Afflerbach and Cho, 2009a; Coiro, 2007; Hartman, Morsink, and Zheng, 2010; IRA, 2009; RAND Reading Study Group, 2002; Zhang and Duke, 2008). The literature seems to suggest that *reading strategies* and *reading skills* are at opposite ends of a continuum. Whereas strategies suggest effortful, goal-directed, and conscious actions on the part of the reader to construct meaning from text; skills are characterized by automaticity, fluency, and effortlessness, often without the explicit conscious control of the reader (Afflerbach, Pearson, and Paris, 2008; Dole, Nokes, and Drits, 2009; Pressley and Harris, 2006). Reading strategies have been described as 'skills under consideration' (Paris, Lipson, and Wixson, 1983, p. 295). Furthermore, it appears that the good reader has the ability to 'shift seamlessly' (Afflerbach *et al.*, 2008, p. 371) between the automatic use of a reading skill to the effortful use of a reading strategy.

The sections that follow explore some of the additional complexities introduced for readers in an online environment and how the interactions between the reader, the text, and the activity within a socio-cultural environment changes in such an online environment.

First, the online reader is more effortful in 'realising and constructing potential texts to read' (Afflerbach and Cho, 2009b, p. 209). It is the reader, rather than the author, who determines a unique pathway through the fluidity of online text. The reader must read selectively and strategically, monitoring the text to be read, while at the same time avoiding unwarranted distractions, such as advertisements. The interaction between the reader, text, and the activity may be more dynamic, opportunistic, and interactive in an online environment (McEneaney, 2006). Although the reader of a print text may choose to read nonfiction or indeed fiction in a nonlinear manner, the text is a stable, fixed entity confined within the bounds of the book cover. The reader is aware of exactly where they are in the print-based text and indeed the physical length of such a text.

Second, the content of hyperlinks is hidden from view and consequently the online reader is less able to construct meaning by drawing on contextual information. Therefore, predictive inferencing becomes necessary to unpack this hidden content (Coiro and Dobler, 2007). Hyperlinks are 'constant decision points' (Kuiper and Volman, 2008, p. 249). Overviewing of text, that is, skimming and scanning, is qualitatively different in an online environment where the online reader must engage in predictions of partially obscured content by navigating within hyperlinks and across web pages engaging in what amounts to 'slightly educated guesses' (Afflerbach and Cho, 2009b, p. 204) to anticipate the relevancy of the information to the task focus.

Third, self-regulation and persistence in an online environment is crucial to avoid the cognitive overload and disorientation often experienced by online readers (Nachmias and Gilad, 2002). The online reader must be involved in active decision-making processes (Duke, Schmar-Dobler, and Zhang, 2006), such as planning, monitoring, predicting, and questioning (Coiro and Dobler, 2007) as he/she moves speedily and efficiently (Leu *et al.*, 2004) across websites 'berrypicking' (Bates, 1989) information and making intertextual (Hartman, 1995) links across and within texts on-the-hoof to assemble ideas, recall, summarize, and synthesize the information retrieved. Learner control and choice is heightened in an online environment. When searching for information online the reader generates search strings and evaluates search results, chooses which hyperlink is pertinent to the task and which is extraneous, judges what information to skim quickly and what information to scan carefully. While this can both empower and liberate the online reader it can also be daunting for those readers with limited online skills. The online environment can be a challenging landscape where McCombs' (1996) notion of self-as-agent is crucially important to develop as readers orient themselves (Hill and Hannafin,

1997), exercise high levels of self-efficacy (Tsai and Tsai, 2003), persistence (Bilal, 2000), resilience (Coiro, forthcoming), and flexibility to take responsibility for their own learning in a dynamic shifting environment (Dalton and Proctor, 2008).

Fourth, the online reader must draw flexibly on a wide range of prior knowledge sources in an online environment. These include the activation of prior knowledge of the *architecture of online informational text structures* (e.g., menu, hyperlinks, and multimodal supports); an ability to draw on *Internet application knowledge* (e.g., navigational Internet browser features); and a facility to engage with domain and topic knowledge while concomitantly connecting with *world knowledge*. What is unclear, at present, is the role of each of these prior knowledge sources as they fuse in an online environment. For example, what level of automaticity of prior knowledge in online informational text structures and Internet application knowledge is required to free up the cognitive energy of the online reader to focus on and connect with prior domain, topic, and world knowledge? (Hill and Hannafin, 1997; Lawless and Kulikowich, 1998; Moos and Azevedo, 2008). What level of domain and topic knowledge is needed to allow online readers to access a sufficiently extensive vocabulary range to generate and revise search strings, investigate search results with a critical eye, and judge the accuracy, authority, relevance, and importance of information in text to the task at hand? (Allington and McGill-Franzen, 2009; Dwyer, 2010). Finally, what is the role of knowledge gathered on-the-hoof by the navigational decisions of online readers across multiple websites where online readers accrue new knowledge and update their prior knowledge sources in the malleable moments of Internet searching? (Coiro, 2007; DeSchryver and Spiro, 2008; Leu *et al.*, 2009).

In sum, the Internet and other information and communications technologies (ICTs) introduce additional complexities to the *acts of reading* for the online reader. Drawing on and extending Pearson's (2009) use of metaphor, the online reader is a *builder* (drawing concurrently on a wider range of prior knowledge sources while developing 'schemas-of-the-moment') (DeSchryver and Spiro, 2008, p. 9); a *fixer* (utilizing metacognitive, self-regulatory, active decision-making processes in a recursive and integrative fashion); an *assembler* (using top-down and bottom-up skills and strategies on-the-hoof; including recall, summarization, and synthesis across a labyrinth of linked texts); a *responder* (both in efferent and aesthetic modes) (Rosenblatt, 1978); and as a critic and a critical evaluator and consumer of text in an ill-structured and un-scrutinized domain (Spiro *et al.*, 2004). These changes present challenges for students in an online environment. In turn, they present challenges for teachers to enable them to construct effective pedagogies and curriculum to accommodate the new literacies into learning in the twenty-first century classroom (Reinking, Labbo, and McKenna, 2000).

Challenges for Students and their Teachers in an Online Environment

There is a dissonance between the in-school and out-of-school literacies experienced by our students (Alvermann, 2008). Our students' literacy and technology lives outside school incorporate social networking, emailing, and texting, uploading and downloading videos, and engaging with gaming applications. However, research has shown that the high level of prowess with technology use afforded to the 'Digital Native' generation (Prensky, 2001) lacks credibility in the research-based literature (Bennett, Matton, and Kervin, 2008; University College London CIBER Group, 2008). Research suggests that students face difficulties in a number of areas related to both reading comprehension and completing information searches in an online environment. For example, students are unlikely to be critical consumers of online information and have difficulty in evaluating online information for quality, credibility, authority, and reliability (Hirsh, 1999; Leu *et al.*, 2008).

The new literacies perspective (Leu *et al.*, 2004; Coiro *et al.*, 2008) posit that searching for information online is a 'problem-based inquiry process' (Leu *et al.*, 2008, p. 323) requiring skills, strategies, and affective dimensions in posing effective questions to structure online inquiry; locating relevant information; critically assessing the currency of that information to the task question; and synthesizing and communicating that information to others. The following sections discuss the challenges for students when searching for information in an online environment.

Planning and setting goals for online information searches

For purposeful reading and inquiry on the Internet it is important that students formulate engaging questions to provide a purpose for their inquiry, set a context for problem solving, and establish a goal for learning (Owens, Hester, and Teale, 2002). Zhang and Duke (2008) also note the difference between reader characteristics depending on the nature of the task. For example, online readers may process text differently if browsing for recreational purposes, searching for specific information, or reading to develop conceptual knowledge.

Studies suggest that students rarely plan or articulate the goal of information-seeking or engage in strategy formulation when conducting Internet inquiry (Burke, 2002; Fidel *et al.*, 1999). This adds to the feelings of frustration encountered by online readers where the expectation that the answer to a poorly articulated question is but a mere 'click' away (Kuiper and Volman, 2008). The feeling of disorientation experienced by online readers has been well documented in the literature, where readers become overwhelmed both by the amount of information retrieved (Foltz, 1996; Treymayne and Dunwoody, 2001) and the feeling of being lost in hyperspace (Edwards and Hardman, 1999).

Generating search terms and investigating search results

The online information inquiry process encompasses both the ability to generate and revise search strings and investigate search results in a critical manner. Both of these gatekeeper skills (Henry, 2006) are necessary for the retrieval of online information. Research indicates that students at elementary (Kafai and Bates, 1997; Fidel *et al.*, 1999; Wallace and Kupperman, 1997) and high school levels (Nahl and Harada, 1996) have difficulties formulating search strings. Factors compounding these difficulties include insufficient prior knowledge of search engine algorithms; inadequate domain and topic knowledge to generate effective keywords; insufficient vocabulary knowledge for synonym and superordination generation; and flexibility at a conditional level of knowledge (Lipson and Wixson, 1986) to generate, monitor, and revise search string keywords (Bilal, 2001; Kuiper and Volman, 2008; Schacter, Chung, and Dorr, 1998).

The ability to investigate search results speedily and with a critical eye is an important Internet skill. Research findings indicate that students rarely venture beyond the first few results; have difficulty with the level of abstraction necessary to successfully construct meaning from the search result paragraph (Bilal, 2000); and seldom use the search result heading to assess the relevance of the search result to the task (Fidel *et al.*, 1999; Hill and Hannafin, 1997; Kafai and Bates, 1997). Emerging research suggests a taxonomy of skills in investigating search results. First, a random (Guinee, Eagleton, and Hall, 2003) '*click and look*' (Leu *et al.*, 2007) strategy with minimal reading of search results. Second, a *limited strategic scrolling* of search results (Dwyer, 2010) where each result, in turn, is systematically investigated. Finally, a *skilful investigation strategy* (Dwyer, 2010) where the relevance of each result is assessed by critiquing evidence provided by the URL and the abstract paragraph, matching this to the task goal and doing so speedily, efficiently and automatically.

Generating and revising search strings and investing search results with a critical eye are crucial skills in the process of locating online information. Both facilitate the online reader to locate information relevant to their task goal. The section that follows considers the challenges for students in locating online information.

Locating online information

Locating information in an online environment has been referred to as 'a nontrivial complex skill' (Nachmias and Gilad, 2002, p. 481). Some of the main challenges experienced by online readers include a capacity to manage an information overload; an inability to evaluate the relevancy of information to the task focus; equating the quantity of information with the quality of that information (i.e., quantity equals quality); and a facility to separate the wheat from the chaff. The ability to self-regulate in an online environment draws on many of the skills associated with print-based skills, such as monitoring, planning, questioning, and evaluating. In an online environment self-regulation acquires a higher level of complexity as the reader filters information across a myriad of texts (Bulger, 2006) and synthesizes that information, thereby 'spinning straw into gold' (Eagleton and Guinee, 2002, p. 52). Students also face the challenge of assessing the quality of the information retrieved for their task goal. Kuiper and Volman (2008, p. 63) have questioned what they call the 'consumerist nature of students' where students find an acceptable answer to a question in the shortest time possible. They are, therefore, engaging in what Agosto (2002) has called 'satisficing' behavior finding sufficient information to satisfy the task set.

Studies have shown that students spend more time on the process of information seeking rather than the product of that search, that is, reading relevant information for the task focus. In the Wallace and Kupperman study (1997), students spent 24 percent of their time actually reading information on websites. The rest of the time was spent on finding a path to that information. Authors (Birkerts, 1994; Purves, 1998) have noted the cursory, superficiality of the information retrieved and the lack of depth in growth of conceptual learning and knowledge development during online activity. It is therefore important that we support our students to grasp the opportunities presented for learning with the Internet and to deepen their learning experiences online.

Evaluation of online information

Evaluation of online information includes critical evaluation skills (e.g., assessing reliability and accuracy of information; critical thinking skills (e.g., a disposition for interrogating the text); critical literacy skills (e.g., assessing author purpose, stance, and bias); and media-savviness and information literacy skills (e.g., establishing trustworthiness and reasonableness of information presented). Critical evaluation of information introduces new complexities for the online reader as the Internet is an un-vetted open network where anyone can publish any information. Evaluation of information draws on exercising one's ability to comprehend, apply, analyze and synthesize information. Previous studies reveal that students face challenges in realizing that misleading and erroneous information can be placed on the web (Schacter *et al.*, 1998); are unaware of the need to challenge the veracity, authority, and reliability of information presented (Shenton and Dixon 2003; Wallace and Kupperman, 1997); are misled by the appearance of a website (Sutherland-Smith, 2002); and struggle to detect hidden author agendas (Fabos, 2008). In addition, students need to draw on a maturity of reflection and a world experience and knowledge that they simply do not have. Therefore, it is important to help our students to read with their antennae raised so that they develop a 'healthy scepticism' (Leu *et al.*, 2007) about what they read in an online environment.

Communication of information

Web 2.0 and beyond introduced new possibilities for all online readers to be online authors and producers of texts (Malloy, Castek, and Leu, 2010). Online platforms are continually emerging and include shared reading, writing, and communication spaces, such as Nings, Wikis and Google Docs; threaded discussion boards; and online social networking sites, such as Facebook, Edmodo, and Twitter. The Internet expands our vision of 'audience' and 'community of learners' beyond the four walls of the classroom to encompass a global classroom network. Here, students can engage in collaborative communities, such as ePals, to co-construct meaning by engaging in socio-collaborative reading of texts (Hartman, Morsink, and Zheng, 2010) to communicate, transact, and respond with others in an online environment.

Challenges for Teachers in an Online Environment

While some teachers are successfully integrating the Internet and other ICTs into the curriculum (Crook *et al.*, 2010) many are not (Hutchinson and Reinking, 2011). The reasons cited by teachers include: a lack of infrastructural and technical support; an insufficient knowledge base; a fear of change; an already overloaded curriculum; and limited opportunities for professional development. Developing content and pedagogical knowledge (Shulman, 1987) is no longer sufficient to meet the needs of the twenty-first century classroom. The Technological Pedagogical Content Knowledge (TPCK) framework proposed by Mishra and Koehler (2006) promotes the flexible orchestration, transaction, and integration of pedagogy, content, and technology. The TPCK framework allows teachers to draw flexibly from, and integrate knowledge of, pedagogy, content, and technology to develop appropriate classroom frameworks, curriculum, and instructional practices to support learning with the new literacies.

Little research has focused on the development of curriculum or instructional contexts in classroom environments that support the development of effective online reading skills (Castek, 2008; Dalton *et al.*, 2011; Eagleton and Dobler, 2007; Leu *et al.*, 2008). The Dwyer (2010) study sought to accommodate the new literacies of the Internet and other ICTs within an inquiry-based integrated curriculum. A brief outline of the study and its findings are presented next and serve as an illustrative, contextual example of the possibilities of accommodating a new literacies framework within the classroom curriculum. Following this, some of the consequences for classroom curriculum, pedagogies, and conceptual learning with the Internet and other ICTs will be presented drawing both on the Dwyer (2010) study and other emerging studies in the field.

Scaffolding Internet reading with struggling readers from disadvantaged communities

The Dwyer (2010) longitudinal study was conducted, with 3rd to 6th grade students, in a high poverty school district in Ireland. The pedagogical goal of the study was to scaffold the development of online literacies with struggling readers from disadvantaged communities within the context of the learning ecology of the classroom. The classroom learning ecology includes the complex, multilevel, dynamic, transactional interplay and interdependency, which is evolving rather than static, between multiple actors (teachers, students, school administrators, parents, the wider community, and policy makers) and multiple variables (curriculum, pedagogies, infrastructure, resources, and technical ICT support) (Zhao and Frank, 2003).

The study was underpinned by a formative and design experimental methodological framework (F&DE) (see Reinking and Bradley, 2008 for a full description). The F&DE framework is sympathetic to the 'multiple realities' and provisionality of the classroom environment (Labbo and Reinking, 1999). The F&DE methodology is interventionist by nature; adaptive and iterative by design; and driven by a theoretically determined, valued, and clearly articulated pedagogical goal in authentic learning environments. The F&DE methodological framework 'serves the central goal of putting theory to work in a way that simultaneously informs and refines or generates useful theory grounded in practice' (Reinking and Bradley, 2008, p. 43); thereby making firm research to practice connections while concomitantly generating theory.

The study was conducted in three interlinked phases: the baseline phase; reading development and critical web literacy development phase; and the main study phase. Each phase built on emerging insights from analysis of preceding phases in a spiral fashion. A range of essentially qualitative data sources were analyzed using inductive and deductive methods (Miles and Huberman, 1994), on both on a micro (weekly basis) and macro basis (at the end of each phase) (Gravemeijer and Cobb, 2006). Data sources included; online recorded Internet activity; think aloud protocols (Pressley and Afflerbach, 1995); semi-structured interviews; digitally recorded group discussions, fieldnotes, lesson samples; and artifacts of students' work.

The design of the study included the development of a series of integrated cross-curricular themed units designed to develop both offline and online literacies. For example, one cross-curricular thematic unit, integrating literacy, science and the Internet, related to *Animals and their Adaptations to their Environments*. Situational interest in this thematic unit was developed by conducting observations, science experiments and fieldtrips, (drawing on and adapting the Concept Oriented Reading Instruction (CORI) model; for a review of the model see Guthrie, 2004). Graded nonfiction texts were added to the class library related to each thematic unit. The teachers adopted a novel also related to the theme as the class reader. For example, *The Butterfly Lion* (Morpurgo, 1996) related to animal adaptations.

The students also worked in mixed-ability triad groups during a series of 25 Internet workshops, conducted across the timeline of the study, in the computer lab in the school. Explicit strategy instruction, using the gradual release of responsibility model (Pearson and Gallagher, 1983), in the form of mini-lessons, modeling, and scaffolding, was utilized to develop online reading comprehension and information-seeking skills and strategies. The students conducted research, primarily on the Internet, on inquiry-based self-chosen topics related to the themed cross-curricular units. They produced online ebooks using RealeWriter software, (www.realewriter.com) to communicate information related to the themed units.

Students adopted leadership roles online in the guise of a questioner, navigator, or summarizer (emulating Palinscar and Brown's 1984 reciprocal teaching model). This provided a structure where students could scaffold each other's online learning activities. Peer-to-peer collaboration was also encouraged through the use of electronic share boards, class discussions, and quick shares where students reflected on their developing online skills and strategies. Across the timeline of the study learner-centered assessment (Tierney, 2000) was utilized to inform future teaching. Students were also presented with Internet inquiry challenges, which they conducted independently, at key points in the study. For example, one inquiry challenge related to finding information on how a Burmese Python can swallow an animal whole without choking. Data from these online inquiry challenges provided a digital portfolio of work, and both summative and formative evidence on the progression of online skills strategies and dispositions. Self-and peer-assessment practices and reflections also allowed the students to become stakeholders with their teachers in the assessment practices in the class (Afflerbach, 2007).

Findings from the study suggested that (a) the development of an ecological learning community within the classroom coupled with an integrated enquiry-based curriculum enhanced engagement and motivation and enabled the students to develop high levels of online reading, writing, and communication skills; (b) new literacies were acquired through explicit instruction, adaptive scaffolding, and peer-to-peer collaboration; and (c) peer-to-peer collaboration supported the development of the cognitive, affective, and social dimensions of learning in such environments.

The sections which follow review the findings from the Dwyer (2010) study, against a backdrop of other emerging studies in the field, and discuss the consequences for classroom curriculum, development of classroom pedagogies, and the development of learning with the Internet and other ICTs.

Consequences for the Development of Classroom Curriculum, Pedagogies, and Learning with the Internet and other ICTs

'The content of new technologies can replicate the past or transform the future. Ultimately it will take a conscientious effort to change ways of thinking, ways of doing, ways of believing' (Young, 2008, p. 352). The instructional environment with the classroom learning ecology evolved considerably across the timeline of the Dwyer (2010) study. The role of the class teacher changed from that of a transmitter of knowledge to that of a co-learner, co-constructor, and ultimately a facilitator of learning. The students' role also changed from passive recipients of knowledge to more active metacognitive constructors of knowledge as they co-constructed their own learning through collaboration with their peers and with the class teacher. The classroom environment promoted mutual respect, dialogue, ownership, a sharing of responsibility, and reciprocity.

This was achieved through the development of an integrated inquiry-based, problem solving, classroom curriculum that created a synergy between literacy, the content areas, and the Internet. The spiral nature of the curriculum, developed over two school years, helped to develop self-efficacy, motivation, and engagement. It enabled the students to develop, deepen and hone their offline and online literacy skills over an extended period of time. The development of curriculum drew on a suite of well researched print-based instructional models, such as the CORI (Guthrie, 2004) model and the Reciprocal Teaching model (Palinscar and Brown, 1984). These models were adapted and transitioned onto an online format. This holds promise for the construction of curriculum and suggests that we do not need to reinvent the wheel or discard all that we hold dear to accommodate the new literacies into the classroom curriculum.

Developing a community of learners within the ecology of learning in classrooms reshapes the contexts for learning within those classrooms. The ability to work collaboratively to co-construct meaning, to problem solve as part of a team, and to develop new understandings by exploring multiple perspectives are valued in the workplace and should be nurtured in the classroom to enhance learning. Collaboration provides 'multiple resources at the reading construction site' (Kucan and Beck, 1997, p. 289) and allows students to draw on their own knowledge and understanding, and on the strengths, insights, and knowledge construction processes of others in the group (Putney *et al.*, 2000). Findings from the Dwyer (2010) study suggest that peer-to-peer collaboration does not occur spontaneously and requires the introduction of structural frameworks, such as online reciprocal roles, share boards, and class discussions to develop the quality of interactions in groups. Further, 'huddling' (Barron, 2003) occurs within the classroom environment when groups of students are presented with a choice of challenging inquiry-based tasks. This leads to an active, group-enhanced self-regulation and a deeper processing of texts. Students can examine, challenge, affirm, and extend one another's thinking and processing of texts. In the Castek (2008) study, challenging activities prompted the students to adopt shifting leadership roles within the groups where students shared emerging insights with other group members.

In the new literacies classroom teachers become 'orchestrators of literacy learning environments' (Leu *et al.*, 2004, p. 1599). Therefore, the teacher's role in designing classroom spaces and challenging curriculum to enhance learning becomes more not less important in a changing and evolving learning and literacy landscape. Traditional forms of professional development, such as summer courses or focus days have largely been unsuccessful in changing practice in classrooms. In the Dwyer (2010) study the researcher worked *in situ*, over an extended period, and in partnership with the class teachers in a professional learning community to provide sustained, customized onsite professional development. In turn, in a ripple effect, the class teachers involved in the study collaborated with and supported other class teachers in the school to accommodate the new literacies into classroom curriculum and pedagogies to support student learning in a school-wide learning ecology (Zhao and Frank, 2003). In a new literacies landscape, where technology tools for literacy are continually emerging, innovative ways, such as incorporating social networking tools, could be utilized to develop global elearning communities where teachers, teacher educators, researchers, experts in content areas and senior scholars in the fields of literacy and technology could collaborate to share understandings of how to develop effective technological, pedagogical content knowledge to accommodate the new literacies framework (Mishra and Koehler, 2006).

The discourse in the digital divide debate has moved from a focus on *physical patterns of access* to technology to *equality of opportunity in access* to technology at home and in school according to socio-economic status (SES) (Hargittai and Hinnant 2008; Livingstone and Helsper, 2007; Warschauer, 2003). Studies show that students from lower SES and those struggling with print-based literacies have either limited access to technology (Karchmer, 2001) or are engaged in decontextualized, drill and practice type software programs (Dalton and Strangman, 2006). This is in marked contrast to their more affluent peers who are engaged in collaborative, problem-solving activities and the development of higher-order thinking skills in their access to technology (Becker, 2000). Therefore, technology compounds the divide between students of different SES, leading to a digitally determined (Dwyer and Harrison, 2008) Matthew effect (Stanovich, 1986). Those who need both quality of, and equality in, access to technology to enhance learning and literacy are 'those receiving it the least' (Leu, 2006). Results from the Dwyer (2010) study show the importance of access to online technologies for all students regardless of their print-based literacy achievements. Findings from the study illustrate the possibilities that the Internet and other ICTs have to actively engage, motivate, and challenge these students on the margins to develop higher-order thinking skills and problem-solving strategies in challenging inquiry-based activities.

Conclusion

This chapter has explored some of the changes, challenges and consequences for literacy, classroom curricula, and pedagogies in twenty-first century classroom communities. It has provided some emerging insights into the potential of the Internet and other ICTs to motivate all students to engage deeply with literacy and learning. Clearly, as teachers, teacher educators, researchers, scholars, and policy makers, we have just embarked on this journey and the road ahead looks promising. There is still much to learn about the new literacies of the Internet and other ICTs.

References

Afflerbach, P. (2007) *Understanding and Using Reading Assessment, K–12.* Newark, DE: International Reading Association.

Afflerbach, P.A., and Cho, B.Y. (2009a) Identifying and describing constructively responsive comprehension strategies in new and traditional forms of reading. In S. Israel and G. Duffy (eds) *Handbook of Reading Comprehension Research.* Mahwah, NJ: Erlbaum, pp. 69–90.

Afflerbach, P., and Cho, B.Y. (2009b) Determining and describing reading strategies: Internet and traditional forms of reading. In H.S. Waters and W. Schneider (eds) *Metacognition, Strategy Use, and Instruction.* New York: Guilford Press, pp. 201–225.

Afflerbach, P., Pearson, P.D., and Paris, S.G. (2008) Clarifying differences between reading skills and reading strategies. *The Reading Teacher,* 61(5): 364–373.

Agosto, D.E. (2002) Bounded rationality and satisficing in young people's Web-based decision-making. *Journal of the American Society for Information Science and Technology,* 53: 16–27.

Allington, R.L., and McGill-Franzen, A. (2009) Comprehension difficulties among struggling readers. In S.E. Israel and G.G. Duffy (eds) *Handbook of Research on Reading Comprehension,* New York: Routledge, pp. 551–568.

Alvermann, D. (2008) Commentary: Why bother theorizing adolescents' online literacies for classroom practice and research? *Journal of Adolescent and Adult Literacy,* 52: 8–19.

Barron, B. (2003) When smart groups fail. *Journal of the Learning Sciences,* 12(3): 307–359.

Bates, M.J. (1989) *The Design of Browsing and Berrypicking Techniques for the Online Search Interface,* accessed November 20, 2012: www.gseis.ucla.edu/faculty/bates/berrypicking.html

Becker, H.J. (2000) Who's wired and who's not: Children's access to and use of computer technology. *The Future of Children,* 10(2): 44–75.

Bennett, S., Matton, K., and Kervin, L. (2008) The 'digital natives' debate: A critical review of the evidence. *British Journal of Educational Technology,* 39(5): 775–786.

Bilal, D. (2000) Children's use of the Yahooligans! Web search engine:1. Cognitive, physical and affective behaviors on fact-based search tasks. *Journal of the American Society for Information Science,* 51(7): 646–665.

Bilal, D. (2001) Children's use of the Yahooligans! Web search engine: II. Cognitive, physical and affective behaviors on research tasks. *Journal of the American Society for Information Science,* 52(2): 118–136.

Birkerts, S. (1994) *The Gutenberg Elegies: The Fate of Reading in an Electronic Age.* Boston: Faber and Faber.

Bolter, J.D. (1998) Hypertext and the question of visual literacy. In D. Reinking, M.C. McKenna, L.D. Labbo, and R.D. Kieffer (eds) *Handbook of Literacy and Technology: Transformations in a Post-Typographic World.* Mahwah, NJ: Lawrence Erlbaum, pp. 3–14.

Bulger, M. (2006) Beyond search: A preliminary skill set for online literacy, accessed November 20, 2012: http://transliteracies.english.ucsb.edu/research-papers/translit-bulger-onlinelit.pdf

Burke, J. (2002) The Internet reader. *Educational Leadership,* 60(3): 38–42.

Castek, J. (2008) How do 4th and 5th grade students acquire the new literacies of online reading comprehension? Exploring the contexts that facilitate learning. Unpublished doctoral dissertation. University of Connecticut, Storrs.

Coiro, J. (2007) Exploring changes to reading comprehension on the Internet: Paradoxes and possibilities for diverse adolescent readers. Unpublished doctoral dissertation, University of Connecticut, Storrs.

Coiro, J. (forthcoming) Purposeful, critical, and flexible: Key dimensions of online reading and learning. In R. Spiro, M. DeSchrvyer, M. Schira-Hagerman, *et al.* (eds) *Reading at a Crossroads? Disjunctures and Continuities in Current Conceptions and Practices.* New York: Routledge.

Coiro, J., and Dobler, E. (2007) Exploring the comprehension strategies used by sixth-grade skilled readers as they search for and locate information on the Internet. *Reading Research Quarterly*, 42: 214–257.

Coiro, J., Knobel, M., Lankshear, C., and Leu, D.J. (2008) Central issues in new literacies and new literacies research. In J. Coiro, M. Knobel, C. Lankshear, and D.J. Leu (eds) *Handbook of Research on New Literacies*. Mahwah, NJ: Lawrence Erlbaum, pp. 1–21.

Crook, C., Harrison, C., Farrington-Flint, L., *et al.* (2010) *Impact 09 final report.* Coventry: BECTA.

Dalton, B., and Proctor, C.P. (2008) The changing landscape of text and comprehension in the age of the new literacies. In J. Coiro, M. Knobel, C. Lankshear, and D.J. Leu (eds) *Handbook of Research on New Literacies*. Mahwah, NJ: Lawrence Erlbaum, pp. 297–324.

Dalton, B., Proctor, C.P., Uccelli, P., *et al.* (2011) Designing for diversity: The role of reading strategies and interactive vocabulary in a digital reading environment for fifth-grade monolingual English and bilingual students. *Journal of Literacy Research*, 43(1): 68–100.

Dalton, B., and Strangman, N. (2006) Improving struggling readers' comprehension through scaffolded hypertexts and other computer-based literacy programs. In M.C. McKenna, L.D. Labbo, R.D. Kieffer, and D. Reinking (eds) *International Handbook of Literacy and Technology*, Vol. II. Mahwah, NJ: Lawrence Erlbaum, pp. 75–93.

DeSchryver, M., and Spiro, R. (2008) New forms of deep learning on the web: Meeting the challenge of cognitive load in conditions of unfettered exploration in online multimedia environments. In R. Zheng (ed.) *Cognitive Effects of Multimedia Environments*. Hershey, PA: IGI Global.

Dole, J.A., Nokes, J.D., and Drits, D. (2009) Cognitive strategy instruction. In S.E. Israel and G.G. Duffy (eds) *Handbook of Research on Reading Comprehension*. New York: Routledge, pp. 347–372.

Dwyer, B. (2010) Scaffolding Internet reading: A study of a disadvantaged school community in Ireland. Unpublished doctoral dissertation, University of Nottingham: U.K.

Dwyer, B., and Harrison, C. (2008) There's no rabbits on the Internet: Scaffolding the development of effective search strategies for struggling readers during Internet inquiry. In Y. Kim and V.J. Risko (eds) *57th Yearbook of the National Reading Conference*. Oak Creek, WI: National Reading Conference, pp. 187–202.

Duke, N.K., Schmar-Dobler, E., and Zhang, S. (2006) Comprehension and technology. In M.C. McKenna, L.D. Labbo, R.D. Kieffer, and D. Reinking (eds) *International Handbook of Literacy and Technology*, Vol. II. Mahwah, NJ: Erlbaum, pp. 317–326.

Eagleton, M.B., and Dobler, E. (2007) *Reading the Web: Strategies for Internet Inquiry*. New York: Guildford.

Eagleton, M.B., and Guinee, K. (2002) Strategies for supporting student Internet inquiry. *New England Reading Association Journal*, 38(2): 39–47.

Edwards, D.M., and Hardman, L. (1999) 'Lost in hyperspace': Cognitive mapping and navigation in a hypertext environment. In R. McAleese (ed.) *Hypertext: Theory into Practice*, 2nd rev. edn. Oxford, UK: Intellect Books, pp. 90–105.

Fabos, B. (2008) The price of information: Critical literacy, education, and today's Internet. In J. Coiro, M. Knobel, D. Leu, and C. Lankshear (eds) *Handbook of Research on New Literacies*. Mahwah, NJ: Erlbaum, pp. 839–870.

Fidel, R., Davies, R.K., Douglass, M.H., *et al.* (1999) A visit to the information mall: Searching behavior of high school students. *Journal of the American Society for Information Science*, 50(1): 24–37.

Flood, J., and Lapp, D. (1995) Broadening the lens: toward an expanded conceptualization of literacy. In K.A. Hinchman, D.J. Leu, and C.K. Kinzer (eds) *Perspectives on Literacy Research and Practice: The 44th Year Book of the National Reading Conference*. Chicago: National Reading Conference, pp. 1–16.

Foltz, P.W. (1996) Comprehension, coherence and strategies in hypertext and linear text. In J.-F. Rouet, J.J. Levonen, A. Dillon, and R. Spiro (eds) *Hypertext and Cognition*. Hillsdale, NJ: Lawrence Erlbaum, pp. 109–136.

Gravemeijer, K., and Cobb, P. (2006) Design research from a learning perspective. In J. van den Akker, K. Gravemeijer, S.S. McKenney, and N. Nieveen (eds) *Educational Design Research*. New York: Routledge, pp. 17–51.

Guinee, K., Eagleton, M.B., and Hall, T.E. (2003) Adolescents' Internet search strategies: Drawing upon familiar paradigms when sourcing electronic information sources. *Journal of Educational Computing Research*, 29(3): 363–374.

Guthrie, J.T. (2004) Classroom contexts for engaged reading: An overview. In J.T. Guthrie, A. Wigfield, and K.C. Perencevich (eds) *Motivating Reading Comprehension. Concept-oriented Reading Instruction*. Mahwah, NJ: Lawrence Erlbaum, pp. 87–112.

Hargittai, E., and Hinnant, A. (2008) Digital inequality: Differences in young adults' use of the Internet. *Communication Research*, 35(5): 602–621.

Harrison, C. (2008) Researching technology and literacy. Thirteen ways of looking at a blackboard. In J. Coiro, M. Knobel, C. Lankshear, and D.J. Leu (eds) *Handbook of Research on New Literacies*. Mahwah, NJ: Lawrence Erlbaum, pp. 1283–1293.

Hartman, D.K. (1995) Eight readers reading: The intertextual links of proficient readers reading multiple passages. *Reading Research Quarterly*, 30(3): 520–561.

Hartman, D.K., Morsink, P.M., and Zheng, J. (2010) From print to pixels: The evolution of cognitive conceptions of reading comprehension. In E.A. Baker (ed.) *The New Literacies: Multiple Perspectives on Research and Practice*. New York: Guilford Press, pp. 131–164.

Henry, L.A. (2006) SEARCHing for an answer: The critical role of new literacies while reading on the Internet. *The Reading Teacher*, 59(7): 614–627.

Hill, J.R., and Hannafin, M.J. (1997) Cognitive strategies and learning on the World Wide Web. *Educational Technology Research and Development*, 45(4): 37–64.

Hirsh, S.G. (1999) Children's relevance criteria and information seeking on electronic resources. *Journal of the American Society for Information Science*, 50(14): 1265–1283.

Hutchinson, A., and Reinking, D. (2011) Teachers' perceptions of integrating Information and Communication Technologies into literacy instruction: A national Survey in the US. *Reading Research Quarterly*, 46(4): 308–329.

IRA (International Reading Association) (2009) *New Literacies and 21st Century Technologies: A Position Statement*. Newark, DE: IRA, accessed November 20, 2012: www.reading.org/General/AboutIRA/PositionStatements/21stCenturyLiteracies.aspx

Kafai, Y., and Bates, M.J. (1997) Internet web-searching instruction in the elementary classroom: Building a foundation for information literacy. *School Library Media Quarterly*, 25(2): 103–111.

Karchmer, K.A. (2001) The journey ahead: Thirteen teachers report how the Internet influences literacy and literacy instruction in their K–12 classrooms. *Reading Research Quarterly*, 36: 442–467.

Kress, G. (2003) *Literacy in the New Media Age*. London: Routledge.

Kress, G. (2010) *Multimodality: A Social Semiotic Approach to Contemporary Communication*. London: Routledge.

Kucan, L., and Beck, I.L. (1997) Thinking aloud and reading comprehension research: Inquiry, instruction and social interaction. *Review of Educational Research*, 67(3): 271–279.

Kuiper, E., and Volman, M. (2008) The web as a source of information for K–12 education. In J. Coiro, M. Knobel, C. Lankshear, and D.J. Leu, (eds) *Handbook of Research on New Literacies*. Mahwah, NJ: Lawrence Erlbaum, pp. 267–296.

Labbo, L.D., and Reinking, D. (1999) Negotiating the multiple realities of technology in literacy research and instruction. *Reading Research Quarterly*, 34(4): 478–492.

Lawless, K.A., and Kulikowich, J.M. (1998) Domain knowledge, interest, and hypertext navigation: A study of individual differences. *Journal of Educational Multimedia and Hypermedia*, 7(1): 51–69.

Leu, D.J. (2006) New literacies, reading research, and the challenges of change: A deictic perspective. In J.V. Hoffman, D.L. Schallert, C.M. Fairbanks, *et al.* (eds) *The 55th Yearbook of the National Reading Conference*. Milwaukee, WI: National Reading Conference, pp. 1–20.

Leu, D.J., Coiro, J., Castek, J., *et al.* (2008) Research on instruction and assessment in the new literacies of online reading comprehension. In C.C. Block and S.R. Parris (eds) *Comprehension Instruction: Research-based Best Practices*, 2nd edn. New York: Guildford Press, pp. 321–346.

Leu, D.J., and Kinzer, C.K. (2000) The convergence of literacy instruction with networked technologies for information and communication. *Reading Research Quarterly*, 35(1): 108–127.

Leu, D.J., Kinzer, C.K., Coiro, J., and Cammack, D. (2004) Towards a theory of new literacies emerging from the Internet and other Information and Communication Technologies. In R.B. Ruddell and N. Unrau (eds) *Theoretical Models and Processes of Reading*, 5th edn. DE: International Reading Association, pp. 1570–1613.

Leu, D.J., O'Byrne, W.I., Zawlinski, L., *et al.* (2009) Expanding the new literacies conversation. *Educational Researcher*, 38: 264–269.

Leu, D.J., Zawlinski, L., Castek, J., *et al.* (2007) What is new about the new literacies of online reading comprehension? In L.S. Rush, A.J. Eakle, and A. Berger (eds) *Secondary School Literacy: What Research Reveals for Classroom Practice*. Urbana, IL: National Council of Teachers of English, pp. 37–68.

Lipson, M.Y., and Wixson, K.K. (1986) Reading disability research: An interactionist perspective. *Review of Educational Research*, 56(1): 111–136.

Livingstone, S., and Helsper, E. (2007) Gradations in digital inclusion: Children, young people and the digital divide. *New Media and Society*, 9(4): 671–696.

Malloy, J., Castek, J., and Leu, D.J. (2010) Silent reading and online reading comprehension. In E. Hiebert and R. Reutzel (eds) *Revisiting Silent Reading*. Newark, DE: International Reading Association, pp. 221–240.

McCombs, B. (1996) Alternative perspectives for motivation. In L. Baker, P. Afflerbach, and D. Reinking (eds) *Developing Engaged Readers in School and Home Communities*. Mahwah, NJ: Lawrence Erlbaum, pp. 67–89.

McEneaney, J.E. (2006) Agent-based literacy theory. *Reading Research Quarterly*, 41(3): 352–371.

Miles, M.B., and Huberman, A.M. (1994) *Qualitative Data Analysis: An Expanded Sourcebook*, 2nd edn. Thousand Oaks, CA: Sage.

Mishra, P., and Koehler, M.J. (2006) Technological pedagogical content knowledge: A new framework for teacher knowledge. *Teachers College Record*, 108(6): 1017–1054.

Moos, D.C., and Azevedo, R. (2008) Self-regulated learning with hypermedia: The role of prior domain knowledge. *Contemporary Educational Psychology*, 33: 270–298.

Morpurgo, M. (1996) *The Butterfly Lion*. London: HarperCollins Children's books.

Nachmias, R., and Gilad, A. (2002) Needle in a hyperstack: Searching for information on the World Wide Web. *Journal of Research on Technology*, 34(4): 475–486.

Nahl, D., and Harada, V.H. (1996) Composing Boolean logic statements: Self-confidence, concept analysis, search logic, and errors. *School Library Media Quarterly*, 24(4): 199–207.

Owens, R.F., Hester, J.L., and Teale, W.H. (2002) Where do you want to go today? Inquiry-based learning and technology integration. *The Reading Teacher*, 55(7): 616–625.

Palinscar, A.S., and Brown, A.L. (1984) Reciprocal teaching of comprehension-fostering and comprehension-monitoring activities. *Cognition and Instruction*, 1(2): 117–175.

Paris, S.G., Lipson, M.Y., and Wixson, K.K. (1983) Becoming a strategic reader. *Contemporary Educational Psychology*, 8: 293–316.

Pearson, P.D. (2009) The roots of reading comprehension instruction. In S.E. Israel and G.G. Duffy (eds) *Handbook of Research on Reading Comprehension*. New York: Routledge, pp. 3–31.

Pearson, P.D., and Gallagher, M.C. (1983) The instruction of reading comprehension. *Contemporary Educational Psychology*, 8: 317–344.

Prensky, M. (2001) Digital natives, digital immigrants. *On the Horizon*, 9(5): 1–6, accessed November 20, 2012: www.marcprensky.com/writing/Prensky%20-%20Digital%20Natives,%20Digital%20Immigrants%20-%20Part1.pdf

Pressley, M., and Afflerbach, P. (1995) *Verbal Protocols for Reading: The Nature of Constructively Responsive Reading*. Hillsdale, NJ: Erlbaum.

Pressley, M., and Harris, K.H. (2006) Cognitive strategy instruction: From basic research to classroom instruction. In P.A. Alexander and P.H. Winne (eds) *Handbook of Educational Psychology*, 2nd edn. Mahwah, NJ: Erlbaum, pp. 265–286.

Purves, A. (1998) Flies in the web of hypertext. In D. Reinking, M.C. McKenna, L.D. Labbo, and R.D. Kieffer (eds) *Handbook of Literacy and Technology: Transformations in a Post-typographic World*. Mahwah, NJ: Lawrence Erlbaum. pp. 235–252.

Putney, L.A.G., Green, J., Dixon, C., *et al.* (2000) Consequential progressions: Exploring collective-individual development in a bilingual classroom. In C.D. Lee and P. Smagorinsky (eds) *Vygotskian Perspectives on Literacy Research: Constructing Meaning through Collaborative Inquiry.* New York: Cambridge University Press, pp. 86–126.

RAND Reading Study Group. (2002) *Reading for Understanding: Toward a Research and Development Program in Reading Comprehension.* Pittsburgh, PA: Office of Educational Research and Improvement.

Reinking, D. (1998) Synthesising technological transformations of literacy in a post-typographic world. In D. Reinking, M. McKenna, L. Labbo, and R. Kieffer (eds) *Handbook of Literacy and Technology: Transformations in a Post-typographic World,* Mahwah, NJ: Erlbaum, pp. xi–xxx.

Reinking, D., and Bradley, B.A. (2008) *On Formative and Design Experiments.* New York: Teachers College Press.

Reinking, D., Labbo, L.D., and McKenna, M.C. (2000) From assimilation to accommodation: A developmental framework for integrating digital technologies into literacy research and instruction. *Journal of Research in Reading,* 23(2): 110–122.

Rosenblatt, L.M. (1978) *The Reader, the Text, the Poem: The Transactional Theory of Literary Work.* Carbondale: Southern Illinois University Press.

Schacter, J., Chung, G.K., and Dorr, A. (1998) Children's Internet searching on complex problems: Performance and process analyses. *Journal of the American Society for Information Science,* 49(9): 840–849.

Shenton, A.K., and Dixon, P. (2003) A comparison of youngsters' use of CD-Rom and the Internet as information resources. *Journal of the American Society for Information Science and Technology,* 54(11): 1029–1049.

Shulman, L.S. (1987) Knowledge and teaching: Foundations of the new reform. *Harvard Educational Review,* 57(1): 1–22.

Spiro, R.J., Coulson, R.L., Feltovich, P.J., and Anderson, D.K. (2004) Cognitive flexibility theory: Advanced knowledge acquisition in ill-structured domains. In R.B. Ruddell and N.J. Unrau (eds) *Theoretical Models and Processes of Reading,* 5th edn. Newark, DE: International Reading Association, pp. 640–654.

Stanovich, K.E. (1986) Matthew effects in reading: Some consequences of individual differences in the acquisition of literacy. *Reading Research Quarterly,* 21(4): 360–407.

Sutherland-Smith, W. (2002) Weaving the literacy web: Changes in reading from page to screen. *The Reading Teacher,* 55(7): 662–669.

Tierney, R.J. (2000) Literacy assessment reform: Shifting beliefs, principled possibilities, and emerging practices In N.D. Padak, *et al.* (eds) *Distinguished Educators on Reading: Contributions that have Shaped Effective Literacy Instruction.* Newark, DE: International Reading Association, pp. 517–541.

Treymayne, M., and Dunwoody, S. (2001) Interactivity, information processing and learning on the World Wide Web. *Science Communication,* 23(2): 111–134.

Tsai, M.-J., and Tsai, C.-C. (2003) Information searching strategies in web-based science learning: The role of Internet self-efficacy. *Innovations in Education and Teaching International,* 40(1): 43–50.

University College London CIBER group (2008) *Information Behaviour of the Researcher of the Future.* London: University College London, accessed November 20, 2012: from www.bl.uk/news/pdf/googlegen.pdf

Wallace, R., and Kupperman, J. (1997) On-line search in the science classroom: Benefits and possibilities. Paper presented at the Annual Meeting of the American Educational Research Association, Chicago, accessed October 18, 2008: www.msu.edu/~mccrory/pubs/online_search.pdf

Warschauer, M. (2003) *Technology and Social Inclusion: Rethinking the Digital Divide.* Cambridge, MA: MIT Press.

Young, P.A. (2008) Exploring culture in the design of new technologies of literacy. In J. Coiro, M. Knobel, C. Lankshear, and D.J. Leu (eds) *Handbook of Research on New Literacies.* Mahwah, NJ: Lawrence Erlbaum, pp. 325–358.

Zhang, S., and Duke, N.K. (2008) Strategies for Internet reading with different reading purposes: A descriptive study of twelve good Internet readers. *Journal of Literacy Research*, 40(1): 128–162.

Zhao, Y., and Frank, K.A. (2003) Factors affecting technology uses in schools: An ecological perspective. *American Educational Research Journal*, 40(4): 807–840.

Chapter 26

Hybrid Literacies in a Post-hybrid World

Making a Case for Navigating

Elizabeth Birr Moje

Introduction

One year, in early spring, I looked out at my garden, eagerly anticipating the glorious riot of color produced by the blooming of our 30 varieties of iris flowers. I was to be disappointed, however, because when I looked out again in late spring, I saw mostly dark purple iris, the color most often associated with the bloom.

> 'Where are the maroon, the peach, and the pale pink iris? What happened to our maize and blue iris?' I petulantly asked our head gardener (also known as my husband). I suspected that he had been moving things around in the garden again.
> 'Purple is dominant,' he replied. 'Those colors are gone.'

I sighed, because I knew he was right. The iris had been in the ground for almost ten years; it was not surprising that those unusual hybrid colors were no longer in evidence. We had seen it time and time again in our garden, and the eclipsing of the recessive by the dominant in hybrids is a well-known phenomenon in biological studies. Being confronted with that phenomenon in nature, however, made me question what it might mean for the desire to apply the metaphor of hybridity to social and cultural studies of literacy, identity, and culture. How powerful is a social or cultural hybrid? Do hybrids even exist in actual practice? And what is the hybrid? Are people hybrid? The spaces they inhabit? The literacies they employ in those spaces?

These questions, which have haunted my work for some time, form the basis for the theoretical musings in this chapter. To address them, I briefly review the concept of *hybrid literacies* by drawing on various theoretical perspectives and empirical studies that have examined or contributed to the conceptualization of literacy practices as hybrids of many different ways of knowing, expressing, and representing meaning.

Although the review of various theories and empirical works is key to unpacking what it means to talk about hybrid literacies, a more pressing goal of the chapter is to focus attention on challenges in theorizing, studying, and teaching hybrid literacy practices. Several questions

International Handbook of Research on Children's Literacy, Learning, and Culture, First Edition.
Edited by Kathy Hall, Teresa Cremin, Barbara Comber, and Luis C. Moll.
© 2013 John Wiley & Sons, Ltd. Published 2013 by John Wiley & Sons, Ltd.

arise, for example, in the pursuit of research on hybrid literacies. First, is hybridity real? That is, are people's practices actually hybrid, or do they simply code switch from one discourse community to another? Second, is hybridity healthy? What is powerful about a concept of hybrid literacy practices, identities, or cultures? On the flip side, what are the potential down sides to hybridity? What does it take to nurture hybridity?

Third, if hybridity needs expansion or reconceptualization as a metaphor for human identities and/or for the spaces in which identities are generated, then what are some alternatives that can capture what has been so compelling about the metaphor and expand it simultaneously? In response to that question, I offer an expansion of the concept of hybridity by considering the idea of *navigating* or navigations as a replacement for hybridity in our thinking about literacy learning, practice, and development. I suggest that the concept of navigations might allow for hybridity in certain contexts, but recognize that people may not always want or be able to take on new practices or habits of mind, or that certain contexts may demand the enactment of particular, rather than hybrid, identities. With navigations as a working metaphor, I then turn to the question of what it might take to study and teach navigations. How are navigations recognized, nurtured, and taught as *skills*? In an era of increasing attempts to standardize curricula and learning experiences, as well as ever-growing demands for accountability through standard measures, how do educators foster teachers' attention to and abilities in developing and nurturing hybridity and navigational skills? Finally, what does studying hybridity or navigations entail? How does one measure, document, or capture hybridity or navigations, especially in light of the question of whether practices are truly hybrid or simply different in varied settings? What are innovative research designs, methods, and tools for documenting hybridity and navigations? What responsibilities do researchers have when studying and representing people's navigations?

Theories of Hybridity

The concept of hybridity implies the bringing together of many influences and this is nowhere more evident than in the conceptualization of hybridity itself. Thus, this brief review includes Peircean semiotics, theories of spatiality, conceptions of third space and hybridity from cultural geography, postcolonial theory, and education theory. I also draw on ethnographic research that has illustrated how children and youths' *funds of knowledge* (Moll and Greenberg, 1990) can be brought into classroom learning environments and how children and youth navigate literacy demands across multiple spaces (e.g., Gutiérrez *et al.*, 1999; Moje *et al.*, 2004). The review I offer here is, of necessity, fairly brief because it stands in service of the theorizing that follows, rather than as a stand-alone review. As a result, the representation of each theory is something of a gloss; readers are encouraged to consult each of the theorists cited herein, as well as Moje *et al.* (2004) and Gutiérrez (2008) for more detail and precision in representation of the different concepts.

Terms of distinction, or, distinguishing among terms

Three related, but not isomorphic, terms or phrases – hybridity, hybrid literacies, and third space – are germane to this chapter and, as such, demand some explicit naming and defining.

Hybridity typically refers either to identities or to contexts, spaces, and cultures. References to hybridity in identity theory often suggest a mingling – sometimes conflicted – of the ways that people identify or are identified by others. Homi Bhabha (1994), in particular, posited hybridity as a phenomenon of a colonial and postcolonial world, wherein two or more ways of knowing in the world come into contact and members of both (or more) worlds are forced to construct new ways of knowing the world – and new identities – as they navigate the 'in-between.'

The concept of *hybrid literacies* stems from such work as various scholars have taken up the ideas from hybridity theory and applied them to the idea that the literate practices valued in home, community, peer groups, and schools can come together in unpredictable ways to produce new literate practices (e.g., Gutiérrez, Rymes, and Larson, 1995; Moll, 1992a) or conventional practices (both everyday and academic) used for unconventional purposes (e.g., Barton, Tan, and Rivet, 2008; Elmesky, 2011). Indeed, the narrative style of the introductory paragraphs to this chapter could be considered an example of the latter sense of hybrid literacies.

The idea of *third space* situates hybrid identities and practices in physical, social, and cultural spaces. The notion of third space is not intended to convey an actual or singular space in which hybridity emerges, but the space of the in-between, the place where different practices collide, where identities are recognized and people are positioned, and where possibilities of new ideas reside. Any given set of interactions can produce multiple third spaces. The central, shared element of all three constructs of hybridity, hybrid literacies, and third space is *multiplicity*, the place where the first and second come together and produce something different, a third.

The concept of 'thirdness' and the hybrid

Hybridity theory recognizes the complexity of the spaces people inhabit on a daily basis and what that complexity means for identities, discourses, and literacies, particularly in a globalized world (Hall, 1995). The theory posits that people in any given community draw on multiple resources or funds (Gonzalez, Moll, and Amanti, 2005; Moll and Greenberg, 1990) to make sense of the world and of oral and written representations of the world. Further, hybridity theory examines how living in-between and having to make sense of several different funds of knowledge and discourses can be both productive and constraining in terms of one's literate, social, and cultural practices and, ultimately, one's identity development. The notion of hybridity can thus apply to the integration of competing knowledges and discourses; to the texts one reads and writes; to the spaces, contexts, and relationships one encounters; and even to a person's identity enactments and sense of self. Hybridity theory connects in important ways to third space, because third spaces are hybrid spaces that bring together any or all of the constructs named above. In effect, all conceptions of hybridity begin with a notion of a plural, and in most theories, they begin with some version of the concept of *thirdness*.

C.S. Peirce (1839–1914) offered the concept of 'thirdness' and his theorization of what he referred to as the *phaneron*, or the idea, as being comprised of three dimensions of firstness, secondness, and thirdness. The first, in Peirce's conceptualization, was an idea in pure form (also known to Peirce as a monad); the second, or dyad, was two subjects or ideas 'brought into oneness.' His argument was that the second was dependent on being distinguished from the first. The third, for Peirce, was,

> the medium or connecting bond between the absolute first and last. The beginning is first, the end second, the middle third. The end is second, the means third . . . A fork in a road is a third, it supposes three ways; a straight road, considered merely as a connection between two places is second, but so far as it implies passing through intermediate places it is third. . . . The positive degree of an adjective is first, the superlative second, the comparative third. All exaggerated language, 'supreme,' 'utter,' 'matchless,' 'root and branch,' is the furniture of minds which think of seconds and forget thirds. Action is second, but conduct is third. Law as an active force is second, but order and legislation are third. Sympathy, flesh and blood, that by which I feel my neighbor's feelings, is third. (Peirce, 1997, p. 170)

Although the third could be construed as a reference to hybridity, with the third being a hybrid of the first and second, such was not Peirce's intention, as he made especially clear with his reference to the superlative and comparative forms of adjectives. As Peirce noted, the third draws on what one knows about the first (the positive) and the second (the extreme) and compares those two, noting their differences and constructing something yet again anew, even transcendent, drawing from Peirce's concept of *abduction*. Peirce's work was marbled throughout with attention to thirds or triads in all forms of reasoning and representation. In particular, Peirce is well known for his conception of abduction as a conception of an idea that transcends the two ends of the inductive-deductive dichotomy, a space in which new ideas were generated.

This notion of the third as something that drew from, but did not simply combine, two dimensions or instantiations of an idea has resonance with Henri LeFebvre's theorizations of space and time, later taken up by cultural geographers, postcolonial theorists, and education researchers alike and translated into the moniker of *third space*. Like Peirce, LeFebvre argued that 'there is always an other' (1980, p. 143), positing a concept of the dynamic relationship between space and time in response to what he critiqued as an overwhelming focus on a linear and causal conception of time. Time, argued LeFebvre, marks itself in space; people act, use, and live in spaces in ways that shape new moments in time. Particularly interested in the concept of difference, especially in contrast to structuralist interpretations of difference as discursively produced, LeFebvre suggested that difference emerges from struggle, rather than from uniqueness of individuals or from the merging of two disparate entities into one new idea, discourse, or entity (LeFebvre, 1970). Like Pratt's notion of contact zones, Lefebvre's conception of the production of difference emphasizes the spaces and points of contact, rather than the end product of difference.

Taking up the idea that spaces bring together sometimes conflicting social and material resources (LeFebvre, 1996), Edward Soja (1996) offered the notion of *third space*. From Soja's perspective, third space demands looking beyond the binary categories of first and second spaces of the physical and social. In third space, what seem to be oppositional categories can actually work together to generate new knowledge, new Discourses, and new forms of literacy. Indeed, a commitment to third space demands a suspicion of binaries; it demands that when one reads phrases such as 'academic *versus* everyday literacies or knowledge,' one wonders about other ways of being literate that are not acknowledged in such simple binary positions.

Acknowledging the third forces one to ask how and when forms of literacy overlap, and whether everyday practices might, at times, look more like so-called academic literacies than they do like everyday literacies. The third also pushes one to ask what lies beneath the simple labels of everyday and academic, recognizing the plurality of ideas available once a third exists.

Homi Bhabha (1994) also used the term 'third space' (p. 36) in his critique of modern notions of culture, but Bhabha argued that third spaces were hybrid spaces, one of the first theorists to enter the word *hybridity* explicitly into conversation with the concept of thirds or third spaces. For Bhabha, third space is produced in and through language as people come together, and particularly as people resist cultural authority, bringing different experiences to bear on the same linguistic signs or cultural symbols and, likewise, different signs and symbols to bear on the same experiences. Bhabha's work was situated in the discourses of postcolonialism, but the privileged position of certain discourses in academic texts is akin to the privilege accorded the ways of knowing of the colonizer (Moje *et al.*, 2004). School texts can act as colonizers, validating only certain knowledge and discourse as legitimate. The struggles students may experience as they try to reconcile competing discourses can result in what Bhabha refers to as a 'splitting' (pp. 98–99, 131) of discourse, of culture, and of consciousness, in which students both take up and resist the privileged language of academic contexts. This splitting could be considered a kind of hybridity, except that hybridity – at least in biological terms – generally produces a wholly new, and new type, of being.

For Bhabha, whose theorizing was addressed to a postcolonial world, such splitting was both problematic and productive. The splitting, or the doubling and tripling of discourse, culture, and consciousness, can result in the anxious subject, a person who struggles to achieve a strong sense of self, but who must always articulate him/herself in response to an Other, and numerous theorists of self and the social would agree (see LeFebvre, 1980; Mead, 1934). At the same time, Bhabha argued, it is in this struggle for identity and selfhood that 'newness enters the world' (1994, p. 212). The struggle over and through different discourse communities and views of knowledge can be made productive, but only if people are not constantly defined in relation to a dominant discourse. Hybridity, then, is productive, rather than anxiety producing or diminishing, only if teachers and students actively incorporate divergent texts in the hope of generating new knowledge and discourse. That is, for hybridity to be a productive product, the goal must be to allow newness to enter the world, rather than to force a different way of being or doing onto an Other.

Re-theorizing Hybrid Literacies: The Case for Navigating

The concepts of *hybridity*, *hybrid literacies*, and *third space* theories have contributed enormously to education research and particularly to literacy education by asking theorists, researchers, and practitioners to consider how conflicts between different ways with words might produce both challenges and affordances for young people learning literacy in and out of school. In applications to education and, specifically, to conceptions of literacy learning and development, hybridity and third space theories have played a critical role in moving theory, research, and practice beyond attention to teaching literacy as an autonomous set of skills (Street, 1984). Attention to how people's literacy *practices*, rather than mere skills, differ by context, culture, and space has demanded that those interested in supporting literacy learning consider the ways that these different practices might come together and inform each other. Gutiérrez and colleagues (1999), for example, argued that the many different discourses to which students have access or with which they are confronted can, with the right nurturance, provide the 'mediational context and tools necessary for future social and cognitive development' (Gutiérrez *et al.*, 1999, p. 92; see also Heath, 1983; Hudicourt-Barnes, 2003; Lee, 1993; Lee and Fradd, 1998; Moje *et al.*, 2004; Moll *et al.*, 1989; Warren *et al.*, 2001). This kind of hybrid literacy practice is important because it provides opportunities for success in traditional school learning while also making a space for typically marginalized voices. Hybrid literacy theories allow educators to consider how new literate practices develop and what those new practices mean for the development and teaching of conventional skills.

The concept of hybrid literacies has also allowed literacy researchers to see beyond the goal of teaching youth to comprehend or compose texts (both important goals) to examine how different kinds of text and literate practice demands might shape readers' and writers' identities as literate beings. And finally, considering hybrid literacies has advanced attention to different ways of doing research in order to capture the multiple ways that youth engage in literate practice. With all of these advantages stemming from the notion of hybrid literacies and identities, as well as the spaces in which these literacies and identities develop, why would one engage in a critique of the concept? Why mess with a good thing?

Hybrid literacies can be used to challenge and reshape both academic content literacy practices and the knowledge and discourses of youths' everyday lives. Only a few studies, however, have documented students' growth in terms of developing new, critical understandings that *integrate* academic and everyday worlds (e.g., Gutiérrez, 2008; Hammond, 2001; Lee, 1993; Moje *et al.*, 2001; Morrell and Collatos, 2003; Seiler, 2001), and we have little information about how robust those practices were for youth. More to the point, we have little evidence that the participants in the studies actually saw themselves as engaging in something hybrid, versus code switching across spaces and contexts that allowed for or constrained the use of such practices. These points raise the question of whether conceptions of a hybrid, third space really do allow 'newness to enter the world' (Bhabha, 1994, p. 212), or whether they produce something new for a single moment in time. More critical, what are the possibilities of that moment of hybridity for people's practices in different spaces? Do the hybrids maintain, or do they fade over time or in different spaces, much like the maroon iris did in my garden? Were they ever really *real?*

Taking the metaphor to its roots in biology, it is clear that hybrids can have highly desirable characteristics, thus making the concept of hybridity appealing. Worth noting, however, is that the linguistic hybridity produced in both instances is both a strength and a potential challenge unless, just as with hybrid plants, their skills and identities are nurtured. Orellana *et al.* (2003), for example, demonstrate that young children who serve as language brokers, or *paraphrasers*, for their parents, experience both the positive consequences of co-constructing meaning with more knowledgeable adults and the potentially negative consequences of being positioned as responsible for tasks far beyond their years.

Indeed, a biological exploration of hybridity as a concept could even suggest more weaknesses than strengths: as suggested in the opening anecdote, biological hybrids are sometimes weaker than nonhybrids, with the dominant gene in a plant hybrid often overtaking and repressing the recessive gene. They can fade as dominance overwhelms them. Worse, they can be sterile, unable to reproduce or generate new possibilities. Thus, something new is generated, but the possibility of newness is confined to the hybrid itself and cannot be made anew.

In addition, the making of hybrids in nature relies heavily on both engineering and nurturing. The characteristics to be hybridized must first be brought together in some equivalent relationship. Gutiérrez and colleagues (Gutiérrez, 2008; Gutiérrez *et al.*, 1999; Gutiérrez, Baquedano-Lopez, and Alvarez, 2001) demonstrate that highly-skilled teachers who are able to hear, both literally and figuratively, their students' counterscripts and incorporate them into the official script of the classroom generate hybrid spaces that increase opportunities to learn. However, that engineering work took great skill and knowledge on the part of those teachers. Following that 'engineering' work, hybrids have to be nurtured. Once the hybrid is made, they must be nurtured through careful attention to building complex, supportive contexts and to folding in a variety of literacy and other social practices. Moll and colleagues (Moll, 1992a, 1992b; Moll and Diaz, 1993; Moll and Gonzalez, 1994) wrote about their work in sending teachers out into the community and parents and community members into classrooms to enrich the available funds of knowledge of classrooms and communities alike (see also Heath, 1983). This kind of nurturing of hybrid spaces, identities, and literacies is critical to making a focus on hybridity productive, rather than repressive. Students moving from a classroom or school where hybridity is recognized as a strength to a space where only certain practices are valued (whether a school or everyday space) may feel their hybridity slipping away (again, the maroon iris become purple).

In addition, although the concept of hybridity is appealing because it generates something new, a third, with multiple possibilities for growth and expansion, it may be the case that it is only those who are not part of the dominant group who are expected to 'be' hybrid, to enact hybrid literacies, or to construct third spaces. Too often, the marginalized must do the work of making hybrids, whereas the dominant maintain their dominance. Bhabha (1994) would argue that even the colonizer is changed in the moment of contact or in-betweenness, but what is evident in literacy theory is that hybrid literacies are typically those employed by the powerless, whereas canonical literacies, texts, and media enjoy continued power. Of greater concern is the loss that the marginalized may experience in taking up a hybrid form of literacy or identity. Although Peirce might argue that the third is transcendent because it merges the first and the second into something wholly new and ultimately more generative than first or second alone, there is a subtractive quality to the language of hybrids once one recognizes that only those who lack power are expected to hybridize their practices. Consider English language learners in the United States, for example. The addition of a second language to their linguistic repertoires could certainly be considered a boon; it is well documented that the merging of two language systems provides greater opportunity to develop metalinguistic awareness, among other skills (Cummins, 2005; Hakuta, 1986). Yet, unless school-aged English language learners experience an additive, rather than subtractive (August and Hakuta, 1997; Valdes, 1998), school environment where their first language is valued and first language development continues, they generally experience a loss of their first language and only a minimal hybridity. Indeed, many English language learners experience not only a linguistic loss, but also a social, emotional, and cultural loss (Rodriguez, 1982) as they maintain only basic forms of their first language and are unable to fully communicate with family and community. Furthermore, many English language learners often are not able to develop *literacy* in both languages even when they develop some level of oral hybridity in first and second languages. This bias toward the dominant is not, of course, a given in the push toward hybridity, but it is a troubling possibility. Were all learners asked to produce and engage in hybrid literacies and identities, then hybridity would be a more powerful concept, but if only the marginalized are expected to hybridize, then the concept loses some of its appeal.

Moreover, the notion of hybridity does not seem accurate at times. One of the most demanding navigations I carry out on a daily basis is that of the space between mothering and scholarship. Even the space names occupy different parts of speech, although one could have used 'motherhood' and 'scholarship,' and yet even rendering both as nouns produces subtly different meanings of the words. Indeed, when I consulted a dictionary to examine the difference in these various parts of speech and word meanings, I discovered this telling example sentence for the definition of mothering: 'Because they are involved in careers and mothering, many women lead exhausting lives' (Bloom, n.d.). The contrast between 'career' and 'mothering' in Bloom's statement is important to considering hybridity as a concept. In this statement, mothering apparently has little to do with one's career (unless, perhaps, one writes self-help books for mothers) and vice versa. Indeed, this separation of the two positions or identities is born out in experience: When one enters the space of scholarship for the academic, everything about such a space pushes away the position as mother. When one takes up the position as mother, the requirements for good scholarship (namely, time alone, deeply invested in reading, writing, and thought) are generally unavailable. Thus, the positions of mother and scholar, occupied by the same individual, could be described not as hybrid but as an artifact of navigation. One might argue that the spaces of academia and the home themselves could be made to be more hybrid and thus would create new positions such as mother-scholar, but ultimately, the work of each is different enough that it seems difficult, at least for this scholar-mother, to conceive of a truly hybrid positionality or identity of mother-scholar.

Does that mean that no new conceptions of either can be produced? To the contrary, it is in the act of navigating the difference, of struggling with the challenge between the need (or desire) to closet oneself away to write and the need (or desire) to be physically and emotionally present for others, that new ways of defining mothering and scholarship can emerge. It is in the navigating the discursive differences of the research presentation and the dance moms that the scholar-mother comes to understand herself as both scholar and mother and to recognize the differences between the two. It is in the moments of holding back a lecture on what she knows about how people learn when confronted with another mother's dismissal of a new mathematics curriculum or school schedule that the mother-scholar recognizes her different positions and identities. These acts of navigating decidedly nonhybrid spaces produce new ways of knowing that can afford change.

The concept of navigating thus acknowledges the roles of space, time, and context in how people engage in literate practice or enact identities in a way that hybridity or hybrid literacies cannot. Hybridity is, in some sense, a stable state; complex and multifaceted, to be sure, but stable, nonetheless. If hybridity is conceived of as living inside a person, rather than as the product of people living in and navigating across spaces, discourses, and demands, then we risk making hybridity a trait of an individual or of a literate practice, rather than about the outcome of a process of navigating. As a noun, hybridity implies a state of being and thus risks playing into a totalizing notion that seeks to transcend difference, rather than embracing and employing difference – and the work of navigating across difference – to make something new. In writing about newness in critical discourse, Bhabha (1994, p. 25, emphases added) argued that:

> The language of critique is effective not because it keeps forever separate the terms of the master and the slave, the mercantilist and the Marxist, but to the extent to which it overcomes the given grounds of opposition and opens up *a space of translation*: a place of hybridity, figuratively speaking, where the construction of a political object that is new, neither the one nor the other, properly alienates our political expectations, and changes, as it must, the very forms of our recognition of the moment of politics. The challenges lie in conceiving of the time of political actions and understanding as opening up a space that can accept and regulate the differential structure of the moment of intervention *without rushing to produce a unity of the social antagonism or contradiction.*

Just as Bhabha argued against an essentialized or unified concept of politics as a product of hybridity, I seek to redefine hybridity as something more unstable, a state of flux. This does not suggest a need to do away with the concept or to diminish the work that has employed it (including my own). Instead this conception of navigating underscores the point that hybridity does not lie in the person, but rather in the experience of navigating and struggling across different spaces, discourses, and demands, what Mary Louise Pratt (1991) labeled 'contact zones.' Literacies and identities are not hybrid; spaces are. People navigate across and within spaces and in so doing experience moments of hybridity as they confront the in-between, the discourse that is neither their own nor the other's, the practice that they both take up and change. They navigate – or need to learn to navigate – the positions in which they find themselves or which are made available to them in various spaces (Holland and Leander, 2004). In the hope of avoiding the production of fragile, or even sterile, hybrids, and given that the work of producing robust and generative hybrids is difficult and that educators cannot control the multiple future contexts their students will traverse, I suggest that a focus on *navigating* and *navigations* might rescue hybridity from becoming a new form of dominance.

That is, perhaps teaching and learning should not be about trying to construct third spaces of learning that produce hybrid beings and literacy practices, but also about teaching children and youth when, how, and why they should engage in different practices valued by the various discourse communities they cross. Navigating is related to, but distinct from, code switching; navigational work depends on the ability to switch linguistic and other codes as one moves across spaces. However, navigating is strategic, planful, and purposeful. Thus, the goal of teaching people navigations becomes one of teaching the processes and practices of navigating, thus requiring attention not only to literacy skills and strategies necessary for reading and writing at basic levels, but also the skills for navigating across various spaces, contexts, and relationships. Delpit (1988) provided an excellent example of a teacher's efforts to help her students learn to navigate when she engaged students in thinking about the spaces and contexts in which it was useful to use dominant forms of language versus the spaces and contexts where their home language codes were valued.

Of course, navigational work also requires that teachers are aware of and willing to traverse the many spaces their students must traverse on a daily basis. Yet, that demand should also be viewed as a strength of a navigations approach because it stands to develop the same sorts of navigations in teachers that they expect of their students. Such work makes the production of hybridity via the process and practice of navigating multiple and conflicting spaces and contexts something in which all should engage, rather than something expected only of those who live on the margins.

One significant challenge to the teaching of navigations presents itself in an era of increasing attempts to standardize curricula and learning experiences, as well as ever-growing demands for accountability through standard measures: how do teachers make the time to help youth navigate? How do teacher educators and researchers foster teachers' attention to and abilities in developing and nurturing navigations? Still, the advantages of working from the concept of navigating, rather than hybridizing, are multiple.

First, it may be easier to teach children and youth how to navigate multiple spaces, and the literacies and discourses contained therein, than it is to produce in them some sort of hybrid practices and, ultimately, hybrid identities. Furthermore, the skills of navigating are skills that are valuable within and across contexts. Specifically, in addition to basic comprehension and composing skills, navigating involves listening, metacognition, meta-awareness, and critical thinking skills. Developing these skills also helps to develop agency among learners, and with the ability to navigate, the learner can decide if, when, and how they want to hybridize their practices and identities. Developing this meta-awareness distinguishes navigating from code switching because it moves from a responsive or tactical act of switching linguistic or other codes as the context demands it to actively navigating contexts in a strategic way as agents who decide how they want to be recognized or positioned.

It might be argued that navigating does not produce agency and instead renders the subject fractured and potentially paralyzed as s/he moves from space to space, always fighting for a voice that feels right or true to the sense of self. Certainly the danger exists for people to navigate by employing false performances of selves, by self-silencing, or by avoiding contested spaces entirely, thus further limiting the possibility for both newness to enter the world and for building a socially just society in which many voices can come together. Luke (pers. comm., February 6, 2012) would argue that such avoidance or self-silencing is impossible in what he refers to as a 'post-hybrid' world. The world and many of its spaces are already hybrid; contact zones abound. People need to be equipped to navigate these contact zones with power.

At the secondary school level, in particular, readers and writers must cross the discursive boundaries of different disciplines as they encounter or seek specialized texts of the subject areas (Hicks, 1995/1996; Hinchman and Zalewski, 1996; Lemke, 1990; Luke, 2001; Moje, *et al.*, 2001; New London Group, 1996). This crossing of boundaries – or entry into contact zones between the disciplines – is navigational work. Studies of such practices indicate that teaching navigational skills via students' everyday knowledge seems linked to students' growth in developing conventional academic knowledge and literacy skill (Barton *et al.*, 2008; Gutiérrez *et al.*, 1999; Hammond, 2001; Lee, 1993; Moje *et al.*, 2004; Morrell and Collatos, 2003; Wong, 1996). These studies also suggest that schools spaces that engage students in explicitly examining the multiple funds of discourse and knowledge they must employ in different spaces can support their abilities to navigate different contexts by drawing from skills they possess across those contexts (see Hammond, 2001). Finally, these studies demonstrate that this kind of work can reshape our understandings of what counts as both academic and everyday literacies, practice, and knowledge (e.g., Gutiérrez, 2008; Moje and Speyer, 2008; Morrell and Collatos, 2003; Tang, 2011). In contrast to a decontextualized, autonomous skills approach, an approach that emphasizes navigating is 'concerned with meaning making, identity, power and authority and foreground[s] the institutional nature of what "counts" as knowledge in any particular academic context' (Street, 2009, p. 3). Understanding what counts as knowledge in different contexts requires, according to Street (2009), that teachers help students learn how to articulate the voice that is meaningful to the writer and recognizable by the reader; take, communicate, and defend a stance; and how to signal what they want readers to understand through a text. Street argues that each of these 'hidden features' (Street, 2009) of academic writing demands a sense of awareness of self and audience; I argue that each demands an ability to navigate those audiences, to recognize the space or context in which the writing (or reading) is being conducted, and to use strategically the linguistic and cultural devices valued by those audiences.

How Should Navigations be Studied?

The first critical element of studying the processes and practices of navigating is that people need to be followed across spaces. This is not a particularly new idea; ethnographers have followed people across spaces throughout the history of the field and education researchers interested in youth literacy in nonschool contexts have made a particular point of emphasizing the need to move across spaces (e.g. Leander, 2004; Leander and Lovvorn, 2006; Leander and McKim, 2003; Stevens, Satwitz, and McCarthy, 2008). What is unique, though, is that I propose that in the act of following people researchers should focus less on the people themselves, and more on how the particular social and physical spaces of their daily lives demand or produce certain kinds of practices and on what people do and think and learn from those interactions and their responses to them. In other words, the unit of analysis should be on how, why, and when people navigate; on what sense they make of those navigations; and on what they *do* with that information as they navigate back and forth across spaces or to new and different spaces.[1] Such research could contribute enormously to the literature because it would help to expose how people take up and employ new ways of reading, writing, and doing, which would provide teachers with information about how to teach those navigations to others.

Such a focus implies not only a need to follow people across spaces, but also across time. To fully understand the practice of navigating, one has to watch the individual navigate multiple contexts, but also watch the person navigate those multiple contexts repeatedly. What's more, to examine how people make sense of the effects of their navigations, researchers need two critical kinds of data: First, they need to observe how people act differently in one context from one moment in time to the next, and second, they need to ask people about why they acted differently. Navigations can be tactical or responsive (e.g., remaining silent in a tricky social or political discussion) or strategic and agentic (e.g., setting up the conversation to unfold in a particular way and being prepared with evidence to support one's position). Observing and interviewing people about what they learn from tactical, responsive navigations and how they bring that learning forward into the same social setting at a later time or how they transfer that learning to a new social setting reveals important information that could guide teachers in thinking about how to teach navigating to young people.

The focus on studying navigating over time might imply that studies of navigating must be conducted over a long term; although there is a certain advantage to long-term studies – on a most basic level, long-term work produces a rich and robust data set – it may not be the case that each and every navigational move requires long-term study. That said, navigating does require attention to the multiplicity of spaces and contexts through which a person moves and thus requires some attention to whether, in fact, the research has navigated with the participants across all the relevant spaces of people's lives that ultimately inform how, why, and when they navigate and how, why, and when they use various literacies in different spaces. Although it seems unlikely that literacy researchers could ever traverse *everywhere* a given set of research participants might navigate, too often research makes claims from a limited set of experiences and fails to acknowledge the partiality of the data collected. Although research efforts could benefit from more attention to their partiality (particularly those that make claims to generalizability), research on navigations and the learning that occurs from navigating seems to demand explicit discussion of the partiality of our research methods because it is all about what people learn from traversing multiple spaces in a 'post-hybrid' world, a place where we can no longer avoid contact zones with multiple Others, where we are always managing hybridity through the process of navigating.

Conclusions: My Own Navigating Work

I have attempted in this chapter to make a case for reconceptualizing hybrid literacies (and many related concepts, such as hybrid identities and third spaces) in terms of navigating and navigations not because I think that the concept of hybridity is flawed, but because I sense a recent tendency in the field to view hybridity as an end goal, an outcome or product, a state of being. It is important to underscore that my own work has emphasized the value of hybridity and hybrid literacy practices; thus, the argument I offer here is by no means intended to dismiss or devalue such work. Instead, by focusing on the navigational aspects of hybridity, I hope to emphasize the active and generative processes from which people can learn in the world I describe above, where contact zones are only a keystroke away. In a world of multiple and ever-present contact zones, hybridity conceptualized in a static way loses meaning and power. Navigating contact zones has become a way of life; as a result, we need to consider what people learn as they navigate those zones and how teachers might leverage research on that learning to teach others powerful navigating processes.

Note

1. For some, this focus may evoke the application of Bruno Latour's (1987) increasingly popular actor-network theory (ANT). Although not conceptualized in opposition to ANT, I do not see what I propose here as isomorphic with ANT. Latour's interest, it seems to me, has been more squarely in the network, its materiality, and how the network itself produces movements and relationships among actors and institutions that are part of the network. Such work is useful in understanding navigations, to be sure, but I am more interested in what the members of the network do with and learn from their navigating practices, whereas Latour seems more interested in the networks.

References

August, D., and Hakuta, K. (1997) *Improving Schooling for Language-Minority Children: A Research Agenda*. Washington, DC: National Academies Press.

Barton, A.C., Tan, E., and Rivet, A. (2008) Creating hybrid spaces for engaging school science among urban middle school girls. *American Educational Research Journal*, 45: 68–103.

Bhabha, H. (1994) *The Location of Culture*. London: Routledge.

Bloom, D.E. (n.d.) Mothering, accessed November 20, 2012: www.thefreedictionary.com/mothering

Cummins, J. (2005) A proposal for action: Strategies for recognizing heritage language competence as a learning resource within the mainstream classroom. *Modern Language Journal*, 89(4): 585–592.

Delpit, L.D. (1988) The silenced dialogue: Pedagogy and power in educating other people's children. *Harvard Educational Review*, 58: 280–298.

Elmesky, R. (2011) Rap as a roadway: Creating creolized forms of science in an era of cultural globalization. *Cultural Studies of Science Education*, 6: 49–76.

Gonzalez, N., Moll, L.C., and Amanti, C. (2005) *Funds of Knowledge: Theorizing Practices in Households, Communities, and Classrooms*. Hillsdale, NJ: Lawrence Erlbaum.

Gutiérrez, K.D. (2008) Developing a sociocritical literacy in the third space. *Reading Research Quarterly*, 43(2): 148–164.

Gutiérrez, K.D., Baquedano-López, P., and Alvarez, H.H. (2001) Literacy as hybridity: Moving beyond bilingualism in urban classrooms. In M. de la Luz Reyes and J.J. Halcon (eds) *The Best for our Children: Critical Perspectives on Literacy for Latino Students. Language and Literacy Series*. New York: Teachers College Press, pp. 122–141.

Gutiérrez, K.D., Baquedano-López, P., Alvarez, H., and Chiu, M.M. (1999) Building a culture of collaboration through hybrid language practices. *Theory into Practice*, 38(2): 87–93.

Gutiérrez, K.D., Rymes, B., and Larson, J. (1995) Script, counterscript, and underlife in the classroom: James Brown versus Brown v. Board of Education. *Harvard Educational Review*, 65: 445–471.

Hakuta, K. (1986) *The Mirror of Language: The Debate on Bilingualism*. New York: Basic Books.

Hall, S. (1995) The meaning of new times. In D. Morley and K.-H. Chen (eds) *Stuart Hall: Critical Dialogues in Cultural Studies*. New York: Routledge, pp. 223–337.

Hammond, L. (2001) Notes from California: An anthropological approach to urban science education for language minority families. *Journal of Research in Science Teaching*, 38(9): 983–999.

Heath, S.B. (1983) *Ways with Words: Language, Life, and Work in Communities and Classrooms*. Cambridge, UK: Cambridge University Press.

Hicks, D. (1995/1996) Discourse, learning, and teaching. In M.W. Apple (ed.) *Review of Research in Education*, vol. 21. Washington, DC: American Educational Research Association, pp. 49–95.

Hinchman, K.A., and Zalewski, P. (1996) Reading for success in a tenth-grade global-studies class: A qualitative study. *Journal of Literacy Research*, 28: 91–106.

Holland, D., and Leander, K. (2004) Ethnographic studies of positioning and subjectivity: An introduction. *ETHOS*, 32(2): 127–139.

Hudicourt-Barnes, J. (2003) The use of argumentation in Haitian Creole science classrooms. *Harvard Educational Review*, 73(1): 73–93.

Latour, B. (1987) *Science in Action*. Cambridge, MA: Harvard University Press.

Leander, K.M. (2004) 'They took out the wrong context': Uses of time-space in the practice of positioning. *ETHOS*, 32(2): 188–213.

Leander, K.M., and Lovvorn, J.F. (2006) Literacy networks: Following the circulation of texts, bodies, and objects in the schooling and online gaming of one youth. *Cognition and Instruction*, 24(3): 291–340.

Leander, K.M., and McKim, K.K. (2003) Tracing the everyday 'sitings' of adolescents on the Internet: A strategic adaptation of ethnography across online and offline spaces. *Education, Communication, and Information*, 3(2): 211–240.

Lee, C.D. (1993) *Signifying as a Scaffold for Literary Interpretation: The Pedagogical Implications of an African American Discourse Genre* (NCTE Research Report, No 26). Urbana, IL: National Council of Teachers of English.

Lee, C.D. (1995) A culturally based cognitive apprenticeship: Teaching African American high school students skills in literary interpretation. *Reading Research Quarterly*, 30(4): 608–630.

Lee, O., and Fradd, S.H. (1998) Science for all, including students from non-English language backgrounds. *Educational Researcher*, 27(3): 12–21.

LeFebvre, H. (1970) *Le manifeste differentialiste*. Paris, France: Gallimard.

LeFebvre, H. (1980) *Le Presence et l'absence*. Paris, France: Casterman.

LeFebvre, H. (1996) *Writings on Cities*, trans. E. Kofman and E. Lebas. Oxford, UK: Blackwell.

Lemke, J.L. (1990) *Talking Science: Language, Learning, and Values*. Norwood, NJ: Ablex.

Luke, A. (2001) Foreword. In E.B. Moje and D.G. O'Brien (eds) *Constructions of Literacy: Studies of Teaching and Learning In and Out of Secondary Schools*. Mahwah, NJ: Lawrence Erlbaum, pp. ix–xii.

Mead, G.H. (1934) *Mind, Self, Society*. Chicago: University of Chicago Press.

Moje, E.B., Ciechanowski, K.M., Kramer, K.E., *et al.* (2004) Working toward third space in content area literacy: An examination of everyday funds of knowledge and discourse. *Reading Research Quarterly*, 39(1): 38–71.

Moje, E.B., Collazo, T., Carrillo, R., and Marx, R.W. (2001) 'Maestro, what is "quality"?' Language, literacy, and discourse in project-based science. *Journal of Research in Science Teaching*, 38(4): 469–496.

Moje, E.B., Peek-Brown, D., Sutherland, L.M., *et al.* (2004) Explaining explanations: Developing scientific literacy in middle-school project-based science reforms. In D. Strickland and D.E. Alvermann (eds) *Bridging the Gap: Improving Literacy Learning for Preadolescent and Adolescent Learners in Grades 4–12*. New York: Carnegie Corporation, pp. 227–251.

Moje, E.B., and Speyer, J. (2008) The reality of challenging texts in high school science and social studies: How teachers can mediate comprehension. In K. Hinchman and H. Thomas (eds) *Best Practices in Adolescent Literacy Instruction*. New York: Guilford Press, pp. 185–211.

Moll, L.C. (1992a) Bilingual classroom studies and community analysis. *Educational Researcher*, 21(2): 20–24.

Moll, L.C. (1992b) Literacy research in community and classrooms: A sociocultural approach. In R. Beach, J.L. Green, M.L. Kamil, and T. Shanahan (eds) *Multidisciplinary Perspectives in Literacy Research*. Urbana, IL: National Conference on Research in English and National Council of Teachers of English, pp. 211–244.

Moll, L.C., and Diaz, S. (1993) Change as the goal of educational research. In E. Jacob and C. Jordan (eds) *Minority Education: Anthropological Perspectives*. Norwood, NJ: Ablex Publishing Company, pp. 67–79.

Moll, L.C., and Gonzalez, N. (1994) Critical issues: Lessons from research with language-minority children. *Journal of Reading Behavior*, 26(4): 439–456.

Moll, L.C., and Greenberg, J. (1990) Creating zones of possibilities: Combining social contexts for instruction. In L.C. Moll (ed.) *Vygotsky and Education*. New York: Cambridge University Press, pp. 319–348.

Moll, L.C., Veléz-Ibañéz, C., and Greenberg, J. (1989) *Year One Progress Report: Community Knowledge and Classroom Practice: Combining Resources for Literacy Instruction*. Tucson, AZ: University of Arizona.

Morrell, E., and Collatos, A. (2003, April) Critical pedagogy in a college access program for students of color. Paper presented at the American Educational Research Association, Chicago, IL.

New, L.G. (1996) A pedagogy of multiliteracies: Designing social futures. *Harvard Educational Review*, 66: 60–92.

Orellana, M.F., Reynolds, J., Dorner, L., and Meza, M. (2003) In other words: Translating or 'paraphrasing' as a family literacy practice in immigrant households. *Reading Research Quarterly*, 38(1): 12–34.

Peirce, C.S. (1997) *The Collected Papers of Charles Sanders Peirce*, vol. 3, chapter 3.

Pratt, M.L. (1991) Arts of the contact zone. *Profession*, 91: 33–40.

Rodriguez, R. (1982) *Hunger of Memory*. Boston, MA: David Grodine.

Seiler, G. (2001) Reversing the 'standard' direction: Science emerging from the lives of African American students. *Journal of Research in Science Teaching*, 38(9): 1000–1014.

Soja, E.W. (1996) *Thirdspace: Journeys to Los Angeles and Other Real-and-imagined Places*. Malden, MA: Blackwell Publishers.

Stevens, R., Satwitz, T., and McCarthy, L. (2008) In-game, in-room, in-world: Reconnecting video game play to the rest of kids' lives. In K. Salen (ed.) *The Ecology of Games: Connecting Youth, Games, and Learning*. Cambridge, MA: MIT Press, pp. 42–66.

Street, B.V. (1984) *Literacy in Theory and Practice*. Cambridge, England: Cambridge University Press.

Street, B.V. (2009) '*Hidden' Features of Academic Paper Writing*. Work Papers in Educational Linguistics. University of Pennsylvania, Philadelphia.

Tang, K.-S. (2011) Hybridizing cultural understandings of the natural world to foster critical science literacy. Unpublished doctoral dissertation. University of Michigan, Ann Arbor.

Valdes, G. (1998) The world outside and inside schools: Language and immigrant children. *Educational Researcher*, 27(6): 4–18.

Warren, B., Ballenger, C., Ogonowski, M., *et al.* (2001) Rethinking diversity in learning science: The logic of everyday languages. *Journal of Research in Science Teaching*, 38, 1–24.

Wong, E.D. (1996) Students' scientific explanations and the contexts in which they occur. *Elementary School Journal*, 96(5): 495–509.

Chapter 27

Official Literacy Practices Co-construct Racialized Bodies

Three Key Ideas to Further Integrate Cultural and 'Racially Literate' Research

Karl Kitching

Introduction: The Social Regulation Function of Official Literacy

New Literacy Studies have explored and debated the connections between literacy and identity, as both are constructed through wider social patterns, since the 1980s. This field broadly views literate behavior and a person's identity as two parts of the same whole: the practice and the expertise of naming, knowing, and living everyday life. Its approaches have generated recognition of multimodal literacies, paying close attention to the social practices that 'author' one's identity implicitly or explicitly as a knowledgeable and competent person in particular contexts. The concept of *figured worlds* captures the interplay between cultural and critical perspectives on everyday literacy very well (Bartlett and Holland, 2002). People use particular frames of reference about the world as they engage in literacy activities. Within 'their' worlds, the practices of creating and using artifacts, symbols, and identities are enmeshed and inextricable. As a result of this, a political question always arises about 'who' it is possible to be within particular literacy worlds – and how freely this repeatedly co-constructed self can navigate these worlds.

Power-laden designations of (il)literacy have historically infused the repertoires of practice and institutional structuring that designates acceptable personhood inside and outside classrooms. The web of practices that co-constructs literacy and acceptable selfhood extends beyond the school, not just to industry and the economy, but also to the criminal justice system, health care, border control, the family, and other institutions (Graff, 1987; Nichols, Nixon and Rowsell, 2009). Socio-cultural views of literacy help us move beyond viewing the 'presence' of conventional, school-based literacy as 'an individual attribute that . . . transforms a person's life chances' and the 'absence' of literacy as something that exists 'as a sign of social and personal failure' (Cook-Gumperz, 2006: 2). However, causal relationships are repeatedly drawn between 'illiteracy' and (usually racially bounded) understandings of 'the nation,' masking the inequalities that hamper particular peoples' opportunities to achieve in officially

International Handbook of Research on Children's Literacy, Learning, and Culture, First Edition.
Edited by Kathy Hall, Teresa Cremin, Barbara Comber, and Luis C. Moll.

desired ways. For example, Ireland's recent literacy and numeracy strategy draws quite overt correlations between the causes of social problems and 'illiteracy':

> We know . . . that children who do not learn to read, write and communicate effectively are more likely to leave school early and in later life to be unemployed or in low skilled jobs, to have poorer emotional and physical health, to have limited earning power, and are more likely to be imprisoned. (DES 2011: 9)[1]

Scholarly pedagogical fields such as funds of knowledge, culturally responsive pedagogy, critical race theory, whiteness studies, and critical poststructuralism demonstrate that practices of 'official literacy' are typically enmeshed in excluding and negatively evaluating the experiences, resources and even the official achievements of poor, working class, and racially minoritized people. The tools used in these fields have cross-pollinated, but their scholars retain different emphases for important strategic reasons (e.g., Au, 2001). While attending to the varying emphases of different analyses, I want to create a more robust conversation between the variety of *cultural* lenses used in some of the above fields and the materialist, *critical* emphases foregrounded in others. In cross-sectioning these fields, I identify three key ideas that I regard productive for research analyses of race and literacy inequalities. The first, already identified field is the *cultural practices* perspective of New Literacy Studies, which argues that literate identities are constructed in reciprocal relation to texts, Others, and to ideologies; these relations are imbued with power struggles. The second is Critical Race Theory (CRT) and Critical Whiteness Studies' understandings of *literacy as white property*, which contends that there is a reality to racial oppression that is historically inscribed and cannot be underestimated; an actively reinforced system of *white supremacy*. I argue in the third section that another key idea, how white and Other *racialized bodies are repeatedly constituted* in social practices and interactions, must be deployed to combat the essentialism of social constructionist literacy and race scholarship (Nayak, 2006; Kitching, 2011a). I then analyze an individual fragment of ethnographic classroom data to exemplify the combined strengths of these ideas. While the fragment of data was generated in a secondary/high school, conceptually, the ideas are entirely relevant to early and children's literacies.

Cultural and Critical Perspectives: From Funds of Knowledge to Whiteness Studies

Scholars researching the marginalized literacies of minority ethnic, language, working class, and immigrant families have fostered a range of inclusionary principles that are generally agreed upon, but differently prioritized. They focus on repertoires of practice, emphasize that teachers need to 'know the culture' and/or listen hard to the voices of their students, that teachers must identify their students' positioning in relation to power and wider social structures, that cultural differences are not individual, fixed traits that a person carries around, and that their students (knowingly or unknowingly) display constrained forms of agency in the context of particular figured worlds (Gutierrez and Rogoff, 2003; González, 2005). The concept of 'funds of knowledge' has risen to prominence in the United States, and has been taken up in the United Kingdom (Andrews and Yee, 2006). Its premise is that 'people are competent, they have knowledge, and their life experiences have given them that knowledge . . . first-hand research experiences with families allows one to document this competence and knowledge' (González, Moll, and Amanti, 2005: ix–x). It has encouraged the examination of informal literacy practices: cultural and cognitive strategies deployed outside of the classroom, for example, in the playground (Grugeon, 2005). Its most characteristic approach is to visit households and student's localities, conduct guided conversation and interviews, and attempt to learn and appreciate how people 'use resources of all kinds . . . to engage life' (González, 2005: xi).[2] The field of culturally responsive pedagogy/schooling[3] also addresses the power-laden 'gap' between personal literacies, numeracies, and languages and literacies, numeracies, and languages of the school (Ladson-Billings, 1995; Gay, 2002; Greer *et al.*, 2009). A key focus in this field is to outline how different and diverse ways of being and living exist, in order to gain space for ethnic and/or racially minoritized communities. In the US context, Gay suggests the following as initial priorities:

> Which ethnic groups give priority to communal living and cooperative problem solving and how these preferences affect educational motivation, aspiration, and task performance; (b) how different ethnic groups' protocols of appropriate ways for children to interact with adults are exhibited in instructional settings; and (c) the implications of gender role socialization in different ethnic groups for implementing equity initiatives in classroom instruction (2002, p. 107).

Gay (2002) asserts that subject area pedagogies need to respond in various ways to how different ethnic and linguistic groups might construct knowledge. They must also acknowledge the contributions made by various minority groups to already existing 'official' knowledge (e.g., in music, politics, discoveries). Culturally responsive pedagogy particularly focuses on developing and employing teachers' cultural competencies to encourage minority student achievement without compromising on high expectations or ignoring power relations (Ladson-Billings 1995).

Clearly, both funds of knowledge and culturally responsive thinking share critical goals, in terms of interrupting official literacy practices that close down particular students' learning and political agency. However, there is constant slippage from the *relational and dialogical* notions of practice that these ideas are based on. Rather than moving beyond understandings of literacy as school-defined and inviting students to co-construct knowledge, the power-laden narrowing of 'multiculturalism' can reduce practice to a focus on 'how to teach' ethnic and racialized minorities. Examples of this include examining typical cultural artifacts (such as food, traditional dress, holidays and customs) that become ways to contain students, rather than addressing the complexity of their lived experiences. As Oughton (2010) describes, further slippages from the tenets of funds of knowledge in adult education include focusing on individual learners as opposed to household and community knowledges, looking at 'metacognition' instead of practical life skills, and the policy appropriation of funds of knowledge into a bland, acultural 'prior knowledge' discourse.

The 'cultural learning styles' field is also well-intentioned in terms of attending to the specificities of difference, and challenging deficit thinking about racialized communities. However, it can tend to treat cultural differences (such as those cited with reference to Gay [2002] above) as static individual traits, 'making it harder to understand the relation of individual learning and the practices of cultural communities' (Gutierrez 2006, p. 45). For example, a child from a particular minority ethnic or racialized group might be assumed to adopt an 'analytic' or 'holistic' style of learning, as if their perceived 'community learning' was carried around as a fixed genetic trait. This practice again denies a view of literacy, language, learning, and identity as relational, that is, situated, co-constructed, and thus open to constant change and readjustment in different worlds of practice. Defining the pedagogical problem with 'cultural learning styles,' Gutierrez argues 'a one-style-per-person assumption based on an individual's membership in a cultural community does not allow for change in individuals, their practices, or the community itself' (Gutierrez, 2006, p. 45). The political problem is that efforts to 'explain minority students' in fixed and singular ways leads to policy responses which attempt to 'fix minority students' (Gutierrez, 2006).[4]

Toward a more Critical Focus on Racism: Literacy as White Property

Castagno and Brayboy's (2008) review reveals how infrequently racism is discussed in the field of culturally responsive schooling for indigenous youth in the United States, and how racisms might in the first instance create the need for, and hamper the effectiveness of, culturally responsive educations (2008, p. 950)[5] Critical Race Theory (CRT) scholars have drawn much greater attention to how the contemporary ordinariness of racism has allowed race to continue to be a real, unequal organizing principle of society in the postcivil rights era. While racisms have an ideological rather than a biological justification, they have seriously infused social relations, shaping institutions, identities and material outcomes in implicit ways that are enforced as normal and natural:

> Social stratification helped to construct literacy education, in the US imagination as well as in the policy and practices of schools, as a right for white children and a privilege for children of color (Prendergast [2003]). As Ladson-Billings (2003) asserted, from a critical race theory perspective, literacy represents a form of property. It is 'property that was traditionally owned and used by whites in the society' (p. ix) (Rogers and Mosley, 2006, p. 462).

Ladson-Billings' (2003) assertion of literacy as 'white property' does not portray white people as ethnically, nationally, or even physically homogenous, or necessarily knowingly oppressive. The idea is to expose how white racial politics strategically work to collectivize and homogenize people constructed as 'white,' to their benefit/use, at particular historical junctures. Minority ethnic and working-class whites may approximate or lose their status as structurally privileged at key moments; 'how the Irish became white' in the United States being a case in point (Ignatiev, 1995). The notion of white property deliberately links to and confronts the histories and realities of slave-ownership and the active, ordinary maintenance of white supremacy.[6] Linking with subaltern perspectives, these ideas also refute the Western notion of knowledge as individual property, and looks to collectivize knowledge as shared and characterized by difference. Drawing on the CRT concept of interest convergence, the desires and successes of racialized minorities are generally recognized only when they benefit whites and/or white ethno-national majorities. Examples include the 'hard-working (Asian) model minorities' to the derogation of other racialized communities (Gillborn, 2008), and PISA evidence, which heralds the successes of 'immigrant populations' while remaining silent on how selective its OECD-member countries are about 'which immigrants' enter its borders (Kitching, 2010).

As these latter examples attest, racial, ethnic, and/or migrant Others are not always constructed as illiterate. The historical and contemporary context of white (middle class) supremacy shows that such constructions are multifaceted and open to strategic alteration. Examining a graph of GCSE results from the British DfES, Gillborn's paper (2010) shows that the vast differences in affluence between white students and the minimal affluence differences among black students are downplayed by British media in order to focus on the differences between white boys receiving free school meals (FSM) and the highest achieving black boys receiving free school meals (FSM). Several examples exist from the United Kingdom and elsewhere of the ways in which race, class, and other oppressions are made to 'compete' against each other at the expense of noticing who stands 'above' this competition.[7] However, while we may legitimately and provisionally differentiate between differing inequalities because of the specificity of how they are constructed (as this chapter does with racism), the notion of competing and/or 'priority' inequalities is itself problematic not just politically, but also empirically. Classed and racialized inequalities are not formed in isolation from each other if we think about how capitalism, colonialism, and whiteness are historically intertwined. They are not structured separately in contemporary times; and as my analysis later demonstrates, nor are such relations enforced in finite, singular ways (Gillborn, 2008; Kitching, 2011b; Leonardo, 2009; Youdell, 2006).

Explaining Race Culturally: Bodies as Repeatedly Co-constituted with Literacies

Racisms can continue to do their 'previous' classificatory work in everyday schooling through the oversimplified recruitment of the language of 'culture' and everyday silencing of power relations (Mirza 1998). In getting away from these everyday conflations of race and culture, and returning to New Literacy Studies, I want to re-emphasize the need to understand identities – literate, racial, and otherwise – as a repertoire of practices, in terms of Culture with a capital 'C' (González, 2005). Our analysis of 'who can be literate' must emphasize the co-constructed nature of how literacy activities are organized, how identities are taken up, and how unequal social positions are maintained. As Leonardo argues (2011a, p. 677):

> Although racism involves a whole range of social processes . . . it never does not involve language, which is always in play. It is not language *qua* language that concerns us, but language as a form of social practice. Subjects do not merely describe the world of race, but actively perform and constitute it through discourse. This establishes the fact that in order to know racism, we must know language intimately.

There are emergent approaches to analyzing racism in the context of literacy education that navigate racism using Cultural/linguistic analysis (from here on I will use a small 'c'). An important exemplar is Rogers and Mosley's (2006) CRT-based critical discourse analysis of how race is silenced and white supremacy/systemic racism enforced in a St Louis literacy classroom. This paper is a key text for me as a teacher and researcher. It extensively and meticulously demonstrates the way in which race and white privilege are enacted, silenced, and disrupted through African American and white working class children's shared interactions around racism in literacy texts.

In my own ethnographic work, I ask subtly different questions to Rogers and Mosley's (2006) quest to uncover 'what ways . . . white students and their white teachers take up race in the literacy curriculum' (2006, p. 465). Even studies that view white identity as an unpredictable, transgressable social construction can continue to write oppressive practices as emanating from static, pre-social, 'simply there' white bodies.[8] Rogers and Mosley (2006) certainly highlight that whiteness is an interactional accomplishment, and they attend to the interplay of meanings evidenced in body language and talk, texts and interactions around skin color, and so forth. However, their analysis is based on particular practices as emanating *from* individual bodies. Repoliticizing race can go beyond 'just' exposing and counter the notion white people should have a guaranteed or predictable set of entitlements and properties. Emerging thinking about race and whiteness suggests we must also recognize that white supremacy is entirely dependent upon, and articulated through the assumption of a pre-social white body. As Leonardo (2009) puts it 'race trouble arrived at the scene precisely at the moment when people started thinking they were white' (Leonardo, 2009, p. 62). Linking back my the earlier discussion of 'traits' projected on to individuals from particular cultural communities, certain race theorists are now asserting that researchers must attend not only to how racial domination happens, but also to how disembodied accounts of racialized behavior inadvertently again reduce political practice to something as inexorably contained 'within' bodies. Such reductions keep the vision of disestablishing racist and essentialist hierarchies of superior/inferior bodies off the horizon (Nayak 2006; Youdell 2006; Leonardo 2009).

Broadening 'practices': Beyond social constructionism and toward the body

Thus, I want to push the literacy research agenda a little further to consider the manner in which white bodies *themselves*, and the bodies of the racial Other are repetitively *constituted as meaningful* in classroom exchanges. To be 'racially literate' we must be concerned now with not only *describing* the world of race; we must also seek to analyze how race is actively performed (Rogers and Mosley, 2006; Leonardo, 2011b). An analysis of the manner in which the racialized body is repeatedly constituted as meaningful looks not 'just' at the social practices that construct and reflect the world through spoken and printed language and visual texts. It also includes:

- An analysis of *bodies as texts*: reading the body as actively *produced* within and through a situated set of wider meanings, rather than simply being surrounded by them, or under the total control of a knowing self.
- An examination of the interplay between literature and how bodies inside and outside the classroom are centralized or ignored through literacy events. More subtly, we can look to the ways in which bodies and their behaviors are represented as being pre-social (or 'simply there') in classroom exchanges, schoolbooks, and research accounts. Refuting the naturalness of the body can involve deconstructing how different bodily habits signify, or are taken to signify the deployment or refutation of particular meanings within racialized contexts (e.g., habits and positionings like sitting at the top of the room, yawning, staying silent, sitting upright).
- How such analyses can extend to show particularly the silenced manner in which racial constructions are marked on, and thus racially authenticating, particular (black/white/Asian) bodies, their social outcomes, and their behaviors. This analysis of racial authentication processes does not seek to further undermine the identities of the racially oppressed. Questioning race attempts to challenge white supremacy before it is 'designed to threaten the status of its victims' (Leonardo, 2009, p. 67).

Changing the Logic of Analytic Representation: *Post*structural Thinking

These analyses require us to rethink the 'simply thereness' not just of bodies, but of all that we attempt to represent in research, and the productive power, or the ordering, framing and regulatory capability that the continued use of such representations have. Practices are performative: they not only give meaning and order to printed texts, talk, institutional and social structures, and self/other categorical identifications (race, class, gender) and bodies: *they also are given meaning and order by them*. Race analyses had legitimately assumed the body to act as a representative vehicle for highlighting racial stratification in society, rather than examining the *constitutive effects of such assumptions*, that is, how ways of politicizing unequal relations requires a set of bodies that are only recognizable and knowable within particular forms of racial stratification. Certain anti-racist scholars have come to cautiously rethink their own representations; otherwise, their work against racism can be undone by failing to imagine racial identity without race oppression, *impossible as that contemporarily is*.

The fragment of data below was taken from a school ethnography I conducted in Termonfort, a suburban area of Dublin that was subject to rapid immigration during the past 15 years. The region became home to almost double the number of 'non-Irish' immigrants during Ireland's Celtic Tiger economic boom (approximately 22 percent, according to census breakdowns). The largest groups of 'non-Irish' residents in the region were Nigerian, Polish, Lithuanian, and British; these groups ranging between 1,000 and 2,000 people approximately. While white-Irish politicians spoke of 'not making the mistakes of other countries' (e.g., the United Kingdom, the Netherlands) with respect to racism and 'ghettoization' during this period, Irish and wider European immigration regulations constructed migrant students along a continuum of desirability from white European economic migrant to black-African asylum seeker. Irish education policies glossed over the deep implications of statements against institutional racism (and religious exclusion), instead inciting schools to help migrant students 'learn English' and make individual successes of themselves (Bryan 2010; Devine 2005; Kitching 2010). I spent a year visiting a mixed-sex second-level school in Termonfort. Prior to mass immigration, this school achieved above average Leaving Certificate (state school-leaving) results despite a shift 'downwards' in its social class profile. Approximately 15 percent of the students in the school were new migrants, coming from the aforementioned countries as well as from the Philippines, DR Congo, India, China, and Pakistan.

As written texts, identities and bodies are as *productive* of social relations as they are *representative* of them, Leander and Wells Rowe (2006) are careful about taking/creating such objects and artifacts as purely representational in literacy events (e.g., naturalizing racial identity), and using these to order and create stable frames within which meanings can be isolated from each other and codified.

> We are less concerned with the relative adequacy or inadequacy of representations and more directly invested in deconstructing the logic of representation as a means to understand literacy performances . . . the problem we encounter is not merely that representations are inadequate or partial, but that performances themselves are not merely or even primarily representational . . . we do not reject representations (or our use of them), but rather consider and critique the effects that representational logic has on understanding difference as it is produced through literacy performances (Leander and Wells Rowe, 2006, p. 432).

This focus forces us to pause before we impose new structures, frames and stabilities about 'how things (categorical identities, bodies, texts) are related,' and to think instead about how the meanings of such things are constantly inscribed or changed, through the constant forming and breaking of relations between them. In the following analysis, I analyze the *performative citations* occurring in a classroom scene. Performatives are identity categories that actively make subjects 'through their deployment in the classificatory systems, categories and names that are used to designate, differentiate and sort people' (Youdell, 2011, p. 42). Counting the number of performative citations in each classroom scene is not the point: data excerpts are nonexhaustive in this view. However, there are familiar and resonating ways in which power relations are cited and inscribed through *practices*. Literacy arrangements and practices like ability grouping, teaching to the test, ethnocentric curricula overtly call up 'literate/illiterate'; 'linguistically proficient/deficient,' 'indigenous/newcomer,' and 'us/them' hierarchical binaries, and as text-body-identity interactions demonstrate, are shot through with the active maintenance and ignoring of unequal societal relations. I follow Youdell's (2006) practice of placing the identities that are taken to politicize these relations at the start of the fragment (e.g., white-working class-female). These categorical identities are written in chained sequence to remind us of the intersectional, rather than the competing nature of oppressions. Again, these categories are not 'simply there'; my concern is to deconstruct how the inequalities they signify are *relationally, performatively cited, and inscribed*. I am also interested in how particular practices might intentionally or unintentionally *rupture* the routine identity/power relations script, and how they may be *recuperated* to the status quo (see Kitching, 2011b; Youdell, 2006).

I had multiple goals with the study, but for the purposes of this chapter, I want to think about what discourses coalesce to extend or deny the possibility of inhabiting *officially literate* and *racially literate* subjectivities, I acknowledge the limitations of this chapter in an Irish context in term of its use of the Anglo-American concept of racism which tends to normalize a white/black, skin-based understanding at the expense of intra-European histories and contemporary politics of migration. Certainly I am implicated in the reciting and inscribing of particular performatives as my analysis creates yet another text. Like Britzman, I approach ethnographic writing as 'an effect of contest of discourses, even if the ethnographer has the power to suggest what is at stake when identities are at stake' (Britzman, 2000, p. 37).

Friday afternoon, 8th period 3rd Year B Band class: Junior Cert English

Generating data in this lesson

KK:	28-year-old white-Irish-middle-class researcher (Speakers)
MS BURKE:	late 30s white-Irish-middle-class-(hetero)-female, teacher
MICHAEL:	15-year-old white-Irish working-class-male student
JASON:	15-year-old white-Irish working-class-male student
TOMA:	16-year-old white-Moldovan-working-class-male student
JACK:	15-year-old white-Irish working-class-male student

(Rest of class does not participate in classroom exchanges. These students are all white and almost all Irish apart from)

JONATHAN:	15-year-old black-Nigerian male student
FEYI:	15-year-old black-Belgian-Congolese female student
CHRISTIAN	15-year-old -black-Congolese-Belgian male student

Ms Burke begins the class 10 minutes late as she waits for some students to turn up. Students trickle casually into the room, and talk loudly long after the bell has gone. I take a free seat near the top of the class on the right hand side. The teacher does not admonish anyone for being late, and she occasionally utters 'come on, let's get started' here and there in a halfhearted way as she prepares herself. The class largely ignores these initial utterances, which makes me feel uncomfortable as the 'other adult' in the room.

The lesson is based on reading through a comprehension exercise from their sample state exam papers; the students' first state exam is in a couple of months. The piece used is from Bill Bryson's novel about an American roadtrip, *The Lost Continent*. Ms Burke suggests several times from the beginning of the lesson that those learning English might have some difficulty with the text; it turns out later on that she is specifically referring to Bryson's use of black English spelling/accents in some of the dialogue.

The vast majority of talk in the lesson centers on the white boys named above and Ms Burke. In fact, it is through the attention given to these chatty 'messers' that the teacher seems to manage the group. The only female voice heard in the entire lesson is that of the teacher, but this is unusual for this group. When Jason volunteers to read, Ms Burke allows him, but quickly takes over as she needs to get though the text quickly and the accents (a black Mississippi woman and an upper-class white British man visiting the area) are difficult to do justice to.

A discussion ensues from the passage about strangers coming to a new town. Ms Burke explains how she was raised in a remote Irish background where everyone could spot a stranger, and describes the city as a more impersonal place. Michael makes the point that on 'the estate,' everyone knows each other, inferring that her theory about parochialism actually extends to more urban or suburban spaces.

MICHAEL: I knew where he (Jason) came from the first time I met him.
JASON: (*Looking around, smiling at Michael*)
MICHAEL: The smell
JACK: Yeah (*under his breath*), Paki

Ms Burke reads on, apparently oblivious (but I don't know how she could be) to the latter remark. She continues to use 'black Mississippi' and 'upper-class English' accents as she reads. All the boys involved in the above exchange (Michael, Toma, and Jack in particular) shake while trying to stifle their laughter.

A separate, 'whole class' conversation begins about two minutes later about racial stereotyping in the text, which includes some of the boys – the teacher asks them to remember 'when we talked about this with *Roll of Thunder Hear my Cry*' (another commonly used text from the state syllabus). Ms Burke concurs with a suggestion from one of the class that there is a little bit of racism going on here.

Later in the class, Ms Burke reads a piece where a character says 'it be's closed now.' She again notes how this incorrect form may be difficult for English language learners. She asks what the character 'should have said' and directs this question at Toma. 'It *is* closed now,' say some of the class in chorus. A conversation then develops about the black woman's accent, and one student suggests how strange the accent is.

JASON: Some people might find *his* (*the Englishman's*) accent funny
MICHAEL: I find Kellyer's accent funny

Ms Burke then describes another personal anecdote on how she has a sister in America who has kept her accent, and not changed to a more US accent. Some cut in again:

STEVE: You know when you're on holiday miss, and they ask you if you're English first,
MICHAEL: (*Recognizing this*) Yeah!
STEVE: But then they find out that you're Irish and you're alright
JASON: Yeah, all Americans love Irish. Why is that?
MICHAEL: 'Cause they all think they're Irish. Anyway, what's not to like about Irish people? 'Cept Jason Kelly.

Analysis

To readers who may be unfamiliar with discourses around race, racism, and education in contemporary Ireland, the uncritical and quite damaging nature of the above exchanges requires little sophisticated unpacking. However, there are plenty of lessons here. As with all literacy and race politics, the wider social context is everything. Color-blindness and racial domination develops in its own specific ways in particular education systems. First, the deracialized construction of migrant students in Ireland as 'solely in need of English language support' pervades how Ms Burke structures her interactions as a 'good teacher.' Attention is drawn three times toward Tomas as a language learner, and to no one else. He is overtly inscribed as an 'almost literate' subject through the national, European and global, Anglophone discourse of English deficit. It is notable how the three black students in the class are not constructed language learners by Ms Burke. Although these students do attend language support classes, this is only due to an exemption from Irish language/literature classes; they speak English as a parallel first language. In the wider ethnography, I encountered confusion around migrant students' language proficiency. There was a silence among teachers about the fact that particular black and (particularly male) migrant students' English support classes were more likely to function as *learning support* classes. At the very least, their placement in these classes acted as disciplinary/containment periods that avoided the restructuring of school timetables and the A/B tiering of learner 'abilities' in the school. This wider, deracialized, nationalist assimilationist policy construction completely refused to engage discussion of indigenous/migrant power relations as legitimate (Kitching, 2010). Entertaining power in this way might simultaneously force a wider need to look at Ireland's individualizing competitive state exams system. The ways in which this system provokes teachers to maximize test-taking ability and 'cover content' pervades how Ms Burke structures engagements with the text above.

One could argue that the teacher directed her comments about understanding the language at Toma because she had a particular relationship or understanding of him. Whatever Ms Burke's individual relationship to Toma, his inscription as the 'speakable' face of language support also needs to be understood within the context of Ms Burke's management of these four boys as a collective here. The teacher's body language, and her low energy indicate quite clearly that this and possibly other lessons with this group, in this school, or at this time are stressful for her. The casual working-class masculinities of four white boys: Michael, Jason, Toma, and Jack dominate her energies. They mostly sit lazily, or sprawled in their desks while interrupting the teacher and entertaining others with their thoughts. Whether she is conscious of the gendered and classed nature of their interactions, Ms Burke tries hard to keep up with, or ignore the boys at particular points. As I have argued elsewhere, the silencing of racialized power relations in Irish education has to be understood in the context of the 'privileged' narrative of classed and gendered inequalities (Kitching, 2011a). The histories and geographies of such inequalities classed and gendered student and family educational subjectivities, some which are self-conscious and that are more tacitly aware of their position; Michael, in his reference to 'the estate' for example, strategically takes up his position as a literate subject of urban working-class consciousness, pointing out Ms Burke's failure to nuance what 'city life' is like. Critical thinking and learning is performed by these boys. They can recognize and play with different accents, and they do make choices, but these choices are not rationally taken within the symbolic terrain of official school literacy. They seem to relate more to the practicing suburban working-class-maleness; to the efforts to submit to and master a subject space that is not always commensurable with officially literate behavior.

The boys' shared practices are also quite clearly racialized, and Ms Burke is made complicit in/coopted into this particular aspect of the teacher–student dynamic. Despite the fact that one of the boys is not indigenously Irish, their interactions with and away from the text mutually constitute each other (and Ms Burke) as *meaningfully white*. It would be easy to argue that because the boys' use of the racially abusive term 'Paki' with *each other* parodies racial constructions, they actually disrupt race and whiteness. But I would argue that the insult was meaningful and laughable *because the boys are citing mutual recognition as having natural and inalienable membership of whiteness.* I witnessed during the ethnography that racist abuse toward migrant and minority ethnic students in the school is met with serious disciplinary sanctions. However, a white boy can relatively safely call another a 'Paki.' Rather than worry about the individual slagging between these white boys *per se*, I want to focus on the fact that ignoring this interaction reiterates the fixities of racial hierarchy. It does this by authorizing the continuance of a racial reality, where it is unthinkable that these boys would slide down the racial ladder, to actually being 'Pakis.' The fact that this can be ignored while acknowledging 'a little bit of racism' in the text indicates the unspeakability, and yet the obviousness, of racialized power relations infusing the lesson. The passing over of 'Paki' in this scene may or may not mean much to many in the room, depending on how students recognize/refute themselves as being constructed through white/black binaries (among others). This and other examples from the lesson are part of a series of ways in which white people constitute themselves as belonging meaningfully to the co-constructed category 'white,' that is, by failing to perform racial Otherness. The most obvious example apart from the 'Paki' utterance is Ms Burke's (and Jason's) failure to embody the black American and white English characters in the text. This failure extends well beyond 'doing the right accent' to meaningfully doing race, ethnicity, gender, nationality, and class identity. While the racially minoritized can and do impersonate and parody whiteness (e.g., publicly in comedy stand-up), these are more intelligible as coping or relief mechanisms than assertions of societal dominance. The fact that the school prohibition on racist speech does not extend to how whites inversely affirm each other's whiteness actually works to maintain white supremacy.

How and whether the black and other minority ethnic students in the class relate to themselves as subjects of a racially bounded, nationalist education regime is unknowable in this particular instance (although it is evidenced in other interviews with these students; Kitching, 2011a). I initially wondered why Christian, Feyi, and Jonathan did not take the opportunity to make a general point to the teacher that refutes her correction of the female character's English, given their trilingual identities, and the English hybridities used in the school by various black African students. Stepping for a moment 'outside' of race, this may or may not require them as individuals to identify with a character and a linguistic repertoire from a completely different historical, colonial and ethnonational context (and one that is written into being by a white man who does not use such language himself). From a literacy-agency perspective, it would require that the opportunity to be viewed as linguistically skilled and knowledgeable were extended to them in an ongoing, established basis in the classroom space. Regardless of whether they wished to make a point about the general need to account for linguistic and dialectic difference in literacy exchanges, such an intervention might impose the authentication of *black subjectivity* upon them; in a 'new migrant' context where critical discussions of race appear unavailable, there is a greater risk that racial residue might stick to them, in a way that parodies cannot stick to white bodies. Feyi, Christian, and Jonathan would become more explicitly collectivized and fixed via culturalist, de-ethnicized discourses of race (how black people speak across history and nations). Furthermore, such an intervention might breach the aforementioned silences regarding black students, language support, and learning support.

To further unpack the specific context of exchanges and silences that mutually constitute text, talk, subjectivities, and bodies in this scene, I want to turn to how Irishness is articulated in ways that intersect with and may trouble white supremacy. Again, in the symbolic classroom terrain, particular types of national identity project and steer (uncritical) textual interactions around the text: Ms Burke provides an insight into her own childhood in a remote part of Ireland; an island which has specific connotations of true Gaelicness. Yet there are strategic disruptions of homogenous Irish identity in certain moments for particular purposes and resealings of that homogeneity in others. In one moment, Michael asserts to Ms Burke that Irishness is cross-sectioned by (sub)urbanness, rurality, and classed differences. In another, unacceptable Englishness is rapidly inscribed as domineering and over-saturated in its relationship to post-independence Irishness. Overpowering Englishness is wearily replayed for Irish holidaymakers in the boys' remarks. English colonization of European holiday resorts is perhaps also underwritten as crass and distinctly different from (respectable working class?) Irishness. However, the privileges associated with successfully becoming white are clear as Michael plays on the shifting meanings of White-Irishness in the United States. White-Irish working class subjectivities have to work strategically here: holding on to an anti-Englishness Irishness, approximating a respectable Irish-USA-ness. What else is to differentiate between diasporic, majority, and minority whites on both sides of the Atlantic?

Conclusion: Practice makes Practice in Creating Racially Literate Analyses

I would argue that unraveling the strategic enforcement, elision, and conflation of race, class, ethno-nationality, and gender *via texts, bodies, identities, and social contexts* in classroom scenes is a form of critical literacy that is critically lacking in Ireland. 'Racial literacy' is particularly lacking, and a useful definition of what it means is worth quoting in full.

> First, racial literacy defines racism as a structural problem rather than as an individual one. Second, racial literacy locates debates about public process, which are often cloaked in the subtext of race, within an explicitly democratic context that is forward looking. Third, the process dimension to racial literacy can be used to guide participatory problem solving. Guinier wrote, 'in order to change the way race is understood, race has to be directly addressed rather than ignored' (p. 207) (Guinier, 2003 quoted in Rogers and Mosley, 2006, p. 465).

I agree entirely with the principles above. First, we must attend to multiple literacies. We must also name racialized power relations and positionings in their various manifestations before we reveal their dependence on the category of race. However, revealing this dependence is also politically important. The figured world of classroom literacy involves not just the interrelationships between artifacts (e.g., exam papers, textbooks, video games) and the manner in which persons (e.g., students and teachers) extend or are extended agency in relation to these artifacts. It does not just extend to institutional structures (e.g., streamed class groups) and the social structures that correlate in patterned, unequal ways with these (e.g., race, class, and gender). It also includes the organization of bodies that cross-section within the above structures, patterns, and interactions. We must unpack the manner in which those bodies are repetitively ascribed particular meanings, how they are related to other bodies and social artifacts, and how bodily practices are mutually ordered and named. Practice *makes practice* when it comes to leaving the space of literacy disembodied: if we do not understand bodies as texts, our language slips into talking about 'girls,' for example, as socially constructed but only because 'they have female bodies.' The politics of social constructionism, in this way becomes entirely negated, as policy makers simply replace the category 'sex' with a 'social' category that deployed in completely essentializing ways: 'gender.' Thus, little reconfiguration actually occurs (see Youdell, 2006, 2011).

Literacy analyses must demonstrate the manner in which the unequal relations within which particular bodies are not just positioned – but constituted – in deeply embedded ways, in relation to categorical identities, texts, specific cultural community practices and social stratifications. Here, we are more concerned with the change, the mistakes, and the new innovations that can occur in the unlimited process of building and destroying interactions between texts, identities, bodies, and society. Analyses of the inherently repetitive and unstable practice of racialization in mundane and exceptional moments can help educate against the guarantees associated with race for whites (Leonardo, 2009). This discernibly Cultural (with a big 'C') lens performs important critical work by supplementing our 'racial literacy' with an anti-racist politics that works laterally and through a process of identifying new possibilities and repeated, inscribed limitations of our current frameworks; this is a politics that works in positive tension with more fixed, hierarchical modes of naming and acting on the world. My politics respectfully do not call this a 'third space' (Gutierrez, 2008) as reinscribing 'how text-body-identity-society exchanges work,' even through the definition of an important and very useful new paradigm, leaves existing relations open to reification, appropriation, and dilution. Speaking from subjugated bodies, voices and experiences in complex ways (e.g., as in CRT thinking) is politically vital, now more than ever. We must also fight the ways productive power works within and beyond modern naming, structuring, and representative literacy and research models, to dynamically reinscribe white, majority ethnic, middle-class, hetero-male, able-bodied subjects.

Notes

1. Little mention is given in the strategy to the political panic that was caused by Ireland's 2009 fall from grace in PISA rankings, the backdrop of financial crisis that accelerated this panic, or of course, the politics of international organizations like PISA/OECD. Most importantly, no mention is made in the strategy of major questions raised by literacy researchers and independent auditors over whether or not the PISA data could confirm young people taking the test were any less formally literate than previous generations of test-takers (ERC and Statistics Canada).

2. Local literacies, according to Mercado (2005) are 'not likely to be visible through typical questions . . . such as "What kinds of things do you read?"' (p. 243). They are also unlikely to take the form of direct, formal instruction. Instead, this approach attempts to recognize the depth of goals, emotions, and symbols embedded in family migratory history, household composition, income-producing and recreational activities (e.g., traditional games and video games), child-rearing practices and beliefs, and tales and modes of resilience in the face of oppression. Within these local literacy repertoires, oral and written practices in English and/or minority languages may include storytelling, note-writing, form-filling, paying bills, keeping calendars (Mercado, 2005).

3. This field fuses aspects of Freirean critical pedagogy, Vygotskian social constructivism, and American multicultural equity perspectives in order to explain and challenge the ways in which certain learners (particularly those of African, Asian, Latino, and Native American backgrounds) are excluded from classroom participation and achievement.

4. Broader pedagogical studies have further nuanced views of teachers' cultural competence in recent years. For example Leonardo (2009) contests the myth of white ignorance when it comes to the racial Other's educational oppression. Making more a cultural than critical pedagogical argument, Lowenstein (2009) reviews and refutes the literature's assumption that white student teachers are deficient learners who lack resources for learning about diversity and equity.

5. Castagno and Brayboy (2008) conduct a wide-ranging review of the literature on Culturally Responsive Schooling (CRS) for the education of Indigenous (Alaskan and Native) American youth. They also note that the failure to move beyond the trivialization and essentialization of culture, and the lack of recognition of students as active meaning-makers means 'systemic, institutional, or lasting changes to schools serving Indigenous youth' are constantly off the agenda (2008, p. 941).

6. While criticisms have been leveled at CRT internationally for 'importing' a theory based on African-American experiences (Rizvi 2009), the use of 'property' is relevant and useful here for a couple of reasons. First, slavery was and is a transatlantic phenomenon. Cities such as Amsterdam and Bristol were built on the profits of slavery. Ireland, where I write from, is both a key destination and gateway for children, women, and men trafficked into prostitution, drugs and other overtly exploitative,

gendered, and racialized forms of work and existence; a fact that failures of state policy-making is complicit in (Kelleher *et al.*, 2009; Martin, Christie, Horgan, and O'Riordan, 2011).

7. As with scholars of gender and sexuality, who have focused on 'which girls and which boys' achieve (Epstein *et al.*, 1998), Gillborn shows how misleading it is to neatly categorize social groups separately (e.g., working-class people, ethnic minorities and boys) in order to measure or 'represent' the dynamics of achievement inequality. Indeed, the largest achievement gaps in GCSE grades relate to *Black Caribbean non-FSM students*. Girls in this group are '9.7 percentage points less likely to achieve the benchmark than their White peers . . . the figure for boys is 17.2 percentage points' (2010, p. 13).

8. In other words, as poststructural thinkers have argued, social constructionism does not move scholarship beyond essentialism (Nayak 2006; Youdell 2006).

References

Andrews, J., and Yee, W.C. (2006) Children's 'funds of knowledge' and their real life activities: Two minority ethnic children learning in out-of-school contexts in the UK. *Educational Review*, 58(4): 435–449.

Au, K.H. (2001) Culturally responsive instruction as a dimension of new literacies. *Reading Online*, 5(1), accessed November 20, 2012: www.readingonline.org/newliteracies/au/index.html

Bartlett, L., and Holland, D. (2002) Theorizing the space of literacy practice. *Ways of Knowing*, 2(1): 10–22.

Britzman, D. (2000) 'The question of belief': Writing poststructural ethnography. In E. St. Pierre and W.S. Pillow (eds) *Working the Ruins: Feminist Poststructural Theory and Methods in Education*. New York: Routledge, pp. 27–40.

Bryan, A. (2010) Corporate multiculturalism, diversity management, and positive interculturalism in Irish schools and society. *Irish Educational Studies*, 29(3): 253–269.

Castagno, A.E., and Brayboy, B.M.J. (2008) Culturally responsive schooling for Indigenous youth: A review of the literature. *Review of Educational Research*, 78(4): 941–993.

Cook-Gumperz, J. (2006) *The Social Construction of Literacy*, 2nd edn. Cambridge: Cambridge University Press.

DES (Department of Education and Skills, Government of Ireland) (2011) *Literacy and Numeracy for Learning and Life*. Dublin: Department of Education and Skills.

Devine, D. (2005) Welcome to the Celtic Tiger? Teacher responses to immigration and increasing ethnic diversity in Irish schools. *International Studies in Sociology of Education*, 15(1): 49–70.

Epstein, D., Elwood, J., Hey, V., and Maw, J. (1998) *Failing Boys? Issues in Gender and Achievement*. Buckingham: Open University Press.

Gay, G. (2002) Preparing for culturally responsive teaching. *Journal of Teacher Education*, 53(2): 106–116.

Gillborn, D. (2008) *Racism and Education: Coincidence or Conspiracy?* London: Routledge.

Gillborn, D. (2010) The white working class, racism and respectability: Victims, degenerates and interest-convergence. *British Journal of Educational Studies*, 58(1): 3–25.

González, N. (2005) Beyond culture: The hybridity of funds of knowledge. In González, N., Moll, C., and Amanti, C. (eds) *Funds of Knowledge: Theorizing Practices in Households, Communities and Classrooms*. London: Lawrence Erlbaum, pp. 29–46.

González, N., Moll, L., and Amanti, C. (2005) Introduction: Theorizing practices. In González, N., Moll, C., and Amanti, C. (eds) *Funds of Knowledge: Theorizing Practices in Households, Communities and Classrooms*. London: Lawrence Erlbaum.

Graff, H.J. (1987) *The Labyrinths of Literacy: Reflections on Literacy Past and Present*. East Sussex: The Falmer Press.

Greer, B., Mukhopadhyay, S., Powell, A.B., and Nelson-Barber, S. (2009) *Culturally Responsive Mathematics Education*. London: Routledge.

Grugeon, E. (2005) Listening to learning outside the classroom: student teachers study playground literacies. *Literacy*, 39(1): 3–9.

Gutierrez, K.D. (2006) *Culture Matters: Rethinking Educational Equity.* New York: Carnegie Foundation.

Gutierrez, K.D. (2008) Developing a socio-cultural literacy in the third space. *Reading Research Quarterly*, 43(2): 148–164.

Gutierrez, K.D., and Rogoff, B. (2003) Cultural ways of learning: Individual traits or repertoires of practice. *Educational Researcher*, 32(5): 19–25.

Ignatiev, N. (1995) *How the Irish Became White.* New York: Routledge.

Kelleher, P., O'Connor, M., Kelleher, C., and Pillinger, J. (2009) *Globalisation, Sex Trafficking and Prostitution: The Experiences of Migrant Women in Ireland.* Dublin: Immigrant Council of Ireland, accessed November 20, 2012: www.immigrantcouncil.ie/images/stories/Trafficking_Report_FULL_LENGTH_FINAL.pdf

Kitching, K. (2010) An excavation of the racialised politics of viability underpinning education policy in Ireland. *Irish Educational Studies*, 29(3): 213–229.

Kitching, K. (2011a) Interrogating the changing inequalities constituting 'popular,' 'deviant' and 'ordinary' subjects of school/subculture in Ireland: new migrant recognition, resistance and recuperation. *Race Ethnicity and Education*, 14(3): 290–311.

Kitching, K. (2011b) Taking responsibility for race inequality and the limitless acts required: beyond 'good/bad whites' to the immeasurably whitened self. *Power and Education*, 3(2): 164.

Ladson-Billings, G. (1995) But that's just good teaching! The case for culturally relevant pedagogy. *Theory into Practice*, 34(3): 161–165.

Leander, K.M., and Wells Rowe, D. (2006) Mapping literacy spaces in motion: A rhizomatic analysis of a classroom literacy performance. *Reading Research Quarterly*, 41(4): 428–460.

Leonardo, Z. (2009) *Race Whiteness and Education.* New York: Routledge.

Leonardo, Z. (2011a) After the glow: Race ambivalence and other educational prognoses. *Educational Philosophy and Theory*, 43(6): 675–698.

Leonardo, Z. (2011b) Intersections between race and class: or, toward a racio-economic analysis of education. Paper presented at the British Educational Research Association Annual Conference. London 7th September 2011.

Martin, S., Christie, A., Horgan, D., and O'Riordan, J. (2011) 'Often they fall through the cracks': Separated children in Ireland and the role of guardians. *Child Abuse Review*, 20(5): 361–373.

Mercado, C. (2005) Reflections on the Study of Households in New York City and Long Island: A Different Route, a Common Destination. In González, N., Moll, C., and Amanti, C. (eds) *Funds of Knowledge: Theorizing Practices in Households, Communities and Classrooms.* London: Lawrence Erlbaum.

Mirza, H.S. (1998) Race, gender and IQ: The Social consequence of pseudo-scientific discourse. *Race, Ethnicity and Education*, 1(1): 109–126.

Nayak, A. (2006) After race: Ethnography, race and post-race theory. *Ethnic and Racial Studies*, 29(3): 411–430.

Nichols, S., Nixon, H., and Rowsell, J. (2009) The good parent in relation to early childhood literacy: Symbolic terrain and lived practice. *Literacy*, 43(2): 65–74.

Oughton, H. (2010) Funds of knowledge: A conceptual critique. *Studies in the Education of Adults*, 42(1): 63–78.

Rizvi, F. (2009) Review Symposium on 'Racism and Education: Coincidence or Conspiracy?' *British Journal of Sociology of Education*, 30(3): 359–371.

Rogers, R., and Mosley, M. (2006) Racial literacy in a second-grade classroom: Critical race theory, whiteness studies, and literacy research. *Reading Research Quarterly*, 41(4): 462–495.

Youdell, D. (2006) *Impossible Bodies, Impossible Selves: Exclusions and Student Subjectivities.* Dordrecht: Springer.

Youdell, D. (2011) *School Trouble: Identity, Power and Politics in Education.* London: Routledge.

Chapter 28

Emotional Investments and Crises of Truth

Gender, Class, and Literacies

Stephanie Jones and Kristy Shackelford

Introduction

Joanie was six years old and beginning her first grade year in a high-poverty urban community in the United States when she committed 30 minutes to a written piece about her mother (see Figure 28.1). Like most mothers in the community, Joanie's had a complicated relationship with school including substantiated fear of school authorities reporting her family to the State Child Protective Services for unfit parenting. Joanie's mother was often harshly judged by middle-class school authorities, a reality reflective of research on working-class and poor mothers in the United States and the United Kingdom (e.g., Jones, 2004, 2007; Osgood, 2011; Steedman, 1986, 1987; Walkerdine, Lucey, and Melody, 2001; White, 2001). In Joanie's text (see Figure 28.1) readers may see 'I (heart) U mom' in three places as well as several variations of 'My and my mom' – or, as Joanie read it, 'Me and my mom.' Additionally, mom is spread throughout the text alongside hearts and Joanie represented through 'me.'

Young children's discursive practices and text production have been studied extensively by scholars committed to disrupting theories of socialization and illuminating the creative and powerful ways children engage socio-cultural tools – including discourses – available to them (e.g., Davies, 2003a; Dyson, 1997; Hicks, 2004; Marsh, 1999; Orellana, 1999). In this chapter we review some of these rich inquiries into children's texts and set them alongside sociological, historical, and psychosocial scholarship on social class, gender, and working-class mother–daughter relationships (e.g., Reay, 2004, 2005; Steedman, 1987; Walkerdine, Lucey and Melody, 2001), and emerging theories and philosophies of emotions and education (e.g., Boler, 1999; Reay, 2004, 2005). Weaving together research on interpreting children's texts and discursive practices, working-class mother–daughter relations, and theories of emotions in education animates our work toward a theory of literacy practices as not only *social* and *ideological* but also *emotional*. This work also contributes to a project of theorizing emotions and histories of girls' and women's emotions as not located in individuals 'but in a subject who is shaped by dominant discourses and ideologies and who also resists those ideologies through emotional knowledge and critical inquiry' (Boler, 1999, p. 20). The young participants in our own projects were well aware of discourses and ideologies operating at the state and school level

International Handbook of Research on Children's Literacy, Learning, and Culture, First Edition.
Edited by Kathy Hall, Teresa Cremin, Barbara Comber, and Luis C. Moll.
© 2013 John Wiley & Sons, Ltd. Published 2013 by John Wiley & Sons, Ltd.

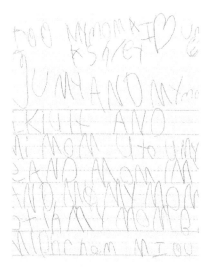

Figure 28.1 I love my Mom, by Joanie (fall, 1st grade)

about working-class mothers, and their textual productions reflected a resistance to dominant discourses and resistance through emotional investment from and in their mothers.

In what follows, we explore how researchers concerned with issues around gender, race, social class, and equity have interpreted children's writing. Next we briefly introduce feminist scholarship focused on psychosocial experiences of social class, gender, and mother–daughter relations to set the stage for our argument that literacy practices are not only *social* but *psychosocial* and bound up with emotions significantly influenced by social class and institutional power. In other words, we take for granted that literacies are *social* practices refracted through the political and spatial (e.g., Comber and Nixon, 2008; Janks, 2000; Vasudevan, 2010) and that the psychic is 'formed in and through the social' (e.g., Luttrell, 2006, p. 48). Thus, literacies impact the psychological and emotional just as the psychological and emotional impact literacies.

On Children's Texts, Discursive Practices, and the Feltness of Literacies

Carolyn Steedman, feminist historian and educator, provides rich analyses of children's writing from the 1800s through the twentieth century in her study of little girls' writing (1987). Steedman's work emphasizes the classed and gendered nature of young girls' writing historically and in contemporary times in the United Kingdom. Steedman's analyses of young working-class girls' writing (and their talking about that writing) in her own classroom in England in the 1970s demonstrated that the girls 'knew that their parents' situation was one of poverty and that the presence of children only increased it . . . that children were longed for, materially desired, but that their presence meant irritation, regret and resentment' (p. 25). Discourses of social class, gender, femininity, and childhood in the working-class girls' writing in Steedman's classroom were complex and disruptive of the dominant discourses surrounding girls and women. A mother's ambivalence toward a child was one theme in the girls' writing that challenged mainstream expectations that good mothers are happy and fully satisfied to sacrifice their personal needs and desires to care for their children. Steedman calls for a commitment for researchers to study young working-class children to get a better sense of through what means they understand their circumstances and come to class-consciousness. She argues that we have substantial evidence of working-class women's *recollections* of childhood and class consciousness in memoirs and through interviews, but that working-class children themselves have so rarely been the focus of critical inquiry that the fields of childhood studies and child development are severely lacking (1987). Part of Steedman's concern is related to overdetermined socialization processes and she argues that her interpretations of working-class children's writing is 'valuable evidence of the fact that children are not the passive subjects of their socialization, but active, thoughtful and frequently resentful participants in the process' (p. 31).

Literacy researchers working from socio-cultural and poststructural perspectives of language, literacy, and subjectivity have written extensively about children's creative use of socio-political tools available to them. This work buttresses the argument that children are not passive subjects of socialization but rather powerful players in their sense-making of sociopolitical discourses through which they live, work, and play (Davies, 2003a, 2003b; Dyson, 1982, 1989, 1993, 1997, 2003; Marsh, 1999, 2000; Millard, 2003; Orellana, 1995, 1999; Wohlwend, 2009). Davies' (2003a) work tends specifically to the constitution of gendered subjects through discourses and she argues that socialization theories are related 'to the individualistic humanist theories of the person that . . . obscure our recognition of the complex and contradictory ways in which we are continually constituting and reconstituting ourselves and the social world through various discourses in which we participate' (2003a, p. 6). Children's discursive practices and text production, these scholars would argue, are creative engagements with available discourses that afford and constrain possible subjectivities – not simple reconstitutions of self and other within binaries that produce a powerful/powerless dichotomy.

Pushing the boundaries of socio-cultural research on literacy as social practice, Hicks (e.g., 2001, 2002, 2004; Hicks and Jones, 2007), Dutro (2008, 2009a, 2009b, 2011), and Jones (2004, 2006b, 2007, 2012a, 2012b) engage scholarship within the nexus of literacies, gender, and/or social class that is most closely aligned with the psychosocial work we attempt here. In two longitudinal ethnographic studies, Hicks situates young children's and young adolescents' literacies within psychosocial lived experiences saturated with feeling and emotion. Hicks draws on cultural understandings of particular literacy practices and poststructural understandings of discourses and subjectivity to argue for literacy research that is embedded in the concreteness of lives and attuned to emotional ways of knowing and feeling. Her multiyear study of two young children (2002) demonstrated the ways that coming to know the world through language and literacies was intractable from coming to know the world *with* intimate others. Dutro grounds her work in the same assumption and enters the conversation around children's and youth's emotions and literacies through feminist literary studies broadly, and the constructs of testimony and witness specifically (e.g., 2009a, 2009b). She argues that children are 'everyday documentarians' and their testimonies about life often lived through struggle and challenging relationships with schools articulated through conversation and written text production need and deserve ethical *response* or *critical witnessing* in the school space.

In addition to the significance of the psychosocial within literacy practices, we ultimately draw implications that challenge assumptions about school literacy acquisition as always positive and productive. Acquiring school literacy, argues Viruru, 'is very much a process of both loss and gain, of contradiction and accommodation, of colonization and agency' (2003, p. 17). For our purposes, this may be especially true for working-class girls forced to adopt literacies that contradict their lived experiences and aim for a hypothetical 'upward mobility' that constitutes them as differently, and 'improved,' classed subjects from their mothers. Viruru's ethnographic research in India (2001) and her review of similar work from a number of countries (2003) emphasize the importance of researchers considering the colonizing work of educational institutions. Scholars such as Hicks, Dutro, and Viruru help foreground emotions and the feltness of literacies, the losses and gains afforded by school literacies, the personal and political nature of literacies, and the intricate ways literacies are embedded in the psychosocial. One way to focus on such losses and gains is through the lens of social class marginalization and mother–daughter relations.

On Working-Class Mothers, Daughters, and Emotions

[T]he fairytale of social mobility has no happy ending. It is always at others' expense. Cinderella becomes a princess but a whole host of young women take her place in the gutter. And what happens to Cinderella's mother? Killed off in the fairy story but alive and slighted in most working class children's lives. Once you put the social back into individual transformation others bear the costs of self-betterment and you are left with guilty gratitude – the dirty pleasures of privilege that have always left me feeling slightly soiled. (Reay, 2004/5, p. 7)

What, indeed, happens to the mother when the little working-class girl beats the odds of class reproduction and finds 'success' in upwardly mobile fashion by aligning herself with school and school authorities? Feminist sociologist Diane Reay challenges the individual trajectory of upward mobility by pointing to the social nature of the transformation of the self, drawing attention to the reality that most people don't experience upward mobility and the cost of 'slighting' family members who are left behind. This slighting may be particularly painful in the mother/daughter relationship and Reay's extensive work with working-class children pointed to a particular theme where mothers were powerful in the home but 'need[ed] her children to stand up for her in the outside world' (2004/5) where a 'multiplicity of discourses produced by a whole series of mechanisms operating in different institutions' (Foucault, 1990, p. 33) to construct the working-class mother as a pathology and in need of surveillance and correction. However, children might not be positioned to defend their mothers if they do not recognize the precarious positioning and potential judgment of the mother, and if the mother had not invested emotional capital in, or demonstrated an overt emotional investment toward, the child.

Reay's critique and extension of Bourdieu's capitals (e.g., Bourdieu, 1990, 2000) to include a theory of emotional capital aligns with other contemporary feminist efforts to theorize embodiment and emotion (e.g., Boler, 1997, 1999; Bordo, 1987; Davies and Gannon, 2009; Dutro, 2008, 2011; Grumet, 1988; Sedgwick, 2003). These scholars and others make the case that emotions and embodiment have been historically undertheorized and blatantly dismissed as 'private' issues, reinscribing men and theories of men as 'public' and the socio-political space of women as 'private,' therefore not worthy of theory or philosophy. For Reay, emotional capital is conceived of as the emotional work invested in a child by the mother toward the child's education. Her assertion that when mothers distance themselves from school, they might actually create more space to devote to the overall emotional care of their children is crucial for us to consider as we analyze the presence of the mother in little girls' school texts juxtaposed with her relative absence in the physical school. Reay would argue this emotional distance *from* school could result in more positive emotions devoted to the child and may well equip the child with the confidence necessary to achieve academically *in* school. This is a direct challenge to a mainstream expectation, in the United States, that children's parents (especially those from working-class and poor backgrounds) must be physically present and closely linked to the school in order for their children to succeed academically.

Boler (1999) argues that emotions 'are experiences in which economic power and dominant culture are deeply invested' (p. 21) and pastoral power and regimes of truth (e.g., Foucault) produce a terrain of feeling power where those investments are felt. She argues that emotions are sites of social control as well as resistance, a powerful force working toward conformity and hegemony on one side and against control on the other. For our purposes it is worth considering how working-class mothers are constructed as either too emotionally involved or not engaged enough (or 'not caring') about their children's success in school and how emotions – perception and judgments about others' emotions – are intimately involved in the constructions of 'truth' about mothers. Further, how children's emotional investments in their mothers are produced, recognized, or dismissed in school as potential disruptions of dominant discourses about deviant mothers.

Building on feminist literary scholars interested in reading practices around trauma narratives, Boler further suggests that a reader of any genre can position herself to be shaken by a text, to reconsider what it is she thought to be truth before the reading, and to be willing to recognize herself implicated in inequitable power relations that produce human suffering and challenges. This orientation toward reading is what Boler calls 'testimonial reading,' or the reader's responsibility to engage with text empathically, to be moved to action, and to 'radically [shift] [her] self-reflective understanding of power relations' (p. 158). Scholarship focused on young working-class girls' writing could benefit from reading the texts *testimonially*, aware of the socio-political context in which the girls were producing texts, and interested in the ways emotional investments between working-class girls and their mothers manifest in discursive practices and text productions in school.

Reading Girls' Texts for Crises of Truth

Resistance to stereotypical gendered discourses

Drawing on feminist theories of emotion, we use Boler's (1999) notion of testimonial reading to situate young girls' texts as 'historically situated in power relationships . . . To enquire about these [testimonial] readings tasks, we might ask, what crisis of truth does this text speak to, and what mass of contradictions and struggles do I become as a result?' (pp. 170–171). Educators and scholars must be willing to embrace a 'mass of contradictions and struggles' when they examine the intersection and frequent contradictions of truths constituted in state institutions with truths produced by students caught up in the webs of those institutions. One way researchers and practitioners might prepare themselves to *experience* crises of truths in their reading of young girls' textual productions is to ask themselves what truths are readily available for making sense of the girls and how those truths are constituted. For example, one readily available truth for researchers and practitioners to access is that stereotypically 'girl' commercial toys and media are potentially socially and psychologically damaging since they are assumed to carry and project gendered ways of being that position girls and women as subordinate to – and in service of – boys and men.

Karen Wohlwend's work (2009) on analyzing the complex ways kindergarten-aged girls consumed and produced gendered identities through their textual play with Disney Princesses is an example of a researcher prepared to experience a crisis of truth in reading just these kinds of texts. While Wohlwend doesn't use theories of emotion to frame her work or call on Boler specifically to situate her work, she resists the carefully constructed and reproduced 'truth' narratives available to her to recognize the girls' play with mass produced commercial princesses as a sedimenting of stereotypical gendered subjectivities. Rather, Wohlwend draws on ethnographic observations, textual artifacts, and classroom conversations to stitch together a transformative portrayal of young girls 'select[ing] from the universe of possible identities and contexts for pretense, [and taking] up disparately empowered subject positions within discourses of emphasized femininity and creative expression' (p. 76).

This creative expression resulted in the girls rewriting and revising scripts and play-roles to position the girl princesses as wielding tremendous power in the fantasy world of castles, dragons, and princes. Their reworking of the well-known gendered scripts from the Disney movies produces a crisis of truth around the notion that young girls are passive consumers of media. The materiality of the toys produced by entertainment conglomerates and presumed stand-ins for stereotypical gendered performances (the Disney princess dolls in this case) 'offered concrete repositories that carried and stabilized story meanings and were paradoxically packed with potential for transformation' (p. 76). In other words, there is a truth operating around girls and 'girl' products that doesn't account for girls' creative and complex engagements with circulating ideologies in texts and society. Socialization of girls doesn't take place without the 'active, thoughtful and frequently resentful participants in the process,' (Steedman, 1987, p. 31). Wohlwend's work offers an empirical example of very young girls recognizing ideological truths circulating in and around princess dolls, and actively resisting those truths through their production of texts in school. Such textual productions are inevitably invested with emotion as the children negotiated who would play what roles with the princess dolls and what the storylines would be, what dialogue characters would speak, and the physical movements characters would make. And with emotional investment, the girls produce possible storylines that may endure and strengthen over time.

As researchers concerned with the mother–daughter relationship and emotional investments in particular storylines aligned with mothers or institutions, we wonder if and how Wohlwend's girl participants explicitly produced their mothers in school texts. If we had access to that kind of data, we might ask ourselves how and if those particular storylines might have influenced their textual play with the Disney princesses. In other words, we would ask about traces of the mother in the girls' productions of subjectivities available for themselves and others. While Wohlwend doesn't describe the social class positioning of the three focus participants in this article, readers can acknowledge that these very young girls are producing texts as resistance to stereotypical femininities and doing so while they are playing with merchandise most adults would believe only constrain gendered possibilities. The contradictions are fierce, and a testimonial reading and crisis of truth affords the contradictions to emerge.

Resistance to stereotypical discourses of working-class mothers

Fierce contradictions emerged in one of our projects as we set out to read for crises of truth in young working-class girls' textual productions of their mothers in school. Looking across data from three separate studies about working-class girls' literacies and identities (Jones, 2004; Jones, 2006b; Jones, 2012b), we were overwhelmed by the explicit presence of the 'mother' in drawings, writings, and oral conversations. The girls were in kindergarten, first, second, and third grades (approximately 5–8 years old), had families that would be considered working-class or poor, had experienced observable marginalization in their classrooms or the school, and all had mothers who were not well respected by school authorities.

Through our analyses, we constructed three ways through which the girls produced their mothers that create a crisis of truth around working-class and poor mothers: (1) Mother as valued worker; (2) Mother as provider of physical and emotional needs; and (3) Mother as vulnerable and needing defending or care. These were not the only ways the girls constructed their mothers, but they were ways through which girls produced positive and powerful portrayals that counter dominant discourses.

While we don't claim to know the girls' intentions or motivations in their writing and conversations around work, we can situate these conversations within regimes of truth – or discourses – about lazy poor mothers who never work hard enough, whether that work is for earning money or for appropriately raising children (e.g., Jones, 2004, 2006a, 2007; Osgood, 2011). These discourses of the undeserving, financially irresponsible, lazy poor mother are legitimized through various state institutions. State welfare agencies require mothers receiving state benefits to live by certain rules regarding work and how food benefits are allowed to be spent; child protective services often evaluate the quality of mothering on the cleanliness of a home and children and therefore on her perceived productivity or her laziness; and authorities in educational institutions often judge a mother's quality of parenting based on her physical presence, appearance, and mannerisms on school property.

These girls, however, produced an alternative discourse of poor mothers, portraying them as hard workers who control the money and wield power in the home, including influence over what the girls imagine as possible futures for themselves:

HEATHER: Can we talk about what we wanna be when we grow up?
STEPHANIE: Let's do that.
CALLIE: Help kids. Like when they're in the nursing home and there're little kids that need help.

Callie's mother worked in a nursing home as an assistant and as a custodial worker. Here Callie merges one desire – to work with kids, with another desire – to be like her mother, and readers can experience another crisis of truth: working-class jobs are valued and even desired. Callie was not the only girl to present her mother's labor as admirable and desirable, and the conversation continued:

TRACY: I wanna work at a nursing home like my mom – or a hospital.
STEPHANIE: Doing what?
TRACY: Helping old people.
MICHELLE: Work in a nursing home cuz you get a lot of money.
TRACY: In a hospital you get more money than in a nursing home.
STEPHANIE: What would you do at the nursing home?
CALLIE: My mom works at a nursing home and she has to change diapers.

Moms reign powerful in the discursive practices of these young girls. While some dads were in jail and other dads constantly pursued more stable employment, it was the mothers who held full-time positions and probably provided the bulk of the family income – meager as it was. Moms have the jobs, moms talk about money, moms have and control the money – and power – and these were popular subjects for the girls' free writing and discussion in and out of the classroom. These realities buttress Reay's argument that working-class mothers are often powerful inside their homes, but experience extreme marginalization and judgment outside their homes by middle-class others. In these examples we can see how mothers' focus on their work and the necessity of paid labor to provide for the girls points to emotional investment in the girls by the mothers, and vice versa as the daughters produce their mothers as productive and powerful, and worthy of becoming.

All the girls brought their mothers into school each day and wrote, drew, and spoke them into existence when they were physically absent. In the piece below Christina, who lived with her mother and grandmother and did not know her father, writes a fictional story about visiting France with an illustration (see Figure 28.2) depicting both a mom and dad

I was in the car in the night.
We parked at the hotel then we went to the fourth floor. I went in the room.
I put on my pajamas and turned on the T.V. and we had popcorn.

Figure 28.2   When we went to France, by Christina (2nd half of Kindergarten)

Christina's inclusion of a 'Dad' in the illustration alongside Christina and her mother might be read as her desire to have a traditional family that includes a mother and a father, or even as a fictional representation of her own family to be more like her friends in the classroom who mostly had two heterosexual married parents in the home. But Christina disrupted both interpretations later in the year when she read the book *What Mommies Do Best/What Daddies Do Best* (Numeroff, 1998) and reported:

CHRISTINA: My mom is my dad.
STEPHANIE: What do you mean?
CHRISTINA: It's the same thing because my mom teach you how to ride a bike and take care of you and that is what dads do best too.
CHRISTINA: Because I don't have a dad but my mom is my dad.
STEPHANIE: She's both.
CHRISTINA: Yeah.
STEPHANIE: How did you know your mom is your dad too?
CHRISTINA: Because she tells me.

Christina's mother is the provider for everything in Christina's life, including an unknown father. During the reading of the book she regularly commented about how her mom performed all the physical acts represented on both sides of the 'Mommies/Daddies' book. Christina's assertion that her mother tells her that she is both the mom and the dad points to her mother's emotional investment in Christina, and Christina's textual production of her mother as *both mother and father* portrays a reciprocal emotional investment on the part of Christina. The mother defies a mainstream narrative in the United States that a single African American mother is a deficit to a child by telling and showing Christina that they are a complete family together – she is both the mom and the dad – a crisis of truth.

We suggest that two dominant discourses – school as providing potential upward mobility and school as judge of working-class mothers – collide and contradict one another when working-class girls' texts are read testimonially, or with a willingness to reimagine one's assumptions about the 'truth' prior to the reading and one's role in inequitable power relations embedded in the text (Boler, 1999). This collision of upward mobility discourses and the judging of mothers positions young working-class and poor girls in an impossible situation and reinscribes social class by not producing alternatives to either choosing loyalty toward their harshly judged mothers or loyalty toward an institution that can potentially lead to upward mobility. This analytic window into little girls' text production illuminates the complexities of social reproduction in-the-making *through* school literacies – ironically the very site through which educators and policymakers claim can catapult working-class and poor children into an upwardly mobile trajectory. Another crisis of truth.

Literacies, Emotions, and Children's Textual Productions

Literacies and emotions are inextricably linked – each producing the other within broad sociopolitical contexts, circulating discourses and regimes of truth, and intimate moments of being with others. Some emotional investments in textual productions might be observable and recognizable as indeed 'emotional' such as the sadness, crying, and anger present in the studies by Dutro and Hicks, or the joy and animated physical activity of role-playing in Wohlwend's work, and the pain of loss in Viruru's work. Other times it may not be possible to observe some emotional change in a child producing a text, such as in the examples from our project, but having access to girls' performances across contexts can provide insight to some of the emotional investments embedded in their seemingly emotion-neutral texts. Inscribing emotion into text through crayons drawing, fingers typing, pencils writing, voices speaking, and bodies acting is an act embodied in the fullest way: social, political, psychological, and material. All textual productions won't carry the same emotional weight over time, but tracing the persistence of particular emotional investments across time might lead researchers to crises of truth and the production of new – and inevitably contradictory – understandings about girls, social class, and identities.

Social class and gender play a central role in the production of literacies and emotions, emotional investments in storylines for one's future, and in implications for educators and scholars. The scholarship included in this chapter can make significant contributions to studies of literacies, identities, gender, and class. We draw on this wide range of work to offer two suggestions here for literacy researchers.

First, the close documentation of young girls' textual productions of classed and gendered lives is important work. This kind of work can answer Steedman's call for studies of gendered and classed childhoods from children's perspectives rather than from adults' recollections. Documentation of this sort can provide opportunities for tracing emotional investments through texts across time and space, and also within particular times and particular places. Close analysis of girls' texts can also challenge simple theories of socialization and reproduction, and offer researchers and education practitioners an opportunity to read their texts testimonially.

Second, while significant work has been conducted on working-class and poor children's literacies and identities, much more work can be taken up. Working-class and poor children (particularly girls and mothers) are still too frequently produced as deficit in one way or another, but mostly because they are simply positioned as always 'having less' of everything compared to their middle-class and affluent peers. Work reviewed in this chapter portrays working-class and poor children and families as resourceful, resilient, insightful about circulating truths and ideologies, and resistant to powerful institutional forces attempting colonization.

Young girls navigate complex terrain between home, school, emotions, and literacies and – knowingly or not – begin to construct gendered and classed storylines for themselves in relation to truths created through state institutions. Emotions and literacies have everything to do with this shaping of oneself as resilient and not dominated by institutional others. Boler (1999, pp. xvi–xvii) believes that,

> By rethinking the absence of emotion, how emotion shapes how we treat other people and informs our moral assumptions and judgments . . . we have the potential to radically change our cultural values and violent practices of cruelty and injustice, which are often rooted in unspoken 'emotional' investments in unexamined ideological beliefs.

Our emotional investments as researchers – commitments to challenge sexism and classism and foreground lived experiences of how working-class children disrupt dominant discourses – shape this work just as much as educators' emotional investments in ideological beliefs shape perceptions of children and children's literacies in school. Rethinking the absence of attention to emotion in research and practice around young children's literacies and considering how emotional investments in people or ideas influence selective seeing, hearing, and believing on the part of adults can prompt us all to be willing to experience crises of truth and move uncertainly toward more inclusive and powerful practices for everyone.

References

Boler, M. (1997) Disciplined emotions: Philosophies of educated feelings. *Educational Theory*, 47(3): 226–246.

Boler, M. (1999) *Feeling Power: Emotions and Education*. New York: Routledge.

Bourdieu, P. (1990) *The Logic of Practice*. Stanford, CA: Stanford University Press.

Bourdieu, P. (2000) *Pascalian Meditations*. Stanford, CA: Stanford University Press.

Bordo, S. (1987) *The Flight to Objectivity: Essays on Cartesianism and Culture*. Albany, NY: SUNY Press.

Comber, B., and Nixon, H. (2008) Spatial literacies, design texts, and emergent pedagogies in purposeful literacy curriculum. *Pedagogies: An International Journal*, 3(2): 221–240.

Davies, B. (2003a) *Frogs and Snails and Feminist Tales*. Cresskill, NJ: Hampton Press.

Davies, B. (2003b) *Shards of Glass: Children Reading and Writing beyond Gendered Identities*. Cresskill, NJ: Hampton Press.

Davies, B., and Gannon, S. (eds) (2009) *Pedagogical Encounters*. New York: Peter Lang.

Dutro, E. (2008) 'That's why I was crying on this book': Trauma as testimony in responses to literature. *Changing English*, 15(4): 423–434.

Dutro, E. (2009a) Children writing 'Hard Times': Lived experiences of poverty and the class-privileged assumptions of a mandated curriculum. *Language Arts*, 87(2): 89–98.

Dutro, E. (2009b) Children's testimony and the necessity of critical witness in urban classrooms. *Theory into Practice*, 48: 231–238.

Dutro, E. (2011) Writing wounded: Trauma, testimony, and critical witness in literacy classrooms. *English Education*, 43(2): 193–211.

Dyson, A.H. (1982) Reading, writing, and language: Young children solving the written language puzzle. *Language Arts*, 59(8): 829–839.

Dyson, A.H. (1989) *Multiple Worlds of Child Writers: Friends Learning to Write*. New York: Teachers College Press.

Dyson, A.H. (1993) *Social Worlds of Children: Learning to Write in an Urban Primary School*. New York: Teachers College Press.

Dyson, A.H. (1997) *Writing Superheroes: Contemporary Childhood, Popular Culture and Classroom Literacy*. New York: Teachers College Press.

Dyson, A.H. (2003) *The Brothers and Sisters Learn to Write: Popular Literacies in Childhood and School Cultures*. New York: Teachers College Press.

Foucault, M. (1990) *The History of Sexuality: An Introduction*, Vol. 1. New York: Vintage Books.

Grumet, M. (1988) *Bitter Milk: Women and Teaching*. Amherst, MA: University of Massachusetts Press.

Hicks, D. (2001) Literacies and masculinities in the life of a young working-class boy. *Language Arts*, 78(3): 217–226.

Hicks, D. (2002) *Reading Lives: Working-class Children and Literacy Learning*. New York: Teachers College Press.

Hicks, D. (2004) Back to Oz? Rethinking the literacy in a critical study of reading. *Research in the Teaching of English*, 39(1): 63–84.

Hicks, D., and Jones, S. (2007) Living class as a girl. In J.A. Van Galen and G.W. Noblit (eds) *Late to Class: Social Class and Schooling in the New Economy*. New York: SUNY Press, pp. 55–85.

Jones, S. (2003) Identities of race, class, and gender inside and outside the math classroom: A girls' math club as a hybrid possibility. *Feminist Teacher*, 14(3): 220–233.

Janks, H. (2000) Domination, access, diversity and design: A synthesis model for critical literacy education. *Educational Review*, 52(2): 175–186.

Jones, S. (2004) Living poverty and literacy learning: Sanctioning the topics of students' lives. *Language Arts*, 81(6): 461–469.

Jones, S. (2006a) Girls, social class, and literacy: What teachers can do to make a difference. Portsmouth, NH: Heinemann.

Jones, S. (2006b) Language with an attitude: White girls performing class. *Language Arts*, 84(2): 114–124.

Jones, S. (2007) Working-poor mothers and middle-class others: Psychosocial considerations in home-school relations and research. *Anthropology and Education Quarterly*, 38(2): 159–177.

Jones, S. (2012a) Critical literacies in the making: Social class and identities in the early reading classroom. *Journal of Early Childhood Literacy*. First published online January 11, 2012, http://ecl.sagepub.com/content/early/2012/01/09/1468798411430102.full.pdf+html

Jones, S. (2012b) Negotiating mothering identities: Ethnographic and intergenerational insights to social class and gender in a high-poverty U.S. context. *Gender and Education*, 24(4): 443–460.

Luttrell, W. (2006) Commentary: 'That place which understands the psychic as formed in and through the social.' *Ethos*, 34(1): 48–54.

Marsh, J. (1999) Batman and Batwoman go to school: Popular culture in the literacy curriculum. *International Journal of Early Years Education*, 7(2): 117–131.

Marsh, J. (2000) 'But I want to fly too!' Girls and superhero play in the infant classroom. *Gender and Education*, 12(2): 209–220.

Millard, E. (2003) Gender and early childhood literacy. In N. Hall, J. Larson, and J. Marsh (eds) *Handbook of Early Childhood Literacy*. London: Sage, pp. 22–33.

Numeroff, L. (1998) *What Mommies do Best/ What Daddies do Best*. New York: Simon and Schuster.

Orellana, M.J. (1995) Literacy as a gendered social practice: Texts, talk, tasks and take-up in two bilingual classrooms. *Reading Research Quarterly*, 30(4): 335–365.

Orellana, M.J. (1999) Good guys and bad girls. In M. Bucholtz, A.C. Liang, and L.A. Sutton (eds) *Reinventing Identities: The Gendered Self in Discourse*. Oxford University Press, pp. 64–82.

Osgood, J. (2011) Paper presentation at the 8th International Gender and Education Association Conference. Exeter, UK. April.

Reay, D. (2004) Gendering Bourdieu's concepts of capitals? Emotional capital, women, and social class. In L. Adkins and B. Skeggs (eds) *Feminism after Bourdieu*. Oxford: Blackwell Publishing/The Sociological Review, pp. 57–74.

Reay, D. (2004/5) On the wild side: Identifications and disidentifications in the research field. Paper presented at the Centre for Psycho-Social Studies, University of the West of England.

Reay, D. (2005) Beyond consciousness? The psychic landscape of social class. *Sociology*, 39(5): 911–928.

Sedgwick, E.K. (2003) *Touching Feeling: Affect, Pedagogy, Performativity*. Durham, NC: Duke University Press.

Steedman, C. (1986) *Landscape for a Good Woman*. New Brunswick, NJ: Rutgers University Press.

Steedman, C. (1987) *The Tidy House: Little Girls Writing*. London: Virago.

Vasudevan, L. (2010) Education remix: New media, literacies, and emerging digital geographies. *Digital Culture and Education*, 2(1): 62–82.

Viruru, R. (2001) *Early Childhood Education: Postcolonial Perspectives from India*. New Delhi: Sage.

Viruru, R. (2003) Postcolonial perspectives on childhood and literacy. In N. Hall, J. Larson, and J. Marsh (eds) *Handbook of Early Childhood Literacy*. London: Sage, pp. 13–21.

Walkerdine, V., Lucey, H., and Melody, J. (2001) *Growing Up Girl: Psycho-Social Explorations of Class and Gender*. New York: SUNY Press

White, C. (2001) Examining poverty and literacy in our schools: Janice's story. In S. Boran and B. Comber (eds) *Critiquing Whole Language and Classroom Inquiry*. Urbana, IL: National Council of Teachers of English, pp. 169–199.

Wohlwend, K.E. (2009) Damsels in discourse: Girls consuming and producing identity texts through Disney Princess play. *Reading Research Quarterly*, 44(1): 57–83.

Chapter 29

What Does Human Geography Have To Do With Classrooms?

Margaret Sheehy

Introduction

Literacy research is enjoying a spatial turn. Research on classroom practices is beginning to explain learning contexts as relational processes that delimit people's (contingent) positions as teachers, students, administrators, and parents. A geographic explanation of context – the social, relational processes, imaginings, and artifacts that distinguish one classroom and one school from another – complicates context and therefore practice. When a human geographic analysis is applied to the literacy practices of classrooms, taken for granted constructs such as agency, place, space, time, and resistance become entangled in relational processes and can no longer be considered separately from them. When we recognize the complexity of people's actions as part of entangled relations played out in time, we have no choice but to wrestle, not only with what students and teachers *can* do but also with what they *can't* do. Whereas, traditionally, explanations of classroom literacy concern what people actually do, Henri Lefebvre (1996) argued that the site for political action is made visible precisely at the line between the 'possible/impossible,' a line made by what people can and can't do. Specifically, human geography asks, 'What resources are available to people in particular places, how do they deploy them, and what are the social processes and artifacts engaged?' A major goal is to reveal people's struggle to achieve as part of the social processes they work within and against. Within this struggle, 'different groups have different resources which give them different capacities to articulate their position, their politics, their identities, and to mobilize communities of resistance' (Keith and Pile, 1993, p. 37).

In this chapter, I argue that we need yet more human geographic explanations of classroom literacy practices in order to be political and effect pedagogies committed to working the ever-changing possible/impossible lines that demarcate people's struggle. I argue that geography compels us to examine literacy practice in ways that will make lines of struggle visible. Geographic analyses draw on a number of theories, from the sociological theories of Henri Lefebvre, Michel Foucault, Pierre Bourdieu, and Michel de Certeau, to activity network theories that explain social practices as the accomplished activity of actors, artifacts, and discourses

International Handbook of Research on Children's Literacy, Learning, and Culture, First Edition.
Edited by Kathy Hall, Teresa Cremin, Barbara Comber, and Luis C. Moll.
© 2013 John Wiley & Sons, Ltd. Published 2013 by John Wiley & Sons, Ltd.

all networked together. I will draw on each of these theories as I discuss some of the ways in which geographic formations play in children's literacy experiences in school.

I begin by examining the formation of broad geographic networks made visible via federal regulations enacted in the United States. I then compare literacy practices in middle schools in two urban areas in New York State where the material resources available to individuals differ and thus influence the kinds of literacy practices available to students. Next, I explain the possibility available in material relations when ideas migrate into classrooms and people use them in ways that effect positive, marginal practices. I then contemplate research methodologies, which may help us understand migration processes more thoroughly. I conclude by pulling all the ideas I developed in the chapter together and asking a series of questions that need further explanation if we want youths, teachers, and administrators to use literacy toward their own ends.

A Glimpse at Some Macro Processes that Shape School Literacy Practices

Education systems create learning standards in order to provide guidance regarding what content knowledge is needed for future jobs and cultural wellbeing. Achieving standards involves literate practices across school disciplines. Creating standards is a cultural process Bourdieu (1977) likened to a struggle over taste. Some countries have succeeded in adopting national standards and the United States is well on its way with nearly all states having adopted 'common core learning standards.' The thinking is that if knowledge domains are pinned down as set concepts and facts to know and as dispositions to emulate, then schools will have a better chance of serving students more equitably. Ideally, standards serve as a map that, if taught, would assure educational equity for all.

While standards-makers mean well, the high stakes attached to the tests that typically accompany standards (disciplining school personnel when students do not perform according to the metrics designed for them, for example) only manage to close down some practices in favor of others. For example, in many US schools, the arts have been eliminated to make more time available to the major disciplinary literacy that get tested: English Language Arts. Schools in which 'the achievement gap' between privileged and underprivileged students is greatest are pressured to raise test scores and, thus, curriculum becomes a year-long, data-driven (test-data driven) obsession with testing. When practices resulting from the No Child Left Behind Act of 2001 didn't close the achievement gap after eight years of testing, the United States Department of Education funded a new program, 'Race to the Top,' under the American Recovery and Reinvestment Act of 2009. Race to the Top provides funding to a few states that have adopted 'common core standards' and can argue that they will turn around low-achieving schools.

New York received Race to the Top funding in 2010. One year later, Race to the Top is radically reorganizing literacy practices in New York's schools. In exchange for the sizable grant, New York promised to reduce the achievement gap, first, by adopting 'common core learning standards' and second, by implementing a performance review of teachers and principals. The common core standards serve to organize curriculum in a standard manner. The performance reviews for teachers and administrators rate their performance, as evidenced by youths' test scores and by evaluations of their day-to-day work. A complicated mathematical equation results in a rating for each teacher and principal, which will determine whether they will continue working or be fired, after a designated period during which they can improve their scores.

Race to the Top is being articulated in different ways by different educational stakeholders. In schools, administrators and teachers are attempting to shape curricular practices that will engage youth in the literacy practices necessary to do well on tests. Policy scholars take up the struggle differently. Some (e.g., Barnes, 2011) question whether Race to the Top will close the achievement gap, because neither of the two federal acts (the Elementary and Secondary Education Act and No Child Left Behind) that provided funding for education programs resulted in increased test scores. Others debate whether the federal government's real interest is to privatize education (e.g., Ravitch, 2011; Manna and Ryan, 2011) since, if school test scores do not increase, they can be taken over by charter schools or other agencies. Policy debates have on-the-ground implications for literacy practices in schools. Barnes (2011) argued that it is not a problem to have standards but that regulating them requires limits. All states had standards prior to the No Child Left Behind Act and, now, Race to the Top. The punishments attached to No Child Left Behind (closing schools) and Race to the Top (firing teachers and administrators and closing schools) however, are a major regulatory force in shaping literacy practices in schools. With so much funding earmarked for Race to the Top, federal funding for other literacy possibilities such as the National Writing Project have been reduced, stalled, or eliminated. In the meantime, youths are attending school and engaging in the current articulations of Race to the Top in New York schools. These articulations are literacy practices. Those in schools where test scores are low are going to focus on the tested literacy practices (Ravitch, 2011).

A Glimpse at Articulating Standards in Two Different Schools: The Significance of Place

Here, I will compare two middle schools – one in Albany, located in Upstate New York, and the other, in New York City, on the main island of Manhattan. Albany is the capital city of New York. Albany has a population of 98,000 and nearly 750,000 live within the 20-mile radius of the Albany region. Euro-Americans account for 57 percent of Albany's residents, 28 percent are African American, about 6 percent are Latina/o, and there is a small Asian population. Albany public schools reflect a different racial profile: of the student body 21 percent is European American, 61 percent African American, 12 percent Latina/o, and 6 percent Asian. Whereas over half the Albany population is European American, not even a quarter of the schools' students are white.

New York City is comprised of five 'boroughs.' Manhattan is the oldest, populated by 1,585,873 people. New York City students attend neighborhood schools; however, they apply to these schools, and the application processes is highly competitive. The middle school considered in this comparison of two city schools is in the 'East Village,' a neighborhood that is about 50 percent European American, 9 percent African American, 25 percent Latina/o and 15 percent Asian. The racial demographics of the middle school, however, are 57 percent European American, 10 percent African American, 12 percent Latina/o, and 21 percent Asian. In Albany, a good number of European Americans do not attend the public schools. In the East Village middle school, representation of Latina/o and Asian students does not parallel the neighborhood demographics for the East Village. Race and social class play central roles in how standardization plays out in practice, in Albany and in New York City.

According to Bourdieu (1977), all social practice is a form of struggle over taste. The struggle looks a million ways, depending on the place where you live. If you live on Manhattan and, just before your sixth grade year, scored well on a battery of tests taken (state tests, a writing sample, an interview) to get into its competitive public schools, the struggle in your sixth grade year will look like students engaged in reading workshops that run quite smoothly. In these classrooms, a person observing a reading workshop will see youths choosing their own books, discussing them with a few selected peers, and keeping a reading log of insights about the book and about language and genres, in general. The kind of independence one observes the youths exhibit is not surprising, since students in Manhattan's more competitive public schools are selected based on test scores, writing, and how they represent themselves in an interview. They are chosen because the moment the school's sixth grade curriculum map unfolds on the first day of school, the majority of the student body (85 percent) will be ready: they have been culled for their readiness to read independently and talk and write 'just so' about books.

Conversely, if you live on the south side of Albany, New York, and go to its neighborhood middle school, a school often identified by the state's education department as a 'School in Need of Improvement' because student test scores were not sufficient, the struggle may look like teachers and students engaged in verbal conflict at various points during a lesson. In the example of the competitive Manhattan public school, 'Most of the children accepted have reading and math scores of level 4 (the highest level) on the 4th grade math and reading tests, but there is no formal cutoff to be considered for admission' (Inside Schools, n.d.). Comparatively, scores in a South Albany classroom will range from low to high, with most of the scores below the 70th percentile and only 31 percent above it (NYS, 2009). Thus, one will see less youth independence with books and writing in the Albany middle school. More direct instruction is needed, and that instruction can run the gamut from helping one child decode words, to providing comprehension support for another, to providing more advanced work for yet another child. Importantly, this will occur in all the class periods a teacher may teach in a day.

Manhattan's competitive public schools look different from South Albany's schools because sorting processes – actually getting into specific schools – assure the practices will be different. Once sorted and accepted into a school segregated for those with the highest test scores, best writing, and the most school-like verbal and bodily presentation, the majority of these students' primary home discourses (Gee, 1996) are extended, further enriched, and developed in the competitive public schools. In other words, home and school discourses – the ways of talking and being in the world as a certain kind of person – are not at odds. Also, a trajectory of expectations (a vision for the future) is clear and unified, for teachers, administrators, parents and students: young people will have a leg up, after three years of middle school, on getting into a similarly competitive public high school where the trajectory is also clear: young people will have every chance, if they work hard enough at their public school, of attending a college where a sorting out process will guarantee them a space of position at Harvard, Brown, Yale – in the Ivy League. Publicly funded, competitive schools are able to compete with private schools.

In South Albany, trajectories are less clear. What is the final stop in a South Albany student's education path? Is it the Ivy League or a state college? Is it a 4-year college or 2-year college? Is it a vocational trade? The trajectory for students in competitive public schools on Manhattan is unified, because sorting process have funneled students into a very narrow category, a college-bound youth. The same funnel, applied to Albany's sorting system, is the top of the funnel, where youth flood in. It is not the narrowed portion, where kids are sorted out. Thus, not only are trajectories for the Albany student multiple, students entering public schools represent a broader range of people, a broader range of home discourses, and a broader range of life trajectories.

On Manhattan, sorting practices create a 'vital conjuncture' for youth at the threshold of their upper-elementary and middle-school years. Johnson-Hanks (2002) recommends examining 'vital conjunctures' in young people's lives as a means of understanding the spatiality of their human development. Vital conjunctures are events in which the forces that created the 'risks' a youth experiences are revealed. In grade five, Manhattan schools sort students in ways that will have vital effects: the schools they are sorted into and out of will set them on a particular course, with particular people, visions, practices, and things available to them to think with. Preparation for sorting – 'bridging' – begins early. Elementary schools prepare children for the middle school vital conjuncture: they know it is coming and prepare for it. As getting into these schools depends on testing, writing, and interviewing well, elementary schools that typically funnel their students into competitive middle schools begin a reading and writing workshop curriculum early. By the time young children reach the middle school vital juncture, they are better prepared to read, write, and think in the ways competitive schools want them to.

Elementary school principals know the trajectories that different schools have in mind for their students and lead their teachers in professional development efforts to influence the kind of teaching that will prepare students for particular trajectories, early. Such preparation is called 'bridging.' Long a concern among school district administrators attempting to make students' transition from middle to high school smooth and effortless, bridging now occurs in younger grades as teachers engage their students in school practices that will result in the high test scores, well-written essays, and the discursive walk and talk needed to bridge students' path into Manhattan's competitive public schools. Learning the right discourses and practices early is necessary for placement in the best public middle schools, which increases chances of getting into prestigious public high schools, which increases chances, finally, of getting into prestigious, private colleges.

Albany's school district does not impose a structural, vital conjuncture for middle school entrants; therefore, students in the public system continue apace from elementary to middle school, without worry of being sorted out so early in their development – at least not sorted into and out of particular school buildings. Within schools, however, countless sorting practices occur that place youth in social relations that might create other vital conjunctures. For example: placement in special education without being disabled; being sorted into upper or lower-level classes based on test scores or classroom performance; or being sorted out, by peers, as an 'other' because of sexual orientation, gender questioning, linguistic difference, religion, or race.

Vital conjunctures can be created by school personnel and by youths, in both prestigious and less prestigious schools. Either way, when youths manage any risks produced at vital junctures, they engage with other people and use whatever material is available to survive the risk. Managing risk occurs within and outside schools. In classrooms, management may look like a youth steadfastly doing his school-work and extending the school boundaries into his home where he continues his labors. Or, it might look like a child who puts her head on her desk, ignoring a reading workshop she is expected to participate in but can't easily for any number of reasons. In one middle school study I conducted (Sheehy, 2010) management of school risk also involved management of home risk when youths were key members of their home economies and stayed home to care for their siblings or help their mothers shop. Management of home risk was a spatial distribution of siblings, single mothers, public transportation, and the grocery store. The city bus made few stops in this particular neighborhood, making shopping take at least three hours. Mothers had their children stay at home to care for their younger siblings while they shopped, or vice versa. Youths missed entire days of school as they helped their mothers manage children, time, and the public transportation system in order to buy food and household goods. Geography clearly influences what literacy practices schools make available, and vital conjunctures reveal that geography.

Public school students in New York, no matter where they attend school and no matter how wide the range of discourses and trajectories at play there, are tested in English Language Arts and Math, yearly, from grade three to eight, and are expected to perform well. What results, across schools and cities where specific schools are composed of radically different relations, histories, and practices, is a bell curve. McDermott, Raley, and Seyer-Ochi (2009) asked us to look closely at this bell because it is both the sign and the effect of people's struggle for position, a struggle that all of us are engaged in. 'Ask not for whom the bell curve tolls,' they warned. 'In a culture that promises equality but delivers hierarchy, everyone is risk rich, everyone a victim and a perpetrator' (p. 103). One person's space of position in the fourth quartile – that very narrow wedge on the bottom-right of the bell – requires that most people occupy spaces in the first three quartiles. The bell, with average scores rounding out the top, represents spaces of position, a graphic display of schools' and youths' 'struggle for position' (Bourdieu, 1983), in a field of politics, expectations, and histories that have a hand in placing them at a particular space on the bell.

Would a person who did not attend one of Manhattan's premiere public schools have a better chance at occupying a position on the fourth quartile of the bell if they had? Probably – Cole (2010) reported that when poor youth move into middle class neighborhoods and attend those schools, school performance increases significantly with no decline in performance by wealthier classmates. Where we live and the social spaces we inhabit influence our experiences and the resources available to us. Our very selves are created in relation to the things and activities available in the places we inhabit.

By using place as a unit of analysis, one can explain literacy practices as a flow of ideas and artifacts in webs of discourses. When one looks closely (in the way that de Certeau (1984) looked at the city and how people used it) one sees the nuances of what Bourdieu's (1983) struggle for position looks like. One might, for example, see a dominant practice being accepted by a fairly homogeneous classroom culture (in a Manhattan case) or thwarted in a heterogeneous one (in an Albany case). One may also see underground literacy practices (Finders, 1997) in concert with these school practices. One may also see long-term, culturally relevant practices in the margins (Nguyen, 2010; Wissman, 2011) or short-lived ones in the center (Gutierrez, Rymes, and Larson, 1995; Sheehy, 2010). Sometimes there are no apparent boundaries around a school at all, and one sees community development efforts moving in and out of schools, emerging from people's interests rather than test scores (Comber *et al.*, 2006). Places, including schools, have a range of thin or thick borders (Sheehy, 2004) and people draw on resources from other places as they participate in the making of a specific geographic locale (Nespor, 1997; Nguyen, 2010). Resources are things, activities, and people. In schools, these are arranged in particular ways and highly influenced by discourses pertaining to what school is supposed to achieve for people and activities occurring in and out of the school. The arrangement of resources has great implications for the development of thinking and the development of selves in all school geographies.

The Promise in Margins and Migrations

When looking closely at a place, permanent *and* permeable boundaries are evident (Rose, 1993; Sheehy, 2004). A close look at a particular place can reveal what mechanisms are boundary-making and what mechanisms open up and even collapse boundaries.

'Marginalization' has such negative undertones that one wouldn't expect to find, upon looking, that marginal geographies can bring esteem to their inhabitants, depending on how those geographies are defined in relation to the centers from which they emerge. Nguyen

(2010) reported that in one Texas school district, a group of English Language Learning teachers whose Vietnamese classes operated in a building separated from the main school were often made aware of their marginalized positions in relation to those who taught 'regular' classes in the main building. After ten years, the 'regular' teachers didn't know the ELL teachers' names, for example, and the very placement of ELL outside the main school was another marginalizing mechanism. While the ELL teachers could have defined themselves as the 'regular' teachers defined them, they did not. Instead, they turned their ELL building into a center for Vietnamese immigrants, working day and night to help new immigrants manage all the paperwork required of them while also holding parties and culturally relevant events that provided space for Vietnamese immigrants to remember Vietnam. They created a center out of a periphery, calling the relationship between center and periphery into question, creating what Foucault (1986) called a 'heterotopia,' an 'other place.'

There are numerous examples of spaces initially created in ostracizing practices that were recuperated and resignified as valuable by their occupants. Vadeboncoeur (2009) found that alternative schools in Australia, Montana, and British Columbia provided an education that students valued because it was different from general education; hooks (1991) reminds us that the home is a powerful center for African Americans; and Wilson (2004) opens our eyes to a completely unexpected understanding about prison life – that even in prison, the most marginal of places imaginable – prisoners find ways to take the artifacts available to them and signify them in ways they value. Vadeboncoeur (2009) cautioned, however, in regard to the alternative education settings in her research, that while alternative spaces do provide new freedoms for students, they may not necessarily rewrite the power relations that spurred their production. Her argument is evident in Hirst's (2004) study of a Language Other Than English (LOTE) classroom in Australia, where a Pakistani teacher, who shared a classroom with a general education teacher, was repeatedly humiliated by the ostracizing practices of this teacher who viewed the classrooms as rightfully hers because she taught the traditional Australian and curriculum and, in that claiming, demarcated the LOTE classroom as an 'other' curriculum outside Australian tradition.

Studies of margins and centers reveal migrations of people, ideas, curricula, and goods. Some borders are thin (Sheehy, 2004), as in Comber *et al.*'s (2006) study of a school in Australia, where several university departments, including an architecture department and an education department, worked with personnel and children at a pre-school to design a child-centered playground. In schools, any time children are asked what they think, there is an opportunity to examine the migration of ideas and people across a classroom or a school's borders. When children are not only asked what they think but also treated as intellectuals and asked to aid in the design of their playgrounds, the boundaries between homes, school, and university departments, in this case, are thin: migrations of ideas, people, and goods into and out of the school are multiple. In the case of Comber and her colleagues' project, a thin border between school and other places created positive activity for numerous players in the playground project. The arrangement of resources opened up possibilities for thinking.

Migration of ideas does not always produce a communal spirit. Some migrations of ideas reveal conflicts emanating from different perspectives and stakes in regard to the ideas. Newspaper accounts of school board and teacher union conflicts exemplify such border and community tensions. When a particular stake in such struggle gains greater public support and administrative sanction, borders can start thickening as practices in schools become inscribed by the ideologies behind one stake, versus many. For example, Diane Ravitch (2011), once a supporter of No Child Left Behind, reversed her support when she saw that this testing system, tied as it is to rewards and punishments, reduced curriculum to test-taking, a reduction that can be likened to thick border-making. Standards do not create the thick borders, practices do. In New York, because teachers and administrators can now be fired and schools closed when students do not perform as expected, curriculum in low-achieving schools becomes test-driven. The time and space needed to teach to tests does not allow for additional practices. Some schools have eliminated the arts to make time and space (practice) for test preparation. Closing down whole disciplines is a migratory problem. Certain practices are narrowed or closed down all together and school borders thicken so that more school space and time are devoted to one literacy practice: test preparation.

Migration of ideas, people, and objects across specific school borders needs further study. We need to know the mechanisms of ideas' routes in and out of schools. We need to know what, if anything, impedes movement in thin places. We need to know what enables movement. We need to know the same of thick places. We need to foreground these processes in our research reports so that the binary of pedagogy/policy that is so tightly wrapped around 'school knowledge' is broken. These fields that currently tangentially inform one another, now need to directly inform one another. Studying migration would provide useful information about how policies are practiced, resisted, and creatively twisted in particular schools. Pedagogy and policy scholarship would benefit from research making this political turn.

How to Study Migration

Place is a necessary unit of analysis for spatial studies because it provides a starting point for analysis. How we demarcate its boundaries influences how we analyze the social making of places. Harvey (1996, p. 316) describes places as relationally complex:

> They are the focus of the imaginary, of beliefs, longings, and desires (most particularly with respect to the psychological pull and push of the idea of 'home'). They are an intense focus of discursive activity, filled with symbolic and representational meanings, and they are a distinctive product of institutionalized social and political-economic power.

Places, besides shaping values and beliefs, are relational and have meaning in relation to other places. Lefebvre (1991), for instance, argued that class struggle was 'inscribed in space through uneven development of the qualities of places' (Harvey, 1996, p. 299). A classic example of this inequality is Willis's (1977) ethnography of adolescent males in Britain's working-class schools, where Willis argued that young men learned to labor as a result of curricular practices that taught them to do as they were told and not to originate ideas. While the young men rejected this curriculum, they did not develop the thinking practices of the professional classes. By default, they learned to be the rote workers necessary for working-class jobs. My description of the culling practices that occur in Manhattan's public school system also exemplifies the inscription of public school space as an uneven development of quality.

Parkes and Thrift (1978) argued that the realization of place lies in the temporal structuring of space: 'Timed space is the essence of a place' (p. 119). Thrift's (1992) explanation of human action as a time/space budgeting process is probably easily grasped by classroom teachers who constantly make choices about what to teach based on how much time they have available:

> The point is that human action takes place in time as a continual time- (and space-) budgeting process and as an irreversible sequence of actions. . . . Yet it is the ad hoc improvisatory strategy imposed on people's practices by the fact that they have limited time in which to carry out particular activities (and limited time in which to decide to do them) that is a crucial part of practice, practical consciousness, and practical meaning. Practice, therefore, is always structured in time and space. (Thrift, 1992, pp. 384–385).

As the social and the spatial produce one another (Massey, 1999) in classrooms and elsewhere, how we conceive of space, and how we demarcate it in our studies, matters. Allen, Massey, and Cochran (1998), in a move away from producing place and its processes as stabilities that can be represented on maps, recommend conceptualizing a region (of any size) as 'a particular space at a particular time' and to focus on two things: (1) whatever it is that is 'core' about an area being studied, and (2) the processes that make it core. These simple guidelines could be particularly useful to classroom teachers doing their own inquiries. They can identify issues in their classroom, building, or district (these may also be national or international issues). They can identify what discourses connect and diverge across that 'core' terrain. They can determine, within the maps they create, any number of things including (1) how they are personally situated on their maps, (2) how the map is affecting their curriculum, and (3) how political action, perhaps in collaboration with peers or other entities identified on the map, might reterritorialize the map. Maps, as such, may demonstrate effects, but they could be mobilized as a tool for organizing new effects.

It is also possible to explain a place with more complicated methods. Parkes and Thrift (1978) account for four levels of society, or four scales: (1) the political economy; (2) the physical (built) environment; (3) activity systems that individuals take part in; and (4) attitudes and perceptions of activity systems. Wolch and Dear (1989) posit a framing of society, using three spheres: (1) an economic sphere organized on capitalist principles; (2) a political sphere, including state apparatuses such as schools and the legal system; and (3) the social sphere, including civil society. Regardless of the structuring system of space used, Wolch and Dear argue that a locale is a complex synthesis of objects, patterns, and processes derived from simultaneous interactions at different scales of a social process. Methodologically, scales of processes are unraveled onto a single terrain, like a classroom or a city. This collapse is a 'geographic puzzle' of unraveling a complex locale into its constituent elements and processes (Wolch and Dear, 1989, p. 7). One way of dealing with this difficulty is to simply lay out a discursive field as the context of a classroom study and try to understand the literacy practices reported as part of that field. Interviewing stakeholders would reveal the discursive field and participants' positions in it.

Depending on method, one can delineate the politics of location as a small-scale locale of a school board or city or include far-reaching scales in the locale. Determining appropriate scales depends on what data is available, what question is being posed, and what emerges in empirical data as core issues. Jan Nespor's (1997) ethnography of a fourth and fifth grade classroom undergoing curricular change is a sophisticated example of a spatial study of classroom practices utilizing actor network theory. He wove together the discourses operating at an elementary school around curriculum and other matters, such as city planning, to demonstrate the multiple ideas that migrated in and out of the school and influenced curriculum planning and implementation. Similarly, I demonstrated how discourses about Appalachians and middle school pedagogy influenced a group of middle school teachers' practices (Sheehy, 2010). Kwek and Luke (2006) were able to demonstrate more global relations in their study of Singapore schools because globality functioned as a core discourse for these schools.

Conclusion

I opened this chapter with a discussion of Race to the Top and the manner in which the punishments attached to it are having a radical effect on literacy practices in classrooms in New York. I moved from the broad issue of a national attempt to standardize practice to local examples of two cities' schools and how literacy plays out differently in them in order to demonstrate that disparity in classroom practices involves geographic processes. In low performing schools, literacy practices have become more and more restricted since the passing of the No Child Left Behind Act and, in New York, with the funding from Race to the Top. Inequality develops when youths in high performing schools engage in the literacy practices that allow them some freedom of movement and thought while those in low-performing schools engage in literacy for tests. No Child Left Behind and now Race to the Top expects these two geographic formations to perform the same: the expectation is that all students will achieve 100 percent accuracy on tests (Ravitch, 2011). As a result of geographic disparity – a difference in the flow of ideas, people, and practices that travel into and out of classrooms and schools –instead of perfection, a bell curve is produced.

Some look to the margins for hope. Examples of how people carve out spaces that allow them to engage practices that make them happy are important. Vadeboncoeur's (2009) cautionary note, that these spaces may not change the forces of power that stimulated their production, suggests that we need research that will help us understand whether that matters or, if it does matter, how these spaces might be mobilized to inform the central spaces that ostracized them.

I suggest that the most important thing we can do is to start tracking what migrates into and out of schools so that we can build a body of knowledge about power relations. We need to know: What enables freedom of movement? When are practices of freedom worth time and when are they not? What are the mechanisms of border-making? What types of borders are useful and which are not? I suggested some different ways studies of migration could be conducted and a few cases of how they have been conducted to date.

In universities and other professional development organizations, we need this and more information in order to learn how to educate teachers to participate effectively and profitably in the power relations that inscribe their practices so deeply. In schools of education, we need to recognize when we don't really understand how or whether one can teach well when freedom of practice is seriously restricted. When we don't know, we too need to politicize and work with teachers and administrators in schools to figure out how, when stakes are so high, to make sure youth can engage in literacy for the sake of learning, not testing. We need to ask today's questions: How can we prepare teachers to teach in schools where resources are seriously restricted? What possibilities are available to these teachers? How can they thin out the borders of their work?

At the same time, when we do know the conditions of good practice, we need to detail them. Good practice has much to do with schools' geographies – the ideas, things, and people that are able to flow in and out of classroom buildings. These flows need to be documented. Migration needs to be brought to the foreground in studies of classroom literacy practices. Knowing how people use resources that flow in and out of their schools will provide a political pedagogical knowledge that, heretofore, has been easy to put off but, as of now, cannot be.

References

Allen, J., Massey, D., and Cochrane, A. (1998) *Rethinking the Region*. London: Routledge.

Barnes, C.R. (2011) 'Race to the top' only benefits big government. *Journal of Law and Education*, 40(2): 393–402.

Bourdieu, P. (1977) *Distinction: A Social Critique of the Judgment of Taste*. Cambridge, MA: Harvard University Press.

Bourdieu, P. (1983) The flied of cultural production, or: Economic world reversed. *Poetics*, 12: 311–356.

Comber, B., Nixon, H., Ashmore, L., *et al.* (2006) Urban renewal from the inside out: Spatial and critical literacies in a low socioeconomic school community. *Mind and Activity*, 13(3): 228–246.

Cole, R. (2010) What's culture got to do with it? Educational research as a necessarily interdisciplinary enterprise. *Educational Researcher*, 39(6): 461–470.

de Certeau, M. (1984) *The Practice of Everyday Life*. Berkeley: University of California Press.

Finders, M.J. (1997) *Just Girls: Hidden Literacies and Life in Junior High*. New York: Teachers College Press.

Foucault, M. (1986) Of other spaces. *Diacritics*, 16(1): 22–27.

Gee, J.P. (1996) *Social Linguistics and Literacies: Ideology in Discourses*. New York: Routledge.

Gutierrez, K., Rymes, B., and Larson, J. (1995) Script, counter-script, and underlife in the classroom: James Brown versus Brown v. Board of Education. *Harvard Educational Review*, 65(3): 445–471.

Harvey, D. (1996) *Justice, Nature and the Geography of Difference*. Malden, MA: Blackwell.

Hirst, E. (2004) Diverse social contexts of a second language classroom and the construction of identity. In K.M. Leander and M. Sheehy (eds) *Spatializing Literacy Research and Practice*. New York: Peter Lang, pp. 39–65.

hooks, b. (1991) *Yearning: Race, Gender, and Cultural Politics*. Boston, MA: South End Press.

Inside Schools (n.d.) M.S. 255 Salk School of Science, accessed November 21, 2012: http://insideschools.org/middle/browse/school/60

Johnson-Hanks, D. (2002) On the limits of life stages in ethnography: towards a theory of vital conjunctures. *American Anthropologist*, 104: 865–880.

Keith, M., and Pile, S. (1993) Introduction part 2: The place of politics. In M. Keith and S. Pile (eds) *Place and the Politics of Identity*. London: Routledge, pp. 22–40.

Kwek, D., and Luke, A. (2006) Spaces of indifference: Asia/Singapore/school/classroom as globalized spaces for pedagogy, discourse and identity. Paper presented to the American Educational Research Association, April 2006, San Francisco, CA.

Lefebvre, H. (1991) *The Production of Space*. Cambridge, MA. Blackwell.

Lefebvre, H. (1996) *Writings on Cities*. Malden, MA: Blackwell.

Manna, P., and Ryan, L. (2011) Competitive grants and educational federalism: President Obama's 'race to the top' in theory and practice. *Publius*, 41(3): 522–546.

Massey, D. (1999) Entanglements of power: reflections. In J.P. Sharp, P. Routledge, C. Philo, and R. Paddison (eds) *Entanglements of Power: Geographies of Domination/Resistance*. London: Routledge, pp. 279–286.

McDermott, R., Raley, J.D., and Seyer-Ochi, I. (2009) Race and class in a culture of risk. *Review of Research in Education*, 33: 101–116.

Nespor, J. (1997) *Tangled up in School. Politics, Space, Bodies and Signs in the Educational Process*. Mahwah, NJ: Lawrence Erlbaum.

Nguyen, T.S. (2010) Vietnamese diasporic placemaking: An ethnographic moment in uneven geographic development. *Education Policy*, 24(1): 159–188.

NYS (New York State) (2009) NYS Report Cardn (see www.nysed.gov)

Parkes, D., and Thrift, N. (1978) Putting time in its place. In T. Carlstein, D. Parkes, and N. Thrift (eds) *Making Sense of Time*. London: Edward Arnold Ltd, pp. 119–129.

Ravitch, D. (2011) Obama's war on schools. *Newsweek*, March 20.

Rose, G. (1993) *Feminism and Geography: The Limits of Geographical Knowledge*. Cambridge: Polity.

Sheehy, M. (2004) Between a thick and a thin place: Changing practices. In K.M. Leander and M. Sheehy (eds) *Spatializing Literacy Research and Practice*. New York: Peter Lang, pp. 91–114.

Sheehy, M. (2010) *Place Stories: Time, Space, and Literacy in Two Classrooms*. Cresskill, NJ: Hampton Press.

Thrift, N. (1992) On the determination of social action in space and time. *Environment and Planning D. Society and Space*, 1: 23–57.

Vadeboncoeur, J.A. (2009) Spaces of difference: The contradictions of alternative educational programs. *Educational Studies*, 45: 280–299.

Willis, P. (1977) *Learning to Labour: How Working Class Kids get Working Class Jobs*. New York: Columbia University Press.

Wilson, A. (2004) Four days and a breakfast: Time, space and literacy/ies in the prison community. In K.M. Leander and M. Sheehy (eds) *Spatializing Literacy Research and Practice*. New York: Peter Lang, pp. 67–90.

Wissman, K.K. (2011) 'Rise Up!' Literacies, lived experiences, and identities within an in-school 'other space'. *Research in the Teaching of English*, 45(4): 405–438.

Wolch, J., and Dear, M. (1989) *The Power of Geography: How Territory Shapes Social Life*. Boston, MA: Unwin Hyman.

Chapter 30

Space, Place, and Power

The Spatial Turn in Literacy Research

Kathy A. Mills and Barbara Comber

Introduction

Place matters to literacy because the meanings of our language and actions are always materially and socially placed in the world (Scollon and Scollon, 2003). We cannot interpret signs, whether an icon, symbol, gesture, word, or action, without taking into account their associations with other meanings and objects in places. This chapter maps an emergent strand of literacy research that foregrounds place and space as constitutive, rather than a backdrop for the real action. Space and place are seen as relational and dynamic, not as fixed and unchanging. Space and place are socially produced, and hence, can be contested, reimagined, and remade. In bringing space and place into the frame of literacy studies we see a subtle shift – a rebalancing of the semiotic with the materiality of lived, embodied, and situated experience.

A caveat is that space and place are not entirely new to literacy studies. Ethnographies of literacy practices have long emphasized the socio-cultural dimensions of context and situated those practices in particular geographic locales with specific communities (Barton and Hamilton, 1998; Gregory and Williams, 2000; Heath, 1983; Street, 1984). Such work stresses that literacy practices are situated and associated within the different dimensions of life, such as workplaces, homes, or schools (Barton, Hamilton, and Ivanic, 2000). However, spatialized or place-based literacy research draws attention to the material locale as integrally connected to literacy practices, rather than to the socio-cultural context alone. The foregrounding of space and place is steadily increasing in literacy research, as evidenced by the naming of spatial terms in titles and abstracts in literacy research – city, urban, rural, river, ghetto, street, environment, and sites. We acknowledge parallel moves toward the dimensions of time and mobility, as literacy scholars grapple with globalization, and its implications for changing populations, places, and communication (see Compton-Lilly, Chapter 7 this volume).

In this chapter we discuss selected research in literacy studies, which in various ways addresses these themes. We begin by discussing studies that foreground the politics of place and literacy in classrooms and introduce the concept of place-conscious pedagogy through illustrative examples. We then explore place and digital spaces in globalized communication networks

International Handbook of Research on Children's Literacy, Learning, and Culture, First Edition.
Edited by Kathy Hall, Teresa Cremin, Barbara Comber, and Luis C. Moll.
© 2013 John Wiley & Sons, Ltd. Published 2013 by John Wiley & Sons, Ltd.

and conclude by considering the potential of new spatial analytical tools for fostering new directions in literacy studies.

The Politics of Place and Literacy in Classrooms

Research that explicitly addresses the spatiality of place, and the associated micro-politics and power relations in classrooms, acknowledges that social and material processes cannot be separated from literacy practices. The critical concerns of race, class, gender, disability, and other categories of marginalization have long been examined, albeit often without a foundation of spatial theorization. For example, four decades ago Rist (1970) researched ability grouping in urban schools, observing how the students' proximity to the teacher and material resources reflected the associated social divisions of race and class. Such work foreshadowed important connections between space, power, and literacy that that have been theorized by literacy scholars in more recent times.

Literacy scholars have argued that all literacy practices are ideological (Luke, 1998; Street, 1999) and must be interpreted in relation to larger social contexts and power relations. Applying these principles to the research of literacy practices both within and across communities has yielded significant evidence of patterns of marginalization that are socially and historically constituted. There is now a growing corpus of research that foregrounds the materiality of marginalization in studies of classroom practices (Hawkins, 2004; Janks, 2000; Stein, 2007).

Spatialized literacy research both in and outside classrooms demonstrates that material spaces and places shape the identity and literate practices of youth. The concept of 'third spaces,' as theorized by Gutiérrez, Rymes, and Larson (1995), provides a useful heuristic for explaining the tensions between the teacher scripts and students' counterscripts and identities in classrooms as social spaces. The term 'third space' describes how other spaces might interanimate and create a more heteroglossic authentic interaction – a new area of negotiation of meaning and representation, where official and unofficial, formal and informal spaces become permeable and create the potential for new kinds of learning. Hirst (2004) draws on this concept to theorize power relations in a second language classroom taught by an Indonesian national in an Australian classroom. There were significant power struggles as students challenged the teacher's space. Hirst (2004) demonstrates how a student called Lilly, mimicked a cartoon character to distort the teacher's mode of being to the amusement of the class. There was little space for cultural difference within the typical language lesson 'chronotopes' – that is, ways in which temporal and spatial reality are typically represented and organized in events or texts (Bakhtin, 1981). Students who were neither of the dominant culture, nor shared the ethnicity of the teacher, demonstrated resistance and constructed counterspaces.

A classroom case study by Leander (2002) similarly explored the materiality and situated nature of space, power, and identity in classrooms. Leander analyzed a 'Derogatory Terms Activity' conducted by two teachers in the school, which engaged students in difficult yet open discussions of race, language, and cultural identity. The students recorded examples of derogatory terms that are used to label certain groups, creating a large graffiti banner for the classroom wall. The teacher read the words aloud to the class, and began a discussion to destabilize identities and social spaces, as it challenged the unhealthy social undercurrents that are present in the classroom, often as a type of 'underlife' (Gutiérrez, Rymes, and Larson, 1995). Micropolitical patterns of marginalization were reflected in both the classroom discourse and the physical positioning of the students to one another. In other words, power relations are enacted through inclusions and exclusions in talk and the material positioning of the students' bodies in the classroom. In particular, students labeled a poor African American student called Latanya as 'ghetto,' and Latanya resisted this identity. Leander's spatial analysis brought together a microgenetic analysis of classroom discourse, an interpretation of the materiality of the seating arrangements, the embodied meanings of the students' gaze and movements, and artifacts in the classroom. The graffiti banner created a highly unstable hybridization of identity stereotypes, making a 'third space' for naming and challenging what is typically unmentionable in an institutional setting (Gutiérrez, Rymes, and Larson, 1995; Soja, 1996). Leander's spatial analysis showed that interactants define and stabilize identity by producing identity artifacts with multimodal means, by constructing configurations of those artifacts, and by using those artifacts to project social space and identity.

Sheehy (1999) coins the term 'in-between spaces' to denote the difficult interactional nego-tiations that can occur when teachers attempt to shift from reproducing literacies that are disembodied from the materiality of students' lives – worksheets, tests, and typical school knowledge – to focus on the meaningful events, objects, literacy practices, and knowledge inherent in students' own lives. These 'in-between spaces' are akin to Gutiérrez's third spaces of authentic learning interactions. Analyzing a project in a seventh grade classroom that engaged students in understanding the socio-political nature of the planned closure of their school build-ing, Sheehy highlights the tensions that were created in the in-between places. The classroom space was destabilized through the community surveys about the school closure, preparing and presenting public speeches, engaging in difficult classroom dialogues, and meeting with the school board (Sheehy, 2004). Creating this in-between space temporarily transformed textual, time, and spatial relations in the classroom, disrupting the daily rhythms of the typical literacy economy in classrooms.

The spatial dimension of power and marginalization in classrooms has afforded new insights in literacy research, including studies theoretically framed by critical theory (Hirst, 2004; Leander, 2002; Sheehy, 2004). Researchers analyzed the organization and structure of the classroom space as a social product, arising from and contributing to the meaning of purposeful social practices. Social space can refer to both individual and collective social action, which converge at specified times and places (Lefebvre, 1991). It is frequently acknowledged that classroom places and spaces are not separate structures that are independent from the wider social framework (Mills, 2010). A recent study by Dixon in post-Apartheid South Africa (2011, p. 7) makes it clear that 'the geographical location of the schools children attend is not neutral. These locations are shaped and colored by histories of class, race and culture.' Using a Foucauldian approach to the visual gaze and the organization of space within the school as a disciplinary institution, Dixon demonstrates that literacy instruction involves the regulation of bodies in time and place; that meaning-making potential can be seriously curtailed when the authorized curriculum leaves little space for children to learn and focuses instead on the display of outcomes. Moreover, Dixon (2011, p. 168) argues that Foucault's approach to space and time 'opens space for analyzing how particular enactments of literacy may become embodied in particular spaces, but not in others, and why this might happen.'

While the terms 'space' and 'place' are sometimes used metaphorically, such as Sheehy's 'old, new and in-between spaces' (Sheehy, 2004), these terms are often tied to tangible or material contexts of action, which are essentially socially produced (Bourdieu, 1998; Harvey, 1993; Mills, 2010). Whether it be the form, content, and distributional patterns of the built classroom space, or the bodily arrangements and orientations of the students to objects, bringing spatial meanings to the fore acknowledges that places and spaces have a social origin, and are constituted with social meaning (Soja, 1989).

These classroom studies illustrate Said's (1993, p. 7) argument that no one is 'completely free from the struggle over geography.' The distribution of material and social resources, while tied to political, social and economic power, is differentiated by place. The spatiality of justice is an integrative and formative component of justice itself, socially constructed and evolving over time (Soja, 2010). A critical pedagogy of place can play a vital role in assisting children to understand and respond to the rapid social and geographical changes that influence their social and material conditions for action. Literacy research that ignores place may become abstract, disembodied, and decontextualized from local and global geographies, with their affordances and constraints for meaningful social action.

Place-Conscious Pedagogies

A growing body of research on literacy and place is located within the broader theory of place-conscious education or place-based pedagogies (Gruenewald, 2003a; Theobald, 1997). Theorizing the nexus between critical literacy on one hand, and place as environment on the other, are pedagogies that pursue decolonization and reinhabitation of physical environments. Place-conscious educators engage learners with problems in their material and ecological contexts tied to their local communities. A critical pedagogy of place is more than an environmental movement. It concerns the critical dimension of consciousness in literacy classrooms that positions children as active agents who transform social, material, and ecological places.

In North America, place-based pedagogies have underpinned rural education writing projects for some time (Brooke, 2003; Smith and Sobel, 2010). Indeed at the college composition level the 'rural' has had a particular history in the study of rhetoric (Donehower, Hogg, and Schell, 2007). Donehower and colleagues argue for problematizing spatial terms which tend to elicit certain ways of thinking that either romanticize or demonize the 'rural,' typically in a problematic binary relationship with the 'urban.' While not located in schools, they make a strong case for building citizenship and pedagogy around sustainability, which is broadly applicable across education. Such an approach begins with a critical approach to rural literacies, examining the assumptions underpinning categories for describing and ways of knowing the rural. Assumptions of the rural as empty or culturally underdeveloped tend to pervade educational bureaucracies, and can result in educational success being understood as achieving the credentials to leave a community to go somewhere better – to escape the rural (Corbett, 2007). Such assumptions are dangerous, and left unexamined, may lead to scripted literacy programs being considered as most appropriate for rural teachers and students, whereby students are assumed to have no useful knowledge or experience to bring to school learning (Eppley, 2011).

Critical literacy and environmental communications are contingent upon developing content knowledge of places and geographies. Consistent with this place-based orientation towards understanding the environment is the River Literacies project. This research centered on developing informed understandings of the Murray-Darling Basin in Australia among teachers and students. The participants came to appreciate this distinctive bioregion, and its contributions to the social, economic, and ecological wellbeing of school communities, including indigenous and non-indigenous groups (Comber, Nixon, and Reid, 2007; Green, Cormack, and Reid, 2006). The aim was to facilitate children's re-engagement with the cultural and ecological contexts of communities in the Basin. Teachers also worked with students to explore the affordances of digital technologies in communicating their findings to local and educational communities (Comber, Nixon, and Reid, 2007). Students and teachers researched endangered indigenous local flora and fauna, the ways in which various species were integrally connected and codependent on each other; the politics of decision-making concerning the use and development of spaces (for example constructing a football ground or preserving historic native trees); and the impact of tourism on both the economic and ecological conditions of a small river community. Key elements of this work were for teachers and students to build knowledge and understandings of the scientific and social aspects of places. This study demonstrated the important potential of a critical orientation towards the natural environment in an age in which environmental sustainability is increasingly a global priority.

Also working in the Murray Darling Basin bioregion, Somerville's (2007) analysis of Aboriginal histories, stories, knowledge, symbolic meanings, and places further illuminates the politics of place and literacy. This work applies place pedagogies with Australian indigenous and nonindigenous local communities to create connections between dominant and alternative meanings of water, focusing on the iconic Narran Lakes. The principles underlying Somerville's work are threefold. First, place learning is necessarily embodied and local, demonstrated, for example, in many Australian indigenous legends of how the river began, blended with everyday accounts from indigenous communities who move, live, remember, paint, story, play, and draw from the river.

Second, one's relationship to place is frequently represented through stories and other material artifacts. Somerville illustrates that literacies and places are mutually constituted in place through storytelling and representation, since the earth does not just shape language, but the land itself is also transformed through our representations.

Third, place learning involves contested stories and accounts of spaces. Somerville's (2007) work traced how dominant, Western storylines of place sometimes deny or obscure our bodily connection to earthly phenomena and construct places as 'sites on a map to be economically exploited' (Gruenewald, 2003b, p. 624). For example, dominant accounts of the Murray River reflect a 'cultural and political narrative of technological and agricultural progress' (Sinclair, 2001, p. 24). The stories of the Narran Lake in Somerville's work show that places are often sites of deep contest, such as between the legends of the lake and its creatures, and Western narratives of cultural progress.

It should not be assumed however that place-based pedagogies are concerned only with the natural world, nor are they restricted to schools located in rural and regional communities. All schools are located in places of historical, political, economic, and environmental contestation, and as such, place-based pedagogies are equally relevant and important in urban locales. Negative representations of the places in which schools are located have long plagued state-funded schools in high poverty areas and continue to do so (Comber, Thompson, and Wells, 2001; Gannon, 2009). Comber and colleagues have investigated how literacy practices in classrooms, particularly those characterized by poverty, mediate local social and material action and places (Comber, Nixon, Ashmore, *et al.*, 2006). The project Urban Renewal from the Inside Out provides one example of the ways in which teachers and students can contest deficit discourses about their school communities and engage in literacy practices to bring about local spatial transformation. Teachers, researchers, and students from the fields of architecture, communications, and literacy studies collaborated with elementary students to redesign an area of the school grounds in a poor suburb of Adelaide, South Australia.

The teachers engaged primary students in a series of text-making practices to transform a barren, unshaded space between the school and the pre-school into a student-designed garden. They designed a curriculum based on local and neighborhood literacies and issues of place in the context of a broader municipal program of urban renewal (Comber *et al.*, 2001). The project aimed to equip students with repertoires of powerful social and semiotic practices, such as spatial design, negotiation, and consultation with experts, to achieve material change of their local place (Comber and Nixon, 2008).

The Grove Gardens project enabled the students to work with real designers and architects to transform some of the oppressive elements of their situational reality (Freire, 1970). The architect used workshop methods to introduce key concepts and terms related to social space and architectonic design elements (Comber *et al.*, 2006). Through a process of imagining, negotiating, and representing their ideas multimodally – through oral discussion, written descriptions, and design concept drawings – a desolate space became a preferred space in the school, both symbolically and materially. Later, a larger proportion of the school was rebuilt – a project that also involved the children in the process of consultation with the local council. Yet the original strip of wasteland that had become 'Grove Garden' remained a place of stability within the wider flow of material, social, and ecological urbanization of the school and local area.

An important feature of this spatializing of literacy practices is that critical consciousness is brought about through the authentic unity of reflection and social action (Freire, 1970). The Grove Gardens project foregrounds the critical dimension of consciousness in literacy classrooms, positioning children as active agents who transform social, material, and ecological places. In so doing, teachers and students can leave behind a 'culture of silence' and passivity to realize a degree of cultural and spatial freedom (Freire, 1970, pp. 64–65).

Opportunities for such in-depth engagement in a project where students literally redesign and remake their school spaces may be rare, but increasingly literacy researchers are working with culturally diverse school communities to make place the object of study in the literacy classroom. For example Wyse and colleagues (2011) recently reported on a project where they investigated children's place-related identities using reading and writing tasks. They examined children's thinking about places they live, their school and neighborhoods, and discourses of place and family.

These place-based pedagogies do not interpret places as stable, homogenous entities, but take into account complex relations between class, gender, race, and extra-local relations of power. Necessary priority is given to how young learners understand the world through their communicative and representational interactions with the immediate environment. This gives logical and developmental priority to the local over against abstract global phenomena. As Gruenewald and Smith (2008, p. xvi) have argued: 'Place-based education . . . introduces . . . youth to the skills and dispositions needed to regenerate and sustain communities. It achieves this end by drawing on local phenomena as the sources of at least a share of children's learning experiences.'

These studies of place-based pedagogies all demonstrate that the organization of places is clearly social and ideological (Cresswell, 1996). Places constrain and enable social practices in the interests of maintaining and reproducing established hierarchies. A critical pedagogy of place emphasizes the need for teachers to guide students in the critical analysis of the material conditions of places and the way they are inhabited. Such pedagogies require the critical analysis of the purposes of education and the different places and spaces students inhabit now and in the future. This includes how place and space are reconfigured when literacy practices are mediated by different technologies to communicate with others for different purposes.

Place and Digital Spaces in Globalized Communication Networks

The increasing role of networked technologies in the global communications environment has significant implications for the way in which place and space are experienced, understood, and theorized in literacy research. The New Literacy Studies tradition has demonstrated that web-based literacy practices such as online gaming in virtual worlds (Barab *et al.*, 2005), blogging (Lankshear and Knobel, 2006), micro-blogging (Mills and Chandra, 2011), online chat (Jacobs, 2004; Lewis and Fabos, 2005), journal communities (Guzzetti and Gamboa, 2005), and fan sites (Thomas, 2007) enable cross-cultural, cross-generational, and transnational connections between people to create new online communities (Lam, 2009).

Online communication practices frequently overlap and yet extend beyond relationships that are forged in a face-to-face materiality. Practices like multiuser online games bring together text users from multiple places to create new social spaces. For example, large-scale ethnographic research by Ito and colleagues has highlighted the way in which collaborative online spaces of youth and adults are tied primarily to friendship-driven or interest-driven social practices that are often situated beyond their local communities (Ito *et al.*, 2009; Ito *et al.*, 2008).

This research is generating useful models for supporting students as globally recognized designers, and critics of digital texts in official and unofficial spaces of learning. Participants have been found to spontaneously transfer certain digital practices from one geographical site to another, such as from school to home, creating media products for intergenerational audiences across diverse social sites (Mercier, Barron, and O'Conner, 2006).

A key example is Moje *et al.*'s (2004) seven-year, ethnographic research of Latino youth in a school and community located in the outskirts of a large city known locally as 'Mexican Town.' A focus of Moje's theoretical work is the tracing of spatial and temporal identities or versions of self that are enacted according to different relations between ones' material conditions, social contexts, times, and spaces. She illustrates how Latino youth used virtual spaces, such as [city name] raza.com and lowrider.com, to unite the Latino community that was geographically dispersed across the city. Textual practices within these virtual sites fulfilled a vital role in maintaining a sense of pride of their Mexican ethnicity and identities associated with their interest-driven literacy practices.

At the level of literacy research in schools, there are new potentials for exploring the changed materiality of classroom space in digital contexts of literacy practice (Leander, 2003). A growing body of work has examined the intersections between students' engagement in multimodal design and transformations of classroom space. Classroom studies of digital practices and social space have tended to focus on one or more of the following dimensions of space: bodily, screen, dialogic, embodied, and architectonic (Mills, 2010).

Changed bodily dispositions of students in the literacy classroom have been examined by Bezemer (2008) and Mills (2010) who examined 'bodily spaces' – the multimodal displays of bodily orientation, such as specific postures, gaze, and gestures of students. These studies demonstrated that individuals appropriated certain multimodal and gestural resources to be successful learners across the curriculum. Students did not appropriate a limited range of postures that are required when students listen to the teacher. Rather, multimodal designing of films allowed individuals to communicate holistic bodily engagement with displays of bodily orientation in multiple different directions, directly coordinated and differentiated by student groups, rather than the teacher.

Jewitt (2006) and Graham and Bellert (2005) have similarly applied multimodal semiotics to the study of children's interactions with different 'screen spaces,' such as when playing computer games in classrooms. These studies demonstrate that knowledge, pedagogies, and learning are reshaped in significant ways with new meaning potentials when screen spaces are embedded in the English curriculum. Norris (2004) and Mills (2010) have both used multimodal analysis to examine the changed speech interactions or 'dialogic spaces' that have been successfully created among students when engaged with screen-based texts. For instance, collaborative multimodal designing of films requires increased horizontal communication between peers, generating new interactional orders among the group. These dialogic spaces differ significantly to didactic teaching methods that emphasize vertical relations between teacher and students.

Stanton and colleagues (2001) researched what Mills (2010) calls the changed 'architectonic spaces' – material qualities of design and structure, such as spatial arrangements of classroom furniture. For example, Stanton *et al.* (2001) observed transformations of the physical space when students used KidPad, an interface that uses large floor mats and video-tracked and barcoded physical props around the classroom to navigate a collaborative digital story. The new architectonic patterns in these studies constituted markedly different spatial and material arrangements and meanings within the classroom.

In relation to 'embodied space,' Stein (2006) and Mills (2010) have examined how students produce identity artifacts, whether as claymation characters in Mills' research, or as African dolls in Stein's study. The three-dimensional figures were more than just objects created by children, but were embodiments of internal acts of meaning – playing a symbolic role in the production of social space.

These recent studies point to significant changed material and interactional relations between text users, objects, and the physical classroom space when multimodal designing becomes integrated into literacy curricula. Soja (2004, pp. x–xi) states: 'When seen as a heterotopia or as fully lived space . . . the classroom becomes an encapsulation of everything and everywhere, a kind of hieroglyphic site that opens up a potentially endless realm of insightful reading and learning.' These studies extend what has emerged from the transdisciplinary focus on place and space by Soja (2010), Lefebvre (1991), Harvey (1993), Massey (1995, 2005), and other social geographers – that space is not merely a container for social action, but a dimension of social relations that offers significant explanatory power beyond attention to the historical or temporal dimension alone.

New Spatial Analysis Tools for Literacy

With the increasing sophistication in digital technologies for analyzing spatial data, there are expanding potentials for managing both quantitative and qualitative data, and new ways of conceptualizing, measuring, visualizing, and representing spatial relationships. Ferrare and Apple (2010, p. 216) have argued that we need to expand our repertoire of methodological tools to 'think spatially.'

The spatial turn in anthropological and ethnographic research methods has seen a renewed emphasis on capturing what Pink (2009) describes as the multisensoriality of emplaced experiences, perception, and knowledge in different environments. Pink calls for a rethinking of the ethnographic process through a theory of place and space that has the capacity to bring together the phenomenology of place and the politics of space (Pink, 2007, 2009). Pink's methodological contributions include new ethnographic approaches – visual and sensory ethnography – that explicitly draw on geographical theories of place, place-making, and space (Massey, 2005), in combination with philosophical and anthropological work on place and perception (Casey, 1996; Ingold, 2007; Pink, 2009). Casey's writing on place is relevant to sensory ethnographers because he sees places and spaces as events, constituted through lived bodies and material and social objects. Massey's (2005) ideas invite ethnographers to consider how the specificity and immediacy of lived experiences and its spatial configurations in local places are inevitably interwoven or entangled with wider geographies and spatial contexts.

Visual, sensory, and 'multimodal ethnography' share an acknowledgement that sensory data plays an important role in the generation of knowledge (see Kress, 2011). These ethnographic methodologies can incorporate widely used visual methods, such as video, visual artifacts, and hypermedia, to represent the materiality of culture and experience in ways that do not privilege one form of knowing over another (Pink, 2009).

Similarly, educational theorists of multimodal semiotics have, throughout the past decade, provided a range of analytic tools for examining the materiality of texts and lived experiences in classrooms. For example, Jewitt (2006, 2008), Kress and Bezemer (2008), Kress and van Leeuwen (1996), van Leeuwen and Jewitt (2001), Unsworth (2001), and others have conceptualized multimodal frameworks and categories to describe the features of two- and three-dimensional material spaces. For example, Jewitt (2006) provides a systematic framework for analyzing social action in classrooms, particularly in relation to technology use, that draws on multimodal semiotics (Kress and van Leeuwen, 2001), and activity theory (Engestrom, 1987). Such theories are specifically oriented towards the materiality of social spaces and places have potentials for exploring new directions in literacy research, in ways that are methodologically and epistemologically compatible with theories of social space.

Conclusion

This chapter has drawn attention to a growing body of literacy studies that take into account space or place as an important feature in understanding literacy practices. Whether implicitly or explicitly acknowledged as 'socio-cultural contexts,' 'places,' 'spaces,' 'spatialized literacy research,' 'place-based pedagogies,' 'literacies of place,' or 'socially-produced spaces,' there is a consensus that place and space matter to literacy practices. While spatial metaphors abound, there is a common recognition that spaces and places are more than simply containers for social action and textual practices. Rather, places and spaces comprise sets of material social relations. Space influences and is influenced by social interactions in the literacy classroom.

Literacy practices and relations between them remain abstractions until they become materialized in some form within places and spaces. Literacy practices and spatiality are mutually constitutive. Foregrounding place and space in literacy studies provides valuable connections between the materiality of literacy and its flows in the new times. What is needed are pedagogies of place and literacy in schools that create new sets of relationships and possibilities in the microcosm of classrooms, by taking into account relevant aspects of spatiality with a view to repositioning students and teachers as agents who can remake inequitable and oppressive social spaces and places in the struggle for better social futures.

References

Bakhtin, M.M. (1981) Forms of time and the chronotype in the novel, trans. C. Emerson. In M. Holquist (ed.) *The Dialogic Imagination: Four Essays*. Austin: University of Texas, pp. 84–258.

Barab, S., Thomas, M., Dodge, T., *et al.* (2005) Making learning fun: Quest Atlantis, a game without guns. *Educational Technology Research and Development*, 53(1): 86–107.

Barton, D., and Hamilton, M. (1998) *Local Literacies: Reading and Writing in One Community*. London: Routledge.

Barton, D., Hamilton, M., and Ivanic, R. (2000) *Situated Literacies: Reading and Writing in Context*. London: Routledge.

Bezemer, J. (2008) Displaying orientation in the classroom: Students' multimodal responses to teacher instructions. *Linguistics and Education*, 19(2): 166–178.

Bourdieu, P. (1998) *Practical Reason*, trans. R. Johnson. Palo Alta, CA: Stanford University Press.

Brooke, A. (2003) *Twentieth-century Attitudes: Literary Power in Uncertain Times*. Chicago: Ivan R. Dee.

Casey, E. (1996) How to get from space to place in a fairly short stretch of time. In S. Feld and K. Basso (eds) *Senses of Place*. Santa Fe, NE: School of American Research Press, pp. 13–52.

Comber, B., and Nixon, H. (2008) Spatial literacies: Emergent pedagogies. *Pedagogies: An International Journal*, 3(2): 221–240.

Comber, B., Nixon, H., Ashmore, L., *et al.* (2006) Urban renewal from the inside out: Spatial and critical literacies in a low socioeconomic school community. *Mind, Culture and Activity*, 13(3): 228–246.

Comber, B. Nixon, H., and Reid, J. (eds) (2007) *Literacies in Place: Teaching Environmental Communications*. Newtown, NSW: Primary English Teaching Association.

Comber, B., Thompson, P., and Wells, M. (2001) Critical literacy finds a place: Writing and social action in a low-income Australian grade 2/3 classroom. *The Elementary School Journal*, 101(4): 451–464.

Corbett, M. (2007) *Learning to Leave: The Irony of Schooling in a Coastal Community*. Halifax, Canada: Fernwood Books.

Cresswell, T. (1996) *In Place-Out of Place: Geography, Ideology, and Transgression*. Minneapolis: University of Minnesota Press.

Dixon, K. (2011) *Literacy, Power, and the Schooled Body: Learning in Time and Space*. Routledge: New York and London.

Donehower, K., Hogg, C., and Schell, E.E. (2007) *Rural Literacies*. Carbondale: South Illinois University Press.

Engestrom, Y. (1987) Learning by expanding: An activity-theoretical approach to developmental work research, accessed November 21, 2012: http://lchc.ucsd.edu/mca/Paper/Engestrom/expanding/toc.htm

Eppley, K. (2011) Reading mastery as pedagogy of erasure. *Journal of Research in Rural Education*, 26(11): 1–5.

Ferrare, J.J., and Apple, M.W. (2010) Spatializing critical education: Progress and cautions. *Critical Studies in Education*, 51(2): 209–221.

Freire, P. (1970) Cultural action and conscientization. *Harvard Educational Review*, 40(3): 452–477.

Gannon, S. (2009) Rewriting 'the road to nowhere': Place pedagogies in Western Sydney. *Urban Education*, 44(5): 608–624.

Graham, L., and Bellert, A. (2005) Reading comprehension difficulties experienced by students with learning disabilities. *Australian Journal of Learning Disabilities*, 10(2): 71–78.

Green, B., Cormack, P., and Reid, J. (2006) River literacies: Discursive constructions of place and environment in children's writing about the Murray-Darling Basin. Paper presented at the 'Senses of Place' Conference: April 5–8, Hobart: University of Tasmania.

Gregory, E., and Williams, A. (2000) *City Literacies: Learning to Read across Generations and Cultures*. London and New York: Routledge.

Gruenewald, D. (2003a) The best of both worlds: A critical pedagogy of place. *Educational Researcher*, 32(4): 3–12.

Gruenewald, D. (2003b) Foundations of place: Multidisciplinary frameworks for place-conscious education. *American Educational Research Journal*, 40(3): 619–654.

Gruenewald, D.A., and Smith, G.A. (2008) Place-based education in the global age. Local Diversity, NY: Lawrence Erlbaum.

Gutiérrez, K., Rymes, B., and Larson, J. (1995) Script, counterscript and underlife in the classroom: James Brown versus Brown versus Board of Education. *Harvard Educational Review*, 65(3): 445–471.

Guzzetti, B.J., and Gamboa, M. (2005) Online journaling: The informal writings of two adolescent girls. *Research in the Teaching of English*, 40(2): 168–206.

Harvey, D. (1993) From space to place and back again: Reflections on the condition of postmodernity. In J. Bird, B. Curtis, T. Putnam, *et al.* (eds) *Mapping the Futures: Local Cultures, Global Change*. London: Routledge.

Hawkins, M.R. (2004) Researching English language and literacy development in schools. *Educational Researcher*, 33(3): 14–25.

Heath, S.B. (1983) *Ways with Words: Language, Life and Work in Communities and Classrooms*. New York: Cambridge University Press.

Hirst, E. (2004) Diverse social contexts of a second-language classroom. In K. Leander and M. Sheehy (eds) *Spatializing Literacy Research and Practice*. New York: Peter Lang Publishing, pp. 39–66.

Ingold, T. (2007) *Lines: A Brief History*. London: Routledge.

Ito, M., Baumer, S., Bittanti, M., *et al.* (2009) *Hanging Out, Messing Around, Geeking Out: Living and Learning with New Media.* Cambridge: MIT Press.

Ito, M., Horst, H.A., Bittanti, M., *et al.* (2008) White Paper – Living and learning with new media: Summary of findings from the Digital Youth Project, Chicago, IL.

Jacobs, G.E. (2004) Complicating contexts: Issues of methodology in researching the language and literacies of instant messaging. *Reading Research Quarterly*, 39(4): 394–406.

Janks, H. (2000) Domination, access, diversity and design: A synthesis for critical literacy education. *Educational Review*, 52(2): 175–186.

Jewitt, C. (2006) *Technology, Literacy and Learning: A Multimodal Approach.* Abingdon: Routledge.

Jewitt, C. (2008) Multimodality and literacy in school classrooms. *Review of Research in Education*, 32(1): 241–267.

Kress, G. (2011) 'Partnerships in research': Multimodality and ethnography. *Qualitative Research*, 11(3): 239–260.

Kress, G., and Bezemer, J. (2008) Writing in multimodal texts: A social semiotic account of designs for learning. *Written Communication*, 25(2): 166–195.

Kress, G., and van Leeuwen, T. (1996) *Reading Images: The Grammar of Visual Design.* London: Routledge.

Kress, G., and van Leeuwen, T. (2001) *Multimodal Discourse: The Modes and Media of Contemporary Communication.* London: Arnold.

Lam, E.W.S. (2009) Multiliteracies on instant messaging in negotiating local, translocal, and transnational affiliations: A case of an adolescent immigrant. *Reading Research Quarterly*, 44(4): 377–397.

Lankshear, C., and Knobel, M. (2006) Blogging as participation: The active sociality of a new literacy. Paper presented at the American Educational Research Association Conference, April 11, San Francisco.

Leander, K.M. (2002) Locating Latanya: The situated production of identity artifacts in classroom interaction. *Research in the Teaching of English*, 37(2): 198–250.

Leander, K.M. (2003) Writing travellers' tales on new literacyscapes. *Reading Research Quarterly*, 38(3): 392–397.

Lefebvre, H. (1991) *The Production of Space*, trans. D. Nicholson-Smith. Cambridge: Blackwell.

Lewis, C., and Fabos, B. (2005) Instant messaging, literacies, and social identities. *Reading Research Quarterly*, 40(4): 470–501.

Luke, A. (ed.) (1998) *Encyclopedia of Language and Education*, 2 vols. Dordrecht: Kluwer.

Massey, D.B. (1995) *Spatial Divisions of Labor: Social Structures and the Geography of Production*, 2nd edn. New York: Routledge.

Massey, D.B. (2005) *For Space.* London: Sage.

Mercier, E., Barron, B., and O'Conner, K. (2006) Images of self and others as computer users: The role of gender and experience. *Journal of Computer Assisted Learning*, 22(5): 335–348.

Mills, K.A. (2010) Filming in progress: New spaces for multimodal designing. *Linguistics and Education*, 21(1): 14–28.

Mills, K.A., and Chandra, V. (2011) Microblogging as a literacy practice for educational communities. *Journal of Adolescent and Adult Literacy*, 55(1): 35–45.

Moje, E.M., McIntosh, K., Kramer, K., *et al.* (2004) Working toward third space in content area literacy: An examination of everyday funds of knowledge and discourse. *Reading Research Quarterly*, 39(1): 38–70.

Norris, S. (2004) *Analysing Multimodal Interaction.* London: RoutledgeFalmer.

Pink, S. (2007) *Doing Visual Ethnography: Images, Media and Representation in Research*, 2nd edn. London: Sage.

Pink, S. (2009) *Doing Sensory Ethnography.* London: Sage.

Rist, R. (1970) Student social class and teacher expectations: The self-fulfilling prophecy in ghetto education. *Harvard Educational Review*, 40(3): 411–451.

Said, E. (1993) *Culture and Imperialism.* Portugal: Vintage.

Scollon, R., and Scollon, S.W. (2003) *Discourses in Place: Language in the Material World.* London: Routledge.

Sheehy, M. (1999) Un/making place: A topological analysis of time and space representation in an urban Aooakacguab seventh grade civics project. The Ohio State University, Ohio.

Sheehy, M. (2004) Between a thick and a thin place. In K. Leander and M. Sheehy (eds) *Spatializing Literacy Research and Practice*. New York: Peter Lang, pp. 91–114.

Sinclair, P. (2001) *The Murray: A River and its People*. Melbourne: Melbourne University Press.

Smith, G., and Sobel, D. (2010) *Place- and Community-Based Education in Schools*. Routledge: New York and London.

Soja, E. (1996) *Thirdspace: Journeys to Los Angeles and Other Real-and-Imagined Places*. Oxford: Basil Blackwell.

Soja, E.W. (1989) *Postmodern Geographies: The Reassertion of Space in Critical Social Theory*. Oxford: Verso.

Soja, E.W. (2004) Preface. In K. Leander and M. Sheehy (eds) *Spatializing Literacy Research and Practice*. New York: Peter Lang, pp. ix–xvi.

Soja, E.W. (2010) *Seeking Spatial Justice*. Minneapolis: University of Minnesota Press.

Somerville, M.J. (2007) Place Literacies. *Australian Journal of Language and Literacy*, 30(2): 149–164.

Stanton, D., Bayon, V., Neale, H., *et al.* (2001) Classroom collaboration in the design of tangible interfaces for storytelling. *CHI2001, ACM Conference on Human Factors in Computing Systems, CHI Letters* 3(1): 482–489.

Stein, P. (2006) The Olifantsvlei fresh stories project: Multimodality, creativity, and fixing in the semiotic chain. In C. Jewitt and G. Kress (eds) *Multimodal Literacy*. New York: Peter Lang, pp. 123–138.

Stein, P. (2007) *Multimodal Pedagogies in Diverse Classrooms: Representation, Rights, and Resources*. Abingdon: Routledge.

Street, B. (1984) *Literacy in Theory and Practice*. Cambridge: Cambridge University Press.

Street, B. (1999) The meaning of literacy. In D. Wagner, R. Venezky, and B. Street (eds) *Literacy: An International Handbook*. Boulder, CO: Westview Press, pp. 34–40.

Theobald, P. (1997) *Teaching the Commons: Place, Pride, and the Renewal of Community*. Boulder, CO: Westview Press.

Thomas, A. (2007) Blurring and breaking through the boundaries of narrative, literacy, and identity in adolescent fan fiction. In M. Knobel and C. Lankshear (eds) *A New Literacies Sampler*. New York: Peter Lang, pp. 137–166.

Unsworth, L. (2001) *Teaching Multiliteracies across the Curriculum*. Philadelphia, PA: Open University Press.

van Leeuwen, T., and Jewitt, C. (2001) *Handbook of Visual Analysis*. London: Sage.

Wyse, D., Nikolajeva, M., Charlton, E., *et al.* (2011) Place-related identity, texts, and transcultural meanings. *British Educational Research Journal*, 59(1): 1–21.

Part III
Teachers, Culture, and Identity

Chapter 31

On Becoming Teachers

Knowing and Believing

Jennifer I. Hathaway and Victoria J. Risko

Introduction

One challenge influencing the learning of prospective teachers (PTs) is disrupting their prior knowledge and beliefs about teaching and learning developed over years spent in classrooms as students, or what Lortie (1975) called an apprenticeship-of-observation. Research has shown us that these understandings are long-lasting (Lortie, 1975; Wideen, Mayer-Smith, and Moon, 1998), can be difficult to change (Richardson, 1996), and impact PTs' learning (Cochran-Smith and Zeichner, 2005). However change, or learning, is indeed possible through teacher preparation programs once we are able to grapple with the difficult task of how to intrude on PTs' perspectives of what teaching is in order to help them be willing to take on new understandings.

In this chapter, we discuss research addressing PTs' knowledge development and how beliefs are associated. As we examine existing research and theoretical arguments, we identify methodologies supporting PTs' growing knowledge and where possible we discuss how acquiring new knowledge about effective instruction is linked to PTs' beliefs about what constitutes effective teaching, their beliefs about their own abilities as teachers, and their beliefs about the capabilities of their students.

Research Perspectives: Knowing and Believing

Researchers in the field of literacy, in general, support the thesis that knowledge acquisition and beliefs can impact each other in powerful ways. For example, Worthy and Patterson (2001) reported that once teachers were able to view themselves as successful teachers of struggling readers, their beliefs in their capabilities as teachers and the capabilities of their students increased in a positive direction. Other researchers substantiate this finding by indicating that teachers' beliefs will ultimately influence their classroom practices (e.g., Grisham, 2000; Mesmer, 2006) as well as student learning (e.g., Reutzel and Sabey, 1996). In this first section, we begin by examining the connections between the constructs of knowledge and

International Handbook of Research on Children's Literacy, Learning, and Culture, First Edition.
Edited by Kathy Hall, Teresa Cremin, Barbara Comber, and Luis C. Moll.
© 2013 John Wiley & Sons, Ltd. Published 2013 by John Wiley & Sons, Ltd.

belief. We then explore conceptual understandings that shape the study of PTs' learning and general principles related to the change of knowledge and beliefs. We end this section by considering the importance of PTs' knowledge and beliefs for sorting out the complexity of the classroom.

Knowledge versus belief

The relationship between knowledge and belief is often a matter of debate within the research literature. Theorists such as Green (1971) and Nespor (1987) posited knowledge and belief as distinct constructs. They argued that knowing is not a psychological phenomenon like believing. However, Green (1971) also acknowledged that knowledge and belief can easily be mistaken for one another. He noted, 'when a person believes something, he believes it to be true or to be a reasonable approximation to the truth' (p. 43). Thus, knowing is a unique type of believing where one believes what is actually true. That truth condition is what most often separates how knowledge and belief are defined – knowledge must be supported by either rigorous proof or consensus within a community whereas beliefs require no agreement regarding their validity or appropriateness (Green, 1971; Pajares, 1992).

In contrast, Kagan (1992) asserted that the constructs of knowledge and belief are so closely related they are virtually indistinguishable. She argued that because teaching itself has no absolute truths, ultimately all knowledge teachers hold is subjective, and therefore, a form of belief. Similarly, Pajares (1992), referencing the work of Nespor (1987) and others (i.e., Ernest, 1989; Nisbett and Ross, 1980), acknowledged that though the cognitive processes involved in believing and knowing may differ, ultimately the concepts are so intertwined they cannot be separated.

Studying prospective teachers' knowledge and beliefs

One way to examine how researchers view the relationship between knowledge and belief is to consider how they study the constructs. In their analysis of how the term knowledge is used in the study of learning and literacy, Alexander, Schallert, and Hare (1991) noted that a clear distinction of knowledge as justified true belief is found most often in the field of epistemology. Within the larger field of education, however, such a distinction is hard to maintain (Calderhead, 1996; Pajares, 1992; Sturtevant, 1996). Richardson (1996) noted that in teaching and teacher education literature, little distinction is made between knowledge and beliefs. Instead, knowledge is most often used as a term for grouping ideas about teaching.

Within the field of literacy, researchers deal with the distinction between knowledge and belief in several different ways. Some acknowledge that the constructs of knowledge and belief may be different; however, they find them to be so closely related that they choose to study them in a parallel manner (e.g., Grisham, 2000; Thomas and Barksdale-Ladd, 1997). For example, Thomas and Barksdale-Ladd's research addressed how teachers' differing professional knowledge and literacy-learning beliefs affected their instructional practices. Others argue knowledge and beliefs cannot be separated and therefore choose to collapse the constructs (e.g., DeFord, 1985; Sturtevant, 1996) as is seen in Sturtevant's study in which she assumed teachers' instructional beliefs included their knowledge related to instruction. Finally, some researchers keep the two constructs separate, using different techniques to measure and examine both PTs' beliefs and knowledge (e.g., Shaw, Dvorak, and Bates, 2007).

The inconsistent conceptualization of knowledge and belief as distinct or intertwined constructs is just one factor contributing to the difficulty of researching the development of PTs' knowledge and beliefs. Another factor is the complexity inherent within teaching. As Nespor (1987) noted, teaching is an entangled domain; multiple forms of knowledge and a multitude of beliefs are often at work simultaneously in teaching settings. Opfer and Pedder (2011) examined the literature addressing teachers' professional learning and found that models of teachers' learning tend to treat learning in the form of changes in beliefs and practice as a linear process. Often, the argument is made that a change in teachers' beliefs will lead to a change in their practice, which will ultimately lead to a change in students' learning (Xu, 2000a, 2000b). Or, the opposite is argued in which a change in practice precedes a change in beliefs (Worthy and Patterson, 2001). There are also researchers who posit there is a dynamic relationship between teachers' beliefs and practice, with each holding the potential to change the other (i.e., Bullough and Baughman, 1997; Richardson, 1996).

Opfer and Pedder (2011) contend that teacher learning is more complex than any linear model can illustrate. They argue that teacher learning is a reciprocal process; there may be many different ways learning occurs. They also note the importance of considering the context in which teacher learning is occurring. Citing Huberman's (1983, 1995) work on the cyclic nature of teacher change, they note,

> Changes in beliefs lead to changes in practice that bring changes in student learning that bring further changes in practice that result in additional changes in belief and so on. The relationship between these processes is also reciprocal with changes in one being contingent on changes in another . . . for learning to occur, change may occur in all three areas, and, as a result, change in only one area may not constitute teacher learning (pp. 395–396).

While knowledge and belief may be conceptualized in different ways, there is general agreement that both influence PTs' learning (Borko and Putnam, 1996; Calderhead, 1996). Indeed, teacher learning is often measured by a change in teachers' knowledge, beliefs, or practice (Opfer and Pedder, 2011).

Potential for change in knowledge and beliefs

While prospective teachers' pre-existing knowledge and beliefs can be powerful mediators of their learning (Cochran-Smith and Zeichner, 2005) and may be difficult to change (Richardson, 1996), change, or learning, does occur. Often, the impetus for new learning is the disequilibrium that arises when one is faced with evidence contrary to existing understandings and beliefs (Kagan, 1992). This type of 'good dissonance' (Lyons and Pinnell, 2001, p. 140) disrupts current knowledge and beliefs and allows teachers to modify their understandings and practice (Lyons and Pinnell, 2001; Olson and Singer, 1994). For teachers, the change process can be gradual and difficult (Guskey, 1986) and can result in frustration and anxiety (Borko *et al.*, 2000).

Though specific findings addressing ways to shift PTs' perspectives about literacy instruction are provided in the next section of this chapter, in general, learning is fostered when new knowledge is connected to prior knowledge. Often learners need support as they search for these connections (Bransford *et al.*, 2005). Similarly, researchers have found there are possibilities for bringing about changes in PTs' belief (i.e., Nierstheimer *et al.*, 2000; Shaw *et al.*, 2007; Wideen, Mayer-Smith, and Moon, 1998).

Wideen, Mayer-Smith, and Moon (1998) identified one particular challenge in addressing prospective teachers' perspectives. Often, teacher educators view PTs' pre-existing understandings and beliefs as problematic, and thus, work to change them. However, the PTs themselves do not share in this change effort because they are not given opportunities to closely examine and problematize their own perspectives (Wideen, Mayer-Smith, and Moon, 1998). As many of the ideas PTs bring into their teacher preparation programs are naïve, it is imperative that teacher educators help PTs make their beliefs explicit. PTs need to spend time examining their beliefs in light of the evidence being presented to them through their teacher education programs (Hammerness, Darling-Hammond, and Bransford, 2005; IRA, 2007; Richardson, 1996). Through this examination, dissonance can be created and PTs' underlying knowledge and beliefs can be disrupted. However, uncovering PTs' beliefs can be a difficult task. Tools and methods for supporting PTs' efforts to elicit their own beliefs will be discussed in the next section of this chapter.

Moving the debate forward

While the debate may continue about the nature of knowledge versus belief, what is evident is that both play vital roles in teacher development. Researchers have examined both the knowledge and beliefs that PTs bring to their teacher education programs and the power of such programs to shape those understandings. Much of the challenge of studying PTs' learning is a result of the complex spaces in which teaching and learning occur. In schools and classrooms, there are no absolute truths; therefore, teachers must work to make sense of the situations (Kagan, 1992), or ill-defined problems, that arise in the classroom. Ill-defined problems require teachers to move beyond a reliance on the information contained in the problems and instead to rely on their own background knowledge or make guesses and assumptions in order to solve them (Nespor, 1987). Kagan (1992) referred to these problems and domains as 'schizophrenic tasks' (p. 79). When teachers encounter such tasks, or uncertainties, in the classroom, they realize they cannot solve such problems by a reliance on clear, indisputable guidelines. Their relevant schemata cannot be accessed, and teachers cannot determine needed information or appropriate behaviors (Pajares, 1992). When this happens, they either acquire new knowledge and associated strategies for applying the knowledge (Bransford, Brown, and Cocking, 1999) required for complex problem solving or they rely on their prior beliefs and experiences that are insufficient for addressing novel problems. With new knowledge come new beliefs, constantly interacting to inform decision making, problem solving, and teaching practices (Opfer and Pedder, 2011).

Instruction that Fosters Knowing and Believing

Having explored the connections between knowledge and belief and the potential impact of each on changes in PTs' learning, we now turn to considering ways to tackle the difficult work of disrupting their sometimes naïve perspectives. PTs often enter teacher education feeling as if they are 'insiders' to teaching because of the time they have spent in classrooms as students (Pajares, 1992). However, while PTs develop affective responses to teaching through these experiences, they do not acquire the technical, pedagogical knowledge of teaching because they are not privy to teachers' intentions and personal reflections as they set goals, prepare for instruction, or analyze the results of their actions (Lortie, 1975). One of the purposes of teacher education is to create the dissonance needed to allow PTs to grow and develop beyond their initial understandings of teaching. Thus, a primary question for literacy teacher educators and researchers focuses attention on what prospective teachers are learning (as seen in changes in knowledge, beliefs, and/or practice) in their teacher education programs (methods courses, field placements, student teaching) and what forms of instruction seem to best facilitate that learning (Clift and Brady, 2005; Risko *et al.*, 2008). In the following section, we first discuss research associated with PTs' knowledge development. Next we present research addressing change in both knowledge and beliefs. Last we share research findings that relate to uses of specific tools for influencing knowledge and beliefs, and for tapping into PTs' beliefs.

The role of demonstrations and explicit teaching moves

In reviews conducted by Clift and Brady (2005) and Risko *et al.* (2008), researchers concluded that structured teaching formats provided positive trajectories toward fostering knowledge and applications of newly learned teaching methods in PTs' classrooms. Characteristics of these structured teaching formats, referred to as explicit teaching methods by Risko *et al.* (2008), were derived by a close examination of eight studies. These studies were conducted by Abrego, Rubin, and Sutterby (2006); Maheady, Mallette, and Harper (1996); Mallette, Maheady, and Harper (1999); Massey (1990, 2006); Morgan *et al.* (1992); Nierstheimer *et al.* (2000); and Worthy and Patterson (2001). Explicit teaching characteristics included (a) demonstrations of teaching strategies within the methods courses with some use of video models to invite analysis of teaching methods; (b) use of a structured lesson planning format that highlighted explicit instructional elements focusing on reading skills and strategies; and (c) careful guidance during teaching with specific feedback on lesson plans prior to the lessons and feedback during and after teaching.

In a separate study, L'Allier (2005) supported this direction when describing impactful instruction for PTs. She learned that reading about teaching methods in the course textbook or watching demonstrations in class without suggested applications to teaching were ineffective to support PTs' use of these strategies. Conversely, methods that were both demonstrated in the methods class and then guided in application in the field placement were more likely to be adopted by future teachers.

Embedded in the above forms of explicit demonstrations and guided applications is the concept of *learning by doing* (Dewey, 1916). When PTs are invited to use instructional strategies to aid their own learning or to witness its success in their own teaching, they come to understand the usefulness of the recommended forms of instructional methods and are more likely to adopt these methods. For example, Fazio (2000, 2003) demonstrated and guided his PTs' use of cognitive reading strategies with the course textbook. He reported that students who used these strategies independently for their own learning came to value them and envisioned their application in their teaching. Stevens (2002) engaged PTs preparing for middle and high school teaching in online collaborative discussions. She demonstrated her use of comprehension strategies and traced the strategies used by her students while reading texts online. She was interested in knowing when and if her students were beginning to use and discuss the demonstrated strategies to aid their comprehension. While participating in online discussions, Stevens was able to clarify misconceptions and redirect her students' ineffective study habits. Stevens observed increased use of strategies and positive beliefs about their power to aid comprehension.

Bean (2001) observed prospective teachers with secondary education and content majors in different school settings and within different content classrooms and further elaborated the earlier hypothesis of seeing usefulness of new forms of instruction. He concluded that strategy selection in classrooms occurred when the strategies were congruent with the structure of disciplinary knowledge and when mentor teachers demonstrated and believed in the use of reading strategies to support student learning. Where there was little congruence with school applications, PTs tended to reject what they learned in college methods courses and adopted the strategies in place in their student teaching classrooms.

Explicit learning conditions associated with belief changes

As we noted above, increased knowledge about effective methods for reading instruction occurs in well-structured teacher education formats with guidance during applications in classrooms. Several researchers noted the additional finding of positive shifts in PTs' beliefs about their ability to teach and the capabilities of their students. These researchers reported added benefits for both knowledge and belief changes when PTs (a) formed personal relationships with their students, (b) had prolonged engagement with their students, and (c) were invited to reflect on their teaching within well-supported learning communities.

Establishing personal relationships with their students (i.e., knowing their interests; knowing how their students approached their reading and writing activities) and teaching in a tutoring setting were identified as important for preparing future teachers to apply newly-acquired knowledge of methods and building positive beliefs about struggling readers and their own capabilities as teachers. These experiences, however, were situated within well supervised tutoring settings that provided expectations for well-structured lesson plans that addressed content and teaching methods and well-structured requirements for self reflection (Abrego, Rubin, and Sutterby, 2006; Maheady, Mallette, and Harper, 1996, 1999; Massey, 1990; Morgan, Timmons, and Shaheen, 2006; Morgan *et al.*, 1992; Niersheimer *et al.*, 2000; Worthy and Patterson, 2001).

Worthy and Patterson (2001), for example, argued for the importance of building caring relationships when PTs are assigned to a tutoring experience with a struggling reader. They explained that tutoring one student was instrumental for fostering personal, caring relationships and that such relationships influenced positive changes in pupil performance and in changes of some (not all) prospective teachers' learning. Researchers, such as Clark and Medina (2000), Kidd, Sanchez and Thorp (2002), Wolf and colleagues (1999, 2000), Xu (2000a, 2000b), and others demonstrated that personal relationships with students enhanced PTs' confidence in teaching struggling readers and/or changed deficit views of students whose culture or language was different from their own.

Multiple studies focus on prospective teachers' use of assessment data to inform their teaching (Lazar, 2001; Mallette *et al.*, 2000; Mora and Grisham, 2001; Wolf, Ballentine, and Hill, 2000; Wolf, Carey, and Mieras, 1996; Wolf, Hill, and Ballentine, 1999). Prolonged engagement with pupils during the assessment and teaching process and instructor feedback that is timely and focused enhanced PTs' accuracy in analyzing and reporting data and confidence in both assessment and teaching methods. Beliefs about the capabilities of students also increased. In addition to enhancing confidence in students' capabilities, Wolf and her colleagues (Wolf *et al.*, 1996, 1999, 2000) and Lazar (2001) noted enhanced critique of school inequities and the goal to implement culturally responsive instruction that optimized connections to children's interests, experiences, and prior knowledge.

Another set of studies focused on the goal of inviting self-reflection and shared learning opportunities, described as creating a sense of community by Akiba (2011). For example, Obidah's (2000) use of reflective self-study engaged 29 PTs in dialogue about multiculturalism to examine the impact of cultures on identity formation and educational experiences. His students began to reconceptualize their own identities, their understandings and expectations of others with different cultural histories, and the challenges of becoming a critical analyst of cultural understandings and misunderstandings. Similarly, Cicchelli and Cho (2007) found that reflection on multicultural attitudes displayed in urban settings and their own personal involvement with students whose culture was different from their own were instrumental in improving multicultural attitudes throughout the program. Akiba (2011) found that attitudes improved when PTs felt they were given sufficient opportunity to discuss their social and cultural histories and their fears about teaching in multicultural settings with their peers, felt that their opinions were respected and valued, and felt that the college classroom atmosphere was comfortable and supportive. This concept of learning as a community is associated with views of learning as a social activity and that learning is deepened with multiple forms of dialogue and the study of others' perspectives (Wertsch, 2002).

Tools for influencing knowledge and beliefs

Personal writing is an additional strategy implemented to change prospective teachers' knowledge and beliefs about cultural diversity. Clark and Medina (2000), for example, asked PTs to write personal narratives patterned after book-length autobiographical narratives (e.g., Luis J. Rodriquez's *Always Running*) that they read in their teacher education classes. They identified changes in their PTs' multicultural attitudes as they began to identify situated events that influence literacy development, express and adopt multicultural perspectives, and acknowledge the importance of their pupils' stories for teaching. Clark and Medina (2000) concluded that the narrative writings enabled their PTs to change their understandings of individuals from cultural backgrounds different from their own.

Similarly, Xu (2000a, 2000b) found positive benefits on prospective teachers' attitudes when they wrote autobiographies (i.e., their personal stories), biographies of their students, and then compared likenesses and differences. While noting positive changes in multicultural attitudes, she learned that changing attitudes alone was insufficient for changing teaching practices. Xu noted that PTs had difficulty knowing how to apply what they were learning about cultural differences to their teaching.

Involving students in collecting and analyzing pupil data was associated with reported changes in knowledge and beliefs. One method, reported on by Kidd *et al.* (2002), is engaging prospective teachers in interviews with families and their children and writing stories about their students. Through this interviewing process, Kidd *et al.* (2002) observed gains in PTs' knowledge of cultural differences and beliefs about the capabilities of their students. Yet almost half of the 14 PTs felt unable to apply their new appreciation of differences in their own teaching. The researchers noted that increased understandings of cultural differences are insufficient if teachers are unable to draw on methods to enact culturally appropriate instruction.

Tools for uncovering beliefs

Earlier in this chapter we discussed the influence prospective teachers' beliefs can have on their learning. We also highlighted the importance of helping PTs explore their beliefs as part of the process of modifying them. Through this exploration, which often includes some of the methods mentioned above such as self-reflection and personal writing, their beliefs can be made visible and perhaps altered. However, simply uncovering these understandings can be difficult because many beliefs are held implicitly (Pajares, 1992). While there are many tools used to research teachers' beliefs including simulations, commentaries, concept mapping, repertory grid techniques, ethnography and case studies, narratives (Calderhead, 1996), and surveys (Fang, 1996), several of these can also serve as tools for helping teacher educators support PTs' efforts to examine their own beliefs.

For example, simulations can be a useful tool for uncovering PTs' beliefs. Simulations typically involve a fictitious problem or context used to bring forth teachers' thinking about practical teaching situations (Calderhead, 1996). For example, Abernathy (2002) used a storybook prompt to elicit PTs' beliefs about struggling readers. After hearing the story *Next Year*

I'll Be Special (Giff, 1980) about Marilyn, a student struggling in first grade who looks forward to a better year in second grade, PTs were asked to write narrative responses describing their own thoughts about what second grade would be like for Marilyn and then to discuss their responses.

Another example is metaphors. Metaphors may be a useful tool for accessing PTs' knowledge and beliefs (Mahlios, Massengill-Shaw, and Barry, 2010) or for identifying shifts in thinking as Bullough and Baughman (1997) note that changing metaphors are often indicators of changing beliefs and practice. Lakoff and Johnson (1980) argued metaphors shape one's understandings of the world, and Munby (1986) found this to be true for teachers as he examined the metaphors they used when talking about their own practice. Metaphors may be a useful way to open conversations with PTs about their own understandings and how those beliefs impact what they understand about teaching (Mahlios, Massengill-Shaw, and Barry, 2010).

Teacher storylines, a method that allows a person's experiences and events to be quantified and compared using a graphic representation (Beijaard, van Driel, and Verloop, 1999), can also be used to trace PTs' beliefs over time. Grisham (2000) utilized this method as part of her study of the impact of undergraduate constructivist literacy coursework on teachers' beliefs and instructional practices. She had participants construct storylines regarding their idea of constructivist teaching from the last year of their teacher education program through their second year of teaching. Through these storylines, participants plotted how congruent they believed their practices to be with constructivist theory noting changes over time and providing explanations for their ratings. The storylines allowed participants to reflect on the differences in their own beliefs and practices and to examine factors influencing those discrepancies.

A final example of a method that holds promise for teacher educators is visioning. The teacher visioning protocol (Hammerness, 1999, 2006) uses five open-ended questions to prompt respondents to describe an ideal day in a classroom, specifically addressing elements such as the role of the teacher and students, instructional materials, and the larger purposes of schooling. This measure can reveal unconsciously held beliefs (Squires and Bliss, 2004) and help teachers develop a greater awareness of their own beliefs (Hammerness, 2003). While this measure has primarily been used with in-service teachers, recent work indicates it can also support PTs' examination of their own beliefs (McElhone *et al.*, 2009).

Concluding Thoughts and Future Directions

While it can be difficult to tease out the differences between the constructs of knowledge and belief, prospective teachers' knowledge and beliefs play a prominent role in their development as teachers (Borko and Putnam, 1996; Calderhead, 1996). The understandings they bring with them into their teacher education programs are durable (Wideen, Mayer-Smith, and Moon, 1998) and must be addressed in order for PTs to learn (Hammerness, Darling-Hammond, and Bransford, 2005; IRA, 2007) as seen through their development of new knowledge, beliefs, or practices. However, that learning is complex. It involves reciprocal cycles of development as old beliefs are re-examined in light of new understandings and practices, and as new beliefs lead to reconsideration of what was previously known about teaching (Opfer and Pedder, 2011).

Though teacher education programs can positively influence changes in PTs' knowledge and beliefs (Risko *et al.*, 2008), one of the difficulties for teacher educators is determining the best ways to create the cognitive dissonance needed to spur that learning. Risko *et al.* (2008) found structured teaching formats to be effective. Specifically, providing PTs with demonstrations and making teaching moves explicit, supporting their lesson planning efforts, and providing guidance before teaching lessons as well as feedback during and after their teaching appeared to enhance PTs' knowledge about teaching literacy.

Along with increases in PTs' knowledge, teacher education can also support positive changes in their beliefs. To foster this type of development, teacher educators can set up instructional situations in which PTs are able to form meaningful relationships with their students during their early teaching experiences and then reflect on these experiences. Supporting PTs' use of assessment data can also encourage this type of learning as can involving PTs in self-reflection and shared learning opportunities.

Finally, there are a variety of tools available to teacher educators as they work to foster PTs' learning. Tools such as personal writing, data analysis, and interviewing have been shown to positively influence prospective teachers' knowledge and beliefs, while tools such as surveys, simulations, metaphors, teacher storylines, and visioning provide teacher educators with ways to tap into PTs' beliefs and help the PTs make those beliefs explicit in order to critically examine them.

While current research provides a starting point for understanding and supporting prospective teachers' learning in the form of changes in knowledge, beliefs, or practice, there are questions that remain. One such question concerns the best way to address PTs' naïve beliefs that may run counter to best practices in teaching. While simply helping PTs uncover their prior knowledge and beliefs is important, to support the process of PTs' learning, successful literacy teacher educators must be able to 'encourage their students to reflect about their own beliefs regarding pedagogical practices while leading discussions regarding those beliefs' (IRA, 2007, p. 9). In order for learning to occur, PTs must work through the dissonance created when they are confronted with new, conflicting ideas. In this way, they are able to reconcile new ideas with their current perspectives (Green, 1971). While the methods discussed in this chapter provide ways for teacher educators to bring about this needed disruption in PTs' prior beliefs, it is common for those beliefs to be viewed as problematic and in need of reform, leading teacher educators to attempt to simply replace them with more desirable beliefs (Wideen, Mayer-Smith, and Moon, 1998). This can lead to what Green (1971) referred to as indoctrination – a situation in which PTs appear to adopt new ideas without attempting to reconcile them with their personal perspectives. This can be problematic because when teaching challenges are faced, PTs' new learning is often abandoned as they fall back on their more tightly held personal perspectives (Grisham, 2000). To avoid this situation, Wideen, Mayer-Smith, and Moon (1998) argued teacher educators should look for ways to build on students' existing beliefs rather than just trying to replace them with more desirable ones. By doing this, prospective teachers become more independent thinkers who are open to change and are active participants in the change process (Duffy, 2002).

A second question that lingers when addressing prospective teachers' learning is how to address the mismatches PTs encounter between the new understandings they develop during their participation in teacher education and the realities they face in schools during their field experiences, student teaching, and beginning teaching positions. As Opfer and Pedder (2011) note, teaching contexts influence teachers' learning just as much as the personal characteristics of individual teachers and the learning activities in which they engage. As a result, some PTs may not experience a change in their understandings, due in part to the lack of congruence between the ideas they receive from their teacher education programs and the field placements in which they find themselves (Clift and Brady, 2005). For other PTs, the shifts in their understandings about teaching may be fleeting. For example, Grisham (2000) found that PTs' teacher preparation programs positively influenced their beliefs and practice during the beginning of their teaching career. However, beyond the first two years of teaching, their development as literacy teachers became more highly influenced by the teaching contexts in which they worked, causing them to revert to their long-held perspectives. There is research indicating that with mentoring in new settings by prior teacher educators, the practices and beliefs established in teacher education can be sustained (Massey, 2006). However, additional research is needed in this area, including longitudinal studies that trace the development of teachers' knowledge and beliefs from teacher education into their teaching careers (Clift and Brady, 2005).

References

Abernathy, T.V. (2002) Using a storybook prompt to uncover inservice and preservice teachers' dispositions toward struggling students. *The Teacher Educator*, 38(2): 78–98.

Abrego, M.H., Rubin, R., and Sutterby, J.A. (2006) They call me 'Maestra': Preservice teachers' interactions with parents in a reading tutoring program. *Action in Teacher Education*, 28(1): 3–12.

Akiba, M. (2011) Identifying program characteristics for preparing pre-service teachers for diversity. *Teachers College Record*, 113(3): 658–697.

Alexander, P.A., Schallert, D.L., and Hare, V.C. (1991) Coming to terms: How researchers in learning and literacy talk about knowledge. *Review of Educational Research*, 61(3): 315–343.

Bean, T.W. (2001) Preservice teachers' selection and use of content area literacy strategies. *Journal of Educational Research*, 90(3): 154–163.

Beijaard, D., van Driel, J., and Verloop, N. (1999) Evaluation of story-line methodology in research on teachers' practical knowledge. *Studies in Educational Evaluation*, 25(1): 47–62.

Borko, H., Davinroy, K.H., Bliem, C.L., and Cumbo, K.B. (2000) Exploring and supporting teacher change: Two third-grade teachers' experiences in a mathematics and literacy staff development project. *The Elementary School Journal*, 100(4): 273–306.

Borko, H., and Putnam, R.T. (1996) Learning to teach. In D.C. Berliner and R.C. Calfee (eds) *Handbook of Educational Psychology*. New York: Macmillan, pp. 673–708.

Bransford, J.D., Brown, A.L., and Cocking, R.R. (eds) (1999) *How People Learn: Bridging Research and Practice*. Washington, DC: National Academy Press.

Bransford, J., Derry, S., Berliner, D., and Hammerness, K. (with Beckett, K.L.) (2005) Theories of learning and their roles in teaching. In L. Darling-Hammond and J. Bransford (eds) *Preparing Teachers for a Changing World: What Teachers Should Learn and be Able to Do*. San Francisco, CA: Jossey-Bass, pp. 40–87.

Bullough, R.V., Jr., and Baughman, K. (1997) *'First Year Teacher' Eight Years Later: An Inquiry into Teacher Development*. New York: Teachers College Press.

Calderhead, J. (1996) Teachers: Beliefs and knowledge. In D.C. Berliner and R.C. Calfee (eds) *Handbook of Educational Psychology*. New York: Macmillan, pp. 709–715.

Cicchelli, T., and Cho, S.J. (2007) Teacher multicultural attitudes: Intern/Teaching fellows in New York City. *Education and Urban Society*, 39(3): 370–381.

Clark, C., and Medina, C. (2000) How reading and writing literacy narratives affect pre–service teachers' understandings of literacy, pedagogy, and multiculturalism. *Journal of Teacher Education*, 51(1): 63–76.

Clift, R.T., and Brady, P. (2005) Research on methods courses and field experiences. In M. Cochran-Smith and K.M. Zeichner (eds) *Studying Teacher Education: The Report of the AERA Panel on Research and Teacher Education*. Mahwah, NJ: Erlbaum, pp. 309–424.

Cochran-Smith, M., and Zeichner, K.M. (eds) (2005) *Studying Teacher Education: The Report of the AERA Panel on Research and Teacher Education*. Mahwah, NJ: Lawrence Erlbaum.

DeFord, D.E. (1985) Validating the construct of theoretical orientation in reading. *Reading Research Quarterly*, 20(3): 351–367.

Dewey, J. (1916) *Democracy and Education: An Introduction to the Philosophy of Education*. New York: Macmillan.

Duffy, G.G. (2002) Visioning and the development of outstanding teachers. *Reading Research and Instruction*, 41(4): 331–344.

Fang, Z. (1996) A review of research on teacher beliefs and practices. *Educational Research*, 38(1): 47–65.

Fazio, M. (2000) Constructive comprehension and metacognitive strategy instruction in a field-based teacher education program. *Yearbook of the College Reading Association*, 22: 177–190.

Fazio, M. (2003) Constructive comprehension and metacognitive strategy reading instruction in a field–based teacher education program: Effecting change in preservice and inservice teachers – participant one. *Yearbook of the College Reading Association*, 25: 23–45.

Ernest, P. (1989) The knowledge, beliefs and attitudes of the mathematics teacher: A model. *Journal of Education for Teaching*, 15(1): 13–33.

Giff, P.R. (1980) *Next Year I'll be Special*. New York: Bantam Doubleday Dell.

Green, T.F. (1971) *The Activities of Teaching*. New York: McGraw–Hill.

Grisham, D.L. (2000) Connecting theoretical conceptions of reading to practice: A longitudinal study of elementary school teachers. *Reading Psychology*, 21: 145–170.

Guskey, T.R. (1986) Staff development and the process of teacher change. *Educational Researcher*, 15(5): 5–12.

Hammerness, K. (1999) Seeing through teachers' eyes: An exploration of the content, character and role of teachers' vision. Unpublished doctoral dissertation, Stanford University, CA.

Hammerness, K. (2003) Learning to hope, or hoping to learn? The role of vision in the early professional lives of teachers. *Journal of Teacher Education*, 54(1): 43–56.

Hammerness, K. (2006) *Seeing through Teachers' Eyes: Professional Ideals and Classroom Practices*. New York: Teachers College Press.

Hammerness, K., Darling-Hammond, L., Bransford, J., *et al.* (2005) How teachers learn and develop. In L. Darling-Hammond and J. Bransford (eds) *Preparing Teachers for a Changing World: What Teachers Should Learn and Be Able To Do*. San Francisco, CA: Jossey-Bass, pp. 358–389.

Huberman, M. (1983) Recipes for busy teachers. *Knowledge: Creation, Diffusion, Utilization*, 4: 478–510.

Huberman, M. (1995) Professional careers and professional development: some intersections. In: T.R. Guskey and M. Huberman (eds) *Professional Development in Education: New Paradigms and Practices*. New York: Teachers College Press, pp. 193–224.

IRA (International Reading Association) (2007) *Teaching Reading Well: A Synthesis of the International Reading Association's Research on Teacher Preparation for Reading Instruction*. Newark, DE: Author.

Kagan, D.M. (1992) Implications of research on teacher belief. *Educational Psychologist*, 27(1): 65–90.

Kidd, J.K., Sanchez, S.Y., and Thorp, E.K. (2002) A focus on family stories: Enhancing pre-service teachers' cultural awareness. *National Reading Conference Yearbook*, 51: 242–252.

Lakoff, G, and Johnson, M. (1980) *Metaphors We Live By*. Chicago, IL: University of Chicago Press.

L'Allier, S. (2005) Using the reflections of preservice teachers to help teacher educators improve their own practice. In P.E. Linder, M.B. Sampson, J.R. Dugan, and B. Brancato (eds) *Building Bridges, The 27th yearbook of the College Reading Association*. Commerce, TX: Texas A&M University, pp. 79–93.

Lazar, A. (2001) Preparing white preservice teachers for urban classrooms: Growth in a Philadelphia-based literacy practicum. *National Reading Conference Yearbook*, 50: 367–381.

Lortie, D.C. (1975) *Schoolteacher: A Sociological Study*. Chicago, IL: The University of Chicago Press.

Lyons, C.A., and Pinnell, G.S. (2001) *Systems for Change in Literacy Education: A Guide to Professional Development*. Portsmouth, NH: Heinemann.

Maheady, L., Mallette, B., and Harper, G.F. (1996) The pair tutoring program: An early field-based experience to prepare preservice general educators to work with students with special learning needs. *Teacher Education and Special Education*, 19(4): 277–297.

Mahlios, M., Massengill-Shaw, D., and Barry, A. (2010) Making sense of teaching through metaphors: A review across three studies. *Teachers and Teaching: Theory and Practice*, 16(1): 49–71.

Mallette, B., Maheady, L., and Harper, G.F. (1999) The effects of reciprocal peer coaching on preservice general educators' instruction of students with special learning needs. *Teacher Education and Special Education*, 22(4): 201–216.

Mallette, M.H., Kile, R.S., Smith, M.M., *et al.* (2000) Constructing meaning about literacy difficulties: Preservice teachers beginning to think about pedagogy. *Teaching and Teacher Education*, 16(5–6): 593–612.

Massey, D.D. (1990) Preservice teachers as tutors: Influences of tutoring on whole-class literacy instruction. *National Reading Conference Yearbook*, 52, 259–271.

Massey, D.D. (2006) 'You teach for me: I've had it!' A first-year teacher's cry for help. *Action in Teacher Education*, 28(3): 73–85.

McElhone, D., Hebard, H., Scott, R., and Juel, C. (2009) The role of vision in trajectories of literacy practice among new teachers. *Studying Teacher Education*, 5(2): 147–158.

Mesmer, H.E. (2006) Beginning reading materials: A national survey of primary teachers' reported uses and beliefs. *Journal of Literacy Research*, 38(4): 389–425.

Mora, J.K., and Grisham, D.L. (2001) !What deliches tortillas!: Preparing teachers for literacy instruction in linguistically diverse classrooms. *Teacher Education Quarterly*, 28(4): 51–70.

Morgan, D.N., Timmons, B., and Shaheen, M. (2006) Tutoring: A personal and professional space for preservice teachers to learn about literacy instruction. In J.V. Hoffman, D.L. Schallert, C.M. Fairbanks, *et al.* (eds) *55th Yearbook of the National Reading Conference*. Oak Creek, WI: NRC, Inc., pp. 212–223.

Morgan, R.L., Gustafson, K.J., Hudson, P.J., and Salzberg, C.L. (1992) Peer coaching in a preservice special education program. *Teacher Education and Special Education*, 15(4): 249–258.

Munby, H. (1986) Metaphor in the thinking of teachers: An exploratory study. *Journal of Curriculum Studies*, 18(2): 197–209.

Nespor, J. (1987) The role of beliefs in the practice of teaching. *Journal of Curriculum Studies*, 19(4): 317–328.

Niersheimer, S.L., Hopkins, C.J., Dillon, D.R., and Schmitt, M.C. (2000) Preservice teachers' shifting beliefs about struggling literacy learners. *Reading Research and Instruction*, 40(1): 1–16.

Nisbett, R., and Ross, L. (1980) *Human Inference: Strategies and Shortcomings of Social Judgment*. Englewood Cliffs, NJ: Prentice-Hall.

Obidah, J.E. (2000) Mediating boundaries of race, class, and professional authority as a critical multiculturalist. *Teachers College Record*, 102(6): 1035–1060.

Olson, J.R., and Singer, M. (1994) Examining teacher beliefs, reflective change, and the teaching of reading. *Reading Research and Instruction*, 34(2): 97–110.

Opfer, V.D., and Pedder, D. (2011) Conceptualizing teacher professional learning. *Review of Educational Research*, 81(3): 376–407.

Pajares, M.F. (1992) Teachers' beliefs and educational research: Cleaning up a messy construct. *Review of Educational Research*, 62(3): 307–332.

Reutzel, D.R., and Sabey, B. (1996) Teacher beliefs and children's concepts about reading: Are they related? *Reading Research and Instruction*, 35(4): 323–342.

Richardson, V. (1996) The role of attitudes and beliefs in learning to teach. In J. Sikula, T.J. Buttery, and E. Guyton (eds) *Handbook of Research on Teacher Education*. New York: Macmillan, pp. 102–119.

Risko, V.J., Roller, C.M., Cummins, C., *et al.* (2008) A critical analysis of research on reading teacher education. *Reading Research Quarterly*, 43(3): 252–288.

Shaw, D.M., Dvorak, M.J., and Bates, K. (2007) Promise and possibility – hope for teacher education: Pre-service literacy instruction can have an impact. *Reading Research and Instruction*, 46(3): 223–254.

Squires, D., and Bliss, T. (2004) Teacher visions: Navigating beliefs about literacy learning. *The Reading Teacher*, 57(8): 756–763.

Stevens, L.P. (2002) Making the road by walking: The transition from content area literacy to adolescent literacy. *Reading Research and Instruction*, 41(3): 267–278.

Sturtevant, E.G. (1996) Lifetime influences on the literacy–based instructional beliefs of experienced high school history teachers: Two comparative case studies. *Journal of Literacy Research*, 28(2): 227–257.

Thomas, K.F., and Barksdale-Ladd, M.A. (1997) Plant a radish, get a radish: Case study of kindergarten teachers' differing literacy belief systems. *Reading Research and Instruction*, 37(1): 39–60.

Wertsch, J.V. (2002) *Voices of Collective Remembering*. Cambridge, UK: Cambridge University Press.

Wideen, M., Mayer-Smith, J., and Moon, B. (1998) A critical analysis of the research on learning to teach: Making the case for an ecological perspective on inquiry. *Review of Educational Research*, 68(2): 130–178.

Wolf, S.A., Ballentine, D., and Hill, L.A. (2000) 'Only connect!': Cross-cultural connections in the reading lives of preservice teachers and children. *Journal of Literacy Research*, 32: 533–569.

Wolf, S.A., Carey, A.A., and Mieras, E.L. (1996) 'What is this literachurch stuff anyway?': Preservice teachers' growth in understanding children's literary response. *Reading Research Quarterly*, 31: 130–157.

Wolf, S.A., Hill, L., and Ballentine, D. (1999) Teaching on fissured ground: Preparing preservice teachers for culturally conscious pedagogy. *National Reading Conference Yearbook*, 48: 423–436.

Worthy, J., and Patterson, E. (2001) 'I can't wait to see Carlos!': Preservice teachers, situated learning, and personal relationships with students. *Journal of Literacy Research*, 33: 303–344.

Xu, S.H. (2000a) Preservice teachers in a literacy methods course consider issues of diversity. *Journal of Literacy Research*, 32: 505–531.

Xu, S.H. (2000b) Preservice teachers integrate understandings of diversity into literacy instruction: An adaptation of the ABC's Model. *Journal of Teacher Education*, 51(2): 135–142.

Chapter 32

Reforming How We Prepare Teachers to Teach Literacy

Why? What? How?

Brian Cambourne and Julie Kiggins

Introduction

This chapter is about reforming the preparation of pre-service teachers to teach literacy. It addresses three specific reform questions:

Why reform how we prepare teachers to teach literacy?
What aspects of this preparation need reform?
How can such reforms be implemented?

In the process of addressing these questions we explore the implications of paradigmatic change to traditional ways of organizing, delivering, and assessing professional knowledge in a typical higher education setting. We draw on a regional Australian university's ten year experiment to reform its pre-service program to inform this exploration.

Background Context

From 1997 to 2006 the Faculty of Education at the University of Wollongong experimented with some radically different organizational structures and conceptual processes in its teacher education program (Cambourne, Ferry, and Kiggins, 2003). Wollongong's purpose was to promote significant change to the traditional structures, delivery, and concept of 'professional knowledge and skills' in its program.

Wollongong's reform agenda involved three components of its program:

* Knowledge organization and mode of delivery; instead of a traditional 'Theory-Into-Practice-campus-based-lecture-plus-tutorial' mode of program organization and delivery (T-I-P), Wollongong shifted to a 'Practice-into-Theory-problem-based-learning-on-a-school-site' mode (P-I-T).

International Handbook of Research on Children's Literacy, Learning, and Culture, First Edition.
Edited by Kathy Hall, Teresa Cremin, Barbara Comber, and Luis C. Moll.
© 2013 John Wiley & Sons, Ltd. Published 2013 by John Wiley & Sons, Ltd.

- The 'field work' and/or 'practicum' experience; instead of the traditional 'clinical supervision' of 'practice teaching' Wollongong developed a 'problem-based-action-learning-mentoring' model.
- The traditional assessment practices; instead of a 'one-size fits all' model of standardized, competitive assessment Wollongong developed an 'integrated-learner-oriented' model.

Although these proposed changes involved significantly different parts of the program they were fundamentally epistemological in nature, reflecting concerns about the structure of professional knowledge and how it is 'best acquired' (i.e., 'learned') and assessed in higher education settings (Cochran-Smith and Lytle, 2009).

Why Reform How We Prepare Teachers To Teach Literacy?

Literacy education and pre-service teacher education are large, complex, domains of inquiry. Over the last half century each has been subjected to intense scrutiny by hundreds of researchers, theorists, educational pundits, media commentators, politicians, educational reformers, and lobbyists. As a consequence they have become targets for programmatic reform and intervention. What is the basis of these calls for reform?

(a) Pressures for reform in pre-service teacher education

For the past quarter of a century providers of pre-service teacher education in western democracies have been under significant pressure to reform the way they prepare teachers. Historically scholars have characterized teacher education programs as a series of disparate, 'stand-alone,' individual 'courses,' or 'subjects' rather than carefully constructed and integrated learning experiences informed by a cohesive vision of teaching and learning (Cochran-Smith and Lytle, 2009; Darling-Hammond 2006a, 2006b, 2010; Hammerness, 2006; Howey and Zimpher, 1989; Korthagen and Kessels, 1999).

In 1991 John Goodlad was demanding a complete redesign of teacher education based on the results of a comprehensive study of the conditions and circumstance involved in educating educators in the United States (p. 2). His conclusions were:

- There was a 'debilitating lack of prestige in the teacher education enterprise';
- teacher education programs lacked 'program coherence';
- there was a 'separation of theory and practice'; and
- teacher education programs were characterized by 'a stifling regulated conformity' (Goodlad, 1991, p. 2).

Goodlad's conclusions were not unique to the United States. Australian teacher education providers were drawing similar conclusions. Both anecdotal and empirical data indicated that a significant proportion of teaching graduates and their employers were dissatisfied with their preparation, citing among other things that new graduates arrived at schools 'unaware of how school and classroom cultures operated' and were 'unable to make connections between the theoretical courses they had completed at university and how these were turned into effective classroom practice' (Armour and Booth, 1999; Grant, 1994). Furthermore, in Australia between 1979 and 2005, 103 state and/or federal government sponsored inquiries were held into different aspects of teacher education (House of Representatives, 2007). Three recurring themes emerged from these inquiries:

- concerns about the quality of the professional experience components in teacher education programs;
- concerns about a weakness in the links between theory and practice; and
- a perceived lack of relevance and/or coherence of the theoretical components included in the programs.

A review of more recent literature shows that little has changed. Recent pressures for reform range from demands for general reform of the whole field (Darling-Hammond, 2006a, 2006b, 2010) to more specific calls to:

- reject traditional 'transmission' models of knowledge/learning (Cochran-Smith and Lytle, 2009; Cope and Kalantzis, 2009; Green, 2009);
- eliminate the 'gap' between theory and practice, thereby increasing overall 'program coherence' (Darling-Hammond, 2006a, 2006b, 2010, Cochran-Smith and Lytle, 2009; Grossman *et al.*, 2009; Reid *et al.*, 2011);
- redesign university/departmental organizational, structural, and learning 'ecologies' (Darling-Hammond, 2006a, 2006b, 2010);
- change traditional epistemological construals of 'knowledge,' 'knowing,' 'teaching,' and 'learning' (Kalantzis, 2006); and
- change the nature and purpose of assessment (Darling-Hammond, 2006b).

Hammerness' (2006) observation that, too often, university-based teacher education programs consist of a set of disconnected individual courses; separate clinical work from coursework; and lack a vision of teaching and learning, succinctly summarizes the current state of the field (p. 1).

Sadly, not much seems to have changed.

(b) Pressures for reform in literacy education

The calls for reform in the literacy education field reflect a similarly contested field of inquiry, characterized by a long history of acrimonious debate about so-called 'best pedagogies' for teaching reading, writing, and other accoutrements of literacy such as spelling and grammar (Pearson, 2004).

The strident tenor of these debates does not mean that there is a lack of consensus in the field. There is a strong consensus that high degrees of literacy are important to nurture and sustain democracy. Most agree with Giroux's assertion that democracies need to develop a vision of schooling dedicated to the cultivation of an informed, critical citizenry capable of actively participating and governing in a democratic society (Giroux, 2010, p. 1). There is also a strong consensus that in an age when human problems facing the planet are rapidly increasing, the ability to read, comprehend and critically respond to complex written texts, (both screen-based or book/paper-based) is essential. Add to this the exponential rate at which information is increasing and the need for citizens who can quickly understand and critically evaluate the truth-value of the multiple textual messages with which they are being continually bombarded, becomes even more urgent. Furthermore there is also an almost universal consensus that this outcome would be significantly enhanced if the profession had a 'scientifically derived pedagogy' for teaching literacy (Pressley and Allington, 1999).

However, any consensus around the importance of literacy as a pre-requisite for democracy dramatically dissipates when it comes to this concept of a 'scientifically derived pedagogy.' Instead we have the so-called 'Reading Wars' (Pearson, 2004), which have a long history.

The literature of the 1950s indicates that these began as 'Method A versus Method B' debates over opposing pedagogies. These debates continued through the 1970s, 1980s, and 1990s under different names such as 'code-based' versus 'meaning-based'; 'whole language' versus direct 'instruction' which in turn spawned several variant strains including 'literature-based' versus 'skills-based,' 'implicit' versus 'explicit' teaching, and 'holistic' versus 'fragmented' teaching.

Irrespective of changes in label the core conflict is fundamentally about how the human mind creates meaning from abstract symbols. On one side are those who argue that when an abstract symbol system is alphabetic readers must first 'decode' the visual display to sounds, blend these sounds together to make words, and only after this has been done can the meaning of the text be accessed. On the other side, are those who argue that meaning can be accessed directly from the visual display without first accessing sound. The pedagogical implications of choosing one side in this conflict are far reaching. Given these trends and half a century of calls for reform from leaders in both fields suggests that the answer to the 'Why' question above is: both fields need to resolve these issues to prepare teachers and students better for the future.

What Aspects of this Preparation need Reforming?

The ranges of issues identified in each field are variations of the same fundamental epistemo-logical issue, namely 'what knowledge and skills are needed for a profession and/or field and how are these best acquired?' Let's explore the concept of 'epistemological reform' in more detail.

Epistemological reform in pre-service teacher education

Epistemological reform is highly debated within pre-service teacher education. These debates range from explicit critiques of transmission models of knowledge and/or learning (Cochran-Smith and Lytle, 2009; Cope and Kalantzis, 2009) to doubts that practical knowledge is indeed teachable (Green, 2009), to calls for the introduction of mandatory philosophy of education/curriculum subjects dealing with epistemological issues (Carr, 2007) to encourage-ment to embrace principles inherent in emerging specializations such as Authentic Learning (Herrington and Herrington, 2006), Integrative Learning (Huber and Hutchings, 2004), and Coherence (Hammerness, 2006). While on the surface these debates seem to range over a multiplicity of epistemological issues, at a deeper level they are variations of long-term pressure for higher education to reject its traditional objectivist tradition of knowledge, pedagogy, and assessment, and replace it with a constructivist epistemological tradition (Birenbaum, 1996; Broadfoot, 1994; Huber and Hutchings, 2004; Lakoff and Johnson, 1999; Shepard, 2001). Table 32.1 compares and summarizes the assumptions of each tradition.

Anyone who has taught or participated in a university-based professional preparation pro-gram will acknowledge that most elements listed in the 'Objectivist' column in Table 32.1 are

Table 32.1   A comparison of constructivist and objectivist epistemological traditions

Aspect of learning culture	*Objectivist tradition*	*Constructivist tradition*
Knowledge	There is an existing body of correctly structured, true, propositional knowledge to be acquired by the learner This correct knowledge is immutable All novices come to the learning setting as blank slates The purpose of a professional course is to impart a finite amount of correct/immutable knowledge This finite amount of immutable knowledge is the basis of plans for professional action	There is a real world which exists but what this real world means is imposed by human thought There are many valid meanings for any event or concept There is no one, final, immutable, correct meaning we are striving to acquire The knowledge that a learner constructs and uses is not independent of, nor can it be separated from, the context in which it was learned There is no ultimate shared reality Reality is the outcome of constructive processes
Pedagogy	Effective teaching is the transmission of true propositional knowledge from an expert source to groups of metaphorical empty slates The best pedagogical approaches for transferring information and knowledge from expert to empty slate are teacher-centered methods of Lecture +Tutorial, supported by prescribed texts	Learning is an active, constructive process through which the learner builds an internal, personal representation of knowledge on the basis of experience This representation is constantly open to change While core knowledge can be specified and agreed upon, learners are encouraged to search for other knowledge domains, which may be relevant to any particular issue or problem
Assessment	Assessment is the universal goal/objective of instruction An exam (or other standardized assessment) task best measures progress toward this goal The combined data from assessment indicate the relative effectiveness of the system Two major purposes of assessment are: i. To grade students along a 100-point scale, ii. Encourage and maintain a competitive approach to learning and study.	The goal is to assess each student's ability to use knowledge in authentic tasks. This means it is the thinking processes, which are assessed and evaluated These include: i. Instrumentality: the degree to which the learner's constructed knowledge permits him/her to function effectively in the field. ii. Justification behavior: the degree to which the student can explain justify and, if necessary, defend decisions.

entrenched in the culture of most higher education institutions. Advocates of constructivism argue that universities:

> are perpetuating a tradition of formal university teaching that has ignored the substantial insights gained from more recent history and research into the way people learn. Typically, university education has been a place to learn theoretical knowledge devoid of context. Essentially for students, this has meant that teachers transmit facts and skills that they are required to regurgitate in exams. Textbooks and lecture notes are the main resources for study, with the practice of 'cramming' for exams a common learning strategy. Retention and transfer of knowledge was assumed but rarely assessed (Herrington and Herrington, 2006, p. 2).

This entrenched culture pervades the whole fabric of most higher education institutions, from the architectural design of university lecture theaters where students face a podium from which the 'expert' transmits knowledge, to the staffing and funding formula based on the number of staff needed to deliver lectures, to the mandatory course/subject outlines that shows that the dominant pedagogy is the weekly mass lecture. Each of these exemplars clearly reflects (and demands) a 'transmission-of-information' (i.e., objectivist) pedagogy.

Another defining characteristic of an objectivist epistemological tradition is the 'Theory-Into-Practice' (T-I-P) directional flow of the learning. In this mode of delivery students are first exposed to the educational theories of others through pre-planned mass lectures, smaller tutorial classes, and the study of prescribed texts. Only after the theories have been introduced do T-I-P programs provide opportunities for students to witness and experience these theories in-action during fieldwork and/or practicum experiences. The discourse associated with T-I-P modes of delivery emphasizes that theory is dominant, and the ultimate outcome is to make links between theory and practice. Inherent in the T-I-P mode of delivery is the perceived need for standardized assessment tasks and/or examinations.

Therefore, the epistemological differences between the entrenched objectivist culture and the constructivist paradigm are so profound that the prospect of implementing the principles of constructivism in a setting which has been designed, built, resourced, and staffed on the basis of an entrenched objectivist epistemology seems both daunting and problematic.

Epistemological reform in literacy education

Epistemological reform is the most highly debated issue within literacy education. The long-standing failure of literacy educators to develop a consensus around the epistemological question 'What knowledge and skills are needed for this profession and/or field and how are these best acquired?' lies at the core of the 'Reading Wars.' After more than 100 years of experimental research and theorizing in the field literacy education should have moved beyond the theoretical squabbling that still pervades it. In other domains new theories evolve and converge toward a single set of derivative, explanatory principles. Theories, which lack either internal and/or external validity, are eliminated from serious consideration in the process. Why has this not happened in literacy education? Such a state of affairs suggests something has hampered literacy education's evolution as a legitimate knowledge domain subject to scientific experimentation. Recent research (Flippo, 2010) indicates this 'something' can be linked to the profession's failure to agree on operational definitions for two key concepts in the field 'effective literate behavior' and 'effective learning behavior.' These are epistemological decisions, which ensure that everyone in the field has similar understandings about how the phenomenon being studied is actually manifested in the world. For example:

> Is effective reading behavior the ability to match and errorlessly reproduce (i.e., pronounce) every word on the page, or is it the ability to match the meanings, which the author of the text intended perhaps using different words (e.g., substituting 'dad' for 'father')?

> Is 'effective learning' the transfer of linear sequences carefully graded and reinforced sub-skills and facts from teacher to learner until mastery is achieved? Or is it the 'knowledge' that learners are continually constructing, deconstructing, and reconstructing through collaborative problem solving and dialogue with others?

Without consensual agreement on how they are operationally defined, the terms effective reading and effective learning mean different things to different literacy educators. Researchers with such different views collect quite different data and conduct research involving different clusters of dependent and independent variables. Without agreement on definitions of such key concepts researchers are forced to use the same general conceptual terms (and their cognates) to describe and measure quite distinctly different things. Thus 'effective reading' can mean 'the ability to sound out and accurately pronounce nonsense words' in some studies and 'comprehension of what the author intended after silent reading' in others. These are epistemological issues, which should have been resolved long ago. Until the profession develops some consensus around these operational definitions the field will continue to be perceived as internally dysfunctional, epistemologically immature, and scientifically naïve.

Given these unresolved epistemological issues in the literacy education field, one wonders if it's possible to design and embed an individual subject (e.g., Literacy 101; see below) that acknowledges the 'disputed status' of knowledge and skills needed to teach and assess literacy effectively, within a broader institutional framework based on a constructivist epistemology. This exploration of 'epistemological reform' in the fields of pre-service education and literacy education raises two questions:

> Is it possible to implement the principles of constructivism into a setting, which has been designed, built, resourced, and staffed on the basis of an entrenched objectivist epistemology?

> Is it possible to embed an individual method-type subject (e.g., 'Literacy 101'), which acknowledges the 'disputed status' of an evidence-based pedagogy in the field within a broader constructivist framework?

While we believe the short answer to each question is 'Yes,' we also realize that there are three 'levels' of implementation.

1 Full faculty-wide implementation: This option is only possible in 'new' institutions and or 'new' faculties. In Australia these have typically been medical faculties who can afford to appoint staff and purchase resources two years before students actually enroll.
2 Full implementation for a sub-group within the faculty: This option involves creating an organizational infrastructure that allows a sub-group of students to trial 'radically different organizational structures and conceptual processes' without major disruption to the extant program.
3 Partial implementation through minor changes to assessment and pedagogy: This option involves 'nibbling' around the edges of the entrenched epistemological traditions and 'tweaking' assessment practices and/or tutorial activities.

Wollongong opted for the second option. In what follows we will draw on this experience to inform others contemplating paradigmatic reform.

How Can Such Reforms Be Implemented?

Wollongong opted for option (2) to address the issue of 'implementing the principles of a constructivist epistemology into a setting that has been designed, built, resourced, and staffed on the basis of an entrenched objectivist epistemology without major disruption to the extant program.' This necessitated the creation of new organizational and conceptual infrastructures. Figure 32.1 provides a visual summary of the organizational infrastructure Wollongong created to support the reforms it wanted to trial. It depicts how the Reform Program group, which comprised approximately 10 percent of the total yearly cohort, was embedded within the faculty and operated in parallel with the other 90 percent of 'mainstream' (i.e., Traditional Program) students. Embedding the sub-group within the faculty in this way made it possible

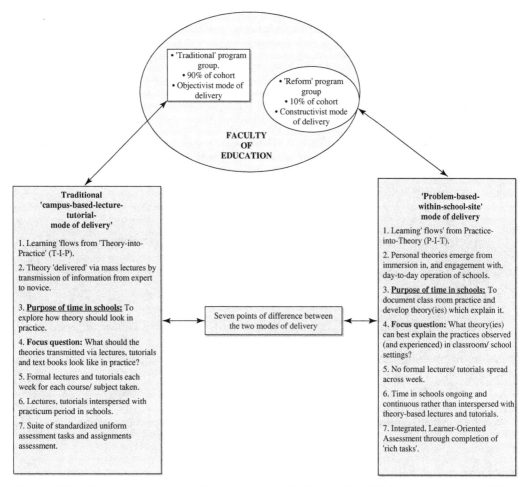

Figure 32.1 Visual summary of simultaneous modes of delivery within Wollongong's Faculty of Education 1997–2006

for them to enroll in the same subjects as their peers and work towards achieving the same outcomes for each of these subjects.

Figure 32.1 summarizes the seven major points of pedagogical difference between each epistemological tradition.

The mean size of this subgroup typically fluctuated between 24–28 students (10 percent of the total yearly intake). This group was organized into smaller cohesive 'research teams' of three to five for the purpose of 'advancing their own collective intellectual growth through sustained, collaborative investigations' (Hewitt *et al.*, 1995). The core feature of this mode of program delivery was 'problem-based-learning-within-a-school-site' and these students did not attend pre-planned lectures or tutorials. Instead each research team of 3–4 students 'lived in schools' for two days per week vacillating between two roles. These two roles included Associate Teacher and Novice Anthropologist. As an Associate teacher the pre-service teachers supported the classroom teachers in the ebb and flow of school and classroom life. In the role of the novice anthropologist the students were using the techniques of scientific anthropology to develop grounded theories of how classrooms and schools 'operated.'

When not in schools (i.e., the other three days per week) these students met in a dedicated campus-based 'Home Room' as members of a Knowledge Building Community (KBC) during which the processes of collaborative or 'Community Learning' (CL) were applied. As members of the KBC they were expected to construct grounded theories of what they witnessed and experienced in schools. The assessment tasks that the students were undertaking were carefully designed to ensure that, in developing these grounded theories, the students were forced to demonstrate deep understanding of the concepts and theories in textbooks and/or papers prescribed and recommended in the course outlines. The Home Room sessions were a continual process of 'making and remaking sense of' both the anthropological data and the information in the prescribed readings through processes of collegial analysis, discussion, debate, and textual interrogation. The KBC Home Room sessions were supported by lecturers skilled in the techniques of problem-based learning (in this case the authors). This organizational infrastructure supported the development of a professional learning culture, which reflected a constructivist epistemology.

Details of the Conceptual Infrastructure Wollongong Created

Research into the development of professional learning cultures identifies four variables that shape them.

1 A theory of cognition, which guides and frames how professional knowledge is developed and used.
2 A set of teaching-learning (i.e., 'pedagogical') structures congruent with this theory of cognition.
3 A set of cognitive processing behaviors to be used in these pedagogical structures.
4 A professionally empowering 'credo' that identifies (and continually reinforces) the desired professional attributes of those who engage in these structures and processes (Flick, 2011; Turbill, 1994).

Figure 32.2 is a visual representation of how Wollongong integrated these four variables into the day-to-day running of the Reform Group's program. It should be read from the centre out.

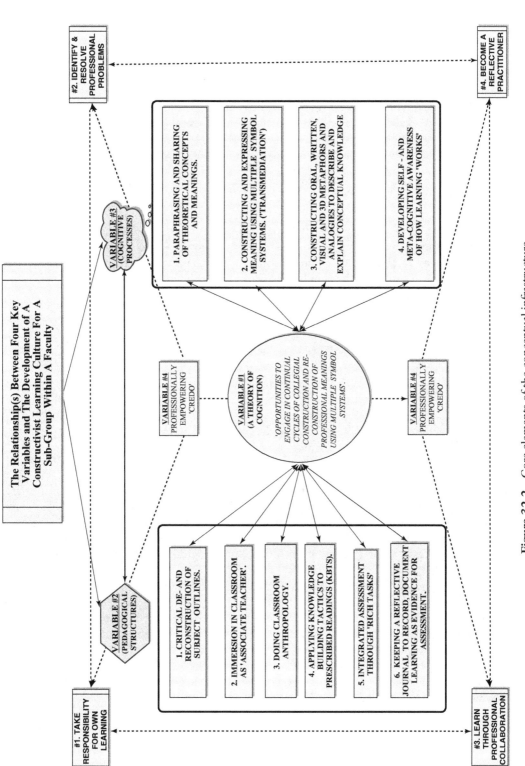

Figure 32.2 Core elements of the conceptual infrastructure

'Unpacking' Figure 32.2

Variable number 1: A theory of cognition At the centre of Figure 32.2 is 'Conceptual Blending Theory' (Fauconnier and Turner, 2002). The three core tenets of this theory are summarized thus:

> The organised 'body' or 'pool' of cognitive knowledge that enables humans to think, solve problems and make sense of their world is the sum of all the meanings they've constructed using symbols. These symbols are 'stored' as integrated 'networks' of connected meanings, which can be encoded using different symbol systems. Humans continually add to, extend, and modify (i.e., 'reorganise') these networks of meaning (i.e., 'knowledge') by engaging in continual cycles of both individual (i.e., 'reflective') and collaborative (i.e., 'collegial') meaning-construction activities using a wide range of symbol systems.

In the context of developing specialist professional knowledge this means implementing a pedagogy, which provides multiple 'opportunities to engage in continual cycles of collegial construction and reconstruction of professional meanings using multiple symbol systems.' In our context this meant providing multiple opportunities for students to construct, share, and compare professional meanings by talking, listening, reading, writing, drawing, constructing models, dramatic performance, etc.

Variables 2 and 3: Pedagogical structures and cognitive processes In Figure 32.2 the principles of conceptual blending theory 'flow outwards' to shape the next two variables, 'pedagogical structures' and 'cognitive processes.' 'Pedagogical structures' are regularly occurring, predetermined 'events' or 'settings,' which encourage students to engage in continual cycles of knowledge-building and problem-solving behaviors. Six pedagogical structures, which were created to support this version of authentic learning are listed in the left hand rectangle.

'Cognitive processes' refers to the range of meaning-making processes that learners are encouraged to use and apply to construct meanings while engaged in the predetermined patterns of behavior associated with each pedagogical structure. These processes are by-products of such behaviors and can include talking, listening, reading, writing, drawing, and performing. Talking, listening, reading, and writing use the oral and/or written language symbol systems. Drawing involves all forms of artistic representation, while performing can include forms of dance, mime, music, and dramatic performance. Four cognitive processes that students were encouraged to apply while engaged in each of the pedagogical structures are listed in the right hand rectangle.

The double-headed arrows linking these three variables represent the theory-practice nexus between them. They also indicate the potential for using all (or any mix of) the four cognitive processes while engaged in any one of the pedagogical structures. For example when engaged in Pedagogical structure 1 ('Critical de- and reconstruction of subject outcomes') students could begin by using Cognitive process 1 ('Paraphrasing and sharing of theoretical concepts and meaning'), and then at other times use any one (or all) of 2, 3, or 4 as they continually 'shaped and tightened' their interpretations of what the mandatory outcomes of each subject in which they were enrolled 'meant.'

Variable number 4: Professionally empowering 'credo' Figure 32.2 shows that Variables 1, 2, and 3 are bounded by four 'statements-of-belief,' which summarize the literature on desired professional characteristics that teachers need to succeed in modern school systems. This credo was clearly displayed in the Home Room, and frequently referred to especially when these behaviors were demonstrated (or ignored) by members of the group. It was not uncommon that this was publicly recognized, discussed, and on some occasions used to 'tweak' final grades.

Embedding Literacy 101 within this Organizational and Conceptual Infrastructure

In this section we address the issue of delivering an individual method-type subject within the organizational and conceptual frameworks depicted in Figures 32.1 and 32.2.

EDUL101: Language and Literacy was one of two mandatory method subjects designed to prepare Wollongong's pre-service teacher education students to teach literacy. In the Faculty Handbook it was described as a 6 credit point subject, requiring 3 contact hours per week, with 2 prescribed textbooks which students were expected to read, know, and understand. The subject outline stated 2 broad aims:

1   Examine theoretical foundations and develop practical strategies for the teaching of reading.
2   Explore the knowledge and strategies readers use to make meaning from both literary and factual texts.

It concluded with the following broad outcome: 'Students will become familiar with the developmental patterns of emergent, beginning and fluent readers and the respective teaching and assessment strategies.'

Embedding this individual subject within the broader organizational and conceptual frameworks described in Figures 32.1 and 32.2 was complicated by an ethical dilemma. The EDUL101 outline contained no hint or acknowledgement of the 'disputed status' of an 'evidence-based pedagogy' raging in the literature. Rather it assumed that 'theoretical foundations,' 'practical strategies for teaching reading,' and 'developmental patterns of emergent, beginning and fluent readers and the respective teaching and assessment strategies' were established and undisputed 'truths' ready for students to learn. This absence of any reference to the 'disputed status' of an appropriate 'evidence-based pedagogy' in EDUL101 was a potential source of confusion for naïve 'underprepared' professionals especially as they engaged in intensive field work in a range of different schools where they would witness the 'disputed status' of reading pedagogy in action. Prolonged exposure to such a plethora of different, often conflicting 'models' of 'appropriate pedagogy' during a four-year program increases the potential for professionally confused graduates.

The ethical challenge Wollongong had to address was: how to honor the content and intent of EDUL101 while simultaneously acknowledging the disputed status of theories and pedagogies raging in the field without compromising the final assessments of the Reform Group's students, or creating professional confusion.

How Wollongong Met This Challenge

It is important to understand that being freed of compulsory attendance at lectures and tutorials meant that the Reform Program sub-group could spend extended periods of time in either their Home Room or their assigned schools engaged in continual cycles of both individual (i.e., 'reflective') and collaborative (i.e., 'collegial') meaning-construction activities, using a range of symbol systems, guided by lecturers with expertise in facilitating these processes (i.e., the authors).

In the first week of semester a significant amount of dedicated Home Room time was devoted to addressing the following three questions *ad seriatim*:

1 What are we expected to 'learn' in EDUL101?
2 How can we 'learn' what is expected in 13 weeks?
3 How can we 'prove' we have learned what is expected?

Our intention was for the responses to each question to 'feed forward' and influence responses to the next question, using this process to introduce students to the pedagogical structures and cognitive processes depicted in Figure 32.2. Responses to these three questions were also used to provide an 'organizational map' for guiding the EDUL101 'learning journey' that this group of students had to complete in 13 weeks. Here's what this 'looked like' in practice.

What are we expected to learn in EDUL101?

Students began by constructing individual paraphrases of the subject outline and the list of its outcomes. These were then shared and discussed in random groups of three to five students. Students were then introduced to the concepts of 'reflection' and 'reflective journal' and invited to reflect on how 'paraphrasing' and 'sharing' influenced their interpretation of the information in the document. These responses were again shared and discussed.

Teams of three to five students were then formed and given the task of designing a group poster, which represented a summary of the group's interpretation of what they believed they had to learn. They were urged to consider the creative use of other symbol systems (art, graphic organizers, collage, etc) to design these posters. On completion these were prominently displayed in the Home Room and groups were invited to 'share and compare.' These posters were considered works-in-progress and over the next weeks were revisited and modified as new insights and information became available.

During the first week this ongoing cycle of revisiting, evaluating, and perhaps modifying both the content and design of these posters, together with documenting and reflecting on the process, ensured that students developed substantive understandings of what they were expected to learn in EDUL101. They were also learning how to apply all four cognitive processes shown in Figure 32.2 to pedagogical structures 1 ('de-and reconstructing subject outlines') through to 6 ('keeping a reflective journal')

How can we learn what's expected in 13 weeks?

Once substantive understanding of what was expected in EDUL101 was evident, this second question was posed. A prerequisite for addressing this second question is having a shared understanding of the nature and purpose of the four pedagogical structures available to support the knowledge-building task, shown in Figure 32.2:

• Immersion in classrooms as associate teachers;
• Classroom anthropology;
• Applying knowledge building tactics to prescribed readings; and
• Integrated assessment through rich tasks.

This shared understanding was achieved through input in the form of 'mini-lectures' and follow-up collegial discussions on how these pedagogical structures could be used to 'Learn what is expected in EDUL101.' When some degree of shared understanding of how all six pedagogical structures shown in Figure 32.2 could be used to support knowledge building was established, the 'How can we learn what's expected in 13 weeks?' question was split into two sub-questions. The first question directed students to ask 'how and why is reading taught at our "practice" school? The second question posed asked the students to investigate 'what theory (or theories) in the prescribed texts best explained "how" and "why" reading was taught in our "practice" school?' Once these questions were posed students could envisage and plan how, as Associate Teachers, they could interview teachers, study school documents and employ the tools of anthropology to answer the first sub-question. They also began to explore how they could apply the knowledge building tactics, which had been previously discussed, to develop deep understanding of the theoretical content in the prescribed texts.

Typically this stage of awareness was achieved by the end of week two of the semester, thus leaving 11 weeks of Home Room and school-based learning to collect data, collegially share, discuss, analyze, and shape these data in ways that addressed the third question.

How can we 'prove' we've learned what's expected?

Figure 32.2 indicates that the obvious answer to this question is by successful completion of a 'Rich Task' (pedagogical structure 5). In our context Rich Tasks were activities, which forced students to acquire, practice, and use a wide range of knowledge, skills and understandings and apply them to the solution of a real-world, authentic problem. The end product had to be something tangible that could be used to make judgments about the degree of learning that had occurred. This product was accompanied by a two to three page document, which presented evidence of achieving each of the subject outcomes listed on their group posters. Sometimes students were invited to develop and negotiate Rich Tasks based on problems or issues encountered at their school-based learning sites. On other occasions lecturer(s) coordinating the program set the Rich Tasks.

Did this way of implementing EDUL101 'work'?

Ten years of data clearly showed that, unlike their mainstream peers, these students quickly became aware of the unspoken and implicit 'disputed status' of literacy pedagogy. They also developed their own grounded theories of effective literacy pedagogy that they could justify and defend. This in turn helped them to deal with the different approaches they encountered in different schools without compromising their own values. Furthermore, the collaborative de- and reconstruction of EDUL101's outcomes made them fully cognizant of what they needed to do in order to be awarded a high grade for the subject. Finally they learned how to apply the 'four pillars' of the professional learning credo (See Figure 32.2) to the multiplicity of issues that their professional futures would present.

Concluding remarks

This chapter describes one university's attempt to reform how pre-service teachers were prepared to teach literacy. It describes how the University of Wollongong applied a constructivist 'Practice-Into-Theory' (P-I-T) approach to knowledge building, which created a professional learning culture that was significantly different from the traditional culture of university teaching and learning. In this culture students engaged in continual cycles of collegial construction and reconstruction of professional meanings using multiple symbol systems. These multiple opportunities to construct, share, and compare professional meanings through talking, listening, reading, writing, drawing, constructing 3D-models, or engaging in dramatic performance meant that students were continually de- and reconstructing professional knowledge, storing it as semantic networks of professional meaning, which were continually extended, modified, and 'reformed' (Fauconnier and Turner 2002).

It needs to be remembered that this experiment was a trial involving only 10 percent of the total student intake. Whether the reforms described could be applied across a whole faculty is problematic in the current climate. Notwithstanding this, we learned a great deal about improving the teaching learning culture of our program from this trial. We hope others find what we did as useful.

References

Armour, L., and Booth, E. (1999) Analysis of a questionnaire to primary educators at schools accepting students for the six week extended practicum. Report for the Faculty of Education, The University of Wollongong, Australia.

Birenbaum, M. (1996) Assessment 2000. In M. Birenbaum and F. Dochy (eds) *Alternatives in Assessment of Achievement, Learning Processes and Prior Knowledge*. Norwell MA: Kluwer, pp. 3–30.

Broadfoot, P.M. (1994) The myth of measurement. Inaugural Address, the University of Bristol.

Cambourne, B.L., Ferry, B., and Kiggins, J. (2003) The knowledge building community odyssey: Reflections on the journey. *Change: Transformations In Education*, 6(2): 57–66.

Carr, D. (2007) Knowledge, mind and the curriculum. *Educational Philosophy and Theory*, 16(1): 12–22.

Cochran-Smith, M., and Lytle, S. (2009) *Inquiry as Stance: Practitioner Research for the Next Generation*. New York. Teachers College Press.

Cope, B., and Kalantzis, M. (2009) Multiliteracies: New literacies, new learning. *Pedagogies: An International Journal*, 4: 164–195.

Darling-Hammond, L. (2006a) Assessing teacher education: The usefulness of multiple measures for assessing program outcomes. *Journal of Teacher Education*, 57(2): 120–138.

Darling-Hammond, L. (2006b) Constructing 21st century teacher education. *Journal of Teacher Education*, 57(3): 300–314.

Darling-Hammond, L. (2010) Teacher education and the American future. *Journal of Teacher Education*, 61(1–2): 35–47.

Fauconnier, G., and Turner. M. (2002) *The Way We Think: Conceptual Blending and the Mind's Hidden Complexities*. New York: Basic Books.

Flick, E. (2011) A responsive evaluation of a NSW disadvantaged school's professional learning program. Unpublished honors thesis, University of Wollongong, NSW Australia.

Flippo, R. (2010) *Reading researchers in search of common ground: The expert study revisited*, 2nd edn. New York: Routledge.

Giroux, H.A. (2010) Lessons to be learned from Paulo Freire as education is being taken over by the mega rich viewpoint, accessed November 22, 2012: www.viewpointonline.net/lessons-to-be-learned-from-paulo-freire-as-education-is-being-taken-over-by-the-mega-rich-henry-a-giroux.html

Goodlad, J. (1991) Why we need a complete redesign of teacher education. *Educational Leadership*, 49(3): 4–6.

Grant, L.M. (1994) An evaluation of the effectiveness of preservice language education in one university. Unpublished honors thesis, Faculty of Education, University of Wollongong, NSW. Australia.

Green, B. (2009) *Understanding and researching professional practice*. Rotterdam: Sense Publishers.

Grossman, P., Compton, C., Shahan, E., *et al.* (2009) Teaching practice across professional perspective. *Teachers College Record*, 111(9): 2055–2100

Hammerness, K. (2006) From coherence in theory to coherence in practice. *Teachers College Record*, 108(7): 1241–1265

Herrington, A., and Herrington, J. (2006) *Authentic Learning Environments in Higher Education*. Melbourne: Information Science Publishing.

Hewitt, J., Brett, C., Scardamalia, M., *et al.* (1995) Schools for thought: Transforming classrooms into learning communities. Paper Presented at the American Educational Research Association Annual Conference. San Francisco.

House of Representatives Standing Committee on Education and Vocational Training (2007) *Top of the class: Report on the inquiry into teacher education*. Canberra: Commonwealth of Australia.

Howey, K., and Zimpher, N. (1989) *Profiles of Preservice Teacher Education*. Albany: SUNY Press.

Huber, M.T., and Hutchings, P. (2004) *Integrative Learning: Mapping the Terrain*. Washington, DC: Association of American Colleges and Universities.

Kalantzis, M. (2006) Changing subjectivities, New learning. *Pedagogies: An International Journal*, 1(1): 7–12

Korthagen, F.A., and Kessels, J.P. (1999) Linking theory and practice: Changing the pedagogy of teacher education. *Educational Researcher*, 28(4): 4–17.

Lakoff, G., and Johnson, M. (1999) *Philosophy in the Flesh: The Embodied Mind and its Challenge to Western Thought*. New York: Basic Books.

Pearson, P.D. (2004) The Reading Wars. *Educational Policy*, 18: 216–252.

Pressley, M., and Allington, R. (1999) What should reading instructional research be research of? *Issues in Education*, 5(1): 1–35.

Reid, J., Singh, S., Santoro, N., and Mayer, D. (2011) What does good teacher education research look like? *Asia-Pacific Journal of Teacher Education*, 39(3): 177–182.

Shepard, L.A. (2001) The role of classroom assessment in teaching and learning. In V. Richardson (ed.) *Handbook of Research on Teaching*. Washington, DC: American Educational Research Association, pp. 1066–1101

Turbill, J. (1994) From a personal theory to a grounded theory of staff development. Unpublished doctoral thesis, University of Wollongong, Wollongong.

Chapter 33

Teachers' Literate Identities

Toni Gennrich and Hilary Janks

Introduction

Imagine a teacher who is used to reading and explaining from the front of the class. She is in charge of the content, pacing and sequencing of the lesson and she directs the amount and nature of students' participation. Two-thirds of all talk is teacher-talk. After ten years of teaching in this way, she is required to change to a learner-centered approach as a result of new policies.

Now consider a different teacher who has based his career on his passion for literature and his ability to enable his students to appreciate the aesthetic in both reading and writing. After ten years of teaching, he is confronted by learners who think all of this is out of touch with the on-screen literacies that they value.

These vignettes are based on real teachers we have encountered in our research and in our involvement with teacher education. This chapter addresses the ways in which changes in the field impact on teachers' embodied literate identities and the implications this has for teacher education.

The work of Pierre Bourdieu will provide the theory that frames the discussion on embodied identity and the possibilities for change. This will be followed by a discussion of literacy underpinned by Freebody and Luke's (1990) work on the four roles of the reader, which we will expand to include the roles of the writer and the roles of both the consumers and producers of digital texts. In combination, these theories work to underpin our notion of 'literate identities.'

This theoretical framework will be used to ground the discussion that follows organized around key questions in the literature pertaining to identities and practices of teachers of literacy. They include:

- Do teachers need to be models of reading and writing?
- What do literacy teachers read and write? What should they read and write?
- How does curriculum impact on teacher identity?

International Handbook of Research on Children's Literacy, Learning, and Culture, First Edition.
Edited by Kathy Hall, Teresa Cremin, Barbara Comber, and Luis C. Moll.
© 2013 John Wiley & Sons, Ltd. Published 2013 by John Wiley & Sons, Ltd.

- What digital practices do literacy teachers engage in and should they engage with these practices?
- How should literacy be taught to students who come to class with diverse funds of knowledge?

Finally, we will consider the implications for teacher training looking particularly at a course to which we contribute at the University of the Witwatersrand, and how it attempts to address the literate identities of future teachers.

Theoretical Framework

Embodied identity and Bourdieu's theory of habitus

Bourdieu's notion of habitus helps to explain how deeply ingrained and unconscious our dispositions are and how this impacts on our perceptions, appreciations and practices (1990, p. 53). Bourdieu explains how habitus is rooted in our early family life (Burroway, 2010) and how it is structured by our past and present circumstances. Operating below the level of consciousness, habitus then structures our actions and our dispositions, including our involvement with and dispositions towards literacy. It is a 'structured and structuring structure' (Bourdieu, 1994, p. 170) that is immensely durable.

For Bourdieu there is a close interlocking of the concepts: habitus, capital and field which result in a particular practice. So one's practice results from 'the relations between one's dispositions (habitus) and one's position in a field (capital), within the current state of play of that social arena (field)' (Maton, 2008, p. 51). It is the *relationship* between these four – practices, habitus, capital and field – that is important.

In attempting to understand how teachers' literate habituses affect their practice, we begin by looking at how their dispositions to literacy are embodied and how this impacts on their teaching. Consider the ways in which teacher-directed lessons, as described in our first vignette, and student-centered lessons require teachers to use their bodies differently. This includes differences in where they stand; whether they stand or sit; whether and how they move; whether they speak or listen; who they speak or listen to; how much they speak; when they speak; where they look and what they look at, as well as how they use their bodies to establish their authority and manage the class. The change in practice requires the teacher to take on a differently embodied teacher identity.

The change in embodiment is different for the teacher in the second vignette. What he was able to take for granted in how he modeled literacy for his students is destabilized. In order to include digital literacy in his teaching repertoire he has to sit or stand at a screen; use his eyes differently to scroll and to manage multiple on-screen texts simultaneously; type rather than write, which requires a different kind of physical and tactile experience; and present information using a range of modes rather than relying primarily on his voice.

Disrupting habitus is extremely difficult but not impossible. It can be interrupted by encounters with other fields, or by changes within the field itself. What this may do is create the desire or need to change. Wanting to change is a necessary but not sufficient condition for shifting habitus, as Janks (2010), using the Alexander Technique as a metaphor, explains. She suggests that change is only achieved by conscious effort and practice together with the ability to recognize and inhibit old ways of being. Burroway (2010) suggests that it is the clash between a durable habitus and a field which creates the possibility of societal change. This chapter will show how the different circumstances of changing curricula and changing literacy demands in a new communication landscape produce a disruption of teachers' 'pedagogic habitus' (Grenfell, 1996). Such disruption may be embraced or resisted.

Despite the durability of habitus, it is also generative and transposable (Bourdieu, 1991, p. 13). The field or the context in which we find ourselves structures our habitus. According to Thomson (2008), practices in the field structure the habitus of individuals working in that field and they, in turn, structure the field. These fields can be particular classrooms, schools, education systems, philosophical standpoints, or even curricula. The field and the individual become mutually constitutive. Habitus is also transposable to other fields and other individuals. Teachers may unconsciously reproduce their habitus in the students they teach.

What do teachers value as symbolic and cultural capital in relation to literacy and how does this influence their literacy and pedagogic practices? Bourdieu distinguishes between three types of cultural capital: embodied, objectified, and institutionalized (2006). Embodied is what is found within people, in their minds and bodies: their talents and competencies. Objectified is material evidence of capital such as cultural artifacts and cultural goods such as literary texts. Finally, institutional cultural capital is what is regarded as important to give one status such as educational qualifications (Bourdieu, 1986). In economic terms all these forms of capital carry value and allow one to control one's own future and that of others.

The notion of distinction is a useful concept with which to make sense of teachers' differing literacy practices. *Distinction*, Bourdieu's (1984) 'social critique of the judgement of taste' shows how the construction of taste is linked to both status and power. Distinction is reinforced by society and is inflicted on those who do not have the dominant cultural resources by those who do. Dominant classes give value to certain types of literature and reading materials and subvert those of others. The reality is that certain literacy practices, pedagogies, and texts are constructed as more prestigious than others, thus giving them greater value in relation to cultural capital.

Literacy and the four roles of the reader: Freebody and Luke (1990)

We link Bourdieu's theory of habitus to Freebody and Luke's (1990) *Four Roles of the Reader* to explain teachers' literate identities. Their framework incorporates different theories of literacy as well as sets out what it means to be literate in each of the four roles: decoder, participant, user, and analyst. To be literate requires the use of all four roles in producing and consuming texts whether in print or online.

The role of the reader as a *decoder* is based on phonic, phonemic, and whole word approaches to literacy, supported by theory that sees reading as a cognitive process that links abstract symbols to semantics (Hill, 1999; Snow and Juel, 2008; Wolf, 2007). Writing using this role involves using the correct conventions of spelling, grammar, punctuation, paragraphing and sentence structure. The ability to decode text has become more complex since texts have become increasingly multimodal (Kress and van Leeuwen, 1990) and web-based (Coiro, 2003; Sutherland-Smith, 2002). On screens the decoder would need to be able to use signs and icons and know how to format a document or slide.

In the role of the *participant*, readers have to know how to interact with a text; how to take and bring meaning to it. They have to be active readers who can relate previously acquired knowledge to the ideas in the text in order to engage with them critically. This role relies on cognition – prediction, comprehension, inference, reflection, and analysis. It is also based on socio-cultural theory that understands reading as a social practice in which meaning is tied to the events in which reading occurs (Barton, Hamilton, and Ivanic, 2000). It is in the creation of texts (in print or online) that heightens one's awareness that particular text types are matched to different purposes.

The role of participant is linked to the role of text *user* because it is easier to be a participant if one understands the social uses of different kinds of texts. As text users, readers engage with a wide range of different kinds of texts and understand the relationship between the content, form, and social function of a text. They know the difference between transactional texts (Britton *et al.*, 1975), what Rosenblatt (1986) calls efferent texts, and aesthetic or literary texts. The role of text user opens up questions of how much use and how many text types qualify one as a literate user.

In these three roles the focus is on the ability to make sense of the text in context. As a *text analyst*, however, one has to go beyond that to consider its social effects. Analysts pay attention to how texts position readers and consider whose interests are served by this positioning. They recognize that texts are instantiations of discourses that shape our identities, our society, our beliefs, and our values. Analysts explain how power works in and through texts (Comber, 2001; Luke, 1995; Vasquez, 2004) and they imagine how they might be redesigned to produce a more equitable society.

Freebody and Luke (1990) enable us to create a picture of what being literate entails. This does not mean that all readers can be expected to be equally literate in all domains (e.g., home, school, and work) and all fields (e.g., education and medicine). Nevertheless, these theorists provide us with a sense of the different roles that literacy teachers and their students should inhabit so that the appropriate skills, dispositions, and practices become part of their durable habitus as literate subjects.

Do Teachers Need to be Models of Reading and Writing?

The literature views teachers' engagement in the role of *users* and *participants* as essential because it allows them to model the value and enjoyment of leading 'a literate life' (Kaufman, 2002). However, there is very little discussion on the need for teachers to be text-analysts. By sharing what they have read and written with their learners teachers embody a disposition to literacy that gives the kind of message that is more powerful than 'the conscious transmission of subject matter' (Kaufman, 2002, p. 51). Teachers' enthusiasm for reading and writing and the pleasure they take in it is believed to motivate students (Arici, 2009; Commeyras *et al.*, 2003; Davis, 1995; Kaufman, 2002; Ngugi, 2009; Sanacore, 2002). Equally, teachers who lack this passion are seen to affect their learners negatively (Applegate and Applegate, 2004; Draper *et al.*, 2000).

In addition to modeling engagement, teachers who lead literate lives are able to share their own reading and writing with students (Bisplinghoff, 2002; Burns and Myhill, 2004; Kaufman, 2002); provide rich literacy environments in the fields of their classrooms (Morrow *et al.*, 1990); and have the kind of insight gained from their own experience of mastering the literacy skills to inform their pedagogies (Calkins, 1993; Commeyras *et al.*, 2003).

Much of the literature assumes that you cannot be a teacher of reading and writing if you do not read and write yourself, despite the fact that the evidence for this claim is not conclusive. Brooks (2007) questions whether the simple link between teachers who read and write themselves and the quality of their teaching of reading and writing can be made. He believes that the hypothesis is too vague. How often do teachers need to read and write to be effective teachers of reading and writing? What, exactly do they need to read and write? Gleeson and Prain (1996) and Frager (1994) ask similar questions: What does it mean to be a writer? Is personal writing sufficient or are only published writers good enough to teach writing?

Brooks' study (2007) with 'excellent' fourth-grade teachers found that they pointed to factors other than their personal reading and writing practices that made them good teachers of reading and writing. It seems that it is teachers' belief in the value of reading and writing, their classroom strategies and their ability to give constructive feedback in a range of different genres that influences their teaching rather than their abilities as readers and writers. Gleeson and Prain (1996) also found that teachers' knowledge of writing did not necessarily increase if they wrote themselves. What does seem to make a difference in students' lives is teachers' ability to inspire them to read and write (Cremin *et al.*, 2008; Dreher, 2003).

An ongoing debate in the research literature has to do with what teachers read and what some say they *should* read. The US research suggests that neither pre-service nor in-service teachers read (Applegate and Applegate, 2004; Nathanson, Pruslow and Levitt, 2008; Sulentic-Dowell *et al.*, 2006). The work of Cremin and her colleagues in England shows that teachers do read (Cremin *et al.*, 2009) and that they read popular fiction but that their knowledge of children's literature is fairly limited. The most important books in teachers' lives are 'religious, spiritual, allegorical and exemplary books' (Cremin *et al.*, 2006–2007, p. 8). Commeyras and Inyega's (2007) literature review shows that Kenyan teachers do not read much beyond newspapers and religious texts. Commeyras and Mazile's work in Botswana (2009) shows the teachers read for information and self-enhancement. Newspapers predominate in Nigeria (Babalola, 2002). A study with trainee teachers of English in Singapore shows that the majority of students read primarily for information rather than pleasure (Cox and Schaetzel's, 2007).

The term 'aliteracy' (Powell-Brown, 2004) refers to people who can read and write but who choose not to. Alliterate teachers are clearly able to decode and comprehend texts but they tend not to be text users and so often have difficulty imagining what to do with reading and writing in their classrooms once their students are able to decode.

Gains' research (2010) with Grade 1 teachers in South Africa reveals that these teachers' prior experiences with literacy affect both how they conceptualize literacy and the ways in which they teach. Teachers' own literacies are related to the fields in which they have grown up as well as those in which they teach. It is these fields that structure their dispositions to literacy. Those teachers who do not themselves engage in the *practices* that require the skills needed for the reading and writing of extended text remain unsure as to the world of possibility that literacy offers and how to give their students access to this world.

One of the concerns, particularly in the early literature (Mour, 1977) and some of the more recent literature (Applegate and Applegate, 2004; Nathanson, Pruslow, and Levitt, 2008), is that teachers do not read high quality literary works, nor do they do much professional reading (Rudland and Kemp, 2004). There is also a conflict between the curriculum requirements and teachers' own reading choices. In some countries, particularly developing countries, there are fewer people who have had benefits that have allowed them to acquire literacy capital in relation to printed texts. Lack of access to reading materials in mother-tongue and few or no libraries have resulted in societies that provide more capital and power to some and less to others. This is an example of what Bourdieu refers to as 'differential access' (1990, p. 133). Furthermore, the dominance of English as a language of learning and teaching further disempowers those whose mother-tongue is not English. These factors combine and result in an 'unequal distribution of the chances of access to the means of production of the legitimate competence, and to the legitimate places of expression' (Bourdieu, 1991, p. 57). Although there are many differing literacy practices that serve the needs of literate subjects in particular domains, not all literacy practices are equally valued in the field of education and in society as a whole. Hence, what makes up a particular literate habitus may not be valued in certain domains.

Clearly there is more than one way to be a literate subject. Aesthetic reading is not the only source of pleasure. Researchers can read for information and ideas and be immensely stimulated. Engineers can enjoy *Popular Mechanics* and motorcar magazines. Students can pay careful attention to the construction of their Facebook pages and adults take pride in their tweets and in the number of their followers. As Brooks (2007, p. 189) asks, 'Are teachers who read children's literature necessarily better teachers of reading than are teachers who read John Grisham, *People* magazine, professional educational journals, or texts that their students write?'

Yet teachers are encouraged to familiarize themselves with a wide variety of children's books in order to motivate young children to become readers for pleasure (Cremin *et al.*, 2006–2007; Dreher, 2003). The literature also indicates the importance of teachers' ability to guide students to be self-directed in their reading choices. At the same time, however, teachers themselves show that they are limited in making their own reading choices, relying on friends' recommendations and the media (Cremin *et al.*, 2008; Gomez, 2005).

The debate around what teachers should read appears to ignore three aspects of teachers' work. First, it ignores the exigencies of the curriculum. Then it disregards the fact that students bring different dispositions to literacy, different 'ways with words' (Heath, 1983), and different out-of-school literacy practices into the classroom. Finally, it does not pay enough attention to the changing communication landscape enabled by new technologies.

The research literature also reports on what teachers write, together with discussion of what they should write (Frager, 1994; Gleeson and Prain, 1996, Jost, 1990; Robbins, 1992, 1996; Whitney, 2009). The findings of these researchers are similar to the findings with regard to reading. The kinds of writing that teachers do – journals, letters, emails, reports, or blogs – are not valued, so teachers do not see themselves as writers. They measure their own writing against what is recognized in the field as distinctive: published professional articles and literary work. This produces feelings of self-doubt despite the fact that the students they teach, like them, will have to learn to use writing in a range of genres for different social purposes.

What is the Relationship between the Curriculum, Policy and Teacher Identity?

In an age of increasingly prescriptive curricula combined with the pressure of standardized tests and accountability, what and how teachers teach is constrained (Cremin *et al.*, 2008). Compelled to cover the required ground, including set texts, they cannot allow themselves to be distracted by students' interests and desire to explore something in greater depth. Nor can they stop for students who need more time to understand the work. The enjoyment and satisfaction that comes from reading and writing is often sacrificed to the goals set far away from actual classrooms and students. Compliance replaces curiosity as teachers play by the 'rules of the game.' They are seldom given the space or time to question the arbitrariness of these rules, in fact these become so internalized that teachers misrecognize them as the truth. The taken-for-granted authority of the curriculum prevents players in the field from recognizing that what is valued is socially constructed. What counts as important in the field, as well as what counts as distinctive, produces, according to Bourdieu and Passeron (1977), a curriculum that favors the cultural capital of the middle class. This is fundamental to ways in which education reproduces the values and dispositions of the elite and disadvantages students who come to school with a different literate habitus. Because the cultural capital needed for schooling is naturalized and seen to be in the interests of all, middle class children are at an advantage.

The curriculum demands that particular texts are read and teachers and students are limited in choice. It focuses on uniformity and does not take into account differences of culture and taste (Moore, 2004). In addition, policies, which result in the constantly changing curricula as is the case in South Africa, complicate teachers' lives even further.

The curriculum itself is determined by overarching policy frameworks over which teachers have little control. These in turn are influenced by privileging some theoretical frameworks over others. In the field of literacy, for example, 'scientific,' quantitative, cognitive paradigms currently prevail over qualitative, social practice theories of literacy.

How Should Literacy be Taught to Students who Come to Class with Diverse Funds of Knowledge?

When children, whose 'funds of knowledge' (Moll *et al.*, 1992) are different from those valued by their schools, fail to succeed at school, they internalize this as their own failure rather than the failure of schools to be institutions where 'all children can achieve, not just children with the "right parents"' (Allington, 1994, p. 3). The structure of the field of education disguises their dispossession. Ironically, teachers play according to the 'rules' required by their field, despite the fact that neither they nor many of their students are inclined to the texts and practices privileged by the curriculum. This is a form of symbolic violence (Bourdieu and Passeron, 1977) in which teachers and students misrecognize the value inherent in their own out-of-school literacies, and overvalue those granted symbolic capital in the field.

An important historical example of the power of the field to produce identities is the formation of teachers' literate habitus in schools for African children and in African teachers' training colleges during the era of apartheid education. Colonial and apartheid practices of using literacy as a form of domestication resulted in a focus on decoding and the ability to recall information from texts in the teaching of reading. The testing of reading comprehension was limited to an ability to make sense of the text and not to question it. Using Freebody and Luke's terms, students were taught to be decoders and comprehenders. They were rarely afforded opportunities to bring their own meanings into relation with the text or to be active participants when reading. Texts were seen as authoritative and were often presented in the form of extracts. As users there were no opportunities for readers to choose what they wanted to read or write about or even to understand the overall purpose of whole texts or the ways in which purpose shapes genre. Education as a field in South Africa constituted learners as docile, unquestioning citizens.

Prinsloo's (2002) genealogical investigation of the curricula for teaching Afrikaans, English, and IsiZulu as home languages in Natal from 1960 to 1994, together with her analysis of matriculation papers, shows how in these different languages students were positioned as different kinds of human subjects. English students were constructed as global subjects; Afrikaans students were constructed in relation to their national identity and IsiZulu students were constructed as tribal subjects.

The practices in the segregated schools under apartheid helped form the early habitus of teachers giving them differential access to literacy based on race, language, and class. For African teachers, this was compounded by training, for only two years after Grade 10 in teachers' training colleges. While many of these teachers have gone on to develop themselves and to requalify, habitus continues to structure many of their practices. Using this local example, we raise the question of how habitus might be working against teacher transformation in other contexts.

What Digital Practices do Literacy Teachers Engage In and How Should They Engage with these Practices?

Perhaps literature – the pleasure of the leisured classes – is not the best preparation for students to take their place in the new knowledge economy. This economy is predicated on the democratization of the production and consumption of information made possible by the new digital technologies and the Internet.

What digital technologies have made possible is the increasing use of other modes for the making of meaning in texts. The ability to design texts with images, graphs, charts, sound, video, hyperlinks, animations, and color are all part of what it now means to be literate. Many students are more at home in this multimodal world than their teachers and may be sophisticated readers and producers of online texts. These new literacies give students a great deal of pleasure – the kind of pleasure that fosters literacy. There is now 'no distinction between playing and learning. They have been learning from playing and have been playing while learning' (Lei, 2009, p. 88). While 'reading' may have declined, students are producing texts for fun more than at any time before and their audience is the global online community. They are also reading and responding to other people's texts. Reading has become more interactive and writing has become more collaborative in fields where there is easy access to digital technologies.

Teachers have to prepare their students to make and interpret meaning using a multiplicity of modes such as visual, spoken, and written (Kress, 1997). The increasing use of digitally produced texts requires different literacies and teachers find themselves having to adapt accordingly. As a result of economic, social, and global trends (Lankshear and Knobel, 2003, in McDougall, 2010), students now need a range of literacies, digital literacy, media literacy, and information literacy among others, in order to make their way successfully in the world.

Teachers are faced with enormous challenges in this regard particularly because of the confusing and contradictory messages they are confronted with (McDougall, 2010). First, teachers are faced with two distinct discourses in relation to digital literacy and the use of technology in the classroom (Willet, 2007). The first constructs digital literacy in a negative light, focusing on the dangers to children of being in cyberspace; the impact of digital technology on thinking skills and the deterioration of language in text messaging. It seems necessary for teachers to protect their students from these risks. The second discourse is positive and positions students as digital natives (Prensky, 2001) who are at home with technology and eager to learn using new technologies. Teachers are unsure what their role is in facilitating learning with students who often know more than they do. They also have to deal with students who have differing levels of digital skills.

Not only are these discourses used in relation to students but teachers themselves are faced with mixed messages about their own use of digital media. Research shows that younger teachers' primary use of digital technology is for social networking (Lei, 2009). However, the pleasure teachers get from this is dampened by the dire warnings of the consequences of using Web 2.0 technologies (Kist, 2008). Teachers are cautioned about the consequences of having students as friends and the care that needs to be taken about what they post on their personal pages. This is enough to keep many of them away from using the technology. Yet in other instances, the possibilities opened up by social networking as a strategy for teaching and learning are encouraged (Kist, 2008; Reid, 2011). With an expanding definition of literacy that includes helping students to negotiate the digital environment and giving them the skills necessary to become users and producers of digital texts, teachers are under pressure to become differently literate themselves (McDougall, 2010).

Another challenge faced by teachers is that they come with a habitus very different from that of many of their students in relation to digital technology. As we have emphasized in this chapter, literacy and literate persons are social constructs formed within the context of dynamic fields. In these fields, agents occupy certain positions according to the cultural capital they have. Teachers now find themselves in a dynamic field in which their cultural capital in relation to digital literacy is often limited. This results in a shift in their roles. Because habitus is an embodied disposition (Bourdieu, 1991) it is difficult for teachers to change. Traditionally teachers have been recognized as authoritative and all-knowing facilitators of learning and this recognition has been tied to their self-belief. Now they find that their positions have shifted as they are often less digitally literate than those they teach. Many of them do not have the technical knowledge and skills necessary to bring digital technology into their teaching. As a result they are anxious about their use of technology (Lei, 2009); negative and skeptical (Bahr *et al.*, 2004; Eteokleous, 2008); concerned that technology will detract from basic literacy skills (Boling, 2008); and often, because of organizational constraints, restricted and traditional in the use of new technology (Eteokleous, 2008).

In fact, education is at a crossroads. Currently schools and teacher training institutions have instructors who are uncomfortable with the use of digital technology as well younger teachers who can be described as 'digital natives' who are more comfortable and positive in the way they value and use digital technology. However, studies show that pre-service teachers are neither as technologically adept nor as comfortable in the use of technology as one would expect (Cameron, 2005; Eteokleous, 2008; Lei, 2009). Teachers use the technology to prepare lessons and activities but do not actively integrate technology into their classroom strategies and pedagogy. Some teachers are positive about using technology in the classroom but are limited by the constraints of time, confidence, and accessibility (Yang and Huang, 2008). Overcoming their negative self-belief is an issue. Dealing with the constraints placed on them by the exam-based curriculum that leaves little space for innovation, is another. Although students and teachers in Africa have until recently been on the wrong side of the digital divide, cell phone penetration, combined with new bandwidth cables and reduced costs are increasing connectivity dramatically (Ledgard, 2011).

What are the Implications for Teacher Training?

If habitus is durable and resistant to change, how might teacher education intervene in the development of literacy teachers? Teachers need a deep understanding of what literacy is for and what it makes possible. As with the teaching of any subject, teachers need to know what their different students are interested in so that they can enable them to use literacy to explore and develop these interests. It *is* possible to encourage students to find their own sources of pleasure from consuming and designing texts, without expecting them to enjoy what adults enjoy. It *is* possible to support creative writers without being one oneself. Knowledge of the new communication landscape and the power of the Internet provide access to many different ways of consuming and creating texts.

The New Literacies for Teachers course to which we contribute at the University of the Witwatersrand provides an example of how teacher education might begin to address the literacy identities of future teachers. This compulsory, first year course for all Bachelor of Education students has four priorities:

1   To develop students' personal literacies, by making a wide range of light reading available to them, particularly for students who have no history of reading books for pleasure and by encouraging peer to peer recommendations in book clubs.
2   To develop students' academic literacies to enable them to succeed in higher education and to use this new domain as an example of literacy as a social practice. Students are given opportunities to develop their abilities in all four of the roles of the reader/writer and to reflect on their own practices in relation to these roles.

3 To undertake an investigation into the literacies needed for school. Different students choose to explore different disciplinary areas or different phases of education to understand the literacy demands made on the learners in schools. Students share the results of these investigations in order to pool the knowledge gained about literacy across the curriculum.
4 To develop students' digital literacies. Many students in South Africa come to university without having used a computer or the Internet. The course requires students to join a closed group tutorial Facebook page; to access information on the course Blog; to construct PowerPoint presentations; to develop wikis for key concepts in the course; to do research using the Internet and to evaluate what they find.

Overall, the course aims to extend students' literacy practices; to encourage them to use and produce texts; to understand the literacy demands of the whole curriculum, not just the subject/s they are responsible for (Draper, Barksdale-Ladd, and Radencich 2000; Fisher and Ivey, 2005) and to develop their ability to reflect on literacy and the practices associated with it. Requiring students to understand their own literacy histories combined with the development of their metacognitive awareness of literacy and its practices is based on the research that sees this as a key component for success as a teacher of literacy (Bisplinghoff, 2002; Ciuffetelli-Parker, 2010; Commeyras *et al.*, 2003; Gomez, 2005).

Habitus is difficult to change and requires constant effort and practice. So the course runs for a year and it is a sustained rather than short-term intervention to help pre-service teachers make conscious decisions about their literate practices.

Conclusion

The rapidly changing demands on peoples' ability to consume and produce texts affects what it means to be literate. This is a moment of real opportunity for teachers and learners to use literacy in more meaningful ways. The field of literacy in the world is changing faster than the field of literacy in schools and many children and young adults who are linked to the Internet are more engaged in reading and writing for their own purposes and pleasure than ever before. One's literate habitus should be constantly evolving. Our job as teachers and teacher educators is to extend our students' horizons of possibility and prowess – allowing them to outpace us as we lead/follow them into the virtual worlds of books, games, videos, and the ideas that entice them. We all need to learn how to open the doors of learning and to run alongside our students as they explore what lies beyond. In doing so, without realizing it, we will find that our own literate habitus will have been transformed along with that of our students in ways that are as yet unimaginable.

References

Allington, R.L. (1994) The schools we have, the schools we need, accessed November 22, 2012: www.albany.edu/cela/reports/allington/allingtonschools.pdf

Applegate, P., and Applegate, M. (2004) The Peter effect: Reading habits and attitudes of preservice teachers. *The Reading Teacher*, 57(6): 554–563.

Arici, A. (2009) Problems in Turkish reading education: Interviews with teachers. *Reading Improvement*, 46: 123–129.

Babalola, E. (2002) Newspapers as instruments for building literate communities: The Nigerian experience. *Nordic Journal of African Studies*, 11(3): 403–410.

Bahr, D.L., Shaha, S.H., Fransworth, B.J., *et al.* (2004) Preparing tomorrow's teachers to use technology: Attitudinal impacts of technology-supported field experience on pre-service teacher candidates. *Journal of Instructional Psychology*, 31(2): 88–97.

Barton, D., Hamilton, M., and Ivanic, R. (2000) *Situated Literacies*. London: Routledge.

Bisplinghoff, B. (2002) Under the wings of writers: A teacher reads to find her way. *The Reading Teacher*, 56(3): 242–252.

Britton, J., Burgess, T., Martin, N., *et al.* (1975) *The Development of Writing Abilities, 11–18*. Houndmills: Macmillan Education.

Boling, E.C. (2008) Learning from teachers' conceptions of technology integration; What do blogs, instant messages, and 3D chat rooms have to do with it? *Research in the Teaching of English*, 43(1): 74–100.

Bourdieu, P., and Passeron, J. (1977) *Reproduction in Education, Society and Culture*. London: Sage.

Bourdieu, P. (1984) *Distinction: A Social Critique of the Judgement of Taste*. Abingdon: Routledge.

Bourdieu, P. (1986) The forms of capital. In J.G. Richardson (ed.) *Handbook of Theory and Research for the Sociology of Education*. New York: Greenwood Press, pp. 241–258.

Bourdieu, P. (1990) *The Logic of Practice*. Stanford, CA: Stanford University Press.

Bourdieu, P. (1991) *Language and Symbolic Power*. Cambridge: Polity Press.

Bourdieu, P. (1994) *In Other Words: Essays towards a Reflexive Sociology*. Cambridge: Polity Press.

Bourdieu, P. (2006) The forms of capital. In H. Lauder, P. Brown, H.-A. Dillabough, and A.H. Halsey (eds) *Education, Globalisation and Social Change*. Oxford: Oxford University Press.

Brooks, G.W. (2007) Teachers as readers and writers and as teachers of reading and writing. *The Journal of Educational Research*, 100(3): 177–190.

Burns, C., and Myhill, D. (2004) Inactive or interactive. *Cambridge Review of Education*, 34(2): 35–49.

Burroway, M. (2010) Eight conversations with Pierre Bourdieu. Lecture series presented at the University of the Witwatersrand.

Calkins, L. (1993) The lifework of writing. *The Australian Journal of Language and Literacy*, 16(1): 32–37.

Cameron, D. (2005) The NetGeneration goes to university. Refereed paper presented at the Journalism Education Association Conference, Surfers Paradise, Queensland, Australia.

Ciuffetelli-Parker, D. (2010) Writing and becoming [a teacher]: Teacher candidates' literacy narratives over four years. *Teacher and Teacher Education*, 26: 1249–1260.

Coiro, J. (2003) Exploring literacy on the Internet: Expanding our understanding of reading comprehension to encompass new literacies. *The Reading Teacher*, 56(5): 458–464.

Comber, B. (2001) Critical literacies and local action: Teacher knowledge and the 'new' research agenda. In B. Comber and A. Simpson (eds) (2001) *Negotiating Critical Literacies in Classrooms*. Mahwah, NJ: Lawrence Erlbaum, pp. 271–282.

Commeyras, M., Bisplinghoff, B.S., and Olson, J. (eds) (2003) *Teachers as Readers: Perspectives on the Importance of Reading in Teachers' Classrooms and Lives*. Newark, DE: International Reading Association.

Commeyras, M., and Inyega, H.N. (2007) An integrative review of teaching reading in Kenyan primary schools. *Reading Research Quarterly*, 42(2): 258–281.

Commeyras, M., and Mazile, B. (2009) On teachers as readers in Botswana. Presentation at the University of the Witwatersrand.

Cox, R., and Schaetzel, K. (2007) A preliminary study of pre-service teachers as readers in Singapore: Prolific, functional, or detached? *Language Teaching Research*, 11(3): 301–317.

Cremin, T., Bearne, E., Mottram, M., and Goodwin, P. (2006–2007) Teachers as readers: Phase 1. Research report for UKLA Web. *UKLA Research 2006–2007*.

Cremin, T., Bearne, E., Mottram, M., and Goodwin, P. (2008) Primary teachers as readers. *English in Education*, 42(1): 8–23.

Cremin, T., Mottram, M., Collins, F., *et al.* (2009) Teachers as readers: Building communities of readers. *Literacy*, 43(1): 11–19.

Davis, C. (1995) Extensive reading: An expensive extravagance? *English Language Teachers Journal*, 49(4): 329–336.

Draper, M.C., Barksdale-Ladd, M.A., and Radencich, M.C. (2000) Reading and writing habits of pre-service teachers. *Reading Horizons*, 40(3): 185–203.

Dreher, M.J. (2003) Motivating teachers to read. *The Reading Teacher*, 56(4): 338–340.

Eteokleous, N. (2008) Evaluating computer technology integration in a centralized school system. *Computers and Education*, 51(2): 669–686.

Fisher, D., and Ivey, G. (2005) Literacy and language as learning in content–area classes: A departure from 'Every teacher a teacher of reading'. *Action in Teacher Education*, 27(2): 3–11.

Frager, A. (1994) Teaching, writing, and identity. *Language Arts*, 71(4): 274–278.

Freebody, P., and Luke, A. (1990) Literacies programmes: Debates and demands in cultural contexts. *Prospect: A Journal of Australian TESOL*, 11: 7–16.

Gains, P. (2010) Learning about literacy: Teachers' conceptualisations and enactments of early literacy pedagogy in South African grade one classrooms. Unpublished doctoral thesis, University of the Witwatersrand, Johannesburg.

Gleeson, A., and Prain, V. (1996) Should teachers of writing write themselves? An Australian contribution to the debate. *The English Journal*, 85(6): 42–49.

Grenfell, M. (1996) Bourdieu and initial teacher education: A post-structuralist approach. *British Educational Research*, 22(3): 287–303.

Gomez, K. (2005) Teachers of literacy, love of reading, and the literate self: A response to Ann Powell-Brown. *Journal of Adolescent and Adult Literacy*, 49(2): 92–96.

Heath, S.B. (1983) *Ways with Words*. Cambridge: Cambridge University Press.

Hill, S. (1999) *Guiding Literacy Learners: Focus on Literacy*. Armadale, Australia: Eleanor Curtain Publishing.

Janks, H. (2010) *Literacy and Power*. New York: Routledge.

Jost, K. (1990) Why high-school writing teachers should not write. *The English Journal*, 79(3): 65–66.

Kaufman, D. (2002) Living a literate life, revisited. *The English Journal*, 91(6): 51–57.

Kist, W. (2008) 'I gave up MySpace for Lent': New teachers and social networking sites. *Journal of Adolescent and Adult Literacy*, 52(3): 245–247.

Kress, G. (1997) *Before Writing: Rethinking the Paths to Literacy*. London: Routledge.

Kress, G., and van Leeuwen, T. (1990) *Reading Images*. Geelong, Australia: Deakin University Press.

Ledgard, J. (2011) Digital Africa. *Intelligent Life*, Spring, accessed November 22, 2012: http://moreintelligentlife.com/content/ideas/jm-ledgard/digital-africa?page=full

Lei, J. (2009) Digital natives as preservice teachers: What technology preparation is needed? *Journal of Computing in Teacher Education*, 25(3): 87–97.

Luke, A. (1995) Text and discourse in education: An introduction to critical discourse analysis. In M. Apple (ed.) *Review of Research in Education, 21, 1995–1996*. AERA, Washington, DC, pp. 3–38.

Maton, K. (2008) Habitus. In M. Grenfell (ed.) *Pierre Bourdieu: Key Concepts*. Stocksfield: Acumen, pp. 49–65.

McDougall, J. (2010) A crisis of professional identity: How primary teachers are coming to terms with changing views of literacy. *Teacher and Teacher Education*, 26: 679–687.

Moll, L., Amanti, C., Neffe, D., and González, N. (1992) Funds of knowledge for teaching: Using a qualitative approach to connect homes and classrooms. *Theory into Practice*, 31(2): 132–141.

Moore, R.A. (2004) Reclaiming the power: Literate identities of students and teachers: An introduction. *Reading and Writing Quarterly: Overcoming Learning Difficulties*, 20(4): 337–342.

Morrow, L.M., O'Connor, E.M., and Smith, J.K. (1990) Effects of a strong reading program on the literacy development of at-risk kindergarten children. *Journal of Reading Behavior*, 22: 255–275.

Mour, S.I. (1977) Do teachers read? *The Reading Teacher*, 30: 397–401.

Nathanson, S., Pruslow, J., and Levitt, R. (2008) The reading habits and literacy attitudes of inservice and prospective teachers. *The Journal of Education*, 59(4): 313–321.

Ngugi, P. (2009) Language and literary education: The state of children's literature in Kiswahili in primary schools in Kenya. Unpublished doctoral thesis, Universität Wien.

Powell-Brown, A. (2004) Can you be a teacher of literacy if you don't love to read? *Journal of Adolescent and Adult Literacy*, 47(4): 284–288.

Prensky, M. (2001) Digital natives, digital immigrants. *On the Horizon*, 9(5): 1–6.

Prinsloo, J. (2002) Possibilities for critical literacy and exploration of schooled literacies in the province of Kwazulu-Natal. Unpublished doctoral thesis, University of the Witwatersrand, Johannesburg.

Reid, J. (2011) 'We don't twitter, we Facebook': An alternative pedagogical space that enables critical practices in relation to writing. *English Teaching Practice and Critique*, 10(1): 58–80.

Robbins, B. (1992) It's not that simple: Some teachers as writers. *The English Journal*, 81(4): 72–74.

Robbins, B. (1996) Teachers as writers: Tensions between theory and practice. *Journal of Teaching Writing*, 15(1): 107–128.

Rosenblatt, L.M. (1986) The aesthetic transaction. *Journal of Aesthetic Education*, 20(4): 122–128.

Rudland, N., and Kemp, C. (2004) The professional reading habits of teachers: Implications for student learning. *Australasian Journal of Special Education*, 28(1): 4–17.

Sanacore, J. (2002) Questions often asked about promoting lifetime literacy efforts. *Intervention in School and Clinic*, 37: 163–168.

Snow, C.E., and Juel, C. (2008) Teaching children to read: What do we know about how to do it? In M.J. Snowling and C. Hulme (eds) *The Science of Reading: A Handbook*. Oxford: Blackwell, pp. 501–520.

Sulentic-Dowell, M., Beal, G.D., and Capraro, R.M. (2006) How do literacy experiences affect the teaching propensities of elementary pre–service teachers? *Reading Psychology*, 27: 235–255.

Sutherland-Smith, W. (2002) Weaving the literacy web: Changes in reading from page and screen. *The Reading Teacher*, 55(7): 662–669.

Thomson, P. (2008) Field. In M. Grenfell (ed.) *Bourdieu: Key Concepts*. Stocksfield: Acumen, pp. 67–81.

Vasquez, V. (2004) *Negotiating Critical Literacies with Young Children*. Mahwah, NJ. Lawrence Erlbaum.

Whitney, A. (2009) National writing project (professional network focused on improvement of writing). *English Education*, 41(3): 236.

Willet, R. (2007) Technology, pedagogy and digital production: A case study of children learning new media skills. *Learning, Media and Technology*, 32(2): 167–181.

Wolf, M. (2007) *Proust and the Squid. The Story and Science of the Reading Brain*. New York: Harper Collins.

Yang, S., and Huang, Y. (2008) A study of high school English teachers' behaviour, concerns and beliefs in integrating information technology into English instruction. *Computers in Human Behavior*, 24: 1085–1103.

Chapter 34

Constructing a Collective Identity

Professional Development for Twenty-first Century Pedagogy

Catherine M. Weber and Taffy E. Raphael

Introduction

Successful teachers of twenty-first century learners must be equipped to teach skills and strategies; guide development of dispositions that create independent learners who can collaborate, problem-solve, and learn how to learn over their lifetimes; and prepare students to use all available resources (Gee, 2000; Goldman, 1997; Kalantzis, Cope, and Harvey, 2003; Lankshear and Knobel, 2007; Leu *et al.*, 2004). For many, however, teaching twenty-first century learners may require a shift in literacy identities, both individually and within the collective, whole-school professional learning community (PLC).

The purpose of this chapter is two-fold: (a) to examine knowledge teachers need to prepare learners for a changing world and (b) to explore schools' collective literacy identities and professional development (PD) needed to shift teachers' literacy conceptions to reflect the twenty-first century's current and future literacy practices. That is, how do teachers conceptualize literacy and how do those conceptions contribute to a school's vision of the successful graduating reader and writer? We first examine the types of knowledge teachers need to prepare twenty-first century literacy learners. We then explore the concept of teachers' individual literacy identities and how these influence curriculum and pedagogy. Third, we discuss the concept of collective identity within a PD model for sustainable school change.

Types of Knowledge Teachers Need to Prepare Twenty-first Century Learners

In high-quality instruction, definitions of literacy for twenty-first century teaching and learning emphasize higher-order thinking skills and multiple literacies that students can control and adapt across contexts. This requires instruction in both long-standing (e.g., phonics, fluency, reading, and writing conventional texts) and twenty-first century literacies (e.g., video, Internet, blogging). Effective teachers prepare their students to apply and adapt literacies to new and continually evolving situations. Thus, effective professional development (PD) considers

International Handbook of Research on Children's Literacy, Learning, and Culture, First Edition.
Edited by Kathy Hall, Teresa Cremin, Barbara Comber, and Luis C. Moll.
© 2013 John Wiley & Sons, Ltd. Published 2013 by John Wiley & Sons, Ltd.

knowledge fundamental to preparing twenty-first century literacy learners for the demands of a changing world: (a) knowledge of literacy, (b) knowledge of societal demands, and (c) knowledge of tools for learning.

Teacher knowledge of literacy

Successful teacher preparation and PD reflects the continuously changing world. How literacy is defined has implications for how we help teachers grapple with differences between new curriculum content and existing approaches to literacy teaching and learning. For decades, scholars have debated what constitutes literacy – what it is, its purpose in our lives, and what it does or does not include (Nixon, 2003). The broad spectrum of literacy conceptions tends to be conceptualized in terms of *functional literacy, conventional literacy,* and *multiple literacies.*

Literacy researchers (see Stanley, 1972) describe *functional literacy* in terms of skills necessary to function in everyday life (e.g., drive a car, shop for groceries). However, Damon (1991) cautions that what it means to function in society changes with societal changes. Literacy scholars describe *conventional literacy* in terms of basic processes for reading, writing, listening, and speaking related to traditional print-based texts (e.g., books, newspapers). For example, Nixon (2003) and others (see Kaestle, 1985) discuss the specific repertoire of skills to be learned and applied to understand the written word.

Literacy scholars (e.g., Damon, 1991) emphasize the concept of *multiple literacies* that are 'each acquired as a functional adaptation to a particular social need . . . Each literacy brings with it its own logical flavor' (p. 48). As cultures change, new literacy skills are needed to be able to interpret the world (Resnick, 1991; Scribner, 1984). The New London Group [NLG] (1996) and others (Goodwyn, 1998; Hull and Nelson, 2005; Kress, 1997; 2000; Kress and van Leeuwen, 1996; Lankshear, Snyder, and Green, 2000; Leu and Kinzer, 2000; Nixon, 2003; Unsworth, 2002, 2006) focus on multimodal meaning-making and the need for schools to reconsider views of teaching and literacy learning to include traditional texts and other media (e.g., diagrams, images, sounds).

Teacher knowledge of societal demands

Teacher knowledge about changing societal demands is central to preparing students for full participation and contributions to public, community, and economic life (NLG, 1996). Students living throughout the twenty-first century must know how to: (a) access, consume, and produce information quickly, (b) communicate effectively across multiple contexts and cultures, and (c) self-direct learning. Teachers need to develop curricula and pedagogy to equip students with the skills and tools needed to navigate new demands successfully.

Access and use information　　The more readily available information becomes, the greater the opportunities for both personal and economic success, if one knows how to access and evaluate this information. Teachers who understand this demand engage students in active and critical inquiry, not passive reception of information. Leu (2006) argues that the Internet and other Information and Communication Technologies (ICTs) define this generation's literacy and learning, requiring new skills, strategies, and dispositions to use it effectively. He and his colleagues (Leu *et al.*, 2004) articulate key skills post-Industrial workers need: (a) quickly identify problems, (b) locate useful information related to the problems, (c) critically evaluate information they find, (d) synthesize the information, and (e) communicate solutions to others.

Communicate effectively　A multiliteracies perspective emphasizes pedagogy that considers cultural and linguistic diversity in a global economy and accounts for the many text forms found in multimedia technologies (NLG, 1996). Effective teachers explicitly and implicitly teach students to navigate multiple cultures and contexts, including how to make meaning through various modalities (e.g., audio, visual, linguistic, spatial, gestural) (Kress, 1997, 2000). They recognize the limitations of using solely traditional texts for learning to navigate the cross-cultural discourses, gestural relationships, and visual and iconic meanings (NLG, 1996). The intertextuality between various modalities has the potential to increase students' abilities to think critically about complex systems and their own interactions within the systems (Fairclough, 1992; NLG, 1996).

Self-directed learning　Schools preparing twenty-first century learners emphasize critical thinking skills and the means for self-directed learning. Historically, education in the United States has been structured along a factory model (Mirel, 2003), where students were taught basic reading, writing, and math skills to enable them to obtain jobs in what were generally top-down organizations. Students, typically passive learners, gained decontextualized knowledge often not applicable to new contexts (Kalantzis *et al.*, 2003).

Today's effective classroom contexts and curricula promote: knowledge production that is both accurate and responsible; access to information and the ability to evaluate the information source and content; and the skills for collaboration, flexibility, change, networking, and niche markets (Kalantzis *et al.*, 2003; NLG, 1996). Teachers teach students to become autonomous, self-directed learners (Gee, 2000; Kalantzis *et al.*, 2003; NLG, 1996), which requires shifting from delivery models of instruction to facilitation models in which teachers engage students in inquiry and equip them with the skills necessary for acquiring new knowledge.

Teacher knowledge of tools for learning

Today's students enter schools with competencies in technological tools, sometimes more advanced than those of their teachers. Effective teachers capitalize on students' competencies and create educative experiences that enhance them by: (a) facilitating social learning opportunities using technology, (b) understanding and using emerging technologies, and (c) identifying skills required to effectively use the technologies. However, Labbo and Reinking (1999) caution that 'what *can be done* with computers needs to be clearly distinguished from what *should be done* based on the goals one has for instruction' (p. 479, italics added). They provide five insights into what today's teachers need to understand about technology. Technology should: (a) be available for literacy instruction, (b) enhance goals of conventional literacy instruction, (c) transform literacy instruction, (d) prepare students for future literacy, and (e) empower students. Educators can create substantive literacy learning experiences when they use technology in meaningful ways rather than add-ons to the curriculum.

Yet, knowledge about technology does not guarantee successful instruction with technology (e.g., Leu *et al.*, 2004; Mishra and Koehler, 2006). Mishra and Koehler (2006) note that, 'knowing how to use technology is not the same as knowing how to teach with it' (p. 1033). For changes in pedagogy to occur, teachers must value this type of instruction and know how to implement it. Such teachers have a well-conceptualized knowledge of literacy, societal demands, and tools for learning to be able to engage students in the high-level literacy tasks required of individuals in the twenty-first century. Their conceptions of literacy form the basis of individual literacy identities, which mediate their understandings of curricula, pedagogical practices, and goals they establish for literacy teaching and learning.

Teachers' Individual Literacy Identities

Effective professional development, like effective teaching, starts from a position of knowledge about learners' needs. To help teachers build individual literacy identities for today's literacy instruction, PD providers begin with teachers' current conceptions of literacy, promoting growth in knowledge, skills, and dispositions. According to scholars (e.g., DeFord, 1985; Richardson *et al.*, 1991), teacher knowledge constructs are powerful predictors of teacher behavior in the classroom. Thus, we must understand teachers' literacy constructs – their individual literacy identity – and the ways in which their identity influences classroom practice. In this section, we examine research about teachers' literacy identities (i.e., knowledge, beliefs, motivations, thought processes) to understand: (a) the importance of literacy identities related to school improvement, (b) the challenge in shifting identities to reflect twenty-first century literacies, and (c) implications for a model of teacher change.

Research on Teachers' Knowledge and Beliefs

Process-product research

While recognizing that teaching includes both thought processes and actions, most research has focused on what can be observed (Clark and Peterson, 1986). These studies of teacher behavior, called process-product research, were most prevalent between the early 1970s and 1990s. The underlying logic of process-product research was that teachers' behavior influences students' behavior (process), which in turn affects student achievement (product) (Fang, 1996). Thus, studying teacher behavior was considered a promising way to affect changes in practices leading to improved achievement.

Despite its long history, process-product research was unable to demonstrate that changing the process (content and pedagogy) improved the product (student achievement and/or behavior). Some researchers (Brousseau, Book, and Byers, 1988) suspected there were mediating elements related to beliefs and theories of those who worked in schools. Research demonstrated that changing teachers' practices was not that direct – faced with new information about teaching, deep and sustainable changes to teaching practices did not occur.

Teacher beliefs research

Missing from process-product research was attention to factors that influence teacher uptake of new concepts and information; how teachers use new knowledge in planning, decision-making, and taking action in their classrooms (Fang, 1996; Nisbett and Ross, 1980). These findings led scholars (e.g., Brophy and Good, 1974) to study teachers' conceptual understandings as a window into effective teachers' practices, creating a stronger basis to affect changes to those practices.

Scholars researched teacher beliefs and theories that comprise literacy identities, suspecting these to be at the heart of what prevented changes in practices. Lortie (1975) introduced the influence of 'apprenticeship of observation,' noting that it was common for educators to rely on the familiar, what they had observed over their years in school. Experiences contribute to our tacit beliefs about what we should and do value. Studying teacher beliefs empirically led to understanding their elusive, tacit, and nonconsensual nature, which makes them challenging to change (Ertmer, 2005). This surfaced the importance of a theory of teacher change that includes belief systems and teacher conceptions of literacy.

Implicit theory research

In recent years, researchers have examined the influence of teachers' implicit theories about students and subject matter on their practice (Ashton, 1990). All teachers have at least an implicit model of what it means to teach (Kamil and Pearson, 1979). Their implicit theories (beliefs) develop from both personal experiences and knowledge they have acquired (DeFord, 1985; Nespor, 1987); in turn, these implicit theories contribute to individuals' literacy identity formation. Beliefs are constituted by cognitive (knowledge), affective, and behavioral components (Rokeach, 1968).

Understanding teachers' individual literacy identities is important when considering professional development and teacher education. Teachers who are teaching in elementary classrooms today began developing their literacy identities – ideas about literacy, teaching, and learning – in the twentieth century through their 'apprenticeship of observation' (Lortie, 1975; Nespor, 1987). While they may have knowledge of multiple literacies and technological tools that can be used in teaching, their underlying beliefs about literacy probably reflect a pre-digital age conception. Prensky (2005) describes students who are 'native speakers of technology, fluent in the digital language of computers, video games, and the Internet' (p. 9) as 'digital natives.' In contrast, 'digital immigrants' are those not born into a digital world. Thus, there can be a disconnect between the longstanding beliefs teachers have about what constitutes cognitive, affective, and behavioral aspects of literacy and their students' experiences. For effective professional development, teacher educators first must understand teachers' beliefs and conceptions, then create learning experiences to support changes in individual identities.

Shifting literacy identities

A promising venue for changing teacher beliefs about literacy, and ultimately their literacy classroom practices, is deepening their understandings about pedagogy and subject matter (Lawless and Pellegrino, 2007; Mishra and Koehler, 2006; Weber, 2010). Recent research has shifted the focus from behaviors to studying teachers' thinking, beliefs, and decision-making processes (Fang, 1996). Brousseau, Book, and Byers (1988) suggest that understanding the values and beliefs of those in the schools is critical to school change efforts.

Given the importance of teachers' literacy identities, we might assume that we could shift conceptions by simply telling teachers how to think differently. However, teachers' identities are long-standing and grounded in their own experiences with literacy and their history of working with schools' curricula; thus, they are challenging to change. Kagan (1992) describes teacher beliefs as 'tacit, often unconsciously held assumptions about students, classrooms, and academic material to be taught' (p. 65). It is difficult to make changes when a person remains unaware of his or her beliefs. Thus, effective PD opportunities recognize the tenacity of beliefs associated with our identities and create opportunities for teachers to shift in directions that aid their twenty-first century teaching.

Theory of Teacher Change

Shifting teachers' literacy identities requires understanding how teachers' identities change and develop and creating contexts to facilitate teacher learning. Clarke and Hollingsworth's (2002) Interconnected Model of Professional Growth conceptualizes the importance of engaging teacher candidates in actual practice while challenging their beliefs with new knowledge. Their model emphasizes the importance of the collective school community in changing individual teacher's beliefs. Thus, effective PD addresses both individual and collective literacy identities. Clarke and Hollingsworth (2002) and others (see Kennedy, 2010; Lawless and Pellegrino, 2007) suggest teachers learn through a mediating process in which they put into action the new idea or practice, then reflect on the experimentation. This mediating process enables teachers to recognize their own literacy identities and use new information and experiences as catalysts for shifting those identities and classroom practices.

Weber (2010) explored a PD model that built upon Clarke and Hollingsworth's (2002) principles for teacher change. In her study of teachers' literacy conceptions, practicing teachers created digital narratives, consisting of digital photographs combined with semi-structured interviews. Participants were asked to take photographs that captured literacy for them; the photos could be taken anywhere, of anything. The teachers then met with a researcher and described what they photographed, why they included particular pictures, and how the pictures captured 'literacy.' This process surfaced teachers' individual literacy identities and enabled both the teachers and researchers to examine participants' beliefs. The photographs served as data to create targeted PD experiences that built on teachers' strengths and addressed specific areas where teachers were thinking about literacy in a solely conventional way. Teachers participating in the study engaged in six PD seminars, focused on multiliteracies and technology, during an academic year. Between sessions they had the opportunity to try new strategies, collaborate with colleagues, and get ongoing feedback from one another about their practice. After the seminars, the teachers created another digital narrative about their literacy conceptions. Findings suggest the targeted PD and opportunities to engage with colleagues within a community of practice began to shift teachers' conceptions and practices of literacy to be more reflective of twenty-first century demands. Successful models for PD honor teachers' individual literacy identities, build on their strengths, and capitalize on the collective expertise of a PLC to make rigorous, sustainable change school-wide. As research suggests, learning occurs through social interactions that are targeted, scaffolded, and provide opportunities to make visible beliefs and practices (Wenger, 1998; Wenger and Snyder, 2000).

Collective Identity as an Integrated Professional Development Approach

Despite several decades and numerous efforts to reform schools, literacy gaps persist (DCSF, 2010; Eivers, Shiel, and Shortt, 2004; Gamse *et al.*, 2008). Results from the 2009 Programme for International Student Assessment (PISA) indicate international trends of decreased student engagement in literacy activities among teens and a disparity in achievement between various groups when data were disaggregated (e.g., male/female, minorities) (IRA, 2010). Many reform efforts have focused on individual teachers or small teams of highly engaged teachers (e.g., 'go with the goers') in which those interested and committed to literacy improvement assume responsibility as change agents, in contrast to whole-school change initiatives. In some cases, the principal or a few key leaders simply direct all teachers to engage in literacy improvement, leading to perceptions (or reality) of a top-down mandate that can lack teacher buy-in. Even with the best of intentions, these models for literacy improvement often fail due to lack of understanding or commitment from all stakeholders (see Taylor, Raphael, and Au, 2011). Schools may experience short-term gains, but sustainability becomes an insurmountable challenge. Schools need to adopt a PD model that empowers individual teachers and creates a productive collective identity.

Creating a collective identity can be challenging because of the 'organic, spontaneous, and informal nature of communities of practice' (Wenger and Snyder, 2000). In this section, we describe five research-based principles critical to creating and sustaining improvements in literacy teaching and learning. For each principle, we describe PD that addresses individual growth and that of the collective PLC. We use the Standards Based Change (SBC) Process as an illustrative example of a PD model that leads to long-term whole school literacy improvement (Au, 2005; Raphael, Au, Goldman, 2009). The five principles are:

1 All stakeholders assume ownership for literacy improvement, collaboratively creating a common vision of success and clear goals for reaching the vision.
2 School leaders create an infrastructure that supports change and enables the PLC to engage in the work necessary for change.
3 Literacy leaders use distributed leadership that draws on the range of staff capacities in literacy teaching and learning, builds on existing strengths, and expands capacity of less confident or knowledgeable members.
4 School faculties develop curricular coherence within and across grade levels and subject areas.
5 The school's PLC engages in systematic ongoing learning that considers individual and collective identity development.

The SBC Process (Au, 2005; Au and Raphael, 2011; Raphael, Au, and Goldman, 2009) is a professional development model that constructs and then builds upon a PLC's collective identity. The process guides schools to develop a collective identity and clear vision of the students they are trying to assist, focusing on one subject area at a time (e.g., comprehension, writing, mathematics). The process supports the school community members by emphasizing multiple levels of development in an iterative and sustainable process of school change. Specific areas of development focus on:

a creating a school infrastructure to support improvement in teaching and learning;
b articulating the school's identity, beliefs, and vision;
c implementing high quality classroom practices (i.e., instruction, curriculum, and assessment) aligned within and across grades that reflect a developmental progression of benchmarks and data-driven instructional decisions; and
d building capacity for sustainable improvement through professional learning opportunities within individual schools and across networks (e.g., leadership, teacher) of participating schools.

The SBC Process works to support schools in creating communities-of-practice (Wenger, 1998); the collaboration empowers teachers and administrators as the enactors of reform.

Principle 1: Common vision and goals

In the past decade, several whole school reform models underscore the importance of shared understandings and collaboratively developed literacy goals and improvement efforts (Raphael *et al.*, 2009; Lai *et al.*, 2009; Timperly and Parr, 2007; Taylor *et al.*, 2011). School change advocates such as Fullan (2008) and Hargreaves (2009) discuss the importance of collective responsibility and distribution of the workload. Given the importance of collective identity, an integrated system for PD is critical to allow each individual to contribute meaningfully toward a coherent goal.

For example, one of the first steps in the SBC Process requires the PLC (faculty and administration) to construct a collective literacy identity revealing a shared vision of the graduating reader or writer. Each school's collective identity depends and capitalizes on individual teachers' strengths, articulating the roles and responsibilities each has in making the vision a reality. Successful schools bring individual teachers' literacy identities to the surface as individuals make their beliefs and expertise public and explicit, and thus available for mutual examination. Copland (2003) argues that a PLC's collective goals are more valuable than the sum of individuals' goals. Through discussion, all stakeholders come together to create their shared vision and consider individual contributions to students achieving that vision.

Schools' literacy improvement efforts are more likely to be effective when each person shares ownership of the vision and understands the role she or he plays in supporting success school wide (Au, 2005; Bryk, Rollow, and Pinnell, 1996; Copland, 2003; Pressley *et al.*, 2007; Purkey and Smith, 1983; Rowan, 1990). The initial construction of a collective identity creates opportunity for all faculty members to understand and commit to school-wide literacy improvement since they are instrumental in developing both the goals and the means for achieving them. Effective PD promoting high-level visions and rigorous goals includes: (a) building knowledge about literacy, societal demands, and tools for learning that reflects twenty-first century literacy demands; and (b) creating opportunities for teachers to examine their own literacy identities and the ways in which they contribute to the collective identity.

Principle 2: Infrastructure to support change

Successful schools have structures that enable faculty members to engage in conversations and work that focuses on twenty-first century literacy improvement. Au (2005) warns schools that the work of school-wide literacy improvement occurs not as a series of 'quick fixes,' but rather, a multiyear strategic plan to implement and sustain change. Successful schools start by determining the degree to which administration and school staff members are ready and willing to engage in the change process that results in a coherent curriculum and continuous improvement for all students. Schools are more likely to be successful when everyone is involved (Bryk *et al.*, 1996; Purkey and Smith, 1983), and the school's infrastructure is key to creating those collaborative spaces fundamental to sustainable improvement efforts.

Effective PLCs operate within schools that have a high-functioning infrastructure to support the collaborative work groups (Cohen, 1995; Gamoran *et al.*, 2000; Newmann, King, and Youngs, 2000; Rowan, 1990). Infrastructure elements include school organization and related norms for participation, time, space, and resources to support school-wide literacy improvement. The successful school's organization focuses on both structures and functions within those structures to support collaborative work groups (e.g., horizontal and vertical teams). The groups meet regularly to work on creating and maintaining a coherent school-wide literacy curriculum. Structures have clear purposes and systems with substantive communication about instructional improvement among all members of the PLC (Bryk *et al.*, 1996; Louis, Marks, and Kruse, 1996; Mason *et al.*, 2005; Newmann *et al.*, 2001). Structures include, but are not limited to: (a) grade level or department team meetings (horizontal), (b) cross grade-level or department meetings (vertical), and (c) whole school sharing time. These structures are dynamic, and adaptable as the needs of the school change.

Moreover, successful schools recognize the importance of PD that makes structures productive. Professional development related to school infrastructure focuses on areas such as strategies for productive meetings (e.g., norms that guarantee equity of voice, creating meaningful agendas, using agendas productively) and effective use of time and resources (e.g., curriculum development or collaborative scoring of assessments).

Principle 3: Distributed literacy leadership

Collective identity is enacted through a distributed leadership model (Spillane, 2006; Timperly, 2009) in which each member of a PLC serves as an agent of change through his or her particular role. In such a model, schools harness the expertise of their entire PLC, including each person's individual skills, knowledge, and competencies (Stoll *et al.*, 2006), and all members of the PLC make a commitment to creating and maintaining lasting change through sustainable leadership (Hargreaves and Fink, 2004; Rowan, 1990). Sustainable leadership is possible when schools have systems in place that enable the continuous regeneration of future leadership (Fullan, 2004). Within these systems, all faculty members have opportunities to grow professionally and take on more responsibility. As Copland (2003) has argued, leadership responsibilities are best distributed based on the task to be undertaken so as to harness the strengths of individual's expertise.

The principal is instrumental in identifying potential leaders and creating both formal and informal means through which the leaders can develop. Leadership teams form one effective way to distribute leadership responsibilities across the school (Bryk *et al.*, 1996; Strahan, 2003; Taylor *et al.*, 2004), establish critical communication lines, and mentor future leaders. Leadership team meetings serve as a forum to generate concerns about the school, make collective decisions, disseminate information, and empower teacher leaders to carry on the work in grade level and vertical team meetings. Hargreaves and Fink's (2004) recommend 'grooming successors' as key to a school's ability to continue forward movement even when key leaders depart.

Fullan (2008) underscores the importance of shared leadership for sustainable change, particularly as it relates to school culture. 'We should not have leadership-development programs for individuals in the absence of parallel strategies focusing on changing the culture of school systems. It will take the combined efforts of both components. Individual and organizational development must go hand in hand' (Fullan, 2008, p. 28). Creating systems of distributed leadership enables individuals and the collective PLC to engage in the substantive work of improving and sustaining literacy achievement for all students across time. Establishing this strong collective identity around core goals reduces the likelihood that staff turnover at any level could undermine continuous improvement.

Professional development related to literacy leadership includes strategies for developing leaders at all levels – principals, coaches, and teachers (see Cantrell and Hughes, 2008; Dole, 2004; Dole *et al.*, 2006). It provides an array of methods for leaders to surface teachers' individual literacy identities to ensure that professional learning experiences target both the individual and collective needs (see Weber, 2010).

Principle 4: Curricular coherence within and across grades

When PLCs are effective levers of school change, participants engage in substantive work that positively impacts classroom practice. They reflect, analyze, diagnose, and implement change based on the school's and its students' specific needs (Copland, 2003). This process of reflection, analysis, and action begins with conversations about instructional coherence and curricular alignment within and across grade levels and/or subject areas (Au and Raphael, 2011; Bryk *et al.*, 1996; Copland, 2003; Mason *et al.*, 2005; Newmann *et al.*, 2000; Rowan, 1990). Success depends upon a 'culture of collaboration' (DuFour, 2004) that emphasizes constructive, collaborative work toward common goals. It involves engaging in substantive, ongoing conversations about literacy improvements. DuFour (2004, p. 8) suggests staff members wrestle with three questions, revisiting them within and across school years.

1   What do we want each student to learn?
2   How will we know when each student has learned it?
3   How will we respond when a student experiences difficulty in learning?

Similarly, Jaeger (1996) suggests that teachers communicate with one another about the specific skills and knowledge they believe their students should have upon entrance to their classroom, as well as their expectations for student achievement upon leaving their classroom at the end of the school year. Grade level team meetings work to build coherence within a grade; however, in order to build coherence across grade levels, teachers from all grade levels must meet on a regular basis to discuss literacy school wide (Au, 2005; Newmann *et al.*, 2001). For example, in the SBC Process, grade level teams meet weekly to engage in literacy improvement work and meet regularly (e.g., monthly or quarterly) with other grade level or subject area teams or the whole school PLC to create vertical coherence. During these vertical conversations, each grade level articulates what is happening at their own meetings and collaborates with colleagues to determine how each group's work will lead to improved achievement for all students.

Scholars suggest schools benefit when they have specific times for whole school sharing to make public the goals for student learning at each grade level (Au *et al.*, 2008; DuFour, 2004). This public sharing creates accountability for student learning by making practice transparent. It deprivatizes practice and puts positive peer pressure on those who do not fully participate in efforts to achieve school-wide goals (Newmann and Wehlage, 1995; Stoll *et al.*, 2006). The deprivatization of practice and the shared responsibility for student learning school wide is at the centre of the PLC's work. It also helps create curricular coherence across grade levels so that there is a developmental progression of goals, rather than a piecemeal approach to instruction (Au and Raphael, 2011). Conversations that take place during these sharing times build the PLC's collective identity and bring coherence to the school-wide curriculum.

Thus, it is critical for teachers and teacher educators to understand individual literacy identities. Effective teachers are aware of their own knowledge and beliefs and thus can share them publicly, open them to examination and critique, or use them to contribute in substantive ways to the collective identity. In the SBC Process, grade level teams utilize weekly meetings to engage in substantive conversations about their collective expectations for end-of-year goals and the contribution their team makes to the collective school vision. They also collaborate with one another around evidence-based teaching to ensure the goals are realized. Professional development focuses on how their individual identities shape their beliefs about what is important for their students to learn, how to align their own beliefs with the collective goals, ways to evaluate students' progress, and instructional decisions that are based on evidence of students' needs.

Principle 5: Systematic ongoing professional learning

A trajectory of continuous literacy improvement for both individual teachers and the school at large requires a strong school-wide PLC that is focused on systematic, contextualized, and sustained professional learning. It includes changes to how PD is envisioned and focuses on analysis of student progress and teachers' own practices.

A first key to systemic ongoing professional learning involves engaging teachers in inquiry. This vision shifts PD from the popular (but ineffective) decontextualized, one-shot workshops to more effective, coherent and long-term approaches (Joyce and Showers, 1983). One-shot workshops cannot provide differentiated, targeted support for teachers and, not surprisingly, are ineffective in substantively changing classroom practices (Joyce and Showers, 1982; IRA,

2004). Effective PD is strategically planned, goal-oriented, aligned with school-wide foci, and connected in a coherent manner over time so that it supports both teacher and student learning (Au, 2005; Newmann *et al.*, 2001; Pressley *et al.*, 2007; Purkey and Smith, 1983; Strahan, 2003). Professional development emphasizing the ability to engage in ongoing inquiry to improve teaching and learning shifts from 'presentation' to 'engagement.' Engaging in PD requires that all members of the PLC develop skills in collecting data, analyzing it, and collaboratively identifying school wide, grade level specific, and individual needs. This cycle applies to both student data and teacher data.

A second key element focuses on student learning, beginning with close examination of student learning and teachers' own practices (Brown, Collins, and Duguid, 1989; John-Steiner and Mahn, 1996; Wenger, 1998), then building on strengths and addressing needs of both individuals and the collective PLC. The cycle of effective PD includes learning new skills/strategies, implementing ideas into classroom practice, reflecting on effectiveness, and collaborating with colleagues (Lawless and Pellegrino, 2007). For example, in the SBC Process, teachers learn to identify key criteria that represent achievement of end-of-year targets. They learn to create a range of formal and informal assessment opportunities to track students' progress. They evaluate their own abilities to provide instruction, based on the assessment results, differentiated to ensure all students progress toward the goal. They also analyze the instructional strategies and curricular resources that can help them meet the goals. The teachers' collaborative investigation of students' needs, within their teacher teams, provides informal venues for ongoing, onsite PD.

A third key element is creating long-term PD plans. Collecting evidence about their own practices and identifying edges of professional growth both engages school faculty in PD and produces further PD plans that strengthens both individual and literacy collective identities. It develops a coherent PD course for teachers as each session builds upon the next. This helps schools maintain a focus and investigate one area (e.g., comprehension or writing) in depth avoiding jumping among topics (which tends to lead to fragmented, shallow understandings). Visscher and Witziers (2004), studying the link between PLCs and student achievement, found that highest achievement occurred in schools where teacher teams:

> consistently translate their shared vision and willingness to cooperate into a system of rules, agreements and goals regarding teaching and instruction, and evolve their professional activities around this by obtaining data on student performance, which in turn serves as a feedback mechanism for improving teaching and learning. This differs from a 'softer' approach stressing reflective dialogue, sharing materials, shared vision and the inner value of professional development (p. 798).

This emphasis on a shared vision within collaborative teams illustrates the positive ways in which effective, strategic PLCs impact student achievement by reconceptualizing PD as iterative feedback cycles of data collection, analysis, reflection, and change of classroom practice (McLaughlin and Talbert, 2001). It focuses on creating systems for diagnosing context-specific needs for ensuring high levels of student achievement. Each school, on its own developmental continuum, recognizes that: (a) they have unique needs that cannot be addressed from wholesale PD; (b) their needs change over time as they move through different stages of reform; and (c) they will benefit from engaging in PD to address authentic problems of practice.

Concluding Comments

For decades, professional development has not achieved anticipated results. International comparisons suggest the achievement gap between students living in poverty and those who are more affluent, and between culturally and linguistically diverse students and mainstream peers, is a concern across nations. Schools unable to achieve adequate yearly progress struggle to raise student achievement, despite adopting new programs and approaches. A continuing demand persists for immediate results. In the United States, a dominant, naïve view suggests that accountability, testing, and deprofessionalizing teaching is the answer to achievement problems (Darling-Hammond, 2008; Tucker, 2011). What we learn from the most effective educational systems in the world is that professionalism of the teaching force – with related high quality, life-long, strategic professional development – is a powerful component for realizing our goal of a competent citizenry, leading useful and fulfilling lives.

References

Ashton, P.T. (1990) Editorial. *Journal of Teacher Education*, 41(1): 2.

Au, K.H. (2005) Negotiating the slippery slope: School change and literacy achievement. *Journal of Literacy Research*, 37(3): 267–288.

Au, K.H., and Raphael, T.E. (2011) The staircase curriculum: Whole-school collaboration to improve literacy achievement. *The New England Reading Association Journal*, 46(2): 1–8.

Au, T., Knightly, L., Jun, S., *et al.* (2008) Salvaging a childhood language. *Journal of Memory and Language*, 58: 998–1011.

Brophy, J.E., and Good, T.L. (1974) *Teacher Student Relationships: Causes and Consequences*. New York: Holt, Rinehart, and Winston.

Brousseau, B.A., Book, C., and Byers, J.L. (1988) Teacher beliefs and the cultures of teaching. *Journal of Teacher Education*, 39(6): 33–39.

Brown, J.S., Collins, A., and Duguid, P. (1989) Situated cognition and the culture of learning. *Educational Researcher*, 18(1): 32–42.

Bryk, A.S., Rollow, S.G., and Pinnell, G.S. (1996) Urban school development: Literacy as a lever for change. *Educational Policy*, 10(2): 172–201.

Cantrell, S.C., and Hughes, H.K. (2008) Teacher efficacy and content literacy implementation: An exploration of the effects of extended professional development with coaching. *Journal of Literacy Research*, 40(1): 95–127.

Clark, C.M., and Peterson, P.L. (1986) Teachers' thought processes. In M.C. Wittrock (ed.) *Handbook of Research on Teaching*. New York: Macmillan.

Clarke, D., and Hollingsworth, H. (2002) Elaborating a model of teacher professional growth. *Teaching and Teacher Education*, 18: 947–967.

Cohen, D.K. (1995) What is the system in systemic reform? *Educational Researcher*, 24(9): 11–17: 31.

Copland, M.A. (2003) Leadership of inquiry: Building and sustaining capacity for school improvement. *Educational Evaluation and Policy Analysis*, 25(4): 375–395.

Damon, W. (1991) Reconciling the literacies of generations. In S. Graubard (ed.) *Literacy: An Overview by Fourteen Experts*. Hill and Wang: New York, pp. 33–53.

Darling-Hammond, L. (2008) Assessment for learning around the world: What would it mean to be internationally competitive? *Phi Delta Kappan*, 90(4): 263–272.

DCSF (Department for Children Schools and Families) (2010) Statistical first release: Attainment by pupil characteristics in England, accessed November 22, 2012: www.education.gov.uk/rsgateway/DB/SFR/index.shtml

DeFord, D.E. (1985) Validating the construct of theoretical orientation in reading instruction. *Reading Research Quarterly*, 20(3): 351–367.

Dole, J. (2004) The changing role of the reading specialist in school reform. *The Reading Teacher*, 57(5): 462–471.

Dole, J., Liang, L.A., Watkins, N., and Wiggins, C.M. (2006) The state of reading professionals in the United States. *The Reading Teacher*, 60(2): 194–199.

DuFour, R. (2004) What is a 'professional learning community'? *Educational Leadership*, 61(8): 6–11.

Eivers, E., Shiel, G., and Shortt, S. (2004) *Reading Literacy in Disadvantaged Primary Schools.* Dublin: Educational Research Centre.

Ertmer, P.A. (2005) Teacher pedagogical beliefs: The final frontier in our quest for technology integration? *Educational Technology Research and Development*, 53(4): 25–39.

Fairclough, N. (1992) Discourse and text: Linguistic and intertextual analysis within discourse analysis. *Discourse and Society*, 3: 193–217.

Fang, Z. (1996) A review of research on teacher beliefs and practices. *Educational Research*, 38(1): 47–65.

Fullan, M. (2004) *Leadership and Sustainability: System Thinkers in Action.* Thousand Oaks, CA: Corwin Press.

Fullan, M. (2008) *The Six Secrets of Change: What the Best Leaders do to Help their Organizations Survive and Thrive.* San Francisco, CA: Jossey–Bass.

Gamoran, A., Secada, W.G., and Marrett, C.A. (2000) The organizational context of teaching and learning: Changing theoretical perspectives. In M.T. Hallinan (ed.) *Handbook of Sociology of Education.* New York: Kluwer Academic, Plenum, pp. 37–64.

Gamse, B.C., Bloom, H.S., Kemple, J.J., and Jacob, R.T. (2008) Reading First impact study: Interim report (NCEE 2008–4016). Washington, DC: National Center for Education Evaluation and Regional Assistance, Institute of Education Sciences, US Department of Education.

Gee, J.P. (2000) The New Literacy Studies; from 'socially situated' to the work of the social In D. Barton, M. Hamilton, and R. Ivanic (2000) *Situated Literacies: Reading and Writing in Context.* Routledge: London, pp. 180–196.

Goldman, S.R. (1997) Learning from text: Reflections on the past and suggestions for the future. *Discourse Processes*, 23: 357–398.

Goodwyn, A. (1998) Adapting to the textual landscape: Bringing print and visual texts together in the classroom. In A. Goodwyn (ed.) *Literary and Media Texts in Secondary English: New Approaches.* London: Cassell, pp. 129–149.

Hargreaves, A. (2009) The fourth way of change. In A. Hargreaves and M. Fullan (eds) *Change Wars.* Bloomington, IN: Solution Tree, pp. 11–43.

Hargreaves, A., and Fink, D. (2004) The seven principles of sustainable leadership. *Educational Leadership*, 61(7): 8–13.

Hull, G.A., and Nelson, M.E. (2005) Locating the semiotic power of multimodality. *Written Communication*, 22(2): 224–261.

IRA (International Reading Association) (2004) The role and qualifications of the reading coach in the United States. A position paper.

IRA (International Reading Association) (2010) PISA 2009 reveals gender disparities, decline in reading engagement [press release], accessed November 22, 2012: www.reading.org/Libraries/Press/PISA-release-FINAL.pdf

Jaeger, E. (1996) The reading specialist as collaborative consultant. *The Reading Teacher*, 49(8): 622–630.

John-Steiner, V., and Mahn, H. (1996) Sociocultural approaches to learning and development: A Vygotskian framework. *Educational Psychologist*, 31(3/4): 191–206.

Joyce, B., and Showers, B. (1982) The coaching of teaching. *Educational Leadership*, October: 4–10.

Joyce, B., and Showers, B. (1983) *Power in Staff Development through Research on Teaching.* Alexandria, VA: Association for Supervision and Curriculum Development.

Kaestle, C.F. (1985) The history of literacy and the history of readers. *Review of Research in Education*, 12: 11–53.

Kagan, D.M. (1992) Implications of research on teacher belief. *Educational Psychologist*, 27(1): 65–90.

Kalantzis, M., Cope, B., and Harvey, A. (2003) Assessing multiliteracies and the new basics. *Assessment in Education*, 10(1): 15–26.

Kamil, M., and Pearson, P.D. (1979) Theory and practice in teaching reading. *New York University Education Quarterly*, 10(2): 10–16.

Kennedy, E. (2010) Narrowing the achievement gap: Motivation, engagement, and self efficacy matter. Annual Proceedings of the Reading Association of Ireland.

Kress, G. (1997) Visual and verbal modes of representation in electronically mediated communication: The potentials of new forms of texts. In I. Snyder (ed.) *Page to Screen: Taking Literacy into the Electronic Age.* London: Routledge, pp. 53–79.

Kress, G. (2000) Multimodality. In B. Cope and M. Kalantzis (eds) *Multiliteracies: Literacy Learning and the Design of Social Futures.* London: Macmillan, pp. 182–202.

Kress, G., and van Leeuwen, T. (1996) *Reading Images: The Grammar of Visual Design.* New York: Routledge.

Labbo, L.D., and Reinking, D. (1999) Negotiating the multiple realities of technology in literacy research and instruction. *Reading Research Quarterly*, 34(4): 478–492.

Lai, M.K., McNaughton, S., Amituanai-Toloa, M., *et al.* (2009) Sustained acceleration of achievement in reading comprehension: The New Zealand experience. *Reading Research Quarterly*, 44(1): 30–56.

Lankshear, C., and Knobel, M. (2007) Sampling 'the new' in new literacies. In C. Lankshear and M. Knobel (eds) *A New Literacies Sampler.* New York: Peter Lang, pp. 1–24.

Lankshear, C., Snyder, I., and Green, B. (2000) *Technology and Technoliteracy: Managing Literacy, Technology, and learning in Schools.* St. Leonards, Australia: Allen & Unwin.

Lawless, K.A., and Pellegrino, J.W. (2007) Professional development in integrating technology into teaching and learning: Knowns, unknowns, and ways to pursue better questions and answers. *Review of Educational Research*, 77(4): 575–614.

Leu, D.J. (2006) New literacies, reading research, and the challenges of change: A deictic perspective (NRC presidential address). In J. Hoffman, C.M. Fairbanks, J. Worthy, and B. Maloch (eds) *The 55th Yearbook of the National Reading Conference.* Milwaukee, WI: National Reading Conference, pp. 1–20.

Leu, D.J., and Kinzer, C.K. (2000) The convergence of literacy instruction with networked technologies for information and communication. *Reading Research Quarterly*, 35(1): 108–127.

Leu, D.J., Kinzer, C.K. Coiro, J.L., and Cammack, D.W. (2004) Toward a theory of new literacies emerging from the Internet and other information and communication technologies. In R.B. Ruddell and N.J. Unrau (eds) *Theoretical Models and Processes of Reading*, 5th edn. Newark, DE: International Reading Association, pp. 1570–1613.

Lortie, D. (1975) *Schoolteacher: A Sociological Study.* London: University of Chicago Press.

Louis, K.S., Marks, H.M., and Kruse, S. (1996) Teachers' professional community in restructuring schools. *American Educational Research Journal*, 33(4): 757–798.

Mason, B., Mason, D.A., Mendez, M., *et al.* (2005) Effects of top-down and bottom-up elementary school standards reform in an underperforming California district. *The Elementary School Journal*, 105(4): 353–376.

McLaughlin, M.W., and Talbert, J.E. (2001) *Professional Communities and the Work of High School Teaching.* Chicago: University of Chicago Press.

Mirel, J. (2003) Old educational ideas, New American Schools: Progressivism and the rhetoric of educational revolution. *Paedagogica Historica*, 39(4): 477–497.

Mishra, P., and Koehler, M.J. (2006) Technological pedagogical content knowledge: A new framework for teacher knowledge. *Teachers College Record*, 108(6): 1017–1054.

Nespor, J. (1987) The role of beliefs in the practice of teaching. *Journal of Curriculum Studies*, 19(4): 317–328.

Newmann, F.M., King, M.B., and Youngs, P. (2000) Professional development that addresses school capacity: Lessons from urban elementary schools. *American Journal of Education*, 108(4): 259–299.

Newmann, F.M., Smith, B., Allensworth, E., and Bryk, A.S. (2001) Instructional program coherence: What it is and why it should guide school improvement policy. *Educational Evaluation and Policy Analysis*, 23(4): 297–321.

Newmann, F.M., and Wehlage, G.H. (1995) *Successful School Restructuring: A Report to the Public and Educators by the Center on Organization and Restructuring of Schools.* Alexandra, VA: Association for Supervision and Curriculum Development.

Nisbett, R., and Ross, L. (1980) *Human Inference: Strategies and Shortcomings of Social Judgment.* Englewood Cliffs, NJ: Prentice-Hall.

Nixon, H. (2003) New research literacies for contemporary research into literacy and new media? *Reading Research Quarterly*, 38(3): 407–413.

NLG (New London Group) (1996) A pedagogy of multiliteracies: Designing social futures. *Harvard Educational Review*, 66(1): 60–91.

Prensky, M. (2005) Listen to the natives. *Educational Leadership*, 63 (4): 8–13.

Pressley, M., Mohan, L., Raphael, L.M., and Fingeret, L. (2007) How does Bennett Woods elementary school produce such high reading and writing achievement? *Journal of Educational Psychology*, 99(2): 221–240.

Purkey, S.C., and Smith, M.S. (1983) Effective schools: A review. *The Elementary School Journal*, 83(4): 426–452.

Raphael, T.E., Au, K.H., and Goldman, S.R. (2009) Whole school instructional improvement through the Standards–Based Change Process: A developmental model. In J. Hoffman and Y. Goodman (eds) *Changing Literacies for Changing Times.* New York: Routledge/Taylor & Francis, pp. 198–229.

Resnick, L.B. (1991) Literacy in school and out. In S. Graubard (ed.) *Literacy: An Overview by Fourteen Experts.* New York: Hill and Wang, pp. 169–185.

Richardson, V., Anders, P., Tidwell, D., and Lloyd, C. (1991) The relationship between teachers' beliefs and practices in reading comprehension instruction. *American Educational Research Journal*, 28(3): 559–586.

Rokeach, M. (1968) *Belief, Attitudes, and Values: A Theory of Organization and Change.* San Francisco: Jossey-Bass.

Rowan, B. (1990) Commitment and control: Alternative strategies for organizational design of schools. *Review of Research in Education*, 16: 353–389.

Scribner, S. (1984) Literacy in three metaphors. *American Journal of Education*, 93: 6–21.

Spillane, J.P. (2006) *Distributed Leadership.* San Francisco: Jossey-Bass.

Stanley, M. (1972) Literacy: The crisis of a conventional wisdom. *School Review*, May, 373–408.

Stoll, L., Bolam, R., McMahon, A., *et al.* (2006) Professional learning communities: A review of the literature. *Journal of Educational Change*, 7: 221–258.

Strahan, D. (2003) Promoting a collaborative professional culture in three elementary schools that have beaten the odds. *The Elementary School Journal*, 104(2): 127–146.

Taylor, B.M., Pearson, P.D., Peterson, D.S., and Rodriguez, M.C. (2004) The CIERA school change framework: An evidence-based approach to professional development and school reading improvement. *Reading Research Quarterly*, 40(1): 40–69.

Taylor, B.M., Raphael, T.E., and Au, K.A. (2011) School reform in literacy. In P.D. Pearson, M. Kamil, P. Afflerbach, and E. Dutrow (eds) *Handbook of Reading Research.* New York: Routledge, pp. 594–628.

Timperly, H. (2009) Distributing leadership to improve outcomes for students. In K. Leithwood, B. Mascall, and T. Strauss (eds) *Distributed Leadership According to the Evidence*, London: Routledge, pp. 197–222.

Timperly, H.S, and Parr, J.M. (2007) Closing the achievement gap through evidence-based inquiry at multiple levels of the education system. *Journal of Advanced Academics*, 19(1): 90–115.

Tucker, M.S. (2011) Standing on the shoulders of giants: An American agenda for education reform. National Centre for Education and the Economy, accessed November 22, 2012: www.ncee.org/wp-content/uploads/2011/05/Standing-on-the-Shoulders-of-Giants-An-American-Agenda-for-Education-Reform.pdf

Unsworth, L. (2002) Changing dimensions of school literacies. *Australian Journal of Language and Literacy*, 25(1): 62–77.

Unsworth, L. (2006) Towards a metalanguage for multiliteracies education: Describing the meaning-making resources of language-image interaction. *English Teaching: Practice and Critique*, 5(1): 55–76.

Visscher, A.J., and Witziers, B. (2004) Subject departments as professional communities? *British Educational Research Journal*, 30(6): 785–800.

Weber, C.M. (2010) Juxtaposing words and images: Using digital narratives to capture teachers' conceptions of literacy. Unpublished doctoral dissertation, University of Illinois at Chicago, IL.

Wenger, E. (1998) *Communities of Practice: Learning, Meaning, and Identity.* New York: Cambridge University Press.

Wenger, E.C., and Snyder, W.M. (2000) Communities of practice: The organizational frontier. *Harvard Business Review*, 78(1): 139–145.

Chapter 35

Raising Literacy Achievement Levels through Collaborative Professional Development

Eithne Kennedy and Gerry Shiel

Introduction

Expertise in teaching reading, acquired through ongoing professional development (PD), has been identified as a key driver of educational reform, both in education generally (Cordingley *et al.*, 2003), and in literacy development in particular (Anders, Hoffman, and Duffy, 2000; Dillon *et al.*, 2010; IRA/International Reading Association, 2010), with PD often being credited with raising the achievement of students attending schools in areas with high levels of socioeconomic disadvantage (Gehsmann and Woodside-Jiron, 2005; Kennedy, 2008), and of enhancing the attractiveness of teaching as a professional activity (Cochran-Smith and Lytle, 2009). First, we define PD as it relates to literacy. Second, we describe four forms of PD – traditional workshops, teacher-as-researcher, coaching, and PD for accreditation and additional qualifications. Third, we characterize effective PD as being embedded in a school context, customized, collaborative, inquiry-based, grounded in content and pedagogical content strategies, and with a focus on ongoing analysis of student data. Fourth, we summarize research on the effectiveness of PD programs in literacy with reference to outcomes for students and their teachers. We conclude by identifying aspects of PD that need further study.

Defining Professional Development

Professional development can be described as 'a systematic structured attempt to generate desired or preferred change in the core business of curriculum, teaching and learning, and thereby to shift patterns of educational outcomes and effects' (Luke, 2005, p. 1). According to MacDonald Grieve and McGinley (2010), it should 'empower teachers and help them to develop a critically reflective approach to teaching and learning. It should encourage teachers to reflect, revitalise and extend their commitment to teaching... it needs to be embedded in practice' (p. 174). Along with curriculum and organizational reform, PD has been identified as a major strategy for improving student achievement (Darling-Hammond *et al.*, 2009; Slavin *et al.*, 2009).

International Handbook of Research on Children's Literacy, Learning, and Culture, First Edition.
Edited by Kathy Hall, Teresa Cremin, Barbara Comber, and Luis C. Moll.
© 2013 John Wiley & Sons, Ltd. Published 2013 by John Wiley & Sons, Ltd.

PD can be viewed as part of a continuum of teacher education that extends over a career-long pathway or framework, within which teachers engage in a process of progressive differentiation as they learn, enact, assess, and reflect on knowledge gleaned at various points along the way (Snow, Griffin, and Burns, 2005). A similar perspective is adopted by the International Reading Association's (IRA, 2010) *Standards for Reading Professionals*, which outlines the knowledge, skills, and dispositions that literacy professionals should have at different points along a literacy-related career trajectory beginning in pre-service and moving to induction to in-service and master teacher. The current chapter focuses on PD for practicing teachers of literacy, with a particular emphasis on interventions that support teachers in instructional decision making and are designed to bring change in both teaching and learning.

Teachers' professional knowledge can be described as comprising content (subject) knowledge and pedagogical content strategies (Shulman, 1987). Together, these represent a 'blending of content and pedagogy into an understanding of how particular topics, problems or issues are organised, presented and adapted to the diverse interests and abilities of the learners and presented for instruction' (p. 8). Combining these two elements, it is argued, can mutually inform and empower professional practice, considerably strengthening the effect of the PD, compared to a focus on content knowledge or pedagogical strategies alone (Showers, Joyce, and Bennett, 1987). Wray *et al.* (1999) have characterized the knowledge of effective teachers of literacy as comprising knowledge of content, knowledge about effective pedagogy, and knowledge about learners and how they learn. According to Wray *et al.*, effective teachers may not have more content knowledge than teachers with less expertise, nor are they always able to define linguistic terminology out of context, but they are more capable of identifying links across aspects of content knowledge, and can communicate key concepts to children in the context of real reading and writing activities.

According to Sigel (2006), the essential task of PD is to support teachers in moving their current instructional practices into closer proximity with evidence-based practices. The change process may involve straightforward enhancements, minor modifications, or a significant reworking or replacement of prevailing practices (Powell and Diamond, 2011). Wide gaps between existing practices and proposed reforms can pose a significant challenge for PD programs, since new ideas may not be viewed by teachers as desirable or 'within reach' of their existing approach. Related to this, Evans (2002) makes a distinction between *functional development*, wherein teachers modify teaching practices in order to comply with national or local requirements, and *attitudinal development*, which is viewed as a key component of effective, sustainable PD.

Forms of Professional Development in Literacy

Professional development in literacy can take many forms ranging from research undertaken by an individual teacher, to informal collaborative learning at school level, to large-scale PD designed to support the implementation of new programs or reforms. In this section, four forms of PD in literacy are described: courses and workshops, teacher as researcher, literacy coaching, and PD for accreditation or qualification. None of these forms is completely independent of the others and some PD programs may include a suite of approaches (e.g., workshops, teacher collaborative study groups, and observation of and feedback on teaching).

A traditional form of PD is the one-off *workshop* or *short course*, typically conducted outside school hours and off-site – something that has been termed a 'hit and run approach' (Darling-Hammond, 1996). This practice has continued in some countries. In a survey of US teachers, Darling-Hammond *et al.* (2009) reported that nine in ten teachers had participated in professional learning consisting primarily of short-term conferences or workshops, leading her to conclude:

> The US is far behind in providing public school teachers with opportunities to participate in extended learning opportunities and productive learning communities: opportunities that allow teachers to work together on issues of instructional planning, learn from one another through mentoring or peer coaching and conduct research on the outcomes of classroom practices, assessment and professional learning decisions (p. 6).

Teachers typically attend courses on topics they are interested in but the content may not be geared to their specific needs, is often transmitted (Villegas-Reimers, 2003), and has a poor record of actually changing teachers' literacy practices (Strickland and Kamil, 2004). Nevertheless, workshops, short courses or summer institutes may be important components of broader PD initiatives (Yoon *et al.*, 2007).

Another form of PD is *teacher as researcher* (also known as action research, teacher reflection or practitioner research), a systematic, intentional inquiry by teachers into their own school and classroom work that privileges their own voices (Cochran-Smith and Lytle, 2009), or, in terms used by Bakhtin, 'the speaking personality, the speaking consciousness' (1981, p. 434). Pappas and Tucker-Raymond (2011) argue that teacher research in literacy fosters 'an explicit awareness of teachers' practices; it represents opportunities [for teachers] to become reflective practitioners and to conduct research in their own classrooms' (p. vii). Cochran-Smith and Lytle (2009) describe this perspective as 'inquiry as stance' whereby teachers develop the tools and habits of mind necessary for making informed choices on selecting effective teaching methods, thereby empowering them as professionals. Theories developed by teachers are grounded in their practice as they develop a conscious understanding of the underlying basis for their actions. Although, in general, the outcomes of action research projects are not published in academic journals, Pappas and Tucker-Raymond (2011) provide several examples of such projects designed to raise achievement levels in literacy.

A form of PD that is particularly prevalent in the United States is *literacy coaching* which is often linked to federally-funded projects that require substantial PD for teachers. According to Neuman and Cunningham (2009), coaching involves ongoing classroom modeling, supportive critiques of practice, and specific observations. Like mentoring (where a novice teacher is paired with a more experienced colleague), it 'involves a collaborative relationship between an expert who may have been working in the field for many years, and a practitioner, to develop specific knowledge and skills related to instructional practice' (p. 538). Marsh *et al.* (2008) describe a range of coaching activities that include modeling lessons and co-teaching with colleagues, conferring, observing and debriefing, facilitating study groups, engaging in action research and reflection, and investigating common interest topics. Given the increase in this form of PD, researchers are seeking to understand the complexity of the processes involved in building relationships between coaches and teachers, and how their roles are utilized to support change in school and teacher practices (Ippolito, 2010). In theory, coaching seems a worthwhile approach. In practice, the effectiveness of coaching depends on a range of factors such as school climate, teacher openness to change, and organizational structures for facilitating the change process (Smith, 2007). This underscores the complexity involved in initiating change and requires a coach who is adept at providing the right level of support and then pressure to encourage teachers to engage with the change process, moving in and out of responsive coaching roles and more directive coaching roles as needed (Ippolito, 2010). A study by Bean *et al.* (2010), based on the self-reports of 20 coaches, provides insights into the range of activities that coaches are routinely engaged in, including working with teachers in small groups or individually (36 percent), management tasks related to their role such as entering assessment data and writing reports (21 percent), school-related tasks such as meeting with the principal or support personnel (21 percent), planning and organization of work to support teachers (14 percent), and working with students (8 percent). Just over a third of the time was spent in direct work with teachers, including modeling, observing, co-teaching and conferencing. In the same study, schools that experienced higher levels of coaching that involved interactions with teachers had more children performing at proficiency level and smaller percentages of at-risk learners. It would seem that the more focused a coach is on the quality of teaching and learning in classrooms, the greater the potential of coaching to deliver on raising achievement. Coburn and Woulfin (2012) report that literacy coaches can have a substantial impact on whether or not teachers make substantial changes in their classroom practices arising from policy reform initiatives, with coaches again supporting teachers to adopt new approaches, while at the same time pressurizing them to do so. Coburn and Woulfin report that coaching can be particularly effective in influencing those aspects of literacy teaching that are most difficult to change.

Reviews of PD involving literacy coaching (e.g., Powell and Diamond, 2011; Henry and Pianta, 2011) describe how technology can also be effective as remote coaches provide individualized feedback to teachers on their implementation of modeled techniques demonstrated in video-taped lessons, and use of hypermedia resources to illustrate evidence-based practice.

A related form of coaching, peer coaching, involves teachers identifying areas of need and working to hone their knowledge and practice by learning from each other. Lauer and Matthews (2007) describe an initiative in a high-poverty school in which teachers analyzed assessment data, decided on which aspects of reading to emphasize during instruction, created a professional learning community, and designed appropriate lessons. Briefing sessions prior to observations allowed teachers to set the agenda for the observations, while debriefing after lessons allowed for further professional dialogue. Lauer and Matthews viewed this approach to PD as honoring teacher individuality and professionalism as well as impacting positively on achievement. However, additional corroborating research is needed to confirm the efficacy of this approach.

A feature of a number of PD initiatives involving partnerships between university personnel and schools to raise achievement is the provision of *accreditation or additional qualifications* such as a diploma or master's degree with an emphasis on literacy (e.g., Au, Raphael and Mooney, 2008; Kennedy, 2008; Wray and Medwell, 2006). As an extension of the university–school relationship, university coursework can enable interested teachers to bridge the gap between the professional and academic worlds and experience professional renewal. MacDonald Grieve and McGinley (2010) note the collaborative nature of university coursework, where teachers can 'construct teacher knowledge based on shared practice, collaborative learning and scholarly reflection on practice' (p. 175). Engagement of teachers in accredited coursework is also consistent with associations between teacher qualifications and student achievement (e.g., Darling-Hammond *et al.*, 2009). However, more research is needed to ascertain the impact of this type of PD on teacher professional knowledge and how such knowledge is transferred to practice.

While it is potentially useful to consider possible effects of different forms of PD for improving teaching and raising literacy levels, Desimone (2009) argues that it is the characteristics of PD in whatever form(s) it takes that defines effectiveness. The next section considers key characteristics of PD designed to raise achievement.

Characteristics of Professional Development that Can Bridge the Gap

This section identifies key characteristics of PD that have been shown to be effective in raising achievement The more of these features that are present in a PD program, the greater the chance that the program will be successful. These elements can create a synergy within schools which can create the climate for sustainable change.

Sustained, customized on-site, whole school approach

Embedding PD within schools is a key feature of educational reform initiatives aimed at maximizing each student's potential. Collective participation provides opportunities to address specific concerns, questions and goals articulated by staff (Fullan, 1991; Strickland and Kamil, 2004). It can bring coherence, continuity, and focus over a multiyear change process (Au, 2005). In high achieving high-poverty schools, it is seen not as an event but a process and a way of life (Lipson *et al.*, 2004). In many studies that report enhanced literacy achievement, duration has varied from one year (Taylor *et al.*, 2003; Kinnucan-Welsch, Rosemary and Grogan, 2006), to two years (Kennedy, 2008) to four or more years (Au, Raphael, and Mooney, 2008), with varying degrees of intensity. While there is debate on the optimum length and distribution of time needed for PD, it is likely to be most effective if it occurs over an extended period, usually a minimum of one year (Garet *et al.*, 2001).

Collaborative inquiry stance within a professional learning community

Increasingly, the research literature reports collaborative partnerships between schools and out-side experts – often researchers and teacher educators (Cordingley *et al.*, 2003; Snow, Burns, and Griffin, 1998; Kennedy, 2010) who develop 'knowledge *of* practice' (Cochran-Smith and Lytle, 2001). Outsiders can help schools evolve into professional learning communities by providing scaffolding as teachers adopt an 'inquiry stance' to identifying the strengths and weaknesses of the school's literacy framework (Kennedy, 2008). This cultivates teacher agency and builds ownership of and commitment to the change process as teachers actively shape its direction from the outset. The 'funds of knowledge' (Moll *et al.*, 1992) of all participants are considered essential, with each of the partners acknowledged as bringing 'separate but complementary bodies of knowledge' (Ross *et al.*, 1999; Kennedy, 2008) to the investigation. As John-Steiner (2000, p. 189) suggests, adults working in collaboration 'create zones of proximal development for each other. Collaboration can be a mirror for each partner – a chance to understand one's habits, styles, working methods and beliefs through the comparison and contrast with one's collaborator.'

   In this model, inquiry involves teachers 'working within communities to generate local knowledge, envision and theorize their practice, and interpret and interrogate the theory and research of others' (Cochran-Smith and Lytle, 2001, p. 50). The approach acknowledges the complexity of teaching, the fact there is 'no quick fix' (Allington and Walmsley, 2007), that the research base is not static but continuously updating and that school-based collaborative partnerships can contribute to and advance this research base (Cordingley *et al.*, 2003). Effective collaboration in disadvantaged schools involves teachers working within and across grade levels and with the special education team, leading to more informed understandings of expectations within the school (Taylor *et al.*, 2003; Lipson *et al.*, 2004; Au, Raphael, and Mooney, 2008) and to the development of a school vision for literacy which everyone is focused on achieving (Lipson *et al.*, 2004).

Ongoing assessment of student achievement

Collaborative forms of continuing PD often link student assessment data to the ongoing design of the PD, which ensures that it is grounded in the complexities and realities of particular school and classroom contexts (Villegas-Reimers 2003; Gehsmann and Woodside-Jiron, 2005; Kinnucan-Welsch, Rosemary, and Grogan, 2006; Kennedy, 2008). When the inquiry stance described above includes ongoing collection and analysis of formative and summative assessment data, teachers probe their own teaching, identify PD needs in relation to literacy content and pedagogy, and monitor the effects of instructional changes on student achievement. Cordingley *et al.* (2003) point out that this kind of professional development is demanding on teachers and that it is important that 'arrangements for creating a distinctive space where it is safe to admit need' are put in place 'as there is often a period of pain and anxiety for teachers in risking new strategies and opening up their practice to observation' (p. 62). Thompson and Zeuli (1999, p. 342) suggest that real change involves 'transformational' learning leading to 'changes in deeply held beliefs, knowledge and habits of practice' and that in order for that to occur teachers need to be involved in a cycle of continuous improvement by identifying new issues that arise, engaging actively to understand them, deciding how to act to address the challenges, reflecting on the effectiveness of the solution and going through the whole process again as a new problem presents itself.

Grounding in pedagogical content strategies

As noted earlier, a dual focus on content and pedagogical strategies is needed to effectively mediate content in the classroom (Garet *et al.*, 2001; Shulman, 1987). With literacy, this implies enhancing teacher pedagogical knowledge in such areas as alphabetics (phonological awareness, letter and word-identification knowledge), fluency, vocabulary, comprehension, writing, assessment, motivation and engagement, and demonstrating a flexible range of methods and assessment tools (Snow, Griffin, and Burns, 2005; IRA, 2010). When this occurs as part of a whole school change process, it can have a powerful effect on the development of a school-wide balanced literacy framework responsive to the needs of diverse learners (Kennedy, 2008). Teachers' knowledge of the content and pedagogy of literacy can be enhanced through the provision of appropriate readings (journal articles, book chapters) which can form the basis for study groups, within professional learning communities in schools (Taylor *et al.*, 2003). It is most useful if the range of professional readings illustrate new methodologies through real classroom vignettes that teachers can read prior to PD sessions. This provides a common language and framework for teachers across the school to discuss content, pedagogy, and assessment for learning practices. It can provide a level of 'cognitive dissonance' (Thompson and Zeuli, 1999), prompting teachers to question their current methods as they see there are other, potentially more effective methods of teaching content. These readings can also provide the 'social persuasion' (Bandura, 1995) necessary to help teachers begin to envision themselves as potential doers of new pedagogy. Vanderburg and Stephens (2010), in a study of the impact of literacy coaches on teachers' knowledge and practice, found that teachers in the study highly valued the opportunity to study research on literacy theory and practice combined with follow-up sessions with their coach on how to implement the research in their own classrooms. The authors note that, for most teachers, 'a shift in theory is what led to a shift in practice' (p. 157).

Use of demonstrations and nonevaluative observations

Another way to build teachers' content and pedagogical content knowledge is to embed demonstrations and nonevaluative observations into the PD process (Cordingley *et al.*, 2003;

Kennedy, 2008). Teachers who observe knowledgeable others modeling new instructional techniques in their classrooms can experience greater confidence in applying the techniques and embedding them in their ongoing practice. In some studies, these supports are provided by teachers functioning as literacy coaches (e.g., Biancarosa, Bryk, and Dexter, 2010) or by an external partner who is collaborating with and supporting the school in developing a research-based approach to literacy (Shanahan, 2002). Teachers who open their practice up to observation conducted as part of PD are more likely to develop a stronger sense of self-efficacy than teachers who do not experience observation or on whom observation is imposed as a monitoring or accountability exercise (Da Costa, 1993). A positive impact for observation is more likely to occur when PD is ongoing, on-site, customized, and collaborative, providing the conditions for 'relational trust' (Hord, 2008) to develop among participants in PD. Trust is a characteristic of professional learning communities, and supports the kinds of experimentation and risk-taking necessary for solving the complex issues involved in teaching literacy (Kennedy and Shiel, 2010; Vanderburg and Stephens, 2010).

Internal structures, phased approach, and early success

The success of PD initiatives is also contingent on the level of 'structural supports' (Hord, 2008) in place in the school, the pace of the change agenda and the level of success teachers experience in the early stages of the change process (Guskey, 1986). Guskey argues that significant changes in teachers' beliefs and attitudes occur only *after* positive changes in student learning outcomes are apparent. This is particularly important in schools that may have experienced low levels of success in changing outcomes over many years despite best efforts of and high levels of commitment from teachers. As a result, teachers can have low expectations for students and be reluctant to change practices (Eivers, Shiel, and Shortt, 2004). However, when teachers are active in the change process from the outset and, together with the professional developer providing support to them, examine assessment data continuously, determine priorities, select goals and adopt a teacher-as-researcher stance within their own classrooms, they can introduce change gradually and closely monitor the effect of change on children's achievement, motivation, and engagement. Guiding teachers to set realistic goals and providing the support necessary to ensure success is a critical component in PD that is endeavoring to enable schools to raise achievement. This early success is a critical element as it not only cements commitment to the change process but also builds teachers' own self-efficacy in their ability to address challenges and dramatically improve achievement (Kennedy, in press).

Change does not occur in a linear fashion but rather in a dialectical manner 'moving back and forth between change in beliefs and change in classroom practice' (Cobb, Wood, and Yackel, 1990, reviewed in Villegas-Reimers, 2003). This can be facilitated further when there is a regularly scheduled time in which participants can support each other, share successes and challenges, reflect on teaching, evaluate progress in terms of student response, debate issues, and consider new goals as each target set is met.

Impact of Professional Development on Teachers and Students

As a basis for evaluating the effectiveness of PD across studies, it is useful to draw on Desimone's (2009) framework which includes (i) core characteristics of PD (whether they are present or not); (ii) changes in teacher knowledge and skills and in teacher attitudes and beliefs; (iii) changes in instruction (i.e., classroom practice); and (iv) changes in student learning. Desimone argues that this framework can be applied across studies of PD that draw on different research methodologies.

An early but influential audit of the effects of PD on student's literacy outcomes was conducted by the US National Reading Panel (NICHHD, 2000). Recognizing only studies that employed experimental research, just 21, all conducted in the US, met the panel's 'evidence-based' criteria. Fifteen studies reported modest improvements for teacher knowledge or practice, while 13 reported significant effects for student achievement, with teacher effects occurring side-by-side with higher student achievement in several studies. Similarly, Yoon *et al.* (2007) identified seven studies involving reading or English language arts that established clear links between nature and quantity of PD and student learning outcomes. The studies showed moderate effects for teacher professional learning on achievement of primary school students – an average effect size of 0.53 after adjusting for clustering within classes and for multiple comparisons. The authors predicted that average control group students would have increased their achievement by 21 percentile points if their teachers had received the same PD as teachers of experimental groups. As a result of the lack of variability in form and much variability in duration and intensity in this small number of studies, it was not possible to discern any clear linkages between characteristics of PD and their effects.

In a large-scale evaluation, Garet *et al.* (2008) assessed the effects of two PD approaches in second grade in 90 urban, high-poverty schools in the US with large numbers of English language learners (ELLs) on the knowledge and practices of 250 teachers and the achievement of their students. One intervention consisted of an eight-day series of content-based in-service institutes and seminars focusing on second grade reading instruction, based on a comprehensive reading and spelling program. The second was the same as the first, but also included intensive in-school coaching from trained literacy coaches. A control group of teachers received their districts' regular PD program. Although there were positive impacts on teachers' knowledge of scientifically-based reading instruction[1] and on one of the three instructional practices promoted by the study (use of explicit instruction),[2] neither PD intervention resulted in significantly higher student test scores at the end of the one-year treatment or at follow-up a year later. Possible reasons for this outcome included: the high turnover of teachers (33 percent over two years), variation in the amount of coaching received by teachers, and the short duration of training for coaches (less than one week). It is also possible that Garet *et al.*'s interventions did not promote ownership of the change process in schools or encourage a sufficiently strong inquiry stance among teachers linked to ongoing assessment of student achievement, or pay sufficient attention to the 'attitudinal development' noted earlier as being an essential element of PD.

In a four-year longitudinal study that used a hierarchical, value-added, cross-level effects model designed to trace effects on achievement of individual coaching in the context of a school reform initiative, Biancarosa, Bryk, and Dexter (2010) demonstrated increasing improvements in reading performance with effect sizes of .22, .37 and .43 over three years (relative to baseline). Effects were also found to persist through summers. The authors attributed these positive impacts to the duration of training for coaches (a full school year before project implementation, including graduate-level coursework), and the coaching model itself, which was underpinned by a comprehensive literacy development program. Gehsmann and Woodside-Jiron (2005) also reported positive effects of a coaching model in a low-performing school over a four-year period. They customized PD with reference to the assessed needs of students in the school. In a study involving early childhood practitioners, Neuman and Wright (2010) studied the impact of two kinds of professional development (off-site coursework or on-site individualized coaching) on teacher knowledge and practice. Coaching was interactive with teacher and coach co-teaching on-site through modeling and demonstration, with reflection on practice a key component. Coaches were asked to focus on nonevaluative feedback and to build a rapport with teachers. Pre- and post-assessments of teacher knowledge and practice revealed no differences in relation to knowledge; however, those who had received coaching had made significant changes to the structural environment during the intervention and sustained them up to 5 months post-intervention but there were only modest changes in teaching strategies. The authors concluded that coaching is an effective form of PD for early childhood educators but that duration, intensity, and focus of coaching sessions needs to be further researched.

In a two-year mixed-methods study employing a multilevel research design that included a significant coaching element, Kennedy (2008, 2010) worked collaboratively with a high-poverty junior school serving 4–8 year olds to design and implement a research-based cognitively challenging balanced literacy framework. PD was customized to particular classroom contexts with a view to accelerating literacy achievement in ways that cultivated children's creativity, agency, and independence. A multifaceted collaborative program, in line with the principles outlined earlier, was put in place. A range of qualitative data was gathered (interviews and observations) and children's achievement in reading, writing, and spelling were tracked throughout. Outcomes included statistically significant improvements in reading, writing and spelling. For example, the numbers of children performing below the 10th percentile between first and second grade on a nationally standardized reading test had reduced by three quarters, while 20 percent were performing above the 80th percentile (no children were at this level at the outset). Overall effect sizes were considered to be large (*Cohen's d*, $d = 1.29$ (Cohen, 1988)), indicating substantive progress.

Teachers attributed this success to the sustained customized professional development that they felt had deepened their expertise in literacy pedagogy and assessment, enabling them to respond effectively to the children's stage of development in ways that built their motivation and engagement. Teachers also reported having higher expectations for the children and higher levels of self-efficacy and confidence in their own ability to address literacy difficulties. Their sense of power and agency had arisen from the early success they had in achieving the first goals they had set and from their continued engagement with the research literature that they felt had helped them re-envision themselves as literacy teachers. This small scale study demonstrates what can be achieved when the research base is utilized in ways that build teachers' professionalism and autonomy over time. Its outcomes are consistent with those of other similar studies (e.g., Gehsmann and Woodside-Jiron, 2005; Au, Raphael, and Mooney, 2008).

In two separate year-long studies employing multimethods, Cremin and colleagues (Cremin, 2006; Cremin *et al.*, 2009; UKLA, 2011) drew attention to teachers' awareness of themselves as readers and writers, and to how this awareness can impact on both teaching and student learning. Cremin (2006) showed how collaborative meetings among teachers helped overcome initial fear and lack of confidence about themselves as writers, and led to enhanced understanding of the challenges faced by their students during writing classes. Cremin *et al.* (2009) looked at teachers' as readers, their knowledge of children's literature, and the effects these had on their pedagogical practices. Again meeting in collaborative groups, the teachers' broadened their own reading, and their interest in and attitude to their students' reading material became more positive. Other outcomes were higher levels of cooperation and discussion among teachers, enhanced perceptions by children of their abilities, and greater than expected improvement in reading achievement, as measured by national tests. These studies and the National Writing Project (NWP) in the United States (Wood and Lieberman, 2000), which involves teachers working collaboratively during a summer institute to develop their own writing as well as their students' writing, underline important and often overlooked relationships among teacher agency, teaching and learning, that should also be addressed in studies designed to raise student achievement. Whitney (2008) attributed the success of the NWP to its transformative power – participating in writing enables teachers to make sense of new experiences, as well as interpret previous experiences (teaching writing) from new perspectives. She shows how epistemological shifts and accompanying shifts in agency and authority occur for teachers participating in NWP summer institutes, and argues that studies of the effects of NWP on teaching writing in classrooms should question the intentions, reasons and understandings that shape teachers' actions, as well as document the actions themselves.

Finally, while most of the research reviewed here has looked at effects of PD interventions on primary school teachers and their students, researchers have begun to consider effects at post-primary level. For example, Slavin *et al.* (2009) reported that the most effective literacy intervention programs for middle-school and high-school students were those that involved cooperative learning and mixed activities. Such programs were found to provide extensive professional development, and to affect teaching practices in positive and significant ways.

Conclusions

A key aspect of PD for literacy concerns what constitutes teachers' professional knowledge. Although Shulman's (1987) distinction between content (subject) knowledge and pedagogical knowledge can form a useful basis for thinking about what should be presented in PD, the work of Wray *et al.* (1999) suggests teachers' knowledge of abstract content may be less important than supporting teachers to communicate important concepts to children in meaningful contexts. Poulson (2001) points to dangers of separating content and practical knowledge, and argues that more attention should be given to understanding the relationship between tacit and formal or explicit knowledge, and how teachers acquire both.

Despite the need for further work in conceptualizing the knowledge base for literacy teaching, there is broad consensus that PD in literacy should include both content knowledge and teaching strategies in such areas as alphabetics, fluency, vocabulary, comprehension, writing, motivation and engagement, and assessment. The work of Cremin and her colleagues (Cremin, 2006; Cremin *et al.*, 2009), as well as the National Writing Project, suggests a need to take teachers' own literacy practices, and, by extension, the literacy practices of children and their communities, into account in designing effective PD and in seeking to improve classroom practice.

The 'best evidence' syntheses of research by the National Reading Panel (NICHHD, 2000) and Yoon *et al.* (2007), and the disappointing outcomes of the Garet *et al.* (2008) study could lead to the conclusion that we know relatively little about how to design and implement effective PD. Fortunately, more recent studies using a range of research methods show that it is possible to design and implement effective PD that can raise student achievement, including the achievements of weaker students. Biancarosa, Bryk, and Dexter's (2010) study illustrates how multilevel modeling can tease out the effects of PD forms such as coaching over a number of years, while studies by Gehsmann and Woodside-Jiron (2005) and Kennedy (2008) illustrate how several characteristics of PD, including nonevaluative coaching, can be combined in a single school-level program to support improved cognitive and attitudinal outcomes for at-risk students, as well as stronger agency and self-efficacy among teachers.

While it is encouraging to see a large body of research emerging on the effectiveness of literacy coaching, there is an obvious risk in limiting research efforts on the effectiveness of PD to coaching alone. There is also a need to look at the effects of other forms of PD including college-based courses that teachers take for credit and action research studies undertaken by teachers in their own classroom settings. It would also be worthwhile to compare college-based experts with literacy coordinators or coaches in terms of their effects of teachers' knowledge about literacy and their effects on student learning.

A difficulty with many of the studies on PD in literacy and in other areas is that they rarely report on both processes and outcomes (Cordingley *et al.*, 2003). In order to improve our understanding of links between PD and student performance, it is important that studies describe the process of PD and rigorously document changes in teachers' knowledge, practices and attitudes, as well as the effects of PD on students' achievement, motivation and engagement.

Finally, we reiterate that there is no 'quick fix' where PD in literacy is concerned. The successful studies reviewed here demonstrate that a long-term commitment to PD (often several years) may be necessary to effect real change in how teachers teach, and in how at-risk students respond to new teaching methods.

Notes

1. A survey of Reading Content and Practices was administered on three occasions during the study.
2. The other practices were: guiding students in independent practice of reading activities, and differentiating instruction to meet individual students' needs.

References

Allington, R.L., and Walmsley, S.A. (2007) *No Quick Fix, the RTI Edition, Rethinking Literacy Programs in America's Elementary Schools*. New York: Teachers College Press.

Anders, P.L., Hoffman, J.V., and Duffy, G.G. (2000) Teaching teachers to teach reading: Paradigm shifts, persistent problems, and challenges. In M.L. Kamil, P.B. Moesenthal, P.D. Pearson, and R. Barr (eds) *Handbook of Reading Research*, Vol. III. Mahwah, NJ: Erlbaum, pp. 719–742.

Au, K. (2005) Negotiating the slippery slope: School change and literacy achievement. *Journal of Literacy Research*, 37(3): 267–288.

Au, K., Raphael, T., and Mooney, K.C. (2008) What we have learned about teacher education to improve literacy achievement in urban schools. In V. Chou, L. Morrow, and L. Wilkinson (eds) *Improving Literacy Achievement in Urban Schools: Critical Elements in Teacher Preparation*. Newark, DE: International Reading Association, pp. 159–184.

Bakhtin, M.M. (1981) *The Dialogic Imagination: Four Essays by M.M. Bakhtin*, (ed. M. Holquist; trans, C. Emerson and M. Holquist). Austin, TX: University of Texas Press.

Bandura, A. (1995) Exercise of personal and collective efficacy in changing societies. In A. Bandura (ed.) *Self-Efficacy in Changing Societies*. Cambridge, UK: Cambridge University Press, pp. 1–45.

Bean, R.M., Draper, J.A., Hall, V., *et al.* (2010) Coaches and coaching in Reading First schools. *The Elementary School Journal*, 111(1): 87–114.

Biancarosa, G., Bryk, A.S., and Dexter, E.R. (2010) Assessing the value-added effects of literacy collaborative professional development on student learning. *Elementary School Journal*, 111(1): 7–34.

Coburn, C.E., and Woulfin, S.L. (2012) Reading coaches and the relationship between policy and practice. *Reading Research Quarterly*, 47(1): 5–30.

Cochran-Smith, M., and Lytle, S.L. (2001) Beyond certainty: Taking an inquiry stance on practice. In A. Leiberman and L. Miller (eds) *Teachers Caught in the Action: Professional Development that Matters*. New York: Teachers College Press, pp. 45–58.

Cochran-Smith, M., and Lytle, S.L. (2009) *Inquiry as Stance. Practitioner Research for a New Generation*. New York: Teachers' College Press.

Cohen, J. (1988) *Statistical Power Analysis for the Behavioral Sciences*. Hillsdale, NJ: Lawrence Erlbaum.

Cordingley, P., Bell, M., Rundell, B., and Evans, D. (2003) The impact of collaborative CPD on classroom teaching and learning. London: EPPI-Centre, Social Science Research Unit, Institute of Education, University of London, accessed November 23, 2012: http://eppi.ioe.ac.uk/cms/Default.aspx?tabid=132

Cremin, T. (2006) Creativity, uncertainty and discomfort: Teachers as writers. *Cambridge Journal of Education*, 36(3): 415–433.

Cremin, T., Mottram, M., Collins, F., *et al.* (2009) Teachers as readers: Building communities of readers. *Literacy*, 43(1): 11–19.

Da Costa, J. L. (1993) A study of teacher collaboration in terms of teaching-learning performance. Paper given at the American Educational Research Association Annual Meeting, April 12–16, Atlanta, GA.

Darling-Hammond, L. (1996) What matters most: A competent teacher for every child. *Phi-Delta Kappan*, 78(3): 193–200.

Darling-Hammond, L., Chung Wei, R., Andreee, A., *et al.* (2009) *Professional Learning in the Learning Profession: A Status Report on Teacher Development in the United States and Abroad*. Dallas, TX: National Staff Development Council.

Desimone, L.M. (2009) Improving impact studies of teachers' professional development: Towards better conceptualisations and measures. *Educational Researcher*, 38(3): 181–199.

Dillon, D.R., O'Brien, D.G., Sato, M., and Kelly, C.M. (2010) Professional development and teacher education for reading instruction. In M.L. Kamil, P.D. Pearson, E.B. Moje, and P. Afflerbach (eds) *Handbook of Reading Research*, Vol. 4. Mahwah, NJ: Lawrence Erlbaum, pp. 629–659.

Eivers, E., Shiel, G., and Shortt, S. (2004) *Reading Literacy in Disadvantaged Primary Schools*. Dublin: Educational Research Centre.

Evans, L. (2002) 'What is teacher development?' *Oxford Review of Education*, 28(1): 123–137.

Fullan, M. (1991) *The New Meaning of Educational Change*. New York: Teachers College Press.

Garet, M.S., Cronen, S., Eaton, M., *et al.* (2008) *The Impact of Two Professional Development Interventions on Early Reading Instruction and Achievement*, (NCEE 2008–4030). Washington, DC: National Center for Education Evaluation and Regional Assistance, Institute of Education Sciences, U.S. Department of Education.

Garet, M.S., Porter, A.C., Desimone, L., *et al.* (2001) What makes professional development effective? Results from a national sample of teachers. *American Educational Research Journal*, 38(4): 915–945.

Gehsmann, K.M., and Woodside-Jiron, H.W. (2005) Becoming more effective in the age of school accountability: A high-poverty school narrows the literacy achievement gap. In B. Maloch, J. Hoffman, D.L. Schallert, *et al.* (eds) *Fifty-Fourth Yearbook of the National Reading Conference*. Oak Creek, WI: National Reading Conference, pp. 182–197.

Guskey, T.R. (1986) Staff development and the process of teacher change. *Educational Researcher*, 15(5): 5–12.

Henry, A.E., and Pianta, R.C. (2011) Effective teacher–child interactions and children's literacy: Evidence for scalable, aligned approaches to professional development. In S.B. Neuman and D.K. Dickinson (eds) *Handbook of Early Literacy Research*, Vol. 3. New York: Guilford Press, pp. 308–321.

Hord, S.M. (2008) Evolution of the learning community. *Journal of Staff Development*, 29(3): 10–13.

Ippolito, J. (2010) Three ways that literacy coaches balance response and directive relationships with teachers. *Elementary School Journal*, 111(1): 164–190.

IRA (International Reading Association) (2010) *Standards for Reading Professionals. Revised 2010*. Newark, DE: Author.

John-Steiner, V. (2000) *Creative Collaboration*. New York: Oxford University Press.

Kennedy, E. (2008) Improving literacy achievement in a disadvantaged primary school: Empowering classroom teachers through professional development. Unpublished doctoral dissertation, St Patrick's College, Dublin, Ireland.

Kennedy, E. (2010) Improving literacy achievement in a high-poverty school: Empowering classroom teachers through professional development. *Reading Research Quarterly*, 44(5): 384–387.

Kennedy, E. (in press) *Raising Literacy Achievement in High-poverty Schools: An Evidence-based Approach*. New York: Routledge.

Kennedy, E., and Shiel, G. (2010) Raising literacy levels with collaborative onsite professional development in an urban disadvantaged school. *The Reading Teacher*, 63(5): 372–383.

Kinnucan-Welsch, K., Rosemary, C.A., and Grogan, P.R. (2006) Accountability by design in literacy professional development. *The Reading Teacher*, 59(5): 426–435.

Lauer, D., and Matthews, M. (2007) Teachers steer their own learning. *Journal of Professional Development*, 28(2): 36–41.

Lipson, M.Y., Mosenthal, J.H., Mekkelson, J., and Russ, B. (2004) Building knowledge and fashioning success one school at a time. *The Reading Teacher*, 57(6): 534–545.

Luke, A. (2005) CRPP intervention plan: Moving from the core to pedagogic change. Unpublished technical report. Singapore: Centre for Research and Pedagogic Support.

MacDonald Grieve, A., and McGinley, B.P. (2010) Enhancing professionalism? Teachers' voices on continuing professional development in Scotland. *Teaching Education*, 21(2): 171–184.

Marsh, J., Sloan-McCombs, J., Jockwood, J.R., *et al.* (2008) Supporting literacy across the sunshine state: A study of Florida middle-school reading coaches. Santa Monica, CA: Rand, accessed November 23, 2012: www.rand.org/pubs/monographs/2008/RAND_MG762.pdf

Moll, L.C., Amanti, C., Neff, D., and Gonzalez, N. (1992) Funds of knowledge for teaching: Using a qualitative approach to connect homes and classrooms. *Theory into Practice*, 31(2): 32–141.

Neuman, S., and Cunningham, L. (2009) The impact of professional development and coaching on early language and literacy instructional practices. *American Educational Research Journal*, 46: 532–566.

Neuman, S., and Wright, T. (2010) Promoting language and literacy development for early childhood educators. *Elementary School Journal*, 111(1): 63–86.

NICHHD (National Institute of Child Health and Human Development) (2000) *Report of the National Reading Panel. Teaching Children to Read: An Evidence-Based Assessment of the Scientific Research Literature on Reading and its Implications for Reading Instruction: Reports of the Subgroups*. Washington: US Government Printing Office.

Pappas, C., and Tucker-Raymond, E. (2011) *Becoming a Teacher Researcher in Literacy Teaching and Learning: Strategies and Tools for the Inquiry Process*. New York: Routledge.

Poulson, L. (2001) Paradigm lost: Subject knowledge, primary teachers and educational policy. *British Journal of Educational Studies*, 49(1): 40–55.

Powell, D.R., and Diamond, K.E. (2011) Improving the outcomes of coaching-based professional development interventions. In S.B. Neuman and D.K. Dickinson (eds) *Handbook of Literacy Research*, Vol. 3. New York: Guilford, pp. 295–307.

Ross, J.A., Rolheiser, C., and Hogaboam-Gray, A. (1999) Effects of collaborative action-research on the knowledge of five Canadian teacher researchers. *The Elementary School Journal*, 99(3): 255–275.

Shanahan, T. (2002) Research synthesis: Making sense of the accumulation of knowledge in reading. In M.L. Kamil, P.B. Mosenthal, P.D. Pearson, and R. Barr (eds) *Methods of Literacy Research*. Mahwah, NJ: Erlbaum, pp. 133–150.

Showers, B., Joyce, B., and Bennett, B. (1987) Synthesis of research on staff development: A framework for future study and state of the art analysis. *Educational Leadership*, 45(3): 77–87.

Shulman, L.S. (1987) Knowledge and teaching: Foundations of the new reform. *Harvard Educational Review*, 57(1): 1–22.

Sigel, I.E. (2006) Research to practice redefined. In W. Damon and R.M. Lerner (series eds) and K.A. Renninger and I.E. Sigel (vol. eds) *Handbook of Child Psychology:* Vol. 4. *Child Psychology in Practice*, 6th edn. Hoboken, NJ: Wiley, pp. 1017–1023.

Slavin, R.E., Lake, C., Chambers, B., *et al.* (2009) Effective reading programs for the elementary grades: A best evidence synthesis. *Review of Educational Research*, 79(4): 1391–1466.

Smith, A.T. (2007) The middle school literacy coach: considering roles in context. In D.W. Rowe, R.T. Jimenez, D.L. Compton, *et al.* (eds) *56th Yearbook of the National Reading Conference*. Oak Creek, WI: National Reading Conference, pp. 53–67.

Snow, C., Burns, S.M., and Griffin, P. (eds) (1998) *Preventing Reading Difficulties in Young Children*. Washington: National Academy Press.

Snow, C., Griffin, P., and Burns, S.M. (eds) (2005) *Knowledge to Support the Teaching of Reading: Preparing Teachers for a Changing World*. San Francisco, CA: Jossey-Bass.

Strickland, D., and Kamil, M.L. (2004) *Improving Reading Achievement through Professional Development*. Norwood, MA: Christopher-Gordon Publishers.

Taylor, B.M., Pearson, D.P., Peterson, D.S., and Rodriguez, M.C. (2003) Reading growth in high-poverty classrooms: The influence of teacher practices that encourage cognitive engagement in literacy learning. *The Elementary School Journal*, 104(1): 3–28.

Thompson, C.L., and Zeuli, J.S. (1999) The frame and the tapestry: Standards-based reform and professional development. In L. Darling-Hammond and G. Sykes (eds) *Teaching as the Learning Profession: Handbook of Policy and Practice*. San Francisco: Jossey-Bass, pp. 341–375.

UKLA (United Kingdom Literacy Association) (2011) Building communities: Researching literacy lives 2009–10. Draft executive summary.

Vanderburg, M., and Stephens, D. (2010) The impact of literacy coaches: What teachers value and how teachers change. *Elementary School Journal*, 111(1): 141–163.

Villegas-Reimers, E. (2003) *Teacher Professional Development: An International Review of the Evidence*. UNESCO: International Institute for Educational Planning.

Whitney, A. (2008) Teacher transformation in the National Writing Project. *Research in the Teaching of English*, 43(2): 144–187.

Wood, D.R., and Lieberman, A. (2000) Teachers as authors: the National Writing Project's approach to professional development. *International Journal of Leadership in Education*, 3(3): 255–273.

Wray, D., and Medwell, J. (2006) Professional development for literacy teaching: the evidence from effective teachers. *Journal of In-service Education*, 26(3): 487–498.

Wray, D., Medwell, J., Fox, R., and Poulson, L. (1999) Teaching reading: Lessons from experts. *Reading*, 33(1): 17–22.

Yoon, K.S., Duncan, T., Lee, S.W.-Y., *et al.* (2007) Reviewing the evidence on how teacher professional development affects student achievement. Issues and Answers Report, REL 2007–No. 033. Washington, DC: US Department of Education, Institute of Education Sciences, National Center for Education Evaluation and Regional Assistance, Regional Educational Laboratory Southwest.

Chapter 36

Teacher Research on Literacy

Turning Around to Students and Technology

Christopher S. Walsh and Barbara Kamler

Introduction

Over the past 30 years, we have seen 'moral panics' over literacy education fuelled by the media in the British, Australian, Canadian, and American press (Barton, 2000). 'Moral panics' as a rhetorical strategy promote deficit thinking and construct literacy crises that require expedient political solutions. Too often children are blamed for poor attention, disruptive behavior or disinterest; parents are blamed for disorderly family routines and turmoil in the home; teachers are blamed for failing to teach traditional values and get their students to perform; and teacher educators are blamed for failing to impart the necessary knowledge to teach children who lack mainstream social values and literacy practices. As long-time researchers of literacy, we know it is no easy matter to disrupt discourses of blame that attend literacy failure and underachievement.

In recent times, we have seen the emergence of increased and pervasive accountability regimes that monitor literacy teachers' performance. The pressure to perform and produce quality outcomes has been accompanied by a greater reliance on standardized testing and normative assessments of literacy curriculum – and a devaluing of the professional judgment of teachers. At the same time literacy, and what it means to be literate in the twenty-first century, is changing due to the communicative affordances of digital and mobile technologies. Against this backdrop of top-down prescriptive standardization, micro-management of teachers' work, and the changing nature of literacy, it is timely to think about the role of teacher research and its relationship to children's literacy education.

We argue that in current times, teacher research is more significant than ever. Facilitating a researcher disposition in pre-service and in-service teachers is crucial not only in confronting deficit assumptions about children's literacy, but in dealing with the provocative challenges of the twenty-first century. While teacher research has a long history of providing spaces of inquiry that sustain teachers' professional learning, we worry that it may be under threat given reductions in spending and a global inclination to quick political fixes for educational problems. By contrast, teacher research takes time, requires trust and a sustained commitment to working collaboratively to question, observe, analyze, and problem-solve in local communities. It can be, however, a key methodology for confronting deficit thinking, and more fully engaging

International Handbook of Research on Children's Literacy, Learning, and Culture, First Edition.
Edited by Kathy Hall, Teresa Cremin, Barbara Comber, and Luis C. Moll.
© 2013 John Wiley & Sons, Ltd. Published 2013 by John Wiley & Sons, Ltd.

students as literate learners (Comber and Kamler, 2004) who explore 'new possibilities for knowledge-building, action and communication' (Comber, Nixon, and Reid, 2007, p. 12).

In this chapter, we first review the evolution of teacher research that links inquiry to democracy, social justice, and educational change. We then examine key moves in teacher research in and on children's literacy education. Using the metaphor of teachers 'turning around' (Comber and Kamler 2005) to students as researchers and to technology (Beavis *et al.*, 2009; Walsh, 2007, 2009, 2010), we explore productive directions for future teacher research, given the strengths of past research and opportunities of the present.

Teacher Research, Democracy, and Social Justice

The history of teacher research can be traced back to John Dewey who called for significant reforms in teacher education. Dewey saw reflection and inquiry as always tied to the ideal of democracy with the purpose of bringing about personal, social, and educational change (Dewey 1933/1985). So too, Freire's *Pedagogy of the Oppressed* (1970), Schön's *The Reflective Practitioner* (1983) as well as Habermas' *Knowledge and Human Interests* (1971) posit strong links between reflection and inquiry and democracy and social justice. The ethos of teacher research that stems from these influential texts has inspired educators to engage in research that interrogates teacher viewpoints and considers the needs of students within the contextualized histories of schools (Cochran-Smith and Lytle, 1999).

In the 1960s in the United Kingdom, Stenhouse strongly advocated that teachers engage in research (Cochran-Smith and Lytle 1990) when curriculum and professional development were merged into a single activity that engaged teachers as active agents (Craig, 2009). In the 1970s, Schwab's (1969) influential work in the United States on practical inquiry also called for teachers to play a central role in curriculum development and to engage in reflection by paying close attention to the lived experience of children and teachers in classrooms (Elbaz-Luwisch, 2006). This provided the momentum for the teacher research movement in the United States in the 1980s that emphasized action research and reflective practice.

Cochran-Smith and Lytle (2009) trace a variety of theoretical and intellectual influences on teacher research. These include: writings about language, learning and literacy that brought about a paradigm shift in the way teachers research, teach and assess writing (1970s and 1980s); critical democratic social theory where teachers worked actively to bring about social change (1980s); alternate modes of understanding learning and teacher development (1970s and 1980s); and ethnographic research that challenged the hegemony of an exclusively university-generated knowledge base for teaching (1980s). Common across these more recent traditions of teacher research is the positioning of the teacher as knower and change agent in his/her classroom or school (Cochran-Smith and Lytle, 1993, 1999).

A key strength of teacher research is that it generates both local and public knowledge (Cochran-Smith and Lytle, 1993, 1999; Lytle and Cochran-Smith, 1994) through a dialectical relationship or stance with theories of teaching and learning (Cochran-Smith and Lytle, 2009). Over the past four decades, teacher research has taken on numerous forms (action research, lesson study, self-study, narrative or autobiographical study). Nonetheless, it has been primarily conducted by teachers with the goal of understanding teaching and learning in context and from the perspective of those who interact daily in the classroom (Meier and Henderson, 2007; Zeichner, 1999). Notwithstanding different methodologies, advocates of teacher research generally concede it must be grounded in the 'dialectic of inquiry and practice rather than in one particular theoretical tradition or framework' (Cochran-Smith and Lytle, 2009, p. 42). When teacher researchers publicly share their findings, they add to the knowledge base on teaching and learning (Borko, Liston, and Whitcomb, 2007; Freeman *et al.*, 2007; Shulman *et al.*,

1999; Zeichner and Noffke, 2001) with the goal of improving the life chances of their students (Lytle, 2008).

From our point of view, this positioning of teachers as knowers is a significant move to counter deficit discourses that diminish teacher agency. It allows teachers to be viewed as actors and learners rather than minions who follow orders. Teacher research provides teachers with the knowledge and means to challenge standardized top-down approaches to curriculum reflective of technical standards. It stands in opposition to limited forms of practitioner research where teachers are only guided to try trial something new (Somekh, 2006) or reflect upon their pedagogy where the scope of reflection is primarily technical (Kemmis, 2006). This kind of 'technical inquiry' does not touch upon the ways 'globalization can marginalize or even exploit deeply rooted local specificities' (Weis, Fine, and Dimitriadis, 2009, p. 439).

When, by contrast, the work of teacher research communities is understood to be both social and political, teachers have questioned and challenged current arrangements of schooling they find unjust, inequitable or exclusionary. Whether it be investigating how a law like 'No Child Left Behind' in the United States brings about an increase in mandated testing (Karp, 2003) driving certain forms of literacy instruction; or assessing the ways knowledge is constructed, evaluated, and used (Cochran-Smith, 2004); or critiquing the larger purposes of schools (Lyons, 2010), teacher research requires a dialectical relationship between theory and action to bring about social justice and equity.

> Much practitioner inquiry remains radical and passionate, deeply personal and profoundly political – richly embedded in situations where teachers have agency around their own practice and where their commitments to educational access and equity remain clear in spite of these 'trying times' (Lytle, 2008, p. 373).

Not surprisingly, teacher research has been recognized for its potential to drive school reform. In Australia, for example, the Commonwealth Government funded the *Innovative Links between Schools and Universities for Teacher Professional Development* project in the 1990s to generate school-based teacher research and reform across the country. Seventeen universities established a 'Roundtable' with several surrounding schools to facilitate school-based action research (See for example Hogan and Strickland 1998, which charted attempts to build a collaborative learning community through writing narratives about teacher research.) Professional associations such as the Primary English Teaching Association (PETA) and the Australian Association of Teachers of English (AATE) have a history of supporting innovative teacher research on a smaller scale (Comber, Nixon, and Reid, 2007; Doecke and Gill, 2001).

While practitioner inquiry and teacher research has also become a goal for some pre-service and in-service teacher education in the United States (Liston and Zeichner, 1990); Canada (Clarke, 2006; Nielsen *et al.*, 2010; Mitchell, Clarke, and Nutall, 2007); New Zealand (Limbrick *et al.*, 2010); and to some extent the United Kingdom (McArdle and Coutts, 2010), this remains exceptional, suggesting the need to provide more enduring spaces in schools, and support structures (through unions, national policies, teaching councils and accreditation agencies) where teachers reflect and share successful research practices, particularly in regards to children's literacy (Hamston, Risko, and Ellis, 2006).

Teacher Research on Children's Literacy

When it comes to teachers researching literacy, we find a strong commitment to social justice and political action. Since the 1980s, in particular, much teacher research has been informed by critical literacy pedagogies which foreground the 'non-neutrality of literacy, the non-innocence of young children's textual work and play, and their potential for complex analytical practice' (Comber, 2003, p. 355) whether they be 'reading' texts, people, places, or events.

A key move in this type of teacher research has been the repositioning of teachers and students as researchers of language and discourse. In a three-year study from New York City, teacher researchers repositioned their students as co-researchers by explicitly teaching them transdisciplinary semiotic modes of textual and visual analysis (Albright, Purohit, and Walsh, 2007). This approach to literacy curricula and pedagogy enabled students to locate themselves in texts, learn the semiotic grammars for understanding meaning making, and use this learning to analyze, discuss, recreate, and redesign texts (The New London Group, 1996). By accessing a toolbox of semiotic strategies, students were empowered to uncover discriminatory discourses across school subjects.

O'Neil (2010) proposes literacy teachers use postmodern picture books to reposition students as researchers who consider alternative points of views to those provided by authors. This approach expands understandings of equity by allowing students to engage in classroom debates that move beyond the usual examination of character and plot. They learn to 'see both themselves and others, explore constraints and underpinnings of social expectations, and perhaps even imagine a different way of being' (O'Neil, 2010, p. 51). Pre-adolescent Serbian and Bosnian girls attending literacy workshops at a summer camp in Bosnia were provided the opportunity to write, illustrate, and construct their own books about peace, friendship, and the preservation of nature (Darvin, 2009). The girls hosted a 'story hour' for younger children at the camp and read stories aloud and then discussed them. These were powerful literacy events and an example of children's complex analytical practice. The act of authoring and sharing stories provided an opportunity to unite and heal disparate groups by collectively imagining a more hopeful future. The project exemplifies the critical role played by teachers to help these young girls use language and other semiotic modes as a means of constructing and seeing themselves in relation to others, evaluating themselves and their experiences in light of significant religious and ethnic differences.

This kind of practice fosters collective action to bring about social change and generate new knowledge emerging from everyday literacy teaching. It engages students and teachers in significant roles as researchers – who gain proficiency in critical research methods to challenge authoritarian, racist, and gendered discourses encountered in school, media texts, and their lived experience (Albright and Walsh, 2003; Purohit and Walsh, 2003). Comber and Kamler (2005) intentionally built teacher research communities to challenge deficit views of children from marginalized and low socio-economic groups and thus 'turn around' unequal literacy outcomes.

They brought together twenty early- and late-career teachers – using their different generational knowledge's – to re-engage their most at-risk students. Teacher researchers engaged in intellectual work; reading theory, learning methods for data analysis, and writing about their findings. They engaged in a variety of data-gathering activities including home visits, interviews, and conversations where they turned to children and families to listen, watch, observe, and identify their funds of knowledge (Moll *et al.*, 1992); and used this knowledge to redesign their literacy curriculum. By researching their own literacy practices and its effects on students and tailoring the literacy curriculum for individual children's needs, they 'turned around' the literacy performance of the students they were most worried about (Kamler and Comber, 2008).

A significant aspect of this research was the expectation that teacher researchers document their analyses and make public their findings. In the volume *Turn around Pedagogies: Literacy Interventions for At-Risk Students* (Comber and Kamler, 2005), nine teachers detail the multiple ways they turned around student literacy achievement using a wide array of visual and print technologies. For example, Duck and Hutchison (2005) explore how computer-mediated animation was used to reconnect disenchanted grade 5/6 writers and develop their writing abilities. In another study Petersen (2005) examines the technology-infused curriculum and social networks he built in order to allow students to develop and display a richer range of literate practices.

The point we wish to emphasize here is that the term 'turn around pedagogies' was coined as a pedagogical model for supporting teachers to connect children with improved literacy outcomes better. Implicit in the metaphor of 'turning around' is a commitment to acknowledging students' proficiencies with different literacy practices that emerge from their funds of knowledge (Moll *et al.*, 1992) and their engagements with popular culture.

A further example of using popular culture to turn around even the youngest school children is seen in an action research study by Salmon (2010) in the United States, who used musical activities to promote literacy development. Her study shows how engaging with children's popular music culture allows them to translate their thinking into successful reading and writing practices. When children heard their own music in the classroom related to their ethnicity or culture, they were inspired to author vibrant stories rich in details related to their lifeworlds.

Viewing students and their funds of knowledge as resourceful contests deficit assumptions about them, their families, and their communities. 'Turning around' to students allows them to reconsider their own experiences and develop strategies for new subjectivities where they can interrogate things that matter to them. This usage is distinguished from the more common accountability-driven 'turn around,' proffered by politicians to signal the miracle cure their governments will deliver through standardization, benchmarks, and quality assurance. 'Turn around' as we understand it, is a process and a commitment to the pedagogic, curriculum, and people work 'that may not be as easy to measure, but which is certainly no less profound' (Comber and Kamler 2005, p. 7).

In the remainder of this chapter we utilize the 'turn around' metaphor to emphasize our belief that teachers need to engage in research for their own well-being and that of their students and communities. We look, in particular, at recent research that 'turns around' to the capacities of digital and mobile literacies and to students as researchers. We find here new directions that may enhance teacher research on literacy – its long-standing commitment to social justice, teacher learning and student engagement.

Teachers 'Turning Around' to Technology

It is widely understood that profound shifts in what it means to be literate in the twenty-first century require teacher researchers to develop competency in rapidly developing technologies to promote quality literacy learning for all students (Beavis *et al.*, 2009; Hagood, Stevens, and Reinking, 2003; Lankshear and Knobel, 2008; Walsh, 2009, 2010). However, it is less clear that teacher research is being used as a powerful methodology for extending teacher knowledge and practice with digital technologies. Only recently has teacher research 'turned around' to technology to connect and reconnect students with literacy learning. While many literacy teachers are incorporating digital technologies into their teaching practice, these technologies need to be viewed as more than a tool for reading, writing, and viewing.

A recent project that focuses on 'turning around' to technology is *Literacy in the Digital World of the Twenty-First Century: Learning from Computer Games* (Apperley and Beavis, 2011; Beavis *et al.*, 2009, Walsh, 2010) where teacher researchers investigated digital games as new forms of text and literacy in English classrooms. The project brought together teachers from five urban and suburban schools in Victoria, Australia who leveraged young people's interest in digital games and the culture of gaming to strengthen existing school-based literacies and identify new forms of literacy practice. Teacher researchers met regularly to play digital games, read and discuss research related to digital games and literacy.

The teachers' projects were diverse in the types of digital games they incorporated into their classrooms; genres ranged from narrative, quest-based epics to sandbox, serious and fantasy sports games. In some classrooms, students researched, played, critiqued, and designed digital games. In others, students designed multimodal presentations and/or authored game reviews on wikis that allowed them to incorporate multiple semiotic modes in their argumentative writing. Students also engaged in retrospective reflections on themselves as players, researched a comprehensive historical digital games exhibition, engaged in digital games-related writing, drama, and reviews (Apperley and Beavis, 2011).

By integrating and researching the impact of digital games on their literacy teaching practices, teacher researchers learned to tailor the literacy curriculum to students' lifeworlds and increase their engagement with more traditional school-based literacies. They also documented their research in the edited book, *Digital Games: Literacy in Action* (Beavis, O'Mara, and McNeice, 2012), which includes chapters from six of the participating teacher researchers. For example, Byrne (2012) who taught English to a small cohort of Year 7 students struggling with traditional print-based literacies, adapted Freebody and Luke's (1990) four resources model to his digital games project. As code breakers, students explored how they played the digital game and its rules. As text users, students compared different games and gameplay across different digital platforms. As text participants, they interrogated the digital game's purpose, narrative, genre, and their own role(s) in the game. Finally, as text analysts, they explored why certain games were enjoyed over others and how the gameplay experience could be improved. Their final assessment, an oral presentation and PowerPoint slide presentation, provided many of Byrne's struggling students with their first positive and successful literacy achievement.

In another project, a group of Year 7 boys joined a wiki that focused on their individual gaming practices and research (Cann, 2012). The wiki offered students a virtual space that drew on their proficiencies as gamers by engaging, exploring, and extending their print and multimodal literacies. Students authored wiki pages on elements of game design: character development, color, genre, iconography, movement, plot, point of view, and sound. In the project's final assignment students designed their own digital game using Microsoft PowerPoint. Their digital games were interactive, with well-developed storylines and high quality student designed and imported graphics. Students' games drew on diverse programming, technical, artistic, cognitive, social and linguistic practices and knowledge of how to configure systems (Walsh, 2010).

These action research projects show teachers 'turning around' to technology and 'turning around' the literacy performance of their students. In a study from the United States, a teacher researcher encouraged his students to use digital technologies to disrupt racist and exclusionary discourses they encountered in school texts and their lived experience (Walsh, 2009). The project was a school-museum collaboration that worked with a digital artist in residence to teach students web design skills. Students explored questions of Chinese-American and immigrant identities through a discourse analysis of history texts and primary documents. Then, drawing on a digital gothic and hip-hop cartoon web project at the museum, they challenged the negative ways their ethnic identities were positioned by drawing political satire cartoons about immigration to the United States. The project concluded with a public and virtual exhibition of students' artwork, using HTML and Flash to create the online exhibition. The redesigned websites represent a new set of multimodal literacy practices that allowed students to not only disrupt racist discourses, but to reach a much wider audience than is usually possible in literacy classrooms.

In an attempt to raise boys' attainment in literacy, a study in England turned to technology and designed a literacy-rich 3D virtual world in which primary students explored avatar-based game play (Merchant, 2009). The project recognized that when children were playfully engaged through their exploration of the 3D world, it worked as a stimulus for more traditional literacy work. Teachers observed improvements in students' print literacy practices as well as their speaking and listening abilities. The project suggests that literacy teachers need time and training to build their confidence and to experiment with new approaches to teaching literacy using a variety of digital tools.

In South East Asia and the Global South current attempts to train large numbers of teachers have turned to technology in an attempt to encourage teacher research and reflection on practice. For example, English in Action (EIA), a large collaborative international development project (Walsh, 2011; Walsh, Shrestha, and Hedges, in press) is using low cost mobile phones within a program of work-based professional development to train 80,000 teachers over nine years in Bangladesh (2009–2017). While not formulated within a teacher research paradigm, EIA suggests how teacher research might foster reflexivity among larger numbers of teachers at scale. Within EIA's 16-month cycle of professional development, teachers are required to reflect on and illustrate how they have implemented new teaching strategies into their English classrooms. Teachers use the video recorder on their mobile phones to document their changed teaching practices, and these are shared, discussed, and critiqued in professional development meetings.

In designing EIA's teacher professional development modules, a variety of media are used: print, short films on communicative English language teaching (CLT) techniques that teachers view on low cost mobile phones provided by the project, audio files, or a 'talking head' to explain the rationale behind different CLT strategies that work in tandem with the professional development modules. All of these resources, with an additional 700 audio files explicitly aligned with the national textbook (used in every English classroom nationwide), are provided on inexpensive micro secure digital (SD) cards (4GB) that can be used across most mobile phone platforms.

In an earlier study, The Digital Education Enhancement Project (DEEP) investigated the use of information communication technologies (ICT) for teaching and learning in Sub-Saharan Africa classrooms (Leach *et al.*, 2004). Each teacher was provided with a hand-held computer and pocket camera for use throughout the project. The project's findings indicate that the use of ICT enhanced teacher professional capability because it widened opportunities for professional planning, extended their range of pedagogic practices and subject knowledge and permitted new forms of teacher-to-teacher cooperation. The Teacher Education in Sub-Saharan Africa (TESSA) research and development network similarly aims to improve the quality of, and extend access to, teacher education in Sub-Saharan Africa across nine countries. TESSA supports the exploration and development of school-based modes of teacher education where teachers develop their competencies and skills to meet students' needs. TESSA materials are all Open Educational Resources (OERs) available in digital format on CD-ROM or from their website. These materials can be freely downloaded, adapted, translated, and integrated with other materials. This comprehensive turn to technology exemplifies the significance OERs can play in providing large number of teachers with access to knowledge about teacher research they can use productively to design projects aimed at improving their practice.

These examples point to the future possibility of making teacher research widely available to everyday teachers across developed and developing nation states using inexpensive tech-nologies. As open distance learning (ODL) platforms are increasingly designed for handheld devices, the methodology and rationale for engaging in teacher research can also be made available more widely on mobile platforms. Mobile technologies have the potential to reshape teacher research, making it more accessible with the potential to not only improve the literacy achievement of students, but to turn around their lives as well.

Teachers 'Turning Around' To Students as Researchers

While the 'turning around to technology' work illustrates the multiple ways teachers might work *with* students as research participants, an additional step, not explicitly explored in most teacher research, is to reposition students *as* researchers themselves. There is, as Thomson (2008) points out, in some states in Australia and in England a growing tradition of research with children and young people at school, called students-as-researchers.

> A students-as-researchers approach means that children and young people conduct a specifically designed inquiry, about a topic they have decided on, to provide data to inform recommendations for change (Atweh and Burton, 1995; Edwards, 2000; Fielding and Bragg, 2003.) . . . Students might survey their peers, or conduct a range of focus groups across year levels or interview a representative sample of the school. Such an investigation . . . allows them to speak about the views of all students, rather than simply giving their own opinions. (Thomson, 2008, p. 7)

Thomson and Gunter (2007) draw fascinating parallels between teacher research and research with students in schools, arguing that both can be seen as 'standpoint research'; where researchers are located in the context they are researching; have unique access to school events and histories; foreground views that may not be heard in mainstream research; and are committed to a change agenda. More specifically, student standpoint research can be seen as

- addressing issues of importance to students and is thus research in the interests of students;
- working with students' (subjugated) knowledges about the way in which the school works;
- allowing marginalized perspectives and voices to come center stage;
- using students' subjectivities and experiences to develop approaches, tools, representations and validities;
- interrupting the power relations in school including, but not confined to, those which are age related; and
- being geared to making a difference. (Thomson and Gunter, 2007, p. 331.)

These criteria can apply to any situation where children are researchers in their own right or co-researchers with teachers and/or other adult social scientists. A shift to more deliberately positioning students within teacher literacy research seems to us a productive direction that should be explored more widely. The Creative Spaces project in the United Kingdom (CapeUK, 2009) worked explicitly with children as co-researchers in the design of museum and gallery learning. The project recognizes young people as experts in their own lives and therefore in a prime position to shape research about the learning opportunities that are designed for them.

A student co-researcher project in the United States also encouraged high school students to become active partners in educational reform (Yonezawa and Jones, 2009). The student co-researchers changed and influenced the kinds of questions teachers asked themselves and altered the discussions adults had within their schools. This kind of collaboration helped teachers in low-performing urban schools analyze academic strengths and weaknesses in a timely fashion and develop a more complete portrait of students' needs and the kinds of classroom practices that best support students' learning and academic success.

In an ethnographic study from Argentina, a teacher researcher positioned children as co-researchers to understand better aspects of school politicization (Milstein, 2012). She realized that not seeing or listening to children kept them invisible and hid an integral part of the reality she was hoping to uncover. By including children as co-researchers she consciously overcame her tendency to either romanticize or demonize them. Rather, turning to students as researchers, she drew on their data collection of photographs, interviews, observations, readings, and field notes. This collage of data showcased their views on school politicization and provided the distance needed to successfully conduct ethnographic research that transcended pervading adult opinions. Simultaneously it legitimized children's viewpoints concerning the social and cultural life in which they take part.

An Australian project (Comber, Nixon, and Reid, 2007) provides a further example of bringing together teacher and student researchers. Using the resources of multimodality and place-based education, they explored new ways of sustaining the environment, in particular the Murray-Darling Basin where their schools were located. Teachers focused on the local and bioregional environment in their science/literacy curriculum and designed learning experiences that allowed students to be active creators of knowledge. Teachers acted as experienced guides and co-learners, brokers of community resources, allowing the boundaries between school and community to become more permeable. In an edited volume called *Literacies in Place: Teaching Environmental Communications* (Comber, Nixon, and Reid, 2007), eight teachers document their research with students. Five key pedagogical principles drawn from this place-based teacher research might serve as a framework for other teacher researchers who wish to 'turn around' to students as researchers of place.

1 Start with research about subjects that matter to students and their community.
2 Build conceptual and knowledge resources over an extended period of time.
3 Students and teachers work in the 'field' and document those experiences.
4 Introduce students to a range of genres, media, and communications technologies (thus expanding their capacity to interpret and produce multisemiotic texts).
5 Ensure time for the production and dissemination of student-produced texts and findings (e.g., through film or slide shows for the community, radio presentations) that can often be impeded by resource limitations in schools. (Comber, Nixon, and Reid, 2007, pp. 17–21)

As exciting as this work is, the researchers warn that normative understandings of literacy education continue to limit the scope of teachers' decision making in the classroom and can impact negatively on research with students. Challenges to producing what they call a *pedagogy of responsibility* include addressing: teacher workload and the commitment, time and energy needed to do this work; the complexity of local politics and issues that are emotionally charged in local communities; acquiring adequate environmental knowledge to support and plan for student learning; and sustaining commitment over time. (Comber, Nixon, and Reid, 2007, pp. 147–153)

Yet, to us, the need to position our students as researchers of their worlds, to engage with the complexities in ways that make a difference is the only kind of literacy education worth pursuing.

A Future Agenda for Teacher Research?

Teacher research in and on children's literacy is well established, yet not a regular feature in most pre-service education programs. The fact also remains that many in-service teachers don't have time to engage in teacher research due to the demands of mandated programs and standardized testing regimes. Currently lesson study, an ongoing form of teacher research popular in Japan since the 1990s (Watanabe, 2002), is gaining momentum in the United States (Marble, 2006), Hong Kong (Lee, 2008), Singapore (Fang *et al.*, 2009), Sweden and Iran (Cheng, 2011). Lesson study is a research process in which teachers jointly plan, observe, analyze, and refine actual classroom lessons called research lessons. Lesson study is widely credited for the steady improvement of Japanese elementary mathematics and science instruction (Lewis and Hurd, 2011) and is seen as ongoing and easy to integrate into most school structures. Self-study (Loughran *et al.*, 2004; Lassonde, Galman, and Kosnik, 2009) is another existing trend in teacher research that emerged from the Self-Study of Teacher Education Practices (S-STEP) (Hamilton *et al.*, 1998) in the early 1990s. Self-study encourages teachers to take control of their profession by placing greater importance on the knowledge and learning derived from researching their own practice. As both approaches appear to work presently in multiple global contexts, a practicable way forward is to rethink lesson study and self-study in ways that emphasize social justice, democracy, and turning to students as researchers.

We know from what has been done, that teacher research can question assumptions and challenge the status quo when committed to social justice and political action. The successful examples in the literature need to be problematized to some extent because many come from funded research projects where university-based educators work in collaboration with teachers at nearby schools. These kinds of partnerships – while critical to the field – cannot always be sustained financially. If we want to see teacher research become central and commonplace to literacy teachers' everyday practice, globally, then changes to existing policy, pre-service, and continuing teacher education is timely and paramount.

Perhaps those who sit comfortably (or uncomfortably) in faculties of education need to take it upon themselves to lead the charge to mobilize teacher unions, national and international teacher organizations, and teachers themselves. Arguably, this could challenge the current arrangements of schooling that impede teacher research on literacy. A first step might be to challenge the hegemony of publishers and demand that *all* educational research, literacy and otherwise, be available via Open Access or Creative Commons licensing in a digital format. In the short term, this would provide many teachers access to teacher research related to their day-to-day work, regardless of their ability to pay or lack of affiliation to an organization with access. Lack of access disempowers teachers and should be viewed as inequitable in terms of missed opportunities for greater student achievement in literacy and other subjects. Additionally, schools of teacher education and professional organizations could earmark funds to design smart phone applications that deliver methodologies, examples and resources about teacher research – free of charge. These resources could then be connected to online research communities where teachers share resources, practices, and success stories from the field.

We might also conduct large-scale analyses of successful teacher research on children's literacy education that challenges fundamental educational practices like tracking, standardized curricula, testing, and assessment. Also needed are microanalyses of how literacy teachers incorporate successful teacher research practices within the very real constraints of their routine work. Pre-service teacher curricula needs to be explored to determine the extent to which it does or does not prepare teachers to be active consumers of teacher research and become researchers themselves in ways analogous to the legal and medical profession. Taking the best examples of pre-service curricula that support an embodiment of inquiry and reflection is timely and certainly integral to the future profession of teaching. A further step would be to reform teacher credentialing to ensure teacher research and inquiry were viewed as essential and necessary across the life span of the profession.

It is important to look systematically at what constitutes good teacher research across different nation states with the aim of designing a series of OERs specifically related to teacher research. Currently, on the Open Education Resources Commons website (www.oercommons.org) out of just under 40,000 free resources, there is only one solely devoted to teacher research. These OERs could include overviews of successful projects but also be designed to specifically encourage teachers to engage in teacher research to 'rethink, resist and reform the ways we think about, and take action regarding the arrangements and purposes of schools and schooling' (Cochran-Smith and Lytle, 2009, p. 39). A variety of OERs specifically related to research methods, data collection and analysis and to developing a theoretical disposition grounded in the ideals of social justice, access, and equity would also be important. Additional resources could be developed specifically around teacher research in children's literacy education and other school subjects.

The research in this chapter demonstrates that engaging in teacher research has the potential to change teachers' work and their subjectivities. It also has the potential to change the knowledge base of literacy education warehoused in theory-driven teacher education curricula and programs of professional development. However, there is still critical work to be done to empower educators to view teacher research as integral across the life span of their professional lives – rather than as time-bound professional development projects. The extent to which any of the above recommendations will be taken up is questionable. Yet, recent examples of literacy teachers taking it upon themselves to study their own practices and initiate teacher research aimed at 'turning around' to students and technology, to contest deficit discourses, are inspiring. This is because these teachers, like so many others, are taking it upon themselves to make their daily practice a critical site of inquiry. In doing so, their literacy teaching practices improve and make tangible differences to the lives of children.

We know that many teachers enter the profession to 'do some good.' Without a doubt, engaging in teacher research will help them achieve this goal continuously throughout their professional career. The successful work of teacher researchers around the world who have improved literacy outcomes for children continues to inspire us and give us hope that there is still time to 'turn around' inequitable literacy practices and outcomes.

References

Albright, J., Purohit, K., and Walsh, C. (2007) Hybridity, globalisation and literacy education in the context of New York City. *Pedagogies: An International Journal*, 1(4) (2006): 221–242.

Albright, J., and Walsh, C. (2003) Jamming visual culture. *Literacy Learning in the Middle Years*, 11(2): 15–22.

Apperley, T., and Beavis, C. (2011) Literacy into action: Digital games as action and text in the English and Literacy classroom. *Pedagogies: An International Journal*, 6(2): 130–143.

Atweh, W., and Burton, L. (1995) Students as researchers: Rationale and critique. *British Educational Research Journal*, 21(5): 561–575.

Barton, D. (2000) Moral panics about literacy. Centre for Language in Social Life, Working Paper Series, accessed November 23, 2012: www.ling.lancs.ac.uk/pubs/clsl/clsl116.pdf

Beavis, C., Bradford, C., O'Mara, J., and Walsh, C.S. (2009) Researching literacy in the digital age: Learning from computer games. *English in Education*, 43(2): 162–175.

Beavis, C., O'Mara, J., and McNeice, L. (2012) *Digital Games: Literacy in Action*. Australia: Wakefield Press/The Australian Association for the Teaching of English.

Borko, H., Liston, D., and Whitcomb, J. (2007) Genres of empirical research in teacher education. *Journal of Teacher Education*, 58(3): 1, 3–11.

Byrne, P. (2012) Game plan: Using computer games in English class to engage the disengaged. In C. Beavis, J. O'Mara, and L. McNeice (eds) *Digital Games: Literacy in Action*. Australia: Wakefield Press/The Australian Association for the Teaching of English, pp. 51–57.

Cann, M. (2012) Game-O-Rama! In C. Beavis, J. O'Mara, and L. McNeice (eds) *Digital Games: Literacy in Action*. Australia: Wakefield Press/The Australian Association for the Teaching of English, pp. 51–57.

CapeUK (2009) *Creative Spaces: Children as Co-researchers in the Design of Museum and Gallery Learning*. London: MLA.

Cheng, E. (2011) How lesson study develops pre-service teachers' instructional design competency. *The International Journal of Research and Review*, 7(1): 67–79.

Clarke, A. (2006) The nature and substance of cooperating teacher reflection. *Teaching and Teacher Education*, 17(5): 599–611.

Cochran-Smith, M. (2004) Taking stock in 2004: Teacher education in dangerous times. *Journal of Teacher Education*, 55: 3–7.

Cochran-Smith, M., and Lytle, S. (1990) Research on teaching and teacher research: The issues that divide. *Educational Researcher*, 19(2): 2–11.

Cochran-Smith, M., and Lytle, S. (1993) *Inside-outside: Teacher Research and Knowledge*. New York: Teachers College Press.

Cochran-Smith, M., and Lytle, S. (1999) Relationship of knowledge and practice: Teacher learning in communities In A. Iran-Nejad and C. Pearson (eds) *Review of Research in Education*, Vol. 24. Washington, DC: American Educational Research Association, pp. 249–306.

Cochran-Smith, M., and Lytle, S. (2009) Teacher research as stance. In B. Somekh and S. Noffke (eds) *Handbook of Educational Action Research*. London: Sage, pp. 39–49.

Comber, B. (2003) Critical Literacy: What does it look like in the early years? In N. Hall, J. Larson, and J. Marsh (eds) *Handbook of Research in Early Childhood Literacy*. United Kingdom: Sage/Paul Chapman, pp. 355–368.

Comber, B., and Kamler, B. (2004) Getting out of deficit: Pedagogies of reconnection. *Teaching Education*, 15(3): 293–210.

Comber, B., and Kamler, B. (2005) *Turn-Around Pedagogies: Literacy Interventions for At-Risk Students*. Newtown, Australia: PETA.

Comber, B., Nixon, H., and Reid, J. (eds) (2007) *Literacies in Place: Teaching Environmental Communications*. Newtown, Australia: PETA.

Craig, C.J. (2009) Teacher research and teacher as researcher. In L.J. Saha and A.G. Dworkin (eds) *The New International Handbook of Teachers and Teaching*. New York: Springer Science and Business Media, Inc, pp. 61–70.

Darvin, D. (2009) Make books, not war: Workshops at a summer camp in Bosnia. *Literacy*, 43(1): 50–59.

Dewey, J. (1933/1985) *How We Think, A Restatement of the Relation of Reflective Thinking to the Educative Process*. Boston: Heath.

Doecke, B., and Gill, M. (2001) Setting standards: Confronting paradox, STELLA. A combined issue of *English in Australia*, December 2000–February 2001, 129–130, and Literacy Learning: *The Middle Years*, 9(1): 5–15.

Duck, C., and Hutchison, K. (2005) Animating disenchanted writers. In B. Comber and B. Kamler (eds) *Turn-around pedagogies: Literacy interventions for at-risk students*. Newtown, Australia: PETA, pp. 15–30.

Edwards, J. (2000) *Students-as-Researchers*. Adelaide, SA: South Australian Department for Children's Services.

Elbaz-Luwisch, F. (2006) Studying teachers' lives and experiences: Narrative inquiry in K-12 teaching. In D.J. Clandinin (ed.) *Handbook of Narrative Inquiry*. Thousand Oaks, CA: Sage, pp. 357–382.

Fang, Y., Lee, C., Lim, E., and Syed Haron, S.T. (2009) Innovation of teacher development through lesson study in Singapore – Cases of teacher learning and continuous improvement via mathematics research lessons. In K.Y. Wong, P.Y. Lee, B. Kaur, *et al.* (eds) *Mathematics Education: The Singapore Journey.* Singapore: World Scientific, pp. 101–126.

Fielding, M., and Bragg, S. (2003) *Students as Researchers: Making a Difference.* Cambridge: Pearson Publishing.

Freebody, P., and Luke, A. (1990) Literacies programs: Debates and demands in cultural context. *Prospect: Australian Journal of TESOL,* 5(7): 7–16.

Freeman, M., deMarrais, K., Preissle, J., *et al.* (2007) Standards of evidence in qualitative research: An incitement to discourse. *Educational Researcher,* 36(1): 25–32.

Freire, P. (1970) *The Pedagogy of the Oppressed.* New York: Seabury.

Habermas, J. (1971) *Knowledge and Human Interests.* London: Heinemann.

Hagood, M.C., Stevens, L.P., and Reinking, D. (2003) 'What do THEY have to teach US? Talkin' 'cross generations!' In D. Alvermann (ed.) *Adolescents and Literacies in a Digital World.* New York: Peter Lang, pp. 68–83.

Hamilton, M.L., Pinnegar, S., Russell, T., *et al.* (eds) (1998) *Reconceptualizing Teaching Practice: Self-Study in Teacher Education.* London: Falmer Press.

Hamston, J., Risko, V., and Ellis, V. (2006) Introduction: Mapping the challenges and possibilities in teacher education. *Literacy,* 40 (2): 63–65.

Hogan, C., and Strickland, L. (eds) (1998) *Learning Journeys: Working Together for School Changes.* Murdoch, WA: Centre for Curriculum and Professional Development, School of Education, Murdoch University.

Kamler, B., and Comber, B. (2008) Making a difference: Early career English teachers research their practice. *Changing English: Studies in Culture and Education,* 15(1): 65–76.

Karp, S. (2003) Equity claims for NCLB don't pass the test. *Rethinking Schools,* accessed November 23, 2012: www.rethinkingschools.org/special_reports/bushplan/ESEA173.shtml

Kemmis, S. (2006) Participatory action research and the public sphere. *Educational Action Research,* 14(4): 459–476.

Lankshear, C.J., and Knobel, M. (2008) Introduction: Digital literacies: concepts, policies and practices. In C.J. Lamkshear and M. Knobel (eds) *Digital Literacies: Concepts, Policies and Practices.* New York: Peter Lang, pp. 1–16.

Lassonde, C.A., Galman, S., and Kosnik, C. (eds) (2009) *Self-Study Research Methodologies for Teacher Educators.* Rotterdam: Sense Publishers.

Leach, J., Patel, R., Peters, A., *et al.* (2004) Deep impact: A study of the use of hand–held computers for teacher professional development in primary schools in the Global South. *European Journal of Teacher Education,* 27(1): 5–28.

Lee, J.F.K. (2008) A Hong Kong case of lesson study – Benefits and concerns. *Teaching and Teacher Education,* 24: 1115–1124.

Lewis, C.C., and Hurd, J. (2011) *Lesson Study Step by Step: How Teacher Learning Communities Improve Instruction.* Portsmouth, NH: Heinemann.

Limbrick, L., Buchanan.P., Goodwin, M., and Schwarcz, H. (2010) Doing things differently. The outcomes of teachers researching their own practice in teaching writing. *Canadian Journal of Education,* 33(4): 897–924.

Liston, D.P., and Zeichner, K.M. (1990) Reflective teaching and action research in preservice teacher education. *Journal of Education for Teaching,* 16(3): 3–20.

Loughran, J.J., Hamilton, M.L., LaBoskey, V.K., and Russell, T. (eds) (2004) *International Handbook of Self-Study of Teaching and Teacher Education Practices.* Dordrecht: Kluwer Academic Publishers.

Lyons, N. (2010) Reflection and reflective inquiry: Critical issues, evolving conceptualisations, contemporary claims and future possibilities. In N. Lyons (ed.) *Handbook of Reflective Inquiry.* New York: Springer, pp. 3–22.

Lytle, S. (2008) At last: Practitioner inquiry and the practice of teaching: Some thoughts on better. *Journal of Research in Teaching,* 42(3): 373–379.

Lytle, S., and Cochran-Smith, M. (1994) Teacher research as a way of knowing. *Harvard Educational Review*, 64: 447–474.

Marble, S. (2006) Learning to teach through lesson study. *Action in Teacher Education*, (28)3: 86–96.

McArdle, K., and Coutts, N. (2010) Taking teachers' continuous professional development (CPD) beyond reflection: adding shared sense-making and collaborative engagement for professional renewal. *Studies in Continuing Education*, 32(3): 201–215.

Meier, D.R., and Henderson, B. (2007) *Learning from Young Children in the Classroom: The Art and Science of Teacher Research*. New York: Teachers College Press.

Merchant, G. (2009) Literacy in virtual worlds. *Journal of Research in Reading*, 32(1): 38–56.

Milstein, D. (2012) Children as co-researchers in anthropological narratives in education. *Ethnography and Education*, 5(1): 1–15.

Mitchell, J., Clarke, A., and Nutall, J. (2007) Cooperating teachers' perspectives under scrutiny: A comparative analysis of Australia and Canada. *Asia-Pacific Journal of Teacher Education*, 35(1): 5–25.

Moll, L.C., Amanti, C., Neff, D., and Gonzalez, N. (1992) Funds of knowledge for teaching: Using a qualitative approach to connect homes and classrooms. *Theory and Practice*, 31: 132–141.

New London Group (1996) A pedagogy of multiliteracies: Designing social futures. *Harvard Educational Review*, 66(1): 60–92.

Nielsen, W.S., Triggs, V., Clarke, A., and Collins, J. (2010) The teacher education conversation: A network of cooperating teachers. *Canadian Journal of Education*, 33(4): 837–868.

O'Neil, K. (2010) Once upon today: Teaching for social justice with postmodern picturebooks. *Children's Literature in Education*, 41: 40–51.

Petersen, C. (2005) Teacher-student networks: Using technology-infused curricula to turn around students at risk. In B. Comber and B. Kamler (eds) *Turn-around pedagogies: Literacy interventions for at-risk students*. Newtown, Australia: PETA, pp. 47–62.

Purohit, K., and Walsh, C. (2003) Interrupting discourses around gender through collective memory work and collaborative curriculum research. *Sex Education*, 3(2): 171–183.

Salmon, A. (2010) Using music to promote children's thinking and enhance their literacy development. *Early Child Development and Care*, 180(7): 937–945.

Schön, D. (1983) *The Reflective Practitioner: How Professionals Think in Action*. New York: Basic Books.

Schwab, J.J. (1969) The practical: A language for curriculum. *School Review*, 78: 1–23.

Shulman, L., Lieberman, A., Hatch, T., and Lew, M. (1999) The Carnegie Foundation builds the scholarship of teaching with K-12 teachers and teacher educators. *Teaching and Teacher Education: Division K Newsletter*, American Educational Research Association: 1–5.

Somekh, B. (2006) *Action Research: A Methodology for Change and Development*. Maidenhead: Open University Press.

Thomson, P. (ed.) (2008) *Doing Visual Research with Children and Young People*. London and New York: Routledge.

Thomson, P., and Gunter, H. (2007) The methodology of students-as-researchers: Valuing and using experience and expertise to develop methods. *Discourse*, 28(3): 327–342.

Walsh, C.S. (2007) Creativity as capital in the literacy classroom: Youth as multimodal designers. *Literacy*, 41(2): 79–85.

Walsh, C.S. (2009) The multimodal redesign of school texts. *The Journal of Research in Reading – Special Issue on Literacy and Technology*, 32(1): 126–136.

Walsh, C.S. (2010) Systems-based literacy practices: Digital games research, gameplay and design. *Australian Journal of Language and Literacy Education*, 33(1): 24–40.

Walsh, C.S. (2011) e-Learning in Bangladesh: The 'trainer in your pocket'. In IADIS International Conference e-Learning 2011, a part of the IADIS Multi Conference on Computer Science and Information Systems 2011, 20–23 July, Rome, Italy.

Walsh, C.S., Shrestha, P.N., and Hedges, C. (in press) Mobile phones for professional development and English teaching in Bangladesh. *International Journal of Innovation and Learning*.

Watanabe, T. (2002) Learning from Japanese lesson study. *Educational Leadership*, 59(6): 36–39.

Weis, L., Fine, M., and Dimitriadis, G. (2009) Towards a critical theory of method in shifting times. In M.W. Apple, W.U. Au, and L.A. Gandin (eds) *The Routledge International Handbook of Critical Education*. New York: Routledge, pp. 437–448.

Yonezawa, S., and Jones, M. (2009) Student voices: Generating reform from the inside out. *Theory into Practice*, 48: 205–212.

Zeichner, K. (1999) The new scholarship in teacher education. *Educational Researcher*, 28(9): 4–15.

Zeichner, K.M., and Noffke, S.E. (2001) Practitioner research. In V. Richardson (ed.) *Handbook of Research on Teaching*, 4th edn. Washington, DC: American Educational Research Association, pp. 298–330.

Index

References to tables are given in bold type and to figures in italic type.

CPSIA information can be obtained
at www.ICGtesting.com
Printed in the USA
BVHW062015090121
597415BV00007B/75

9 780470 975978